D1518195

Istvan Anhalt
Pathways and Memory

Istvan Anhalt, born into a Jewish family in Budapest in 1919, studied with Zoltán Kodály before being conscripted into a forced labour camp during World War II. In the late 1940s he studied under Nadia Boulanger and Soulima Stravinsky before emigrating to Canada in 1949, where he has been an important figure in the Canadian music scene for the last fifty years.

Based on a wealth of experience and first-hand knowledge, *Istvan Anhalt* provides biographical information on Anhalt's life in Europe and Canada, as well as critical articles on his music and writings. Previously unpublished writings by Anhalt as well as a commentary on his most recent opera are also included.

Contributors include Istvan Anhalt, composer and writer John Beckwith (Toronto), music theorist and critic William Benjamin (British Columbia), specialist in twentieth-century music Austin Clarkson (York), Robin Elliott, music historian Helmut Kallmann, David Keane, founder of the Electroacoustic Music Studio at Queen's, Carl Morey, editor of the musical works of Glenn Gould and professor at Queen's, composer George Rochberg, and Gordon E. Smith.

ROBIN ELLIOTT, a former student of Anhalt's, is the author of *Counterpoint to a City: The Centennial History of the Women's Music Club of Toronto.* GORDON E. SMITH is associate professor in Queen's University's School of Music.

Photograph of Istvan Anhalt by Walter Curtin (1988)

Istvan Anhalt

Pathways and Memory

Edited by

ROBIN ELLIOTT AND
GORDON E. SMITH

McGill-Queen's University Press
Montreal & Kingston · London · Ithaca

© McGill-Queen's University Press 2001
ISBN 0-7735-2102-X

Legal deposit fourth quarter 2001
Bibliothèque nationale du Québec

Printed in Canada on acid-free paper

Publication of this book has been made possible by
grants from the Institute for Canadian Music at the
Faculty of Music, University of Toronto, the Office of
Funded Research Support Services, University
College, Dublin, and the Academic Vice-Principal
(Research), the Office of Research Services, the
Faculty of Arts and Science, and the School of Music
at Queen's University.

McGill-Queen's University Press acknowledges the
financial support of the Government of Canada
through the Book Publishing Industry Development
Program (BPIDP) for its activities. It also
acknowledges the support of the Canada Council for
the Arts for its publishing program.

Canadian Cataloguing in Publication Data

Main entry under title:
Istvan Anhalt: pathways and memory
Includes bibliographical references.
ISBN 0-7735-2102-X
1. Anhalt, István, 1919–   I. Elliott, Robin, 1956–
II. Smith, Gordon Ernest, 1950–
ML410.A59188 2001   780.'92   C00-901499-3

This book was typeset by Dynagram inc.
in 10/12 Baskerville.

Is someone here ... speaking?
I'm listening ...

Istvan Anhalt, *Traces (Tikkun)*

Contents

Figure and Tables

Contributors

ISTVAN ANHALT, the subject of this book, is a composer and author, and professor emeritus of music at Queen's University. Anhalt's musical works embody a wide range of twentieth-century stylistic idioms, and his most recent opera, *Millennial Mall (Lady Diotima's Walk)* (1999), received its premiere in January 2000 in Winnipeg, Manitoba.

JOHN BECKWITH, composer, writer, and former dean of the Faculty of Music at the University of Toronto, is the author of *Music Papers: Articles and Talks by a Canadian Composer* (1997). His recent compositions include *Round and Round* for orchestra, the opera *Taptoo!* and *Eureka*, an "action piece" for nine winds.

WILLIAM BENJAMIN is a music theorist and critic. A music faculty member at the University of British Columbia, his published work deals with harmonic theory, music of the early twentieth century, and the philosophical foundations of analysis. Among his recent publications are technical and aesthetic studies of Bruckner's Symphony No. 8 (1996) and Schoenberg's *Five Orchestral Pieces*, Op. 16 (1999).

AUSTIN CLARKSON is professor emeritus of music at York University. A specialist in twentieth-century music, he is the general editor of the music and writings of Stefan Wolpe and has published *On the Music of Stefan Wolpe: Essays and Recollections of Stefan Wolpe.*

ROBIN ELLIOTT completed a Ph.D. in musicology at the University of Toronto (1990). A specialist in Canadian music, he served as an associate editor for the second edition of the *Encyclopedia of Music in Canada* (1992), edited three volumes for the Canadian Musical Heritage Society (1989, 1992, 1998), and wrote the book *Counterpoint to a City: The Centennial History of the Women's Musical Club of Toronto* (1997). In 1996 he joined the faculty of the Department of Music at University College, Dublin. When at Queen's as an undergraduate, Elliott was a student of Anhalt and has continued to follow the musical evolution of his former teacher.

HELMUT KALLMANN, music librarian and pioneer historian of music in Canada, was the head of the Music Division of the National Library of Canada (1970–87). He is the author of *A History of Music in Canada 1534–1914* (1960; 1987), co-editor of the *Encyclopedia of Music in Canada* (1981; 2nd ed. 1992), and the editor of two volumes for the Canadian Musical Heritage Society (1990, 1998).

DAVID KEANE, professor emeritus at Queen's University, founded the Queen's Electroacoustic Music Studios in 1970 and directed them for twenty-seven years. He is the author of the book *Tape Music Composition* (1970), and many articles on the composition, aesthetics, and history of electroacoustic composition. Recently he was the keynote speaker and guest composer at the Australian Computer Music Conference (Auckland, New Zealand), and a juror for the 25^e Concours Internationaux de Bourges (France). He has had works featured at the Bourges festival, Primavera en La Habana (Cuba), and Metafonie: Cinquanta anni di musica elettroacustica (Italy).

CARL MOREY occupied the Jean A. Chalmers Chair in Canadian Music at the University of Toronto from 1991 until his retirement on 1 July 2000. He became a professor of musicology there in 1970 and was dean of the Faculty of Music from 1984 to 90. Among his publications are *Music in Canada: A Research and Information Guide* (1997). He is the editor of the musical works of Glenn Gould (Schott).

GEORGE ROCHBERG has been a close friend of Istvan Anhalt since 1960. A professor emeritus at the University of Pennsylvania, Rochberg is a noted composer whose musical works encompass a wide range of twentieth-century idioms. His book, entitled *The Aesthetics of Survival: A Composer's View of Twentieth-Century Music* (1984), is a representative collection of Rochberg's thoughts on music.

GORDON E. SMITH is an associate professor of Canadian music studies and ethnomusicology at Queen's University. He has published on traditional music based on fieldwork in Quebec and the Canadian Maritime provinces, and has written articles on Canadian and American music for the forthcoming edition of the *New Grove Dictionary of Music and Musicians*, and the United States and Canada volume of the *Garland Encyclopedia of World Music*. The author of an article on his colleague, Istvan Anhalt (*Queen's Quarterly* 1991), he has continued his research in the music of Anhalt.

Acknowledgments

We would like to thank those who have contributed so generously to the production of this book through their financial aid: the Institute for Canadian Music and the Charles Jordan Fund at the Faculty of Music of the University of Toronto, as well as the Academic Vice-Principal (Research), the Office of Research Services, and the School of Music at Queen's University, and the Office of Funded Research Support Services at University College, Dublin, Ireland. We are also grateful to Lin Good, former associate librarian at Queen's University, for her generous support of this project.

In addition, thanks is due to the many individuals who helped with the book's research and preparation. Personnel in the Music Division of the National Library of Canada, especially Jannine Barriault, Stéphane Jean, and Maureen Nevins, generously aided a number of the book's contributors. Vivien Taylor as well as her staff in the music library at Queen's University was of special help in researching aspects of Anhalt's life and work. We would like to thank Marjan Mozetich for his fine work on the musical examples in chapter 5 and Gillian Akenson for her generous assistance with the book's index. Thanks also to Walter Curtin for permission to use his photograph of Anhalt as a frontispiece, as well as his photograph taken following the premiere of *Winthrop*.

Sincere thanks go to the staff of McGill-Queen's University Press, including Joan Harcourt, Roger Martin, and Joan McGilvray for their advice and support. We are also most fortunate to have had a splendid copy editor, Rebecca Green, whose combined expertise as a musicologist and as an editor was reflected in her constructive suggestions and thorough fine tuning of the text.

The final word of thanks for this book must go to our subject, Istvan Anhalt, whose continued support, and advice helped us along the long pathway toward making this book a reality. For his knowledge, inspiration, and friendship, we are truly grateful.

Introduction

GORDON E. SMITH

Musician, writer, composer, teacher, and colleague – Istvan[1] Anhalt has been a major figure on the Canadian music scene for five decades. Born into a Jewish family in Budapest in 1919, Anhalt studied at the Franz Liszt Academy of Music with Zoltán Kodály before being conscripted into a forced labour camp during the war. In the late 1940s he studied in Paris with Louis Fourestier, Nadia Boulanger, and Soulima Stravinsky, and emigrated to Canada in 1949, sponsored by a Lady Davis Fellowship for displaced European intellectuals and artists. Settling first in Montreal, he taught at McGill University for twenty-two years, where he established the electronic music studio and built up the theory and composition department, as well as composing a group of seminal musical works. In 1971 he accepted a position as head of the Department of Music at Queen's University, a position he held until 1981, continuing to teach at Queen's until his retirement in 1984. During the Queen's period, Anhalt continued to establish a reputation as a composer, author, administrator, and teacher. In his retirement years he has continued to produce major new compositions, as well as scholarly articles and miscellaneous writings.

Istvan Anhalt: Pathways and Memory is the first comprehensive study of Anhalt. A major aim of the book is to provide wide-ranging discussion about a major individual in Canadian music, as well as the multi-layered contexts of his life and work. The collaborative nature of the book derives from the editors' idea of selecting expert authors to write different sections, thereby drawing on experience and knowledge, as well as providing a range of different voices. The first part of the book examines Anhalt's life in detail, beginning with the European period (1919–49), followed by the Montreal years (1949–71), and then the Kingston period from 1971 to 2000. Written by the editors (the first two by Robin Elliott and the third by Gordon E. Smith), these essays describe Anhalt's life within the context of his family background, musical education, war experiences, emigration from Europe to Canada, life as a newcomer in Canada in the 1950s, and they discuss his work in the Faculty of Music at McGill University, his decision to leave Montreal and start a new life in Kingston, his years at Queen's University as an administrator and teacher, and his continuing active, productive retirement period. Throughout, Elliott and Smith weave Anhalt's life experience with his work as a composer. It is far from a secret that they consider Anhalt's creative instincts as a composer and writer to be integrally linked to his life experiences.

Part 2, "Compositions," contains four essays, beginning with Robin Elliott's survey of the chamber music. Elliott observes that nearly all of Anhalt's chamber pieces were composed before 1954. As Elliott shows, these early pieces variously reflect influences of Anhalt's composition teachers (Zoltán Kodály in Budapest, and later Nadia Boulanger in Paris), as well as his emerging interest in dodecaphonic idioms. In the following essay, John Beckwith studies Anhalt's orchestral repertoire, beginning with *Concerto in stilo di Handel*, which Anhalt wrote when he was a student of Nadia Boulanger, through *Funeral Music* (1951), the *Symphony* (1958), and *Symphony of Modules* (1967) to the large orchestral triptych Anhalt composed in the late 1980s: *Simulacrum*; *SparkskrapS*; *Sonance•Resonance (Welche Töne?)*. With customary precision and probing, Beckwith discusses the compositional frameworks for each piece.

David Keane's essay explains how electroacoustic music was introduced into Canada in the late 1950s and discusses Anhalt's fact-finding visits to Paris and Cologne (1958, 1960) and his association with Hugh Le Caine. He also analyzes Anhalt's electronic compositions from the first part of the 1960s through to *Cento* and *Foci* later in the same decade. Keane also describes Anhalt's concerted efforts to promote what was considered then an experimental, avant-garde musical idiom. In his essay, William Benjamin discusses two of Anhalt's orchestral pieces composed some thirty years apart, the Symphony (1958) and *SparkskrapS* (1988), suggesting that in textless music such as this, Anhalt probes even deeper levels of meaning. With many musical examples and invoking different theoretical models, Benjamin explains in detail the compositional processes at work in this music. In his essay, Benjamin also locates these processes within the broader scope of such recurrent deep themes in Anhalt's work as the human life cycle, transformative experience (traumatic and epiphanic), good and evil, and the Divine.

Part 3, "Writings," contains four essays. Carl Morey deals with Anhalt's approach to text in a large selection of his music. Disparate sources, ideas of borrowing, collage, and linguistic features are discussed within the context of chamber works from the 1940s and 1950s through to *Traces (Tikkun)* in the 1990s. As Morey observes, in Anhalt's recent texted works (from the mid-1980s), the composer has turned to writing his own words rather than reworking assemblages from other sources. Austin Clarkson next discusses Anhalt's analytical writings with particular reference to *Alternative Voices* (1984), what Clarkson views as a pioneering study in that it is the first book-length theoretical treatment of music from the 1960s and 1970s to explore extended vocal techniques. As Clarkson observes, in its multidisciplinary theoretical approach, as well as with respect to the large repertory of music it analyzes, the book is a record of a search through the "intellectual byways of the last thirty years for a context for musical ideas that for the most part have been ignored by music theorists." Clarkson discusses these frameworks, leading the reader through the book and providing valuable interpretive exegesis. Both Morey and Clarkson confirm the idea that understanding Anhalt's work has as much to do with words as with music. On a different but no less interesting plane, Helmut Kallmann provides an informative description of the Anhalt fonds at the National Library of Canada (NLC). As Kallmann demonstrates, the NLC fonds (one of the largest in the Music Division, containing papers and documentation spanning Anhalt's entire life) is not only an invaluable resource for Anhaltian research, but a creative work in itself. Part 3 concludes with a text by Anhalt's longtime friend and colleague, American composer George Rochberg. Here Rochberg comments on his own and Anhalt's roots and creative pathways, as well as Jewish identity.

Part 4 contains a number of writings by Anhalt. For the most part these have not been previously published. The first chapter deals with Anhalt's first three operas, their genesis, and content. This is followed by two talks given by Anhalt – one, a "dialogue with the self" on *Traces (Tikkan),* and the other, reflections on ideas of memory and his orchestral piece, *Simulacrum.* We have then included two texts in which Anhalt describes, respectively, the background and "terrain" of three vocal pieces, and an ideological thread from some of his early works through to the present. This part concludes with the libretto of Anhalt's fourth opera, *Millennial Mall (Lady Diotima's Walk),* followed by the composer's commentary. The book ends with a list of Anhalt's compositions and writings, both published and unpublished.

Pathways and Memory consists of articles of varied lengths, modes of perspective and styles of writing. To facilitate reading the book in different ways, we have provided complete bibliographic listings in endnote format for each essay, rather than a single bibliography at the end of the book. Unless otherwise specified, the dates of Anhalt's compositions refer throughout the book to a work's completion, not its first performance. The diverse mix of styles in the book (including Anhalt's own voice) is deliberate, in a sense testing the borders of scholarly discourse in Canadian music. Important also, the inclusion of Anhalt's voice acknowledges that writing about his own music, thereby elucidating crucial stylistic and contextual patterns, is a vital part of Anhalt's creative process. *Istvan Anhalt: Pathways and Memory* can be read in different ways, inviting juxtapositions and evoking alternative models of location and analysis. Homogenized historical patterns in both Western and Canadian art music may be disrupted, or at least challenged through these textual processes. It is our hope that the book fulfills some of these aims, and that in offering this particular way of looking at Anhalt's life and music, we might rediscover (in the words of Simon Schama) "not just what we already have, but also that which eludes our recognition."[2] In such an interpretation, *Pathways and Memory* can be read as more than collective explanations of what has come before. Inspired by Anhalt's ongoing probing into sites of the past, the not so distant past, and the present, these texts also may be considered as explorations leading to new landscapes of music and meaning.

NOTES

1 The spelling Istvan has been adopted throughout the book in preference to István, reflecting Anhalt's own usage in more recent years.

2 Simon Schama, *Landscape and Memory* (New York: Alfred A. Knopf, 1995), 18.

Istvan Anhalt with his maternal grandmother, Helén Herzfeld, 1923
(Gerberholin Photographer; Istvan Anhalt Fonds, National Library of
Canada, no. 17512)

Family photograph, with friends, Budapest, 1922. Left to right: Fanny Dénes, Ödön Dénes, Katalin Herzfeld (mother), Imre Dénes, Istvan Anhalt, Lajos Heller, Magda Dénes, Béla and Helén Herzfeld (maternal grandparents)

Arnold Anhalt (father of Istvan Anhalt), Budapest, 1922

Istvan Anhalt during student days at the Franz Liszt Academy
of Music, Budapest, 1938 (Istvan Anhalt Fonds, National
Library of Canada, no. 22174)

Istvan Anhalt and Beate Frankenberg; wedding picture in the
Frankenberg home, Montreal, 6 January 1952

Istvan Anhalt checking parts of the Symphony before the premiere, Montreal, 1959
(Istvan Anhalt Fonds, National Library of Canada, no. 22177)

Istvan and Beate Anhalt with their daughters, Helen (age 3; right) and
Carol (age 1; left), Montreal, 1956

Istvan Anhalt with Marius Constant in 1975 at the time of the premiere of *La Tourangelle*

Istvan Anhalt with Theresa de Kerpely, Cape Cod, 1981 (Istvan Anhalt Fonds, National Library of Canada, no. 22175)

Istvan Anhalt with Elmer Iseler at the reception following the premiere of *Winthrop*, Kitchener, Ont., 6 September 1986 (to the right is Louis Applebaum) (Photograph by Walter Curtin)

Istvan Anhalt with Valdine Anderson (soprano) and Bramwell Tovey (conductor) at the premiere of *Millennial Mall (Lady Diotima's Walk)*, Winnipeg, 30 January 2000

Istvan Anhalt with his grandchildren
Left to right: Claudia Greaves, Walker Jordan, and Astrid Greaves

PART ONE

Life Lines

1 Life in Europe (1919–49)

ROBIN ELLIOTT

Anhalt is an uncommon family name, and among people of Jewish origin it is exceptionally rare. In the course of his own casual but fairly extensive genealogical research into his family origins, Istvan Anhalt uncovered only one other Jewish family of that name in Europe, located in Poland.[1] According to an unsubstantiated and likely unprovable story told to Anhalt by his father, the family ancestors came from Dessau, the town where the princes of Anhalt-Dessau had their residence.[2] As the name Anhalt was reserved for members of the ruling family in Dessau, it must have been adopted by Anhalt's ancestors only after they left Germany at some undetermined point in the past, perhaps as recently as the middle of the nineteenth century.[3]

It is certain that by 1865 Anhalt's ancestors on his father's side had arrived in Hungary. The birth registry of the Budapest Israelite Community records that Anhalt's paternal grandfather, Simon Anhalt, was born on 24 January 1867 to Philipp Anhalt and his wife Betty Kontes.[4] Simon became a *shochet* (kosher butcher) for the Jewish community of Budapest. He and his wife Berta (née Weisz) lived in the Jewish quarter, near the Great Synagogue on Dohány Street.[5] Simon did not worship at the Dohány Street synagogue though, because it was home to the Neolog community (Hungarian Reform Jews), while he was a member of the smaller Orthodox community.[6] He worshipped at a synagogue in his neighbourhood. Anhalt as a ten- or twelve-year-old child also attended on occasion: "I recall visits, during the High Holidays, to my paternal grandfather, as he, clad in his white death-shroud, was praying, chanting, swaying in the tiny, smelly, orthodox synagogue, with the cantor belting out coloraturas and everyone vocalising individually."[7] Anhalt has described Simon and Berta Anhalt as "working-class, more-or-less poor, devoutly Jewish ... with little cultural vista beyond things orthodoxly Jewish."[8]

Anhalt's maternal grandparents both came to Budapest from the Hungarian countryside. His maternal grandmother, Helén Weinberger, was born in 1877 in Bajmok in south-central Hungary. Her family was thoroughly assimilated. Four of her five siblings converted to Catholicism and married Catholics, but Helén married a Jewish man, as did her sister Berta. Béla Herzfeld, Helén's husband, was born in 1870 in the village of Látrány in Somogy county in southwestern Hungary.[9] He was a grain merchant in Budapest, which in the 1890s had become the largest flour-milling centre in Europe. Anhalt recalls him as a generous and passionate but also loud and volatile man.[10] Béla and Helén Herzfeld lived in Pest at 1 Rudolf Square, near the Danube River shore and the bridge to Margaret Island. Katalin, their only child, "was persuaded to change her maiden name Herzfeld to the Gentile/Hungarian-sounding Harmat (dew), perhaps 'on the way' to conversion."[11] The Herzfelds, unlike Anhalt's paternal grandparents, were Neolog Jews and non-observant in their religious attitudes.[12]

Anhalt's father, Arnold, was born on 3 February 1894 in Budapest. Arnold Anhalt did not follow the example of his parents in matters of religion; in fact, he was not at all religious, although he did observe the High Holidays and saw to it that his son had a proper bar mitzvah. He was an avid reader, and a keen amateur musician. After completing his high school education, he worked for much of his life as a modestly paid bookkeeper. For a time he held a job with Lajos Heller, a broker at the Budapest Grain Exchange and an intimate friend of and boarder with the Herzfelds. Arnold Anhalt married Katalin Herzfeld/Harmat in 1916, and the newlyweds moved into a flat in the same apartment building as the Herzfelds, at 1 Rudolf Square. Arnold, with his poor, Orthodox Jewish background, seems not to have gotten along very well with the more urbane, middle-class Herzfelds. His in-laws felt that Arnold did not provide well enough for his family (he was poorly paid, yet not infrequently gave money to his financially hard-pressed siblings), and this led to arguments, flaring tempers, and soon enough to separation and divorce. One shouting match between Arnold and his father-in-law was interrupted by the infant Istvan, who retrieved a tube of toothpaste from the bathroom and squirted it on the men's trousers.[13] Arnold moved back in with his parents and was unemployed for a while, but eventually got a job with a Mr Steinitz, who was to become his second father-in-law as well as employer.

Katalin was the same age as Arnold (she was born in Budapest on
26 October 1894). After the separation, she remained in the Rudolf
Square flat. Still a young and attractive woman, she received the atten-
tions of various suitors, and then, in the summer of 1925, remarried.[14] Her second husband was Sándor Somló, who had been born
into an Orthodox family in Munkács in the eastern Carpathians, but
later moved to Budapest and joined the milieu of the assimilated
Neolog Jews of the capital. He operated a law practice out of the flat,
with Katalin acting as his legal secretary. The couple had no children.

The Budapest in which Anhalt's grandparents and parents lived and
worked was home to a flourishing Jewish community. Jews had begun
to settle in Pest after Joseph II's Edict of Toleration in 1782, and they
acquired equality of rights in the year that the Austro-Hungarian Empire was formed, under the terms of the Emancipation Law of 22 December 1867. Budapest itself was formed in 1872 from the union of
Buda, the old city built on the hills of the right bank of the Danube,
with Pest, a modern, rapidly growing commercial centre on the flat expanses of the river's left bank.[15] By 1910 Budapest's 200,000 Jews
made up just over 23 per cent of the city's population.

Although serfdom had been abolished in 1848, Hungary was still a
semifeudal society. Most of the people were rural peasant farmers, or
landless sharecroppers living in poverty, while a small number of aris-
tocratic landowners, some of whose estates encompassed hundreds of
thousands of acres, owned a huge proportion of the land. The population of Budapest doubled between 1870 and 1900, but 95 per cent
of Hungary's population was still rural. Only 45 per cent were Magyar,
5 per cent were Jewish, and the rest belonged to other minority national groups. The middle class was concentrated in Budapest, and
many of its members were Jews. Jewish aristocrats were not unheard
of, as titles of nobility in the Austro-Hungarian Empire were sold to
wealthy Jews because the Magyar ruling class needed their voting support to maintain the existing political and social structures of Hungarian society.[16]

This whole edifice collapsed like a house of cards in the year before
Anhalt's birth. At the end of the First World War the tie to Austria was
severed, the Hapsburg emperor abdicated, and in November 1918 a
centrist coalition government under Count Mihály Károlyi proclaimed
Hungary a liberal republic.[17] Early in 1919 the population of Budapest
was swollen by returning soldiers, and refugees from the provinces. A
shortage of food led to discontent, looting, and violence, and the fail-
ure of the Károlyi government to obtain a peace treaty led to its fall. In
March 1919 the communists under Béla Kun came to power. During
five months of communist rule, Hungary became a Soviet-style socialist

republic: titles and rank were abolished, large industries were national-
ized, land was confiscated, and so on. In August 1919 the Kun government in turn collapsed when the Romanian army entered Budapest.
The next government, under István Friedrich, lasted less than four
months before it too was swept from power by an army under Admiral
Miklós Horthy.

On 1 March 1920 Horthy was installed as regent, and promptly set
about turning the clock back. As George Gabori has written, "he was
the regent of a nonexistent monarch, an admiral without a navy in a
country with no seacoast. It was all a far cry from Western democ-
racy."[18] Indeed, Horthy wielded virtually dictatorial powers as the head
of the armed forces and also the head of state, with the power to ap-
point prime ministers. The hierarchical social structures and outward
trappings of the Hapsburg monarchy were restored, but it all rang
somewhat hollow. As the writer Sándor Márai noted, it was "an *ersatz-
hierarchy* ... artificial, hence lamentable and laughable."[19]

Though Horthy was all-powerful within Hungary, he was unable to
defend the country's interests when the peace treaty was finally signed
on 4 June 1920 at the Trianon Palace in Versailles. Under the terms of
the Treaty of Trianon, Hungary lost over two-thirds of its prewar land
area and three-fifths of its population. Political life in Hungary for the
next two decades was driven by irredentism, the relentless drive to
undo the terms of the Treaty of Trianon in order to restore Hungary's
lost territory. This ceaseless quest would eventually drive the country
into the arms of Nazi Germany.

Jews occupied many of the leading positions in the Károlyi and Kun
governments, and extremists held them to be responsible for all of the
troubles in the immediate postwar period. The accepted and in some
instances even privileged position that Jews had held in the Austro-
Hungarian empire quickly came to an end. When Horthy's counter-
revolutionary forces took over, a period of terrorist reprisals claimed
an estimated 3,000 Jewish victims. Arthur Koestler noted that the beginning of the Horthy era, "with its organized pogroms, with its bombs
thrown into synagogues, its torture chambers and man-hunts, [gave] a
nasty foretaste of things to come."[20]

It was in the midst of this era of unprecedented political and civic
turbulence that Istvan Anhalt was born in Budapest on 12 April 1919,
during the Kun regime. Anhalt's parents separated when he was still
an infant.[21] According to the terms of the divorce settlement, he was to
remain with his mother until he was eight, and then move in with his
father,[22] but in the event things worked out differently. When his father finally remarried in 1931 – his second wife was Elisabeth (Bözsi)
Steinitz, the stepdaughter of his boss – Anhalt did leave his mother's

home to live with his father for a while (at age twelve rather than eight). A few years later, though, he moved again, to live with his maternal grandparents, the Herzfelds, at 10 Pozsonyi út, where he stayed until he was called up for labour service duty in December 1942. Close quarters and financial troubles at his father's household, combined with a strained relationship with his stepmother and the birth of his half sister Judit in 1935, all contributed to Anhalt's decision to move in with his grandparents.[23]

Despite family upheavals and financial difficulties, Anhalt remembers his childhood as a happy and secure time.[24] There were regular visits to Margaret Island, a 200-acre island park in the middle of the Danube, which has been a summer playground since ancient Roman times.[25] Annual trips were made to the resort town of Siófok on Lake Balaton. On occasion holiday journeys took him further afield, to the North Sea and to visit relatives in Transylvania and in Berlin. And visits to the Beketoff Circus in Budapest introduced the young Anhalt to the inspired antics of the famous Swiss musician and clown Grock.[26]

Anhalt attended elementary school from 1925 to 1929. By his own report, he was a rather indifferent pupil during those years.[27] Essays dating from the spring of 1929, during Anhalt's last term of elementary school, give an indication of the kind of education he was receiving. The ascendant Hungarian policy of irredentism is evident even here in the microcosm of a schoolboy's essay. Alongside innocuous offerings such as "The Animals of the Forest" and "How to Protect Ourselves from the Flu," is an essay entitled "Our Flag," which states "I hope that soon the red-white-green flag will flutter across the whole of Greater Hungary." An essay about Fiume, an Adriatic seaport that once belonged to Hungary, notes that "the peace treaty of Trianon attached Fiume to Italy. But we shall never abide this. Never, never, never."[28] The extent to which the nine-year-old schoolboy was influenced by this transparent attempt at indoctrination is now impossible to judge, but soon enough it would be made clear to him that the goals of the Hungarian establishment in no way coincided with his own. For the time being, he managed to please the educational authorities sufficiently well in order to get the marks needed to enter the Dániel Berzsenyi Secondary School on Markó Street.[29] He began his studies there at the age of ten, the usual age for a boy to start gymnasium.

Educational standards in Budapest were extraordinarily high at the time; minimum standards for secondary schools were set by law, and it was a fiercely competitive environment. Many writers have observed that a disproportionately large number of accomplished intellectuals came from the ranks of the Budapest middle class in the early part of the twentieth century, and more particularly from the ranks of the assimilated Jewish population of the city.[30] Science and music, being internationally transportable disciplines, were especially cultivated. Raphael Patai theorizes that Jews had to excel in order to prove themselves indispensable to Hungarian society at large; they could achieve this "by demonstrating that they were able to make valuable contributions to all aspects of Hungarian life ... and that therefore they amply deserved to be accepted by Gentile Hungary as equals in every respect."[31] He adds that "these circumstances placed a premium on ability and performance; they constituted a challenge to achieve excellence, and the Hungarian Jews responded to it by actually rising to preeminence." Patai also notes that "once this pattern was established, many of them could not resist the lure of the West with its broader horizons, greater opportunities, and richer economic and intellectual rewards."[32] This was the path that so many followed, among them the scientists Dennis Gabor, Leo Szilard, Edward Teller, John (János) von Neumann, and Eugene (Jenö) Wigner, and the conductors Antal Doráti, Eugene Ormandy (Jenö Blau), Fritz Reiner, Georg Solti (György Stern),[33] and George Szell. It was also the path that would eventually lead Istvan Anhalt to Canada.

There were three types of secondary schools for pupils from ages ten to eighteen: the *Gymnasium*, which emphasized Latin and Greek as preparation for a career in the humanities; the *Realschule*, which specialized in science and modern languages; and the *Real-Gymnasium*, a mixture of the two. The official name of the school Anhalt attended was Berzsenyi Dániel Real-Gimnázium, and Anhalt has referred to it as "a compromise between the 'classical' gymnasium and ... the 'real' school."[34] The Dániel Berzsenyi school, founded in 1858, was not considered to be one of Budapest's top schools, but it still took good marks and some influence to be admitted. Anhalt's mother and stepfather "somehow found 'access' to a higher government functionary, who agreed to 'put in a good word' "[35] for Anhalt, and he was admitted to the school, where he remained for all eight years of his secondary school education.

It was while attending the Dániel Berzsenyi school that Anhalt became aware of the growing anti-Semitic tendencies in Hungarian society. The first law with anti-Jewish content had been passed as early as 1920 – it was the *Numerus Clausus* Act of 1920, which restricted the admission of Jews into institutions of higher learning to 5 per cent.[36] No such restrictions governed secondary schools, though. In the Dániel Berzsenyi school, Anhalt has estimated that about 30 per cent of the boys in his form were Jewish.[37] It was a boys' school, and the pupils were all given weekly military training.[38] The Jewish boys were segregated and they exercised with shovels, while the Christian boys were given wooden rifles.[39] It was uncannily prophetic of the labour service system introduced in 1939.

Nevertheless, Anhalt's memories of his school days are positive, and he has stated that he never heard an anti-Semitic remark from any of his classmates.[40] The friendships he made at the school (e.g., with Tamás Földesi, who became an electrical engineer and worked in Moscow and later in Budapest, and with Aristides Vértes, who became an entrepreneur and worked in Egypt and South America before settling in New York) were of great importance to him, although his closest friendship during those years was with László Gyopár, who was from a nearby school.[41]

Anhalt's secondary school studies came to an end when he graduated in 1937. His career at the Dániel Berzsenyi school had been an uneven one; at the lowest point, he had received failing marks at midterm one year in art and religion,[42] but thereafter he recovered his standing and even excelled in history, geography, and Italian. Given the exacting standards that were in place at the time, it is perhaps no exaggeration to state that a first-rate intellect was shaped during these years. And music was already the absorbing interest of this lively mind.

Anhalt's mother was not particularly musical, although she did have some interest in opera and serious music, and there was always a piano in her flat. Anhalt's father "had a deep sensitivity and love for music ... He was a self-taught violin player and had an 'ear' for harmony,"[43] but did not have the opportunity for proper musical training. Anhalt has written evocatively of his own childhood musical fantasies and interests, which preceded any practical instruction.[44] Some of his earliest memories are of pretending to control the flow of the music while listening to outdoor concerts on Margaret Island. The child was indeed the father of the man, if one can judge from an early experiment on the household piano: "But one day, I clearly recall it, I brought a knife to the piano and poked the blade into the slot between two adjacent keys to find the sound that must be there. Instead, a dull thud only ... No *real* sound was to be found in the crack ... Disappointing ... There *ought* to be something, I thought. Perhaps one could find it in another way, perhaps on another day."[45] Piano lessons began at about age six with a teacher in the neighbourhood.[46] The studies continued with another teacher who was a friend of the family (Anhalt recalls that "she was an uninspiring teacher who taught me an unchallenging, old-fashioned repertoire"),[47] but the lessons ended at age twelve because of a lack of money and interest.

A serious engagement with music was kindled four years later by a chance meeting with a peer whose attainments in composition far surpassed Anhalt's own, arousing his admiration. At an interschool cultural meeting, Anhalt heard a boy from a neighbouring school play on the piano a piece that he had written himself in the style and idiom of a Bach two-part invention. In an instant, Anhalt's own immature musical efforts and his dream, fuelled in part by his stepfather's enthusiasm, of becoming a Broadway musical composer were set aside, and a new resolve was formed. Anhalt would meet this young performer and learn how to write music like he did. The young man's name was László Gyopár, and the two became fast friends.[48]

Soon after meeting Gyopár, Anhalt began taking private harmony lessons twice a week for an hour with Géza Falk.[49] He also audited Zoltán Kodály's class for a year (1936–37) before sitting the Franz Liszt Academy of Music's entrance exam, which was administered by Kodály and his colleague Albert Siklós. Gyopár, who was a year older than Anhalt, had already passed the exam and was a pupil in Kodály's class. In the fall of 1937, Anhalt also passed the exam and joined his friend as a pupil at the academy.[50]

The National Royal Hungarian Academy of Music opened in 1875, in the same building in Pest where its first president, Franz Liszt, and its director, Ferenc Erkel, had apartments. In 1907 it moved to its present location at Liszt Ferenc tér and was renamed the Franz Liszt Academy of Music. University status was granted in 1919. The academy's most influential composition teacher of the older generation was the Bavarian musician Hans (János) Koessler (1853–1926), a cousin of Max Reger and a disciple of Brahms. He taught in Budapest from 1882 to 1908 and again from 1920 to 1925. Two of Koessler's pupils were the guiding lights of the academy during Anhalt's years there: Ernö Dohnányi, who was the director from 1934 to 1941, and Kodály, who had taken over the first-year composition class from Koessler himself in 1908. (Kodály in turn relinquished the class in 1940; Anhalt was one of his last composition students.) A third Koessler pupil, Béla Bartók, was appointed to a piano professorship in 1907, but left the academy in 1934. Albert Siklós, who until his death in 1942 shared the composition teaching duties with Kodály at the academy, was another Koessler pupil. (Anhalt, during his final year as a pupil at the academy, also studied composition with Siklós, and remembers him as a fine teacher.)

Koessler and many of his colleagues at the academy, such as Robert Volkmann and Viktor Herzfeld, were not only German-born but also taught in German; indeed, Koessler never learned Hungarian. The next generation of teachers was Hungarian, and they reshaped the course of instruction to reflect Magyar musical traditions. Early in his teaching career, Kodály outlined his educational principles: "We have to assimilate all that is best in the musical heritage of Western Europe.

I am doing my best to help my students to master the polyphonic style … Indeed, in this, I go further than anyone has ever done in this country, or even than is customary abroad. But our job is to turn out musicians who are not only European, but also Hungarian … It is only by a fusion of the traditions of both Europe and Hungary that we shall obtain results that are valid for Hungarians … Unless we are content for it to be confined to a small circle of people versed in foreign culture, the musical life of our country must be steeped in folk music."[51]

Anhalt has explained that Kodály's aims and goals, though lofty and praiseworthy in the abstract, nevertheless were not ones that he felt he himself could share in: "While I greatly admired him for what he stood for, early enough it became clear to me that his programme could not have the same relevance for me as it held for most of my fellow students … In the centre of Kodály's life-work stood the ideal of Hungary's cultural renaissance. Unquestionably a most admirable goal, I thought. But for me this presented a problem. How could I, I told myself, regarded, as I was at the time, in the country where I was born, as a person not fully acceptable in the political sense (and soon after increasingly also in the social sense), for the sole reason of belonging to a certain minority religious faith, how could I make this goal also mine?"[52]

Anhalt's ambivalence about adopting Kodály's vision of a Magyar musical identity, then, arose in large measure from the increasingly anti-Semitic nature of Magyar society at large. The Hungarian Parliament passed its first blatantly anti-Jewish law in May 1938. Kodály, whose first wife Emma (?1863–1958) was Jewish, was among those who protested against this law.[53] Kodály presumably regarded anti-Semitism as an unwelcome growth that was alien to Hungarian society, but for Anhalt it was an endemic part of it. In any event, protests against the first law were futile, for further anti-Jewish laws were enacted in May 1939 and August 1941 (these were the very years of Anhalt's studies at the Academy of Music). Dohnányi was also opposed to these measures, and resigned his post as the director of the Academy of Music in 1941 rather than follow the edicts of the third anti-Jewish law.

Despite these abhorrent laws, many Jews continued to think of themselves as Hungarians first and Jews second. Anhalt has written that his own mother regarded the events of those years as an aberration, and throughout her life regarded herself as "a real, bona fide Hungarian."[54] Many Jews, including Anhalt's mother, stepfather, father, stepmother, and half sister, converted to Christianity in an attempt at avoiding persecution during these years.[55] (Under the terms of the third anti-Jewish law, however, all recent Christian converts were classified as "racial" Jews.) In his youth Anhalt himself wished to distance himself from his own Jewish background,[56] but he did not convert to Christianity. Nevertheless, it was becoming impossible for him to ignore or escape from his status in Hungarian society at large.

Although he did not share Kodály's large-scale cultural and educational vision, Anhalt did find intellectual nourishment and stimulating company elsewhere during his student years. At the centre of his circle of friends was the young poet Gábor Devecseri, a star pupil of the brilliant classical scholar Károly (Carl) Kerényi, who lectured at Pázmány University. Devecseri's fiancée Klára was a music education student at the Academy of Music, and it was through her that Anhalt was drawn into this group of young intellectuals and artists. Other members included János-György Szilagyi (later head of the antiquities section at the Museum of Fine Arts in Budapest, and a world authority on Etruscan art), who became a lifelong friend,[57] and, on the periphery of the circle, the poet Sándor Weöres, whose poetry Anhalt – along with Kodály, György Ligeti, and András Szöllösy – set to music. Anhalt felt it was "a charmed circle" and "close to the best that then existed in Hungarian culture."[58] He also found pleasure at this time in intimate relationships with women, first with Marika Hoffman, a violinist and fellow student at the Academy of Music (and later the concertmaster of the Honolulu Symphony), and then with Genevra Gorst, a stepdaughter of the eminent cellist Jenö de Kerpely, who was co-founder of the famous Waldbauer-Kerpely Quartet and taught at the Academy of Music.

After completing the course of studies at the Academy of Music, Anhalt received his diploma on 14 June 1941, with first-class marks in all subjects. He then prolonged his studies for a year and a half by taking classes in folklore and Turkish linguistics at Pázmány University and attending a conductor's seminar given by János Ferencsik. It is from this period that Anhalt's earliest preserved compositions date (*Six Songs from Na Conxy Pan / Hat Dal Na Conxy Panból*), a song cycle for baritone and piano to poems by Sándor Weöres, was begun in 1941, though not completed until 1947 in Paris. The second song is dedicated to Klára Devecseri. *Ünnepek (Feasts)*, a choral suite in three movements, was also begun in 1941 and completed the next year. The second movement of the work (the only one which has been performed to date, by an amateur choir in Budapest) is a setting of a poem by Gábor Devecseri, who in 1945 dedicated his poem " *Szél*" (Wind) to Anhalt.[59] During this period Anhalt also completed a string trio, a fugue for solo violin, a suite for piano, and a solo cello sonata, but these works were all subsequently lost.

Anhalt's student life suddenly came to an end on 1 December 1942, when he received a notice in the mail summoning him immediately to labour service duty. This odious but mandatory slavery would last for two years and almost cost him his life.

The Hungarian labour service system had gone into effect on 1 July 1939.[60] At first it was planned as an alternative to military duty for young men who were deemed to be in some way unfit for regular service. Then in August 1940, the Ministry of Defence issued a secret decree making the labour service system mandatory for all Jewish men, and in August 1941 the term of duty was set at two years. In the meantime, though, the political and military situation in Hungary changed drastically. With the assistance of Nazi Germany, Hungary had acquired land from Czechoslovakia in 1938, Slovakia in 1939, Romania in 1940, and Yugoslavia in 1941. In return, Hungary aligned its foreign and domestic policies ever more closely with Nazi Germany, and in June 1941 it declared war on the Soviet Union, just five days after the Germans had done so.

The fate of Jewish men assigned to labour service duty varied greatly, but was in no case enviable. In the worst instance, the servicemen were sent to the front lines to provide logistical support for fighting units. Some 50,000 labour servicemen were sent to the Ukraine with the Second Hungarian Army, for example; most were killed when the Soviets attacked at Voronezh on 12 January 1943 and decimated the Hungarian forces. Anhalt's unit was based at Bereck in the southeast Carpathian mountains, near the Romanian border.[61] It was sent to Elöpatak in Transylvania (where Anhalt wrote his first poem, "Mirage in Elöpatak," on 1 August 1943),[62] then to Volóc in Ruthenia, and finally in March 1944 to Stanislau, Poland (now Ivano-Frankovsk in the Ukraine). The work involved heavy physical labour for ten to twelve hours per day, six or seven days per week. Despite the hardships, Anhalt was able to stay in contact with his family in Budapest, sending postcards to them regularly and receiving from them clothing and food packages.[63] He was even able to visit with them a few times, either when on leave in Budapest or when they travelled to the Carpathians to visit him there.

Anhalt's company of about 250 to 300 men included several who, like him, survived the war and later emigrated to North America: to Montreal, Paul Rubinyi (a chartered accountant), András Gábor (an obstetrician), and Gábor Komáromi (who later became Anhalt's mother's personal physician); George Webber (an eminent cancer researcher) to Indianapolis; and László Birek (a doctor) to Toronto in retirement. Others were not so fortunate; Anhalt's close friend László Gyopár was stricken with uremia and died in Poland during a forced march, either from illness and exhaustion, or possibly after

being shot by a guard. Years later, Anhalt paid a special tribute to the
memory of Gyopár. After emigrating to Canada, he asked Gyopár's
father to have a professional copy made of Gyopár's *Missa* (1942), a
substantial work of over one hour's duration for soloists, chorus, and
orchestra. (Gyopár, though of Jewish birth, had converted to Christianity.) Anhalt held onto the score over the decades and, finally,
after the momentous political changes that occurred in Hungary in
the 1990s, was able to arrange for a performance of the work. This
was achieved with the assistance of various people in Hungary, notably the musicologist and composer András Szöllösy, who had been a
fellow student with Gyopár and Anhalt and later a teacher at the
Academy of Music. The premiere of Gyopár's *Missa* took place at the
Mátyás Church in Budapest in 1994, within the framework of the
Budapest Spring Festival. It was the fiftieth anniversary of Gyopár's
death.[64]

It was while Anhalt was doing labour service duty that the genocide
of Hungarian Jewry began. Having learned that the Hungarian government was secretly conferring with the Allies about the possibility of
making a separate peace and extricating the country from the war,
Germany occupied Hungary on 19 March 1944. Two days later Adolf
Eichmann arrived in Budapest to oversee the extermination of the
Hungarian Jews. The systematic mass deportation of the Jews began
on 15 May 1944. About 95 per cent were sent to Auschwitz, where the
camp commandant Rudolf Hoess had made large-scale preparations
for their mass murder. By 7 July 1944, when Admiral Horthy suspended the deportations, 437,000 Jews, including 50,000 from
Budapest, had been sent to Auschwitz.

The summer of 1944 was a temporary reprieve for the Hungarian
Jews. Horthy dismissed the most outspoken pro-Nazi members of his
government on 17 August, and a week later Eichmann left Hungary.
On 22 September, the Red Army broke through into the Hungarian
plain, and on 11 October Hungary concluded a preliminary armistice
with the Soviet Union. On 15 October 1944, Horthy broadcast news of
the armistice, but before it could take effect the Germans, along with
the Nyilas (the Hungarian Fascist Party), staged a coup. The Nyilas
leader Ferenc Szálasi was made prime minister, and Horthy was exiled
to Germany. Eichmann returned to Budapest, and the deportations resumed. Although the Red Army was closing in on Budapest, the persecution of the Jews continued. When it was no longer possible to send
the Jews to Auschwitz, they were used as slave labourers to build
ditches and fortifications for the defence of Budapest. Even as Budapest was falling to the Soviets, thousands of Jews were sent on forced
death marches to Austria to dig trenches for the defence of Vienna.

The siege of Budapest began on 24 December 1944. While Soviet troops attacked the city mercilessly, unparalleled terror reigned within the city. Nyilas thugs roamed the streets and took the law into their own hands, summarily executing any Jews that they could round up. Pest fell to the Soviets and the Jewish ghetto was liberated on 18 January 1945, but Buda held out for nearly another month before it finally fell on 13 February. When the last German troops left Hungary on 4 April 1945, there were 144,000 Jews remaining in Budapest and about 50,000 to 60,000 in the provinces. (The European campaign of the war ended a little over a month later, with Germany's unconditional surrender on 7 May 1945.) Randolph L. Braham has estimated that the overall losses of Hungarian Jewry during the war amounted to 564,507.[65]

It is likely that actions taken by Anhalt in the summer of 1944 saved his life. His labour service unit had retreated from Poland into Hungary. It was stationed in the eastern Carpathians and the Red Army was not far away. Finding himself alone in a wooded region of the Carpathian foothills as the straggler at the end of the marching column one day, Anhalt threw himself into a water-filled ditch and hid there for hours, finding refuge with a peasant couple that evening. A few days later, though, he was forced to go to a nearby military hospital for medical treatment, as he feared that the pain in his lower limbs (caused by infected lacerated skin on both legs) might be a sign of blood poisoning. After convalescing for a month in the hospital, Anhalt was sent under escort to another more humane labour service unit.[66]

While marching to the Austrian border in the late fall of 1944, Anhalt's new unit passed through Esztergom, a town on the Danube River north of Budapest. On the night of 30 November, Anhalt escaped from the barn in which his unit was billeted and fled to a nearby monastery of the Salesian order of St John Bosco. There he was provided with papers and a train ticket to Budapest. After staying for one night with the de Kerpely family (the parents of his former girlfriend Genevra Gorst, who was now married to Károly de Csipkay), he found his way to the central home of the Salesian order in Rákospalota in the southeast corner of Pest. There he met Pater János Antal, the superior of the order, who provided him not only with temporary accommodation, but also a priest's cassock and better identity papers.[67] Now disguised as a Salesian priest, Anhalt was free to find his way around Budapest and contact family and friends.

After leaving the Salesian house, Anhalt returned to the de Kerpely home on the Rózsadomb (Mount of Roses) at the northern end of Buda for refuge. The de Kerpelys provided safe haven under the most dangerous of circumstances for the remainder of the war. The household at that time included Jenö de Kerpely, his British-born second wife Theresa, Genevra Gorst de Csipkay (Theresa's daughter by her first husband) with her husband and two young children, and Genevra's younger sister Nina. Years later Theresa de Kerpely described the household's wartime experiences in her novel *A Crown for Ashes* (in which Anhalt figures as a Jewish music student named Andrew Marton) and in her autobiography *Of Love and Wars*.[68]

Over the years, Anhalt kept in touch with the de Kerpelys and with Pater Antal. The de Kerpelys emigrated to the United States in 1948, and Jenö joined the faculty at the University of Redlands in California, where he was a member of a piano trio. Anhalt wrote his Piano Trio (1953) for Jenö's ensemble and dedicated the work to the de Kerpelys. Jenö died in 1954, but Theresa lived on until August 1993 and became a frequent correspondent and intimate friend of Anhalt. Pater Antal was transferred after the war to the Salesian order's central house in Turin, Italy, and until his death exchanged letters with Anhalt. In gratitude for Pater Antal's courageous assistance during the war, Anhalt dedicated the musical tableau *La Tourangelle* (1975) to his memory.

During a visit to Israel in 1992, Anhalt learned about the Yad Vashem memorial institute,[69] which bestows recognition upon righteous Gentiles who saved Jewish lives at great personal risk to themselves during the Second World War. He made application to have the de Kerpelys and Pater Antal receive this recognition. This was duly granted to Pater Antal posthumously, and to Theresa de Kerpely in a ceremony held in Boise, Idaho (where she was then living, at age 94) on 2 April 1993.[70]

Anhalt's wartime experiences, incidentally, were very similar to those of the composer György Ligeti, who is four years his junior. Ligeti was conscripted into labour service duty in January 1944, and he deserted from his unit a month or so before Anhalt did. Ligeti's opportunity came during a battle in October 1944, when he fled and escaped on foot to Transylvania, which was then under Russian occupation. He spent the remainder of the war in Cluj, and was ill for much of the time with pleurisy, a recurrent illness that he picked up while in forced labour service.[71] The two men did not know each other at the time, though; they first met in Cologne in 1958.

After nearly three years of musical silence enforced by his wartime experiences, Anhalt found early in 1945 that he could once again attempt to make music:

On the day the war ended for me I found myself in a house, close to the top of one of the scenic hills that constitute much of Buda. On the second floor of that house, that bore the scars of the just ended battle, there was a grand piano that remained incongruously intact amidst the rubble. I sat down in front of it. First, for a while, I savoured the silence around me ... Then I began to play, trying to give expression to an incipient sense of relief and hope, but, at the same time, still feeling the anxiety that was my steady companion for so long. I began to improvise. What I wanted to hear was this: an excited, almost ecstatic, chirping and cackling of soaring birds and a symphony of tolling bells, at times quasi-human in character, speaking of jubilation and also of tears. Alas, my fingers were stiff and my musical mind not in tune as yet either, and the actual sounds that emerged from that piano were a disappointment ... I stopped ... hoping for another occasion, on another day, when I might succeed in finding the right tones ... (After fifteen years, and in a new country, Canada, I did manage to realize the piece: it is my *Electronic Composition No. 3*, subtitled *Birds and Bells*.)[72]

A few days later Anhalt came across a sight that became engraved upon his mind permanently. While walking through the bombed-out streets of Buda, he was stopped dead in his tracks by a grim scene: "On the roadway, half buried in the mud, lay the quasi-two-dimensional distortion of what must have been a man. He was wearing the uniform of a German soldier."[73] Although profoundly shaken and revolted by the sight, Anhalt also reflected on its significance and meaning: "What did he do to deserve this? Who was he? I found myself *wanting* to believe that he was an ss murderer who was lying here, flattened to a 'pancake' by a passing tank ... But I couldn't, I still am not, cannot be certain of this. How much choice did this 'pancake man' have in doing what he did in the course of the war? How much was it up to him to chose *not* to do what was alien to his nature, mind, values, beliefs? ... I often thought of that terrible sight which ... I came to associate in my mind with *decision and the consequences that may accrue from it*."[74] From the pancake man Anhalt learned to reflect carefully on every action, as sometimes even simple actions have grim consequences.

People slowly began to resume their lives amidst the rubble and ruins to which Budapest had been reduced as a result of the war. Most of Anhalt's immediate family survived the horrors of those years, with the exception of his paternal grandfather Simon, who died, possibly of starvation, in the Budapest ghetto on 9 January 1945. (His paternal grandmother had died of natural causes in 1936, as did his maternal grandfather in 1944.) Bözsi Anhalt, his stepmother, had been deported to Bergen-Belsen, but survived and returned to Budapest in 1945. Anhalt's father and half sister, and his mother, stepfather, and maternal grandmother all went into hiding in Budapest and survived the war. By the end of February 1945, Anhalt was living again with his grandmother and Lajos Heller in the flat at 10 Pozsonyi út.

The experience of living through the persecution and hardships of life as a Jew in Second World War Hungary transformed Anhalt in ways that can scarcely be imagined, much less understood. His account of a recurring nightmare about finding himself back in a forced labour camp under Nazi supervision is one indication of how the experience has left its mark.[75] More positively, he has found a way to exorcise the demons of those years through various creative endeavours – in the widest sense, in his life's work as a composer, but more narrowly, in his allegorical writings about persecution and times of tribulation, such as his fictional works "The Bridge" and "Indictment (An Old Story)," and the texts of his musical works *Thisness* and *Traces (Tikkun).*[76]

As the war was drawing to a conclusion, an opportunity for employment, or at least work experience, materialized. The Royal Hungarian Opera House, which had been renamed the Hungarian State Opera House, was rising up like a phoenix from the ashes of the ruined city. János Ferencsik, with whom Anhalt had briefly studied conducting, offered him a job as an unpaid *répétiteur* in February 1945. Dreams of rising through the ranks to become an opera conductor soon faded, however, when his short-term contract was not renewed in the summer of 1945. Anhalt learned that political reasons (i.e., his not belonging to the Communist Party) may well have contributed to his lack of success at the Opera.[77] This gave him pause to reconsider his future in Hungary.

Anhalt was not alone in weighing his options in the wake of the great changes that were taking place across Eastern Europe at the end of the Second World War. The writer Sándor Márai noted in his memoirs that when he first saw a Red Army soldier in 1945, he realized that this man represented a new dispensation that was rapidly evolving in Hungary, and that soon everyone would have cause to question their future: "Something had ended, an impossible situation had dissolved into a new, equally dangerous but entirely different state of affairs ... I understood that we must now answer a question. I couldn't put the question into words, but on this particular night, when a warrior from the East entered a dark Hungarian village – we 'understand' only what we see and touch – I felt in my bones that this young Soviet soldier had brought a question to Europe with him ... A power had appeared in Europe, and the Red Army was only the military expression of this power. What was this power? What was Communism? The Slavs? The East?"[78]

For most Hungarians, these questions boiled down to one immediate and pressing query, namely whether or not they could find a way to fit into the new society that was arising. For the vast majority of the population, the answer was yes – however qualified an assertion that turned out to be in the long run. Anhalt's father and stepfather, for example, soon joined the Communist Party and continued their pre-war lives and occupations as best they could under the new system that was materializing. Anhalt himself, though, came to the opposite conclusion. Sporadic but persistent outbursts of anti-Semitic agitation after the war, combined with his own sense that the political and so-cial system that was emerging was inimical to his hopes for freedom of choice and opportunity, led Anhalt to seek his fortune abroad.

The decision was more easily made than acted upon. Anhalt did not have a passport and so could not leave Hungary by official chan-nels. He had neither the money nor the connections to make a life for himself abroad, even if he could find a way of getting out of the country. If he were going to attempt to emigrate, clearly he would need some help. He turned to a Zionist organization, and soon found that he could leave as an adult "staff member" accompanying a small group of young orphaned children on a train to Austria. It would mean leaving behind his family, including his grandmother who was very ill, but it was a rare opportunity and he seized it. And so on the night of 22 January 1946,[79] with a small amount of money from his relatives and such of his possessions as he could fit into two suitcases, Anhalt set out from the South Railway Station in Budapest to begin a new life in the West. Although the future was fraught with uncer-tainty, the hope for freedom and the expectation of better opportuni-ties abroad led him on.

After a moment of uncertainty when the train was stopped at the border, the trip continued uneventfully, and a few hours later Anhalt arrived in Vienna. A stay of a few days at the Rothschild Hospital (the main screening station for displaced persons on the way to refuges in Germany, Austria, and Italy) afforded the opportunity to attend two performances by the Vienna State Opera which, like its Budapest counterpart, had been resurrected and was giving performances at the Theater an der Wien. Next Anhalt was taken by truck across the border into the U.S.-occupied part of Germany and relocated in a camp for displaced persons in Ainring, near Berchtesgaden (where Hitler had had his Eagle's Nest retreat). Despite his unsettled circumstances, An-halt enjoyed his new-found sense of freedom, and even managed to write some music: a Capriccio for piano on two manuscript pages dated 1 March 1946 was the first music he sketched after leaving Hun-gary.[80] He also put the time to good use by giving English lessons to fellow displaced persons (he had studied English for two years in Budapest and had put it to use in the de Kerpely-Gorst household) while improving his own command of the language by writing out a small Hungarian-English dictionary.[81]

Although his situation at Ainring was comparatively comfortable, Anhalt realized that he needed to leave there to begin his real life in the West. But how? He decided to give a piano recital, hoping that it might help in some way. And so it did; the concert caught the attention of a French officer of the United Nations Relief and Rehabilitation Administration, who asked Anhalt about his plans for the future. Anhalt replied that he hoped to travel to Paris to resume his musical studies. In the middle of March the official, on the way to a home leave in France, agreed to drive Anhalt to Strasbourg, and there he supplied him with a train ticket to Paris. A few days later Anhalt managed to obtain a *carte d'identité*, which legalized his presence in France.

Anhalt spoke scarcely a word of French, but fortunately he was not entirely without contacts in Paris. His stepfather's sister lived there with her husband and two grown children, and Anhalt stayed with them for a few days while finding his feet. He quickly received permission to audit classes at the Paris Conservatoire, and on the strength of this tenuous but semi-official student status, he became eligible to receive a small monthly stipend from the Union des étudiants juifs de France. The Union in turn arranged for him to have an interview at the Cité universitaire, as a result of which he was granted a residential place in the Maison de Monaco at 47, boulevard Jourdan.

Anhalt's objective in coming to Paris had been to study with Igor Stravinsky, but Stravinsky had decided to remain in California after the war. Nadia Boulanger, Stravinsky's friend and close professional associate, was accepting pupils, though, and Anhalt quickly arranged to study with her. By the middle of April he had begun private composition lessons with Boulanger, and she became a second notable influence on his development as a composer. In an interview Anhalt once reflected upon the differences between his two famous teachers: "Kodály was very aloof, almost to the extent of being unapproachable, but he was a great man and a profound scholar. Boulanger was entirely different. She was very approachable, very warm, understanding and interested in the students. The great musical mother."[82]

Boulanger had only just returned to Paris herself when Anhalt began his lessons with her. In July 1940 she had left France to spend the war years in the United States. Upon her return in January 1946, she immediately moved back into her apartment at 36, rue Ballu and resumed giving private lessons and holding her famous Wednesdy afternoon classes in analysis and sight-singing. During the war, her old friend Claude Delvincourt had become the director of the Paris Conservatoire, and thanks to him she now began teaching there for the first time. (Before the war she had taught at the École normale de musique.)

Boulanger's biographer Léonie Rosenstiel noted that "Nadia dogmatically divided all music students into three categories – talented pupils with no money, moneyed pupils with no talent, and pupils with both talent and money – always adding ruefully, 'And *those* I never get.'"[83] Anhalt fell into the first category, and it is to her credit that Boulanger taught him for nearly three years without ever charging any fee. Despite her negative feelings about Jews and her belief that they had little talent for creative ability, she was warm, open, and an encouraging and helpful teacher to Anhalt, as she had been to her previous Jewish pupils.[84]

Boulanger was still an internationally respected teacher after the war, but she was no longer the shaping force in music that she had been between 1920 and 1940. Olivier Messiaen (who coincidentally was Boulanger's parish organist) had begun teaching at the Conservatoire in 1942, and many leading figures of the younger generation were flocking to him rather than to Boulanger. Pierre Boulez was emphatic and polemical in his view: "After the war, Messiaen and Leibowitz were the important figures and no one had any use for Boulanger."[85] Boulanger, for her part, had no use for Schoenberg and his school (Anhalt quickly learned to keep his own interest in Schoenberg to himself); Stravinsky continued to be her guiding light, and her resistance to twelve-tone music and its practitioners was unshakable. Nevertheless, she continued to attract much new talent, including Claudio Santoro from Brazil, Gian Carlo Menotti from the United States, Pierre Mercure from Canada, Karel Husa and Anhalt from Eastern Europe, and Henry-Louis de La Grange (one of her rare pupils with both talent and money) from France.

Anhalt had been well trained in traditional compositional techniques under Kodály, and so after just a few set assignments, his lessons with Boulanger were given over to "free" composition. Under her tutelage, he produced *Concerto in stilo di Handel* in 1946. The work was in the nature of a pastiche, but Anhalt soon became disenchanted with its idiom and discouraged performances of the concerto (successfully so to date; the work has never been performed). He also completed a string quartet under her direction (Boulanger referred to it as *"très remarquable"*),[86] and a piano sonata, which was reworked in 1951.[87] In 1947 he completed the *Six Songs from Na Conxy Pan*, a work to which Boulanger reacted very positively. She arranged for the noted bass-baritone Doda Conrad to sing the premiere of the work, which took place in a semi-public concert-broadcast for the Radiodiffusion Française program "Tribune des jeunes compositeurs" in May 1948.[88] Anhalt accompanied Conrad at the piano. The event was mounted like a legal trial, with the composition as the evidence, music critics putting the case for the defence and the prosecution, and the audience as the jury. Among those in attendance was Pierre Boulez. Shortly after this event, the *Six Songs from Na Conxy Pan* were sung by Anhalt, accompanied by a Conservatoire colleague, in a private concert that also featured Boulez performing his Piano Sonata No. 1.

But Anhalt's studies with Boulanger were not all that occupied him during his Paris sojourn. He still wanted to keep as many options open as possible, and so continued his piano and conducting studies. (Anhalt had no ambitions to become a concert pianist, but he recognized that any good conductor, or indeed composer, should attain a degree of proficiency at the instrument.) On Boulanger's advice, he went to Soulima Stravinsky (Igor's son) for piano lessons. Soulima Stravinsky was also something of a composer, and so the piano lessons soon turned into discussions of contemporary music and composition rather than piano technique.

Conducting he pursued rather more seriously. In October 1946 he took part in a competitive entrance exam at the Conservatoire and won one of the two places available for foreigners in the class of the eminent French conductor Louis Fourestier. For a time conducting vied with composition as a possible career choice. Early in 1947 Anhalt seriously considered emigrating to South Africa and got a letter of recommendation from Fourestier for a conducting post there, but nothing came of that opportunity. Nevertheless the conducting studies continued, and on 14 April 1948 Anhalt took part in a UNESCO-sponsored concert by student conductors, with a Conservatoire orchestra; his chosen work was Mozart's *Don Giovanni* overture. On 13 July 1948 he received a diploma *"premier accessit"* in orchestral conducting from the Conservatoire.

The taste of freedom that Paris offered, combined with successful progress in his studies and optimistic hopes for a good career in music, brought concomitant benefits to Anhalt in his personal life. The young music student quickly found his feet and made many new friends and acquaintances. Among those in his circle were the French composer Raymond Depraz, the Hungarian-Jewish pianist Pierre Mosonyi, and André Schimmerling, who was at the beginning of his career as an architect. There were also intimate relationships with women – he enjoyed reciprocal friendships of varying kinds and intensity with at least half a dozen young women during the thirty-three months that he spent in Paris. Two of these women became especially close friends:

Eveline Accart and Gaby Ly thi Ty. Accart became a composer and worked for many years in the ORTF (Office de radiodiffusion-télévision française); Anhalt spent two pleasant Christmas vacations at her parents' home in the south of France. Ly, a dentistry student from Saigon, lived with her twin sister at the Cité universitaire. Anhalt's relationship with her lasted the better part of two years, but ended amicably when she gave up the idea of marrying Anhalt and acquired a French boyfriend instead. About the only dark cloud during these years for Anhalt personally was the passing away of his beloved grandmother Helén Herzfeld on 15 June 1947.

The state of Israel was founded on 14 May 1948, two years after Anhalt arrived in Paris. For many Jews who had survived persecution and hardship in Europe during the war, it was an opportunity to work together to build security for the future and help to create a Jewish state where the fear of anti-Semitism would never again be an issue. Mosonyi argued with Anhalt that the two of them ought to go to Palestine in 1947 and help work for the founding of the state of Israel. Anhalt wrestled with his conscience for a while, but in the end decided that Israel could manage without him, and that his own destiny lay elsewhere. Mosonyi, incidentally, came to the same decision.

In the fall of 1947 Anhalt's small but indispensable stipend from the Union des étudiants juifs de France was discontinued and he had to find another source of income. He learned that his friend Mosonyi was making money by singing in a vocal quartet in an orthodox synagogue on the rue Pavée, and Anhalt decided to apply for a position there. The cantor of the synagogue hired Anhalt to be the conductor of the little group, and this provided a modest but sufficient living income for the remainder of his stay in France.

The extra money came in particularly handy when Anhalt's father visited him for three weeks in the late summer or early fall of 1948. Arnold Anhalt stayed on a spare bed in his son's room in the Maison de Monaco, and the two had a wonderful time together getting caught up on each other's lives and interests. Sadly it was to be the last time that Anhalt would see his father. In 1955, while living in Montreal, he received a letter in the mail from his stepmother and half-sister informing him that his father had died of a heart attack at the age of 61. Bözsi Anhalt and Judit Anhalt have continued to live and work (until their retirements) in Budapest. Judit had an office job and in 1966 visited Anhalt for two months in Montreal. She retired in 1991 but has continued to work occasionally as a tourist guide.

By his second year in Paris, it was becoming clear to Anhalt that France had enough talented musicians of its own, and that for the sake of his career he should look into emigrating to another less musically developed country. As mentioned, an application for a conducting post in South Africa came to naught, as did inquiries into emigrating to Paraguay (the consul in Paris dissuaded him from emigrating there, saying it was not the right place for him). The fear of being stranded as a displaced person in Paris and the urgings of his stepfather led him to briefly consider returning to Hungary, but in the end that idea proved even less appealing than emigrating to Israel. As it turned out, events that were happening three thousand miles away would help to determine his future in an unexpected way.

In March 1948 Henriette Davis established the Lady Davis Foundation in Montreal; its stated aim was "to facilitate the entry into academic life in Canada of outstanding European scholars and scientists desiring to domicile themselves in this Dominion."[89] The intention was to assist displaced persons and refugee scholars in postwar Europe to find a new home in Canada. Beatrice R. Hayes, the wife of Saul Hayes (the executive director of the Canadian Jewish Congress at the time) was named the secretary of the foundation, and an advisory committee was set up, consisting of F. Cyril James, Vincent Massey, Ross Clarkson, and Lazarus Phillips. Outside advice was sought from various eminent people, including Albert Einstein. In the first 18 months of its operation, the foundation received 400 applications and gave out nearly $200,000 in grants and awards to a total of 64 refugee scholars, most of whom were scientists. Individual scholars or Canadian universities could make an application; for successful candidates, the foundation would pay for the scholar to travel to Canada and would also contribute $5,000 to $10,000 towards his or her salary. The university for its part had to offer a three-year academic appointment. A.L. Jolliffe, the director of the immigration branch of the federal Department of Mines and Resources, personally took charge of the immigration aspects of the foundation's candidates. (The foundation ceased to exist sometime in the 1950s.)

Anhalt learned of the Lady Davis Foundation through Lottie Levinson, who was representing the Canadian Jewish Congress in Paris through the offices of the Hebrew Immigrants Aid Society. Beginning in 1947, Anhalt visited Levinson every six to eight weeks, inquiring whether there was a chance of emigrating to Canada. The visits were without success until April 1948, when Anhalt invited Levinson to attend the concert in which he conducted the *Don Giovanni* overture. She came, and a few weeks later invited him to come to her office to fill out an application for the Lady Davis Fellowship.

In addition to the application form, Anhalt needed three letters of reference. A year earlier, Zoltán Kodály had visited Paris, and Anhalt had wisely used the opportunity to solicit a letter of reference from him. Nadia Boulanger and Louis Fourestier supplied the other two. The final page of the application required Anhalt to explain his plans for the work that he hoped to undertake in Canada. With the assistance of Lottie Levinson, who put his ideas into proper English, Anhalt outlined his hopes for the future: "In the first place the Fellowship would enable me to continue my composing. If I should be asked to teach in a Canadian school of Music, I would be able to teach the theory of music, counterpoint, fugue and composition ... My musical education is based on classical principles, in the meantime impregnated by progressive contemporary music (Béla Bartók; Igor Stravinsky). I wish to develop the unity of those in my work."[90] The completed application was sent off, and Anhalt proceeded to put the matter out of his mind.

The good news arrived via telegram, appropriately enough on Dominion Day, 1948: "LADY DAVIS FELLOWSHIP OF DLRS 5,000 PLUS FARE FROM PARIS AWARDED TODAY STOP LET ME KNOW WHAT FUNDS YOU NEED FOR TRAVEL EXPENSES STOP CANADIAN IMMIGRATION AUTHORITIES BEING INFORMED LETTER FOLLOWING = BEATRICE R. HAYES SECRETARY."[91] A letter was sent the next day confirming the cable, and a second letter sent on 18 August contained the added information that there was a place waiting for Anhalt on the staff of the Faculty of Music at McGill University. A delay of a few months ensued, as a routine medical exam at the Canadian Embassy in Paris unexpectedly produced a kink in the proceedings by showing evidence of a rheumatic heart. The file was submitted to London, but evidently did not alarm the authorities, for on 3 December 1948 a visa was issued by the Department of National Health and Welfare allowing Anhalt to travel to Canada.

At last everything was in order. The goodbyes to family and friends were made, Anhalt's modest belongings were packed up, and he set sail from Paris on board the ship *Scythia*. On 23 January 1949 he arrived at Halifax and was immediately granted landed immigrant status. A new life was about to begin in the New World.

NOTES

1 Istvan Anhalt, "An Interim Account of My Search for Genealogical Information Pertaining to My Family's Background" (Kingston, 1995, manuscript), 60–65. The Polish Anhalt family is from Ostrowo; its relationship (or lack thereof) to Istvan Anhalt's family has not yet been determined (ibid., 70).

2 Dessau (pop. 91,000) is the third-largest town in the German *Land* of Saxony-Anhalt. It was the birthplace of Kurt Weill (1900–50), whose father was chief Cantor at the local synagogue.

3 Documentary evidence places the Polish branch of Anhalts in Ostrowo as early as 1836–38 (Anhalt, "An Interim Account," 60–6).

4 Anhalt, "An Interim Account," 51, reproduces the birth certificate. According to information Anhalt found in the Mormon Family History Centre microfilms (nos. 064 2986 and 064 2987), Simon was one of nine siblings. Berta, the eldest child, was born in 1865 (ibid., 51a).

5 Construction of the Nagy Zsinagóga (Great Synagogue) on Dohány Street, the largest synagogue in Europe, was begun in 1844 and completed in 1859. See Raphael Patai, *The Jews of Hungary: History, Culture, Psychology* (Detroit: Wayne State University Press, 1996), 299–300 for the ground plan and pictures of the interior and exterior of the Dohány Street synagogue.

6 According to *Encyclopedia Judaica*, s.v. "Hungary," the Budapest Jewish community in the interwar period was 65 per cent Neolog, 29 per cent Orthodox, and 5 per cent status quo. The Hungarian Orthodox community was larger outside of Budapest, but many of the Orthodox centres of the period before the First World War were in areas ceded to neighbouring countries by the Treaty of Trianon.

7 Istvan Anhalt, letter to Alan M. Gillmor, 2 November 1987, quoted in Gillmor's "Echoes of Time and the River," in *Taking a Stand: Essays in Honour of John Beckwith*, ed. Timothy J. McGee (Toronto: University of Toronto Press, 1995), 38. The same recollection is told in a slightly different fashion in Anhalt's "From 'Mirage' to *Simulacrum* and Afterthought," a talk given at the University of Toronto on 5 January 1988, which is inserted in Anhalt's "A Weave of Life Lines" (Kingston, 1992, manuscript) on unnumbered pages after p. 302; the text of this talk is also contained in part 4 of this volume. The memory of these childhood visits helped to shape Anhalt's orchestral work *Simulacrum* (1986).

8 Anhalt, "A Weave of Life Lines," 38.

9 In Anhalt, "An Interim Account," 33, Anhalt notes that his Herzfeld ancestors were not, as far as he is aware, related to Viktor Herzfeld (1856–1919), a German-born musician who taught at the Franz Liszt Academy of Music in Budapest. Anhalt's Herzfeld ancestors likely came from the city of Pozsony (Bratislava; Pressburg) early in the nineteenth century (Anhalt, letter to the author, 28 August 1997). Béla Herzfeld's maternal ancestors, however, had resided in Látrány since the mid-eighteenth century (Anhalt, "An Interim Account," 13–29).

10 Anhalt, "A Weave of Life Lines," 67–8.

11 Anhalt, "An Interim Account," 40.

12 Anhalt, "A Weave of Life Lines," 393.

13 Ibid., 67. One is reminded of the incident that Mahler related to Freud about fleeing from his home as a child during a violent argument between his parents and hearing an organ grinder playing "O du lieber Augustin" in the street. This incident is often cited to explain why Mahler ironically juxtaposes intensely passionate music and simple folklike tunes in his compositions. For Anhalt, witnessing a loud family argument seems to have had personal rather than musical consequences, for it led to a lifelong desire to avoid scenes of violent confrontation.

14 The date of the remarriage is taken from Istvan Anhalt, letter to the author of 2 February 1996.

15 The Obuda suburb and Margaret Island were also amalgamated into Budapest in 1872.

16 After 1918, in smaller postwar Hungary, there was no longer need for Jewish support to assert a Magyar majority; this was one factor that may have contributed to the growth of anti-Semitism.

17 Anhalt, "A Weave of Life Lines," 121–3 provides a brief outline of historical events in Hungary from 1914 to 1945, mixed in with family history.

18 George Gabori, *When Evils Were Most Free*, trans. Eric Johnson with George Faludy (N.p.: Deneau Publishers, 1981), 3. Horthy's title of admiral had been earned in the service of the Austro-Hungarian empire.

19 Sándor Márai, *Memoir of Hungary 1944–1948*, trans. with introduction and notes by Albert Tezla (Budapest: Corvina / Central European University Press, 1996), 168.

20 Arthur Koestler, *Arrow in the Blue: The First Volume of an Autobiography: 1905–31* (London: Hutchinson & Co., 1969), 91.

21 In various autobiographical writings, Anhalt states that his parents separated after about six years of marriage when he was about four years old, but the judgment of the royal tribunal which dissolved the marriage is in the Anhalt fonds at the National Library of Canada, Ottawa (folder C1.1); it is dated 3 December 1920. For a description of the Anhalt fonds, see Helmut Kallmann's essay in this volume.

22 Anhalt, "A Weave of Life Lines," 69.

23 Ibid., 82.

24 Ibid., 108.

25 Raphael Patai, *Apprentice in Budapest: Memories of a World That Is No More* (Salt Lake City: University of Utah Press, 1988), 8–12 describes Margitsziget (Margaret Island) at the time Anhalt would have visited it as a child. Anhalt himself writes of his visits there in "What Tack to Take? An Autobiographical Sketch (Life in Progress …)," *Queen's Quarterly* 92,1 (spring 1985), 96–7, and in "A Weave of Life Lines," 488–9.

26 Istvan Anhalt, letter to Luciano Berio, 6 August 1974, Anhalt fonds, folder H2.18. Grock, whose real name was Charles Adrien Wettach (1880–1959), could play twenty-four musical instruments and often built his comic routines around musical performances.

27 Anhalt, "A Weave of Life Lines," 113–14.

28 Anhalt's translations of these essays are in the Anhalt fonds, Accession June 1993, folder 31.

29 Dániel Berzsenyi (1776–1836), after whom Anhalt's school was named, was a Hungarian author with romantic tendencies who wrote poetry in Greek and Latin verse forms. Zoltán Kodály set a poem by Berzsenyi, "The Approaching Winter," for voice and orchestra as the first part of his *Two Songs*, Op. 5.

30 See William O. McCagg, Jr, *Jewish Nobles and Geniuses in Modern Hungary* (Boulder, Col.: East European Quarterly; distributed by New York: Columbia University Press, 1972).

31 Raphael Patai, "The Cultural Losses of Hungarian Jewry," in *The Holocaust in Hungary: Forty Years Later*, ed. Randolph L. Braham and Bela Vago, East European Monographs, no. 190 (New York: Social Science Monographs, and Institute for Holocaust Studies of the City University of New York, and Institute for Holocaust Studies of the University of Haifa, 1985), 173.

32 Ibid.

33 Sir Georg Solti, with assistance from Harvey Sachs, *Solti on Solti: A Memoir* (London: Chatto & Windus, 1997), 1–44 provides a description of life in Budapest, including music studies at the Franz Liszt Academy of Music, during the period when Anhalt was growing up there. Anhalt met Solti, who was seven years his senior, at a Lake Balaton resort shortly before Solti left Hungary (Anhalt, "A Weave of Life Lines," 3; Anhalt dates the encounter in 1939 or 1940, but it must have been earlier, as Solti left Hungary in 1938).

34 Anhalt, "A Weave of Life Lines," 228–9.

35 Ibid., 231.

36 *Encyclopedia Judaica*, s.v. "Hungary." Patai, "The Cultural Losses," 166 notes that "the *Numerus Clausus* in the long run proved a blessing in disguise, since it forced many Hungarian Jewish high school graduates to seek higher education abroad in schools whose academic level was often higher than that of their Hungarian equivalents."

37 Anhalt, "A Weave of Life Lines," 230.

38 The training did not take place in the school; it was held in a separate location once a week for about two hours, after the school day was over (Anhalt, letter to the author, 28 August 1997).

39 Anhalt, "A Weave of Life Lines," 88.

40 Ibid., 235.

41 Gyopár attended the Bólyai Realschule, which was also on Markó Street, about half a block away from Anhalt's school.

42 Anhalt notes that the failing mark in religion may have been due at least in part to a class prank in which he participated that was perpetrated at the expense of the teacher, an elderly rabbi (Anhalt, letter to the author, 28 August 1997).

43 Ibid.

44 Anhalt, "What Tack to Take?" 96–7.

45 Ibid.; ellipses in original.

46 An early c.v. in the Anhalt fonds (folder C2.1) states that he began musical studies at age eight, but another early c.v. (folder C1.3) states that he had private musical studies from 1925 to 1938, and most of his later autobiographical writings state that the studies began at age six.

47 Anhalt, "A Weave of Life Lines," 413.

48 Anhalt, "What Tack to Take?" 99–100 and Anhalt, "A Weave of Life Lines," 2–28 describe Anhalt's relationship with Gyopár.

49 Anhalt has described Falk as "a little-known composer, but popular author [of] *The All-Knowing Musical Notebook* " (Anhalt, "A Weave of Life Lines," 83).

50 According to a recent account, Anhalt states that he was an auditor in Kodály's class in 1936 and that he was one of two pupils accepted into Kodály's class in 1937, the other being Pál Járdányi (Anhalt, "A Weave of Life Lines," 87, 238). But Járdányi seems to have entered Kodály's class in 1938 (John S. Weissman, "Pál Járdányi," *The New Grove Dictionary of Music and Musicians*, 9:555), and autobiographical materials in the Anhalt fonds (folders C1.3 and C2.1) dating from the late 1940s state that Anhalt began his studies with Kodály in 1938. Despite this inconsistency, Anhalt is quite sure that he began formal studies at the Academy of Music in 1937.

51 As quoted in László Eösze, *Zoltán Kodály: His Life and Work* , trans. István Farkas and Gyula Gulyás (London: Collet's, in cooperation with Corvina Press, Budapest, 1962), 67; ellipses in original.

52 Anhalt, "What Tack to Take?" 101.

53 Patai, *The Jews of Hungary*, 536.

54 Anhalt, "A Weave of Life Lines," 155.

55 Ibid., 393.

56 Ibid., 41–2.

57 Szilagyi, like Anhalt, was forced to enlist in a labour service unit during the Second World War. He spent several years in Russia as a prisoner of war before returning to Hungary and resuming his career.

58 Anhalt, "A Weave of Life Lines," 203.

59 Anhalt translated "Szél" into English in April 1997.

60 See Randolph Braham, *The Hungarian Labor Service System 1938–1945* (Boulder, Col.: East European Quarterly, 1977). A shorter, revised, and updated

version of this study appears as chapter 10 of Braham's *The Politics of Genocide: The Holocaust in Hungary*, rev. ed., vol. 1 (New York and Boulder, Co.: The Rosenthal Institute for Holocaust Studies, Graduate Center / The City University of New York, and Social Science Monographs, 1994), 295–380.

61 Istvan Anhalt, "About the 'Unidentifiable Righteous among the Nations' (A Personal Account)" (Kingston, 1999, typescript), 2–3 describes the humane actions of one of the conscripts in charge of this labour service unit, and the inhumane behaviour that was more characteristic of the other guards.

62 Anhalt translated the poem into English in 1985; it is reproduced in Anhalt, "A Weave of Life Lines," as an insert after p. 132.

63 The Anhalt fonds (folder H1.1) includes 88 postcards that Anhalt wrote while he was on labour service duty; 49 are addressed to Béla Herzfeld, 38 to Sándor Somló, and 1 to Arnold Anhalt.

64 Substantial documentation about this work, including the score, correspondence and press material pertaining to the premiere performance, and a video cassette of the premiere, are in the Anhalt fonds.

65 Randolph L. Braham, "The Losses of Hungarian Jewry: A Statistical Overview," in his *The Politics of Genocide*, 1,296–1,301.

66 This escape is described in detail in Anhalt's "A Brief Account of My Four Escapes (or Were There Five?)" (Kingston, 1995, manuscript), 1–11 and in Anhalt, "About the 'Unidentifiable Righteous,'" 4–7.

67 Uri Asaf, "Christian Support for Jews during the Holocaust in Hungary," in *Studies on the Holocaust in Hungary*, ed. Randolph L. Braham, East European Monographs, no. 301 (Boulder, Col. and New York: Social Science Monographs and the Csengeri Institute for Holocaust Studies of the Graduate School and University Center of the City University of New York, 1990), 65–112 lists ca 465 Christians who came to the aid of Jews (including those recognized by Yad Vashem) as "righteous Gentiles" by the end of 1987. The entry for János Antal (p. 68) reads: "Head of the Salesian house in Rákospalota. In that house many persecuted were sheltered and provided with Vatican safe conduct documents. Mr Antal was arrested but set free after the intervention of the Papal Nuncio."

68 Teresa Kay (pseud.), *A Crown for Ashes* (Milwaukee: The Bruce Publishing Co., 1952); Theresa de Kerpely, *Of Love and Wars* (New York: Stein and Day, 1984). See also Gillmor, "Echoes of Time and the River," 18–23. Gillmor notes that the character Andrew Marton is also partly based on Anhalt's friend László Gyopár.

69 Yad Vashem is "a 'multipurpose' institution: memorial, archive, research centre for Holocaust studies, and 'more'" (Anhalt, letter to the author, 28 August 1997).

70 Istvan Anhalt, "Memorandum RE: Pater János Antal" (Kingston, 18 November 1992, typescript), a document prepared for Yad Vashem; and Anhalt, "A Weave of Life Lines," 530–6. Anhalt subsequently applied to Yad

Vashem to have their Righteous among the Nations honour awarded to several other people who assisted him during his wartime experiences and escapes, but whose identities remain unknown. See Anhalt, "About the 'Unidentifiable Righteous among the Nations,'" 1–12.

71 Robert W. Richart, *György Ligeti: A Bio-Bibliography*, Bio-Bibliographies in Music, no. 30 (Westport, Conn.: Greenwood Press, 1990), 3–4. Ligeti describes his experiences as a Jew during the Second World War in "György Ligeti," in *Mein Judentum*, ed. Hans Jürgen Schultz (Stuttgart: Kreuz Verlag, 1978), 234–47.

72 Anhalt, "What Tack to Take?" 102; ellipses in the original. This experience took place on or about 13 February 1945; Anhalt was still living with the de Kerpely family at the time, in their home on Mandula Street, on the Rózsadomb (Mount of Roses).

73 Anhalt, "A Weave of Life Lines," 475.

74 Ibid.; ellipses in original. The financier George Soros has recounted a similar experience, though he does not seem to have reflected on it as deeply as Anhalt did: "immediately after the siege of Budapest ... there were lots of corpses lying about. There was one with its skull bashed in. I felt sick for a few days afterward." *Soros on Soros: Staying Ahead of the Curve* (New York: John Wiley & Sons, 1995), 30.

75 Anhalt, "A Weave of Life Lines," 413.

76 "The Bridge" was written under the pseudonym Tomás Couture-Smith and is in Anhalt, "A Weave of Life Lines," as an insert after p. 328; "Indictment (An Old Story)" is in Anhalt, "A Weave of Life Lines," 510–11.

77 Anhalt, "A Weave of Life Lines," 471.

78 Márai, *Memoir of Hungary*, 32–3.

79 In Anhalt, "A Weave of Life Lines," 100, Anhalt states that he left Hungary on "January 19th, 1946 (I think)," but an early c.v. in the Anhalt fonds (folder C2.1) states that he left Budapest on 22 January 1946 and arrived in Vienna the next day.

80 Capriccio is preserved in the Anhalt fonds folder 6.0.1.

81 The dictionary is preserved in the Anhalt fonds, folder C1.9. For more on this period of Anhalt's life, see Anhalt, "A Brief Account," 12–23.

82 In Leslie Thompson, "The Inspiration of a Composer," *Music Magazine* 3, 2 (March / April 1980), 25.

83 Léonie Rosenstiel, *Nadia Boulanger: A Life in Music* (New York and London: W.W. Norton & Co., 1982), 193.

84 Ibid., 197 states that "Nadia's self-control was so remarkable that apparently none of her Jewish students ever noticed any tinge of anti-Semitism in her behavior."

85 Boulez in conversation with Carlos Moseley, as quoted in ibid., 353.

86 Nadia Boulanger, letter of recommendation dated 3 September 1947, Anhalt fonds folder H2.20. An 83-page holograph manuscript score of the string quartet is in the Anhalt fonds, folder 3.1.7.

87 The 1947 version of the Piano Sonata (a 49-page score) is in the Anhalt fonds, folder 6.0.16; the 1951 version of the Piano Sonata (a 33-page score) is in folder 6.0.17.

88 Anhalt, "A Weave of Life Lines," 191, and p. 3 of Anhalt's Lady Davis Fellowship application (see n90).

89 "Report (1949) of the Lady Davis Foundation," located in the Anhalt fonds, folder C2.1.

90 Istvan Anhalt, Lady Davis Fellowship application, June 1948; ellipsis added. The original application is in Anhalt's staff file at McGill University; Anhalt was supplied with a copy of it in 1993.

91 The telegram is in the Anhalt fonds, folder C1.12.

2 Life in Montreal (1949–71)

ROBIN ELLIOTT

Anhalt's emigration to Canada was part of a significant postwar demographic movement. In 1946 the Canadian government approved emergency measures to allow the immigration of refugees and displaced persons in a belated attempt to make amends for having done so little to provide safe haven for the oppressed of Europe during the war. Between 1947 and 1952, over 165,000 people arrived in Canada under the terms of these emergency measures. Like Anhalt, the majority of them came by boat from Europe and were processed through Halifax's Pier 21, a large two-storey immigration building with barred windows on the waterfront in the south end of the city.[1] Pier 21 resembled a prison, both outside and inside – hardly an encouraging sight for frightened, tired, and disoriented immigrants – but for the 1.5 million people who passed through its doors from 1928 until it closed in 1971, any welcome was better than none. The *Scythia*, the ship on which Anhalt arrived, had seen much service during the war as a transport vessel for troops, war brides, refugees, orphans, and guest children. Anhalt was only too glad to leave it (and Pier 21) behind and begin his new life in Canada.

Anhalt arrived in Halifax on 23 January 1949 and immediately received landed immigrant status,[2] which allowed him to travel on to Montreal in order to begin his employment with McGill University. He travelled by train, and the experience seems to have left its mark; decades later Anhalt explained to Murray Schafer that the trip took on a kind of symbolic importance and even became linked in his mind much later with the musical style of his adopted country. Schafer related the story as follows: "I am reminded of a story István Anhalt told me about how he first became aware of the Canadian style in music. When he arrived from Hungary ... he took a train from Halifax to Montreal. All day he travelled through the woods of New Brunswick, seeing nothing but trees. Here and there he passed a grubby clearing with perhaps a sawmill or a gas station and a few squat houses, then more trees. When he first heard the music of John Beckwith his mind connected back to that experience. Here were bars of repetitious *ostinati* followed by a sudden wild modulation, then the relentless repetitions again. The music and the forest were companions; they intensified one another."[3] Anhalt carried with him on that journey his few material belongings, a small amount of money, a handful of his compositions and sketches, and great hopes for the future.

Upon arriving in Montreal, Anhalt checked into a rooming house on St Catherine Street, and the next day he visited Beatrice R. Hayes, the secretary of the Lady Davis Foundation. Hayes lent Anhalt, who had five dollars to his name, forty dollars to help him get started, and on that same day he moved into temporary quarters in the McGill Faculty Club on McTavish Street. When his first paycheque arrived, he rented a room on Van Horne Boulevard in Outremont, a predominantly French-speaking district of Montreal on the north side of Mount Royal. About a year later he sublet an apartment on Sherbrooke Street in Westmount, and then in 1951 he moved into an apartment over a dentist's office on Park Avenue, just east of the McGill campus.

Although Anhalt enjoyed the rank of assistant professor at McGill and was drawing a salary as a Lady Davis fellow, he had no teaching duties until September 1949, and so he had time to get settled in and acclimatized to his new environment. Anhalt has written about his initial impressions of the New World: "I remember my first days in Montreal, in that cold January of 1949. The city looked so different, so picturesque, unlike any other I had known before. For hours, I just kept walking the streets, hopping over mounds of snow, with an eye on the ever-present mountain, and another on the traffic. The neon lights gave the downtown a festive character that I associated in the old countries only with fairgrounds, public celebrations and the exterior of night-clubs. And there were the many churches, the numerous banks and the cornucopia in the stores."[4] Anhalt enjoyed a sense of security in this new environment: "I immediately felt very good here. At that time there was no flag, no national anthem that everybody could sing. Also, people made fun of nationalism in those days, which was very refreshing, and I felt that nobody could really do any harm to me under these conditions."[5] Given what Anhalt had recently lived through in Europe, and the terrible conditions he had experienced as a result of rampant nationalism in Hungary, the impact of these first impressions was all the more powerful.

The Montreal that greeted Anhalt in 1949 was a very different city from the one of today. It had celebrated the tercentenary of its founding in 1942, and was still enjoying what to all appearances seemed to be a permanent and divinely ordained status as Canada's largest city and economic powerhouse. The city's mayor, Camille Houde, had been arrested for treason during the war, but was returned to office for a further decade's service in 1944. Houde was loyal to the British crown and was made a CBE in 1935, but he had also been a fan of Mussolini and of Marshal Pétain's Vichy government.[6] The novelist Hugh MacLennan felt that Houde was the personification of Montreal, in all its contradictions: "No public figure has ever equalled Houde in his capacity to express Montreal's spirit of wit, tolerance, perversity, cynicism, gaiety, bawdiness, gallantry, delight in living and – make no error here – dignity."[7]

The political life of Quebec was in a scandalous state. In 1944 Maurice Duplessis had been elected to his second term as premier of Quebec, which lasted until 1959.[8] During Duplessis' dictatorial regime, known as La Grande Noirceur (the Great Darkness), political patronage grew to legendary levels, trade unions and civil liberties were subverted, and corruption was rife among politicians, the press, and the police. The Catholic Church exercised great power over people's lives in Quebec: it rigorously censored films, saw to it that the index of prescribed books was faithfully adhered to, and made it impossible to obtain a divorce unless a special act of the federal Parliament was obtained. Anti-Semitism was still quite widespread, although less prominent than it had been in the 1930s.[9] Yet despite it all, this was a period of prosperity and optimism, by and large, and most people were happy with their lot.

When Anhalt arrived in 1949, the population of Montreal was just over one million, about two-thirds French speaking and one-third English speaking. The English minority controlled business and finance in the city, and most did not bother to learn to speak French, a fact that was reflected in the predominance of English signs in the downtown area. As William Weintraub has noted, "An ambitious young person would have no need to speak French; in the Montreal of the time, anything one wanted to accomplish in life could be accomplished in English."[10] This included, of course, a university education, which was available in English at McGill.

McGill University was named after the Scottish-born fur trader James McGill (1744–1813), who in his will left forty-six acres of land on the southern slopes of Mount Royal and a sum of money as an endowment to found a university, stipulating that one college of the institution was to be named after him. A royal charter was obtained in 1821; Stanley Brice Frost notes that the charter came with a bill for £221.05, "so that devoid of funds as it was, the university commenced its career in debt."[11] (The money problems McGill experienced during Anhalt's time there had an impressively long history.) The charter named the new entity McGill College; it was expected that this would become a constituent part of a parent university with other colleges, but that never happened. The common designation for the institution was University of McGill College until 1885, when the name was changed to McGill University.

Music instruction at McGill began in 1884, but at first was offered to women only. The McGill Conservatorium of Music was founded in 1904, with Charles A.E. Harriss as the director and twenty-six instructors who were paid on an hourly basis to teach composition, theory, and performance. In 1908 the English cathedral organist Harry Crane Perrin succeeded Harriss as the director of the Conservatorium and at the same time became McGill's first professor of music. Under Perrin, a Faculty of Music was established at McGill in 1920, but it shared its budget, premises, and teaching staff with the Conservatorium. Douglas Clarke succeeded Perrin as the director of the Conservatorium in 1929 and as the professor of music in 1930, and he continued to serve in both of these capacities at the time of Anhalt's arrival.

When Anhalt reported for duty in 1949, the Faculty of Music was housed in the Workman mansion, a large, dilapidated Victorian house on the northwest corner of Sherbrooke and University Streets that had been in use for music instruction since the Conservatorium had opened in 1904. The university newspaper reported on the conditions there at the end of 1948: "To add to the already big problem of inadequate space, the building itself is settling in its foundations and is slowly slipping out into University street. The walls on this side of the building crumble regularly and have to be replaced at considerable cost to the University and considerable inconvenience to those using the building who must double up in their already crowded quarters during the alterations ... As for the equipment in the building itself, no one at present in the building remembers when the last piano was bought. The pianos made available to students in the basement for practice purposes are so old that the tuner claims he is unable to do anything with them."[12] The article was accompanied by numerous photographs of the crowded, dangerous conditions in the building. Shortly after this bad press, the Workman mansion was torn down (the Otto Maass Chemistry Building, erected in 1964, stands on the site today) and the Faculty of Music moved into Shaughnessy House on Drummond Street, north of Sherbrooke.

The music instruction available at McGill in 1949 must have seemed to Anhalt as peculiar and outdated as the building in which it was being offered. Clarke was still the only full-time member of staff, and he was a broken man suffering from alcoholism and shattered dreams. His main contribution to the musical life of Montreal had been to serve without remuneration as the conductor of the Montreal Orchestra from 1930 to 1941. As Eric McLean noted, though, Clarke "did not succeed in identifying with Canada, regarding himself instead as an Englishman residing abroad."[13] In particular, he did nothing to ingratiate himself with the city's French-speaking musical public, and so a rival orchestra was founded.[14] The city could not support two orchestras indefinitely, and with the collapse of his orchestra after the 1940–41 season, Clarke retreated to the safe harbour of his McGill professorship. He saw to it that the music curriculum at McGill remained firmly patterned on the example of the Cambridge University of his youth. However pertinent that model may have been to England in the 1920s, it was hardly what was needed for music education in postwar Canada.

When Anhalt began teaching at McGill in September 1949, his only duty was to give a one-hour composition class to the fourth-year B.Mus. students each week. As Anhalt recalls, there were five pupils in the class, and the total enrolment in all four years of the B.Mus. program at McGill was just twelve students.[15] With Clarke in charge, nothing was done to expand the numbers or improve the quality and relevance of the curriculum. Those tasks would fall to Anhalt and to three slightly older colleagues who were already in place at McGill when Anhalt arrived, and would still be there when he left: Helmut Blume, Alexander Brott, and Marvin Duchow.

Blume, a pianist and broadcaster, was born in Berlin in 1914 (five years, to the day, before Anhalt) and studied in his native city with Hindemith and in England with the Hungarian-born pianist Louis (Lajos) Kentner. He moved to Canada in 1940 and became an instructor at McGill's Faculty of Music in 1946, remaining for thirty years. Brott and Duchow were both born in Montreal, the former in 1915 and the latter in 1914. Brott, a violinist, conductor, and composer, was a graduate of the McGill Conservatorium and the Juilliard School; he joined the staff at McGill in 1939 and stayed there until he retired in 1985. Duchow, a musicologist and composer, was also a McGill Conservatorium graduate and had studied at the Curtis Institute and New York University. He was on staff at McGill from 1944 to 1978. All three men, like Anhalt, were more attuned than Clarke was to the growing and changing needs of McGill's Faculty of Music, but they were unable to act until Clarke retired in 1955.

Anhalt's term as a Lady Davis fellow lasted for three and a half years, from January 1949 to August 1952 (this included a one-year extension of the fellowship). His teaching duties remained the same during that period: a one-hour composition class each week. He also formed and conducted a small choir, which gave a few concerts, but his ambition to conduct professionally was laid to rest upon arriving in Montreal, in favour of pursuing his career as a teacher and composer. The light teaching schedule at McGill left him with a good deal of time on his hands, which he put to good use. In a newspaper interview given less than a month after his arrival, Anhalt said that his future plans included "the giving of concerts featuring contemporary French, English and Hungarian compositions."[16] He was not long in putting this plan into operation.

On 20 January 1950 Anhalt organized and participated in a concert that was given at Moyse Hall in McGill's old Arts Building. Anhalt took part in two works on the program: Stravinsky's Sonata for Two Pianos (1943–44) and Bartók's Sonata for Two Pianos and Percussion (1937), both receiving their local premieres. Anhalt and Jean-Marie Beaudet played the Stravinsky work, while Anhalt conducted Beaudet with Jeanne Landry and the percussionists Louis Charbonneau (just seventeen years old at the time) and John Nadeau in the Bartók performance. Anhalt recalls that the musicians had many rehearsals for the concert, without any remuneration.[17] Gilles Potvin in his review noted that Anhalt "led the musicians with meticulous precision," that the concert was "felt to be a milestone in musical experience here," and that the "reaction of the audience was very favourable."[18]

Anhalt returned to Moyse Hall on 20 March 1952 for a concert entirely devoted to his own compositions, all but one of them written or revised in Canada. The concert opened with "Journey of the Magi" for baritone and piano, a seven-minute setting of the poem written by T.S. Eliot in 1927. The work, completed less than two months earlier, was sung by Fadlou Shehadi, accompanied by Anhalt. (Shehadi was a Lebanese Ph.D. student in philosophy at McGill who had a well-trained lyric baritone voice.) The second piece on the program was *Funeral Music* (1951), which is dedicated to László Gyopár, Anhalt's close friend and fellow musician who had died in the forced labour service during the war. The work is scored for flute, clarinet, bassoon, horn, and two each of violins, violas, and cellos (for this concert the strings were not doubled).[19] Next came the first two of the *Three Songs of Love* (1951) for two sopranos and alto, sung by Jeanne Desjardins, Lucille

Gauvin, and Maureen Forrester (who was twenty-one years old at the time and still a student).[20] Before the intermission came *L'Arc-en-ciel* (The Rainbow) – ballet in three lights (1951) – a thirty-five-minute piece for two pianos, played by Dorothy Morton and Luba Sluzar. Though the ballet has never been performed on stage, there is a scenario, which revolves around the ancient Greek myth of the judgment of Paris. The musical idiom is indebted to Stravinsky, and the work was a kind of farewell to the influence of Nadia Boulanger. After the intermission, Charles Reiner played the 1951 revised version of the three-movement Piano Sonata that Anhalt had written in Paris, and Shehadi sang the *Six Songs from Na Conxy Pan.*

Ambitious as this concert was, it did not represent all of Anhalt's work as a composer during his first three years in Canada. At the end of 1949 he had completed a piece begun in Paris entitled Interludium, scored for strings, piano, and timpani. He sent a copy of the score to Henriette Davis and was pleased when she wrote back to say that she was "delighted to accept the dedication of the Interludium."[21] Another composition with a Lady Davis connection is "Sonnet" for mezzo-soprano and piano, completed on 8 February 1951; the text is by Beatrice Hayes. A cantata to texts by Walt Whitman for SATB choir was begun in 1949, but was left incomplete after twenty-six pages of score had been composed. Finally, two shorter pieces were written in 1951: "Seu Scheorim" for SATB choir and organ, and "Psalm XIX – A Benediction" for baritone and piano, to a text by A.M. Klein from *The Psalter of Avram Haktani.*[22] These works resulted from Anhalt's contact with Temple Emanuel on Sherbrooke Street, and the second piece is dedicated to the synagogue's cantor, Otto O. Staeren.

Personal contacts were proliferating as quickly as compositions during these years. The first friendship that Anhalt made in Montreal came about as a result of an errand that Nadia Boulanger had asked him to perform. Boulanger had given Anhalt two small presents and asked him to deliver them to her godchildren, Nadia and Ghilaine Papineau-Couture, the children of the composer Jean Papineau-Couture and his wife Isabelle.[23] Within days of arriving in Montreal, Anhalt travelled to the Papineau-Couture home on Coolbrook Avenue in Notre-Dame-de-Grâce, and was accepted with open arms into the family. As Anhalt has noted, Boulanger "might have wanted to give me also a present: an introduction to one of the oldest and most prestigious families" of Quebec.[24] Through his contact with Papineau-Couture, Anhalt established good collegial relationships with two other important francophone composers in Montreal, Pierre Mercure and François Morel.[25] As a member of what would later be called the allophone community, Anhalt lived principally in an English language milieu, but with his Parisian educational background and fluent command of French, he functioned comfortably in both francophone and anglophone environments.

It was through Cantor Staeren, a Viennese-born, classically trained singer, that Anhalt made his most important contact during these years. Staeren invited Anhalt to dinner to meet Emma Frankenberg, a friend of his who was an artist and restaurateur, and a few months later, Frankenberg in turn introduced Anhalt to her daughter Beate. Emma Frankenberg had fled Nazi Germany with her husband Paul (who had owned a private bank in Berlin) and their two children, Beate and Herbert, early in 1939. After spending six months in Sweden, the Frankenbergs arrived in Montreal in August 1939, just one month before the war began. A year or so later Paul Frankenberg opened the Old Mill restaurant on Sherbrooke Street, which he operated, together with a partner, until his death in 1944.[26] Emma Frankenberg carried on the business until 1951.

Beate Frankenberg was born in Düsseldorf in 1924, but moved with her family to Berlin at age two. After emigrating to Canada, she completed her secondary school education in Montreal and went on to do an honours degree in science at McGill from 1942 to 1946, specializing in biochemistry. After graduating from McGill, she began working at Veteran's Hospital.[27] She met Anhalt late in 1949, but almost immediately left for three and a half months on a long trip to Europe. Upon her return, the two got together again, and after a courtship of about a year and a half they were married on 6 January 1952. Anhalt notes simply but sincerely that the marriage was "the happiest and most important event in my life,"[28] and that his relationship with Beate is "the foundation on which everything else in my life could be, and was, undertaken."[29] On their wedding day, the Anhalts moved into a home at 4921 Clanranald Avenue in Notre-Dame-de-Grâce, which they rented from Emma Frankenberg, who had bought the house for that purpose. Exactly one year after the wedding, their first daughter, Helen, was born, and in 1955 a second daughter, Carol, arrived. On 20 May 1955, just a little over a month after the birth of Carol, Anhalt became a Canadian citizen.[30] In 1958 the house on Clanranald Avenue was sold and the family moved into a more spacious house at 464 Claremont Avenue in Westmount, which they again rented from Emma Frankenberg.

Meanwhile, with the expiry of his Lady Davis Fellowship in August 1952, Anhalt was faced with the task of finding a way to support his wife and growing young family. On the advice of Douglas Clarke, he kept his toe in the door at McGill by serving as a part-time instructor of composition and piano between 1952 and 1956, but that did not pay enough to make ends meet. (Ironically, when a better position did become available, it went to Octavia Wilson, who had been Anhalt's pupil at McGill.[31]) To bring in some sorely needed extra income, Anhalt taught piano privately for a few years, travelling to his pupils' homes to give the lessons. To facilitate this peripatetic vocation, he bought his first car in 1953, a second-hand two-door Pontiac. He drove this beauty home after receiving a thirty-minute driving lesson, his first and only such instruction, from the salesman who had sold the car to him.[32] A year or so later he borrowed the money for another large purchase, a 7'2" Steinway grand piano, which he still owns.

Anhalt put on a third concert at Moyse Hall on 6 December 1954, once again devoted entirely to his own compositions, all of them completed within the previous two and a half years. This concert was the penultimate event in a festival that took place in November and December 1954 to celebrate the fiftieth anniversary of the founding of the McGill Conservatorium. The program opened with Anhalt playing his own Fantasia for piano. George Little then conducted members of the Montreal Bach Choir in the first two of the *Three Songs of Death*. Next came the Piano Trio, played by the violinist Eugene Kash, the cellist Walter Joachim, and the pianist Charles Reiner. The concert ended with *Comments*, performed by Maureen Forrester with the same musicians that played the Piano Trio. With the exception of *Three Songs of Death*, the works were all receiving their first performance.

Three Songs of Death for SATB choir was written in the summer of 1952 and is dedicated to the memory of the Herzfelds, Anhalt's maternal grandparents. The first song is to a text by William Davenant, and the last two are to poems by Robert Herrick. (The second song, "The Bell-Man," was subsequently arranged separately for SATB choir, bells, and organ.) The Piano Trio, written in March 1953, is dedicated to the de Kerpelys, while *Comments*, written in August 1954, is dedicated to Maureen Forrester. The Fantasia for piano, Anhalt's first work to use twelve-tone techniques, became one of his most frequently performed pieces. In 1967 Anhalt dedicated the work to its most famous proponent, Glenn Gould, who had just recorded it for Columbia Records.[33]

All of the works featured in this concert, with the partial exception of *Comments*, looked backwards to Anhalt's experiences in Europe, and were rather sombre in mood. Indeed Thomas Archer in his review noted that "the whole mood of the concert ... was one of unremitting depression."[34] Ted Brown agreed with this judgment, writing that "the general impression was weighted with gloom," but added "this was by far the most consistently interesting evening so far in the festival; it has brought a remarkable composer into the public's eye."[35] Eric McLean wrote a detailed and thoughtful critique of the concert for *the Montreal*

Star. His review of *Comments* (performed in the original version, which consisted of five songs; two of the songs were later cut) started as follows: "The cleverest item in this concert seemed to be the final group of five songs sung by Maureen Forrester with cello, violin, and piano accompaniment. This paper unwittingly contributed to the creation of these 'Comments' as they were called. Mr. Anhalt chose the texts from wire-service stories which appeared in *The Star* over the past year or so. Though this combination of words and music at first appeared as consciously nonsensical as the Dada movement, a closer study of the texts shows that a highly developed sense of the dramatic and the bizarre has governed the welding of the two."[36] McLean continued with perceptive observations about three of the songs, singling out the one about the death of Bali's leading dancer and the synopsis of the weather in Quebec and Ontario as the two strongest songs in the set.

Anhalt's exploration of twelve-tone techniques continued with his next two compositions – the Violin Sonata, completed on 21 November 1954 and dedicated to his father (who died the next year), and *Chansons d'aurore* for soprano, flute, and piano, written 13–19 June 1955. The song cycle, a setting of four texts by the French poet André Verdet,[37] was premiered in Montreal in 1955 by the soprano Marguerite Lavergne, the flautist Mario Duschenes, and the pianist Jeanne Landry. The second song of the cycle was later used (in a reorchestrated version) in Anhalt's Symphony. The Violin Sonata was not heard until 1957, when a performance by the violinist François D'Albert and the pianist Samuel Levitan was broadcast on the CBC radio program "Premieres." On the strength of these two works and the *Fantasia*, Anhalt was winning for himself a reputation as one of the leading Canadian practitioners of twelve-tone techniques.

Douglas Clarke's retirement from McGill in the spring of 1955 led to a long overdue reorganization of the Faculty of Music that would soon bring about an improvement in Anhalt's position there. Duchow, though neither as ambitious nor as forward as Blume or Brott, had planned wisely for Clarke's retirement. He had taken a year's leave of absence to do graduate studies at the Eastman School of Music in Rochester, New York, and was awarded an M.A. degree for his efforts in 1951. This made him the only one of the three pretenders to the throne with a graduate degree, and as a result he was made the acting dean in 1955, and went on to serve as the dean from 1957 to 1963. Duchow immediately North Americanized the Faculty of Music's administration and curriculum. Three separate departments were created within the faculty: theory, headed by Duchow; keyboard and vocal music, headed by Blume; and orchestral instruments, headed by Brott. Then in 1956, the McGill Opera Studio was founded, and in that same year the Faculty of Music began to offer three different specializations within the B.Mus. degree program: performance, composition, and school music.[38] The old British-style D.Mus. in composition, which had been offered since 1904, was dropped in 1955 (it would reappear in a new guise in 1974).

The most important development, as far as Anhalt was concerned, was that Duchow reappointed him to the rank of assistant professor in 1956. He was now on a year-round salary, making almost three times what he had been earning before as a part-time instructor on an hourly rate of pay. The days of giving door-to-door piano lessons were over.

In the same year as his reappointment, Anhalt worried about the consequences of the unsuccessful October uprising in Hungary against Soviet domination. None of his relatives left or were harmed, but among the 190,000 other Hungarians who fled the country at that time were several of his friends from the forced labour service, including four who arrived in Montreal: András Gábor, Gábor Komáromi, Paul Rubinyi, and George Webber (Webber later settled in Indianapolis).

Anhalt was grateful to Duchow for the improvement in his professional position, but at the same time he began to have some doubts about whether his own academic credentials were sufficient to ensure the further advancement of his career at McGill. Should he take the same route that Duchow had, and get a graduate degree? With this thought in mind, Anhalt travelled to Eastman to find out more about the graduate program there. But financially it was not feasible for him to take a year off to do a master's degree, and the thought of spending a year in Rochester provided further disincentive. Anhalt quickly hit upon an alternative plan: he would write a substantial work for full orchestra to prove his mettle, instead of pursuing graduate studies. All of his works to date had been scored for chamber forces. They had brought him to the notice of musical cognoscenti, but perhaps an orchestral piece would make his name known to the wider musical public, and at the same time solidify and enhance his growing reputation as one of Canada's leading composers working in a modern idiom.

The new plan was no shortcut to success; Anhalt worked on the orchestral piece for four years, from 1954 to 1958. The final manuscript copy of the work, in Anhalt's neat, meticulous hand, is 102 pages long, with up to 30 staves on each page. The 24-minute work is in a single movement of 629 bars, divided in the score into 13 sections. Yolande Rivard wrote that it "is essentially a series of variations. Indeed, the composer had first titled this work *Variations*. The music, written using serial techniques, is lively and expressive, and shows that the composer has easily mastered a difficult technique."[39] The Symphony is scored for triple winds, timpani, a battery of percussion instruments requiring three performers, celesta, piano, harp, and strings. John Beckwith concluded an analysis of the piece in 1960 by observing, "the work ... is commanding, difficult, original, deeply disturbing. It sets a high standard for orchestral production of the 1960's in this country."[40]

It was one thing to have completed a work of such scope and difficulty; it was quite another to get it performed. Orchestral programs in Canada (as elsewhere) were entirely dominated by music written before the war; as far as contemporary music was concerned, the philosophy was "the shorter the better." The chance of getting a full-length symphony for large forces in a demanding modern idiom scheduled as part of a regular concert program by one of Canada's leading orchestras was slim indeed.

Anhalt did get his Symphony performed, but not as part of a regular orchestral series. The performance came about in part because of his Lady Davis Foundation contacts. Saul Hayes, the husband of Beatrice Hayes, was the executive director of the Canadian Jewish Congress, which was planning to celebrate the bicentennial of Canadian Jewry.[41] As part of the celebrations, it was decided to give an orchestral concert in Plateau Hall, a concert auditorium that seated 1,300 people and was the home of the Montreal Symphony Orchestra.[42] It was further decided that the concert would feature the premiere of Anhalt's Symphony, conducted by the composer.

The first rehearsal for the concert took place in the big hall of the Jewish Public Library on 5 November 1959, just four days before the concert. Nearly forty years later, Anhalt recalled the excitement of that first run-through: "I immediately realized that ... the Symphony 'worked' ... actualizing [the] thought and feeling which I stored in its symbols. Musicians of the orchestra, a dozen or more, surrounded me in the intermission of that first rehearsal, shaking my hand, smiling ... it was wonderful."[43] But once the euphoria of that first rehearsal wore off, Anhalt realized that an extra hour of rehearsal time beyond what was planned would be needed in order to ensure a successful performance. There was no money in the budget for the concert to pay for that extra hour, so Anhalt contributed $800 of his own money for the rehearsal, even though his annual salary at the time was just $5,000. It was a difficult decision, but Anhalt felt that it was a make or break moment in his career and that the money spent would in the long run be a good investment.[44]

The strain of conducting the Symphony took a heavy physical toll. Anhalt wrote to John Beckwith that during the rehearsals "I conducted so arduously that ... [I] developed a terrific shoulder pain"; by the day of the concert, he added, "I could hardly lift my right elbow ... I spent the best part of [the day] in the Montreal General Hospital with x-rays, heat treatment and being massaged."[45] It is difficult to know whether Anhalt's condition was due to physical problems resulting from his conducting technique, or simply a result of strain and nervous exhaustion, but in any event he recovered in time to conduct the premiere on 9 November.

The investment did indeed pay dividends, as the Symphony was soon taken up by other conductors and was heard nationwide on radio broadcasts. The first of these took place on 18 May 1960 on the CBC program "Music of Today," when the work was performed by the Montreal Symphony Orchestra under the baton of Jean-Marie Beaudet. Then the work was offered international exposure when it was performed by the CBC Symphony Orchestra under Walter Susskind on 14 August 1960 in the fifth and final concert given during the International Conference of Composers held in Stratford, Ontario. The CBC orchestra was outstanding in the performance of new music, and the concert, which also included works by Otar Taktakishvili, John Weinzweig, Olivier Messiaen, and Wallingford Riegger, was recorded by Radio Canada International for distribution abroad. Marvin Duchow in an article about the conference for the *Canadian Music Journal* singled out the Anhalt piece for special praise:

In terms of the resources called for, and in terms of content and scope of expression, Istvan Anhalt's *Symphony* turned out to be one of the most impressive works of these concerts. Achieving textures and densities of an almost turgid richness, the work has, in my experience at any rate, an oddly protean quality. Thus, what had impressed me particularly in a previous performance of the *Symphony* was the total submergence and coalescence of its myriad thematic details into a sonorous unity of monumental proportions. Great was my surprise, then, when it revealed an equally impressive – but totally different, and almost Gallic – profile in the incisively outlined interpretation of Mr. Walter Susskind and the CBC Symphony Orchestra. Whatever the reading, however, this work must be accounted one of the very few substantial compositions of symphonic dimensions from the pen of a Canadian composer. [46]

The Stratford performance led to several important developments. In the first place, it brought Anhalt's Symphony to the attention of the delegates from twenty different countries who were attending the conference. The music critic Alfred Frankenstein singled out Anhalt as one of the composers whose music he especially liked.[47] George Rochberg, who developed a close friendship with Anhalt after meeting him at the conference, was so taken with Anhalt's Symphony that he included a quotation from it in his own Symphony No. 3.[48] Perhaps most importantly, Claude Champagne was also present for the performance and, in his capacity as editor for BMI Canada's series of publications by Canadian composers, was responsible for recommending that the composer's manuscript of the score be published.[49] This led to further international exposure for the work, including a positive review in the U.S. periodical *Notes*.[50] In 1967 Alexander Brott conducted a performance of the Symphony in Montreal, and the CBC International Service planned to make a recording of the work under Brott at this time, but Anhalt felt that the rehearsal time was inadequate and the project was abandoned.[51]

Anhalt made a number of other valuable contacts at the Stratford conference; in addition to Rochberg, he established friendly relations with the composers Joseph Tal of Israel, Aurelio de la Vega of Cuba (he had recently moved to California), and Edgard Varèse, whom Anhalt visited in 1962 at his Sullivan Street home in New York.[52] Luciano Berio, whose *Sequenza III* Anhalt was later to write about so perceptively, also attended the conference with his first wife, Cathy Berberian, but Anhalt seems not to have established contact with the couple at this time. A second piece by Anhalt was heard at the conference, in the session on synthetic means, when the Canadian engineer and musician Hugh Le Caine of the National Research Council (NRC) in Ottawa played an excerpt from *Electronic Composition No. 3* at the end of his presentation.[53] This piece, which Anhalt had only just completed, represented a compositional field that he was very preoccupied with at the time, namely electronic music.

Anhalt's first experience of electronic music occurred in 1957 when he heard a CBC broadcast of Karlheinz Stockhausen's early experiments in the field. As Anhalt later told Le Caine's biographer Gayle Young, "It was one of the strongest and most fascinating music experiences I ever had. It was so strong that I told myself, 'Well I really must see the place where this is made and I must meet the person who made that.' "[54] Before travelling to Europe, Anhalt was able to visit an electronic music studio closer to home. His mother-in-law told him that she had read in the *Montreal Gazette* of an electronic music studio in Ottawa. Learning that Le Caine had set this studio up, Anhalt arranged for a short visit to the NRC in the spring of 1958.

In the summer of 1958, Anhalt visited the two leading European electronic music studios of the day, the *musique concrète* studio headed by Pierre Schaeffer in Paris, and the Studio für elektronische Musik at the Westdeutscher Rundfunk (WDR) in Cologne, where Stockhausen was working. In Paris, Anhalt had also arranged for a reunion with his mother, whom he had not seen since leaving Budapest in 1946. Within days of Anhalt's arrival in Paris from Montreal and his mother's arrival from Budapest, however, the political situation in France grew very tense. A right-wing military and civilian revolt in the French colony of Algeria was threatening to spread to Paris. This led to the fall of the Fourth Republic, and General Charles De Gaulle was installed as premier with dictatorial powers for six months to deal with the situation. It was all quite unsettling, and after a brief and not very informative meeting with Pierre Schaeffer, Anhalt and his mother quickly travelled on to Germany.[55]

The week that Anhalt spent in Cologne was much more productive, both professionally and personally. He spent a lot of time in the WDR studio learning about the intricacies of manipulating sound on tape, and made friendly contacts with Stockhausen, György Ligeti, Gottfried Michael Koenig, and Hans Helms, all of whom he corresponded with after returning to Canada. Koenig in particular spent a lot of time in the studio with Anhalt, explaining and demonstrating various ideas about electronic music and playing for him Stockhausen's *Gesang der Jünglinge* (1957) in the studio where it had been created.[56] Anhalt found Helms, a poet, author, composer, and linguist, to be the friendliest of the group around Stockhausen. Helms's letters to Anhalt are full of multilingual wordplay and are peppered with shrewd comments on the European avant-garde artistic circles of the day.[57] The entire experience was so stimulating that Anhalt returned to Cologne in 1960 for a second visit.

Meanwhile, in the summer of 1959, Anhalt was appointed to the position of "visiting scientist" by the National Research Council (NRC), which entitled him to a small salary and full access to the NRC Elmus lab. The Ottawa facilities were measurably superior to what was available in Europe, but still had something of a makeshift nature about them. When Anhalt needed an echo chamber, for instance, the NRC staff rigged up a loudspeaker and microphone connection in a large washroom. The catch was that this facility could only be used after 5:00 P.M., when the other NRC employees had left for the day and the automatic flushing mechanism could be disconnected![58] Anhalt returned to the NRC studio for more creative work in the summers of 1960 and 1961, but without the visiting scientist designation, which in any event had only been a bureaucratic solution to allow a non-NRC employee to have access to the facilities.

In the summer of 1961 Anhalt visited two other leading facilities, the Columbia-Princeton Electronic Music Center, located on the campus of Columbia University in New York City, and the Bell Telephone Laboratories in Murray Hill, New Jersey. He then made his fourth visit to the NRC studio. Earlier that year he had written a short but engaging account of the history and nature of electronic music, including Canadian contributions to the field. In that article, Anhalt's sense of the artistic limitations of pure electronic music is already evident:

> In the early "Fifties" composers, engaged in work with electronic music, were enthusiastic about the prospects of the field. The talk was of marvelous and novel sounds in abundance: truly, the sky seemed to be the limit. When, however, it was found that "novel" sounds are, indeed, very difficult to come by and the limited output of the workers in the field already showed heavy reliance on clichés, a more sober outlook has been adopted with respect to the potential of the thus far employed means and techniques. The experiencing of these very difficulties was of great importance: it demonstrated that natural noises, traditional musical and speech sounds are of hitherto unsuspected complexity. In comparison to natural sounds most electronic sounds seemed, indeed, rigid, and lacking "expression." These insights are giving, at present, an impetus to research in the field of electronic music, and also bring about a new understanding of certain aspects of music by traditional means. [59]

This was a statement of Anhalt's own beliefs as much as an objective statement of fact. After completing four studies in *elektronische Musik* (*Electronic Compositions Nos. 1–4*) Anhalt turned in his next four compositions to a fusion of *elektronische Musik* and *musique concrète* principles and the combination of tape music with live performers; after that he retired from the field of electronic music altogether. The effort of keeping up with the rapidly evolving technological changes in the field after 1975, in particular the early developments in the field of computer generated music, was simply not paying enough artistic dividends to warrant the investment of time and energy required. In addition, during the 1960s Anhalt's research interests shifted from electronic music to the interaction of music with language. The first substantial document reflecting the latter field of inquiry is "Music: Mode of Human Communication," the text of a talk about linguistics, semiotics, and music that he gave at McGill on 5 March 1962.[60] This preoccupation with music and language led eventually to the book *Alternative Voices*,[61] and would also have a profound effect on his work as a composer.

    Electronic Compositions Nos. 1 and 2 (both 1959) were given the subtitles "*Sine Nomine I*" and "*Sine Nomine II*," likely in punning reference to the use of sine tones in these works, and also to the English "*in nomine*" instrumental repertoire of the sixteenth and seventeenth centuries.[62] The first study has never been available on recording, and Anhalt now regards it as "worth next to nil."[63] No. 2 is a charming exercise in the manipulation of sine tones and filtered white noise, producing effects familiar from any number of 1960s science fiction films or television shows. Anhalt sent a copy to Stockhausen, who featured the work in a radio broadcast.[64] *Electronic Composition No. 3* (1960) is programmatic both in inspiration and in realization. The idea for the work goes back to an experience Anhalt had among the ruins of Budapest in 1945 (discussed in chapter 1). Subtitled "Birds and Bells," it features startlingly realistic electronic imitations of bells, and jubilant, otherworldly sounds that are reminiscent of birdsong. *Electronic Composition No. 4* (1961) is sparsely textured, like No. 2. The sonic materials are harsh, but framed by the poignant use of silence. The overall effect of the piece is surprisingly tame, given that it was inspired by, and took its subtitle from, Nevil Shute's science fiction novel *On the Beach* (1957), which predicts the atomic destruction of the entire world.

Anhalt's activities in electronic music were not confined to visiting studios and composing. Indeed, perhaps his most significant contribution in this field was the establishment of an electronic music studio at McGill University. But while McGill had been cooperative when Anhalt had proposed Canada's first tape music concert, which took place at Moyse Hall on 30 November 1959,[65] the idea of providing the money and facilities to set up a studio was another matter. Finally, though, after several years of foot dragging and lack of interest, the go-ahead for the studio was given in the spring of 1964. Earlier that year, the Faculty of Music had relocated to 3500 Redpath Street, a three-floor, twenty-room Victorian house. In the extensive garden behind the house was a coach house, which now became the home of the McGill Electronic Music Studio. Most of the instruments for the studio, including many that were specially designed by Hugh Le Caine, were in fact given to the university on permanent loan from the NRC.[66]

The McGill studio was at first only available to staff members and qualified visitors. Among the early projects realized in the studio were the tape parts of R. Murray Schafer's opera *Toi / Loving* (1965) and Anhalt's *Cento* (tape parts, 1966), and other tape works by Schafer, Pierre Mercure, and Paul Pedersen. In September 1968 the studio became a teaching facility to introduce graduate students to electronic music composition. Kevin Austin, who was one of the first students to work in the studio, reflected back on the experience nearly twenty-five years later:

Equipment was expensive (and often unstable!); composers worked with cumbersome and usually unique devices ... Distortion and tape hiss were our ever-present working friends ... [in] this strange-noise factory hidden behind two padlocked doors ... They were fun and possibly over-sentimentalized times. Frank and Charlie, the janitors, shook their heads and brooms, and shrugged their shoulders as the odd student and occasional well-known composer made the pilgrimage to the Faculty of Music's out-house studio. Even before regular classes were given, the studio was populated by a number of people anxious to experience the future, including painters, film makers and writers. Some of the sound tracks for the World's Fair, Expo 67, were created in this early studio, and Charlie would later recount being asked to play his vacuum cleaner for one of the composers to record. [67]

The creation of the Electronic Music Studio was one of many changes that took place at McGill's Faculty of Music during the 1960s. Duchow stepped down as dean and resigned as chair of the theory department in 1963. Blume took over as acting dean in 1963 and served as dean from 1964 until his retirement in 1976. Anhalt became the chair of the theory department in 1963 and served in that capacity to 1969, in addition to acting as the director of the Electronic Music Studio from 1964 to 1971. (He became an associate professor at McGill on 1 September 1962 and a full professor on 1 January 1967.) The Conservatorium was supplanted by the McGill Preparatory School of Music in 1966, but continued to share its budget and teaching staff with the Faculty of Music until the two institutions were separated in 1970.

It was a period of unprecedented expansion for McGill's Faculty of Music. During the 1960s, the enrolment grew about 500 per cent,[68] and the theory department grew from three to thirteen full-time staff members. To the three existing B.Mus. specializations, three new ones were added in 1966 – in theory, music history, and conducting. Two new master's programs were created in 1968, in composition and musicology, and a third in theory was added in 1970. Pressures on space grew to an unbearable extent during this period, until the Faculty of Music was given the Hurlbatt and Reynolds wings of the Royal Victoria College in 1971. By the time the Faculty of Music moved into these new quarters, which were renamed the Strathcona Music Building, Anhalt had left McGill to take up his duties at Queen's University.

Curiously enough, with all of this expansion going on and new staff being hired every year, there was no appointments committee in place. Anhalt was simply given free reign to offer positions to whomever he chose, and he had mixed success in that regard. Bruce Mather and Paul Pedersen, both hired in 1966, went on to make significant contributions to McGill. Israel J. Katz and Otto E. Laske, appointed in 1968 and 1969 respectively, were strong choices, but each left after a year at McGill, Katz for Columbia University and Laske to teach in Europe. Anhalt also made some imaginative overtures that were not accepted.

He offered the eminent Polish composer Witold Lutoslawski a one-year teaching contract in 1968, but Lutoslawski was not interested in devoting so much time to teaching composition. Anhalt also tried to entice Murray Schafer away from Simon Fraser University in 1968, but again without success.

Many eminent composers visited Montreal in the 1950s and 1960s, some of them at Anhalt's invitation. Stockhausen gave a talk at McGill on "New Electronic and Instrumental Music" on 9 December 1958, and he and his wife Doris stayed with the Anhalts. The friendship was renewed during subsequent visits Stockhausen made to Montreal.[69] John Cage and David Tudor, in town for the International Week of Today's Music/Semaine internationale de la musique actuelle (during which Cage's *Atlas Eclipticalis* was premiered on 3 August 1961),[70] also stayed with the Anhalts, whom they had met and befriended in Manhattan in 1960. Other visitors during this period included Milton Babbitt, Lejaren Hiller, and Toru Takemitsu. Nor were Canadians neglected; Schafer lectured at McGill in 1966, and John Beckwith gave a colloquium on his choral works in 1970, both at Anhalt's invitation.

Anhalt's teaching schedule throughout the 1960s was heavy, ranging from nineteen hours per week in 1962 (the year before he assumed extra administrative obligations), to about nine hours per week by the end of the decade. His duties included teaching harmony and keyboard harmony, and giving class and individual composition lessons. Anhalt outlined his pedagogical philosophy in an interview that he gave in 1968: "There are two important factors in the teaching of composition. The first resides in the fact that each young composer is a unique person. It is my task to help that person to find their identity through their compositional efforts ... [Secondly] it is necessary to help the student to make decisions. A composition is created by the elimination or the adoption of many possibilities ... This second factor pushes me to help the student to develop the power to make decisions quickly and confidently, and to revise them if his memory or perception advises him to do so."[71] Later in the interview, Anhalt stressed the importance of the composers workshops at McGill, which enabled student composers to hear their works performed: "The intensity of information which is obtained there is different from what is obtained in the composition class; the one is verbal and the other is entirely based on musical language: the two complement each other. This activity is for us, as composers, what lab work is for our chemistry or physics students."[72]

Anhalt's excellence as a teacher is attested to by the fact that many of his pupils at McGill during the 1960s went on to prominent careers at universities across Canada. These include Alan Heard (B.Mus. 1962), who taught at McGill from 1967 to 1971 and then at the University of Western Ontario beginning in 1976; Donald Patriquin (B.Mus. 1964), on staff at McGill from 1978; William Benjamin (B.Mus. 1965), on the faculty of the University of Michigan from 1972 to 1978 before moving to the University of British Columbia; Hugh Hartwell (B.Mus. 1967), who joined the staff at McMaster University in 1976; John Hawkins (B.Mus. 1967), appointed to the University of Toronto in 1970; and Kevin Austin (B.Mus. 1970), who began teaching at Concordia University in 1970.

Anhalt found relief from his heavy teaching and administrative duties during the 1960s by taking time out for vacations, a welcome break given that he never had a single sabbatical leave during his twenty-two years at McGill. The family travelled to Cape Cod for four consecutive summer vacations from 1960 to 1963, visited Prince Edward Island in 1964, holidayed in England in 1965, went to Sanibel Island in Florida for Christmas of 1966, and spent three summers in the late 1960s on a farm near Barton in Vermont. Anhalt's mother arrived from Budapest for a visit in 1962, but while she was in Montreal her second husband, Sándor Somló, suffered a stroke. She returned to Budapest immediately, and her husband died just two weeks later. In 1963 she decided to emigrate to Canada to live with Anhalt, who now found himself outnumbered four to one at home by three generations of Anhalt women (and five to one during his mother-in-law's frequent visits).

Outside professional activities kept Anhalt busy during the decade as well. He had joined the Canadian League of Composers already in the 1950s shortly after it was founded,[73] and in 1963 he joined the organization's executive committee, serving as the treasurer. In July 1964 he was invited by the Canada Council to a meeting at Stanley House, near New Richmond in the Gaspé peninsula, to discuss the formation of a Canadian academic music committee along the lines of the American National Association of Schools of Music, which had been in existence since 1924. As a result of this meeting, the Canadian Association of University Schools of Music was formed in 1965 and held its first meeting that year at the University of British Columbia as part of the Learned Societies Conference.[74] In April 1966 Anhalt travelled to New York to attend the first annual conference of the American Society of University Composers. He was back in Europe for eleven weeks in 1968 to visit European electronic music studios and to give a talk on *Cento* for the Congress of Experimental Centers for Electronic Music, which was meeting in Florence during the Maggio Musicale. And finally, in the fall of 1969 he began commuting to Buffalo to teach a seminar on contemporary composition for voice at the State University of New York at Buffalo as the visiting Frederick Slee Professor of Composition. He also had a few individual composition students at SUNY Buffalo, including Michael Horwood, who later settled in Toronto.

The major composition that preoccupied Anhalt during these years, from 1962 to 1967 or 1968, was *Symphony of Modules*. Work was well under way when he accepted a commission to complete the symphony in time for a premiere performance by the Vancouver Symphony Orchestra (VSO) at Simon Fraser University in 1967.[75] The commission came from the Canadian Music Centre (CMC) but was engineered by Murray Schafer and was granted under the auspices of the Centennial Commission. Schafer had mentioned the possibility of commissioning the work as early as January 1965; Keith MacMillan, the executive director of the CMC, came on board in June 1966; and Anhalt accepted the commission in August 1966. The performance was still planned for Simon Fraser in 1967 when Anhalt wrote to Schafer to enumerate the forces required: an orchestra of roughly 95 people (minimum; more string players to be added if available), including 8 percussionists covering 64 instruments; 3 people operating 2 two-channel stereo tape recorders and a mixing console that would control the levels of the multiple contact microphones needed for some instruments ("perhaps additional 'assistants' will be needed" Anhalt cautioned); and 2 conductors, a principal and an associate, to share between them the 18 to 20 hours of rehearsal time that Anhalt requested.[76] Even in the halcyon days of Canada's centennial year, with generous budgets and goodwill towards the arts, this was clearly going to be a production that would be difficult to get off the ground.

Nothing came of the planned centennial premiere, but the hope of having the work performed by the VSO dragged on for nearly two years. At the end of 1968, at the suggestion of Keith MacMillan, Anhalt wrote to Meredith Davies, the conductor of the VSO, to say that the work could probably be done by just one conductor, and that the amount of rehearsal time he had originally asked for "may have been a bit high."[77] Davies cautiously replied that he could not see doing the symphony as part of the orchestra's regular series, and that a CBC or Canada Council subsidy would be needed for a studio performance. Just to make matters perfectly clear, Victor White, the VSO's general manager, wrote to Keith MacMillan to say that $10,195 would be required to cover extra expenses for a planned performance in May 1970. Public funding of this order was just not available, and while Anhalt had been willing to dig deep into his pockets to pay for an extra hour's rehearsal for his first symphony, he was not about to bankrupt himself for *Symphony of Modules*. A performance of the work in Buffalo under Lukas Foss was discussed, but that too came to naught, as did a proposal from John Beckwith to have the University of Toronto Symphony Orchestra do the work in 1976. It remains unperformed to this day.

There is some doubt as to whether the tape parts for *Symphony of Modules* were ever completed. Anhalt certainly worked on them at the McGill Electronic Music Studio, and in a pamphlet published to advertise the studio there is a list of work completed there, which includes the entry "*Symphony of Modules* (tape parts, 1968)."[78] Even if they had been completed, though, they would scarcely be of good enough quality to be used in a contemporary performance, should one be planned.

The final compositions to be completed during Anhalt's Montreal years were *Cento* ("Cantata Urbana") on Eldon Grier's *An Ecstasy* of 1967 and *Foci* of 1969. *Cento* was commissioned by the University of British Columbia Chamber Singers for Canada's centennial, and was premiered by that choir under Cortland Hultberg on 9 February 1967. Anhalt travelled to Vancouver for the premiere, and Schafer was in the audience too. Schafer was so impressed with the work that he dedicated to Anhalt a setting of a Babylonian psalm that he composed, saying that *Cento* had inspired in him new ideas about choral writing.[79] Beckwith also wrote to say that his work *Gas!* (1969) was influenced by *Cento*, which he had heard performed on 5 March 1967 in Toronto as part of the Ten Centuries concert series.[80] *Foci* was written for the new music group at SUNY Buffalo while Anhalt was the visiting Slee professor there. The first performance took place on 13 December 1969 at the Albright-Knox Art Gallery Auditorium, with Anhalt conducting, and repeat performances were given at Rutgers University and in Manhattan in January 1970. The work received its Canadian premiere on 2 April 1970 at McGill, and was first heard in Toronto on 21 May 1971.[81]

Cento was subtitled "Cantata Urbana" as a reference to, and in admiration of, Bartók's *Cantata Profana*, a work that Anhalt had lectured on in Budapest in 1945.[82] It is dedicated to Paul Rochberg, George Rochberg's son.[83] The text consists of an assemblage of ninety-nine words drawn from the poem *An Ecstasy* by the poet and painter Eldon Grier, who with his second wife, the painter Sylvia Tait, is a good friend of the Anhalts. One literary critic's interpretation of Grier's poem perhaps provides a clue as to why Anhalt was drawn to it: "[The] long twenty-part poem 'An Ecstasy' (actually numbered to 21 but with part 11 missing) reflects a dominant Grier theme in its ambivalent attitude to the inevitable transition from the old world to the new, mingling nostalgic regret with courageous optimism."[84] Anhalt reordered the ninety-nine words to create what is in effect a new poem, an exact literary equivalent of the centonization process by which Gregorian chant was created (giving one explanation of the title of the work). *Cento* is scored for a twelve-voice SATB choir and a second choir of equal size on tape (there are also electronic sounds on the tape).[85] Neither the live nor taped choir sings; instead they give an inflected recitation of the text. The work opens with a clear, homorhythmic declamation of the words, rather in the manner of the speech-choirs of the 1920s and 1930s.[86] As the eleven-minute work progresses, the electronic sounds become increasingly intrusive and the text grows ever more fragmentary and distorted. The progress from order to chaos made for a rather wry commentary on the Canadian centennial celebrations.

Foci was an inspired leap into altogether new creative territory for Anhalt. Perhaps the experience of having recently turned fifty freed up a new spirit of adventure in the composer, or maybe it was the stimulus of having a work premiered in the United States. In any event, the work is electrifyingly dramatic, even on recording; with the addition of the intended visual, lighting, and action effects, it must be an overwhelming experience in live performance. *Foci* is one of those rare works that manages to be completely evocative of its own time and place, yet still timeless and universal in its appeal. It is scored for soprano, instrumental ensemble (electric harpsichord, electric organ, celesta, piano, flute, clarinet, trombone, violin, cello, double bass, percussion), and tape (there are electronic sounds and twenty-nine spoken voices on the tape). The soprano appears only in the last of the work's nine movements, which is a thrilling and virtuosic aria. The text is a heterogeneous assemblage culled by Anhalt from an extraordinary range of sources, including a dictionary of psychological terms (which provides the text for the first, fourth, seventh, and ninth movements), the Odyssey, the New Testament, voodoo texts, newspaper reports, and so on. The texts are primarily in English and French, though German, Italian, Yiddish, Aramaic, Greek, Hungarian, and Creole are also used; it is the linguistic environment, in short, of Anhalt's daily experience in Montreal.[87]

Anhalt made an interesting observation about the use of taped voices in *Cento* and *Foci*: "In both works the persons whose voices are on the tape were carefully chosen for their age, native tongue, dialect, timbre, and for the vocal character(s) they were able to impersonate. These people are, thus, not interchangeable, as may be, for example, two competent violinists, each of whom may equally well perform a given part in a chamber work. The tape medium allows for this non-interchangeability. It also makes certain that the same 'performers' are always available, in top form, wherever, and whenever, a performance takes place."[88] Among the twenty-nine carefully chosen voices on the tape of *Foci* is Anhalt himself, whose attractive speaking voice, with its precise, lightly accented, careful English diction, is clearly audible in several of the movements.

The inspired achievement of *Foci* is all the more remarkable considering that it was partly written in the Montreal General Hospital, where Anhalt spent a week in October 1969 under observation for high blood pressure and hypertension.[89] Many factors contributed to this medical condition: financial worries (these contributed to Anhalt's decision to accept Lejaren Hiller's invitation to teach at SUNY Buffalo, but the improvement in the financial situation was offset by the stress of commuting to Buffalo once a fortnight while continuing to teach at McGill); overwork (Anhalt was under the gun to complete *Foci* by the imposed deadline of 1 November); and perhaps most of all, a growing feeling of unease about the political situation in Quebec.

The Quiet Revolution had altered Quebec almost beyond recognition during the 1960s. The election of a provincial Liberal government in 1960 brought about sea changes in the economic, social, and cultural life of the province, and the philosophy of *maîtres chez nous* led to an upsurge in francophone Québécois nationalism. Bill 63 was passed in November 1969, forcing English schoolchildren and immigrants to learn French. The English minority felt that Bill 63 went too far, but the French majority thought that it did not go far enough. The extremist fringe of the nationalist movement was represented by the Front de libération du Québec (FLQ), founded in 1963. The FLQ was responsible for 200 bombings, including one at McGill University and one in a mailbox just a block away from the school that Anhalt's daughters attended.[90] It was all too reminiscent of Anhalt's worst memories of life in Hungary. Gradually but inevitably, the determination to leave Quebec built up in his mind.

By 1969 at the latest, Anhalt began seriously looking for an academic position outside of Quebec. He had discussed the matter with John Beckwith, and when the latter was named the dean of the Faculty of Music at the University of Toronto in January 1970 (to take effect from 1 July), the prospect of moving to Toronto was raised. In the event, internal considerations in the Faculty of Music at Toronto prevented Beckwith from making an immediate offer.[91] Then the head position at the recently established music department at Queen's University in Kingston was advertised; Anhalt applied (Beckwith was one of his referees) and was the chosen candidate.

There were a number of difficult decisions to make before accepting the job at Queen's. First of all, Anhalt did not want to burn his bridges at McGill, and so he tried to get a two-year unpaid leave of absence in case things did not work out at Queen's. Without Blume's support this was not forthcoming, but in the end this did not deter Anhalt.[92] Family considerations also had to be weighed. Anhalt's mother-in-law did not want to leave the city where she had lived happily for over thirty years, and his mother also did not want to disrupt her life yet again. Beate did not feel as strongly about the situation in Quebec, and was not happy with the idea of moving to Kingston and leaving the two elderly mothers behind. Helen had just completed a year of studies at McGill and also did not want to leave. Only Anhalt himself and Carol seemed happy with the idea. Eventually, however, compromises were worked out. The two older women stayed in Montreal, Emma Frankenberg until her death in 1984, and Katalin Somló until 1977, when she rejoined the family in Kingston. The rest of the family moved to Kingston, although after a year at Queen's, Helen moved back to Montreal to complete her studies at McGill.

From the first day, Anhalt "easily settled into the Queen's routine,"[93] and the rest of the family also eventually became acclimatized to the slower pace of life and different cultural patterns of Kingston. A pleasant postscript to Anhalt's career at McGill came on 9 June 1982, when the university conferred upon him the degree of Doctor of Music, *honoris causa*. It was a fitting recognition of his twenty-two years of dedicated service to McGill.

NOTES

1 See Peter C. Newman, "Pier 21: The Place Where We Became Canadians," *Maclean's* (22 July 1996). After being closed for many years, Pier 21 was renovated and reopened as a museum of Canadian immigration on 1 July 1999. Information about Pier 21 is available on the Pier 21 Web site at http://www.pier21.ns.ca.

2 Anhalt's immigration card is in the Anhalt fonds, National Library of Canada, Ottawa, folder C1.11.

3 R. Murray Schafer, "Canadian Culture: Colonial Culture," *On Canadian Music* (Bancroft: Arcana Editions, 1984), 80. Anhalt arrived from France rather than Hungary.

4 Istvan Anhalt, "What Tack to Take? An Autobiographical Sketch (Life in Progress ...)," *Queen's Quarterly* 92, 1 (spring 1985), 103.

5 Leslie Thompson, "The Inspiration of a Composer," *Music Magazine* 3, 2 (March / April 1980), 26.

6 According to William Weintraub, *City Unique: Montreal Days and Nights in the 1940s and '50s* (Toronto: McClelland & Stewart, 1996), 262, a July 1942 opinion poll showed that the Vichy government enjoyed an approval rating of 75 per cent in Quebec.

7 Hugh MacLennan, as quoted in Weintraub, *City Unique*, 90.

8 Duplessis, frequently referred to as "le Chef," was born one year to the day after Hitler.

9 See Weintraub, "A Third Solitude: The Jews," in *City Unique*, 183–202. Weintraub notes (202) that "Jewish high-school graduates had to have higher marks than gentiles to be admitted to McGill." It was almost reminiscent of the *Numerus Clausus* laws of prewar Budapest.

10 Weintraub, *City Unique*, 178.

11 Stanley Brice Frost, *McGill University: For the Advancement of Learning*, vol. 1, *1801–1895* (Montreal: McGill-Queen's University Press, 1980), 49.

12 "Meet the McGill University Faculty of Music," *McGill Daily* (15 December 1948), 1; clipping in the Anhalt fonds, folder D3.1.1.

13 Eric McLean, "The Montreal Orchestra," *Encyclopedia of Music in Canada*, 2nd ed. 877.

14 Graham George noted that "for a number of years the city had a single group of musicians, both francophones and anglophones, with two conductors using separate languages, working alternatively in the first and second halves of the week, and, if I remember rightly, two different concert-masters" ("Composers' Panel," in *Canadian Music in the 1930s and 1940s*, ed. Beverley Cavanagh, CanMus Handbooks no. 2 [Kingston: Queen's University School of Music, 1987]: 39).

15 Istvan Anhalt, letter to the author, 29 October 1997. Recalling an earlier period at McGill (ca 1930), Graham George spoke of Dean Clarke's "anglophile oddities" and noted that "the total of undergraduate students in music numbered six" ("Composers' Panel," 39).

16 "Prof. Anhalt of McGill Discusses Music Plans," *Montreal Gazette* (14 February 1949); clipping in the Anhalt fonds, folder C3.1.

17 "Composers' Panel," 45. There is a sheet in the Anhalt fonds, folder C3.2, which proposes a budget of $135 for the event, but the money may not have been forthcoming or it may have been for expenses other than musicians' fees.

18 G[illes] P[otvin], "McGill Stages Unusual Concert: Impressive Program of Contemporary Music Given in Moyse Hall," *Montreal Gazette* (23 January 1950); clipping in the Anhalt fonds, folder C3.1. This same folder contains equally positive reviews of this concert, by Eric McLean for the *Montreal Star* (21 January 1950) and by Brian Macdonald for the *Montreal Herald* (21 January 1950).

19 *Funeral Music* was also performed on 29 July 1961 at the Stratford Festival, conducted by Mario Bernardi, and on 13 April 1967 by the Miskolci Kamarazenekar in Hungary.

20 *Three Songs of Love* was written in August 1951 and revised in 1997 with the addition of an accompaniment for flute and clarinet. The titles (and text sources) are "The Song of the Mad Prince" (Walter de la Mare), "The Maid of the Moor" (anonymous), and "The Two Magicians" (folk song). The three songs are dedicated to Agi Berkovics, Jean and Isabelle Papineau-

Couture, and Beate Frankenberg respectively. Berkovics was a Hungarian
friend who died in Auschwitz in 1944.

21 Henriette Davis, letter to Istvan Anhalt; undated, but the envelope is
franked "Montreal Dec. 29 12:30 p.m. 1949 PQ"; Anhalt fonds, folder
C1.12. Lady Davis lived at 9 Chelsea Place in Montreal.

22 The Montreal writer Abraham Moses Klein (1909–72), best known for his
novel *The Second Scroll* (1951), was "the first distinctive Jewish voice in Canadian literature and the most influential Jewish writer of his generation."
See "Introduction," in *Renewing Our Days: Montreal Jews in the Twentieth
Century*, ed. Ira Robinson Mervin Butovsky (Montreal: Véhicule Press,
1995), 23.

23 Nadia was born in 1945 and Ghilaine in 1946; a third child, François, was
born in 1953.

24 Anhalt, "A Weave of Life Lines" (Kingston, 1992, manuscript), 315–16.

25 Istvan Anhalt, letter to the author, 14 January 1998.

26 Paul Frankenberg was born in Bigge, near Dortmund, in 1891 and died in
Montreal of a heart attack in 1944. Emma Frankenberg (née Gottschalk)
was born in Dortmund in 1896 and died in Montreal in 1984. Her brother-
in-law was related to the composer Kurt Weill. Beate's younger brother
Herbert became a librarian in Montreal.

27 She quit her job at Veteran's Hospital after her first child, Helen, was born
in 1955, but resumed working on a part-time basis in a research lab at the
Royal Victoria Hospital in the early 1960s.

28 Anhalt, "A Weave of Life Lines," 427.

29 Istvan Anhalt, letter to the author, 29 October 1997.

30 His Certificate of Canadian Citizenship is in the Anhalt fonds, folder C4.1.

31 Istvan Anhalt, interview with the author, 3 September 1997. Octavia Wilson
later married Douglas Clarke and moved with him to England when he
retired in 1955.

32 Istvan Anhalt, letter to the author, 29 October 1997.

33 Gould had become acquainted with Anhalt's work when he met the composer in Montreal in 1955. He later requested a copy of the Fantasia,
saying "how deeply impressed I was with your work, particularly the Piano
Fantasy, which has been sufficient in itself to restore my flagging faith in
that idiom" (Glenn Gould, letter to Istvan Anhalt, 23 August 1955; Anhalt
fonds, folder H2.61). Anhalt proposed dedicating the work to Gould in a
letter to the pianist dated 26 September 1967 (Anhalt fonds, folder
H2.61) and Gould accepted the dedication in a letter to the composer of
16 November 1967. Gould recorded the Fantasia in New York on 25 July
1967; the LP was released on Columbia Masterworks 32–110046 in
November 1967. The recording was reissued in CD format on Sony SMK
52 677 in 1992.

34 Thomas Archer, "The Anhalt Concert," *Montreal Gazette* (7 December 1954); clipping in Anhalt fonds, folder B1.3.

35 Ted Brown, "The Music of Anhalt," unidentified newspaper clipping in Anhalt fonds, folder C3.1.

36 Eric McLean, "Anhalt Works Performed in McGill Series," *Montreal Star* (7 December 1954); clipping in Anhalt fonds, folder B1.3. McLean notes that *Three Songs of Death* "has been performed here before," but it has not yet been possible to trace the first performance of this work.

37 The texts are from Verdet's *Les Jours, les nuits et puis l'aurore*, a collection of poems written in 1944 and 1945 while the poet was in various prison camps, including Auschwitz and Buchenwald.

38 J. Paul Green and Nancy F. Vogan, *Music Education in Canada: A Historical Account* (Toronto: University of Toronto Press, 1991), 407, state that "this flexible arrangement was implemented by Marvin Duchow, who had encountered such features in the United States. The impact of these initiatives was not widespread, however, for McGill's enrolment in the 1950s was modest, and as a music school it did not attract widespread attention."

39 Yolande Rivard, "L'enseignement de la composition à l'Université McGill," *Vie musicale* 8 (May 1968), 11; author's translation. The original reads "[Cette symphonie, qui se devise en treize parties,] est essentiellement une série de variations. Le compositeur avait d'ailleurs d'abord intitulé cette oeuvre *Variations*. La musique, écrite d'après les données sérielles, est vivante et expressive, et dénote que le compositeur manie habilement une technique difficile."

40 John Beckwith, "Recent Orchestral Works by Champagne, Morel, and Anhalt," *Canadian Music Journal* 4, 4 (summer 1960), 48.

41 It would be more accurate to say that the bicentennial of the toleration of the Jewish presence in Quebec was being celebrated. Jews had been banned from New France by a 1627 edict that was reinforced by the *Code Noir* of 1685, which stated, "We charge all our officers with driving from our Islands any Jews who have settled there." The edict would hardly have been necessary unless Jews were already living in Quebec. With the fall of New France and the establishment of the English regime, Jewish families began to settle in Quebec in 1760. See Jacques Langlais and David Rome, *Juifs et Québécois français: 200 ans d'histoire commune* (Montreal: Éditions Fides, 1986); translated by Barbara Young as *Jews and French Quebecers: Two Hundred Years of Shared History* (Waterloo, Ont.: Wilfrid Laurier University Press, 1991), 154 and 161n4.

42 The hall was renamed Salle Jean-Deslauriers in 1975; see s.v. "Plateau Hall," *Encyclopedia of Music in Canada*, 2nd ed.

43 Istvan Anhalt, letter to the author, 29 October 1997; ellipses in original.

44 Istvan Anhalt, interview with the author, 3 September 1997.

45 Istvan Anhalt, letter to John Beckwith, 15 November 1959; John Beckwith
   Papers, University of Toronto Music Library, Rare Book Room.
46 Marvin Duchow, "The International Conference of Composers at Stratford," *Canadian Music Journal* 5, 1 (autumn 1960), 9.
47 Alfred Frankenstein, guest review for the *Toronto Daily Star*, as quoted in *The
   Modern Composer and His World* , ed. John Beckwith and Udo Kasemets
   (Toronto: University of Toronto Press, 1961), 170.
48 Istvan Anhalt, interview with the author, 6 August 1995. The closeness of
   the Rochberg-Anhalt friendship is attested to by the correspondence files
   in the Anhalt fonds, which contain hundreds of letters both ways between
   the two men, touching on almost every aspect of their lives from 1961 on.
   It is the largest body of correspondence in the Anhalt fonds.
49 Istvan Anhalt, Symphony (Toronto: BMI Canada, 1963).
50 Robert Schallenberg, "Orchestral Music," *Notes*, 21, 4 (fall 1964), 625. The
   review concludes "one must be grateful for a composition of such truly
   symphonic scope, such integrity of style, and such vigor."
51 In a letter to John Beckwith, 15 November 1967, Beckwith Papers, Anhalt
   stated, "It is better to have *no* recording … than have one which is
   untrue."
52 Earlier, Anhalt had sent Varèse his *Electronic Composition No. 3* upon request,
   and Varèse wrote, "It was a pleasure for my wife to get acquainted with your
   fine work and for me to hear it again – We are enjoying it over and over"
   (Edgard Varèse, letter to Anhalt, 2 October 1960; Anhalt fonds, folder
   H2.177).
53 See Beckwith and Kasemets, *The Modern Composer and His World* , 115–16.
54 Gayle Young, *The Sackbut Blues: Hugh Le Caine Pioneer in Electronic Music*
   (Ottawa: National Museum of Science and Technology, 1989), 106.
55 The Algerian troubles would, in a sense, follow Anhalt to Montreal; the
   terrorist group Front de libération du Québec, founded in March 1963,
   was inspired in part by the decolonization of Algeria.
56 Anhalt, "A Weave of Life Lines," 254.
57 The correspondence is in the Anhalt fonds, folder H2.72. One short
   excerpt from a letter written by Helms to Anhalt (24 November 1958): "In
   Darmstadt Cage has been the dominating person; next year all the young
   and younger composers will probably be cageing. It's bound to be quite
   awful, people imitating something that's nothing abstracted from the person who originated it. Even Stockhausen was impressed and, I think, now is
   a little influenced."
58 Anhalt, "A Weave of Life Lines," 287–8.
59 Istvan Anhalt, "Electronic music: A New Experience in Sound," *JMC*
   [Jeunesses musicales of Canada] *Chronicle*, 7, 4 (February 1961): 3.
60 A forty-page typescript of the talk is in the Anhalt fonds, folder F-25.

61 Istvan Anhalt, *Alternative Voices: Essays on Contemporary Vocal and Choral Composition* (Toronto: University of Toronto Press, 1984).

62 Anhalt explained that the subtitle reflected a desire to humanize the strange sonic materials with which he was working. See liner notes for *Anthology of Canadian Music*, vol. 22, Radio Canada International, 1985, Sound recording, 8; hereafter, *ACM 22*.

63 Anhalt, "A Weave of Life Lines," 288. *Electronic Composition No. 1* was broadcast on the CBC radio program "World of Music" on 10 November 1959.

64 Anhalt, "A Weave of Life Lines," 288. Stockhausen, in a letter to Anhalt of 22 December 1959 (Anhalt fonds, folder H2.164), says that he received a tape of *Electronic Composition No. 2*, but there is no mention of a broadcast. The work was released on LP in *ACM 22*.

65 The program for this event is in the Anhalt fonds, folder G17.1; it states, in part, "several works on the programme are stereophonic compositions and will be presented in that manner. The concert will be followed by a question-answer period. Admission free." The concert cost McGill virtually nothing, as the NRC loaned the necessary equipment and shipped it to Montreal.

66 In 1987 Le Caine's instruments were donated to the National Museum of Science and Technology in Ottawa.

67 Kevin Austin, "Chronicle: Classical Period, 1964-c1970," Electronic Music Festival de musique électroacoustique program (McGill University Faculty of Music, 7–8 December, 1990), 5–6.

68 Green and Vogan, *Music education in Canada*, 408.

69 Marie-Thérèse Lefebvre, *Serge Garant et la révolution musicale au Québec* (Montreal: Louise Courteau éditrice, 1986), 59, reproduces a photo of Stockhausen in Montreal in January 1964. Unacknowledged in the photo caption and cast into the background by the francophone musicians surrounding Stockhausen, Anhalt peeks out at the camera from behind Serge Garant and Maryvonne Kendergi.

70 The third oboe part of *Atlas Eclipticalis* is dedicated to the Anhalts (see John Cage, letter to Istvan Anhalt, 18 December 1961; Anhalt fonds, folder H2.23). The International Week was organized by Pierre Mercure as an avant-garde response to the Stratford conference of 1960. Anhalt's *Electronic Composition No. 3* was on the program for a concert on 6 August, and Anhalt acted as a bilingual moderator for a public forum at Redpath Hall on 8 August.

71 Yolande Rivard, "L'enseignement de la composition à l'Université McGill," *Vie musicale* 8 (May 1968), 6; author's translation. The original reads, "Il existe deux facteurs importants dans l'enseignement de la composition. Le premier réside dans le fait que chaque jeune compositeur est un être unique. C'est mon devoir de l'aider à trouver son identité par le truchement de son travail en composition … Il est nécessaire d'aider l'étudiant à

prendre des décisions. Une composition se crée par l'élimination ou l'adoption de plusieurs possibilités ... Ce deuxième facteur me pousse à aider l'élève à développer son pouvoir de prendre des décisions rapidement avec sûreté, à les reviser si sa mémoire ou sa perception le lui conseille."

72 Ibid., 11; author's translation. The original reads, "L'intensité de l'information qui y est obtenue est différente de celle obtenue aux cours de composition; l'une est verbale et l'autre est entièrement basée sur le langage musical: les deux se complètent. Cette activité est à nos compositeurs ce que le travail de laboratoire est à nos étudiants en chimie ou en physique."

73 Helmut Kallmann, "The Canadian League of Composers in the 1950s: The Heroic Years," in *Célébration*, ed. Godfrey Ridout and Talivaldis Kenins (Toronto: Canadian Music Centre, 1984), 102.

74 The name of the organization was changed to Canadian University Music Society in 1981.

75 The information in this paragraph about the commissioning process is taken from the file of correspondence with Murray Schafer, in the Anhalt fonds, folder H2.150.

76 Istvan Anhalt, letter to Murray Schafer, 15 May 1967; Anhalt fonds, folder H2.151.

77 Information in this paragraph is taken from correspondence in the Anhalt fonds, folder G9.2.

78 McGill University Faculty of Music Electronic Music Studio pamphlet, (ca spring 1968); Anhalt fonds, folder G17.2.

79 Murray Schafer, letter to Istvan Anhalt, 26 December 1967; Anhalt fonds, folder H2.150. Schafer's Babylonian psalm, for 32-voice choir, string quartet, and tape, was incorporated into *Patria 1*. Anhalt in turn used a Babylonian text in the fifth movement of *Foci*. Schafer's setting may have reawakened in Anhalt an interest in the Ishtar legend, which Anhalt had first come across in the 1930s in a Hungarian translation by Sándor Weöres.

80 John Beckwith, letter to Istvan Anhalt, 10 January 1970; Anhalt fonds, folder H2.8. The reviews in the Toronto papers of this performance of *Cento* were particularly unkind; John Kraglund in the *Globe and Mail* (6 March 1967), for instance, wrote, "The effect was rather like intermission at the Women's Musical Club." Beckwith forwarded the reviews to Anhalt anyway, "in case of a shortage of bathroom commodities" (Beckwith, letter to Anhalt, 11 March 1967, Anhalt fonds, folder H2.8).

81 Once again, the Toronto critics were unkind. Anhalt wrote to Beckwith, "I would be lying if I would say that some of the Toronto press comments did not shock me. Fortunately I was forewarned, and I got over it rather fast." (Anhalt, letter to Beckwith, 8 June 1971; Beckwith Papers).

82 Anhalt, letter to Beckwith, 13 December 1988; Beckwith Papers.

83 Paul Rochberg, a gifted young poet, died in 1964 at the age of 20. Anhalt has written, "I was so moved [by Paul's death] that I dedicated *Cento*, a young person's piece, I felt, to Paul. It is still 'Paul's piece.'" (Anhalt, "A Weave of Life Lines," 341).

84 Barbara Pell, "Eldon Grier," in *Canadian Writers, 1920–1959: Second Series*, ed. W.H. New, Dictionary of Literary Biography, vol. 88 (Detroit: Gale Research Inc., 1989), 96. *An Ecstasy* is from *A Friction of Lights* (Toronto: Contact Press, 1963), a selection of the poet's earlier work that was widely greeted with positive reviews.

85 The live and the taped choir are supposed to "blend indistinguishably into a single ensemble" in a live performance of the work (Anhalt, *ACM* 22, 12); in a recording of the piece, the two choirs are of course entirely undifferentiable.

86 For a brief history of the speech-choir movement, see Anhalt, *Alternative Voices*, 14–15. Anhalt does not mention *Cento* in that section of his book, but he does discuss his treatment of text in the work on p. 221.

87 It is possible that Anhalt was influenced in assembling the texts for *Foci* by the writings of A.M. Klein, who "developed a unique lexicon – a brilliant melange of Yiddish and Hebrew terms, English renaissance diction recalling the King James Version of the Bible, and local French patois – to evoke the polyglot world of his Montreal." See "Introduction," Robinson and Butovsky, *Renewing Our Days*, 23. Anhalt had certainly read Klein's work, and set one of his texts in "Psalm XIX – A Benediction" (1951).

88 Istvan Anhalt, "Language as Music on Tape (Notes on *Cento* and *Foci*)" (paper presented at the annual meeting of the College Music Society and the American Musicological Society, Toronto, November 1970); typescript in Anhalt fonds, folder F14.

89 Anhalt, "A Weave of Life Lines," 258–9.

90 Istvan Anhalt, letter to the author, 29 October 1997.

91 John Beckwith, letter to Istvan Anhalt, 10 January 1970: "the Faculty can't right now afford a person of your stature … my replacement will not be primarily a composition person or a senior-echelon person, but rather a junior, with promotions for several present department members at the same time" (Anhalt fonds, folder H2.8).

92 Istvan Anhalt, interview with the author, 3 September 1997.

93 Anhalt, "A Weave of Life Lines," 153.

3 The Kingston Years (1971–present)

GORDON E. SMITH

If that's what you need: well ... then rest.
Stretch out your limbs in the hollows of hills
By the edge of the darkly pensive woods
Where you just might catch, unexpectedly,
A few words resounding from a generous spring:

"On the grassy plains you feed me, my Lord,
And even by the rim of the abyss you are my shepherd ... "
Comes from a distance.
Then ... silence
The voiceless word echoes as long as you hear the thought.

Istvan Anhalt, from "Mirage in Elöpatak"

The pathway that led Istvan Anhalt from McGill to Queen's appeared only after much reflection. As seen in chapter 2, Anhalt's decision to leave his full-time professorship at McGill University for Queen's in 1971 did not come easily. He had worked at McGill since his arrival in Canada in 1949 with good results, building up the theory and composition department, establishing the Electronic Music Studio, and forming his reputation as a teacher and a composer. Over the twenty-two year period in Montreal, Anhalt had also found a stimulating circle of colleagues and friends, both English and French speaking. As an immigrant to Quebec with a Jewish background, Anhalt might have felt perplexed by an apparently tense political climate; it might have reminded him – and perhaps it continues to remind him – of similar politically charged situations in Europe before his arrival in Canada. The observed silence of some of his Québécois colleagues and friends in related conversations might have intensified Anhalt's unease and subsequent resolve toward a move from Quebec. Anhalt also experienced a sense of loss upon leaving his many colleagues and friends in Montreal – not to mention the city itself, which had been his adopted Canadian home for over twenty years, a place of which he had grown fond after putting down new roots, and the scene of his professional accomplishments and personal experience.

The epigraph of this chapter is from a poem ("Mirage in Elöpatak") written originally in Hungarian by Anhalt in August 1943 during the period he was in a forced labour camp in Elöpatak, Transylvania. (He translated it into English in the 1980s; the full text appears in chapter 14, this volume.) In this poem, the first he ever wrote and one which was written during one of the most difficult periods in his life, Anhalt describes ideals of contentment and place. Anhalt's memory of writing these lines is vivid, as is his interpretation of their resonance with the context of his life more than fifty years later. In conversations with Anhalt he has related that he found inner peace and productive tranquility in the small city of Kingston. After Budapest, Paris, and Montreal, Kingston was different both in its size and apparent cultural and ethnic homogeneity. It also seems to fit with the imaginary landscape of contentment described in the poem.

Professionally, Anhalt was pleased with the Kingston move from the beginning: "From the first day on, I fairly easily settled into the Queen's routine and I came to like my involvement there. This has never changed. To this day I regard Queen's as an academic home, as much as this appellation has any grounding in reality. Somehow the atmosphere, the life, and the ease of establishing stimulating contacts with colleagues in a diversity of disciplines made my associations there very pleasant, in other words conducive to what I regard fruitful work."[1]

COMPOSITION AND RESEARCH DURING THE QUEEN'S YEARS (1971–84)

When Anhalt moved to Kingston from Montreal in 1971, he was already working on his first opera, the "musical tableau" *La Tourangelle.* Deeply interested in finding out about the history of his adopted country, Anhalt was drawn to the idea of composing a work related to the Canadian heritage. In response to a commission from John P.L. Roberts, on behalf of CBC Radio (Anhalt quotes Roberts on the title page of the score: "You will recall the idea we discussed was the search for order and meaning in life through the focus of religion – the search for God in other words."), the idea of writing a piece on the subject of Marie de l'Incarnation, founder of the Ursuline order in New France in the seventeenth century, was suggested to Anhalt by the well-known Québécois writer and commentator Laurier La Pierre in 1969. Anhalt was especially interested in exploring French Canadian history, perhaps as a means of understanding some of the early historical events that ultimately led to the current tensions between French and English Canada. Anhalt maintains that his research on Marie de l'Incarnation was "an extended lesson on the history of

French Canada. Through this, I also began to see in a fresh light certain contemporary issues and attitudes."[2] Anhalt recounts further that Kingston, like Quebec City, is a city steeped in history and as such, was a fitting place in which to think and write about Marie de l'Incarnation.[3] Considered within Anhalt's overall compositional corpus, which I have interpreted elsewhere in five stages based on chronology, shifts of creative and intellectual interest, and broad genre considerations,[4] *La Tourangelle* represents Anhalt's largest stylistic break. Subtitled "a musical tableau," it does not present a tightly woven narrative. Rather it is a set of stylized situations that describe various attitudes, relationships, emotions, and moments of decision. Its subtext is the historical narrative, which is told through commentators and certain "characters" who reflect on a given situation. In its exploration of the human voice as a dramatic instrument (cf., *Cento*, 1967, and *Foci*, 1969), its use of multimedia devices, bilingualism, and perhaps most importantly, the work's interpretive dimensions (which challenge the listener and emphasize the human response) Anhalt was seeking new creative pathways in *La Tourangelle*, pathways which, consciously or unconsciously, offer a striking parallel with his move from Montreal to Kingston, and before that with his immigration to Canada in 1949. Significantly, *La Tourangelle* is dedicated to Pater János Antal, the superior of the Salesian order of St John Bosco in Budapest, who sheltered Anhalt when he escaped the forced labour camp in 1944.

La Tourangelle received its premiere as a concert performance in the MacMillan Theatre at the University of Toronto in the CBC summer festival of 1975. The work was generally well received by the critics (e.g., reviews by John Kraglund in the *Globe and Mail*, 18 July 1975, and Louis Appelbaum in the *Kingston Whig Standard*, 19 July 1975), and also by Anhalt's colleagues, both at Queen's and in the wider musical community. One Queen's staff member at the time relates that "we all went to Toronto for the premiere of Istvan's opera [*La Tourangelle*] ... I guess you could say that it was a kind of event – one that showed how we stuck together in those days and, of course, how much we respected the boss" (personal communication). *La Tourangelle* was quickly recognized for its importance as an innovative avant-garde piece by a thoughtful, imaginative composer. In its original stylistic dimensions and historical subject matter, *La Tourangelle* is considered a major contribution to the small but significant repertory of musical works that combine Canadian content with artistic modernism (e.g., Harry Somers's *Louis Riel*, 1967; and parts of R. Murray Schafer's *Patria* cycle). Discussing "Canadianisms" in music, John Beckwith has suggested that "perhaps the most profound musical treatment of a subject from the era of New France is by a composer born in Hungary who spent the first twenty years of his Canadian career in Montreal: I refer to Istvan Anhalt's *La Tourangelle* ... This reminds us that the 'overt and conscious' Canadianisms are a matter of commitment in particular pieces and by individual composers, many of whom were not native to the country."[5]

Anhalt relates that *La Tourangelle* had to end with Marie's arrival in Canada in 1639 for a number of reasons. Chief among these was that he did not feel qualified to portray the interactions between Marie and the native population in New France, which was central to Marie's work. Thus, instead of continuing Marie de l'Incarnation's story, soon after the premiere of *La Tourangelle*, Anhalt began contemplating a second piece, which could be considered its "twin." As with *La Tourangelle*, Anhalt was led to a historical subject – in this case, John Winthrop, the first governor of the Massachusetts Bay Colony and the founder of the city of Boston. The idea for *Winthrop* emerged in a conversation with a colleague, the late George Rawlyk from the history department at Queen's. In the person of John Winthrop, Anhalt found a subject who, because of his English Protestant background, his period, place of activity, and historical importance, made a fitting complement to Marie de l'Incarnation. In the frame of their different religious backgrounds, each of these New World protagonists was committed to a strict religious and moral code and each had a powerful sense of mission: "Both were strong and good persons, builders with outstanding records of achievement, yet, at the same time also fallible and groping individuals, like the rest of us, when having to cope with difficult problems. In my mind they stand as examples for the best one can hope to find in the early history of our country."[6] The opera received its premiere in concert performance by the Kitchener-Waterloo Symphony Orchestra, the Elmer Iseler Singers, and the Stratford Boychoir, with Raffi; Armenian, conductor, in the fall of 1986 in Kitchener's splendid Centre in the Square concert space.

The composition of *Winthrop* (completed in 1984) coincided with the latter stages of Anhalt's research on *Alternative Voices*, which was published in the same year. During his sabbatical leave in 1976–77, the first of two during his entire university career, Anhalt worked on both projects, even though some of the work that is contained in the book had been done before this time (see the book's preface).[7] Anhalt's sabbatical research included studying linguistics (prosody and phonetics) as a means of gaining insights into the potential of the human voice in a contemporary vocal and choral compositional context. To this end he attended Professor J.L.M. Trim's classes in articulatory phonetics and prosody at Cambridge University; and during his stay in Cambridge, England, he also visited, among others, Dr John Laver of the University of Edinburgh, an expert on voice quality, and Dr David Crystal of Reading University, an eminent authority on prosody.

Both the book and the opera were received favourably. *Winthrop* was singled out for its inventiveness and, like *La Tourangelle,* for its innovative uses of the voice.[8] *Alternative Voices* was the subject of a number of favourable reviews, and was selected as one of the 1984 outstanding academic books by *Choice* (a publication of the Association of College and Research Libraries). The completion of *Winthrop* and the publication of *Alternative Voices* in the same year as his retirement from university teaching represents a fitting coincidence[9] in Anhalt's career, as landmarks of his devotion to composition, scholarship, and teaching.

ADMINISTRATION AND TEACHING AT QUEEN'S

When Anhalt arrived at Queen's in the fall of 1971 as head of the music department, the B.Mus. degree program was in its third year of operation.[10] The recently established music department was housed in Goodwin House on Queen's Crescent, east of the present Victoria Hall residence, as well as in 32 Stuart Street. Before the establishment of the B.Mus. program in 1969, music study at Queen's had consisted of various course offerings within the Faculty of Arts and Science. Dating back to 1935, the curriculum had consisted of courses in music history and theory, as well as music appreciation, and ensembles such as the Queen's Glee Club. Faculty included Frank Llewelyn Harrison (at Queen's 1935–45) and Graham George (1946–77), F.R.C. Clarke (1967–91), David Smith (1969–82), Wilbur Maust (1969–76), Duane Bates (1969–present), David Keane (1970–96), Margaret McClellan (1970–95), and Rudi Schnitzler (1971–96).[11]

Anhalt's appointment to Queen's was the result of a search conducted by an advisory committee to the dean of the Faculty of Arts and Science. Other candidates who were interviewed for the position included the current department head, Graham George. Conversations with several colleagues of Dr George reveal that, at the time of Anhalt's appointment, George might have been "somewhat disappointed" he was not offered the position, and, in the first year of Anhalt's tenure, there was some tension between the two. Anhalt was sensitive to this situation, but he was also cognizant of the extraordinary contribution George had made to the study of music at Queen's, as reflected in his remarks at an inaugural assembly of staff and students on 22 September 1971: "My introductions will be the briefest with the exception of that of Dr George. Dr George has been at Queen's University for the past twenty-six years. He in fact introduced the study of music at the university. Without his purposeful and sustained efforts there would be no B.Mus. program at Queen's and you and I wouldn't be here this afternoon. Dr. George's accomplishments range of course far beyond his achievements at Queen's ... knowing just how modest a man he is ... you will have to prod him for this information ... It will be well worth your while, though, to learn closely about this fine musician and dedicated teacher."[12] As Anhalt recalls, a cordial professional relationship evolved between himself and George.

Anhalt was committed to developing the finest B.Mus. program at Queen's, one which would be distinguished by the breadth of its curriculum and by its excellence in each of the areas (music education, theory and composition, performance, and music history and literature). In the spring of 1972 he combined a trip to Hungary (his first since the war), where he was invited by the Hungarian Academy of Music to give three lectures on contemporary music for the voice,[13] with a trip to England, where he interviewed individuals for faculty positions in the Queen's music department. The England trip resulted in two appointments: Denise Narcisse-Mair and Clifford Crawley (at Queen's 1972–83 and 1973–92, respectively). Both appointments were intended to (and did) bolster the original music education mandate of the B.Mus. program. In addition, Narcisse-Mair's choral conducting expertise was an asset to the new department. Crawley's knowledge of twentieth-century music and his work as a composer – along with Clarke's and Keane's, and of course Anhalt's – created particular strength in this area over the years.

Anhalt was head of the music department for two five-year terms (1971–81), at which time F.R.C. Clarke took over the position (1981–91), and Anhalt taught as a regular professor until his retirement in 1984. Anhalt's work at Queen's was characterized by a keen sense of the balance between teaching and research, as well as a commitment to establishing a collegial, professional environment in the department.

A major event, and one which Anhalt oversaw, was the completion of the music building in 1974, plans for which were underway when Anhalt arrived in 1971; as he acknowledged in his inaugural comments to students, faculty, and staff in the fall of 1971, others, notably Professors George and David Smith, had worked very hard to gain approval for the new building.[14] The music department moved into the new building in the summer of 1974, and it was officially opened by the governor general of Canada, Roland Michener, on 9 November 1974. The opening was marked by two concerts, one by faculty held in Dunning Hall on 8 November, and the other by student ensembles, which was held in Grant Hall on 9 November. The Harrison-Le Caine building was named after the eminent British musicologist Frank

Llewelyn Harrison (1905–87), and one of Canada's foremost experts in electronic music, Hugh Le Caine (1914–77). Le Caine received his M.Sc. from Queen's in 1939, helped to establish the first Canadian electronic music studio at the University of Toronto in 1959, and after receiving his Ph.D. at the University of Birmingham, he joined the National Research Council where he worked on different projects before turning his attention to electronic music instruments.[15] A medieval music specialist and later an ethnomusicologist, Harrison earned his D.Mus. from Trinity College, University of Dublin, and in 1935, on the invitation of Principal Hamilton Fyfe, came to Queen's, where he worked (until 1945) as resident musician at the university.[16] The naming of the new music building after Harrison and Le Caine not only served to honour their respective affiliations with Queen's,[17] but also symbolized the qualities of creative activity and academic excellence which, under Anhalt's direction, became anchors of music study at the university.

In addition to his duties as department head, Anhalt taught regularly and took an active interest in students' progress. His teaching was, for the most part, in the theory and composition area, but he also taught courses in twentieth-century music and Canadian music. Many of his outlines and lecture notes for these courses are now part of the Anhalt fonds at the National Library of Canada.[18] Of particular interest are the student course evaluations from the later period of Anhalt's career. Generally, Anhalt was regarded by students as "sometimes hard to understand," but always "erudite – he really knows his stuff," and "committed to his students." The records of Anhalt's teaching reveal an informed, imaginative, and most thorough instructor; on the latter, impressive indeed is the substantial content in his courses, especially for the undergraduate level.

Two examples serve as illustrations of Anhalt's teaching at Queen's. In Anhalt's final academic year at Queen's before his retirement (1983–84), he taught a course on twentieth-century Canadian music since 1930. In addition to the regular course lectures, there were guest lectures by six visitors: F.R.C. Clarke (composer, Queen's), Gail Dixon (theorist, University of Western Ontario), Jean Papineau-Couture (composer, Université de Montréal), John Beckwith (composer, University of Toronto), Gilles Tremblay (Conservatoire de Montréal), and Harry Somers (composer, Toronto) – an impressive list of visitors indeed, and one which demonstrates the extent of Anhalt's connections and the high regard he commanded in both English and French Canada. The documentation for this course includes extensive bibliographies and two typically comprehensive Anhaltian lists; the first is a list of twenty-nine "'Themes' in Canadian Composition since 1930: A

First Approximation," and the second is a list of twenty-three "Compositional Techniques and Procedures Observable in Canadian Composition since 1930." The imposing depth of these lists reveals Anhalt's extensive knowledge of Canadian music within twentieth-century Western art music. It is no coincidence that his book, *Alternative Voices*, a project with which Anhalt had been occupied since his arrival at Queen's in 1971 (and even before), was published around the time Anhalt taught this course on Canadian music. In *Alternative Voices*, he makes frequent reference to Canadian composers and their music.

Another of Anhalt's final courses was the introductory composition class for B.Mus. students, which, Anhalt recalls, was one of his best teaching experiences: "We spent the first hour discussing structure in music, interacting as a group; and then in the second hour we moved to a larger room where the students performed their compositions as if in a laboratory. This was truly a rewarding experience for all of us. If I remember correctly, of the 8–10 students in the course, two went on to study composition at the graduate level" (personal communication). Anhalt's knowledge and integrity as a teacher is summarized compellingly by William Benjamin, one of Anhalt's former composition students at McGill, and a contributor to this book: "There are obvious traits, essential to good teaching if not all that rare: dedication, organization, deep understanding of the subject matter, and true involvement with the student. These he certainly had, but there was also his willingness – far from common – to roll up his sleeves and attend to the nuts and bolts of a student composition. Even more important, there was on his part a capacity to give ardent support and to show genuine warmth, without favoritism, to those students whom he felt had begun to pay their dues ... He has been our special exemplar (if at times our rebuke), but his achievement is a touchstone for all artists."[19]

The importance Anhalt attached to teaching was also reflected in the number of judicious appointments he made to the growing music department at Queen's. These served to bolster the theory and composition area (Bruce Pennycook, at Queen's 1978–87), and also to diversify the history and literature area (Beverley Cavanagh [now Diamond], ethnomusicology and Canadian music, at Queen's 1975–88; and Robert Toft, medieval music, at Queen's 1984–86). Responding to a need to bolster performance (applied music), as well as foster strong student interest, Anhalt also expanded this sector through the appointment of adjunct instructors, including Elaine Keillor, Pierre Jasmin, Ireneus Zuk (piano); Mary Lou Fallis, Patricia Rideout (voice); Gordon Craig, Donelda Hunter, Michael Namer (woodwinds); and Gerrit Tetenburg (historical period instruments). From this list of applied music instructors, Ireneus Zuk is currently a professor of piano and director of the School of Music, and Gordon Craig and Donelda Gartshore (Hunter) are adjunct assistant professors of woodwinds.

During Anhalt's tenure as head of the music department at Queen's, he also enriched the pedagogical and research environment by inviting a series of distinguished visitors to give lectures or teach. These included the ethnomusicologist and specialist in Oceanic music Dr Mervyn McLean, the pianist and musicologist Dr Eva Badura-Skoda, the British composer Trevor Wishart, the Quebec composers Serge Garant, Jean Papineau-Couture, and Gilles Tremblay, as well as English Canadian composers John Beckwith, R. Murray Schafer, and Harry Somers. As Anhalt remembers, he really wanted to "open windows" to the world of music – Western (including Canadian) and non-Western – and in this he was supported by colleagues and students alike. One might consider that his influence in this respect bore fruit in the large conference on many diverse aspects of Canadian music held at Queen's in 1986 to recognize the International Year of Canadian Music. Anhalt's participation on a conference panel dealing with contemporary Canadian music shows his continuing activity in the university music scene in his retirement period (see below under "Composition and Research after Retiring from Queen's").

Anhalt's stature as a teacher in the wider university community is reflected in his participation on a panel session on composition, chaired by John Beckwith, at the annual meeting of the Canadian Association of University Schools of Music (CAUSM, now the Canadian University Music Society) held at Laval University in Quebec City in 1976. Anhalt was asked to speak on the second of four topics: "Directions in the Teaching of Composition at Canadian Universities: Which Way are We Going?" In preparation for this presentation, Anhalt sent a questionnaire to thirty-one institutions listed in the CAUSM directory; from this he received twenty-eight replies and made a number of collated observations in his remarks. He commented that, although the quality of teaching is difficult to evaluate, it is clear that good work is being done, since the country seems to be producing its share of promising composers, based on results of national and international competitions held over the last ten to fifteen years. And in a comment that perhaps reflects the lingering heyday of the university from the 1950s-60s, Anhalt pointed out to his audience "that the young composer in Canada, whether a student at a university or not, is no longer a neglected worker. Apart from scholarships tenable at the different universities, there are numerous awards available to him or to her on a competitive basis."[20]

COMPOSITION AND RESEARCH AFTER
RETIRING FROM QUEEN'S (1984–PRESENT)

In his autobiographical sketch, written at the request of Radio Canada International as part of the Anhalt volume (no. 22) in the *Anthology of Canadian Music* (and subsequently published in the *Queen's Quarterly* the year following his retirement), Anhalt's wrote of leaving Queen's "with the memory of a rewarding and happy experience ... I am looking forward to a period (whatever time is left) of reading, writing, more extended walks, and a little bit more leisurely thinking, as long as ideas keep flowing. Certain questions, long simmering on the back burner, can perhaps now be brought closer to the fore."[21] Anhalt's productivity during the years since he departed from his position at Queen's has been anything but leisurely. Since his retirement in July 1984, Anhalt has remained very active, writing and lecturing, as well as composing three large orchestral compositions – *Simulacrum* (1987) *SparkskrapS* (1987), and *Sonance•Resonance (Welche Töne?)* (1989) – the dramatic chamber composition *Thisness* (1985), the string quartet movement *Doors ... shadows (Glenn Gould in memory)* (1992), and his third and fourth operas *Traces (Tikkun)* (1995), and *Millennial Mall (Lady Diotima's Walk)* (1999).

The "tack" Anhalt has taken has led him to examine further, in both music and words, a number of the topics related to contemporary vocal and choral composition discussed in *Alternative Voices*. In addition, he has explored difficult questions concerning religion and aspects of human existence, and how they might be manifested in different musical genres, including abstract, textless contexts of orchestral music. Central ideas (or "deep themes," to use Anhalt's expression) are for him, and many others, the catalytic forces behind a composer's creative processes, and the presentation of culture patterns and a worldview. Possible deep themes are examined in the sixth chapter of *Alternative Voices*: "[1] hallowed names and cursed names; [2] repetition as a mythical or mystical technique; [3] the arcane ... ; [4] magical elements in music and language; [5] the hierophany of childhood; [6] the hierophany of the victim and the substitute celebration of the absurd; [7] the performance of music as spectacle or celebration; and [8] the search for the past."[22]

In keeping with the subject of the book, Anhalt's text contains discussions of contemporary compositions as illustrations of these themes: [1] in Luciano Berio's *Sinfonia*, Anhalt's *La Tourangelle*; [2] in Karlheinz Stockhausen's *Stimmung*, Steve Reich's *Come Out*; [3] in Mauricio Kagel's *Anagrama*, Murray Schafer's *La Testa d'Adriana*; [4] in Stockhausen's *Am Himmel wandre ich ...* , Harry Somers's *Kyrie*; [5] in

George Crumb's *Ancient Voices of Children*, Claude Vivier's *Chants*; [6] György Ligeti's *Requiem*; Kagel's *Anagrama*; [7] in John Cage's *4'33"*, Peter Maxwell Davies' *Eight Songs for a Mad King*, Schafer's *Patria* series; [8] in John Beckwith's *The Shivaree*, Kagel's *Aus Deutschland*, and so on. The integration of works by Canadian composers in this list is indicative of Anhalt's approach in *Alternative Voices*. Indeed, the book stands out as a major text on contemporary Western art music in which Canadian music is not simply mentioned, but discussed within the context of contemporary thought in philosophy, art, and music.

During the summer of 1985 Anhalt interrupted work on the piano/vocal score of *Winthrop* in order to fulfill a commitment he had made to write a piece ("a few songs") for mezzo-soprano Phyllis Mailing. A commission of the Vancouver New Music Society and premiered during one of the society's concerts in 1986 by Phyllis Mailing and Richard Epp (piano), *Thisness*, subtitled "a duo-drama," is a ten-part dramatic work in which the singer and the pianist are required to wear costumes and act out roles. Anhalt wrote the text himself (nine poems and the description of a short pantomime). The narrative is a journey of retrospection that is played out on psychological, emotional, historical, and even physical levels. *Thisness* represents an exploration of certain deep themes: the search for the past; the mysteries of childhood; personal identity; the root causes of cruelty; reason, unreason; dreaming and the absurd; performance of music as a spectacle; beauty and peace.[23]

Three Orchestral Works

Following the premiere of *Winthrop* in September of 1986, Anhalt and his wife took a vacation in England (Devon, Yorkshire, and "Winthrop country" in East Anglia, on the way back to London). On returning home Anhalt relates that he was looking forward to "some leisurely 'looking around'" before starting another project.[24] Within a couple of weeks, however, Anhalt was invited (coincidentally) to compose two orchestral works. The first of these commissions was from Alex Pauk, conductor of the Esprit Orchestra in Toronto, and the second was from Gabriel Chmura, the conductor designate of the National Arts Centre Orchestra (NACO). Anhalt decided to compose the NACO work first, and the result several months later was *Simulacrum* (Ottawa premiere, 1987). Anhalt then composed the second work, entitled *Spark-skrapS*, which received its premiere by the Esprit Orchestra in March 1988 at a concert celebrating the seventy-fifth birthday of Toronto composer John Weinzweig. The third work in Anhalt's 1980s orchestral triptych, *Sonance•Resonance (Welche Töne?)*, was a commission of the

Toronto Symphony Orchestra [TSO], the Montreal Symphony Orchestra, and the Calgary Symphony Orchestra, and received its premiere by the TSO in September 1989 at the inaugural concert of the orchestra's new music director, the German-born Gunther Herbig.

Each of Anhalt's three orchestral works continues the composer's exploration of certain deep themes. Even in textless music (and perhaps in yet more profound ways) Anhalt continued to search out links and meanings behind the mystery of human existence – in particular, memory, remembering, contexts, backgrounds, and the multidimensional ways we approach the past. Of the three pieces, *Simulacrum* is probably the most personal; it deals with layers of Anhalt's own past and probes the relationships of that past with the present. This is born out in Anhalt's unpublished essay on *Simulacrum* which is included in the present volume, and in Alan Gillmor's article on Anhalt and *Simulacrum* (1995). In "Echoes of Time and the River," Gillmor observes that "If there is an overriding 'deep theme' in *Simulacrum* it is that the notion of time as a linear construct is an illusion, a mirage, for the past, present, and future are unravelable 'organic tangles' or 'interlocking chains of memory cells' [quoting from Anhalt]."[25] In Anhalt's words, the title of the work *Simulacrum* means "an image, a portrait, a reflection in a mirror, in water, a shadow, something imagined, the recollection of a thing (and this aspect of it intrigued me greatly), an imitation, a mirage, perhaps, and other things besides."[26] The work contains a series of quotations from past music, underlining the "recollection" aspect, as well as personal links with Anhalt's past. These quotations include, among others, J.S. Bach's *St Matthew Passion*, Verdi's *Aïda* and *Otello*, and a well-known waltz tune from Richard Strauss's *Der Rosenkavalier*, which Anhalt remembers his father playing (or trying to play) on the piano when Anhalt was a child. Referring to his father's favourite instrument, the violin, Anhalt adds: "My father and his violin remain a permanent image in my memory, a recollection that includes much sweetness, despite the tenseness and the harshness of the 1930s and 1940s we shared in Budapest."[27]

Soon after this quotation Anhalt moves towards another "memory event," by citing two traditional Sephardic tunes, which leads to thoughts of his paternal grandfather, an orthodox Jew, who Anhalt remembers celebrating the Day of Atonement at his small synagogue in the Jewish quarter of Budapest. The two concluding sentences in his description of this memory underline two somewhat confused responses Anhalt has experienced as a Jew – both as a youth and as an adult more than sixty years later: "I recall the [synagogue] was hot, smelly, intense, and despite the occasional silent smiles my grandfather gave me, I was glad when the moment to leave came. For over six decades this was but a faint memory – until *Simulacrum* came along, that is, and demanded that I send a much belated message to my grandfather, a kind of reciprocal gesture for his gentle smile that would say: now, after much delay, I am beginning to understand you ... "[28] Indeed, the quotations Anhalt weaves throughout *Simulacrum* are not only embedded in but also integrated into the compositional fabric of the music, in much the same way – metaphorically speaking – that patterns of recall (remembering) are embedded in human consciousness.

Like *Simulacrum*, *Sonance•Resonance (Welche Töne?)* evokes dimensions of memory and various searches for the past. In *Sonance•Resonance (Welche Töne?)*, the search for a moment in the past is articulated through what Anhalt seemingly envisaged as a possible train of thought in the mind of Beethoven as he wrestled with the difficult transition in his Ninth Symphony from the end of the third movement to the beginning of the setting of Schiller's "Ode to Joy" in the fourth movement. This idea was the result of an invitation to Anhalt by Maestro Gunther Herbig of the Toronto Symphony to compose a work that would share the program with the Beethoven symphony at the inaugural concert of the 1989–90 season. After debating whether or not to ignore the Beethoven work while composing the new piece, he decided to focus on the bass recitative that prefaces the famous "Ode to Joy." This begins with the line "*O Freunde, nicht diese Töne*" (O Friends, not these sounds). The text also appears in a different form in one of Beethoven's sketches: "*Nein diese ... erinnern an unsere Verzweifl*" (No, these [sounds] recall our despair). Both forms appear on one of the front pages of Anhalt's score. Anhalt holds that both statements are likely linked to the powerful fanfare opening of the symphony's last movement, which Wagner referred to as the *Schreckensfanfare* or "fanfare of terror." This led Anhalt to an idea expressed in the subtitle: "*Welche Töne?*" or "which sounds" did Beethoven wish to stifle? Behind all this was the acknowledgment that the attempt to suppress some particularly unpleasant thoughts is a common human trait.

In the work's title the word "sonance" means the "sound" of Beethoven's opus, and "resonance" refers to the memory of this sound, as well as its incorporation or presence in memory. With the associations related to this piece also must be included his memory of Beethoven's symphony as a personal inspiration from the time he first heard it at the age of eighteen as a first-year student at the Academy of Music in Budapest: "I took along the score and was completely overwhelmed by the work. I remember the Ninth now as one of those peak experiences that belongs to my personal museum" (personal communication). As with much of Anhalt's music, this personal interpretive layer is an intrinsic link in understanding *Sonance•Resonance (Welche Töne?)*.

In *SparkskrapS*, Anhalt's third orchestral work of the triptych under discussion here, the palindrome title invites us to see "sparks" and "skraps" (Anhalt uses the old Norse spelling here) as mirror images of each other. The work's many shifts of mood and musical substance parallel what Anhalt calls "a very old timeless theme: the struggle between conflicting urges within us [good and evil]." His perspective on this theme stems from Jewish kabbalistic thought, especially that of Isaac Luria, the rabbi of Safed (Anhalt learned of Luria through the writings of Gershom Scholem, the late eminent scholar of Jewish mysticism). Unlike *Simulacrum* and *Sonance•Resonance (Welche Töne?)*, each of which contains references to older musical works, *SparkskrapS* resonates with the past as an abstract yet compelling theme in Jewish mysticism and identity. This theme also proved to remain a fruitful one, as Anhalt explored it further within other contexts and reference points, notably in his third opera, *Traces (Tikkun)*.

Traces (Tikkun) *and Other Activities in the 1990s*

In the late 1980s Anhalt turned increasingly to studying religious thought, in particular that of his own Judaic heritage. This interest was motivated partly by certain recollections of his childhood and youth.[29] Anhalt has documented memories of his life in Hungary before and during the war years in considerable detail in both published and unpublished writings (see the reference list of Anhalt's writings). On the surface in these texts, one finds a cautious approach to recording aspects of his Jewish background. Writing through the eyes and ears of a young boy, for example, Anhalt has given vivid accounts of some rituals surrounding Jewish holy days, and the deaths of certain family members. On a less conspicuous level, there is a sense of uncertainty and perhaps also reserve in the way Anhalt responds to things Jewish in his background (e.g., the passage dealing with the Day of Atonement, cited above; see also Anhalt's account of his experience as a schoolboy singing during Friday afternoon services in the large Dohány Street synagogue in Budapest in the 1930s).[30] To say that this ambivalence is understandable given the complex and eventually threatening political situation in Europe in the 1930s and 1940s would appear to be a frivolous, overly general explanation. As a young Jew in Budapest, Anhalt's own experiences of the ethnic tensions in the 1930s, and later the unspeakable horrors of the war in the early 1940s, were part of the reality of human existence for Jews in eastern Europe. Understandably, these experiences function variously as critical subtext and "deep theme" in his writings and compositions.

Another reason for Anhalt's recent interest (in the last ten years or so) in his Jewish heritage is linked to his desire to explore and compare monotheistic religions, a topic he has read about extensively in the writings of Mircea Eliade (*Patterns of Comparative Religion*, 1958), among others. In the composition of *La Tourangelle* and *Winthrop*, Anhalt had researched the respective religious backgrounds of the heroes of the operas: Marie de l'Incarnation, a Roman Catholic of French origin, and John Winthrop, a Protestant of English origin. On a personal level, Anhalt had experienced what he refers to as the "best in Christian charity and virtue" shown in his rescue by the Salesian fathers, especially Pater János Antal, the superior of the Salesian order of St John Bosco in Hungary in 1944, and the de Kerpely family in Budapest, close to the end of the war.[31] As well, his thirty-five years of teaching at two universities with strong Scottish Presbyterian foundations had also brought him into contact with many colleagues of Christian backgrounds. He found in these colleagues (many of whom were of English, Scottish, and Irish origin) integrity, wittiness, open-mindedness, and sophistication. With tongue in cheek, Anhalt explains this comment by noting that he might have been "lucky," given that he was working with people at universities "as good as McGill and Queen's, and both within historical and societal contexts with relevance to Canada."[32]

After researching Catholicism and Calvinism for his two operas – in both cases, within historical and societal contexts with respect to Canada – not surprisingly, Anhalt came to realize that he should find out more about his own religious foundation. He had already probed this background when he was working on *Alternative Voices*, at which time he began to discover the world of Jewish mysticism through the writings of Gershom Scholem.[33] Anhalt's gradual pursuit of knowledge about his religious roots included subtle allusions to Judaism in his three orchestral pieces of the late 1980s, as explained earlier, and a trip to Israel in 1992. In 1991 it also led to his work on an opera libretto about the Jewish scientist J.R. Oppenheimer. Pressured by a stringent time frame set by the Canadian Opera Company for the commission to compose the opera, this project was eventually abandoned for a series of reasons, so far not made public knowledge.[34]

Developing an understanding of what constitutes Judaism and being a Jew in relation to "being/remaining an individual"[35] may be considered a motivation behind the Oppenheimer project, as it was behind Anhalt's third opera, *Traces (Tikkun)*, completed in 1995. The Oppenheimer libretto might also be considered as Anhalt's probe into the world of a deep thinker whose faith, compared to the religions of the other operas, was of a more pragmatic nature, rooted in the religion of science. In the composer's interpretation, *Traces (Tikkun)* may be considered a continuation of the hermeneutic pathway on which he had embarked with *La Tourangelle* and *Winthrop*.[36] Within this context, the genesis of *Traces (Tikkun)* took place over a twenty-five year period (from 1970), and in some respects, may be understood as part of Anhalt's personal memory of the past, and the most recent public phase of his search for a sense of identity as an individual Jew. Significantly, *Traces (Tikkun)* is dedicated to the memory of László Gyopár, István Székely, Ödön Taubner, and Lászlo Weiner, who were fellow students of Anhalt's at the Franz Liszt Academy of Music during 1937–40, and who lost their lives in forced labour camps for Jews in the Hungarian Army in the Second World War. Notwithstanding such important links with Anhalt's past, it would be an oversimplification to say that the work is autobiographical. Rather, one might consider it as a series of dialogues with distant and not-so-distant voices, including among numerous others that of the composer himself. Like Anhalt's two earlier operas, *Traces (Tikkun)* focuses on one protagonist. Anhalt explains that the single character in this opera is nameless: "he is probably a much-travelled European-born Jew who settled and set down roots in Canada after his experience in, and survival of, the years between, say, 1920 and 1950 in Europe. While he is an eager learner of things North American, he is also hanging on to his European memories, which slowly, ever so slowly, he begins to understand. In reality, he swings back and forth between an involvement in the late-twentieth-century scene in Canada and the rich storehouse of his memories. Slowly these two strands start making sense to him *in relation to each other*.[37]

The dialogic aspect of *Traces (Tikkun)* is tied to Anhalt's expression "pluri-drama," which he uses as a subtitle to describe the opera. The protagonist, a lyric baritone, displays signs of diverse influences of different people, situations, and events from a long life. The role requires that the soloist portray, in soliloquies and pseudodialogues in a variety of singsong intonations, the minds and voices of about a dozen people.

Unlike the librettos of *La Tourangelle* and *Winthrop*, which Anhalt compiled mostly from pre-existing texts, the libretto of *Traces (Tikkun)* was written by the composer, with allusions to diverse situations, as well as from exposure to various types of expressions found in different sources, including, the *Globe and Mail* and the *Toronto Star*. The ten continuous sections of the piece include, for example, "Metropolis" (section 6) – a scene on a busy street in a modern city – leading to "In the Highdome" (section 7), a rock concert with obvious reference to Toronto's Skydome. The idea of "implied situations," as well as the dialogic aspect of the work, derives in part from Anhalt's study of recent critical theory, notably the writings of the Russian scholar, Mikhail Bakhtin. Bakhtin challenges monological ideas of authorial control, urging rethinking of language in terms of specific discursive situations. He writes that, in language, there are no "'neutral' words and forms – words and forms that can belong to 'no one'; language has been completely taken over, shot through with intentions and accents."[38] Bakhtin's dialogism (or what some postmodern writers, such as James Clifford, have referred to as discursive paradigms of dialogue and polyphony) resonates with Anhalt's creative instincts in *Traces (Tikkun)*.

Anhalt's interest in the dialogic (exchanges of various kinds) dates back to his work in the late 1960s and 1970s, at which time he began exploring possibilities of the human voice from linguistic and musical perspectives, resulting in several compositions (*Cento, Foci, La Tourangelle*), and of course his book *Alternative Voices*. Aside from *Traces (Tikkun)*, another recent manifestation of this interest is the accompanying lecture Anhalt wrote for this work. Entitled "On the Way to *Traces*: A Dialogue with the Self," this talk was presented – or, rather, performed – by the author at Queen's University in March 1996, two months before the Toronto premiere of the opera. Included in part 4 of the present volume, this previously unpublished lecture is constructed as a series of questions and answers, or an imaginary exchange between two persons, and unfolds as an intriguing exposé of Anhalt's ideas behind the composition. In breaking down the monologic (one voice) barrier of the lecture format, Anhalt's performance of this text was fresh and engaging.

Over the last several years, Anhalt has delved into his genealogical roots, revealing a continuing desire to explore his family's background in central Europe, spread over six countries. Behind this may be his desire to leave a genealogical record for his children and grandchildren. During a trip to Hungary and Austria in the fall of 1995, Anhalt visited a number of places related to this past and wrote a detailed diary account of the trip. In May 1995, Anhalt also completed a text entitled "An Interim Account of My Search for Genealogical Information Pertaining to My Family's Background," nearly one hundred itemized pages (with tables and relevant photocopied material) of this research.

In conjunction with his creative work (composing and writing), Anhalt's search for the past – a deep theme noted earlier – continues to occupy much of his time and energy. This search is aimed at a fuller awareness of personal and group identity, as well as a deeper understanding of the mystery of human existence, both in a philosophical and religious sense, and against the backdrop of an increasingly technological, depersonalized global society. In a talk for a class of students at Queen's to whom he was speaking about *Traces (Tikkun)* (following the 1996 premiere), Anhalt made reference to the Austrian writer Robert Musil by asking, "How did I come to be myself?" In the diverse manifestations of our individual as well as collective searching, Musil's question is a fitting probe, especially with respect to Anhalt's recent work.

Millennial Mall (Lady Diotima's Walk) *and Ongoing Deep Themes*

Throughout his academic career, and increasingly in his retirement years, Anhalt has remained a wide-ranging reader of literature, and has maintained mutually enriching associations with colleagues from other disciplines. These connections, both professional and personal, have provided Anhalt with intellectual stimulation, as well as inspiration for his work. Over the years at Queen's, for example, Anhalt's close colleagues have included James Leith and Gerald Tulchinsky (history), the late George Whalley[39] and John Stedmond (English), John Meisel and David Easton (political studies), the late Felix Letemendia (medicine, psychiatry), Merlin Donald (pyschology), Anthony Riley (German), Ross Kilpatrick and Frederick Schroeder (classics), and Robert Bater (religious studies). In Anhalt's most recent composition, *Millennial Mall (Lady Diotima's Walk)*, as with many of his earlier works, a number of personal influences came into play, including several of his colleagues and friends who, at certain points during the genesis of the composition, have been important sources of consultation for the composer.

Millennial Mall (Lady Diotoma's Walk), subtitled A Voice-Drama for the Imagination, was completed in February 1999. It received two highly successful premiere performances by the Winnipeg Symphony Orchestra, the Elmer Iseler Singers, soprano Valdine Anderson (as Lady Diotima), and conductor Bramwell Tovey in the opening concerts of the Winnipeg New Music Festival on 28–29 January 2000.[40] In *Millennial Mall (Lady Diotoma's Walk)*, Anhalt continues his exploration of the pragmatic dimension in language,[41] the idea of what is behind a text, subtext, dialogic aspects of texts and dramatic situations, among other deep themes. He had already delved into these areas in various wide-ranging ways in earlier dramatic works (*La Tourangelle, Winthrop, Traces (Tikkun), Thisness*), as well as the orchestral compositions from the late 1980s, and for that matter some works from the earlier periods (cf., "A Continuing Thread? Perhaps," and also *Alternative Voices* and Anhalt's other prose works, especially from the 1980s). The new work is scored for a lyric soprano, two choirs, and full orchestra. Each choir is divided into six parts (soprano, mezzo-soprano, alto, tenor, baritone, bass); one of the choirs is an ensemble of six soloists, and the other is a full choir of at least eighteen voices. Anhalt was inspired to write a work with a strong component for choir after he heard on radio the superb Danish and Swedish radio choirs in June 1997. He balanced this with the solo soprano, a voice he was "longing to hear" after writing *Traces (Tikkun)* for baritone. As with *Thisness* and *Traces (Tikkun)*, the libretto of *Millennial Mall (Lady Diotima's Walk)* (in twelve scenes) is by the composer. After exploring ideas of Roman Catholicism, Protestant Puritanism, and Judaism in his first three operas, Anhalt steps outside the boundaries of religion proper in *Millenial Mall (Lady Diotima's Walk)* and explores the antireligious, hedonistic, and self-absorbed societal "religion" of the end of the twentieth century.

Anhalt was motivated and perhaps even *disturbed* (rather than inspired) to write this libretto by some aspects of contemporary societal realities as presented in the mass media: the obsession with technology, the growing emphasis on the processing of information, the overbearing weight of market economics, the commercialization of the arts (e.g., popular music and the megamusical), the ubiquitous use of advertising, and the agitated agenda of youth. In conjunction with his references to contemporary popular culture with its manifestations of near-idolatry and hedonism, in *Millennial Mall (Lady Diotima's Walk)* Anhalt also refers to certain parallels in the Bible and in the Greco-Roman world, thereby suggesting a connection between customs in contemporary and ancient societies. Anhalt's juxtaposition of the ancient and the modern resonates with the recent study of the Bible and the Talmuds by historian Donald Akenson, who has compared the hegemonic impact of (Hellenistic) culture on parts of the ancient Jewish world with the pervasive global spread of contemporary American popular culture in the second half of the twentieth century: "American culture was the Hellenistic culture of a later age, in the sense that it – like the Hellenistic – became ubiquitous, was seductive to most members of contact societies, while distrusted by traditionalists and some local cultural elites … It had some common features determined by America's heritage as a republic and as a sometime New World, but mostly it was merely what happened to the U.S.A. first, a stage of modernization (p. 122)."[42]

The interface between old and new, or past and present, often in multiple layers (an ongoing deep theme in Anhalt's work), is represented in the two parts of the title, *Millennial Mall (Lady Diotima's Walk)*. Reminiscent of Anhalt's reference to Bakhtin's "chronotope" concept in relation to other of his compositions,[43] *Millennial Mall* has a metaphorical dimension in that Anhalt is using the present time (the millennium) and a contemporary place (the mall) as a means of

"getting into the soul/gut of contemporary North American society."
The mall is a frequent site of the cult of youth, where one can observe
physical prowess and beauty (the Greek goddess of love and beauty,
Aphrodite comes to mind) often mixed with an uncertain, anxious
energy.

The words in the title's parenthesis were inspired by three disparate
yet connected Diotima models in literature. The first is the Diotima in
Plato's *Symposium*, a personage who made pronouncements on love;
the second is a woman in the German city of Tübingen, Susette Gon-
tard, the mother of a pupil of the German writer, Friedrich Hölderlin
(Anhalt learned of this Diotima through Anthony Riley); and the third
is the beautiful Viennese woman, Diotima Tuzzi, in Robert Musil's *The
Man Without Qualities*. In Plato's *Symposium*, for example, Diotima is a
prophetess who acts as Socrates' teacher. Diotima's extended analysis
begins with "a complex definition of love, *eros*, as an intermediary between gods and human beings, and as a desire for the creation of im-
mortal good in something beautiful."[44] Through Diotima's words,
Plato advocates an increasingly complex series of manifestations of
beauty and love.

Diotima's role in Anhalt's work is an important one. She is a "psy-
chopomp" (a term borrowed from comparative religion studies, especially the writings of Mircea Eliade), a kind of supreme guide who
engages the audience on different levels, escorts them in the mall, and
casts her spell on everyone and everything she touches. Indeed, in
Millennial Mall (Lady Diotima's Walk), Anhalt has created his own version of Diotima – a symbol of love, a spiritual companion, who takes us
to illuminating places where we might gain understanding about love's
mysteries. Diotima moves in and out of character in that she is variously part of the mall, as well as its critic; in the composer's words, "she
mirrors the situation of the writer/composer." In creating this role,
Anhalt maintains Diotima had to (and did) evolve during the course of
writing the libretto, with its numerous revisions, as well as during the
course of the composition of the music. At times, and in subtle ways,
one gets the feeling that Diotima is guiding the composer.

An illustration of Diotima's varied roles, as well as a combinative reference to the present and the past, is scene 7 entitled "The Fashion
Show." In this scene, one of Diotima's "arias," she describes and comments on the scene, while also enacting it. Taking the contemporary
site of a fashion show, Anhalt refers in his text to the feminine beauty
ideal as "birds of paradise." Partway through we are reminded of an ancient analogy from the Book of Genesis (6:1–4) – the sons of God who
descended to earth and married the beautiful daughters of men and
procreated with them. (In conversation Anhalt has observed that,

significantly, this is followed by the story of the Flood. As Anhalt puts it, "the parallel is not unknown today: the powerful sons of man marrying the beautiful daughters of man.") The movement concludes somewhat surprisingly with a reference to the tragic death of the Italian-American designer, Giovanni Versace, who was shot outside his Florida home by a former acquaintance. This reference leaves the audience searching for some causal connection.

The subtitle of *Millennial Mall (Lady Diotima's Walk)*, A Voice-Drama for the Imagination, emphasizes that Anhalt aims to create dramatic situations through text and music, without visual aspects such as staging, choreography, or costumes. In placing the central thrust of the work on the imaginative response(s) of the listener, and moving in and out of the drama himself as the author/composer ("double perspective"), Anhalt follows a pattern established in his other operas, beginning with *La Tourangelle*. Importantly, each of Anhalt's four operas has a subtitle that refers to a creative adaptation of the composer's musical-dramatic ideas (a musical tableau; a historical pageant; a pluri-drama; a voice-drama for the imagination). A point of difference, however, is that unlike *La Tourangelle* and *Winthrop*, both of which are centred around certain aspects of the life story of a historical personage, *Millennial Mall (Lady Diotima's Walk)* presents Diotima, a legendary or fictional figure, who defies explanation in conventional dramatic terms.

Throughout the four operas, there is a decentralizing movement toward alternative modes of dramatic representation, expressed in increasingly personalized textual and musical tropes. Underlying all of the operas there is what one could call an "ethical quest," which is connected to the selection of the operas' themes and the belief systems of their protagonists and their respective societal contexts. The thread between Anhalt's compositions is woven in and around his continuing probe of the mystery of existence and the human condition through different moments and places in time. The wonder of this search is reflected in the feeling that surrounds the concluding poem in the libretto of *Millennial Mall (Lady Diotima's Walk)*. The poem also resonates with the lines from Anhalt's much earlier poem ("Mirage in Elöpatak") which opened this chapter.

Diotima's Song of Love's Gifts

The gift of silence
reserved for words of a friend ...

The gift of touch
for someone in need of reassurance ...

The gift of a smile
to one who is short of hope ...

The gift of support
by an unseen hand ...

The gift of selfless love for a child
... and the love of a child
for someone who is ripe with years ...

Companions for life in love ...

The awe in sight of
nature's wonders ...

marvelling at the
mystery of existence ...

surrender to the
enigmas of the cosmos ...

and of thought thinking itself ... [45]

A conclusion here seems inappropriate. Anhalt's creative and intellectual activities are very much an ongoing project. Nonetheless, through this examination one can observe ever-increasing links between the inspirational forces that have shaped his work over the last thirty years.

NOTES

1 Istvan Anhalt, "A Weave of Life Lines" (Kingston, 1992, manuscript), 153. This detailed handwritten account of experiences and personal relationships in Anhalt's life from childhood through a large part of the Kingston period was written "in a short spurt" in 1992. "A Weave of Life Lines" is a personal, open-ended (i.e., ongoing) account and remains unpublished. I am grateful to Professor Anhalt for sharing this document with me.

2 Istvan Anhalt, "What Tack to Take? An Autobiographical Sketch (Life in Progress ...)" *Queen's Quarterly* 92, 1 (spring 1985): 105–6.

3 Since 1973 Anhalt and his wife, Beate, have lived in a "historically designated" home across the street from Kingston's St Mary's Cathedral. The view from Anhalt's study shows the entire facade of this imposing

pseudobaroque edifice – a suggestive environment indeed for a composer working on an opera centring on an early-seventeenth-century religious personage in France.

4 Gordon E. Smith, " 'Deep Themes' Not So Hidden in the Music of István Anhalt," *Queen's Quarterly* 98,1 (spring 1991): 102.

5 John Beckwith, *Music Papers: Articles and Talks by a Canadian Composer* (Ottawa: Golden Dog Press, 1997), 127.

6 Anhalt, "What Tack to Take?" 106. See also Anhalt's comments on the relevance of *Winthrop* to Canadian history in part 4, pp. 375.

7 In the fall of 1969 Anhalt was a visiting professor at the State University of New York in Buffalo, where he gave a seminar on contemporary vocal and choral composition. Some of the ideas discussed in *Alternative Voices* first came to mind in that class. See Istvan Anhalt, *Alternative Voices: Essays on Contemporary Vocal and Choral Composition* (Toronto: University of Toronto Press, 1984), 269. The input of students and the teaching environment in general were, in this project as well as others, important in the genesis of Anhalt's creative and intellectual work.

8 The CBC Radio publicity department assembled a full documentation package on the premiere of *Winthrop*, which is in the Anhalt fonds at the National Library of Canada, Ottawa. See note 22, below.

9 Note the avoidance of the word "conclusion" here. With Anhalt, one has the impression that his work – musical compositions, scholarly writings, lectures, and even conversations – is integrated and ongoing, or, in a metaphorical interpretation, a mirror of human existence.

10 Anhalt observes that music was, and remains, an integral part of Arts and Science at Queen's. This, he maintains, is conducive to academic/collegial contact in as "wide" a manner as one could hope for. In contrast, the Faculty of Music at McGill during Anhalt's years there was physically (locationally) set apart, administratively autonomous, and only its dean met colleagues from other disciplines. This changed for Anhalt when he was appointed to the senate at McGill in 1968, and during his final three years there he made numerous contacts with colleagues in other departments. At Queen's, he maintains, collegiality was a "given" from the first day of his time there.

11 For more details about music study at Queen's before Anhalt's arrival in 1971, see Graham George, "Music at Queen's – The First Forty Years [1932–72]" (Queen's University School of Music, n.d.).

12 Anhalt fonds, National Library of Canada, folder E3.1.3 (see note 18 below). Graham George certainly knew Anhalt and his music before Anhalt's appointment at Queen's. See the biographical sketch of Anhalt by V.I. Rajewsky (International Service, CBC Montreal, 1961) in which Rajewsky quotes Dr George's positive commentary on Anhalt's Symphony: "here is a complex, sophisticated idiom capable of very refined expression when the composer [Anhalt] reaches the point at which he will want to express

something more than the satisfaction of sound-relations, and this is no small achievement at a time when nearly all his contemporaries are engaged in the same pursuit."

13 A modifed version of one of these lectures was later published. See Istvan Anhalt, "Luciano Berio's *Sequenza III, The Canada Music Book* 7 (autumn-winter 1973): 23–60. Contemporary music for the voice was a topic of particular interest to Anhalt, resulting also in his book *Alternative Voices*.

14 Anhalt fonds, folder E3.1.3.

15 Gayle Young's *The Sackbut Blues: Hugh Le Caine Pioneer in Electronic Music* (Ottawa: National Museum of Science and Technology, 1989) is a detailed study of Le Caine's life and work. The book contains descriptions of Le Caine's connections to Queen's, as well as referenccs to Anhalt's work in electronic music.

16 See Harry White, "Frank Llewellyn Harrison and the Development of Post-war Musicological Thought," *Hermanthena (Trinity College Review)* 146 (1989): 39–47, for an assessment of Harrison's work as a musicologist. Within the Queen's context, Harrison made a return "guest" visit in the late 1970s, during which he taught and gave lectures for a term.

17 Le Caine and Harrison were both present at the official opening ceremonies of the new building, and they also received honorary degrees at the November convocation.

18 Anhalt fonds, folders E3.2.11 and E3.2.9. Described in detail in Helmut Kallmann's article in this volume, itemized in a 1994 catalogue, the Anhalt fonds is one of the largest in the National Library of Canada (NLC), ranking in size with those of Glenn Gould, Sir Ernest MacMillan, and R. Murray Schafer. Anhalt relates the story that he wanted "a better home" for the contents of more than one hundred cardboard boxes in the garage of his Kingston home. After inspection by Helmut Kallmann, there was a series of "transfers" to the NLC. Anhalt has come to regard the fonds, which documents in words, music, and pictures almost all phases of his life, as a kind of "ancestral home."

19 William E. Benjamin, "István Anhalt: A Tribute and an Appreciation," *The Music Scene* 340 (Nov./Dec. 1984): 10–11.

20 Istvan Anhalt, "Directions in the Teaching of Composition at Canadian Universities: Which Way are We Going?" (typescript, 1976), 6, Anhalt fonds, folder F9.

21 Anhalt, "What Tack to Take?" 107.

22 Anhalt, *Alternative Voices*, 176–7. Anhalt adds to this list of "deep themes" in a later article: "myth, mythopoiesis; Freud's theories about the individual psyche, sexuality; individuation ('growth, decay'); the 'quest'; the Jungian archetypes; madness; the collective; religion, utopia; political revolt; fragmentation, montage ambiguity, ambivalence, serendipity, indeterminacy, deconstruction; man and evil; visions of the 'end'" among others.

See Anhalt, "Music: Context, Text, Counter-text," *Contemporary Music Review* 5 (1989): 109, 123–5.

23 Anhalt provides an examination of the compositional processes and contexts of *Thisness* in an article published in *Musical Canada: Words and Music Honouring Helmut Kallmann,* ed. John Beckwith and Frederick A. Hall (Toronto: University of Toronto Press, 1988), 211–31. This "companion" essay is typical of an aspect of Anhalt's creative activity. For many of his compositions there are extended commentaries in which Anhalt discusses and explains various aspects of the particular work's "terrain" (see essays in part 4 of this volume, as well as the appendix, which lists Anhalt's writings). Alan M. Gillmor has suggested that there is often "a fascinating interplay between the writings and the music" in "Echoes of Time and the River," in *Taking a Stand: Essays in Honour of John Beckwith* , ed. Timothy J. McGee (Toronto: University of Toronto Press, 1995), 32.

24 Istvan Anhalt, "From 'Mirage' to *Simulacrum* and 'Afterthought,' " this volume, 413.

25 Gillmor, "Echoes," 32. Gillmor draws attention also to Anhalt's relationship with the de Kerpely family in Budapest at the end of the war (and thereafter), also discussed in chapter 1 of this volume. Jenö de Kerpely was a cellist and co-founder of the Waldbauer-Kerpely String Quartet and a teacher at the Franz Liszt Academy of Music when Anhalt was a student there. His second wife, Theresa de Kerpely, was a writer and in 1952 published her first novel, entitled *A Crown for Ashes*, under the pseudonym Teresa Kay. Based to a large extent on the author's wartime experiences in Budapest, one of the book's leading characters is a young Jewish music student conscripted into a forced labour camp, Andrew Marton, or Anhalt in fictional disguise. As Gillmor points out, this novel is a significant, unusually revealing text: "Considering that *A Crown for Ashes* appeared just seven years after the war's end, it would not be unreasonable to assume that some of the thoughts and feelings Kerpely places in the mind of Marton reflect to a considerable degree Anhalt's own inner turmoil as a young man torn between his race and his country in the face of rejection and monstrous betrayal" ("Echoes," 21).

26 Anhalt, "From 'Mirage' to *Simulacrum*," this volume, 414.

27 Ibid., 417.

28 Ibid., 417; ellipsis in original.

29 Another influence, if not a prod, might have been a "reminder" offered to him by his close colleague and friend John Beckwith, who once asked him, When will you write an opera on a Jewish subject? As it turned out this had to wait, because it turned out to be the hardest enterprise to find a theme, a context, and a musical language for it. Finally by 1992 the pieces for this "came together" and the way was clear toward *Traces (Tikkun)* (personal communication).

30 Anhalt, "What Tack to Take?" 99.

31 Anhalt, "A Weave of Life Lines," 402.

32 Ibid., 369.

33 Anhalt relates that during his work on *Alternative Voices* he also became more sensitized to the religious worlds of two of his musical colleagues and friends, each of whom was working on a project with strong spiritual roots: R. Murray Schafer (Eastern religions) and John Beckwith (Christian hymnody) Anhalt, "A Weave of Life Lines," 404. On a more personal level, in 1984, Anhalt and his wife, who had had no synagogue affiliation in Kingston, joined the Reform synagogue Ihr Ha Melech in order to secure a burial place for his ailing mother; as well, he purchased burial plots for himself and his wife.

34 Anhalt's completed libretto, entitled *Oppenheimer*, is in the Anhalt fonds, in the National Library. After the libretto was considered "not acceptable" by the Canadian Opera Company, Anhalt began a collaboration on the project with John Murrell in 1993, with Canadian Opera Company approval. Murrell did write a libretto outline, but it was never completed. Murrell's role in the venture came to an end at the same time as the whole project was abandoned. Now Anhalt is thinking of his three-act libretto as a potential play. He has received some supportive comments about this idea from theatre professionals.

35 Anhalt, "A Weave of Life Lines," 480.

36 For important links with Anhalt's earlier compositions, see his "A Continuing Thread? Perhaps," included in part 4 of this volume.

37 Istvan Anhalt, "An Operatic Triptych in Multiple Texts," in part 4 of this volume, 371.

38 Mikhail Bahktin, "Discourse in the Novel," in *The Dialogic Imagination*, ed. Michael Holquist and trans. Caryl Emerson and Michael Holquist (Austin: University of Texas Press, 1981), 293.

39 As with many of the individuals in this list, Whalley was a close friend as well as a university colleague. Following Whalley's death in 1989, Anhalt wrote a short essay about his friendship with Whalley ("Remembering George Whalley," in "A Weave of Life Lines"; published as "Remembrance," in *George Whalley Rembrances*, ed. Michael D. Moore (Kingston: Quarry Press, 1989), 142–7.

40 This discussion of *Millennial Mall (Lady Diotima's Walk)* is based on the libretto, and Anhalt's commentary (both in part 4 of this volume), and conversations with the composer. Regarding *Millennial Mall*, see also David Parsons, "A Sprightly Walk through a Mythical Mall," *Globe and Mail* (28 January 2000): R6; and the review by Robert Everett-Green, "In the Bleak Midwinter, Music to Thaw to," *Globe and Mail* (31 January 2000): R4.

41 Here Anhalt has been influenced by the writings of the American philosopher and one of the founders of the semiotic movement, Charles W. Morris

(*The Pragmatic Movement in American Philosophy* [New York: G. Brazilier, 1970]), who explains "pragmatics" as the aim of defining conditions of linguistic communication, for example, the way two interlocutors have an effect on each other. In many if not all of Anhalt's works involving voice(s), the composer has explored "pragmatic" communication levels. To facilitate an understanding of this aspect of these compositions, in 1996 he formulated a "pragmatic hexagram" (a "conceptualization of the pragmatic world"), a series of six focuses or dimensions (history, individual, society, language, situation, role) which can be interpreted separately and in various combinations when applied to Anhalt's music.

42 Donald Harmon Akenson, *Surpassing Wonder: The Invention of the Bible and the Talmuds* (Montreal & Kingston: McGill-Queen's University Press, 1998), 122. Akenson develops this idea with a discussion of the situation between the struggle of the Jews against the Hellenizers, or those spreading "evil" ideas, several centuries B.C.E. (pp. 120–2).

43 This is an important concept in Anhalt's work, and one which he uses as a theme in his text "A Continuing Thread? Perhaps" (included in part 4). "Chronotope" means literally "time-space" with no priority to either dimension. As Bakhtin puts it, "in the literary artistic chronotope, spatial and temporal indicators are fused into one carefully thought-out concrete whole. Time, as it were, thickens, takes on flesh, becomes artistically visible; likewise space becomes charged and responsive to movements of time, plot and history" (in *The Dialogic Imagination*, 84).

44 *The Cambridge Companion to Plato*, ed. Richard Kraut (Cambridge and N.Y.: Cambridge University Press, 1992), 344. See also pp. 344–7 for a critical discussion of Diotima's role in Plato's *Symposium*. A complete English translation of the text is in *The Symposium and the Phaedrus: Plato's Erotic Dialogues*, translated with introduction and commentaries by William S. Cobb (New York: State University of New York, 1993).

45 The complete libretto is given in chapter 17.

PART TWO
Compositions

4 The Instrumental Solo and Chamber Music

ROBIN ELLIOTT

Anhalt's purely instrumental solo and chamber music dates, with one important exception, from early in his career. Most of the music he composed in Europe falls into this category, as do the works he wrote during his first six years in Canada. The only chamber music work to date that reflects the style of Anhalt's later operatic, vocal, and orchestral compositions is *Doors … shadows (Glenn Gould in memory)*. The works under consideration here, with place and date of completion in parentheses, are as follows:

Capriccio for solo piano (Ainring, Germany, 1 March 1946)
String Quartet (Paris, ?1946–47)
Piano Sonata (Paris, 1947; revised Montreal, 1951)
L'Arc-en-ciel (The Rainbow) for two pianos (Montreal, 8 May 1951)
Piano Trio (violin, cello, and piano) (Montreal, March 1953)
Fantasia for piano (Montreal, 1954)
Violin Sonata (violin and piano) (Montreal, 21 November 1954)
"La Fuite" for piano, from *La Tourangelle* (Kingston, 1974)
Doors … shadows (Glenn Gould in memory) for string quartet (Kingston, 1 April 1992; revised 1 October 1992)

Funeral Music (Montreal, 1951; dedicated to László Gyopár) exists on the boundary between the chamber and orchestral repertoires, as it is scored for ten instruments (flute, clarinet, bassoon, French horn, two violins, two violas, and two cellos). Its first performance (Montreal, 20 March 1952) was given as chamber music (solo string scoring, no

Example 4.1   String Quartet, fourth movement, violin 1, mm. 1–3

conductor), but it was subsequently performed with conductor as a chamber orchestra work, and is treated in the following essay, "Orchestral Works," by John Beckwith. The student works from Anhalt's Hungarian years, which included a string trio, a fugue for solo violin, a suite for piano, and a solo cello sonata in three movements, are now lost. The violin fugue (1940) was written in the style of J.S. Bach, the piano suite (1940 or 1941) was influenced by Stravinsky and Balinese music, and the solo cello work (1941 or 1942) owed much to Kodály's Sonata, op. 8, for solo cello (1915).[1] The rest of the works dealt with here are available from the Canadian Music Centre and/or the Anhalt fonds at the National Library of Canada.

The first two works in the above list share a slender or nonexistent performance history and are available only as holograph manuscript unica in the Anhalt fonds. Capriccio is a three-page single movement of 164 bars; it is broadly tonal and for the most part is in a simple two-part texture.[2] Its chief interest lies in the fact that it is the first piece Anhalt wrote after he left Hungary and, together with the *Six Songs from Na Conxy Pan* and *Ünnepek (Feasts)*, is among his earliest preserved works. It is very similar in texture, though not in sound, to "La Fuite" from *La Tourangelle*, written twenty-eight years later.

The String Quartet is considerably more ambitious in scope and achievement than Capriccio. The score is undated but was written in Paris under the guidance of Nadia Boulanger; it is headed "*et in terra*" and so, if one may guess from this reference to peace, likely dates from 1946 or 1947.[3] The quartet is in four movements – Solenne, Calmo, Giocoso, and Appassionato – and is about twenty-three minutes in duration. It is written in a neoclassical tonal style characteristic of the work of so many Boulanger pupils and, like many string quartet composers of the period, Anhalt pays homage here to the Bartók quartets. The Bartók influence is most evident in the style, though not the form, of the last movement, which is entitled *Tema in stilo ungherese con variazioni* and consists of a theme (the opening is given in example 4.1) with five variations and a coda. The care with which the score and a set of parts for the String Quartet were copied out in ink would seem to indicate that a performance of the work was anticipated, but in fact the work has not been performed to date.[4]

Example 4.2 Piano Sonata, first movement, mm. 97–103

The Piano Sonata is a transitional work, as it was one of the last pieces that Anhalt completed in Paris, and a thorough revision of the work was one of the first tasks that the composer completed in Montreal. The Paris version of the work is available for consultation in the Anhalt fonds,[5] but only the revised, Montreal version has been heard in Canada, and it will be the version discussed here.[6] The sonata is in three movements – Andante, Con moto, and Allegro – but there is an *attacca* indication between the last two movements, which are in fact in the same tempo.[7] Indeed, the second movement is so short that it functions as an introduction to the last movement, and is only four bars longer than the introduction to the first movement.

The Bartók influence, which was only mildly evident in the String Quartet, is more pervasive in the Piano Sonata. In the quartet, this influence was confined to the use of string playing techniques and to some extent the rhythmic properties of certain sections of the piece,

Example 4.3   Piano Sonata, third movement, mm. 1–5

whereas in the sonata it extends to the melodic, harmonic, and metric organization of the entire work. Nevertheless, the first movement shows considerable allegiance to tonal procedures; the introduction ends on the dominant of A minor, and the movement closes with a V–I cadence in that key. But semitonal clashes abound, and these are frequently combined with ostinato figures. Bulgarian-style metres such as irregular groupings of eighth notes (3 2 3 and 3 3 2 3) are also used in the manner of Bartók. After a lengthy introduction (Andante, 40 bars), the first movement proper is labelled "Marcia funebre." A lovely pentatonic tune, with the antecedent and consequent phrases presented in strikingly different harmonizations, provides a decided contrast to the funeral march. The movement is not in a traditional sonata-form structure, but after the tune quoted in example 4.2 there is a section in which earlier ideas are developed, followed by a thirty-bar coda, rather than a recapitulation.

The brief second movement is a bitonal study in thirds and sixths with constantly changing metres. This leads directly into the third movement, which opens with a subject that is the most overtly tonal thematic statement of the entire work (see example 4.3). This is developed into a statement of forty-eight bars, which is followed by a second, longer paragraph in a slower tempo. A varied return of the opening section begins at bar 139 and ends on an A-major chord at bar 196, after which there is a lengthy and varied coda.

L'Arc-en-ciel (The Rainbow) was conceived as a "ballet in three lights," on the subject of the judgment of Paris, but to date has only been presented as a concert work for two pianos. The holograph ink score of the work states that the two-piano version is a reduction, but this appears to be the only form in which the piece was completed (there are copious sketches for the work in the Anhalt fonds).[8] The sections of the score are Preamble (First Light – Paris), Second Light (The Rainbow – Pallas Athene – Hera – Aphrodite), Change of Light (Pas de quatre), First Light (Paris). The idea of writing a ballet on a subject from classical Greek mythology was no doubt suggested by Igor Stravinsky's ballets on such themes (*Apollon musagète, Perséphone, Orpheus*), and *L'arc-en-ciel* is indeed in the neoclassical style of Stravinsky. Anhalt became well acquainted with Stravinsky's music through his lessons in Paris with Nadia Boulanger and with Soulima Stravinsky, the composer's son. He remembers in particular having been given a copy of the score of *Perséphone* by Nadia Boulanger to study.[9] The sheer industry required to produce a work of the scope of *L'Arc-en-ciel* is impressive, but in light of the fact that the ballet has never been produced on stage, one is forced to conclude that the creative energy might perhaps have been put to better use.

Anhalt could easily have continued to produce more compositions in the style of Stravinsky and Bartók along the lines of the works discussed so far. But already in Paris he had become aware of the works of Arnold Schoenberg and his pupils, and although Anhalt did not write atonal or twelve-tone music while studying with Boulanger (who was firmly opposed to the Second Viennese School), his curiosity was nevertheless piqued. In the Piano Trio of 1953 he began to explore a markedly more complex harmonic idiom than he had used hitherto, although he did not yet make use of twelve-tone techniques.

The immediate impetus for the composition of the Piano Trio was a suggestion from Anhalt's friend and mentor Jenö de Kerpely, who was the cellist of a piano trio then in residence at the University of Redlands in California. The trio is dedicated to Theresa and Jenö (Eugene) de Kerpely, but the latter's ensemble did not ever perform the work, as the pianist found it to be too difficult. The first performance took place in Montreal on 6 December 1954, and was given by Eugene Kash, violin, Walter Joachim, cello, and Charles Reiner, piano. The trio was later taken into the repertoire of the Halifax Trio (Francis Chaplin, violin, Edward Bisha, cello, and Gordon Macpherson, piano); that trio gave a broadcast performance of the work on the CBC on 20 November 1961[10] and recorded the work in 1966.[11] Kurt Stone, in his review of the Halifax Trio's recording of the work, stated that Anhalt's trio "is music of strong gestures, highstrung activity, and youthful vitality" and that it "shows a good deal of imaginative originality of expression and form, and a convincing inner consistency."[12]

Anhalt himself has drawn attention to four different influences that are evident in the trio: baroque music, Brahms, Bartók, and jazz.[13] The influence of baroque music is largely confined to melodic ideas (especially a turn figure which becomes prominent in the last movement) and textures (the opening of the second movement, for instance, shows a polarization of melodic interest that owes something to the baroque trio sonata). The Brahms influence is also confined to textural features, such as in example 4.4, where the right hand of the piano is in octaves and thirds, the strings are in octaves, and the left hand of the piano has a chordal accompaniment. The influence of Bartók is actually less in evidence in the Piano Trio than it was in the Piano Sonata or even in the String Quartet, and the jazz element is confined to one outburst (bars 96–105) in the second movement.[14]

Anhalt all but abandons tonality in the Piano Trio. The first movement begins and ends with octave sonorities on the pitch G, and the last movement ends with a G-major triad in the piano (very oddly spaced, with the root and third deep in the bass clef and the fifth very high in the treble clef), but there is no sense of tonal resolution anywhere in the work. The pitch content is highly chromatic throughout, and the frequent use of pedal and ostinato figures does not create a feeling of tonality, but rather undermines it. The first movement, for instance, ends with an eightfold repetition of a short phrase (bars 348–55) that simply brings the forward momentum of the work to a complete halt. This repeated phrase is then arbitrarily cut short by a loud eruption, which ends the movement.

The structural organization of the trio is not created by the repetition of earlier sections or the varied restatement of musical features; instead the work evolves as a continuously unfolding succession of independent ideas. This is why a large section of the first movement (bars 233–306, approximately one-fifth of the movement) can be indicated as a cut in the score (and is omitted from the recording of the work) without seriously damaging the work's formal plan.[15] This somewhat arbitrary approach to organizing musical ideas (melodically, harmonically, and formally) was replaced in Anhalt's next work by the rigorous logic of twelve-tone techniques.

Like many composers of his generation, Anhalt never received any formal instruction in twelve-tone techniques. He learned what he knew of the method in part from the standard textbooks by René Leibowitz and Ernst Krenek, but more importantly by studying the scores for himself. Ever the autodidact, Anhalt quickly became highly trained in the principles of twelve-tone composition, and his very first completed work using that method, the Fantasia for piano, remains one of his most admired compositions. It is also, together with the Piano Sonata, Anhalt's only larger independent work for piano solo, which is somewhat surprising given that the piano is his own instrument. Anhalt himself gave the premiere of the Fantasia in Montreal on 6 December 1954.

There are two complete holograph copies of the score of the Fantasia in the Anhalt fonds; one is in pencil and the other is an ink transparency. Both are identical with the final published version of the score,[16] except that in the pencil score the tempo indication Lento is

Example 4.4   Piano Trio, first movement, mm. 183–6

given at the beginning (in addition to the metronome marking of
quarter note = 52–56), and the ink score is dated "Montreal 1954" at
the end. On a separate page at the end of the ink copy of the score
Anhalt wrote out a twelve-tone row, but curiously enough it is not the
basic form of the row used in the Fantasia; the first four pitches are the
same, but the order of the last eight pitches is rearranged.[17] The basic
form of the row used in the Fantasia appears immediately in the first
bar of the piece, as shown in example 4.5. John Beckwith has commented on the opening of the Fantasia that it "gives unsuspecting listeners a rather unpleasant shock; and they would hardly be comforted
if the composer told them, as I imagine he would, that his purpose is to
create as quickly and as radically as possible a climate for what is to follow."[18] The row contains no major thirds or minor sixths, and indeed
those warm, tonal intervals are largely (though not completely) absent
from the piece.

Other kinds of tonal references (or at least departures from strict serial procedures) do crop up in the Fantasia, often involving the pitches
C, B-flat, and B (the first three pitches of the inversion of the row).
These pitches appear (with C emphasized) as a kind of pedal point in
the opening six bars of the work, and occur again in a repeated figure
in the right hand from bar 47 to bar 51. Anhalt not infrequently repeats dyads drawn from the various row forms (for example, in the
right hand at bars 4–5, 20–1, 54–7 and 57–8). Two earlier writers,
Beckwith and Udo Kasemets, nevertheless felt that Anhalt's approach
to twelve-tone composition in the Fantasia is orthodox. Beckwith described it as "athematic music along the lines of some strictly conceived 12-note works of Schoenberg, say the Violin Concerto,"[19] while

Example 4.5 Fantasia, m. 1

Kasemets called it "a perfect example of athematic twelve-tone writing where continual transformation rather than development of thematic ideas is the main form-giving process."[20] Glenn Gould and Norman B. Chapman, on the other hand, have emphasized Anhalt's freedom of approach in the work. Gould wrote that although "in some respects it acknowledges a debt to the later style of Schoenberg ... it delivers its timely homilies in an accent that is both arresting and spontaneous,"[21] while Chapman wrote that in the Fantasia "attention is focused less on the formal application of serialism than on the creation of musical shape and mood."[22]

Although notated throughout with a 4/4 time signature, the Fantasia does not have a regularly recurring pulse to emphasize the metre; indeed, nearly every bar in the piece is marked by some degree of syncopation. Anhalt has commented as follows on his procedure with regard to the notation of rhythm: "I find it 'practical' to notate the rhythm in easily decipherable metric frameworks. However complex the 'inwardly-heard' rhythms, I most often find it feasible [to] notate them in 'simple' metres. (This is especially helpful in ensemble music.)"[23] Fantasia does nevertheless have a clearly articulated formal structure, which consists, in the composer's words, of "a curve of pitch and dynamics with two peaks."[24] The peaks occur at bars 16 and 51 (there are 87 bars in the piece). The opening builds in dynamic and textural intensity to the first climax, after which the tension subsides. A second buildup then follows, marked *sempre accelerando e crescendo*, which reaches a climax at bar 48 that is sustained to bar 51. In the long final section of the work, there is a rallentando and diminuendo that lasts, with some ebb and flow, until the end of the piece. This final section includes a three-voice mirror canon at bars 69 to 75.

Anhalt has stated that the inspiration for the composition of fantasia was a performance of a fantasia by Sweelinck given in Montreal by Glenn Gould.[25] Gould in turn became interested in Anhalt's Fantasia soon after it was written, and wrote to Anhalt in the summer of 1955 to request a copy of the score.[26] Gould kept abreast of Anhalt's works over the years, including *Funeral Music*[27] and the Symphony. He asked Anhalt to act as a commentator on Schoenberg's music for a radio documentary that he prepared in 1962,[28] and he interviewed Anhalt about *Cento* for a radio program in 1969.[29] The most lasting document of Gould's interest in Anhalt's music is the recording he made in 1967 of the Fantasia.[30] Upon hearing Gould's recording of the work, Anhalt wrote to the pianist to say "I now realize the true depth, integrity and over-all-control of form of your reading. In brief: you have played the piece marvellously."[31] Anhalt added that Gould played the first eighteen bars a little too slowly, but that this was a minor issue compared to the linear clarity of his reading of the work. The U.S. critic Alfred Frankenstein, reviewing Gould's recording (which also included the Variations by Jacques Hétu and the Fantasia in D minor by Oskar Morawetz), wrote that Anhalt's Fantasia "has the urgency, the singularity of profile, the economy, and the eloquence of a genuine musical statement," and added that Anhalt is "a 12-tone composer who really has something to say and says it as well as any composer now alive."[32]

The Violin Sonata (dedicated to the composer's father) was completed in 1954 but was not heard until 1957, when it was played by François D'Albert, violin, and Samuel Levitan, piano, for the CBC radio program "Premieres." The first concert performance of the work took place as part of a concert sponsored by the Canadian League of Composers at the Hermitage in Montreal on 5 April 1960; the performers were Hyman Bress, violin, and Charles Reiner, piano.[33] For that performance, and also for a subsequent one on 21 April 1960 that was sponsored by the Montreal Jewish Music Council, the score of the sonata was projected onto a screen while the music was being played, at the suggestion of Bress.

There are two ink transparency score and part sets for the sonata in the Anhalt fonds. One is an undated, incomplete score, and the other is the complete score, which is dated "21.11.1954 / Montreal" at the end (this is the transparency from which the score in the Canadian Music Centre was made).[34] The incomplete score is evidently the earlier of the two versions; it contains only pages 1 to 10 and 20 to 23 (the last page or two is missing). It seems reasonable to suggest that the missing pages were reused for the transparencies of the final version of the sonata, but the beginning and ending of the work were rewritten so thoroughly that the earlier version of these sections could not be reused. (In the final, complete version of the sonata, many of the transparency pages have had the corners cut off, presumably because the old page numbers had to be removed.) The two versions are

Example 4.6 Violin Sonata: basic row

recognizably the same piece, but markedly different with regard to octave register, rhythms, and frequently even choice of pitches.

The sonata is written predominantly in a three-voice texture, with the violin and the right and left hands of the piano part each being given a single melodic line most of the time. This is in contrast to the piano writing in the Piano Trio, which is frequently chordal in texture (as in example 4.4). Anhalt explained the reason for this choice of texture in a note about the sonata: "As far as the role of the piano is concerned here, my intention was to provide such a part, which would allow for as much fusion of timbres as the contrasting qualities of the two instruments permit. In order to reach this goal I used contrapuntal textures throughout the work."[35] This texture also simplified the use of twelve-tone techniques, because each of the three melodic strands typically is based on a separate permutation of the basic row for the piece.

The basic row of the Violin Sonata, which is given in example 4.6, is stated in the right hand of the piano part in the opening three bars of the work. This row can be divided into two hexachords, the second of which (H2) is the inversion of the first (H1), transposed up nine semitones. It can also be divided into four trichords (T1 to T4); the first and last notes of each trichord are a semitone apart, and the interval of a second or a third separates the middle note of each trichord from each of the outer notes.[36] The trichord division features more significantly in the sonata than the hexachord division. The opening trichord of the basic row given in example 4.6, for instance, recurs dozens of times throughout the first movement, including the obsessive ostinato-type treatments of it in the violin part from bar 66 to bar 76 and in the piano left hand from bar 76 to bar 82.

William Lister has noted that throughout this work, "Anhalt avoids any rhythmic, metric or melodic periodicity which might make the notes coalesce into a 'theme' in the classical sense."[37] Although both Beckwith[38] and Lister[39] regard the last movement of the sonata as a variation form, it follows such a pattern only very loosely. Perhaps more helpful is Anhalt's observation that "the division of the Sonata into three movements is but a way of indicating the major articulation points in a form which aims at unfolding in a single curve."[40] The three movements are to be played without pause, and Anhalt gives only a metronome marking, rather than a descriptive tempo designation, for each movement (the Piano Trio also follows this procedure).[41] The Violin Sonata is thus similar in form to the Fantasia, which also unfolds in a single curve with two points of division.

After completing the Violin Sonata in 1954, Anhalt did not write another instrumental chamber music work until nearly four decades later. In the meantime, however, he did write a work for piano solo, which was actually a by product of his large-scale dramatic work *La Tourangelle*, for three sopranos, two reciters, tape, and instrumental ensemble. This is the seven-minute piece known as "La Fuite,"[42] which is drawn from section 4, ("Isaac") that deals with Marie de l'Incarnation's decision to abandon her son Isaac and pursue life as a missionary in the New World.[43] In *La Tourangelle*, the piano is barely audible beneath the complex web of superimposed tape, vocal, and orchestral layers; it is not meant in any way to have a *concertante* solo role. Instead, the piano portrays the thought in Marie de l'Incarnation's mind of fleeing (hence "La Fuite") to the New World, while the other layers represent the complex emotional and psychological situation in which she finds herself at that point in her life. When heard as a piano solo, "La Fuite" stands revealed as a delicate, airy, and charming *moto perpetuo* etude. It is predominantly in a simple two-voice texture, and until the final dozen bars has a consistently high tessitura, with both the right and left hands written in the treble clef. With its frequent use of short repeated patterns, slow harmonic rhythm, and virtually continuous sixteenth-note figuration, "La Fuite" resembles the style of minimalism, although Anhalt has stated that his intention was to evoke the keyboard style of a much earlier age, namely that of Ramcau and Couperin.[44]

Anhalt's last chamber music composition to date was commissioned by the CBC as part of the events marking the tenth anniversary of Glenn Gould's death (and the sixtieth of his birth). As part of the Glenn Gould Conference (held in Toronto, 23–27 September 1992), the CBC offered a concert series in the Glenn Gould Studio, located in the brand new CBC building in Toronto. For one of these concerts, on 24 September, the CBC producer Neil Crory asked the three Canadian composers whose piano pieces Gould had recorded to contribute a movement for string quartet.[45] Crory asked the composers for a movement of five to eight minutes in duration that "should deal, in some fashion, with Glenn Gould" and would be combined with the contributions of Jacques Hétu and Oskar Morawetz into a suite, tentatively to be called "Vignettes of Glenn Gould."[46] The title was later dropped, although the three works were performed in the sequence Morawetz, Anhalt, Hétu by the Glenn Gould String Quartet, an ad hoc group formed for the occasion.[47] Anhalt's movement ended up being approximately twelve minutes in duration.

As a way of paying tribute to Gould, Morawetz and Hétu both used themes from pieces by Bach that Gould had recorded. Morawetz contributed *Improvisation on Four Inventions by J.S. Bach*, which draws on themes from the two- and three-part inventions for keyboard by Bach, and Hétu used the first two bars of the aria from Bach's *Goldberg Variations* as melodic material in his Scherzo, op. 54, along with the first six notes of the row from his own Variations for piano (which Gould had recorded). In the program note for *Doors ... shadows (Glenn Gould in memory)*, Anhalt stated that the connection of his quartet movement to Gould was loose, but concluded that what the piece added up to was "fantasy ... fantasies about someone who left a rare mark and who left much too early ... memories ... blurred shadows behind half open doors."[48]

Anhalt's movement is indeed fantasia-like in its structure, which was only appropriate, given that the Anhalt work that Gould had recorded was the Fantasia. In an introductory note to the score of *Doors ... shadows*, Anhalt stated that "the piece consists of a succession of 'events' of differing character," and that the progression from one event to the next "may imply relatedness, development, new departure, contrast, surprise, etc."[49] The work is often thickly scored, for a quartet; there are numerous sections where eight notes sound at a time. The harmonic language is freely atonal, and the rhythmic structure is characteristically complex and subtle, with the pervasive use of syncopation, frequent changes of tempo and metre, and sections of improvisatory unmeasured rhythms. A wide range of string playing techniques is called for, including microtones, controlled glissandi, varied vibrato effects, artificial harmonics, and tremolo. A remarkably wide palette of string quartet colours is featured, and this, rather than formal considerations, is what lies at the heart of the piece, which is a musical portrait of unusual richness and depth.[50] Anhalt, after reading the above passage, commented further about his quartet movement and its relation to Gould: "*Doors ... shadows* is a quasi-surreal drama of this complex man and great artist/virtuoso pianist ... and the unfathomable secrets that lived within him and, in part, departed with his death. I never forget our exchanges ... I still hear his voice ... Yes: my *Doors ... shadows* is a sort of portrait, but even more so it is a dirge."[51]

Aside from a fairly intense period of preoccupation with instrumental solo and chamber music composition from 1946 to 1954, Anhalt has shown slight interest in working with small performing ensembles. But, characteristically, he has given thoughtful consideration to the reasons and thought processes underlying this shift:

Did this fact (leaving the "chamber" &/or solo "voice" behind) stem from some desire to aim for a hidden "larger scale?" If so what is the "realm of this scale?" The need for a large scale "architecture" to say what? The desire to tell a "story" in "depth," with numerous angles? Does this come from unwilling-ness to ignore significant interconnectednesses, which to "treat fairly" requires longer durations? Whatever the reason(s), the "intimate voice" is now (and since a while) reserved for *selected parts* of a larger/longer piece, where it is put "in context" or, better, in a "context of a situation" (following *here* the wording of B. Malinowsky). Shall I ever return to intimate (chamber, etc.) formats in my 80+ age? Will there be time? Health? Interest? I, simply, (?) don't know. [52]

Although they do not by any means form a major part of Anhalt's oeuvre, the instrumental solo and chamber music works do represent an impressively wide range of compositional idioms and a high degree of artistic accomplishment. It is reasonable to suggest that they will stand the test of time and continue to merit further study and repeat performances in the future.

NOTES

1 Istvan Anhalt, letter to the author, 10 September 1998.
2 Capriccio is preserved in the Anhalt fonds, National Library of Canada, Ottawa, folder 6.0.1, and is dated "1946 III 1 Ainring" at the end. Except where otherwise mentioned, all references to Anhalt fonds files in this chapter refer to series A.
3 The score, which is entitled "Quartetto" by Anhalt, is available in an ink holograph manuscript (83 pages), in the Anhalt fonds, folder 3.1.7. A corresponding set of ink holograph parts is in folders 3.1.8 through 3.1.11.
4 Istvan Anhalt, letter to the author, 10 September 1998.
5 Anhalt fonds, folder 6.0.16 (49 pages).
6 The Montreal version is in the Anhalt fonds, folder 6.0.17 (33 pages), and is also available from the library of the Canadian Music Centre.
7 The last movement is actually designated "Lo stesso movimento" (i.e., Con moto) in the score, and has the same metronome marking as the second movement (quarter note = 100), but in the program for the first perfor-mance of the work (by Charles Reiner in Montreal on 20 March 1952) the last movement is given as Allegro.

8 The holograph ink score is in the Anhalt fonds, folder 6.0.14 (92 pages).
There is an ink transparency of the score in folder 6.0.15. A one-page
sketch of the story of the ballet, in Hungarian, is in folder 6.0.5, and the
drafts and sketches for the work are in folders 6.0.6 through 6.0.13.

9 Istvan Anhalt, letter to the author, 10 September 1998.

10 *CBC Times*, 14, 20 (18–24 November 1961): 13.

11 *Music and Musicians of Canada*, vol. 17, RCI 229/RCI CCS-1023. The recording was reissued in *Anthology of Canadian Music*, vol. 22, Radio Canada
International, 1985 (hereafter cited as ACM 22).

12 Kurt Stone, "Reviews of Records," *Musical Quarterly*, 53, 3 (July 1967): 446.

13 Anhalt, liner notes for *ACM 22*.

14 Section 8 ("Preparation") of *Foci* is based, in part, on the second movement
of the Piano Trio. Istvan Anhalt, letter to the author, 10 September 1998.

15 The cut is indicated in the copy of the score in the library of the Canadian
Music Centre. The original ink transparency of the score is in the Anhalt
fonds, folder 3.1.18 (violin part), 3.1.19 (cello part), and 3.1.20–21 (piano
score); folders 3.1.14–17 contain sketches for the work.

16 Istvan Anhalt, *Fantasia for Piano* (Toronto, Ont.: Berandol Music, 1972).

17 The order of pitches in this row is C, D, D-flat, E, B, D-sharp, F-sharp, B-flat,
F, A-flat, G, and A.

18 John Beckwith, "Composers in Toronto and Montreal," *University of Toronto
Quarterly* 26, 1 (October 1956): 167n4.

19 Ibid., 63.

20 Udo Kasemets, "István Anhalt," in *Contemporary Canadian Composers*, ed. Keith
MacMillan and John Beckwith (Toronto: Oxford University Press, 1975), 8.

21 Glenn Gould, liner notes to his recording *Canadian Music in the 20th Cen-
tury*, Columbia Masterworks 32110046, 1967 (which includes the Anhalt
Fantasia); reprinted in *The Glenn Gould Reader*, ed. Tim Page (Toronto:
Lester & Orpen Dennys, 1984), 206.

22 Norman B. Chapman, "Piano Music by Canadian Composers, 1940–1965,"
(Ph.D. diss., Case Western Reserve University, 1972), 172–80.

23 Istvan Anhalt, letter to the author, 10 September 1998.

24 Anhalt, as quoted in Beckwith, "Composers," 63.

25 Istvan Anhalt, letter to Glenn Gould, 26 September 1967; Anhalt fonds,
folder H2.61. This information is restated in Anhalt, "A Weave of Life
Lines" (Kingston, 1992, manuscript), 246, and in Anhalt, letter to the
author, 29 October 1997.

26 Glenn Gould, letter to Istvan Anhalt, 23 August 1955; Anhalt fonds, folder
H2.61.

27 Gould heard *Funeral Music* performed at Stratford, Ontario, in 1961 and
wrote to Anhalt, "I think that it is the most impressive work of chamber
music by a Canadian that I have heard in many years." Gould, letter to
Anhalt, 8 September 1961; Anhalt fonds, folder H2.61.

28 "Arnold Schoenberg: The Man Who Changed Music," *CBC Wednesday Night*, 8 August 1962.

29 "The Art of Glenn Gould: Take Seven," CBC broadcast, 31 June 1969. The program began with a recital by Gould, which included a performance of Anhalt's Fantasia.

30 Gould, *Canadian Music*; reissued in 1992 in CD format on Sony SMK 52 677.

31 Istvan Anhalt, letter to Glenn Gould, 26 September 1967; Anhalt fonds, folder H2.61.

32 Alfred Frankenstein, "If This Were the Music of Canada, God Save the Queen and *Les Canadiens!*" *High Fidelity* 18, 3 (March 1968): 86.

33 Bress and Reiner also recorded the sonata in 1966 on *Music and Musicians of Canada*, vol. 8, RCI 220/RCI CCS-1014. The recording was reissued in ACM 22.

34 The complete piano score is in the Anhalt fonds, folder 3.1.3, and the corresponding violin part is in folder 3.1.6; the incomplete piano score is in file 3.1.5, with the corresponding violin part in folder 3.1.4.

35 Anhalt, program note about the Violin Sonata, 21 April 1960 (Anhalt fonds, folder B1.2).

36 Beckwith, "Composers," 61 notes that rows of this type feature in works by Webern and Krenek. John Weinzweig also used a similar row in his Wood- wind Quintet (1964).

37 William Warwick Lister, "The Contemporary Sonata for Violin and Piano by Canadian Composers," (D.M.A. thesis, Boston University, School of Fine and Applied Arts, 1970), 133.

38 Beckwith, "Composers," 62.

39 Lister, "Contemporary Sonata," 89.

40 Anhalt, liner notes for ACM 22.

41 The last movement of the Violin Sonata does not even have a metronome marking in the final version of the score; the earlier version gives the indi- cation dotted quarter note = 48 (the movement is in 3/8 time).

42 Antonín Kubálek recorded "La Fuite" from *La Tourangelle* on Centrediscs CMC 0382 in 1982.

43 In the published holograph full score of *La Tourangelle* (Toronto: Berandol Music, 1982), "La Fuite" begins on page 112 and runs to bar 173. This version of "La Fuite" is slightly different from the composer's holograph version for piano solo that is available in the Canadian Music Centre. Some repeated bars or beats in the full score version are omitted in the piano solo version. Otherwise, the piano solo version is simply taken from the piano part for *La Tourangelle*, and includes a separate line which gives the duration in one-second increments and indicates cue lines for the vocal, tape, and orchestral parts. (The durations and cue lines are of course unnecessary when the work is performed as a piano solo.)

44 Anhalt, letter to the author, 10 September 1998.
45 These included Anhalt, Oskar Morawetz, and Jacques Hétu. Gould also
recorded a work by the Canadian composer Barbara Pentland; it was not
released on the original LP recording, but did appear in the CD reissue
(see note 30 for details). Pentland was also approached about contributing
a string quartet movement, but was too ill to participate in the project.
46 Neil Crory, letter to Anhalt, 17 February 1992; Anhalt fonds, Accession
June 1993, folder 19.
47 The members of the quartet were supposed to have been violinists
Malcolm Lowe and Mayumi Seiler, violist Steve Dann, and cellist Fred
Sherry. Lowe, however, was unable to attend and was replaced at the last
minute by Nai-Xian Hu.
48 Istvan Anhalt, program note for *Doors ... shadows (Glenn Gould in memory)*
(April 1992, insert in "A Weave of Life Lines," in after p. 248); ellipses in
original.
49 Istvan Anhalt, *Doors ... shadows (Glenn Gould in memory)* , holograph score,
[p. iii]. A copy of the score is available from the Canadian Music Centre;
the original is in the Anhalt fonds, Accession June 1993, folder 243. Alan
Clark prepared a computer-typeset version of the score, which is also
available in the Anhalt fonds, for the performance by the Glenn Gould
String Quartet.
50 Parts of *Doors ... shadows (Glenn Gould in memory)* appear near the end of
Traces. This is one of several instances of self-borrowing in Anhalt's oeuvre
(Anhalt, letter to the author, 10 September 1998).
51 Istvan Anhalt, letter to the author, 10 September 1998; ellipses in original.
52 Ibid.

5 Orchestral Works

JOHN BECKWITH

Istvan Anhalt's orchestral oeuvre contains eight works: *Concerto in stilo di Handel*, a neobaroque concerto composed during his studies in Paris; Interludium and *Funeral Music*, two short works from his first years in Montreal; Symphony, his major work of the 1950s; *Symphony of Modules*, his major work of the 1960s; and then, in a sudden creative burst of the late 1980s, a triptych of large-scale orchestral essays – *Simulacrum*, *SparkskrapS*, and *Sonance•Resonance (Welche Töne?)*.

The first two pieces have remained unperformed; scores are preserved in the Anhalt fonds of the National Library of Canada. The fonds also contains sketches and eighty-two pages of draft score for a *Concerto per orchestra*, signed "Steven Anhalt." This work for large orchestra was begun in Budapest in 1945, developed further in Paris in 1947–48, but never finished. The existing materials include a completed draft of the first movement ("Capriccio," Andante misterioso) and an extended draft of the second ("Suonata" [sic], Allegro molto); the latter is fully scored at the start and in its last three pages, breaking off without an ending, but the central twenty or so pages are sparse, as if further elaboration was intended. The atmospheric low-string colours of the principal theme in the "Capriccio" (to which bells are added towards the end) and the irregular fast eighth-note energies of the "Suonata" suggest that the young composer had studied Bartók works such as the Divertimento for strings.

In 1946, when Anhalt produced the *Concerto in stilo di Handel*, he was studying with Nadia Boulanger and, as he has said recently, "trying to find my voice." He had discussed with Boulanger a number of works by

Stravinsky and, sharing her admiration for them, completed the first movement of a neoclassic piano sonata, but was unsatisfied with it. The "pastiche" of Handel (as he now calls it) was written in a week; he showed it to Boulanger and she was quite enthusiastic. The concerto calls for strings, a few winds, and cembalo. There are four movements: Ouverture, Air, Sarabande/Variazione, and Tempo ordinario. The main tonality is D major. The "Ouverture" recalls the French overture style: a maestoso section with characteristic dotted rhythms and thirty-second-note flourishes; a fast fugato with interesting cross-rhythms (beamed in the score more in Bartók's manner than in Handel's); a reprise of the maestoso. The concluding "Tempo ordinario" alternates rapid string figures with flourishes from the winds; as a Handelian pastiche it seems closer to the *Water Music* than to the concertios. There have been periodic proposals to perform the work, but Anhalt has discouraged these. Only in his immediately subsequent work, the *Six Songs from Na Conxy Pan*, did Anhalt feel he "found his voice." [1]

The title of Interludium refers to Anhalt's Paris sojourn as a transition in his life. (A coincidental parallel is the title of John Weinzweig's 1943 work for string orchestra, *Interlude in an Artist's Life*, memorializing that composer's period of service in the Royal Canadian Air Force.) When Interludium was written, Anhalt had been in Montreal for nearly a year, and had formed a decision to settle there. The work is dedicated to Lady Davis, sponsor of the fellowship that brought Anhalt to Canada. The Anhalt fonds preserves pencil sketches and three completed versions: a draft in short score dated "Paris-Montreal 1948–49 (1949 julius 30)"; an undated draft in full score for strings, piano, and timpani; and a fair copy in full score, dated "16 xii 1949, Montréal," in which the piano and timpani parts are considerably more elaborate. An arch form in slow tempo, the twenty-nine-bar piece begins and ends in a sombre C minor (Andante tranquillo); a central free rhapsody ventures into nontonal formations and a certain urgency of expression, which the solo and chamber works of the early 1950s would develop further.

Funeral Music, composed in 1951 and scored for a quasi-orchestral grouping of four solo winds and a string sextet, was first performed in Montreal in 1954. Though not initially intended so, this intense seven-minute work took on an elegiac expression; hence the title. The dedication reads "to László Gyopár." Hearing Gyopár's composition in the style of a Bach invention, produced at age sixteen ("an astounding achievement"), reinforced Anhalt's early decision to become a composer. As poignantly related by Anhalt in 1985,[2] the two became close friends, fellow students in Kodály's class, and later, during the war, fellow members of a forced labour brigade of young Jews. Anhalt escaped, while Gyopár met a tragic death in 1944. The memory of his young friend has remained with Anhalt, and forty years after *Funeral Music* Gyopár's name appears as one of the four dedicatees of *Traces (Tikkun)*. A letter of 1 June 1992 relates Anhalt's efforts to arrange a performance in Hungary of the *Missa* composed by Gyopár (a convert to Christianity) in the early 1940s. The score, now part of the Anhalt fonds, "seems to be the only copy extant." These efforts met with success in March 1994, when the *Missa*, minus only its Credo, received a full-scale performance, one hour in length, as part of the Budapest Spring Festival. The locale was the Coronation Church in Buda, and the conductor was László Tardy. Anhalt later viewed a videotape: "You can imagine how moved I was."

The sombre low-register opening bars of *Funeral Music* in fact are marked "*intenso.*" The spirit of a dirge might be expected – the endings of two later works, *Sonance•Resonance* and *Simulacrum*, both suggest this character, the latter deliberately marked "Quasi una marcia funebre" – but there are no such rhythms. The music is continuous, marked by long melodic lines that often exhibit the "singing" expressiveness of baroque ornamentation (mordents, turns, trills) and recall the rhythms and close dovetailing of baroque counterpoint (see example 5.1). Though chromatic and atonal, the work could be seen as a residue both of Gyopár's example and of the neoclassic phase of Anhalt's evolution.

The Symphony – scored for triple woodwinds (with the usual doublings), four horns, three trumpets, three trombones, tuba, timpani, three percussionists, celesta, piano, harp, and strings – derives from twelve-tone principles. Anhalt's interest in Schoenbergian dodecaphony developed during his early Montreal years. He had been profoundly impressed by a live performance of Schoenberg's Piano Concerto, op. 42, in Paris, and knew other works of that composer, including the Variations for Orchestra, op. 31; but Boulanger was an opponent of the Schoenberg school. Later Anhalt read the two monographs of René Leibowitz;[3] the chamber works of the early 1950s reflect Anhalt's new interests. By 1954 he felt ready to compose a piece for large orchestra utilizing his experience.

Along with Milton Babbitt, George Rochberg, and others in those years, Anhalt was excited by the possibilities of "complementation," and by the concept of "metamorphosis," whereby part of the basic twelve-note set could remain stable while the rest would undergo systematic transformation. Thus in the Symphony of 1958 the raw pitch materials are a four-note set, treated in the usual serial ways, and a complementary eight-note conglomerate that is constantly "metamorphosed."

Example 5.1 *Funeral Music*, flute and clarinet, mm. 26–31

In an earlier report I noted two traits of Anhalt's first dodecaphonic compositions: their athematic construction and their habit of beginning as if with a head-first plunge.[4] These were associated with the Symphony in an analytical review[5] that went on to describe the "metamorphosis" feature and also the "density scale" by which Anhalt said he had regulated the wavelike succession of ideas in this uninterrupted structure. (The score identifies thirteen tempo-sections; the review suggested that these tend to coalesce into six "movements.") Despite the dancelike pulsations of sections 5, 6, and 10, and the whirling accelerando of the ending, this music spurns folkloric or motoristic continuity in favour of a freely rhetorical (and at times highly dramatic) kind. Moreover the textures are symphonic – truly orchestral, rather than *concertante*: the first flute and first horn may have demanding lines to play, but these do not obtrude in ways that would call for a solo bow.

The Canadian repertoire in earlier generations is not especially rich in works called symphonies. The second edition of the *Encyclopedia of Music in Canada*[6] has an entry under "Orchestral composition," but no separate entry under "Symphonies," despite the separate entries for cantatas, concertos, operas, oratorios, and other genres. In the 1930s just two symphonies were written and performed in Canada, but between 1939 and 1954 (the date Anhalt started writing his Symphony) at least fifteen works with this designation were composed, and of these, twelve achieved at least one performance.

Anhalt's Symphony – a "landmark" of Canadian symphonic composition[7] – was first performed in Montreal in November 1959 at a concert sponsored by the Canadian Jewish Congress, part of that organization's celebration of the bicentenary of the arrival of the first Jewish settlers in Canada (at Trois Rivières and Montreal, 1760). Four further performances followed in the early 1960s, two of them broadcast by the CBC; the score was published by BMI Canada (now Berandol) in 1963.

If the Symphony culminates Anhalt's experience with Schoenbergian dodecaphony in the 1950s, the *Symphony of Modules* correspondingly culminates his experience with electroacoustic techniques in the 1960s. The following extracts from letters trace its genesis:

At present I am thinking of writing for orchestra again ... the piece will show that I spent considerable time with electronic sound in the past 3–4 years. (16 October 1961)

I feel very strongly about this work: it leads me into a musical world which has that quality of the "half-known – half-unknown," that quality of "delicious riskiness," which eggs [me] on ... The piece will be long and so far I have written about 35% of it. (29 August 1964; ellipses added)

My new orchestral piece comes along slowly ... It will be very complicated and bulky, often harsh and angular. It will require an enormous amount of rehearsal time ... but I just *have* to write it this way, the devil may care for the rest. (24 December 1965; ellipses added)

Completed in July 1967, the *Symphony of Modules* is indeed a "complicated and bulky" score, though at an estimated twenty-eight minutes not as long as the composer had predicted. Its performance history is, however, both long and (at this writing) incomplete. R. Murray Schafer, then living in Vancouver, persuaded the Vancouver Symphony Orchestra to undertake the premiere, and support to that end was secured from the Centennial Commission and Simon Fraser University. Correspondence from Anhalt to the author reports that the work was "scheduled in the spring of 1968" (15 November 1967), but uncertainties arose: "there is some difficulty with obtaining the necessary rehearsal time." By 14 January 1969, "a première by [Lukas] Foss in the spring of 1970 is a strong likelihood. On the same programme would be a work of [Lejaren] Hiller's in première. (I hope Foss will have 50 hrs. of rehearsals.)" When neither of these efforts materialized, the prospect arose of a premiere by the University of Toronto Symphony Orchestra, with Anhalt conducting. This excellent student group under its musical director Victor Feldbrill had recently performed such demanding works as Schafer's *Divan i Shams i Tabriz*, Weinzweig's *Dummiyah*, and Serge Garant's *Phrases II*. Anhalt accepted the invitation "eagerly, and with pleasure" (9 March 1976), but after discussions, suggested a postponement. "I need to retouch the score

... After having re-read it, it seems to me, at places, harsh in a way that requires change ... The tapes, also, need scrutiny. They were done before voltage controlled equipment became available ... I was very impressed with [the orchestra's] quality. However I find the amount of rehearsal time I could count [on] is ... not quite sufficient." (5 May 1976; ellipses added). Later correspondence provides a temporary epilogue to the story (11 March 1995): "the possibility exists that the tape parts ... are *not* needed at all, with the exception of a few." The same letter reveals that Kevin Austin, Anhalt's former student in Montreal, was to help revise the tape parts using state-of-the-art equipment – indications of tape sounds appear on not quite half of the present score's fifty-one pages – however the work remains unperformed.

For the time being the work must be appreciated visually. In this connection we possess not only the outsize score, one of Anhalt's most precisely drawn, but a large number of graphs, also drafted with exceptional imagination and precision of detail, in which the "modules" (small motivic building units of the work) were developed. To give an idea of the extent of this material, the sources for the Symphony occupy at least four outsize boxes in the Anhalt fonds. One file contains eleven sheets of diagrams, some in coloured pencil, mainly referring to timbre effects in the strings; among these is a chart headed "Dynamic curves, lattices." Another file contains twenty-five sheets of graphs, diagrams, and charts; two multicoloured charts are headed "Division" and "Transformation," while a third is labelled "Tessitura-saturation Diagram." Elsewhere eight typewritten pages provide "Performance Notes," including an explanation of the "tablature" notation used in one cello passage. One huge drawing, outlining in colour the proposed movement of instrumental clusters, suggests some wild DNA experiment. Five large files show manuscript sketch pages and transparent cut-outs in various patterns. Here is evidence of a compositional lab working at full tilt.

The *Symphony of Modules* belongs to its age, the age of so many other graphically or spatially notated large works – one thinks of the equally outsize scores of Iannis Xenakis's *Pithoprakta* (1955–56), Karlheinz Stockhausen's *Gruppen* for three orchestras (1955–57), Györgi Ligeti's *Atmosphères* (1961), Earle Brown's *Available Forms II* for two orchestras (1961–62), and Schafer's opera *Loving/Toi* (1965), and of the emphasis on new approaches to performance and especially to notation evidenced in the eye-popping illustrations in books by Erhardt Karkoschka[8] and John Cage[9] (the latter includes one of the *Symphony of Modules* sketches).

The orchestral forces demanded are also outsize: four each of flutes, clarinets, and bassoons, and three oboes (all with the usual ancillary

woodwind doublings; the first and second flutes also double on recorders at one point), six horns, four trumpets, three trombones, two
tubas, two timpanists, six percussionists, harp, guitar, accordion, celesta, harpsichord, piano, and strings. A chart prescribes seating and
equipment for the percussionists (thirty-two separate instruments are
specified, many in multiples); another chart shows a special seating
plan for the (outsize) string sections. An enormous concentration of
creative energy is depicted; no orchestra could expect to cope with
these demands in a normal rehearsal-time allocation.

Pages 42 and 50 of the score provide two contrasting examples of
Anhalt's modular construction in this work: the first is a full-orchestra
passage of continuous small musical actions, adding up, as far as one
can imagine, to a dense and busy thicket of sound; while the second
(from near the end) offers a sparse succession of many unrelated small
actions separated by silence. In both passages one might think for
comparison of a film sequence with a hundred people all behaving differently – though all rather intensely and nervously – with frantic
energy on page 42 but more falteringly on page 50 (see example 5.2).

Extended performance techniques may be more prevalent here
than in any other Anhalt work, and, by their tendency to broaden the
spectra of both pitch and timbre, they confirm that the composer
indeed "spent considerable time with electronic sound." Furthermore,
they imply a link to the tape part: devices include glissandi and the use
of felt beaters on the piano strings; twanging pedal shifts on the harp;
cluster glides, tremolos behind the bridge, and left-hand fingerboard
attacks in the strings; a variety of brass mutes; and staffless, stemless,
and "unstable" pitch indications in both strings and brass.

The course of the music is continuous (as in all of Anhalt's symphonic pieces), but is broken by four "cadenzas" of differing lengths.
Again typical of the 1960s, these are areas of indeterminate or random
coordination, in contrast to the regulated tempos and ensemble elsewhere in the score. Cadenza 1 lasts 30 to 34 seconds and uses the entire orchestra minus only the violins and violas. Of the large quantity of
modules shown, the composer envisions varying amounts to be actually heard, according to the circumstances of each performance; similarly the dynamic range within each part is open to choice according
to a given scheme. In Cadenza 2 (33 seconds long), for percussion and
tape, the two timpanists are allotted three drums each – more or less
high, medium, and low – but precise tunings are not specified; here
several modules, unrelated to each other in time, are to be repeated
until an agreed-upon signal, a procedure familiar from Witold Lutoslawski's works of this period. Cadenza 3, lasting 60 seconds, is a quiet
moment with separated modules for low woodwind, percussion, piano,

Example 5.2a *Symphony of Modules* manuscript, mm. 365–81, page 48 (wind parts only)

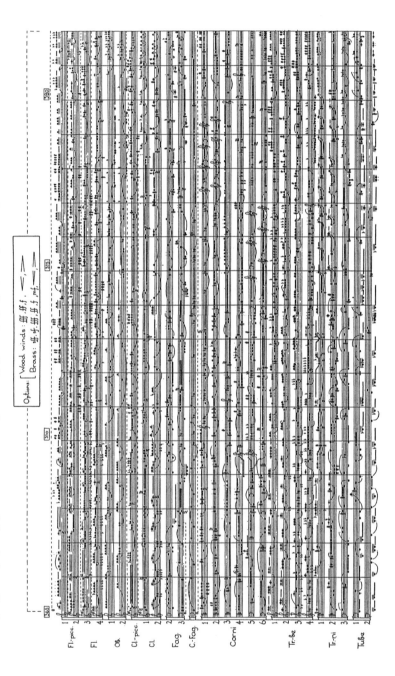

Example 5.2b *Symphony of Modules* manuscript, mm. 446–63, page 50

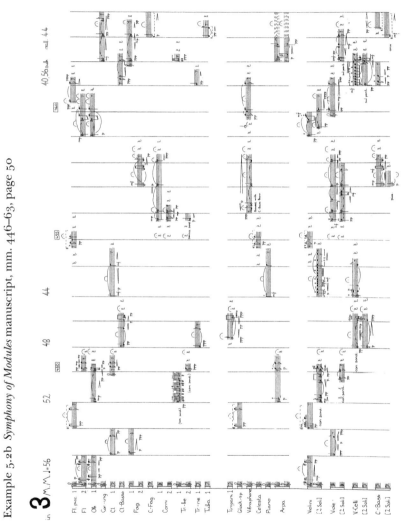

accordion, and guitar, together with a tape part shown as "30% sound, 70% silence." Cadenza 4, the shortest, at 26 seconds, centres in the high strings, especially a violin solo outlined in a graphic contour only, rather than in definite pitches (see example 5.3).

Besides its relationship to electroacoustics, to graphic notation devices, to new instrumental performing resources, and to indeterminacy, the *Symphony of Modules* aligns itself with the 1960s theme of quotation and assemblage, as exemplified in works of Anhalt's good friend George Rochberg such as *Nach Bach* (1966). Early in Anhalt's score, there is a strongly underlined phrase from Strauss's *Till Eulenspiegel*; somewhat later, brief references to Musorgsky and Mozart occur; and at a still later point the tape plays the final sixteen bars of part 4 of Brahms's *Ein deutsches Requiem*, the chorus "*Wie lieblich sind deine Wohnungen*" ("How lovely are thy dwellings," Psalm 84). Though characterizing the work as "harsh and angular," Anhalt appears to have imbued it with an exceptional variety of images and feelings; amid all the fascinating novelties of construction, the Brahms excerpt (especially) may be a useful reminder of this. Describing a summer visit to England in 1965, Anhalt wrote: "I took home with me an unexplainable inspiration from these cathedral towns (especially Salisbury) which seems to have a close bearing on my new work. The immense expanses of grey stone and structural lines … so unfussy and serene … How to translate this into music?" (17 November 1965; ellipses in original).

Will *Symphony of Modules* ever be performed? It clearly deserves to be, as many other equally large and complex works in the repertoire have been. Composers' demands for rehearsal time are always regarded by the rest of humanity as unreasonable. That Anhalt modified his views on rehearsal practicalities after experience with several Canadian orchestras in the late 1980s is suggested when he writes apropos of *Symphony of Modules* that "we should think in terms of 5–6 hrs. of effective rehearsal time. 7–8 hrs. would be quite extra-ordinarily generous" (letter to Kevin Austin, 20 June 1995). We may recall that the Fourth Symphony of Ives, completed in 1916, waited until 1965 for *its* premiere.

The Symphony had occupied Anhalt over a period of four to five years, 1954–58, and *Symphony of Modules* over a similar or even longer period, 1962–67. For the ensuing twenty years his composing energies were concentrated on areas other than the orchestra: expanded vocal techniques, mixed media, theatre. Some projects of those years nevertheless did incorporate "orchestral" elements: an example is the opera *Winthrop*.

Anhalt's resumption of orchestral composition in an exceptionally productive spurt in the late 1980s – completing three major works in

Example 5.3 *Symphony of Modules* manuscript, cadenza 4, page 48

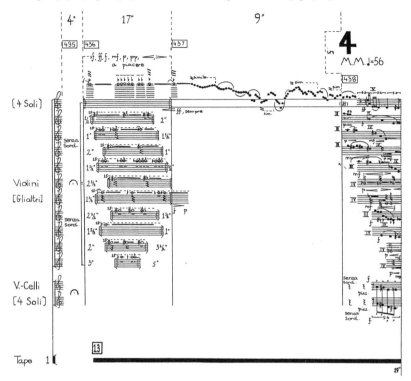

less than two and a one-half years – may be attributed to several things: his freedom from teaching and administrative duties after his 1984 retirement from Queen's; his apparent eagerness to connect his readings and ruminations of those years with a large instrumental-music format; and finally, on a purely practical level, three commissions – one from the National Arts Centre Orchestra, Ottawa, and its newly appointed music director, Gabriel Chmura; one from the Esprit Orchestra, Toronto, and its music director, Alex Pauk; and one from the Toronto Symphony Orchestra and its music director, Gunther Herbig, also then newly appointed. The commissioners are also the dedicatees of the remarkable trilogy of works that resulted: *Simulacrum, SparkskrapS,* and *Sonance•Resonance (Welche Töne?)*. *Simulacrum* (begun 1 December 1986, completed 10 March 1987) is a memory piece sprinkled with brief quotations, among them one self-quotation; *Sparksraps* (begun 15 May 1987, completed 2 December 1987) has specific cultural and philosophical connections; *Sonance•Resonance (Welche Töne?)* (begun 18 December 1988, completed 12 April 1989) refers to, or is virtually a palimpsest on, a specific musical classic.

The three works are distinct musical statements, but obviously come from the same voice, and, because of their proximate position in Anhalt's output, form a trilogy. However, each uses a notably distinct instrumentation. *Simulacrum* calls for the basic late-eighteenth-century forces of the National Arts Centre Orchestra: double woodwinds, two horns, two trumpets, one percussionist, strings. But it stretches these (almost all the woodwind players double on second instruments, the percussionist manages both timpani and a quite extensive *batterie*) and even envisions a number of "optional" extras: two extra horns, an extra trumpet, a pair of trombones, a keyboardist (piano, harpsichord, electronic organ), a harp (offstage, for six bars only), and a second percussionist. *SparkskrapS* also accommodates the moderate size of the commissioning group, in this case Toronto's Esprit Orchestra. It requires double woodwinds, two horns, two trumpets, two trombones, a tuba (doubling on baritone), timpani, percussion, keyboard, harp, and strings. Again, cues in the score suggest "optional" extras – a third flute, two more horns, another trumpet, another trombone. For *Sonance•Resonance* (whose commission in fact was a joint one by three Canadian orchestras, those of Toronto, Montreal, and Calgary), Anhalt was able to work with a fuller ensemble: triple woodwinds (all players doubling), four horns, three trumpets, three trombones, a baritone, a tuba, timpani, five percussionists, keyboard, strings. The baritone, or euphonium, is an unusual addition to the brass, playing some telling solo lines in *SparkskrapS* and acting in *Sonance•Resonance* sometimes as a sixth member of the horn-tuba group, sometimes as a fifth member of the trombone-tuba group, and, once only, penetrating with a highly charged descending solo line.

The title *Simulacrum* is, according to an unsympathetic reviewer, "an obscure English word" (*Toronto Star*, 7 January 1988). "Shadowy likeness" is a useful meaning found in the *Concise Oxford Dictionary*. One of the meanings Anhalt has suggested, "mirage," happens to coincide with the title of a poem he wrote in Hungary in 1943 – his first. As Anhalt noted when providing an English translation, "Mirage in Elöpatak" (naming the forced labour camp he was then confined in) looked towards the future, just as forty-five years later *Simulacrum* looked back on the past. The piece would be, he reflected, "an amalgam of the present and the past" – not only his own past but the performer's past also: "I knew that [Chmura] was born to Jewish parents in Poland in 1946. Were his parents survivors of a concentration camp? As it turned out, they escaped that experience, because they spent the war years in Russia. Then I found out that his father was an opera singer. Suddenly the thought occurred to me that I could be the father of Gabriel Chmura; I share some of the same experiences his parents had. Should he be my son, he who now conducts opera, I could also tell him about my brief stint at the Hungarian Opera as a *répétiteur* ... in Budapest in 1945."[10]

Note-name equivalents to the title word, and to the conductor's surname, influenced Anhalt in his formation of the work's pitch content, as noted in Alan Gillmor's study of the sketches.[11] Moreover, "the last five letters of the word very nearly form an anagram for the dedicatee's surname: 'acrum' equals 'c(h)mura,' hence 'simul-acrum' equals 'Simul-cmura' or 'like Chmura' (that is to say, Anhalt is like Chmura)."[12] That some of the fragmentary quotations in *Simulacrum* connect with the operatic repertoire Anhalt assimilated during his time with the Hungarian Opera is clearly significant. In an interview, Anhalt called the quotations "islands in the river of sound."[13]

The work begins and ends with quiet, vaguely disturbing stop-and-start phrases; the quotations emerge as in a dream. The first is from a chorus in part 2 of J.S. Bach's *St Matthew Passion*. In answer to Pilate's question which prisoner is to be let go, the crowd replies in a unanimous shout, "*Barabbam!*" (Barabbas!). But when Pilate asks what should be done with Jesus, the response, as Anhalt noted in analyzing this passage, is not so unanimous; it comes first from "an *agent provocateur* (or a few of them) – the basses in the choir – who intone brutally, '*Lasst ihn kreuzigen*' (Let him be crucified). Others – the tenors, the altos, and finally the sopranos – thinking this is a fitting idea, echo the dreadful suggestion in that confusing, complex ensemble which Bach composed as a fugato, portraying what we might call today a psychic epidemic taking hold of an excitable crowd."[14] In Bach's manuscript, this astonishing page is written in the form of a cross. Anhalt's recollection is slower and quieter than the original, its effect understated rather than climactic. It starts in the fourth bar (i.e., midway in the alto entry) and surrounds Bach's "confusing" and "complex" modulations with extra chromatic wisps of counterpoint, breaking off abruptly before the cadence.

The second quotation is a familiar waltz from Strauss's *Der Rosenkavalier*. The melody is played *dolce* by two solo violins, reinforced by upper woodwinds and a vibraphone; other violins, divided, softly undulate; lower strings (in harmonics) and an electronic organ sustain a few quiet high-register notes, creating a "shadowy likeness" of the original. This inclusion, says the composer, is "a little personal," and "has to do with my father's love of this tune, which he tried to 'find' – that is, to play by ear ... I remember him sitting, on numerous occasions, in front of the keyboard trying to play the elusive melody with its even more elusive accompaniment ... He also played the violin – not very well, but that did not seem to bother him greatly, because it gave him so much pleasure over the years."[15] The third quotation, or pair of quotations, derives from Abraham Zvi Idelsohn's *Thesaurus of Hebrew Oriental Melodies*: two traditional Sephardic tunes, both "sung" here in the guttural G-string colour of the violins, and exuberantly intertwined. For the composer this further epitomizes family memories, namely "of my paternal grandfather ... whom I did not see very frequently, but whom I always 'visited' with my father on the Day of Atonement."[16]

Shortly a strumming offstage harp heralds another quotation, the chorus of Egyptian priestesses ("*Possente Fthà*" / "Hail, mighty Ptha") from Act I, scene 2 of Verdi's *Aïda*. Verdi's foreground melody (the voice of the solo priestess) is not played; instead, a solo oboe wails a phrase from one of the Sephardic tunes, which closely resembles the Verdi (see Example 5.4). Above and below the harp and oboe, a soft texture of flute, glockenspiel, violin harmonics, and double basses provides again a blurry, dreamlike setting. As a young professional, Anhalt probably rehearsed the *Aïda* passage a few times. Considering it in the present creative context, he noted: "I was quite taken by the mutual affinity, if not overt resemblance, between the two Jewish melodies and Verdi's inspiration of this 'Egyptian' tune. I need only add that I am a regular reader of news reports from the Near East, and this momentary harmony between Jewish and 'Egyptian' melodies appealed to me to the extent that I felt I ought to put them side by side."[17]

Soon we hear another Verdi quote – the climax of the opening storm scene in *Otello*, "*Dio, fulgor della bufera*." The chorus prays that God, the "sparkle" or "shimmer" of the gale, may lead Othello and his fellow Venetians safely through it. To Verdi's powerful full-orchestra gesture in A minor, Anhalt adds a contradictory neutralizing E-flat in the basses and organ, and, in the fourth bar, he replaces Verdi's falling sixth chords in A minor with falling triads in the same rhythm, alternating A and E-flat. While recollections of operatic choral moments from his youth may again be part of Anhalt's thinking, no doubt the implications of the text here ("Save us from the storm") intrude strongly.[18] Indeed, the final brief quotation, from Anhalt's own music, is complementary to the *Otello* fragment in *its* implications. This is part of section 7 of *Thisness*, where the composer-author summons his hatred for voices of unreason in the world: a jailor screams at his victim, "You must be exorcised!" It is a loud and violent moment. "May the gods save us," this music pleads, not only from "the storm" but also from despicable rabble-rousing elements such as the *Passion*'s basses who incite to crucifixion. But in an epilogue the waves of violence subside into the waves of memory's river, where the piece began.

A letter written just after completion of *SparkskrapS*[19] describes it as "jagged," in contrast to *Simulacrum*'s "long, flowing lines," adding: "the

Example 5.4 Melodic derivations in *Simulacrum*: (a) violin 1, mm. 242–4, after
Sephardic tune (Idelsohn vol. 4, 253); (b) oboe 1, mm. 261–3;
(c) Verdi, *Aïda*, Act I, sc. 2, soprano solo

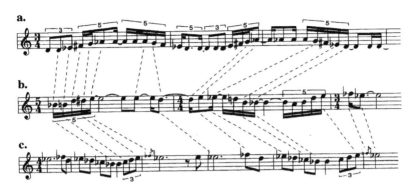

idea of contrast, high/low, dark/light, slow/fast, harsh/sweet, etc. is at
the core of the piece, which reflects the Kabbalistic notions about the
divine sparks (splinters of the divine essence) shattered and intermin-
gled with the 'shells,' the 'husks,' the 'shards,' the 'scraps' … the
organic – it seems – with the inorganic, the good with evil, etc. *yet the
two inextricably belonging together*" (4 December 1987). As early as 1976
Anhalt had envisioned a Jewish theme for a third work in the trilogy
with *La Tourangelle* and *Winthrop*, which eventually emerged as *Oppenheimer*. To this end he invested extensive study time in Jewish lore, corresponded with scientists and scholars, and visited New Mexico in early
1991 and Israel in early 1992. For a period of about fifteen years such
preoccupations persisted with him, and *SparkskrapS* was the first of several creative results. Three extracts from Gershom Scholem appear as
the score's epigraph. The following is a slightly shortened version:

The sparks of Adam's soul and the sparks of the *Shekhinah* [Divine presence]
disperse, fall and go into exile where they will be dominated by the "shells,"
the *Kelippoth* …
The realms of good and evil are to an extent commingled and man's mission is
to separate them.
Every man who acts in accordance with this law [that of the *tikkun* – "restoration" or "reintegration"] brings home the fallen sparks of the *Shekhinah* and
his soul as well.[20]

The image of "sparks" dominates the opening of the piece and, by
recurring helps unify the many disparate elements. (Is this a musical
equivalent to the "reintegration" alluded to?) Darting upward glints
are shared initially by two solo violins, E-flat clarinet, flute, xylophone,

high registers of harp and piano, and cymbal. The percussion colours are central here, and in much of the rest of the piece, too: clanging chords in piano (doubled by vibraphone, high crotales, and low harp) suggest gamelanlike sonorities; later, reiterated permutations of the pitches A, C-sharp, D, and F-sharp, over a B-flat pedal, evoke the tolling of some ritual bell; Balinese gongs are included in the *batterie*, to be selected, Anhalt specifies in the score, for their "massive, brilliant, and very resonant sounds."

SparkskrapS incorporates six sections of "free," unmetred music reminiscent of, but much shorter than, the cadenzas of *Symphony of Modules* (the shortest lasts six seconds; the longest, sixteen). These feature "improvisation" for the percussion on given pitches and/or timbres and repetition of given short motives, and, for the strings, separate (i.e., uncoordinated) parts. They may be taken as jumbled or confused "scraps" opposing the brightly flickering "sparks." The work's general pace is slow, perhaps phantomlike. There is one brief but exhilarating full-orchestra accelerando – essentially a chromatic ascent set against the almost theatrical brilliance of a cymbal tremolo. After this, the peroration, one of Anhalt's most eloquent, moves in a series of sighs separated by pauses; the final sounds are a melodic fragment low in the contrabassoon and a cluster in the piano bass underlined by the tamtam, left to die away.

The third commission, from Gunther Herbig, had a special association that Anhalt found impossible to ignore: for his initial concert as music director of the Toronto Symphony Orchestra (he had conducted it previously several times as a guest), Herbig would lead Beethoven's Ninth Symphony; the proposed work by Anhalt would form the preliminary, "curtain-raising" part of the program. Anhalt re-examined the Beethoven score, an "icon" in the Western classical repertoire, as he noted, and a work he had known well since his student days. His attention focused on the introduction to the finale. It begins with a "chaotic storm" (as D.F. Tovey calls it) in the winds and timpani, to which the low strings respond with a phrase clearly imitative of a vocal recitative. Later, these two phrases are repeated; this time the strings amplify the loud "chaos" gesture and a baritone soloist sings the recitative. Beethoven composed the baritone's words himself as a prelude to the setting of Schiller's "Ode to Joy," which forms the remainder of this epoch-making finale.

"*O Freunde, nicht diese Töne*" (O Friends, not these sounds), the soloist exhorts. Clearly a similar thought, as yet unexpressed in words, underlies the first recitative phrase, the one played by the cellos and basses at the start of the movement. In one of his sketches for the Ninth (the work had an exceptionally long gestation of more than twenty years), Beethoven adds the note "*nein diese ... erinnern an unsere Verzweifl*" (no, these [sounds] recall our despair), and Anhalt has used both these phrases as epigraphs to the score of *Sonance•Resonance* (*Welche Töne?*). The bracketed subtitle asks, Which sounds? The question could mean, Which sounds does Beethoven want us to reject? or Which sounds should we hear instead? – a good question either way.

When Beethoven follows the instrumental recitative with a succession of brief quotations from the first three movements of the Ninth, his own expression may also have several interpretations: "not these sounds" could mean (a) let's not have that chaotic flurry in the wind instruments, of which the echo has scarcely died away; or (b) let's not dwell on the music of movements 1, 2, and 3, as recalled briefly; or (c) (less likely but still possible, since here voices are about to be introduced into the symphonic genre for the first time) let's not have any more abstract instrumental symphonies, a literature stretching from Sammartini and Stamitz right up to Beethoven's own Eighth. Though Beethoven may not have intended (c), it more or less represents Wagner's view of the Ninth. Most analysts of the work would espouse (b). But Anhalt looks at interpretation (a) and ponders the implied *SparkskrapS*-like dichotomy between the *Verzweifl* (despair) that the wind instruments seem to be violently flinging themselves away from and the *Freude* (joy) that eventually will follow.

The "curtain raiser" would not want to intrude on the paean to joy, but can prepare it with sounds (sonance) and responses (resonances): the two most prominent references from the Beethoven work to be found in Anhalt's score are in fact an immediately recognizable version of the opening attention-getter of the winds and timpani (the finale's initial "sonance") and a paraphrase of the following few bars of instrumental recitative (its answering "resonance"). The wind and timpani phrase is quoted not at the start of *Sonance•Resonance* but about one-third of the way into the work. It is moreover transposed from the original D minor to F minor, and played against sustained B naturals in low strings (the timpani are also tuned to B instead of the expected C, the dominant of F minor). The recitative is not quoted immediately, but only after considerable intervening musical discourse (leading up to it is the euphonium solo already alluded to). Starting in E minor, rather than D minor, it twists gradually into the lower tonality, but breaks off before completing the implied 4–3 cadence. The intention is evidently to recall the original in a blurred tonal setting. For comparison, example 5.5 shows the Beethoven recitative alongside Anhalt's "remembrance" of it.

These two passages will mean more to listeners already familiar with the Ninth, but may conceivably rouse interest for those hearing it

Example 5.5 Beethoven's Ninth Symphony and Anhalt's *Sonance•Resonance*:
(a) Ninth Symphony, fourth movement, mm. 8–16; (b)
paraphrase in *Sonance•Resonance*, mm. 523–38

afresh or for the first time. Anhalt's work offers further resonances of
Beethoven's third-period music, and of the Ninth in particular. One
section unmistakably refers to the tenor soloist's "military march" variation. The reference is timbral and rhythmic rather than tonal or harmonic: Anhalt picks up the marching pulse in the same percussion
instruments used by Beethoven (triangle, clash cymbals, bass drum);
and, while the wind instruments he uses are horns and trumpets rather
than Beethoven's shrill upper woodwinds, their rhythm is similar,
albeit exaggerated (quick dotted eighths and sixteenths as opposed to
Beethoven's moderate 6/8 motion).

Without overt quotation, the opening of *Sonance•Resonance* evokes
a third-period Beethoven mood of melodic warmth and serenity,
through an elegant succession of phrases in swaying 6/8. This closely
parallels the opening of the Piano Sonata, op. 101, often regarded as
the gateway to the third-period style. The most extended section of
dramatic tension in Anhalt's work is a vigorous fugato. Such stretches
of contrapuntal animation are frequent in Beethoven's third period:
the fugato in the development section of the first movement and the

Example 5.6   *Sonance•Resonance*, mm. 375–84: fugato

double fugue in the finale are two examples in the Ninth; the fugue in the *Consecration of the House* overture, and the finale of the piano sonata just mentioned are among the many others which might be cited. The subject of Anhalt's fugue (see example 5.6) connects intervalically with several portions of the Ninth (the opening of the first movement, the theme of the Scherzo, the already mentioned opening burst of the finale) without quoting any of them explicitly. The fugue is highly chromatic and forceful in expression (semitones and the falling sequence of the motive marked *y* in example 5.6 constantly recur in both foreground and background voices). While its formation and shape are fully modern, it draws on traditional fugue writing devices such as inversion of the subject. The first gesture of the subject, *x*, is highly traditional, with its fifths and octaves, but tonally oblique in its immediate semitonal continuation; the entries relate by the ambiguous interval of the tritone (G answered by D-flat, D answered by G-sharp) rather than the traditional fifths or fourths. A more accurate echo, creative reflection, or "resonance" of third-period Beethoven *ohne Parodie* (without parody, to borrow a phrase from Mahler), would be hard to imagine.

Even though other features of *Sonance•Resonance* are apparently more freely devised, they are striking in their ability to act as stimuli to the auditory sense and to the imagination as a prelude to the special experience that a good performance of the Ninth always affords. The nervous uncertainty of a piano solo midway in the work recalls classical passagework figures. Anhalt surrounds this line with rhythmically vague gestures in the rest of the orchestra (phrases from a sonatina in adolescent piano studies could be the "resonance" here, perhaps).

One may well associate the twice-repeated long progression of three-voiced trumpet chords near the end with a chorale, perhaps as heard in a dream (the dream atmosphere is suggested by the tonally contradictory soft surroundings). The trumpets subside on a major triad, but other instruments (among them gently tolling high crotales) superimpose a smudge of five other notes. The feeling is that we have resolved our musical thoughts momentarily, but that clearly more is to follow: to wit, the Ninth of Beethoven, no less. But this eloquent ending may also ask us "*welche Töne?*" – whether, in a larger sense, we ever really resolve our musical ideas.

A high-ranking executive of Sony is said to have decreed the standard size for compact discs to be circa seventy minutes – the time it takes to play Beethoven's Ninth Symphony. Approximately one hundred versions of that work are available on CD as this is written. What a fine gift to future generations would be a double CD containing both the Ninth and this splendid trio of orchestral works from late-period Anhalt! Their respective timings are twenty-four minutes, twenty-three minutes, and twenty-three minutes – a total of seventy minutes.

NOTES

1 Direct quotations here and elsewhere in this chapter are from telephone conversations between Anhalt and the author, 22 August and 25 August 1995 and 7 June 1998. Unless otherwise stated, letters quoted are from Istvan Anhalt to the author; originals are in the John Beckwith Papers, University of Toronto Music Library.

2 Istvan Anhalt, "What Tack to Take? An Autobiographical Sketch (Life in Progress ...)," *Queen's Quarterly* 92, 1 (spring 1985).

3 René Leibowitz, *Introduction à la musique de douze sons* (Paris: L'Arche, 1949), and *Schoenberg et son école* (Paris: Janin, 1946).

4 John Beckwith, "Composers in Toronto and Montreal," *University of Toronto Quarterly* 26, 1 (October 1956): 62–3.

5 John Beckwith, "Recent Orchestral Works by Champagne, Morel, and Anhalt," *Canadian Music Journal* 4, 4 (summer 1960): 46–8.

6 *Encyclopedia of Music in Canada* , ed. Helmut Kallmann et al., 2nd ed. (Toronto: University of Toronto Press, 1992).

7 Udo Kasemets, "Anhalt, Istvan," in *Contemporary Canadian Composers* , ed. Keith MacMillan and John Beckwith (Toronto: Oxford University Press, 1975), 9.

8 Erhard Karkoschka, *Das Schriftbild der neuen Musik* (Celle: Hermann Moeck, Verlag 1966).

9 John Cage, *Notations* (New York: Something Else Press, 1969).

10 Anhalt, "From 'Mirage' to *Simulacrum* and 'Afterthought,' " (talk presented at the Faculty of Music, University of Toronto, 5 January 1988). This paper is included in part 4 of the present volume, and the reference here is on p. 414; ellipsis added.

11 Alan M. Gillmor, "Echoes of Time and the River," in *Taking a Stand: Essays in Honour of John Beckwith*, ed. Timothy J. McGee (Toronto: University of Toronto Press, 1995), 15–44.

12 Ibid., 31.

13 The image "river of sound" also occurs in Anhalt's autobiographical article "What Tack to Take?" 97.

14 Anhalt, "From 'Mirage' to *Simulacrum*," this volume, 416. Anhalt also analyzes *Simulacrum* in his article "Pst ... Pst ... Are You Listening? Hearing Voices from Yesterday," *Queen's Quarterly* 93, 1 (spring 1986): 71–84.

15 Anhalt, "From 'Mirage' to *Simulacrum*," this volume, 416–17; ellipses added.

16 Ibid, 417; ellipsis added.

17 Ibid, 418.

18 Anhalt analyzes this scene in "Pst ... Pst ... Are You Listening?"

19 The title appears in some sources (though not in the program of the premiere nor the label of the compact disc) as *SparkskrapS*: the Norse spelling of the second of the two fused words, and the capitalization of the final *S* together draw attention to the title's palindromic shape. On the title page of the score, the word appears in full capitals. [The spelling *SparkskrapS* has been adopted for this book. Eds.]

20 Gershom Scholem, *On the Kabbalah and Its Symbolism* (London: Routledge and Kegan Paul, 1965), 115, 125, 116.

6 Electroacoustic Music

DAVID KEANE

Istvan Anhalt first heard electronic music during a broadcast in the late 1950s on CBC radio, hosted by Helmut Blume. Blume often travelled in Europe, and he had acquired, in Germany, broadcast tapes of two works by Karlheinz Stockhausen. One of the works Anhalt heard was *Studie II* (1954), a work created from white noise[1] carefully filtered to produce striking contrasts in timbre. The second and more recent work was *Gesang der Jünglinge* (1955–56), a remarkable piece created through transformations of the voice of a boy soprano mixed with electronically produced sounds. This latter work remains one of the masterpieces of electroacoustic music, perhaps of twentieth-century music as a whole. Of it Anhalt later wrote, "This work turned out to be a turning point in my musical life."[2] Listening to these works made Anhalt aware of the fact that the means to fulfilling compositional ambitions were now actually becoming available in electronic music. Anhalt promptly went to the CBC and asked to listen further to *Gesang der Jünglinge*. He then set about finding out how he could learn more.

ANHALT MEETS HUGH LE CAINE

Early in 1958 Anhalt's attention was drawn to an article in the Montreal *Gazette* about an experimenter in electronic music at the National Research Council (NRC) in Ottawa.[3] This musician/engineer, Hugh Le Caine, had been developing electrical and electronic instruments as an avocation all his life. His senior project in the engineering physics program at Queen's University in the mid-1930s was a touch-sensitive organ. Since graduation in 1939, Le Caine had been a researcher in nonmusical electronic instrumentation at the NRC and was inventing electronic musical devices on his own time, but in 1954 he was assigned to work on music projects for the NRC. In the spring of that year, the El-mus lab was established and Le Caine moved his projects in touch-sensitive keyboards and a myriad of other novel synthesizer components from his home to the NRC. By the time Anhalt learned of Le Caine's work, Le Caine had developed other projects such as a more advanced touch-sensitive organ, a specialized bank of oscillators, an optical coding device for controlling the oscillators, and an exceptionally flexible multitrack tape recorder.[4] Le Caine had been giving private and public lectures and demonstrations for some years and had developed a love for telling people about his work and for showing off – with great musicianship – his devices. It was Stuart Marshall, a physicist at McGill, who, at Anhalt's request, actually introduced Anhalt to Le Caine by telephone.[5] Anhalt wrote to Le Caine in April of 1958 and promptly received an invitation to visit the NRC lab later that spring.

This was Anhalt's immediate impression on arrival: "There was this big room, and lo and behold, there was an electronic music studio in 1958 in Canada! I didn't believe it! That's incredible. And I had a very stimulating conversation with [Le Caine] – as much as I can call it a conversation because I had great difficulty understanding the man … he talked rather softly and talked away from you, and talked at a monotone. I had a really hard time understanding what he was talking about … [Moreover] I wasn't prepared and also my knowledge of the field was so scanty that I really had a very hard time."[6] He describes his first impression of the lab itself as "a creative confusion. Parts, components, (in various stages of assembly), (some) often discontinued, projects, lose wiring, miscellaneous 'bits and pieces' filled that large room. The two technicians worked in a small corner. Hugh Le Caine's desk was along the opposite wall. My workstation was close to Hugh's space. Plants on the window-sills gave cheer."[7]

Le Caine played *Dripsody* for Anhalt and gave him copies of translations from French and German (prepared at Le Caine's instigation by the NRC) of technical papers relating to electronic music. And of course Anhalt got an elaborate tour of the work that Le Caine had been doing. So, despite the obstacles, both Anhalt and Le Caine came away from the experience stimulated. Anhalt had a substantial first immersion in electronic music making and Le Caine felt for the first time strongly supported by a professional composer for the work in which he (Le Caine) had become increasingly involved over the past years. This meeting led to a deep and fervent correspondence between the two for nearly twenty years. For Anhalt, Le Caine opened many doors into the mysteries of acoustics and electronics and provided both the means and the encouragement that smoothed the way for Anhalt to emerge as Canada's first major composer of electroacoustic music. But before Anhalt was ready to begin composing, he had more research to do. He had by this time heard on the CBC the works of Pierre Schaeffer, made by means of tape recorders at a Paris radio studio and his attention was redoubled by Le Caine's comments.[8] Moreover, Anhalt continued to be deeply impressed by the work of Stockhausen in Cologne. So, in the summer of 1958, Anhalt set out for Europe, supported by a Canada Council travel grant, to visit the electronic music studios of Paris and Cologne.

PARIS RADIO, 1958

Pierre Schaeffer was trained as a communications engineer, but during the 1940s (while he was in his thirties), he evolved into a writer of essays and novels, an aesthetician, and a composer. He was attracted to experiments in transforming recorded sound by mechanically manipulating phonograph discs and, when tape recorders became available, audiotape. By 1951 he found himself responsible for the Group de Recherche de Musique Concrète (GRMC) within the Radiodiffusion Française in Paris. Schaeffer and his colleagues in the GRMC soon disseminated the products of their work throughout Europe via the various national radio broadcasting systems (among them the BBC), and the GRMC became the central focus for the music of the future.

Schaeffer had more experience in all aspects of the field than anyone else and he had a great deal to impart to Anhalt. However, a Russian scientist was visiting Schaeffer on the same day that Anhalt had arranged to be at the GRMC to meet with Schaeffer. Schaeffer gave a good deal more attention to the Russian, so Anhalt was forced to learn what he could by listening to their conversation. He was given a copy of a journal and $33\frac{1}{3}$ rpm recordings of works by Schaeffer and his colleague Pierre Henri. These recordings offered, among other things, Anhalt's first experience of *poésie sonore*, or "sound text," an art form that bridged electroacoustic music and poetry. This was the extent of Anhalt's Paris research.

COLOGNE RADIO, 1958

Anhalt had a far more rewarding experience in Cologne. He spent a week at the Studio for Electronic Music at the Westdeutscher Rundfunk (WDR). This studio was set up under the direction of Herbert Eimert in 1951. Here Anhalt had the full attention of Karlheinz Stockhausen, but he found Gottfried Michael Koenig even more useful. Koenig, then thirty-two, had been in Cologne since 1954 and had helped many composers to realize their electronic works, including Stockhausen, with whom he had worked on *Gesang der Jünglinge* and whom he was currently assisting with *Kontakte*. Koenig had written articles about the composers Bo Nilsson and Henri Pousseur that year in *Die Reihe*[9] and was finishing his own composition, *Essay*, for tape (1957–58). Anhalt was never clear what Koenig's status was at the WDR, but Koenig worked every day with Anhalt and, in particular, talked extensively about the calculations for his own work, *Klangfiguren II* (1955–56). These calculations influenced, in a general way, Anhalt's ideas about oscillator tuning several years later when he created *Electronic Composition No. 3*.

Anhalt was not exactly overwhelmed, however, by the technology he saw in Cologne. He had read a good deal about the work being carried out in this studio and, having already experienced an impressive, if chaotic, array of equipment in Ottawa (where he had not expected to see much at all), he had come to Cologne expecting to be astounded by highly sophisticated and specialized instrumentation. In fact, by comparison with Le Caine's studio, the Cologne studio was very modest. It was only a small room that contained a four-track and a five-track tape recorder, as well as several stereo machines, a few audio generators, some filters of various types, a white noise generator, and some speakers.[10] The works that had been produced in the studio of the WDR were the products of fairly simple equipment and an enormous amount of tedious recording, cutting, and splicing of tape.

The imaginative people that Anhalt met and the fresh ideas that he encountered, however, made a profound and indelible impression on him. Anhalt not only met these people around the studio, but was also invited to a rehearsal of Stockhausen's *Zeitmasse* (for woodwind quintet without electronics), which was in preparation for a tour of Italy. He also went with the people he met, in varying combinations, for coffee and to restaurants (Chinese, in particular). In addition to Stockhausen and Koenig, Anhalt made a number of new acquaintances.

Hans Helms, twenty-six, a German music journalist, novelist, and composer, was experimenting with vocal compositions manipulating speech sounds (though he was not using tape). Mauricio Kagel, twenty-seven, an Argentine composer who had settled in Cologne in 1957, is now best known for his theatre works. He had just completed *Transición I* for tape and was currently working on *Transición II* for piano, percussion, and two tape recorders. Like Anhalt, György Ligeti, thirty-five was of Hungarian Jewish parentage. He was born in Dicsőszentmárton (now Tîrnăveni), Transylvania, and had studied at the Academy of Music in Budapest from 1947 to 1949, ten years after Anhalt's time at the academy. Ligeti moved to Vienna in 1956 and was invited by Eimert to work at the WDR electronic music studios. Here Ligeti realized *Glissandi* for one-track tape (1957) and *Artikulation* for four-track tape. He was also finishing, in the period of Anhalt's visit, an article for *Die Reihe* on structural procedures in the music of Pierre Boulez.[11]

Herbert Eimert, sixty-one, a German composer, theorist, and critic, working since 1945 for the WDR, became director of the late-night music programs (1948–65) and, later, director of the Studio for Electronic Music, which he founded in 1951 and headed until 1962.[12] Eimert gave Anhalt a gift of an LP recording of *Epitaph for Aikichi Kuboyama*[13] for speaker and speech sounds on tape, a work Eimert had just recently completed.

ELECTRONIC COMPOSITION NO. 1

Anhalt left Cologne with new insights about creating music with electronics: "The central impression focused on (1) the scope of generating *assumed* new timbres, (2) the flexibility of the process, (3) the realization of how much painstaking work is needed for producing something worthwhile in the new medium."[14] This conception totally changed his approach to composition, orchestration, and musical aesthetics. He returned to Montreal a man full of ideas and energy. He renewed his contact with Hugh Le Caine and shortly thereafter was introduced to Dr Guy Ballard, the president of the NRC. Anhalt, much to his own surprised amusement, was appointed "visiting scientist" to the NRC for a three-month period in the summer of 1959. This gave Anhalt a small honorarium and unlimited access to Le Caine and his laboratory. But all the while that Anhalt was using the NRC resources to study electronic music, Le Caine was availing himself of the opportunity to study Anhalt – a real composer!

In Le Caine's lab was a technician who had worked with Le Caine since the early 1940s. This was Gordie Ellis. He was assisted by a very young technician called René Farley. Anhalt found in these two men a very practical resource for explaining the technical resources and also for translating the more arcane aspects of Le Caine's discourse. In addition, Anhalt made the acquaintance of Le Caine's section head, Geoffrey Miller, whom Anhalt found over the years to be a great facilitator – always ready to listen and always prepared to smooth the way for Anhalt. Miller was Le Caine's chief supporter and it is no coincidence that, upon Miller's retirement, Le Caine chose to retire himself.

Anhalt continued to value the electronic resources of Le Caine's lab as the means to experiment deeply with sound and structure. In particular he found he had a penchant for making and using tape loops and combining them in various ways, phasing them, and manipulating their relative intensities. [15] Anhalt worked in a corner of Le Caine's lab, usually using earphones from 11:00 A.M. to 5:00 or 6:00 P.M. so as not to disturb Le Caine and his assistants, who were working in the same space. After dinner Anhalt went back to an otherwise unpopulated lab and worked until 2:00 or 3:00 A.M. in the blissful condition of not having to use earphones.

Anhalt's manner of work was influenced by that of Hugh Le Caine, of course, but even more so by his experience in Cologne. A principal difference in working methods between Le Caine and Anhalt was the choice of source material. Le Caine had been largely influenced by his exposure to *musique concrète* on radio broadcasts in Birmingham, and all of his own short works[16] were based on acoustically recorded sounds (variously, a drop of water, an electronic organ, a piano, orchestral recordings, a scream, breaking glass, and a ping-pong ball). Anhalt, on the other hand, confined himself to working with a pulse-wave generator and then editing his work, as he had seen Stockhausen doing. Anhalt's initial production was called *Electronic Composition No.1* and subtitled "*Sine Nomine I.*" Although the original tape is preserved in the Anhalt fonds at the National Library of Canada and the piece is listed in his catalogue of works, Anhalt consistently describes it as a "primitive study." We shall not concern ourselves further with it here other than to note that the making of it provided a foundation of knowledge and experience that informed future works – and not only the electronic ones.

ELECTRONIC COMPOSITION NO. 2

Electronic Composition No. 2, subtitled "*Sine Nomine II*," is one of seven works in volume 22 (devoted to Anhalt) of the Radio Canada International series *Anthology of Canadian Music*. Anhalt recognizes *Electronic Composition No. 2* as a fully representative work, and has written the following about it: "For sound production I used two approaches: sine tone synthesis and noise bands of various registers and width."[17] His noise bands were, like those used by Stockhausen in *Studie II*, created by filtering white noise.[18] A sine tone, on the other hand, is energy concentrated in a single frequency. Consequently, these are conceptually – and to some extent, auditory – opposites. Anhalt's objective was to establish the identity of each pole and then use these elements in ways that would merge those identities. The noise can be filtered so finely that an effervescent near-sine tone can be suggested, and the sine tones in turn can be combined into thick combinations that suggest noise bands. Moreover, the treatment of both to tape reproduction with shifted and varying playback speeds produces a commonality in the materials regardless of source.

As a normal aspect of their functioning, analogue tape recorders apply increases in amplitude to the high and low ranges of any recording to compensate for the strengths and weaknesses of the ability of tape to accurately encode and play back audio. When one changes the speed, not only are the tape's own characteristics modified, but these adjustments (called "equalization") cease to be transparent and become a manifest element of the sound. These make clearly *distorted* results when playing back familiar things such as voices or musical instruments, but the effect of the process on synthetic material actually provides a rich and interesting enhancement of the timbre. Finally, the application of treatments such as tremolo playback of tape source material, tape echo effects, and instantaneous attacks accruing from tape splices or a key attack also create points of similarity in the products of the disparate sources.

With the resources available to Anhalt, pitches could be organized by means of (1) a keyboard that controlled oscillator pitches; (2) a different keyboard that controlled tape playback speed; and (3) cutting out short pieces of pre-recorded tape containing various pitches and assembling these into a string when the composite tape is played back. Near the end of *Electronic Composition No. 2* (at approximately 7:20 into the piece, following a silence) is a progressive pattern of pitches that consists of two high tones (ca two octaves above middle C) alternating with two low tones (ca three octaves below middle C). This sequence stands out because it is the clearest pitch pattern in the piece. The other pitches have lower fidelity (likely owing to a number of tape transfers of the material before it reached the final stage and the extensive use of noise bands), frequently have portamenti that reduce the pitch clarity (owing to generation via continuously variable-speed playback), or are somewhat obscured by simultaneous material or treatments (such as tremolo, echo, and layering, among other).

In addition to standing out from the rest of the piece (though it can be seen to be related to, or even the culmination of, earlier pitch patterns) this brief excerpt is notable because it anticipated a future development: Le Caine's Serial Sound Structure Generator (1965–70) that, among its capabilities, facilitated passages exactly like this one.[19] Other synthesizer designers (such as Robert Moog and Donald Buchla) would also incorporate this facility into their equipment, and by the mid-1970s almost every composer would have such passages in their compositions. The characteristics of this pitch pattern were described in an article published in 1971 by Albert Bregman (a music psychologist at McGill University) and J. Campbell.[20] Bregman and Campbell explained why patterns of this sort divide into two distinct streams, making analytical perception of both streams at the same time difficult. Rapid, accurate, highly repetitive patterns made of sine tones are impossible to create in any way except synthetically. Anhalt's application of this idea is the first in the literature of electroacoustic music.

Electronic Composition No. 2 represents two important features that have come to characterize most Canadian electronic music, though such trends were rare, if not altogether absent from the electronic music of the period. The first is that the musical gestures in this work are expressive and "musical" in the fashion of traditional concert music, despite the entirely modern materials and means. This is to say that there is a sense of phrase, that any given phrase allows a listener to anticipate, to some degree, the nature of the subsequent phrase, and that there is a strong sense of emotional involvement. I use "emotional" here to refer to the element in music that elicits a physiological response to musical stimuli. The music of Schaeffer approaches this, but is also imbued with a strong sense of humour and caprice. Le Caine, of course, treated humour extensively in his music, while Stockhausen and his colleagues (at this time) strongly subordinated emotion to calculated structures.

The second feature is the use of subtle gestures and very quiet dynamics. Composers in mid-twentieth century and after have been strongly tempted by the bombastic potential of the electroacoustic medium, and few have resisted. But the medium has as much potential for the quiet, delicate end of the spectrum as for its opposite. Anhalt was one of the first composers to exploit this potential of electronics, and that delicacy is already in evidence in this 1959 work. There are whole sections of quiet textures and several segments where silence is incorporated in such a way that the ear strains to determine whether the moment is truly silent or whether the activity is at the very threshold of audition.[21]

SOME "FIRSTS" IN CANADIAN ELECTROACOUSTIC MUSIC

Anhalt was not the first composer in Canada to work in the electronic medium, but he was the first to move well beyond the novelty of the new medium and produce extended pieces for concert presentation. Serge Garant, a composer, conductor, and tireless champion of the avant-garde in Montreal is credited with the performance of the first work of tape music in Canada. In 1955 Garant presented, as part of a concert in honour of the tenth anniversary of the death of Anton Webern, *Nucléogame* for six instruments and tape. The tape for *Nucléogame* appears to be no longer extant, and in later years Garant himself thought of the tape contents as being of little consequence.[22] That same year (1955), Hugh Le Caine produced the first work for tape alone, called *Dripsody*. Though this work was subsequently performed in numerous concerts and broadcasts all over the world and was included on several internationally distributed LP recordings, the first concert performance did not take place until 1959.[23] Moreover, the piece was less than one minute and one-half in length, and Le Caine did not think very highly of himself as a composer.[24]

Le Caine is nevertheless the most important personality, after Anhalt, in our story. Lacking contact with composers interested in electronic music, Le Caine began composing short tape pieces in order to better understand what a composer might want in the way of electronic tools. Despite the fact that Le Caine had created seven short pieces with his instruments before he met Anhalt, he did not have access to a concert-going public. While Le Caine gave Anhalt access to the electronic tools and expertise that Anhalt required, Anhalt opened the door to that public for Le Caine.

Although we have already seen that electroacoustic music had been broadcast on the CBC from time to time, Anhalt was responsible for organizing the first program of tape music presented in an auditorium to an audience. This first concert in Canada entirely of tape music was presented in Moyse Hall at McGill University in the autumn of 1959. An Ampex stereo tape recorder was borrowed from Le Caine's laboratory and the amplifiers and speakers were provided by McGill. Le Caine has described the event: "The stage was bare except for a tape recorder on which each composer played his composition telling the audience something about it first ... at least on some occasions ... [the concert] was well attended (though the hall was not crowded). The audience were on the whole quite interested, although I did hear a few nasty remarks."[25] This passage is from an autobiographical typescript; at this point, Le Caine added the handwritten comment "no rocks or fruit thrown though, and no riots!"[26] He was referring to European reactions to some avant-garde concerts in the early part of the century and also in the early 1950s.

Le Caine did not list the works, but he did state that there were "several distinguished compositions by Europeans whose names were well-known to the new music concert audiences (which were small in number)."[27] However, only one European electronic work (*Gesang der Jünglinge*) was on the program.[28]

Electronic Composition No. 1 (1959)   Istvan Anhalt

99 Generators (1956)   Hugh Le Caine
A Noisome Pestilence (1958)
Invocation (1957)

Textures (1958)
Dripsody (1955)
The Burning Deck (1958)

Electronic Composition No. 2 (1959)   Istvan Anhalt

Intermission

Gesang der Jünglinge (1955–56)   Karlheinz Stockhausen

Sonata pian'e forte (1597)   G. Gabrieli, arr. John Bowsher [29]

SECOND VISIT TO COLOGNE

A second Canada Council grant was awarded to Anhalt in 1960 to enable him to return to the WDR for further interaction with Karlheinz Stockhausen and the bright young artists around him. He had the opportunity to renew his friendship with Gottfried Michael Koenig and Hans Helms, spending hours with each to learn about their current work. One afternoon Anhalt attended a fascinating work session where Stockhausen and his assistant, the twenty-four-year-old British composer Cornelius Cardew, were methodically experimenting with electronic sounds. Following Stockhausen's precise notes, they individually recorded each timbre and loudness on tape and cut it to the prescribed length. Sometimes these segments were satisfactory, and sometimes Stockhausen rejected them and another means was tried. This process impressed Anhalt and he became aware of the value of the electronic music studio as a place for trying out new and radical ideas "in a lab-like setting, with compliant machines which can be counted upon not to resist extreme demands made on them. (While this is so, machines don't *add* to a result, as it often happens with gifted 'live' musicians.)"[30]

ELECTRONIC COMPOSITION NO. 3

Anhalt returned to the National Research Council in the summer of 1960 to continue his work in electroacoustic music, this time at his own expense. The electronic resources of the lab were essentially the same as they had been the year before, as were the human resources: Le Caine, senior technician Gordie Ellis, and junior technician René Farley. These men were of inestimable assistance to Anhalt, explaining everything from the theoretical basis for a piece of equipment to matters of industrial safety. For example, Anhalt was told not to touch two pieces of equipment at the same time. Given a room full of prototypes and breadboard circuits, this was very practical advice.

A significant difference between Anhalt's first work period and his return in 1960 was that he had had a year to mull over ideas for his next composition, and had gained a working knowledge of the equipment. This time he worked primarily with the multitrack tape recorder and with the spectrogram controlling nine to twenty-five of the oscillators in the oscillator bank. Anhalt used the spectrogram's motor to drive the paper with its inked patterns through the reader, but at times he also went beyond that by rocking the paper back and forth by hand or by freely activating the photocells by means of direct hand movements.[31] The oscillators were tuned, using a frequency counter, to four sets of relatively simple ratio (harmonic) intervals and five sets of inharmonic intervals.[32] The objective was to suggest "bell and cymbal-like sounds."[33]

Anhalt has written the following about the work, which he subtitled "Birds and Bells": "I have synthesized a number of bell-like and cymbal-like sounds, using published data as models. These were not to be realistically sounding simulations, but dream-like, imaginary, quasi-human sounding ones on account of the artificially exaggerated and easily perceivable spectral changes that were made to occur after the respective pseudo-attacks of these sound mixtures."[34] "Some of these sounds are very loud, some barely audible. This large dynamic range is an important characteristic of the piece. Many of the sounds appear static at first, but upon close listening turn out to be constantly moving. The small changes which create this illusion of motion were of particular interest to me while I was working [on] the piece."[35] There is a striking degree of coherence and tight control in this piece.[36] Many of the works of the time (I am referring to the international scene here, since there was virtually nothing in Canada with which to compare Anhalt's work) were quite manic and often playful in a childish way.

Certainly Hugh Le Caine was impressed with the work. Le Caine was one of twenty-three experts from fifteen countries invited to speak at the International Conference of Composers held at the Stratford Festival in August of 1960. He concluded his talk, in which he described both his thoughts on and some of his contributions to electronic musical instruments, by playing an excerpt from Anhalt's *Electronic Composition No. 3*. After announcing what the piece was, he said, "what I would like you to listen to is the tonal material. I'm sure even from these short fragments you will be able to hear what [Anhalt] has done in the nature of a plastic control of the tone structure. This plastic control arises from the ability to modify the patterns which are presented to the photo-cell machine, and to produce in an economical way a fine spectrum. The tones have, as opposed to some electronic compositions, a continuously varying, scintillating quality. I thought when I first heard the composition that these were sounds that I had always wanted to hear."[37]

THE COLUMBIA-PRINCETON ELECTRONIC MUSIC CENTER

Anhalt had learned a great deal from his visits to the Paris and, in particular, Cologne studios in 1958, but he also discovered that there were several centres in the United States that offered new and very different approaches to electronic music making. One of these was the Columbia-Princeton Electronic Music Center in Manhattan. Vladimir Ussachevsky, one of its four founders (the others were Milton Babbitt, Otto Luening, and Roger Sessions), had first contacted Hugh Le Caine about his work as early as 1956 and had remained in close contact after that time. In the summer of 1959, Ussachevsky wrote to Le Caine to say that Columbia-Princeton had leased the RCA synthesizer Mark 2 from RCA and arranged to have it installed in their studio.[38] Although Ussachevsky had visited Le Caine's lab, Le Caine had not made a return visit. However, the NRC/Columbia-Princeton relationship did lead to a grant from the center that allowed Anhalt to be a visiting composer.

Anhalt went to Columbia University for a month-long visit in the summer of 1961 to work with "what was to be at that time the most advanced and versatile instrument for the production of electronic music."[39] The Mark 2 was of special interest to Anhalt because it was designed by Herbert Belar and Harry Olson. The latter was the author of the acoustics text that had been particularly valuable to Anhalt in designing the pitch structure of *Electronic Composition No. 3*. The Mark 2 was a set of sawtooth and white noise generators, amplifiers, and filters. What made the Mark 2 so interesting was that, like Le Caine's spectrogram, it was controlled by a prepared paper roll. In this case the input roll was a punched tape, prepared while the operator listened to the various effects that were possible and then permanently selected some of them by marking the tape. Unlike Le Caine's spectrogram, the device went well beyond controlling loudness. The composer could specify sequences of pitches, registers, timbres, and articulation. The filters were particularly important in that they were used to subtractively sculpt the timbres from the raw materials of the sawtooth wave and the white noise.[40] The device was quite complex to use; it is reported that for many years "only Babbitt truly understood the RCA synthesizer, to the point of composing at it without the aid of an engineer."[41]

Anhalt described his experience with the Mark 2: "It was by far the largest instrument of its kind I have ever seen ... To learn how to make this cumbersome machine 'speak,' took me a longer time that expected. No doubt due to my lack of familiarity with it I often ended a day's work by getting out of it nothing more than trite sequences, reminding me of mechanically activated electric pianos. Only towards the end of my stay there did I find alternate ways to make sounds with it, which were closer to what I was looking for."[42] Anhalt was given a manual and not much instruction. This is perhaps not surprising in view of the fact that the device was still quite new and little had been generated on it by anyone, with the exception of Milton Babbitt. What Anhalt managed to produce, however, found its way into his next composition, *Electronic Composition No. 4*. Moreover, the visit gave him the opportunity to acquaint himself personally with several more composers whose work was to have major importance in the coming decade: Bülent Arel, forty-one, was a Turkish composer and engineer who had been appointed a technician at Columbia-Princeton in 1959. While Anhalt was there, Arel was working on his first piece using the Mark 2, *Stereo Electronic Music No. 1* for tape.[43] Milton Babbitt, thirty-seven, an American composer and mathematician, had recently been named the Conant Professor of Music at Princeton. He had a long involvement with serial music but only a short experience with electronic music at this time. He was the first composer to work with the Mark 2, producing both *Composition for Synthesizer* (which he played for Anhalt) and *Vision and Prayer* for soprano and synthesizer in the year of Anhalt's visit.[44] Vladimir Ussachevsky, fifty, a composer of Russian birth, had moved to the United States in 1931. Although he was the chairman of the Committee of Direction of the Columbia-Princeton Center, he made little use of the Mark 2 at this time or any other. At the time of Anhalt's visit he was completing *Creation Prologue*, a work for four choruses and tape produced in the "classical" manner, which he had begun as early as 1951.[45]

BELL TELEPHONE LABORATORIES

Upon the conclusion of his work at Columbia-Princeton, Anhalt travelled to nearby Murray Hill, New Jersey (about 50 km west of New York City), where Bell Telephone Laboratories is located. The laboratories comprise a very large research centre dealing with electroacoustics in various forms. Bell had developed the first analogue-to-digital and digital-to-analogue converters, which permitted (among other things) the digital representation of the audio world. In 1957 Max Matthews began work on a series of computer programs that would permit a composer to design a composition that would be performed by the computer directly to speakers or tape. At about the time of Anhalt's visit, Matthews and James Tenney[46] began creating their first major compositions.[47] The principle was similar to the Mark 2 synthesizer as far as the idea of the composer preparing instructions was concerned. However, no sound was heard until (1) the completed set of instructions was prepared on data cards (a large stack of them was necessary for even the simplest series of instructions); (2) the cards were read into an IBM 7094 mainframe computer; and then (3) the digital tape output of the IBM 7094 was run through a smaller computer with a digital-to-analogue converter.

However, because the sound source was not a piece of hardware, but rather a series of instructions about how the vibrations that would produce the sound would behave, the potential for producing novel, complex sound behaviour was considerable. By the time Anhalt arrived at Bell Labs in 1961, Matthews had produced the first comprehensive direct music synthesis program, called Music III.[48] Matthews himself explained the principles for using the system to Anhalt, and Anhalt planned a short experiment lasting forty-five seconds, to be executed by the system. In time, he managed to produce what he described as a "cute, saccharine-sweet 45-second output." Anhalt employed this in his composition *Foci*, written in 1969.

ELECTRONIC COMPOSITION NO. 4

Immediately after his investigations in New York and New Jersey, Anhalt again installed himself in Le Caine's lab to produce *Electronic Composition No. 4*. Two things loomed large at this point in his creative career: the fresh experience of synthesizer and computer aids to composition, and a book that impressed him deeply. "At that time I was reading Nevil Shute's novel *On the Beach*, which made a strong impression on me. It was much on my mind as I was working on the new piece, and its terrible theme and dark imagery found their way into it. I am thinking of the angular chordal gestures, the almost feverish sine tone mixtures, pulsating in a strange way, the very low rumbles (perhaps an auditory analogue of poisonous mushroom clouds), the sound sequences resembling rising bubbles bursting on the water's surface, suggesting perhaps that something indispensable for life is in the process of escaping unchecked. All these I associated with the book and its theme of thermonuclear annihilation."[49]

The work is more chaotic, harsh, and aggressive than *Electronic Composition No. 2* or *No. 3*. The gestures are less coherent and have markedly shorter trajectories. One can easily see what Anhalt means when he applies the words "angular" and "feverish" to the piece and when he describes the piece as "an auditory analogue of poisonous mushroom clouds." On the other hand, there is a more conspicuous, foreground use of reverberation.[50] This counters the harshness somewhat by reducing the dynamic range and placing all of the sounds in the distinct matrix of an implied vast, resonant space.

Anhalt utilized nine of the brief fragments of music that he had managed to produce with the RCA synthesizer Mark 2 at the Columbia-Princeton Electronic Music Center. It was not possible to create an entire piece from these rudimentary fragments, but the materials worked easily into the kinds of textures Anhalt more easily extracted from the NRC studio. Once one has familiarity with Anhalt's use of the NRC instruments, one can hear the Mark 2 sources rather easily. The Ottawa sound clusters tend to have softer attacks and are relatively long, whereas the Mark 2 sounds are more rapidly articulated. Despite the distinctness of source materials, there is a very successful amalgamation of the two.

THE MCGILL ELECTRONIC MUSIC STUDIO

During the years from 1958 to 1961 Anhalt had embarked upon a change of direction in his work and immersed himself deeply in the field of electronic music. He had visited the four most important centres in the world for electronic music (for some reason, Le Caine's lab is never included in lists of the major centres, but it makes the fifth and most important centre for Anhalt). He had met some of the most significant composers and inventors in the field – Stockhausen and Schaeffer were already important figures at the time, but others, such as Koenig, Ligeti, and Matthews, would emerge as major figures some years later. Most importantly, Anhalt produced four works, three of which still stand today as major contributions to the repertoire.

The next six years seem to have been a period of reflection and preparation. In a list, dated 1970 and entitled "A Chronology of Involvement with Electronic Music,"[51] Anhalt describes the period from 1960 to 1963 as "Preparing the establishment of an Electronic Music Studio at McGill University in Montreal." The year 1964 is listed as "The McGill E.M.S. begins operation in 1964. Appointed Director of the new studio." Until 1967 no new pieces are completed, and no other involvement with electronic music is indicated, though visits to European centres continue. However, in 1967, Anhalt finished two extensive and ambitious scores – but of that, more later.

After Anhalt's intense involvement with electronic music, it is only natural that he would consider establishing a facility at McGill University, where he was working. In this matter, he was encouraged and supported by both Hugh Le Caine and by Le Caine's superior, Geoffrey Miller. Not only was moral support offered, but it was also suggested that some pieces of Le Caine's equipment might be placed at McGill. This money saving possibility seemed the key to realizing Anhalt's ambition of opening a studio at McGill.

A university is a sufficiently complex place that there are many levels of administration. Each level must be convinced of the wisdom of launching the Faculty of Music into the radical world of electronic technology, but the first and most important step is to enlist the support of the dean. The dean of the Faculty of Music at McGill during the period 1957–63 was Marvin Duchow. Duchow was a musicologist and composer, but a composer who wrote in a relatively conservative style for the period.[52] Duchow demonstrated little sympathy for the potential of an electronic music studio and offered no support during his tenure.

Meanwhile, Le Caine had met Arnold Walter, who from 1952 to 1968 was the director of the Faculty of Music at the University of Toronto. Walter was a major progressive force in the musical world of Toronto and a man of considerable ambition. One of his ambitions was to involve his faculty in electronic music. After Walter visited Le Caine's lab in 1958, he swiftly gained the support of both the University of Toronto and the NRC to establish an electronic music studio at Toronto. The NRC agreed to provide on "permanent loan" most of the components of the studio and in June of 1959, the studio was operational. The University of Toronto Electronic Music Studio (UTEMS) was the second electronic music studio to be established in North America[53] and the first in Canada.

After Le Caine, Anhalt was the most experienced person in electronic music in Canada, even in 1959. So it is somewhat ironic that a musicologist (Arnold Walter), rather than a composer or an engineer, should found the first studio in Canada.[54] It is true that Le Caine was heavily involved in the Toronto studio as an advisor, technical supervisor, and frequent visiting lecturer, but the first director of the studio (Myron Schaeffer) was also a musicologist, as was his successor (Harvey Olnick). It must have been frustrating in the extreme to Anhalt that, owing to a lack of the administrative support that was so abundant in Toronto, no such studio was going to be available to him in Montreal – for the time being. This is not to say, however, that Toronto did not earn its studio. Toronto quickly became a major world centre for electronic music, largely owing to Le Caine, although the inventiveness of Schaeffer, together with the efforts of Walter and Olnick, significantly extended the technical and human power of the Toronto studio.

In 1963 Helmut Blume became acting dean as successor to Duchow. Blume, a pianist and well-known classical music broadcaster for the CBC, provided progressive energy of the sort Walter brought to Toronto. Blume initiated major changes in course structure in the faculty and propelled plans for the new Pollack Hall.[55] Moreover, Blume was the man who had first acquainted Anhalt with electronic music. It is not surprising, then, that arrangements for an electronic music studio at McGill were completed rather quickly once Blume was in charge.

Thus, the McGill Electronic Music Studio was established in 1964 in cooperation with the NRC, which supplied McGill with the multitrack tape recorder,[56] the oscillator bank, the spectrogram, and keyboard controllers on a long-term loan basis. The equipment was delivered by truck on 16 June 1964 to the small stone coach house that had been reserved by the university for the studio. Anhalt then had the beginnings of his studio, but as he had no technical staff on hand, he had to rely on Le Caine for basic reconfigurations and modifications for the purposes of utility and safety.[57]

Tape recorders, a filter, and a mixer were added soon after, and later a Moog voltage-controlled synthesizer filled out the studio complement. In a few years' time, the studio evolved into three voltage-controlled laboratories, a montage studio, and listening facilities. Some of these were equipped with a few more Le Caine devices and provision for quadraphonic recording and playback.[58]

CENTO

Cento was Anhalt's first production in the new McGill studio. It is a work for twelve-part mixed choir (SSS/AAA/TTT/BBB) and stereophonic analogue tape. The source for the speech contents of the tape is the same as the source for the live speech: Anhalt's fragmentation of a poem by Eldon Grier, called *An Ecstasy*.[59]

The word *Cento* is, among other things, Italian for "one hundred," and this was fitting, as the piece was commissioned by the University of British Columbia Chamber Singers to mark the centennial of Canada in 1967. But the same word, *cento*, in Latin refers, literally, to a "cloak of rags." The term is characteristically applied to a literary or musical work made up of passages from other compositions. Anhalt has defined his use of the term as "an assemblage of fragments,"[60] since all of the materials derive from a single work. Anhalt not only selects words and phrases from *An Ecstasy*, but also reduces some of the text to "syllables, morphemes, phonemes." Some of these, in turn, are "reassembled" into "pseudo-words."[61]

Because *Cento* was the first work requiring electronics that Anhalt was able to produce in his own studio at McGill, he was free from time, space, and sound constraints. He was able to record sounds via microphone, for example, at any time. This may well be the reason that Anhalt chose in this work to record and edit, laboriously, a great wealth of microphone-gathered material rather than confine himself to synthetic material only, as in his previous electronic works. Other factors, however, certainly contributed to the decision to use voices. One of these factors was that Anhalt was deeply moved by Stockhausen's use of the voice of his son in *Gesang der Jünglinge*, one of the earliest examples of electronic music in Anhalt's experience. Another influence was likely the compositions, and also the writings on using speech in composition, by Luciano Berio, Hans Helms, Mauricio Kagel, Luigi Nono, Györgi Ligeti, Witold Lutoslawski, and others.[62]

One of Anhalt's ideas on the use of text in music was that "words should be understood most of the time";[63] he felt that the elongation of vowels, though indispensable for sustained singing of notes, undermined the level of intelligibility. On the other hand, Anhalt has written about the influence of the "cocktail-party effect" on *Cento*.[64] This term is used by psychologists to describe the fact that an individual is able to concentrate on a single conversation even though many other conversations are taking place at the same time. This phenomenon depends to a large degree on the spatial distribution of the various sources. The ability to localize a specific source is lost when the "cocktail party" is recorded monophonically.[65] The loss of the ability to separate out a single source usually results in an unattractive mélange of largely indecipherable speech. However, it was precisely the rich complexity of the undifferentiated mix that attracted Anhalt. The cocktail-party effect "made me listen afresh, and with increased awareness to simultaneous speech. I derived a great delight from listening to groups of people speaking. I listened to them from diverse vantage points ... The sound patterns ... often had the character, the intensity of expression, and the complexity which strongly attracted me as a composer. In fact some of these sound events seemed to me as being very close approximations of certain structures that I wanted to compose for *Cento*."[66]

Anhalt did not record cocktail parties, however. He built up the speech material on the tape out of separate recordings of single individuals. He chose ten people, on the basis of personality, voice character, responsiveness to suggestions, ability to mimic, and imagination. Anhalt then cut up the tape recordings into lengths of various sizes and spliced them into about one thousand tape loops with which he experimented extensively. One of the early problems that he encountered was that various aggregations "comprising three or more words per voice, especially when each voice was of a different timbre, added up more often than not to a grey, indistinct mass."[67] This was, of course, the downside of the cocktail-party effect, exacerbated by the limited signal-to-noise ratio of 1960s microphones and tape recorders and its effect on dynamic and frequency range.[68] In addition, there was some loss of signal with each transfer of audio from one analogue tape to another. Anhalt found that he had to limit the length of the segments and temper the use of longer structures by reducing the density of multiple layers. Live voices, however, do not have these particular problems, so mixing live and recorded, treated voices offers a very rich range of possibilities.

The prepared tape is a major component of the performance of *Cento*, because Anhalt conceived the piece as being for two choirs – "one live on stage and another on tape."[69] The synchronicity of the two choirs is critical. Anhalt has said that "temporal deviations from the score would be tolerable only within the limits of $\pm \frac{1}{2}$ [seconds], and at certain places the greatest possible precision would have to be aimed at."[70] The tape speeds of the time were 7.5 inches per second (ips) and 15 ips, but Anhalt tended to use 7.5 ips speeds. Consequently, the required precision in terms of the tape length would be plus or minus 3.75 inches.

No dynamic levels are marked in the score. Rather, Anhalt asks that the performers develop dynamics empirically on the basis of rehearsals with the tape. The individual controlling the tape levels is not a technician, but rather a musician who understands the work and who adjusts the levels on a musical basis during the performance, while sitting at controls located in the audience area.[71] This style of control is one that appears to have been established by Stockhausen – although Stockhausen insisted that during performances he himself be the person controlling the levels from the audience. This practice is now the standard one throughout the world of electroacoustic music, though Stockhausen and, in Canada, Anhalt were very much the pioneers of the approach.

The sounds on the accompaniment tape for *Cento* are, for the most part, speech sounds that are edited, mixed, and treated to reverberation, filtering, and more sophisticated processing such as loudness modulation at various rates, producing sculptural textures in the speech. The electronic timbres are very like those used in earlier pieces, except that the temporal envelopes tend toward the percussive rather than the sustained and evolving – as occur in, particularly, *Electronic Composition No. 2* and *No. 3*. For the earlier electronic pieces, there were no scores, but here, where live performers had to be coordinated with the tape within a tight tolerance, it was necessary to have some indication of what was on the tape. Rather than the graphic notation coming into vogue at the time,[72] Anhalt used words to describe the character of the electronic sounds at a given point (e.g., bouncing, breaking, crackling, crashing, gliding, gurgling, heaving, popping, pulsating, shooting, surging, vibrating, and whistling).

Cento has a freshness, even after thirty years, owing to the distinctive way in which the speaking choir is carefully integrated with the one on tape. The synthetic sounds are especially effectively blended and mixed with the voice, sometimes sounding like voices and at other times sounding distinctively electronic. There is nothing particularly new for Anhalt or the electronic medium in the specific electronic sounds that are used, but the highly effective interaction of those sounds with the voices is the real achievement of the work.

FOCI

Two years later, Anhalt produced a second mixed-media work of even larger proportions. That work is *Foci*, for soprano and a chamber orchestra of flute, clarinet, trombone, violin, cello, double bass, two keyboard players (piano, celesta, electric organ, and electric harpsichord), and two percussionists (playing more that thirty-eight instruments or sets of instruments), plus four operators (for three stereo tape recorders and *mixage*). In addition, slide projections of voodoo drawings are seen on a screen at the back of the stage, and movement and lighting further enhance the performance.

Foci was composed in preparation for Anhalt's term of teaching at the State University of New York, Buffalo. It was first performed at the Albright-Knox Gallery in Buffalo by the resident new music ensemble, and the same ensemble presented subsequent performances at Rutgers University in New Brunswick, New Jersey, and in Manhattan, New York.[73]

The title (pronounced *fo-kee*) is a plural form of *focus* (though the plural is more commonly rendered *focuses*). *Focus, foci* in Latin originally meant "fireplace" or "hearth." At the time of the coining of this Latin word, and for many centuries after, the hearth was the centre of family life. Writers such as Cicero and Virgil used the term metonymically to mean "house, family, home." Of course, the English word *hearth* has been used extensively in more recent times in the same way. Consequently, the etymology of the word would suggest that Anhalt may have had another level in mind beyond the more obvious "multiple focal points."[74]

Despite the fact that *Foci* has much more varied forces than *Cento*, the texture is generally much thinner, though it is thick and intense enough in sections 6 ("Group") and 9 ("Testament"). Section 6 consists of a dense interplay between streams of pre-recorded, very rapid, brief, English spoken phrases and of five instrumental duets, the latter being cued "in" and "out" by the conductor. Section 9 is the only movement that has no tape parts. One is tempted to suggest that Anhalt wanted to allow sufficient sonic space for the soprano to be perceived as the sole vocal "focus."

The texts articulated by the voices are drawn from at least ten different languages, including Aramaic, Creole, and Hebrew. And the texts are taken from at least nine sources, including the Ishtar legend, voodoo texts, and the Zohar. In selecting the twenty-nine individual voices for the speech source materials, Anhalt's criteria were "the person's mother-tongue, dialect, accent, timbre, age, special vocal characteristics, and the ability to be himself, or herself, during the recordings. These people are, thus, not interchangeable as, for example, two similarly competent violinists, each of whom may perform equally well in a chamber composition may be. Only in the tape medium is it possible to achieve this non-interchangeable quality over a long stretch of time."[75] Anhalt has further explained that his primary objective was to exploit the ability of the tape medium to focus on the uniqueness of the individual.[76] Here he means the individual as defined by each and every one of his/her speech characteristics. Anhalt has a tremendous interest in and respect for such individuality.

For the most part, the texts in *Foci* are spoken on tape, but the live soprano *sings* her part. There is a distinctive style among the tasks allocated to the soprano. For example, a striking voice treatment involving rapid glides over wide leaps is found on page 103 of the score in the performance of the words "to be untrue" (see example 6.1). In a similar style, there is one low male voice on the tape (Anhalt's own voice, I believe) that sings in the deep, overrich, ritualistic manner quite reminiscent of Halim El-Dabh's *Leiyla and the Poet*, which El-Dabh produced at the Columbia-Princeton Electronic Music Center in the period 1959–61. Although Anhalt never encountered this striking, emotional work, and did not meet El-Dabh himself when visiting Columbia-Princeton, there was perhaps something in the environment of the Center or of the times that urged this expression. (El-Dabh's and Anhalt's vocalizations have only a sense of character in common; the material is otherwise entirely distinct.)

In addition to the recorded and altered speech sounds, the tape parts consist of a variety of electronic timbres generated at the McGill studio. Among these synthetic sounds is a segment at the beginning and another at 52 seconds into the piece drawn from the 45 seconds of material that Anhalt generated using Max Matthew's MUSIC III computer program at Bell Telephone Laboratories during his visit there six years earlier. This material has a sound something like a "chiffy" calliope merged with an alto flute. This timbre is more or less a Mark 2 cliché when heard on its own, but mixed (initially with

Example 6.1 *Foci*, section 9, soprano, m. 59

TO BE   UN - TRUE

percussion, and in the second instance adding bass clarinet, cello, and double bass) it contributes to a fresh and engaging quality.

One of the things that Anhalt gleaned from his first effort to make use of microphone-gathered source material in *Cento* was the problem mentioned earlier regarding the loss of fidelity when attempting to encode too many individual recordings on one tape. In *Foci*, he addresses this problem by distributing the playback of his recorded materials over six discrete channels from three separate stereophonic tapes rather than the single stereophonic tape used in *Cento*. The multiple machine approach allows the materials from the various tracks to mix in the acoustic space rather than on the limited bandwidth of one tape. This results in a dynamic capacity six times greater than a single monophonic tape, not to mention the greater richness of sounds emanating from speakers located at the front, middle, and back of each side of the hall – again, six altogether.

Three tape recorders, however, require synchronization and a significant increase in operators where a single multitrack machine would have greatly simplified the task of providing the electronic portion of the performance. Multitrack tape recorders had been available since at least 1956, and a single multitrack capable of six or more channels would have reduced Anhalt's personnel list from four to one – since only one tape recorder would have to be started and stopped, and one mixer operator could easily manage that. However, the only multitrack available to Anhalt was Le Caine's special purpose playback device and this was far too large and unwieldy – not to mention temperamental and noisy – to place in a concert performance. Anhalt makes good use of the number of operators, however, by giving them a quasi-ritualistic entrance and exit.

OTHER WORKS USING TAPE

Going back briefly to 1967, Anhalt's second production that year (after *Cento*) was *Symphony of Modules*. The work is intended for a large complement of string and percussion instruments plus tape. Although the score is most intriguing, the tape portion of the piece is indicated only by timings in the score. Anhalt has written: "For some reason, I have not 'realized' the tape parts in 1967 ... After a few unsuccessful tries to have these completed (recently), I consider it a favourable development that Kevin Austin has recently agreed to help me achieve this."[77] Since no tape is yet extant, there is nothing more that can be said of the piece, from the point of view of electroacoustic music.[78]

Anhalt employed tape resources similar to those in *Foci* in his 1975 musical tableau, entitled *La Tourangelle*. He again uses three stereo tape recorders, each with its own operator, plus a mixer operator. This time, however, he adds a fifth person to the "operator" group and the function of this fifth person is to cue the operators of the tape recorders while following the conductor. Again there are six speakers for the six channels of tape playback, but this time, instead of the speakers being distributed around the entire hall, they are lined up across the stage apron in front of the conductor and performers. Also, in this line of speakers, one is provided for amplification of the three sopranos, and another for the tenor and baritone. Figure 6.1 is a representation of the speaker positions. Note that the speakers facing each other in the front row are stage monitors for the conductor's use only. Aside from the electronic resources, the forces for *La Tourangelle* consist of five solo voices (sss/t/b), sixteen instrumentalists – flute/piccolo, oboe, two clarinets, two bassoons, trumpet/crotales, horn/baritone/crotales, tuba, violin, viola, cello, double bass, harp, two keyboard players (amplified piano, celesta, electric organ, and ondes martenot[79], and two percussionists (playing nineteen instruments or sets of instruments). The complexity of speech/song – live and on tape – and of the instruments is much greater in this work than in *Foci*, although the synthetic material in *La Tourangelle* is less frequent.

Thus, we have seen a progressive decrease in the importance of electronics in Anhalt's final three electroacoustic works, *Cento* (1967), *Foci* (1968), and *La Tourangelle* (1975). The eventual disappearance of synthesizer or computer material in Anhalt's output is presaged in each of these works by the progressive decrease in importance of the electronic material, and counterbalanced by the progressive increase in numbers of forces and greater complexity in the use of those forces, as well as longer performance durations. *La Tourangelle* is the last work – so far – in which Anhalt has made use of prepared tapes.

Once Anhalt completed *Electronic Composition No. 4*, he had a sense of having learned a great deal from those four tape works, but he did not feel that there was a great deal to be gained by continuing to produce more tape pieces. The use of tape continued, as we have seen, for well over a decade, but the shift away from tape had begun. A primary motivation was that Anhalt was simply tired of the tedious process of

Figure 6.1
Speaker distribution for La Tourangelle

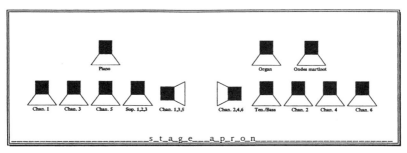

Source: Istvan Anhalt, *La Tourangelle* (Toronto: Berandol Music, 1982), vii.

cutting and splicing tape. The promise of digital synthesis offered similar or better results through more elegant means, though it would be at least another two decades before digital music making was both practical and affordable. Perhaps the most significant deterrent to tape music making was Anhalt's ever increasing interest in the musical use of language and the human voice. Anhalt's initial interest came from Stockhausen and, through Stockhausen, Werner Meyer-Eppler. *Cento* was Anhalt's first big experiment in language-music and it confirmed that this was the true realm of his future. *Foci, La Tourangelle, Winthrop,* and *Traces (Tikkun)* have only confirmed this.

This preference for language-music does not necessarily mean that Anhalt's involvement with electronics is over, however. As mentioned earlier, he still has a desire to see the electronic portion of *Symphony of Modules* (1967) completed. As recently as 1996, he considered the possibility of including a small electronic passage in *Traces (Tikkun),* but in rehearsal he decided that the electronic portion was not appropriate. Though he has no plans for a work with electronics at the moment, the possibility certainly still remains.

NOTES

1 "White noise" refers to a signal comprised of random occurrences of all audio frequencies in equal proportion. Such a signal is readily available as radio frequencies naturally occurring in the universe, detected by the simplest of radio receivers (such as a noisy electron tube in Stockhausen's day).

2 Istvan Anhalt, "La musique électronique," in *Musiques du Kébêk*, ed. Raoul Duguay (Montreal: Éditions du Jour, 1972), 16. The original French reads, "Cette oeuvre s'est révélée être un tournant dans ma vie musicale."

3 Curiously, Hugh Le Caine had presented a lecture on his work with electronic musical instruments at an event sponsored by the American Institute of Electrical and Electronics Engineers (now the IEEE) and the Engineering Institute of Canada in Montreal in 1957, and even earlier (1954) at McGill University itself, but Montreal was a sizable city and Anhalt had no reason to be looking for such lectures in those years.

4 The term "synthesizer" is used to describe a collection of audio generating and processing components to be variously combined to provide a flexible means of audio synthesis. Le Caine had a very successful version of such a device (probably the first worldwide); it was the Electronic Sackbut, named after an obsolete medieval brass slide instrument. Le Caine anticipated the phenomenon that we in the computer age now know all too well – "if it is built, it is already obsolete."

5 Istvan Anhalt, personal interview with the author, 8 February 1996.

6 Gayle Young, *The Sackbut Blues: Hugh Le Caine Pioneer in Electronic Music* (Ottawa: National Museum of Science and Technology, 1989), 106.

7 Istvan Anhalt, personal communication, 20 June 1996.

8 Le Caine had spent 1948–51 in Birmingham, England, completing a doctorate in nuclear physics. During that time he had been deeply influenced by the work of Pierre Schaeffer, about whom he had learned through BBC Third Programme broadcasts. In particular, he began to realize the significance of the tape recorder for electroacoustic music. (See Young, *Sackbut Blues*, 47.)

9 Gottfried Michael Koenig, "Bo Nilsson," and "Henri Pousseur," *Die Reihe* 4 (1958): 85, 18.

10 Anhalt, interview with the author; see also Young, *Sackbut Blues*, 111.

11 György Ligeti, "Pierre Boulez," *Die Reihe* 4 (1958): 38–63.

12 Rudolf Lück, "Eimert, Herbert," *The New Grove Dictionary of Music and Musicians*, 6:83.

13 Anhalt recalls that the theme of *Epitaph for Aikichi Kuboyama* was "the first H-bomb explosion by the US in the Pacific which contaminated the crew of a Japanese fishing boat with tragic results." (Anhalt, personal communication.) We can assume that the imaginative use of live and pre-recorded text in this work was filed away in Anhalt's mind for reference during the preparation of *Cento*, and that the sense of a looming nuclear holocaust that informed *Electronic Composition No. 4* may also relate in some way to the theme of Eimert's work.

14 Anhalt, personal communication.

15 Young, *Sackbut Blues*, 111–12.

16 Le Caine had produced nine works on tape, ranging in length from just over one minute to just under five minutes: *Dripsody* (1955), *Ninety-nine Generators, This Thing Called Key, Arcane Presents Lulu* (1956), *Invocation,*

Study No. 1 for Player Piano and Tape (1957), *The Burning Deck* (1958), *A Noisome Pestilence*, and *Textures* (1959).

17 Istvan Anhalt, liner notes to *Anthology of Canadian Music*, vol. 22, Radio Canada International, 1985 (hereafter ACM 22).

18 See note 1 for a definition of white noise.

19 Young, *Sackbut Blues*, 214–15.

20 A.S. Bregman and J. Campbell, "Primary Auditory Stream Segregation and the Perception of Order in Rapid Sequences of Tones," *Journal of Experimental Psychology* 89, 92 (1971): 244–9.

21 The devices that Anhalt employed in Le Caine's laboratory for work on *Electronic Composition No. 2* and *No. 3* were the following:

Oscillator bank: an array of 108 handmade oscillators capable of 20 Hz – 20 kHz (± .001). These produced individually tunable sine, square, or sawtooth waves and could be combined to produce virtually any spectrum (though the time-varying amplitudes and/or pitch changes that are important in distinguishing one type of sound from another had to be generated by some external means). Each oscillator required about sixty seconds to tune, so the whole bank could take nearly two hours, and the oscillators tuned first likely would have drifted by that time. The laboriousness of the tuning is likely among the reasons that Anhalt chose to employ only twenty-four of the oscillators for his work (developed by Le Caine, 1957–59).

Spectrogram: this was a controller for the oscillator bank (capable of controlling the loudness of up to one hundred individual oscillator modules). It had a drive that would move chart paper across a light source. On the other side of the paper were detectors that interpreted markings on the paper. Where it blocked the light, an oscillator was turned on (the tuning being predetermined by the oscillator itself). The usual use of this system was not to generate harmonies, but to create complex timbres that were capable of changing over time. This capability could not be achieved by any other practical means. This is an example of *additive* synthesis; that is, one can selectively combine the sine tones at specified relative loudnesses to build up a complex timbre (developed by Le Caine, 1959–62).

Coded music apparatus: this device, mentioned in some sources, is one Le Caine developed to work with the Electronic Sackbut (see note 4) over the period 1952–55. He abandoned the work and then returned to the idea in 1959, but the later version was much less complicated and was designed to work with the oscillator bank (Young, *Sackbut Blues*, 182–5, 200–1). Since Le Caine was still developing the spectrogram in 1959, it is possible that he was still calling the device by the earlier name at that time.

Variable and fixed bandwidth filters : these were capable of severely attenuating certain specified frequency ranges while allowing others to pass. This is the means of *subtractive* synthesis; that is, one can selectively remove portions of the audio spectrum to alter the timbre of the original sound (commercial device).

White noise generator: this would have been a component not uncommonly found as part of the test apparatus of an electronics lab. It provided excellent sources for subtractive synthesis treatments (commercial device).

Ampex stereo (two-track) tape recorder (2): professional tape recorders of this sort, by 1959, would be found as standard items in recording studios and broadcast operations. These were of a much higher quality than what one would find in "consumer" settings (commercial device).

Multitrack tape recorder: although called a "tape recorder," the machine did not record. Rather it was a precise but variable-speed playback device that permitted the operator to select and direct multiple outputs with considerable power and flexibility. The version that Anhalt used in the NRC lab had the capability to play back six pre-recorded stereo tapes simultaneously. One keyboard on the device allowed the operator to select one or more of the twelve sources and a second fine-tunable keyboard was used to select the playback speed (i.e., determine the playback pitch) in a manner suited to some predetermined musical pitch structure. While all of these individual capabilities were available elsewhere, no other device of the time provided as many functions in one place, nor did other devices allow for such precise and convenient control (developed by Le Caine, 1955–64).

22 This sentiment was conveyed to the author in a conversation that took place in the early 1980s.

23 The first concert presentation of *Dripsody* was organized by Istvan Anhalt. Details of that concert are given elsewhere in this chapter.

24 Le Caine wrote: "I must explain that I did not regard myself as a composer. However, I felt that the only way to understand the composer's interest in the apparatus was to try and use the equipment myself in the various current musical forms." Hugh Le Caine, " *Recherches au Temps Perdu* : Some Personal Recollections of My Work in Electronic Music Written at the Request of a History Student, Queen's University" (1966, typescript), [53].

25 Le Caine, " *Recherches*," 60.

26 Ibid.

27 Ibid.

28 The program of the concert is in the Anhalt fonds, folder B 10.3.

29 The famous work by Giovanni Gabrieli (from *Sacrae symphoniae*, 1597) may seem out of place in this concert. However, John Bowsher, a British physicist and avocational trombonist who worked in Le Caine's laboratory during the years 1958–59, filtered white noise so narrowly that it created the impression of a specific pitch. He then laboriously reproduced the Gabrieli work in white noise filtered in this way – faithful to both pitch and

dynamics. Although the work could not be considered in the same light as the remainder of the 1959 concert, the Gabrieli work was an interesting curiosity of the potential of electronics for music.

30 Anhalt, interview with the author; Anhalt, personal communication.

31 Anhalt, interview with the author.

32 The oscillator bank tunings used in *Electronic Composition No. 3* are described (and the specific pitches are listed in most cases) in Istvan Anhalt, "Electronic Composition No. III," Anhalt fonds, folder B 10.2. The tunings are summarized as follows:

No. 1: 6/5, 16/15 in alternation, producing a series of just minor thirds alternating with just diatonic semitones

No. 2: 5/4, 7/5, 16/15 twice followed by nearly the reverse (15/16, 7/5, 5/4, 16/15, 7/5, 5/4) – two series of just, small major thirds, augmented fourths, and semitones, but note the inversion of the first interval (15/16) in the second series

No. 3: 4/3, 6/5 in alternation, producing a series of just, perfect fourths alternating with small major thirds

No. 4: 4/3, 7/5 in alternation, producing a series of just, perfect fourths alternating with augmented fourths

No. 5: a series of 25 pitches from 415 to 2,349 Hz separated by equal-sized intervals one-fifth larger than the standard equal temperament used in tuning pianos

Nos. 6–8: three different series of inharmonic numbers designed to suggest "bell-like" timbres

No. 9: an approximation of the spectrum of a cymbal as represented in fig. 6.33 in Harry F. Olson's *Musical Engineering* (New York: Dover Publications, 1952).

Note: in tunings 1–4, Anhalt tuned oscillators 2 and 14–25 "a few cycles off" the calculated tunings in order to produce beats. The other tunings would produce beats without any need to deviate from the calculations, owing to their inharmonicity. Moreover, the instability of the oscillators of the time would have given rise to some additional complex interaction among the tones in any of the series.

33 Anhalt, "Electronic Composition No. III," 1.

34 Anhalt, liner notes to ACM 22.

35 Anhalt, "Electronic Composition No. III," 1.

36 I have presented *Electronic Composition No. 3* in concerts and lectures to many audiences in many countries between 1979 and about 1988. On each hearing, numerous audience members conveyed their amazement at the degree of control Anhalt exhibited (for this period) and their pleasure at hearing the work regardless of its provenance. Credit for this goes to Le Caine for providing the tools, and to Anhalt for having the imagination and sensitivity to make optimum use of those tools.

37 Quoted from John Beckwith and Udo Kasemets eds., *The Modern Composer and His World* (Toronto: University of Toronto Press, 1961), 115–16.

38 Young, *Sackbut Blues*, 91, 107, 114.

39 Anhalt, liner notes to ACM 22.

40 Elliott Schwartz, *Electronic Music: A Listener's Guide* (New York: Praeger Publishers, 1975), 58–9.

41 Ibid., 62.

42 Istvan Anhalt, liner notes to ACM 22.

43 Brian Fennelly, "Arel, Bülent," *The New Grove Dictionary of Music and Musicians*, 1:560.

44 Elaine Barkin, "Babbitt, Milton," *The New Grove Dictionary of Music and Musicians*, 1:765–7.

45 Charles Wuorinen, "Ussachevsky, Vladimir (Alexis)," *The New Grove Dictionary of Music and Musicians*, 19:478.

46 James Tenney subsequently came to Canada and has spent the greater part of his career teaching composition and music technology at York University.

47 Young, *Sackbut Blues*, 145.

48 Max Matthews, a research engineer at Bell Telephone Laboratories, had worked with the very first IBM computer (701) to produce two experimental programs: MUSIC I in 1957 and MUSIC II early in 1958. Both were rudimentary and cumbersome. However, after taking delivery of a much more powerful IBM (7094) in 1959, Matthews was able to produce MUSIC III. This was a program that enabled the composer to describe the target sounds more easily and completely in a manner more accessible to composers. Matthews, along with Joan Miller, produced MUSIC IV in 1962, and it was this version that was the foundation for versions that have been ported to many different machines and/or languages: MUSIC IV BF (1966–67, in Fortran, by Hubert Howe), MUSIC V (1968, a more efficient Fortran version by Matthews), MUSIC 360 (1968, for the IBM 360, by Vercoe), MUSIC 11 (1970, for the PDP 11, by Barry Vercoe), MUSIC 10 (1975, for the much larger PDP 10, by John Chowning and James Moorer), and CMUSIC (1985, for the "C" language, by Moorer), which, along with CSOUND (1986, also for "C," by Vercoe) are still very much in use today. For all of the above information, I am indebted to Peter Manning, *Electronic and Computer Music*, 2nd ed. (Oxford: Clarendon Press, 1993), 219–21.

49 Anhalt, liner notes to ACM 22.

50 Reverberation of the "Real" variety called for the use of large, extremely quiet, and acoustically ideal rooms and these generally were available only to large-budget recording projects such as those for commercial record companies. In the 1950s and early 1960s there were only two types of artificial reverberation available: spring and plate. The reverberation plate was a large sheet of acoustically insulated steel. Audio signals were converted to

mechanical energy on the steel plate's surface and converted back again, along with the myriad reflections of the original signal, to electrical energy at several locations elsewhere on that surface. Reverberation springs used essentially the same concept, except that a spring replaced the plate and, normally, there was only one transducer to convert the spring's vibrations back to electrical energy. Rooms, plates, and springs each have their own distinct qualities. In *Electronic Composition No. 4*, a spring reverberation creates the disproportionate amount of high frequency activity and gives the flaccid but pinched sound that characterizes the implied sonic space of this piece. (This type of reverberation can also be heard in some of Le Caine's own works, such as *Dripsody*.)

51 Istvan Anhalt, "A Chronology of Involvement with Electronic Music," Anhalt fonds, folder C 2.1.

52 Nadia Turbide, "Duchow, Marvin," *Encyclopedia of Music in Canada*, 2nd ed., 386.

53 The first electronic studio to be established in North America was the Columbia-Princeton Electronic Music Center. Varying dates are found in print sources, but the most convincing is a statement in Peter Manning's history of computer music in which he states "a grant of $175,000 was advanced [by the Rockefeller Foundation] in January 1959 for a Columbia-Princeton Electronic Music Center, to be situated at Columbia University, and based upon the RCA synthesizer, which was to be purchased from the manufacturers. Delivery of the original Mark 1 version was soon arranged, pending its replacement by an improved Mark 2 version, delivered later in the year." Manning, *Electronic and Computer Music*, 97. Le Caine delivered the NRC equipment in the late spring of 1959 and the studio was functional sometime in June. So, Toronto was second only by a matter of months, at most.

54 Walter did compose occasionally, in a late-Romantic style, but he was primarily known as an educator and musicologist.

55 Nadia Turbide et al., "Blume, Helmut," *Encyclopedia of Music in Canada*, 2nd ed., 135.

56 The multitrack tape recorder had, in fact, been provided by the NRC on loan to McGill in 1963 to assist Anhalt's work on his composition *Cento*. Young, *Sackbut Blues* 135, 241n16.

57 Young, *Sackbut Blues*, 138.

58 Nadia Turbide, "McGill University," *Encyclopedia of Music in Canada*, 2nd ed., 831.

59 Eldon Grier, *A Friction of Lights* (Toronto: Contact Press, 1963), 11–26.

60 Istvan Anhalt, "The Making of *Cento*," *Canada Music Book* 1 (spring-summer 1970): 81.

61 See Anhalt, "The Making of *Cento*," 85, for further explanation of this derivation process.

62 See Istvan Anhalt, "Composing with Speech," in *Proceedings of the Seventh International Congress of Phonetic Science* (Paris: Mouton, 1972), 447.

63 Anhalt, "The Making of *Cento*," 81.

64 Ibid., 81–9.

65 Alec Nisbett, *The Sound Studio*, 6th ed. (Oxford: Focal Press, 1995), 233.

66 Anhalt, "The Making of *Cento*," 83; ellipses added. It is interesting to compare Anhalt's use of the tape recorder to that of an (ethno-) musicologist like Anhalt's studio director counterpart at the University of Toronto, Myron Schaeffer. Schaeffer had first made use of the tape recorder, prior to his arrival at the University of Toronto in 1958, to record field-gathered folk music in South America. Keane, "Electroacoustic Music in Canada, 1950–1984," in *Célébration* ed. Godfrey Ridout and Talivaldis Kenins (Toronto: Canadian Music Centre, 1984), 66. To Schaeffer, then, the tape recorder functioned to reduce multidimensionality to replicable simplicity for study. Anhalt uses the tape recorder to *create* multidimensionality – to rise above the simplification that Schaeffer sought.

67 Anhalt, "The Making of *Cento*," 86.

68 The resources of the McGill studio in the mid-1960s, all of which were used in the creation of *Cento*, were as follows (from Anhalt, "The Making of *Cento*," 86): *Sound Sources*: standard periodic waveform generators (sine, triangle, sawtooth, staircase, square and pulse); 24 sine tone generators with keyboard controller (a Le Caine device); tone-burst generator; white noise generator; Hammond Novachord. *Treatment*: ring modulator, variable bandpass filter, 6-channel band of octave filters (a Le Caine device); spring-type reverberation devices; Multitrack Tape Recorder (a Le Caine device); 24-channel Spectrogram (a Le Caine device). *Tape Recorders*: Ampex 351 half-track stereo; Ampex AG-350 half-track stereo.

69 Anhalt, "The Making of *Cento*," 83.

70 Ibid.

71 Ibid., 88.

72 For example, Stockhausen, in *Studie II*, uses graph paper to indicate frequency and time rather precisely with a geometric notation.

73 Anhalt, personal communication.

74 It was the German astronomer Johannes Kepler who adopted the term *focus* for use in its present day sense: "the point where rays or waves come together, or from which they issue."

75 Istvan Anhalt, "About *Foci*," *Artscanada* 28 (April-May 1971): 57.

76 Anhalt, personal communication.

77 Istvan Anhalt, letter to the author, 29 May 1995. Kevin Austin, a composer who studied under Anhalt at McGill University, was appointed to Concordia University in 1970 and founded that university's electroacoustic studio in 1971. François Guértin, "Austin, Kevin," *Encyclopedia of Music in Canada*, 2nd ed., 58.

78 See, however, John Beckwith's discussion of *Symphony of Modules* in "Orchestral Works," this volume, pp. 115–20.

79 The ondes martenot is the more frequently used name of the instrument Maurice Martenot introduced in Paris in 1928 as the ondes musicales. It is a monophonic electronic instrument that produces a sine tone that can be controlled very musically via keyboard and ribbon controller. The ondes martenot can be made to produce a sound similar to the human voice, but the range and the precision of controllability is very much greater. Darius Milhaud, Florent Schmitt, Jacques Ibert, Arthur Honegger, Olivier Messiaen, Pierre Boulez, Claude Champagne, Clermont Pépin, Gilles Tremblay, and Gabriel Charpentier, among others, have also written for this instrument. (See Richard Orton, "Ondes Martenot," *The New Grove Dictionary of Music and Musicians*, 13:540–1; and Pierre Rochon, "Ondes Martenot," *Encyclopedia of Music in Canada*, 2nd ed., 964.

7 Alternatives of Voice: Anhalt's Odyssey from Personalized Style to Symbolic Expression

WILLIAM E. BENJAMIN

Over the past half-century, Istvan Anhalt has produced a body of work as technically refined, as rich in meaning, and as fully engaged with musicality as any other from this period. There are reasons why it does not enjoy the wide recognition accorded other oeuvres, of which many have less potential to reward the discerning listener. The professional cost of reaching full production only after the age of fifty can be cited – if easily explained by way of thirty-five years of unstinting devotion to teaching – as can the fractured state of musical politics (like all politics) in Canada, not to mention the dismally fragmented condition of non-commercial music itself. Lamentable as these factors surely are, I prefer to think of qualities that will recommend Anhalt's music to a future in which assessment, however biased, is untainted by the interests that warp our judgments. One such quality is the importance of the recurring themes with which his music is concerned: the human life cycle, transformative experience (traumatic and epiphanic), memory, sexuality, good and evil, and the Divine. Another consists in the music's deep and subtle implication of its wide-ranging traditions, which, by promoting the sharp characterization of detail, affords the acute ear continual delight in being able to grasp this detail intimately, so that it can be remembered – represented to creative consciousness. A third and potentially most decisive trait is the music's inner source of integrity, the way it fixes its materials and structures them with rigour, honouring its self-imposed obligations without compromising an instinct for rapturous freedom.

That these qualities will influence the music's prospects is due, in no small part, to the openings they create for criticism. For now, more than ever, when everything survives in digital storage, special efforts are required to shape canons, to determine what survives in people's ears. Ultimately, performers play the crucial roles in these determinations, but the present state of musical culture – a landscape profusely strewn with ephemera as blatantly inflated in reputation as they are thin in substance – demands the interventions of informed critics on behalf of works that offer delights for the mind and body, and rich possibilities for commentary and musical education. A need to respond has motivated this study which explores music I have long advocated to students and colleagues as among the best of our time and that I now wish to champion in more explicit terms with respect to the qualities introduced above (meaning, the uses of tradition, and structure) and their modes of interaction.

In what follows I will treat extensively only two of Anhalt's works, the Symphony (1958) and *SparkskrapS* (1987). While representing just two of the four phases of Anhalt's composing to date (to be discussed below), and sidestepping the problems of composing for the voice and with language (which have preoccupied him so centrally), this pair of works affords an ideal basis for comparisons that show Anhalt's creative evolution and the ways in which he has participated in and contributed to crucial movements and transformations of recent musical history. Each is a work for full orchestra, of approximately twenty-five minutes in length, and the interval of nearly thirty years between them allows for a clear view of the composer's changing ideas about possibilities, proscriptions, and limits: the possibilities of music to refer outside itself *without invoking language*; the proscription against so-called derivative art in high modernist circles; and the limits of structural and stylistic heterogeneity within an artistic product conceived as a work, that is, as singular, fixed, and somehow of a piece. Both works, then, respond to questions of meaning, of derivation from sources, and of diversity within unity (or freedom within constraints), but each does so within a distinct ideological framework. Notwithstanding the persistence of compositional traits across the decades of Anhalt's career, these frameworks are dissimilar enough to allow for different interpretations of these qualities and a quite different balance among them.

Dating from the later 1950s, the Symphony is a product of Anhalt's second career phase (1954–58),[1] in which he was concerned chiefly with incorporating and personalizing the achievements of classical serialism and, like other leading modernists, with reconstructing aspects of pitch organization from the ground up. This is the shortest of the four phases, and includes only *Three Songs of Death* (1952), *Comments* (1954), the Fantasia for solo piano (1954), the Violin Sonata (1954), the Symphony, on which Anhalt worked for four years, and the four *Chansons d'aurore* for voice, flute, and piano (1955), in which he first tried out serial patterns later used in the Symphony.[2] The second phase follows upon a longer, neoclassical phase (1941–53), which culminates in the Piano Trio (1953). Anhalt's explorations in this first phase are wideranging: he assimilates and makes his own a variety of approaches to dissonant tonality, motivic post-tonality, and chromatic neomodality, producing works – even movements – in immediate succession that differ considerably from one another in rhythmic style and harmonic sound. The Piano Trio, for example, offers the tough-minded Bartók of the 1920s, Stravinsky's later neoclassicism, and a synthesis of early Bartókian expressionism with neobaroque and neoclassical elements as the primary sources of its first, second, and last movements, respectively. At the same time, its first movement manages at one point to allude quite specifically to Brahms (example 7.1).[3] Throughout this work traditional formal syntax is a vestigial presence, as is evident in the use of distinctive themes and their varied restatements, of thematic contrast, and of typical developmental textures; but this presence is subverted in surprising ways which, if not always fully integrated into their stylistic environment, comment on it with extreme irony and point provocatively to Anhalt's much later music.[4]

With his second phase, Anhalt's music sheds all trace of the element of pastiche that sometimes gives his first-phase works, no matter how impressive, an aura of apprenticeship. But this does not mean that the music acquires an oppressive uniformity, or loses all ties with tradition, as is the case with so much music of the 1950s, once considered avant-garde. On the contrary, each of the works of this period has its own personality, and preserves its own links with the past. The magnificent Fantasia, for example, while making use of twelve-tone procedures, is *sui generis* in form and owes little in spirit to the Second Viennese School. Moreover, it is a thoroughly tonical work, deploying quasi-traditional and contextual means to tonicize D (almost unremittingly) in a resolutely dissonant milieu. The Symphony, on the other hand, is essentially a music of ordered and unordered pitch-class (pc) sets, and it charts the 12-pc universe with bold and far-reaching strokes, displaying a synoptic grasp of the resources of the chromatic scale that is, at the very least, remarkable for its time. But, as I shall show, it is also a work that assiduously cultivates traditional terrain: it is consistently metric and in many places richly polymetric; it uses harmonic rhythm and, at times, quasi-functional bass line patterns and related tonal simulacra to produce metre; and it refers both to European symphonic

Example 7.1 Piano Trio, first movement: a Brahmsian moment

archetypes – formal and topical – and to culturally normative functional processes – of progression (intensification) and recession (détente) – at various levels of structure.

SparkskrapS is a product of Anhalt's fourth phase, his last to date and certainly his most prolific. Where this phase is said to begin depends of course on how one conceptualizes its predecessor. The third phase begins in 1959, with three years' immersion in electronic music. Anhalt's electronic pieces are best viewed as attempts to retrain his ear and to prepare himself for rethinking music's expressive possibilities. Indeed, expression is the key value here, as the composer turns away from the strongest attributes of his earlier music – its harmonic subtlety, metric vitality, combinational virtuosity, and empassioned lyricism – apparently believing their expressive potential to be depleted. All his compositions of the 1960s use a combination of live and recorded sound and invite a conception of music that is much more encompassing than anything invoked by the earlier work. As with much music of that decade, their relevant sonic dimensions are essentially timbral; their rhythmic character is ametric, continuous; and their aesthetic is predominantly referential (at times naturalistic) and characteristically rhetorical, even didactic. This is a music of commenting on, of being about, and its primary vehicle is the human voice, employed in its full range of timbral and articulative possibilities, and with reference to comprehensive fields of utterance that are socially and/or instinctively based. I must confess to a less-than-total enthusiasm for the music of this period. *Cento* (1967) and *Foci* (1969), for example, are marred despite their fine moments by overly drawn-out and obvious gestures, and by a foregrounding of linguistic-ideological elements that is less than engaging, with a concomitant suppression of musical substance.[5]

Foci might be viewed as marking the end of the third phase, but the latter's intellectual preoccupations extend into the next decade, culminating in the treatise on new directions in vocal music, *Alternative Voices*, published only in 1984. Also, stylistic features of the music of the late 1960s persist in *La Tourangelle* (1975), notably the mixture of live and recorded sound, and the multitracking of vocal material in contrasting modes of delivery. However, this first of a trilogy of dramatic works on the theme of life-passage – the second being *Winthrop* (1986) and the third, *Traces (Tikkun)* (1995) – demarcates something else as well: the beginning of a remarkable process of reintegration, whereby harmony – understood as made up of chords defined by relationships of resonance that extend registrally and temporally between and even beyond the pitches by which they are expressed – is brought back, to hollow out tone-spaces (and time-spans) in which heterogeneously expressive vocal and instrumental strands are connected and made to resound more deeply, as if by an encompassing medium. This recovery of the harmonic dimension, assuming an importance it had not enjoyed in Anhalt's music since the early 1950s, is all the more remarkable for *not* neutralizing the powers of commentary and dramatization that the music had acquired after 1959. Without blunting these powers, it grounds them in something not of their nature – continuities of sonic substance appealing directly to musical receptivity, as cultivated over several hundred years of tradition. In this way, and in the manner characteristic of all dramatic and interpretive music worthy of our attention, this reinvoked harmony confers an ennobling pathos on discursive content that may not, in itself, enlist our aesthetic sympathies.

If *La Tourangelle* is to be seen as a transitional work, the fourth phase of Anhalt's trajectory as a composer must be said to begin in the late 1970s, with work on *Winthrop*. The latter perseveres in the direction of "re-musicalization," that is, of passing discursive material through a series of harmonic-metric filters to produce musical forms that stand on their own, in traditional terms. It is, without doubt I think, Anhalt's masterpiece of dramatic composition, in which he achieves the most perfect synthesis of music and message.

After *Winthrop*, and the immediately following *Thisness* (1986) for soprano and piano, a comparatively less interesting dramatic essay, Anhalt embarked upon the trilogy of major orchestral works composed in the late 1980s: *Simulacrum* (1986–87), *SparkskrapS* (1987), and *Sonance•Resonance (Welche Töne?)* (1989). It is here that he consolidates the technical and expressive achievements of the fourth phase, in an only partly precedented genre of instrumental music. Not purely symphonic, because of its through-composed, episodic nature, this is a ruminative kind of music, perhaps having antecedents in some of the later chamber works by Schoenberg.[6] Being part musical description, part musical free association, these are fantasia-like tone-records of mental and physical states, and of personal memories (including intertextual memories of music), as well as musical translations of images and concepts, in the tradition of the tone poem, but with none of the latter's paraphernalia of thematic transformation or – as hardly needs saying – its heroics. By referring to a trilogy of works, I do not mean to imply that these pieces are part of a single project, nor even that they are stages in the exploration of a single theme, in the manner of the three dramatic works referred to earlier. In fact, each of the three orchestral works has very much its own personality and technical identity. *Simulacrum*, for example, incorporates quotations from earlier music and adopts, in part, a neoclassical attitude to form, with recapitulative passages and a climactic use of fugal exposition; *SparkskrapS* does neither. *Sonance•Resonance (Welche Töne?)*, on the other hand, is largely a fantasia on musical material derived from Beethoven's Ninth Symphony, and so is more tightly integrated from a motivic standpoint than its forerunners. However, all three share a certain atmosphere – of harmonic plenitude and density of parts, of a prevailingly slow tempo, of contrast between smooth and disrupted continuity, of heterophonic enrichment of homo- and polyphonic textures, of stylistic allusiveness and heterogeneity. And all three convey a sense of reverence and spirituality tinged with some sadness, even horror. They are collectively a music of looking back, and therefore of later life, and yet the products of a mind still enormously fertile and full of vibrant sonic imagery.

I will not extend this preliminary survey to comment on Anhalt's latest works, since my purpose has been only to situate the two compositions that are the subject of the main (analytical-descriptive and critical-comparative) parts of this essay. Besides, the fact that with the music of the 1980s (or perhaps with *La Tourangelle*) Anhalt found an absolutely distinctive voice for the first time, one in which he has since continued to address us, obviates the need for such an extension. Perhaps his career has not taken its final turn, and will close with yet a further stage, but if this is the case, it cannot be foreseen now. Let me turn, therefore, to separate discussions of the Symphony and of *SparkskrapS* as representatives of Anhalt's responses to postwar modernism and the postmodern reaction, respectively; and as resplendent examples of what it has been possible to achieve in the art music of our time.

SYMPHONY (1958)[7]

Reference as Form and Meaning in the Work as a Whole

Writing in 1959, Anhalt described his first work for full orchestra, entitled Symphony, as "a composite of variations of a four-note motif and its eight-note complement, as well as of divers tempi, rhythms, dynamics, instrumental combinations and their correlations."[8] If this description, later echoed by others,[9] does little to justify the title, neither does the appearance of the score, which is divided into thirteen sections. Yet the work's genre affiliation is very much to the symphony as it developed from 1850 onwards, and not to the variation set for orchestra. The variations Anhalt speaks of are there, to be sure: each is a short segment of music of from two to perhaps twelve bars, and is unified (as the composer tells us) with respect to a particular process of pitch-class derivation and a particular texture, or correlation of rhythms, registers, and dynamics with instrumental parts. The textures of these variations are relatively static in some cases, more directed in others, which is to say that the variations are phrases of various kinds, some of which are more thematic or expository, others more processive or developmental. The description "variations of a four-note motive" is confusing, however. The work employs a profusion of motives, in the normal sense of the term, but it is also true that every variation features, in an important role, one or more, and often all, of the six content-distinct transpositions of the set (11,0,5,6), which is shown in example 7.2, and their eight-tone complements, variously partitioned. Thus, "variations on a class of ways of partitioning the aggregate" would have been more accurate, albeit inadvisable in a program note written in 1959.

The thirteen sections are likewise of differing kinds. Many are units comprised of several variations that cohere in terms of a larger functional purpose, expressed as a path of textural progression, textural détente, textural stasis, or some combination of these. Among these, some are units with respect to an archetype of symphonic form at the movement level, such as "scherzo," or of intramovement formal syntax, such as "imitative developmental passage." Still others are assemblages of topical archetypes – for example, an off-balance attempt at a stately march or processional issuing in a breezy simulation of carefree athleticism. Then too, among the thirteen sections, some are not musical units at all, having been packaged as "a convenience for rehearsal purposes."[10] Because the sections are defined across these disparate categories, the work is in no sense a fantasia in thirteen parts; nor is it a set of variations any more than any work composed of perhaps one hundred phrases with motivic interconnections (including a single pitch-class motive in common) is such a set.

An obvious, if question-begging, response to the problem of the work's form is that it is a through-composed whole, and this accords with the composer's point of view. He writes of the work having as its "objective" structure a "fever chart" that plots in two dimensions – intensity against time – a path connecting numerical values that represent successive variations. Each value represents the intensity of a variation, somehow integrated over its time span and reducing its mul-

tidimensionality of energies (loudness, attack density, textural density,
dissonance level, register, etc.) to a
single number. Anhalt, with characteristic thoroughness, even prepared
a graph of this structure, though at

Example 7.2
Symphony: basic set

what stage in the process of composition (or perhaps afterwards) I do
not know.[11] While not meaningless, this kind of representation is
open to serious question as an indicator of large-scale coherence. The
difficulty with it lies first in the incommensurability of the different
scales along which the variables of intensity must be measured, so that
difference by a factor of two in loudness (even if intersubjectively perceived) may not be reliably equated in effect with a parallel difference
in attack density. And it lies also in the undefined nature of integration (summation) over the course of a segment of music – if two passages are identical except that one is twice as long as the other, is the
longer one more intense than the shorter, and if so, how much more?
Moreover, difference in a musical work is always contextual, and hierarchically so; two passages that integrate and reduce to the same
value, however reliably, will necessarily have differing impacts depending on where they occur and what surrounds them. Consider, for example, how different in effect any repeated passage will sound at
different points in a movement; and if so different in effect, how constant in projected intensity? This problem is much compounded
where different passages are being compared.

These problems lead one to look for other ways of describing the
work's coherence and, in this connection, to take its name more seriously. As a single continuity, the Symphony is clearly not based on
classical models, but there is a clear precedent for it in the single-
movement symphony that developed towards the end of the nineteenth century and that composers cultivated so extensively at the
start of the twentieth. In this genre, a greatly extended and very
loosely interpreted realization of first-movement sonata form acts as a
framework for thematic sections that represent each of the remaining
movements of the classical symphony – the slow movement, the
scherzo, and the finale – and the whole is optionally framed with introduction and coda. Perhaps the foremost examples of the genre are
found in Schoenberg's early works, most notably the First String
Quartet (1907) and the Chamber Symphony (1908).[12] Anhalt's Symphony is scarcely a direct descendant of these works, but its affiliation
with them, across half a century of music, is not to be doubted.

There are three defining aspects of the single-movement symphonic form. It must refer to musical characters associated with thematic materials of each of the classical symphony's four movements,

Table 7.1
Overall form of the Symphony

Unit of formal syntax	Internal structure and general description	Measures	Sections
EXPOSITION Mvt 1	Tripartite, with two allegro sections flanking a moderato	1–151	I–III
• first theme-group	concerto grosso format with tutti/soli alternation, leading to a climactic cantilena over a prominent bass line and resonant harmony	1–80	I
• second theme-group	march in three phrases followed by short quasi-trio	81–92 93–100	II
• third theme-group	two broad parallel waves: the first, of four variations; the second, of three variations	101–29 130–51	III
DEVELOPMENT Mvt 1, part 1	Generally in détente, with the intermezzi as static interruptions of various sorts	152–278	IV–VI and first two variations of VII
• contrapuntal treatment of basic motive	flowing, *espressivo*, linear heterogeneity	152–73	IV
• climax of preceding	rapid progression of texture to three short intensity peaks, followed by two resisting cadential gestures	174–91	IV cont.
• development of rhythmic motive	• rising phase, preparing • falling phase (a scurrying descent that slows and thickens)	192–8 199–210	IV cont.
• transition	high, static scherzando fragment, slowing down and preparing metrically for Intermezzo	211–13	IV concluded
• *Intermezzo* I	Comprising two variations: • delicate waltzlike tracery • gentle canonic dialogue	214–19 220–6	V
• transition	similar to 211–13, but more percussive and accelerating	227–30	V cont.
• resumption of DEVELOPMENTAL processes	thickening descent that is a viscous reprise of 214 ff. and a continuation of 199–210	231–4	V concluded
• *Intermezzo* II	Simulation of a set of four gongs, struck at varying places, in varying ways	235–60	V
• transition (codetta and echo)	comprising two variations: • varied reprise of 220–6 • sinister scherzando-type transformation of the gongs	261–71 272–8	VII beginning

Table 7.1
(continued)

Slow Movement	*Sparse textures, largely homophonic:*		
Mvt 2	• *recessive opening variation*	*279–89*	
	• *menacing calm in low and middle registers punctuated by descending sequences,* <u>*dolce*</u>	*290–311*	*VII remainder*
	• <u>*espressivo*</u> *melody with quasi-Alberti-bass accomp.*	*311–15*	
	• *descending sequences, interrupted by high bell sounds, leading to nadir of the composition*	*316–28*	
DEVELOPMENT Mvt 1, part 2	Intensifying contrapuntal treatment of 6-tone series	329–364	VIII
Scherzo Mvt 3	*Four periods (a, b, c, a′), flying into highest regions*	*365–403*	*IX*
DEVELOPMENT Mvt 1, part 3	Based on rhythmic motives, progressing toward climax	404–36	first part of X
RECAPITULATION of work as a whole	Finale is integrated into the reprise of various topics from earlier sections	437–629	rest of X through XIII
• reprise of topic from first theme-group	*espressivo* cantilena over walking bass, climactic	437–49	rest of X
• reprise of topic and pitch material of *Intermezzo* I	"ambling waltz," but more chorale-like; *dolce*	450–461	first part of XI
• reprise of *Intermezzo* II	identical texture, but fragmentary	462–7	conclusion of XI
Finale Mvt 4	*Two distinct groups, the second constituting the emotional climax of the entire work*		
	• *rhythmic canons, textural buildup*	*468–85*	*XII*
	• *massive tutti, with rise to and staggered chromatic descent from a textural climax*	*486–501*	
• reprise of Scherzo topic	airy texture, same motives as in scherzo, and similar phrase structure, but predominantly in middle register	502–35	first part of XIII
• transition	compression and liquidation of preceding; ²/₈ instead of ³/₈	536–58	XIII cont.
• reprise of Slow Movement topics	• rapid thienning out to intense high-register monophony	559–79	XIII cont.
	• menacing calm	580–9	
CODA	Very fast; one enormous wave, rapidly cresting at the end, with intensity values going off the scale	590–629	XIII concluded

in one of their correct orderings. It must include sections that are metrically and motivically of "tight" construction, as well as those that are comparatively "loose" – quasi-thematic and quasi-developmental sections, in other words. And it must include elements of large-scale reprise coming after extended digression. The preceding diagram indicates how Anhalt's Symphony meets these requirements.

Because the information in this table is extremely compressed, some words of explanation are in order. The leftmost column lists the work's divisions, in three ways. Major divisions of the overall (sonata) form are in capital letters and are left-justified. The subdivisions of these are also left-justified, but are in plain text, and are preceded by bullets. All left-justified entries pertain, therefore, to the work conceived as a first-movement form. Interpolated into this design are the second, third, and final movements of a four-movement symphony. These are italicized, and are right-justified. To be sure, the movements thus networked to the first are not stand-alone structures, though the slow movement is elaborate enough to encompass a beginning, middle, and end. The scherzo, a rounded-binary succession of four short periods, lacks any trio or large-scale reprise; and the finale is fragmentary, a bipartite exposition of new material that, because of its location, sounds like the recapitulation of an exposition group that never was. All the same, these "movements" contain some of the work's most important moments: the slow movement ends with its nadir and strongest reference to a traditional cadence; the scherzo has its clearest use of traditional phrase structure; and the finale, its most extended and most emotionally gripping climax.

The functions of the second, third, and fourth columns of the table are obvious. The second lists important surface features of corresponding divisions, also indicating (by separately bulleted entries) lower-level subdivisions where these seem worth noting. The third column is self-explanatory, and the fourth shows how the form as I have analyzed it intersects with Anhalt's thirteen sections.

I don't wish to overstate the resemblances between sonata form as represented in the Symphony and its classical (or romantic) sources. For one thing, the distinction between exposition and development in the Symphony is nothing if not subtle. I call the first three sections a tripartite exposition because each of them is structured as a discernible whole, each employs distinctive topics in an intelligible succession, and each has a clear phrase structure involving the use of phrase-level contrast and reprise. The first section begins as an alternation of tutti and soli. The tutti subsections explore a "chaos" topic, realized in terms of streams of three-tone chords cycling in unpredictable orderings over much more slowly cycling linear three-tone patterns in the bass (see example 7.12). The soli subsections, by contrast, present the beginnings of a melody of the *unendliche* type, reaching towards and gradually attaining the upper registers. At about the middle of the section, tutti and soli textures merge into a highly expressive cantilena duet over a ponderous bass in octaves, harmonized richly by resonant quasi-tertian harmonies (see example 7.13). The overall result is very much in line with the Hebrew Bible's representation of the Genesis topic, in which the Creator's heroically accumulating acts (the soli) generate, from previously inert strata of matter (the tutti), a radiant, fully occupied world in which each part reflects all of the others, but human will (the melody) dominates. The second section is a march or processional, described by Anhalt as "odd" – though "quaint, self-regarding, and somewhat esoteric" would be more precise, in view of the irregular phrase lengths and emphatic but rhythmically off-balance cadences. This is followed by the expected trio, which in the breezy indifference (to the march) of its Webernesque canonic athleticism is suitably ironic in tone. This combination of march and trio provides comic distance from the high seriousness of sections I and III, the outer panels of my expository triptych. There is no return to the march; instead the trio makes a transition to section III, which is in two halves, each beginning with highly organized, rapidly unfolding canonic activity in 5/4 time (see example 7.6). In both instances this activity represents effusive, effective optimism, and in both it is brought down, tragically overcome by struggles with contrary forces so as to culminate in a counterpoint of two slow, thickly doubled parts, painfully converging on the middle register in a brutal cadence.

I won't speculate on what this triptych might mean as a whole, though it is not difficult to imagine how the humanist rhetoric I have invoked to describe the first section might be extended to cover the second and third. My intention in going this far has been to substantiate the designation of its sections as thematic. I trust it is understood that, in referring to phrases and cadences, I am speaking imprecisely, or in terms that will only become precise when detailed analyses are provided. And that the topics I am calling upon are of many kinds, some perfectly obvious ("march"), and others requiring hermeneutic accounts of long cultural traditions that cross musical style boundaries ("Genesis"), accounts that are beyond the scope of this essay. Nevertheless, I hope to have indicated why I think it is correct to speak of the opening sections of the Symphony as an exposition, a laying out of ideas, in both formal and referential senses.

The development section of the Symphony begins with section IV and ends in the middle of section x. It is interrupted at one level by the slow movement and the scherzo, and at another by two intermezzi.

The latter are short sections of a relatively static nature, which stand apart from the musical (developmental) flow, both by resisting the directions in which the latter is headed and in terms of the special topics they represent – topics connected with distance from ordinary reality, and therefore with dreams, visions, memories, secrets, and other "unreal" experiences. Both intermezzi occur in part 1 of the development, which is by far the longest of three. This part begins with section IV, and its lengthy opening passage (mm. 152–73) is marked by extremely intricate six-part counterpoint, based entirely on transformations of the set in example 7.2, the work's Ur-motive. At least three qualities mark this passage (see example 7.14) as archetypally developmental: its obsessive concentration on diverse but easily heard transformations of a small referential collection; its lack of obvious internal punctuation; and its relative neutrality with respect to topic, which, insofar as it has one, might be compositional virtuosity itself.[13] To these, the next passage (mm. 174–91) adds a fourth: a clear pattern of intensification toward climax, which, when reached, takes the form of three brief tutti eruptions separated by pauses, followed by two even shorter gestures that somehow react, as if applying the brakes to the preceding surge, or (to mix metaphors) even pulling the rug out from underneath it, since they sound curiously like orchestrated laughs. (Anhalt's notes refer only to "a question [the three eruptions] and two answers.") The rest of part 1 of the development is generally in recession – dynamically, texturally, registrally, and with respect to tempo. It features a rhythmic motive – two slurred sixteenth notes, a sixteenth rest, and a sixteenth note identical in pitch to the second of the slurred notes – one that, again, is obsessively repeated, in developmental mode. It is interrupted first by intermezzo I, which begins as a gentle dreamlike waltz (see example 7.11) and continues as a melancholy Bartókian canon in two voices, freely accompanied, the whole suggesting a *temps perdu* as experienced by a constructed subject. The second interruption, intermezzo II (see example 7.18), is of an entirely different nature. Anhalt calls it "the Gong," but it is more accurately represented as a cyclic activation of four sonorous bodies, each with its fundamental frequency and associated inharmonic partials (the latter changing with each activation), as if an imaginary set of four gongs were being struck in a cyclic sequence, with a different mallet and stroke placement for each cycle. The effect of this interruption is totally different from that of intermezzo I. It seems to invoke a vision and, from a temporal standpoint, something in the future, something envisioned. In fact, as I shall demonstrate, this passage anticipates compositional techniques developed some years later by another composer of Hungarian Jewish origin, György Ligeti.

The second and third parts of the development follow upon the slow movement and the scherzo, respectively. Part 2 of the development (see example 7.4), a four-voiced imitative treatment of an ordered hexachord, has perhaps the most conventional texture of any passage in the work. Part 3, which I associate with the dances in Stravinsky's *Agon*, is once again based on a rhythmic motive, this time a pair of slurred sixteenth notes followed by an eighth note that is pitch identical to the second of the slurred sixteenth notes. The parallel between this passage (mm. 404–36) and that at mm. 192–210, in part 1 of the development, is obvious. Both are based on rhythmic motives, and these motives are complementary. Since there is an only slightly less obvious parallel between part 2 and the passage (mm. 152–73) that opens part 1 (both are contrapuntal treatments of a single motive), it is clear that parts 2 and 3 together revisit the content of most of part 1. The main difference is that while part 1 of the development is recessive, parts 2 and 3, although separated by the scherzo, progressively reactivate tempo, texture, and upper registers in preparation for the recapitulation at m. 437.

The Symphony's recapitulation is, of all parts of the form, the most unlike its classical models. In the first place, it does not offer in most instances a reprise of literal (or even of varied) content; instead, it gives us reprises of many of the expository *topics* encountered thus far in the work. Moreover, it serves as a recapitulation of the integrated symphonic form as a whole, drawing its topics not only from the first-movement exposition, but from the intermezzi, the slow movement, and the scherzo. It begins with a cantilena that recalls the climactic passage of the first theme-group in the exposition, and continues (in section XI) with a *dolce* passage that functions much like intermezzo I, in fact using the same aggregate partitioning to generate motives and the same interval class of transposition to generate sequentially related phrases (T_{11} in intermezzo I and T_1 in the recap). Section XI ends with a much more literal reprise of the visionary intermezzo II, occurring here as a fragmentary reference to the original. At this point the finale of the four-movement plan is worked in (section XII). It is brief but extremely moving, beginning with an intense canon in three parts that expands into a double canon in six, which in turn accelerates toward the massive tutti that serves as the work's expressive and dramatic climax. One knows that this section is an incorporated movement, and not part of the first-movement framework, by the entirely new topics it introduces: (1) frenzied ritual leading through compulsive repetition and textural accretion to an orgasmic climax; followed by (2) spiritual apotheosis and release. The process of recapitulation is now resumed, this time with respect to the first two interpolated movements. They

are referenced in reverse order, the scherzo at the start of section
XIII, then the slow movement. Once again, it is topics that recur rather
than literal content, but their reappearance is unmistakable. The tying
up of loose ends is now accomplished and there remains only the coda
to discuss. As the table indicates, this is one long wave-segment, starting at a trough and progressing in an accelerating manner to a peak of
intensity reached nowhere else in the work. The topic here is *feux-
follets*, a sonic spectacular that brings the work to an effective finish
while deferring, in terms of emotional power, to the affective climax in
section XII.

   This completes my brief overview of the Symphony. It is not intended primarily as a verbal précis of the music, but as a demonstration of the roles of reference in this profoundly structured and deeply
meaningful work. By "reference" I mean a relationship of the work as
a whole, or a part of the work, to something outside itself, as well as a
relationship of one part of the work to another part. All such relationships are references. As I have shown, the Symphony as a whole relates
formally to a tradition of symphonies that goes back to Haydn, and
of one-movement symphonies that culminates in the early works of
Schoenberg. Passages of the Symphony relate to music by earlier
twentieth-century composers and, in one case, to later music. At the
same time, most passages in the Symphony do symbolic work by engaging European cultural topics in terms of their musical tropes,
which are understood widely, if not always consciously. Finally, with respect to these topics, but not usually to specific content, later passages
in the work recapitulate earlier ones. Reference is therefore both the
source of form and of meaning in this work, as in all art that commu-
nicates. Of course, my brief attempts at symbolic interpretation hardly
constitute a full exploration of this layer of the work's meaning. One
might well proceed from these preliminary assays in the direction of a
full-fledged narrative reading. I will return to consider this possibility
at the end of my study, but in general I leave it to future discourse.

Detailed Analysis

Having surveyed the Symphony from start to finish, I will now examine
a number of passages in detail, with a view to laying out some of the
bases of their coherence and relatedness to one another. The reader
will see that I use a mixed approach, which may disturb those who persist in viewing tonality as incompatible with aggregate-based and freely
dissonant methods of pitch organization. However, I do not view tonality as a system, but as a set of possibilities inherent in intervals and
chords when these are presented in time to suitably acculturated lis-

teners – possibilities they may chose to ignore but which, if taken seriously, provide the surest basis for acquiring a rich and stable mental
representation (audiation) of the score, the only valid basis for performance, analysis, or satisfying listening. In my view, these possibilities
are in no way cancelled out if the intervals and chords figure, at the
same time, in pitch configurations that are totally independent of any
tonal phenomena. Putting it more simply, I see it as appropriate and
indeed necessary to treat the atonal structures in Anhalt's music, and
indeed in most of the twentieth-century music I care about, as motivic
content situated within a pitch-time space hierarchically organized by
progressions of quasi-tonal harmony. Lying behind this conviction is
another, namely, that the complementary concepts of harmony and
harmonic prolongation are too deep, psychologically and culturally, to
be adequately captured in any completely consistent theory. In other
words, in theorizing polyphonic music of any complexity, it is not possible to partition the range of available pitch structures into those that
can and cannot be prolonged; there will always be structures of ambivalent status in this respect, be they pitch intervals, pitch-class (pc) intervals, or chords.[14] For this reason, I am compelled to take a flexible,
open-ended view of harmonic prolongation, and to let factors of presentation override predetermined theoretical distinctions in deciding
what is and what is not a harmony at this or that level.

I am also guided by a second principle, namely, that any way of theorizing about, and therefore analyzing, some music can only be judged
in relation to the purpose for which that music is being studied. If the
intent is to explain the record of compositional process, one kind of
theory may be suitable; if to give an account of score data that is as procedurally objective as possible, another theory may be needed; and if
to promote rich and stable audiation, the need may be for quite a different theory still. Although it is the third of these that interests me
most, I also feel some duty toward the first two. And it happens that, in
the case of the Symphony, a procedurally objective account of most of
the score data is quite achievable and is well supported by documents
that record the compositional process. The Anhalt fonds in the National Library of Canada include, for the Symphony, a large number of
precompositional charts, some sketches, and a draft of the score in
particella form.[15] The charts are all about the ways of partitioning the
aggregate around the set (11,0,5,6) and its transpositions. Because the
draft is, on many pages, cross-referenced to the charts, it is possible to
infer which sets and set transformations were the starting point, at
least, for particular passages. In all cases, the results of studying the apparent compositional process corroborate those of procedurally objective score segmentation and, to this extent, further objectify or validate

the latter. This makes the set-structure of the composition a secure place to start, and a convenient basis for ordering my analyses. Accordingly, I do not proceed chronologically, but begin with passages that are strictly and thoroughly formed out of standard transformations of pc sets, and therefore quite exhaustively describable in set-theoretic terms. I continue in the direction of passages that are less completely determined by apparent rules (*obblighi*) that force note-to-note, set-to-set, or set-upon-set relationships, and therefore demand other kinds of description. Even where there is clarity in the domain of sets and their transformations, however, it soon becomes necessary, in attempting to provide a thorough and convincing account, to go well beyond any objective layer and to consider, first, levels of set structure not explicit in the sketch material, and then, levels of harmonic and linear progression, as well as the manifold interactions of these planes of discourse.

Section VIII (development, part 2)

Examples 7.3 and 7.4 deal with the first half of section VIII, this section being part 2 of the development, in which the music regroups after the slow movement and begins to press toward a climax in section x. All is based here on a six-note series (T) its retrograde (RT) and those of three variants of the series (T*, T†, and T§, to be explained presently). The series is an ordering of set-class (0,1,2,6,7,8), represented in example 7.3b as beginning on E-flat. This highly symmetrical (all-combinatorial) set-class contains two instances of (0,1,6,7), one of which begins T. If we give the version of T beginning on B the name T$_0$ (because its first four elements are the work's Ur-motive), the transposition beginning on E becomes T$_5$ (see ex. 7.3a) and it is seen to have the same pc content as its transposition by 6 (= T$_{11}$; see ex. 7.3c), and to be complemented in content by T$_2$ and T$_8$ (ex. 7.3d). The variant T* is arrived at by reversing the first two elements of T, as in the first segment of ex. 7.3e; T†, by reversing both the first and the last dyads of T, as in ex. 7.3e's last segment; and T§, by reversing the order of the last trichord in T, as is done with RT (producing R§T) in the middle segment of ex. 7.3f. As the middle segment of ex. 7.3e and the last of 7.3f show, these variants are in turn subject to transposition, while the last segment of ex. 7.3f shows that the operations *, †, and § may also be sequentially applied.

The intensifying character of the passage is readily seen in example 7.4. It begins with two sets in counterpoint, continues with three (m. 335), and concludes with four (m. 344). The pair of sets at the beginning (T$_5$ and RT*$_{11}$) are identical in content, as is the next pair (which introduces only two new pcs), but the trio of sets in mm. 335 ff. produces two aggregates, between the upper and the outer voices, and

Example 7.3 Symphony, section VIII (development, part 2), opening:
set-structure

a. T_5 **b.** $(0, 1, 2, 6, 7, 8)$ **c.** T_{11}

$(0, 1, 6, 7)$

d. aggregates generated by transposition

$T_5 + T_8$ $T_5 + T_2$

e. T^*_5 T^*_9 $T\dagger_5$

f. RT_5 $R\S T_5$ $R\S T^*_9$

the quartet in mm. 344 ff. introduces four, between the lower two, upper two, outer two, and inner two. This increase in densities and activity is complemented by a widening of, and steady rise in the upper
limit of, the registral envelope, and at the end of the passage by a crescendo. At the same time, the richness of Anhalt's pitch language allows, as we shall see, for a sequential descent to be perceived in the
harmonic dimension.

The harmonic interpretation given underneath the score in example 7.4 uses white notes to indicate tonicized pitch classes, which are
also spelled out below the staff. Tonicization is accomplished in the traditional way, by associating a pc with the members of the major and/or
minor triad of which it is the root (as well as secondary tones), and

Example 7.4 Symphony, section VIII (development, part 2), opening: serial
            and harmonic analysis

approaching (and occasionally following) it with one or more upper
fifths, the last of which is strengthened if conjoined to a $^{7}_{\sharp 3}$, or approaching it with a leading tone conjoined to other half-step neighbours of the triad. The tonicized pc is given the label I, its upper fifths,
V, II, etc., and its leading tone, VII, as in standard practice. This nomenclature is not intended to imply more than the presence of surface

Example 7.4 *(continued)*

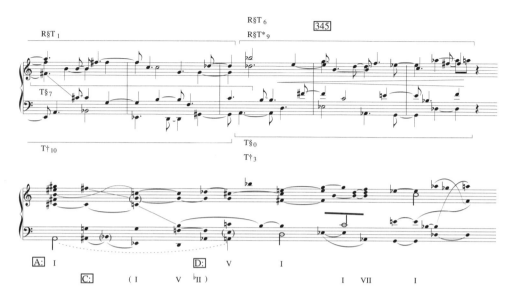

phenomena – there is no assumption of a prevailing diatony and none of prevailing keys. Instead of "tonicized," one might say "harmonically emphasized," or "harmonically prolonged," but these are cumbersome and nonspecific, as well as seeming to me apologetic, when no apology for the use of traditional formations is needed. Still, it has to be emphasized that the purpose of tonicization here is not to create a tonal space in which a passage moves, but to *delineate* a higher-level pc succession, where the verb is to be taken in its root sense as "creating a line (of elements)." It is a line-fortifying circumstance that the successive pcs thus delineated are semitone- and, in one case, fifth-related, but it is their being tonicized that makes of them a line.

The passage divides into four groups, of which the first (mm. 329–32) is so short and tentative that it may be combined with the second (mm. 332–36) as a single phrase. From this standpoint, the first large phrase has as a guiding motion, and for all intents and purposes as a middleground bass line, the pc line <E,E♭,D>, broken into descending seconds: <E,E♭> and <E♭,D>. In effect, the chromatic trichord that underlies the (0,1,2,6,7,8) hexachord is used to shape phraselike units. The next phrase, consisting of mm. 337–41, is a very audible sequence composed of a model and two copies, and is governed by the pc line <E♭,D,D♭>, which as T_{-1} of <E,E♭,D> reproduces at a higher level the transformation connecting successive set statements in each voice. It should be noted that this line occurs in two octaves (continuing a

pattern initiated in the first phrase), and that its appearance as
<$E\flat4,D4,D\flat4$> will prove to have a special significance. The final phrase
begins with the V of A on the last beat of m. 341 and has two limbs –
the second, T_5 of the first, but with a fourth set added to the counterpoint. The tonal plan of this phrase is a little more complex than those
of its predecessors. To be sure, D is tonicized in m. 344 just as A was
in 342, but in m. 343 a sense of C as tonic develops retrospectively,
through the root succession I–V–$\flat$II. This is confirmed in the second
limb, in mm. 344–5, where I–VII–I emerges unmistakably, the I represented by C4. The latter pitch of course realizes an implication of continued descent generated in the first two phrases, an effect made
stronger by the use of the 4-octave to place pcs in all three phrases:
<$E,E\flat$> in the first, <$E\flat,D,D\flat$> in the second, and C in the third. All of
these tonics are extremely fleeting (this is after all a developmental
section!), but as they pass through attentive ears they anchor and measure out motion in the textural parameters, while opposing it in direction. The path they form directs us, but bridges nothing and goes
nowhere. C is thus not a goal, only another marker accented by delay.
No sooner is it lit upon than the music swerves off into an encompassing atonal space.

Section III (exposition, third theme-group)
The next three examples (7.5–7.7) concern the opening variation of
section III, which contains the third theme-group of the work's tripartite exposition. Like the passage just discussed, this one employs a contrapuntal texture based on the strict use of an ordered hexachord.
Here, however, rhythmic-motivic properties, regularities of metre, and
phrase symmetries signify thematic rather than developmental statement. The ordered hexachord, or row, is shown in ex. 7.5a, and its
source set (or normally ordered form) in 7.5b. The latter represents
the set class (0,1,3,4,5,8), unique among hexachords in being combinatorial with only one of its transpositions (T_6). The T-form in ex. 7.5a,
because it occurs first in the uppermost voice (see ex. 7.5h), is named
T_0; its inversion about C and F$\sharp$ is correspondingly named T_0I
(ex. 7.5c). The aggregate-forming combination of T_0 and T_6 is shown
in ex. 7.5d. We see here the probable source of Anhalt's interest in this
six-tone row: corresponding dyads in the two rows, taken together,
form the six distinct forms of (0,1,6,7), the work's Ur-set-class. In the
music itself the combinatorial rows appear in canon, with T_6 in retrograde, as in ex. 7.5e. As a result, two transpositions of the basic tetrachord assume particular salience: the "tonic" transposition (11,0,5,6),
formed by the first dyad of RT_6 and the last dyad of T_0, and (3,4,9,10),
formed in crosswise fashion. Now the last dyad of T_0 and the first of T_2

Example 7.5 Symphony, section III (exposition, third theme-group),
                opening: set-structure

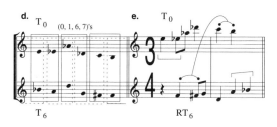

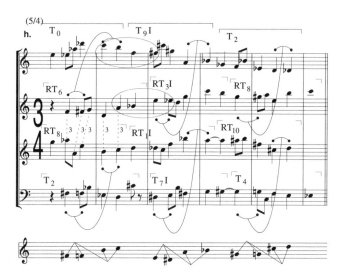

also combine to form (11,0,5,6) and, as ex. 7.5f shows, combining these forms in the same simple canonic relationship – the simplest one possible from a rhythmic standpoint – generates a useful result: a series of interval class (ic) 3s between simultaneous elements. Anhalt uses both pairings, the combinatorial one and that which generates ic 3s, to produce a four-part texture, given in ex. 7.5h. Here, the top two voices are in a combinatorial relationship, as are the bottom two; while the outer voices are in the ic3-forming relationship, as are the inner two. The vertical result is thus highly ordered and, as we shall see in ex. 7.7, symmetrical.

Example 7.5h shows how a phrase is built up out of three statements of the four-voice package. The voice on the top staff executes the row succession $\langle T_0,T_9I,T_2 \rangle$, and the other voices follow suit. The logic of this succession can be described by considering the music to be in $5/4$ time, with bars corresponding to row statements in voices 1 and 3 (from the top). Within the first of these metric units, voices 2 and 4 begin with (F,F$^\sharp$), while voices 1 and 3 end with (C,B); within the second $5/4$ bar (which begins on the last beat of the second notated bar), voice 2 begins RT_3I on $\langle E,E^\flat \rangle$ and voice 4 begins T_7I on $\langle D^\sharp,E \rangle$ while voices 1 and 3 present $\langle A,B^\flat \rangle$ and $\langle B^\flat,A \rangle$ as respective ending dyads. Finally, the third $5/4$ bar gives us (G,G$^\sharp$) as an initial, and (C$^\sharp$,D) as a terminal dyad, each in two voices. The net result is a progression through the aggregate via three forms of the Ur-set-class, as shown in the lowermost staff in the example.

Example 7.5h appears in the particella-score draft of the Symphony, but with a notation to exchange the content of voices 1 and 3 *after* the first row statements are complete. This produces the transformation seen in ex. 7.6, which is how the final version goes. I puzzled a long time over this seemingly arbitrary change before discovering a plausible reason for it, which has to do with how mm. 101–6 sound in relation to mm. 106–11. As ex. 7.6 tries to make clear, there is an implicit polymeter in this passage. The dotted lines partition the music as it was described above into $5/4$ bars. But the solid lines follow a motivic structure that corresponds to the notated $3/4$ metre. This will be heard if the circled dyads (all semitones) are marked for attention: the $\langle E5,E^\flat5 \rangle$ and $\langle C6,B5 \rangle$ in voice 1, mm. 101–2, and the identical dyads in the same metric arrangement in voice 2, mm. 103–4, as well as the $\langle B5,C6 \rangle$ that answers (by reversal) $\langle C6,B5 \rangle$ in voice 2, on the third beat of m. 105 and the first of m. 106. The relations among these suggest a complete six-bar phrase (mm. 101–6) of a type that is not quite classical – (2+2) + 2, instead of the classical (2+2) + 4 – but close enough. The reliance upon the classical model becomes even clearer when the sequel is heard, for it too is a six-bar phrase, elided to the

Example 7.6 Symphony, section III (exposition, third theme-group), opening

first in m. 106. Here the motivic structure just described recurs, and can be followed by regarding the circled dyads in voice 3 (mm. 106–7) and voice 2 (mm. 108–11). The two phrases are paired by their parallelism of structure, but still one more twist transforms them into a parallel period with a classical pedigree. It will have been noted that the

Example 7.7 Symphony, section III (exposition, third
theme-group), opening: harmonic structure

semitonal dyads of voice 1 (in mm. 101–2) were accompanied by those
in voice 3, and similarly that those in voice 3 (mm. 106–7) are accompanied by those in voice 1. By exchanging the content of these voices,
beginning on the third beat of m. 102 (cf., ex. 7.5h), voice 1 gets to
begin the second phrase with <E5,E♭5> and <C5,B4> on the first two
beats of mm. 106 and 107, respectively, thus reproducing almost exactly what it did at the beginning of the first phrase. The same, of
course, holds for voice 3. As a result the players of the parts that sound
these voices will clearly hear that a second phrase begins in m. 106 and
that its relation to the first phrase is of consequent to antecedent,
something not nearly as likely to be apparent to the players in the draft
version.

Finally, example 7.7 provides a close-up look at vertical structures in
this passage. Because of the pairing of rows related vertically (in canon)
by ic 3, the vertical tetrachords of the four-part texture are dominated
by 3s, 9s, and their octave equivalents (shown with dotted lines). The
example notates the set-classes of every simultaneity in the double
canon that begins the passage. Reading these from left to right gives
(0,3) (0,2,3,5) (0,1,3,4) (0,1,2,5) | (0,3,6,9) (0,1,3,4) (0,2,3,5) (0,3,)
– an almost symmetrical succession around the indicated axis. Since
the (0,3) at the end of one formation overlaps with the (0,3) at the
start of the next (see ex. 7.6), producing either another (0,2,3,5) or a
(0,3,4,7), each formation can be heard to get progressively more disso-

Example 7.8a Anhalt's chart for Symphony: D IV a

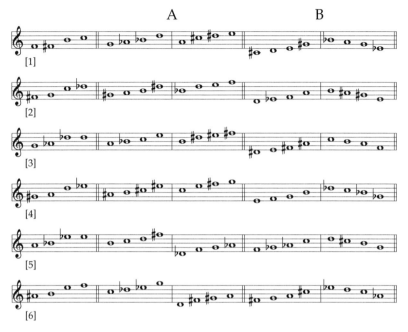

nant towards its central axis, after which the (0,3,6,9) effects a sudden resolution, followed by an upping of dissonance with the (0,1,3,4), and a recession into (0,2,3,5) and either (0,3,4,7) or a further (0,2,3,5), whereupon the next phrase member reinitiates the cycle. This shows how, even in its smallest units, the music is shaped by means of fluctuating intensity.

Section VII (transition to slow movement)

With the next example, we treat, for the first time, a texture of somewhat more complexity, of a type appearing often in the Symphony. Examples 7.8 and 7.9 and tables 7.2a–c are concerned with a passage at the opening of section VII, one that serves as the first part of a transition between part 1 of the development (locally between the "gong" intermezzo) and the slow movement. The mood here is lyrical and pensive, and the material very audibly recapitulates the second variation of intermezzo 1, as if recollecting it. One could call this a codetta. What is new here, both with respect to the passage being recalled and the examples encountered thus far, is the presence of a free solo voice against – in this case, above – a serially and canonically strict group of voices. I call this obbligato vs obbligo, looking at it as a solved compositional problem (and a formidable one) rather than as a textural result.

Example 7.8b Symphony, section VII (transition to slow movement), opening: 8-tone rows

As the latter, it may sound as melody plus accompaniment, or (in this case) as a canon with light descant, or as one of a number of other things. I will concentrate on how the rule-bound part of the texture works, and how the free part is integrated with it.

Example 7.8a shows one of Anhalt's charts for the Symphony, labelled "D IV a," the "D" standing presumably for "diagram." As I noted above, the passage under discussion is cross-referenced to this chart in the draft short score. The chart is typical of those for the work. It has three columns. In the left column are the six distinct forms of the master set-class, numbered in such as way as to reflect the referentiality of $(11,0,5,6)$. In the next two columns, headed A and B, are the two ways of partitioning the complement of the set at the left of a particular row into two forms of set-class $(0,1,3,7)$. The sets listed in columns A and B are to be read as unordered, and no significance need be attached to their presentation as ascending or descending, as far as I know.[16] Example 7.8b shows how Anhalt uses the material of 7.8a to construct the motive on which his canon is based. The two sets in row 1, column A, which I will refer to as 1A, are concatenated to make an eight-tone row, in which they appear in their most compact (normal) order and are related to one another as (ordered) inversions. The row derived from 1A I call T_0 and its inversion about C and F$\sharp$ I call $T_0 I$. The content of the latter is found in the A column of ex. 7.8a, at row 2, and may thus be identified as the (unordered) complement 2A of $(0,1,6,7)$. Experienced readers will see immediately that there are always two rows of the form shown in 7.8b that correspond to any of the complements in columns A and B of 7.8a. (For example, 1A equals $RT_{11}I$ as well T_0, as 7.8b demonstrates.)

In the passage I am about to discuss, Anhalt makes use of the material in his chart "D IV a" to compose a so-called infinite canon, one that, following its apparent rule of construction, could be continued indefinitely, but is cut short once its formal purpose has been satisfied. The starting point of this canon is the listing of unordered eight-tone sets given in table 7.2a. These numbers correspond to the entries in example 7.8a. It will be seen, in the table, that if transposition of columns A and B in example 7.8a is continued beyond row 6, the columns are exchanged: entry 7A, which is T_1 of 6A, is equivalent to 1B, and 7B is equivalent to 1A. Thus, table 7.2a can be extended to any

Table 7.2   Eight-tone sets from Symphony (based on Anhalt's chart D IV a)

Table 7.2a

1A	1B
2A	2B
3A	3B
4A	4B
5A	5B
6A	6B
7A= 1B	1A = 7B
2B	2A
3B	3A
4B	4A
5B	5A
6B	6A
7B = 1A	1B = 7A

Table 7.2b

$$\boxed{1A} \rightarrow 2A \qquad 3A \rightarrow 4A$$

(1A)→2A   3A→4A
↑   ↓   ↑   ↓
(6A)→1B (2B)→3B 4B

Table 7.2c

Top	6A (T$_5$)		1B (RT$_6$)		1A (RT$_{11}$I)		2A (T$_0$I)		2B (T$_7$)
Middle		2B (T$_7$)		3B (RT$_8$)		3A (RT$_1$I)		4A (T$_2$I)	
Bottom	1A (T$_0$)		2A (RT$_1$)		2B (RT$_6$I)		3B (T$_7$I)		3A (T$_2$)

number of rows, but its content repeats with column reversal every six rows, and exactly every twelve rows.

   The box in table 7.2a isolates nine contiguous entries (collections), beginning with 6A and ending with 4B. This block is reproduced, rotated 270 degrees, in table 7.2b, and a path through the block – arguably the simplest because it uses up all entries without skips or diagonals – is indicated with arrows. This is the path followed, from different starting points, by each of the three canonic voices in example 7.9. As table 7.2c illustrates, the top voice begins first, starting at 6A and continuing with 1B, 1A, and 2A, to 2B; the bottom voice begins, a quarter note later, with 1A, the third entry on the path in table 7.2b, and follows that path through to 3A; while the middle voice, entering yet another quarter note later, begins on 2B (the fifth entry in table 7.2b) and moves ahead, pathwise, to 4B. Each of these voices is serially organized in the same way (see example 7.8b for the row used in this variation): first it has a T-form, then an R-form, then an RI-form, then an I-form, and finally, another T-form. Notice that this way of ordering the underlying collections produces a minimally redundant surface result; for example, the bottom voice begins (see table 7.2c) with the collections <1A,2A,2B>, ordered to produce the row succession <T_0,RT_1,RT_6I>; but when the top voice has the same succession of collections (its third, fourth, and fifth), about three bars later (see example 7.9), these are internally ordered to give <RT_{11}I,T_0I,T_7>.

We are now ready to look at example 7.9. Its *obbligo* (strict) voices, on the lower two staves of each system, can be read in conjunction with table 7.2c. Only the first row in each voice is named; the remaining four are marked at their points of initiation with "<." The obbligato voice, or descant, is notated on the top staff of each system. It relates to the canon in an interesting way, using forms of the basic motive (11,0,5,6) that complement the collections lying on the path followed by the canonic voices. In other words, the obbligato voice uses the basic set-class forms 6, 1, 2, and 3, as read from the left column of example 7.8a. The basic-motive form 4 = (2,3,8,9), complementing collections 4A and 4B, used in the middle voice at the end of the canon, was presumably withheld in order to thin out the obbligato part as this passage is brought to a close.

The overall result is strikingly and, for the Symphony, atypically Bartókian. By remembering Bartók it seems to doubly remember everything that he in turn memorializes in densely imitative passages of this type – for not only is his contrapuntal technique recalled, but his much-loved Lydian and Phrygian gapped pentachords as well, by way of normal orderings of sets of the (0,1,3,7) class. And it is the ruminative melancholy of these modal fragments, as the canonic voices wind through them along their paths, that signal not just Bartók, but intricate root systems extending well below the sound of his music. *Root systems.* The metaphor captures the depth of our music-theoretical speech itself, for these pentachords enter posttonal spaces carrying their own fifths, even triads, and therefore their own roots, and it is these that I hear as binding obbligo to obbligato and determining a deeper path, to which the canonic one bears an archaeological relation. This path is harmonic, and is specified by the analysis notated on a system below the short score. Here we see an outer-voice framework filled in with two, at times three, inner voices. The bass moves from E3 (m. 261) to an implied C3 (m. 262), over which the upper voice (shared between the topmost canonic part and the added part) descends in parallel tenths – <G5,F5,E5> – a melodic descending third preceded by A5 (m. 261), which forms a sixth over the bass C#3. This A5 has a longer-range role, ascending to D6 (m. 265) through <B5, B♭5 and C#6>. When D6 is reached, it in turn forms a tenth over B3, which, taking into account the bass line thus far, from the E3 and C3 mentioned above, through the A3 in m. 263 and the A#3 in m. 264,

Example 7.9 Symphony, section VII (transition to slow movement), opening:
canon with obbligato, serving as codetta

can be heard as the V of E. After m. 265, the harmony steps back to the $^{\flat}$II of E, prolonged in mm. 266–8 as V of the key of B$^{\flat}$. Meanwhile, the upper voice drops down to G5, forming a ninth over the bass's F3. The upper voice then descends to E5, reached on the downbeat of m. 269 through F5 in the preceding measure, and tellingly placed over a return of B in the bass (B2), so that a $^{6}_{4}$ chord of dominant function is formed just as the added voice drops out. The structural upper voice, which I repeat is a cooperative venture between the topmost canonic voice and the obbligato part, is thus diminutionally motivic, the opening descent from A5 to E5 in the first two bars being reproduced over the course of the passage as a whole: A5 (m. 261) – G5 (m. 266) – F5 (m. 268) – E5 (m. 269). Of course, this two-levelled descent is a Phrygian tetrachord, and thus confirms the way of hearing instances of (0,1,3,7) adopted in this interpretation.

The notion of tonality as an archaeological presence must be understood, and not only for the sake of this example, since it will be invoked many times in this study. The tonal substratum is not evident to casual perception; it can only be uncovered with patient, careful work, and sensitive instruments. Moreover, it is not a logical precursor of the music, one that determines the music hierarchically through application of the operations of a tonal system. Rather, it bears a historical or genealogical relationship to the musical surface, and can only be heard as the music is aurally peeled away and itself no longer heard. One cannot hear it by way of the music, only by *over* hearing the music, as with any trace of the past in the present. Like all such relationships, some will not need or want to hear it. This approach to Anhalt's music is for those who do.

Section V (intermezzo I)

The next two examples concern the first variation in intermezzo I, which interrupts part 1 of the development. Here we have another example of a thematic structure, a complaisant little waltzlike idyll that appears unexpectedly and dissolves with just as little ado into the next variation, a dialogue that serves as the model for example 7.9. Once again there is an *obbligo* structure with extra voices, but this time there are two separate *obbligo* layers and the extra parts are of secondary importance.

Example 7.10 has a now-familiar format, showing the six transpositions of the basic set-class in the left-hand column, and a particular way of partitioning their eight-tone complements into two equivalent four-tone sets in the two right-hand columns. This is Anhalt's chart "D IV b 3." The sets in the right column are of the class (0,2,5,7); they

Example 7.10 Anhalt's chart for Symphony: D IV b 3

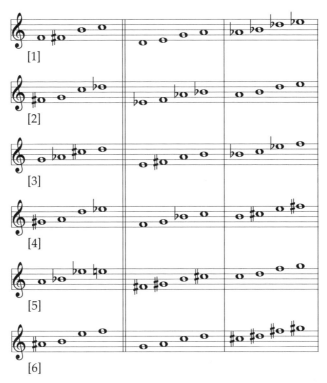

are segments of a circle of fifths, and lend themselves naturally to generating the pale, washed-out sort of harmony that we find here. In
example 7.11 we see one *obbligo* structure in the strings. It is a three-
voice complex, the component voices labelled A, B, and C. The complex is two measures long and is accordingly stated once and repeated
twice in inverted counterpoint and in sequence, successively transposed by T_{11}. This sequential repetition is indicated by dotted lines
through the texture in mm. 215–16 and 217–18. Voice A is a serial hy-
brid, beginning with (3,5,8,10) and (9,11,2,4), the complementary
sets in row 2 of ex. 7.10, and continuing with the basic motive at level
1, its "tonic" transposition (11,0,5,6). Voices B and C, on the other
hand, have closely related twelve-tone rows, formed in each case out
of diatonic hexachords that begin with a form of the class (0,2,5,7)
and close with one of the semitones (1s) in the corresponding transposition of the basic set. For example, voice B is an ordering of
the material of row 1 in example 7.10, namely, (7,4,2,9), (11,0),
(8,1,3,10), (6,5), in which the Ur-motive (11,0,5,6) is partitioned

Example 7.11 Symphony, section v (intermezzo 1), opening: a thematic structure of layered texture

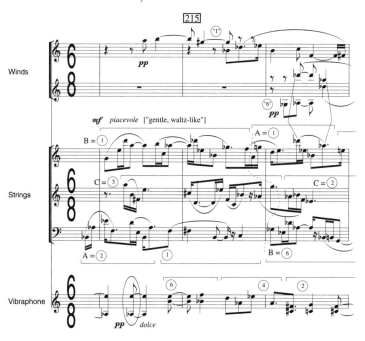

into 1s. Similarly, voice C is an ordering of the material of row 3 of the chart. The derivations of voices A, B, and C in successive transpositions of the complex are indicated in ex. 7.11 by the circled numbers that designate their source rows in ex. 7.10.

It is doubtful if, on its own, the string texture would prove satisfying as a thematic structure since, disguised as it is by contrapuntal inversion, it is still easy to perceive as a sequence descending by semitones, and therefore as a fragment of open-ended process. To create a self-contained effect, Anhalt superimposes a second *obbligo*, or strictly composed voice, which is given to the vibraphone. This is a set palindrome, one consisting of five forms of the basic motive in the transpositional sequence <6,4,2,4,6> (referring to the rows of example 7.10), preceded and followed by the dyad (4,8), the two instances of which are circled in example 7.11. There remain only the wind parts of example 7.11 to account for. These are not really obbligato parts, being more heterophonic than polyphonic in impact. They generally duplicate pitches sounding in the principal voices, either attacking them simultaneously and giving them a different envelope, or else anticipating or echoing principal-voice pitches at very short time intervals. Some of these heterophonic duplications are indicated by solid lines connecting wind-part pitches to their correspondents in the principal voices. It would be possible to explain the wind parts from a different standpoint as having the timbral function of providing a selective and highly differentiated reverberative layer around the primary contrapuntal voices, and thus to describe them in orchestrational rather than pitch-structural terms, but it is also true that they are fully melodic in their own right, even if only perceived as such by their players.

Section 1 (exposition)
Reference was made to example 7.12 above, in the overview of the Symphony. The example presents the work's opening measures, and was described as recalling the tutti/soli or ripieno/concertino contrast of the concerto grosso form, but without any hint of neobaroque style. Instead we have a romantic topical contrast between the churning chaos of the tutti and the striving lyricism of the soli. I have rebarred the music, preserving the triple metre but moving the notated downbeat one quarter note back (in other words, in the score, the opening F1 occurs on the second eighth of the bar), to clarify the metric structures that I believe are involved. This renotation invites the objection that it must be, at the same time, obscuring some relationships that were important to the composer, or that perhaps it makes too evident relationships that the composer, consciously or unconsciously, preferred to leave obscure. This threatens to open up the proverbial can

Example 7.12 Symphony, section I (exposition), opening, rebarred: analysis of metre, unordered-set content, and harmonic implications

Example 7.12 (*continued*)

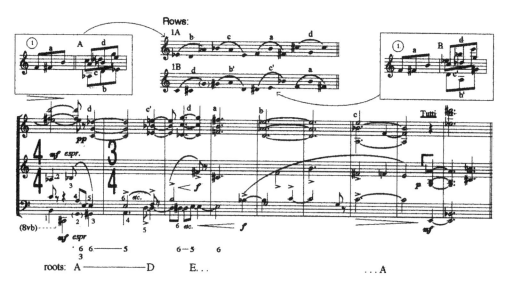

of worms, so I will limit myself to a short defence, which I shall not repeat in the several later instances where I use rebarring. In my opinion, music as complex as this is in no danger of being oversimplified if those aspects of regularity that can provide the listener with points of reference and criteria of measurement are highlighted. To bring out metric regularity, therefore, is not to deny counteractive factors of rhythm, whether themselves metrical or not, nor is it specifically to deny the relevance of the notated metre. With respect to the latter, the composer's intention appears to have been to find a compromise that would accommodate all of section 1's real changes in metre within a single, unvarying 3/4 time, all the while reflecting in the notation at least some aspect of the rhythmic life of the music. In this respect, the notational approach can be linked to that adopted by many composers over the past two hundred years, a decision for stability over structural transparency in notation. The analyst, having no need to think about the former, and every reason to be interested in the latter, is entirely justified in reversing the composer's priorities in such situations.

Example 7.12 divides into two overlapping sections: mm. 1–14 and 13–22. In the first of these, the "ripieno," there are three layers of texture, while the second, the "concertino," has only two. In mm. 1–14 various trichordal subsets of the (11,0,5,6) Ur-motive are expressed in the two lowest voices, while two streams of three-note chords unfold above. These chords are all of two classes – (0,1,4) and (0,1,3) – and the particular forms used are derived from eight ways of partitioning the aggregate into (A) one of the trichords in (11,0,5,6) and three forms of the class (0,1,4,); or (B) one of the trichords in (11,0,5,6), two of the class (0,1,4), and one of the class (0,1,3). The eight partitions are given above the first system of the example, and are labelled 1A, 1B, 2A, 2B, and soon. The integer part of the label indicates one of the four trichordal subsets of (11,0,5,6) while the letters A and B refer to the two ways I have just described of partitioning the other nine tones. Example 7.12 shows how the content of the two chord streams (top two staves in mm. 1–13) is derived from the eight partitions, and in fact moves quite systematically through most of these, while the lower voices begin with trichord 1 = (F,F#,B) and shift at m. 11 to trichord 4 = (F#,B,C). Beginning in m. 13, this texture dissolves and is replaced by a much thinner one in which a pair of *espressivo* string melodies is accompanied by pianissimo trichords in the winds. The pitch material of this concertino has a fascinating relation to that of the preceding bars, as is shown above the second system of the example. Here, the pitch material in the A and B complements of partitions 1A and 1B, described above and appearing at the top left in the example, is transformed in classical twelve-tone fashion, turned on its side, so that instead of a complement to (F,F#,B) of three secondary trichords drawn from classes (0,1,4) and (0,1,3), as in 1A, we get three more trichords of the (0,1,6) class, which I have labelled b, c, and d, while the retained (F,F#,B) gets the label "a." The same transformation applies to 1B. The four equivalent trichords that result in each case are then ordered internally and put in a series to form a row, and two resulting rows are likewise named 1A and 1B. It is these rows that provide the pitch material for the *espressivo* string duet, while the secondary element in the texture, the pianissimo chords, are formed, in a very Schoenbergian way, by recycling the same trichords in a different order to generate local aggregates.

More novel in this passage is the relationship between the string parts, which clearly hint at forming an *Aussensatz* (or two-part contrapuntal framework) that can be described with a figured bass, as shown in ex. 7.12. This patterning continues into m. 17 (as rebarred), where it gives way to various ways of chaining major and minor thirds, an inherently chromatic procedure. But the harmonic implications of the abandoned figured bass, indicated as a progression of prolonged roots below the figures, is not lost, as the chromatic figures of mm. 17–20 come to rest on an A minor triad with added tones in m. 21, the root tone A3 appearing as the lowest tone of wind trichord c in mm. 20–1; as melodies and accompaniment converge in register, so does the tonal functionality of the former spread to the latter. Of course there is no question of a key being established here, in a section of music in which a representation of chaos (the tutti) dominates and any tonal impulse is barely nascent, which is why I have not used Roman numerals for the roots. And yet it is fair to ask how even the most incipient tonality can arise convincingly, how it is made to seem possible in a context that, from a tonal standpoint, begins as unpromisingly as this example – and therefore the Symphony itself – does. It is therefore necessary to ask whether anything that might be heard in terms of tonal hierarchical relationships (or even pointing to such) can be aurally excavated in the opening measures. This is where example 7.12's somewhat complicated sketch of mm. 1–13 comes in. It is based on a hypermetric hearing of these rebarred measures whereby they are grouped in a *ritmo di tre battute*, or three-bar hypermetre. The remarkable clarification of the tutti's melodic and even harmonic content that this hearing affords is self-evident, as it should be, for most of the obviously accented pitches in all three strata of this texture coincide with, or function as obvious anticipations of, the downbeats in 9/4 time thus constructed. Moreover, if we give notational prominence to these accented pitches, which are now hypermetrical downbeat pitches – adding only the metrically unaccented opening pitches of the first two strata, which fall in the initial upbeat segment of the passage – we sense an emergent harmonic logic. There are between three and five higher-level voices at work here. We begin with F_1 in the bass and $B^\flat_4$ (appearing as $B^\flat_3$ in the sketch) in a middle voice, which can be supposed to imply $B^\flat$ as a root. This supposition is confirmed when another middle voice enters with $D^\flat_5$ ($D^\flat_4$ in the sketch), anticipating the downbeat of m. 3, which turns out to be the first hypermetric downbeat. At this downbeat, we also hear an upper voice entering on G_6, so that all four voices now sounding have formed a suggestive but tonally unclear harmony of the $\frac{4}{2}$ type, in figured bass terms. A shift occurs on the next hypermetrical downbeat (m. 7), where F_1 moves to $F^\sharp_1$, $B^\flat_3$ moves to B_3, and a new upper voice enters, on E_6 (E_5 in the sketch). The use of diagonal beams in the middle and upper voice pairs, à la Schenker, is meant to show that at the downbeat of m. 7, there are five voices in action, sounding, from bottom to top, $F^\sharp_1$, B_3, $D^\flat(C^\sharp)_4$, E_5, and G_5, respectively, and therefore harmonizing in a way that implies that $F^\sharp$ is a root and the upper tones are members of a ninth chord in which the third is suspended (B replacing $A^\sharp$), a dominant ninth chord in other words. This would all be the purest fantasy were the musical sequel not to bear it out, which it emphatically does. For on the next big downbeat (m. 10), while $F^\sharp$ is retained (as $F^\sharp_3$), and E_5 leads to $E^\flat_4$, B does in fact resolve to $A^\sharp$, which appears in the highest voice as $B^\flat_6$ ($B^\flat_5$ in the sketch). We are left in this way with a three-voice harmony of the $^{\flat 7}_{\sharp 3}$ type (the fifth and ninth have lost their presence by now), prolonged by octave transfers of the 7 (back to E5) and the $^{\sharp}$3 through the end of m. 12. A strong tonal implication of a harmony rooted on B has thus accumulated and we are rewarded with the appearance of just such an entity in m. 13, where the bass has B1 on the (once again hypermetrical) downbeat, while E$^{\flat}$5 (=D$^{\flat}$5) and F6 (both an octave lower in the sketch) sound simultaneously in middle and upper voices, respectively. This harmony is filled out with A4 (A3 in the sketch) on the second beat of m. 13, and D6, on the first beat of m. 14, by which time the ripieno is dissolving and the concertino taking over. It is clearly a B-rooted harmony, with factors $^{\sharp}$3, 7, $^{\flat}$5, and, to destabilize the expected accent on the downbeat of m. 13 with one at m. 14, as well as for decreased harmonic clarity, an added $^{\natural}$3. The excavation has thus revealed a prototonal stratum in the first 13 bars, one that links quite nicely to that unearthed in mm. 14 ff. Once again, I am not saying that a key is being established in these measures, not A in the concertino, much less B in the tutti, only that a type of harmonic structure basic to tonal music can be heard to emerge, to have a presence, however ghostly, that inhabits a space more overtly determined by twelve-tone structures, or perhaps to determine its own, more subtly insinuated counterspace.

Example 7.13 takes us to the climax of section 1, at which point the concerted forces of the opening (see ex. 7.12) have merged and the texture has coalesced into a recognizable European musical topic, a soaring cantilena-duet over a ponderous, metrically regular bass – as it were a vastly inflated trio-sonata format – filled in with three- and four-part chords, as if realizing the bass's implied continuo. The mood is grand, impassioned, and as I indicated above, signals an affirmation of the music's constructed subject as a source of directed individual will, of striving towards a goal, probably not concrete and posited, but ideal and envisioned.

In this passage, the relation between surface texture (inflated trio sonata) and underlying structural counterpoint is indirect, the latter indifferent to the former, as it were. The structural counterpoint is in six parts, each of which projects a transposition of the Ur-motive (11,0,5,6). These parts are shown in the example, below the reduced score which, once again, is rebarred for metrical clarity. The motive transpositions ascend by 1s in the example's arrangement of parts, a matter of numerical convention that happily produces a result loosely corresponding to the normal arrangement of a score, with higher parts at the top and lower ones at the bottom. To be sure, the parts are not registrally separate – they do overlap, and all six sets are represented in more than one octave – but they are presented according to the most

traditional criteria of clarity: each set is either presented as an uninterrupted linear segment in a most-compact registral arrangement (i.e., as
a kind of stepwise melody) or as a chord (simultaneity), or as some
combination of the two. But unlike the opening of section 1 (see example 7.12), where one can easily hear streams of trichords in counterpoint, this passage does not present its tetrachords for the hearing,
except as the content of the bass and, less obviously, of the paired
upper voices. Instead it offers, for immediate apprehension, a rich bro-
cade of Straussian harmony – worthy of *Salomé*, but leaving more to the
imagination than what its heroine might wear, because of the density of
its sixfold weave. This harmonic fabric is unfolded at the bottom of the
example, almost without analytical interpretation. The only analytical
symbols are the stems attached to the bass notes F$^\sharp$2, G2, G$^\sharp$2, and A2,
which indicate a line that spans the excerpt as far as its penultimate
measure. This line is sufficient for showing what is going on here, as it
too is archetypal: a rising chromatic segment of four tones that begins
on the fifth scale degree (imagine we are in B minor) and progresses to
the natural seventh degree, which is reinterpreted as the fifth of the
relative key (D major). The chords built over this bass-line segment
(here as in Strauss but also as in much of Schoenberg or Stravinsky) are
variously interpretable and seem to invite an efflorescence of colourful
terminology, but they consist in essence of sonorities susceptible to
interpretation as dominants (primary, secondary, substitute, auxiliary)
connected by intricate patterns of chromatic voice leading. Once
again, and at the risk of becoming tiresome, I hasten to say that the
B/D complex is not so much asserted as alluded to here, and the music
is hardly in a key in any normal sense. Nevertheless, the references to B
as a possible tonic at the beginning and end of this theme group (section 1) are not without importance, and of course not unrelated to the
choice of (11,0,5,6) as the work's Ur-motive.

   In example 7.13, then, we see a further instance of a dialectical relationship between atonal and tonal modes of organization. In this case,
it is the atonal patterning that must be teased apart, whereas the suggestions of a tonal hierarchy are apparent, if evanescent. The next example provides another considerably more complex instance of this
dialectic, but one in which a tonal presence is so sustained as to begin
actually to suggest a key.

Section IV (development, part 1)
Example 7.14 takes us to section IV, and to the start of part 1 of the
development of movement 1. Once again we encounter a passage that
yields an abundance of secret wealth, one of closely packed levels of
structure in at least three dimensions: levels defined in terms of the

Example 7.13 Symphony, section 1 (exposition), climax, rebarred: formation out of (0, 1, 6, 7) set-class members

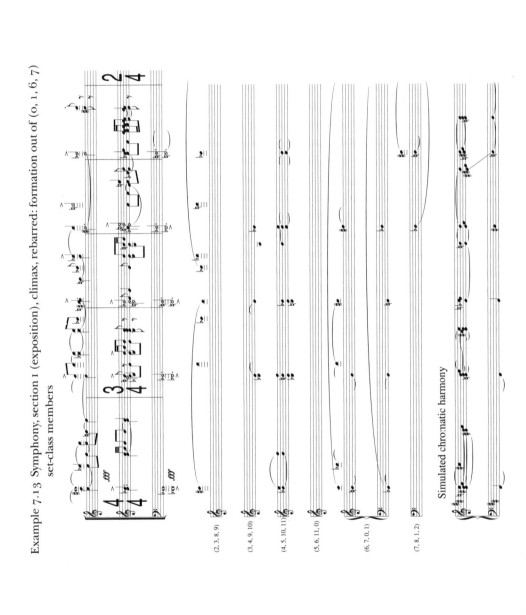

(2, 3, 8, 9)

(3, 4, 9, 10)

(4, 5, 10, 11)

(5, 6, 11, 0)

(6, 7, 0, 1)

(7, 8, 1, 2)

Simulated chromatic harmony

Example 7.13 (*continued*)

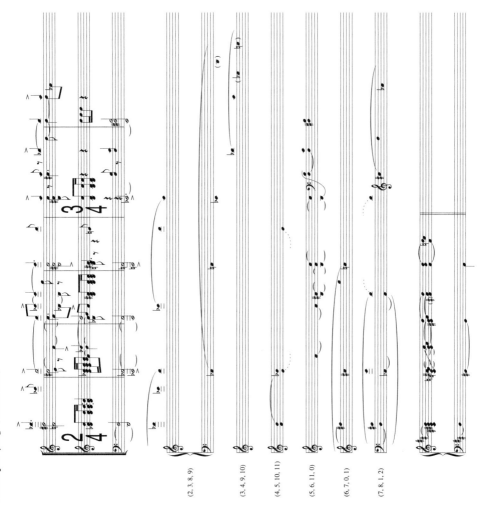

(2, 3, 8, 9)

(3, 4, 9, 10)

(4, 5, 10, 11)

(5, 6, 11, 0)

(6, 7, 0, 1)

(7, 8, 1, 2)

twelve-tone aggregate and expressed orchestrally; levels of overall coherence related in an atonal/tonal dialectic (or from a historical standpoint as levels in a genealogy or at an architectural site); and prolongational levels within the tonal stratum itself. The example attempts to present all of these at once. At the top of the page the score is reduced to show two streams of aggregates going on simultaneously. In the top system is a succession of aggregates partitioned into three forms of the basic motive, which I have labelled [1], [3], and [5], considering (11,0,5,6) as [1] because of its referential status. On the system below it is a parallel succession of aggregates formed out of transpositions [2], [4], and [6]. The bracketed numbers identify the statements of each of the three sets within each system. These are unordered and include pitch-class duplications, but no octaves in chords. In effect, we have another instance of six-part counterpoint, here deployed as two trios. Each voice sounds one of the six transpositions of the Ur-set-class, producing a situation of extreme motivic saturation. Yet the result is anything but "motivic working out," for all that the sets are mostly easy to hear, because the overall effect is of a gentle, meandering, and suavely expressive beauty that has less to do with putting motives through their paces than with putting us in their spaces. Lest there be any misunderstanding, the reduction presented in these strata, while fairly representing the score as far as pitch, rhythm, dynamics, and articulation, in no sense reflects a partitioning of data as far as the orchestration is concerned. The various numbered sets are typically given a timbrally coherent rendering, but neither of the vocal trios is assigned to anything like an orchestral group, and there are many instrumental-part continuities that migrate between the trios. For example, a very clear melody initiated within the [2],[4],[6] trio on the third beat of m. 161, which begins <F#4,G4> in a flute and a clarinet, continues through to A♭4 in those same instruments, at the same time moving over to the [1],[3],[5] trio. There are many other such examples.

This brings us to the second dimension of the analysis, for it is herein that such lines, nonstructural in the atonal sense, acquire their structural meaning. Under each system of the example there is a hierarchical tonal analysis of the data, on two notational levels, each of which can be seen, through attention to standard symbols, to comprehend many levels within itself. Except in its opening bars, which may thus be viewed as preparatory, the passage persists in asserting a single key, something we have not seen thus far in the piece. It is as if the fullness of the music in its twelve-tone identity has called forth a compensating tenacity of tonal commitment. That key is B-flat, and it is of course fully chromatic, with no distinction operating between major and minor and none, therefore, being reflected in the Roman numerals and figured bass under the middleground stratum. The tonal analysis is aligned at its foreground level with the score reduction, from which alignment it is readily seen that most of the notes of the atonally parsed score find their way into the tonal analysis. Notes were left out not because they could not be "explained," but because the density of notation required to give some account of them would have made an already forbidding notational surface increasingly opaque. As things stand, I leave it to the reader, whom I rather expect will want to play these examples repeatedly so as to grasp what they have to say, to do the accounting in the cases of the small note heads. Suffice it to say that they can be fully described using strategies known to musicians experienced in the intricacies of tonal music of the early twentieth century. Specifically, they are either obviously linear notes – passing tones and neighbours, sometimes octave displaced, or chord tones borrowed from other octaves – or added tones that fall into standard categories, more or less – the usual ninths, elevenths, and tertiary harmonic factors such as piles of thirds or fifths between structural outer-voice tones (see mm. 159 and 164–5), or major sevenths added above primary and secondary harmonic elements (e.g., the C$\sharp$2 in m. 160).[17] The real meat of the tonal argument is found at the middleground, where the small note heads are eliminated, and harmonic elements are realigned into chords. This level both obscures and highlights the music's harmonic sound, depending on whether our attention is to immediate experience or to a sense of genealogy. Its content is too consonant, and too unabashedly functional to capture how the music sounds in performance, even upon repeated hearings. Yet it is remarkably revealing of its origins – its mixture of the expected and the sudden, its ardent and sweetly decadent deflection of the obvious, and its accumulating richness of vertical detail proceeding directly from Fauré and the whole train of Conservatoire composers he inaugurated.[18] The indebtedness is evident everywhere in the passage, but no more so than in loving returns to changing forms of the flat-II harmony in mm. 159–163 – the first an underlying major-seventh chord, ballooned out to reveal a diatonic hexachord in the form of piled fifths; the second (in m. 161) a major chord of the sixth to which is added a major seventh above the bass, producing a bittersweetly androgynous tetrachordal mixture that slides up to its natural-II equivalent; and the third (in m. 163) an enharmonically spelled ninth chord. Space prevents me from dwelling at greater length on the harmonic subtleties of this passage, but if they seem to be contradicted by a too deliberate, even bald cadence at m. 168, the reader should recall that we are talking about a genealogical level that in a phenomenological sense is not heard, or is

Example 7.14 Symphony, section IV (development, part 1), opening: developmental passage formed out of paired aggregate partitions, with levelled harmonic analysis

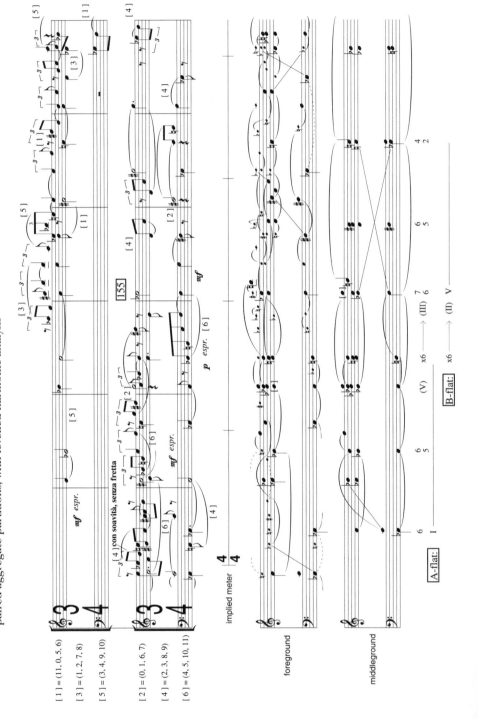

Example 7.14 (continued)

Example 7.14 *(continued)*

heard only in the same sense as any fascinating historical city is seen through the dominating forms of its contemporary successor.[19] Furthermore, this cadence, which occurs at beats 2 and 3 of m. 168, is rhythmically unstable, and is immediately absorbed – as are all of the Symphony's tonal formations, whether real or simulated – in the immediately succeeding discourse, which is tonally neutral. It therefore in no sense blights the music's sound or spoils its effect, and in its way contributes distinctively to solving the problem of the cadence that was first posed by Wagner.[20]

Section XII (finale)

In all the passages examined thus far, primary interest has resided in the dimension of pitch, polymetric complexities notwithstanding. The passage to be examined now is another matter. Examples 7.15 through 7.17 deal with the first part of section XII, which I have identified as the opening of movement 4, the finale. Even after deciding to consider the Symphony as a representative of the single-movement symphony, locating the start of the embedded finale here was not automatic. There are other plausible choices (the start of section X at m. 404, perhaps even m. 437) and there is one problem with the opening of XII – its unmitigatedly processive character, which appears to belong in a development and does not seem to satisfy the requirements of a movement opening, requirements that presumably entail some kind of thematic quality. Without going into all the reasons for rejecting the other possibilities, I can explain the sense in which the opening of XII does qualify, in my opinion. True, it is "developmental" music, in the sense of being composed entirely of sequences, and progressing unblinkingly toward an enormous climax, but it is also so distinctive in tone and in technical means as to stand out from its surroundings as something new. In other words, it becomes thematic almost entirely by virtue of its difference. "Here," we say, as we encounter sonic references as far removed from the Society for Private Performances as from the Conservatoire, "is something else!" What these references are is hard to specify, but I dare say that images of big bands of the late swing era, and their drummers in particular, were active as Anhalt generated this music. The passage turns the whole orchestra into a massive percussion section, or rather, a trio of percussion sections that is multitracked to produce a composite that is then mixed with a second composite of equal complexity. Pitch structure in this music is clear, but it is rudimentary, and it is evident that rhythm, in an extremely visceral sense, is the issue.

Anhalt has not had a profound interest in jazz for many years, much less in varieties of commercial music. But evocations of these styles occur often enough in his work to merit some attention.[21] I do not believe that a single symbolic function can be attributed to all of them, since each refers to a distinctive kind of music, and the contexts in which they occur are unalike. Still, at a very basic level, they all connote the sexual and, more than that, all that has to do with the resources of the body in its identity as fluid power. An old-fashioned term that will do, and that is probably appropriate given Anhalt's background, is the Dionysian. That this is the tone struck here, just before the work's apotheosis at m. 486 ff., is undoubtedly significant. It is as if the music's constructed subject must dig down into his or her physical self to be able to achieve some ultimate transcendence or, less idealistically, to achieve climax and release. Just why this should occur in the embedded fourth movement is another question, and likely relates to cultural codes that I do not propose to examine here. A simpler approach to such questions, even if also a narrower one, is via the accepted history of European musical style. From this standpoint, it does seem appropriate for a symphony to reserve its evocation of a popular idiom for the last movement.

Example 7.15a presents the opening of section XII, completely rebarred to highlight its three-track canonic structure. A small irregularity in this structure, in the segment falling between the 8th and the 13th eighth notes (inclusive) of the excerpt, has been eliminated. The scope of this change can be judged by comparing 7.15a with 7.15b, where the irregularity is restored. I will advance a possible reason for the irregularity below, when discussing example 7.15b. In 7.15a we have a three-part canon, exact in rhythmic and pitch-class terms. Each voice is in compound time (6/8) but the voices enter at a distance of two eighths, if a short percussion segment that introduces the second voice and actually precedes the entry of the first part is overlooked. Each begins on a member of the augmented triad (C,E,G$^\sharp$) marked as "A," and plays a basic repeated-note pattern in 6/8 time on that tone, accenting it on beats 1 and 4, before moving on to play the same pattern on the next tone, which is T_8 of the first. An entire series of tones is thereupon projected in each voice, using a $<T_{11},T_8>$ transformation cycle, so that the first voice has the pc succession $<E,C,B,G,F^\sharp,D,C^\sharp,A...>$, the second $<C,G^\sharp,G,E^\flat,D,B^\flat,A,F...>$ and so on.

Since each voice pursues an independent 6/8 meter, it is necessary to ask what their composite metric result is, if any. This matter is pursued on the fourth staff in the example, labelled "composite line," in which the accented tones in each part, those on *its* beats 1 and 4, are combined into a single succession. I have interpreted this compound line as implying bars of six eighth notes, in which simple triple and compound duple time alternate. This interpretation acquires more

Example 7.15a Symphony, section XII (finale), opening, rebarred: rhythmic analysis, with first two measures (468–9) regularized

Example 7.15b Symphony, section XII (finale), opening: irregularity restored

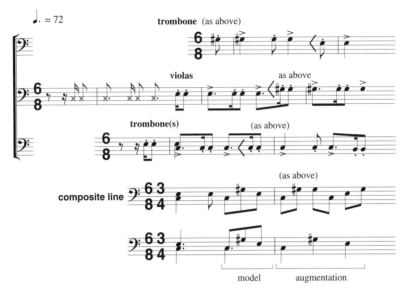

force when one looks at what Anhalt wrote. This is given in example 7.15b. The only difference is that, after starting out on E, just as in 7.15a, voice 1 shifts prematurely to C on its first downbeat, only getting back on track later in its first measure. Correspondingly, voice 2 starts on E instead of C, so that its incipit reads <E,G♯> rather than <C,G♯>, as the regularized version has it. The changes made by Anhalt puzzled me until I realized how they work to project the intended composite meter so much more forcefully than the normalized version in 7.15a. This is evident from the composite line notated on the fourth staff of 7.15b. Its first measure, by virtue of the reiteration of C3 on beats 1 and 4, and on the downbeat of measure 2, clearly projects a 6/8 pattern, whereas its counterpart in 7.15a is, by the same criterion, unclear. If anything, the latter produces more of a 3/4 effect. The second composite-line measure is the same in both examples, presenting the succession <C3,G♯3,G♯3,C3,E3,G♯3>. The note repetition on the second and third eighths makes this hard to hear in 6/8, and the inclination to hear it in 3/4 is reinforced in Anhalt's version when we realize that the pitch succession on beats 1, 2, and 3 of this second bar (heard in 3/4) is an augmentation of the pattern in the second half of the first measure: <C3,G♯3,E3> as shown on the bottom staff of ex. 7.15b. In the normalized version, the indistinctness of the first measure forces us to hear it in 3/4 in hindsight, once the much less equivocal second measure is heard; but in Anhalt's distortion, the <6/8, 3/4>

Example 7.16 (o, 1, 6, 7)s derived from (o, 4, 8)s

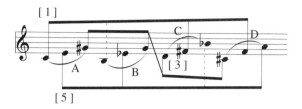

alternation is absolutely clear from the start. To the charge that these are picayune details I would answer that, in a context of absolute regularity such as this, small distortions are heard and do matter; indeed, they signal the control of compositional intelligence and the presence of aesthetic intent.

The material just discussed constitutes one of two three-track complexes in this passage. The second enters five bars after the first in the score, at m. 473. The rhythmic relation between the two can be seen clearly in example 7.17, where the entire passage is given in a durational reduction in which note values are halved, an eighth becoming a sixteenth, a quarter an eighth, and so on. The purpose of the reduction is one of clarification, visual and conceptual: it is much easier to grasp the changes in each complex or stream, and the changing relationships between them, in note values that are half of those in the score. But before discussing example 7.17, I would ask the reader to look at example 7.16, in which the derivation of the three lines (or tracks) of the second stream is explained. In the example, the twelve pitch-classes are arranged in a "descending" succession of augmented triads – (o,4,8)s – labelled A, B, C, and D. This harmonic succession (harmonic in that these triads are to be understood as internally unordered) is melodically partitioned into three Ur-set-class tetrachords, labelled [1], [3], and [5], where [1], as in many previous examples, stands for (11,0,5,6).

We are now ready to look at example 7.17. This opens with the composite line of example 7.15b in durational reduction. As I understand it, this line moves through the four augmented triads in serial rotation: A, B, C, D, where A stands for (C,E,G♯), B for (B,D♯,G), and so on. Each triad occupies two bars at the start of the example, with the small complication of a suspension in odd-numbered (strong) bars (e.g., the E3 in the third bar is "held over" from bar 2 and "resolves" to D♯ in the second half of bar 3; similarly, the B3 in bar 5, the F♯3 in bar 7, etc.). The second stream, derived as in example 7.16, enters with the last sixteenth of the sixth bar of the first stream, where a C2 is

Example 7.17 Symphony, section XII (finale), opening: durational reduction (2:1) and serial analysis

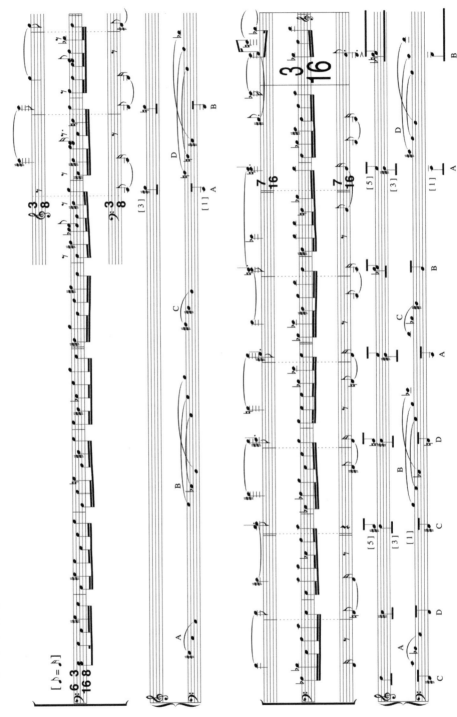

Example 7.17 (continued)

sounded, pizzicato, in the contrabasses. This stream enters with only two of its three constituent lines, marked [1] and [3] on the analytical staffs below the durational reduction in example 7.17. The example makes it clear that the textural relation between the two streams is one of registral enclosure, the second stream emerging as a complex rhythmic reaction, in surrounding pitch space, to the intense goings-on in the first stream – complex because the attack rhythm in the second stream is half as fast as that in the first, but the progression of augmented triad harmonies is *twice as fast* in the second as in the first. The two streams progress regularly for a while, with the second acquiring its full complement of three voices in *its* fifth bar, where the note D6 is sounded (after the first double bar in the top staff of the second system) and the melodic line labelled [5] appears in the analytical reduction. Each stream is seen to consist of four-bar groups (articulated visually by double bars), the bars of which are out of phase by one sixteenth note, the second stream's bars beginning one sixteenth earlier than those of the first stream. Harmonically, the coordination of streams is simple but ingenious: while stream one cycles through the succession <A,B,C,D>, stream two cycles twice as fast through the succession <A,B,C,D,C,D,A,B>. Since stream two begins only where stream one reaches D in its first cycle, a complementary counterpoint is achieved wherein none of the four triads occurs simultaneously in both streams. All this is made quite clear in the analytical reduction.

The rhythmic development of the passage, toward the massive climax at the start of the next subsection of the finale, takes the form of a dramatic acceleration: in the attack rhythm of stream two (at the last sixteenth of the anomalous 7/16 measure); in the rate at which both streams unfold their augmented triads, which rate is doubled in stream two coincident with its doubling of attack rhythm, and doubled in stream one where the metre is marked 6/16; and finally in the metre itself, which involves a compression of bar lengths, toward the end of the example, from six sixteenths to five, to four, and finally to three. This acceleration in the presentation of data is compensated for, with noble reserve, by a simplification of the overall metric situation, because at the point where stream two doubles its rate (at the 3/16 bar of the second system in the example), its "bass" voice begins to sound in sustained octaves, with low string pizzicati doubled by bassoons. This strengthening of the lowest voice imposes a metre to which the first stream conforms, rearranging its harmonic rhythm as if in recognition of the authority of stream two's bass. It will be recalled that the attacks in stream one of example 7.17 are in fact only the accented attacks in that stream (a glance back at example 7.15a will remind the reader of this). By the end of example 7.17, the presentation in stream one has become so compressed that much of the foreground activity in this stream is necessarily suppressed, and single attacks in the reduction actually represent single attacks in the score, instead of groups of three attacks, as at the beginning. The result is that the distinctiveness of stream one is further compromised, and the ensemble sounds as one stream of six-part counterpoint as the passage nears its close.

Section VI (intermezzo II)
As a penultimate object of scrutiny from the Symphony, I have chosen the second intermezzo in the development of movement 1. This is probably the most arresting passage in the entire work, one that seems to me to have no precedent in the literature, and that struck me, when I first heard it in 1963, as a summons to look at music anew. Indeed the term "summons" seems to me to be operative here on another more intimate level. The entire development progresses, in my estimation, from a state of materiality, or objectivity, to one of imaging the unreal, the dreamlike – a progression, to put it another way, from a state of exteriority, in which the subject deals with what is given on the outside, to one of interiority, in which the subject retreats into mental states (memories, projections, fantasies, dreams). The first intermezzo (see examples 7.10 and 7.11, above) is the first such interior state, and it sounds first as a daydream, then as a memory. The prominent part given to the vibraphone in intermezzo I is important in establishing this music a symbol of unreality. We shall see a similar expressive function for bell-like instruments in *SparkskrapS*, and of course intermezzo II is nothing but a gigantic serial cascade of synthesized bell or gong sounds. Here, in section VI, a set of four imaginary metallophones not only images an equally imaginary mental space, but seems veritably to summon it into being. What is summoned does eventually make itself known – not immediately, since the beginning of section VII is a codetta and reminiscence of music from earlier in the development, but in the remainder of section VII, which is the slow movement. Here we have a true representation of interior states: repressed memories, anxious foreboding, even a mystical suspension of the thought process itself. And here, in this slow movement, the Symphony looks ahead to the sister work that took three decades to be born. Of this, more later on. For the present, let us concentrate on the remarkable technical achievement of intermezzo II, which prefigures in a striking way the micropolyphonic technique invented shortly thereafter by Ligeti, whose music Anhalt only came to know about six years after completing this work.

Whereas not many preliminary (predraft) sketches are extant for most of the Symphony – though it may be that some of these were discarded – a great mass of sketch material does remain for this section.[22]

Example 7.18 Symphony, section VI (intermezzo II, "the Gong"), opening: (a) deep structure; (b) surface structure

Example 7.18 *(continued)*

c. realization of surface structure

Anhalt clearly had a certain sound in mind from the start, but before worrying about orchestration, he had to work out a canonic technique that would produce what he wanted in the way of pitches. The sketches sort out this technique at a cost of much time and labour. Rather than recapitulate Anhalt's process for the reader, I have attempted to account for the end result in a logical way. Therefore, examples 17.18a–c, without duplicating any of the relevant sketch material, show how the variegated structure that emerged in the process of composition may be thought to have arisen through transformations of a simple pitch-class array.

Anhalt's basic conception involved using the four augmented triads, this time in a chromatically ascending series, to represent the fundamentals of a series of four bells or gongs. These "instruments" were to be "struck" methodically in a regular rotation: 1, 2, 3, 4, with 1 standing for (C,E,G♯), 2 for (F,A,C♯), and so on. The always changing enharmonic partials of these imaginary metallophones were to be simulated by a six-part canon that was to function as a homophonic complement to the fundamental triads, as one might expect. Anhalt's highly ingenious solution is shown in example 7.18a. The source (augmented) triads are shown on the top staff of the first system. On the bottom staff of the system, these same triads are registrally deployed as in the music, in regularly recurring rotation. The top five of the six intermediate staves present a canon in which each part unfolds a complete chromatic circle of fifths, which it then recycles a number of times in the course of the section. The sixth or lowest of the intermediate staves presents an added voice, the special structure and function of which will be discussed presently. The five canonic circle-of-fifths parts enter one after another, a quarter note apart. The starting tones of the five (and finally, six) canonic voices are of course key to the chordal results, once all nine voices (three in the fundamental, six in the partials) are brought into play. Here Anhalt took advantage of the fact that a series of fifths cycles through the four augmented triads just as does a series of semitones. This is shown in the circle-of-fifths parts by numbering their tones according to membership in the augmented triads of the fundamentals. By carefully choosing the starting points of the canonic voices, Anhalt insured that the partials would always comprise one complete augmented triad in a whole-tone relationship with the fundamental triad, along with single members of each of the remaining two augmented triads, drawn of course from the complementary whole-tone scale. The sixth voice of partials may be termed an added voice, because it does not follow a simple circle of fifths. Instead, it presents the first half of such a circle, but doubles back to repeat the last two tones in this first hexachord as the first two of a second hexachord, proceeding in this way for the whole of the section. The function of this distortion seems to me twofold: on the one hand it introduces a factor of complexity, or incommensurability, into the ensemble, and on the other it acts countermetrically with respect to the fundamentals. These clearly establish a 4/4 metre by virtue of regular recurrence, with triad 2 sounding as a downbeat for reasons of contour; but the added (sixth) partial voice partitions the chordal flow into spans of six chords, or an implied (if hardly apparent) 3/2 metre, which also happens to be the metre notated in the score.

That this is not the end of rhythmic subtlety in this passage is evident from example 7.18b, which moves us one stage closer to the actual music. Here, the five strict circle of fifths give way to a linear surface that is less obviously redundant. Specifically, parts are derived from the abstracted lines of 7.18a by following diagonals within the original array of five circle-of-fifths voices. One of these diagonals is shown in ex. 7.18a and its linear result is the topmost voice in ex. 7.18b. The second voice from the top in 7.18b is similarly derived, by following the next diagonal in 7.18a, beginning on the second tone in the top voice of 7.18a (A), continuing with the second in the next voice down (B♭), the second in the third voice (A♭), and so on. The result is still a five-part canon, but now the voices progress by tones and semitones in both directions, and the hint of Ligeti's micropolyphony is apparent. Interestingly, a new metre of 5/4 now emerges in each of these parts, expressed by a chromatic turn figure that rises by a semitone every five quarter notes. Moreover, the parts now recycle after sixty notes instead of twelve. The added (sixth) partial voice remains as it did in example 7.18a, so the transformation in 7.18b projects a predominating 4/4 metre in the ostinato fundamentals, five different 5/4 metres in the five strictly canonic parts, which now seem to climb slowly against an invariant ground, and the 3/2 metre mentioned above in the quasi-canonic sixth part. Furthermore, as example 7.18b shows, the ostinato, once it gets going, is linearly partitioned into

Example 7.19 Anhalt's chart for Symphony: Extra 3

three forms of the Ur-set-class, as was shown in example 7.17. It may also be mentioned that, owing to the kinds of interval cycles used in all voices, all the nine-note chords in this section belong to the same set-class. The reader can verify this with a brief look at the next example.

Example 7.18c shows the actual registral disposition of all nine voices in the opening measures of section VI. The orchestration of this passage, in which the whole orchestra's resources are brought to bear to create a timbre that varies subtly as if some vast array of partials were being variously filtered over time, deserves a paper in its own right, and I will leave the task of commenting on it to someone more knowledgable in these matters. Of interest to me is the overall shape of this section, which is to some extent a microcosmic reflection of the Symphony's overall shape, which consists in a succession of waves. There are three waves in the "gong" section, each peaking in a pronounced dynamic climax, and there are three waves in the Symphony as a whole, the difference being that the work as a whole begins and ends with a peak, resulting in four peaks in all.[23]

Section IX (scherzo)
The matter of overall shape provides a suitable entrée to the final passage to be discussed. In example 7.20 I will try to give some feeling for how an entire section, one that also functions as a self-contained large-scale unit in the work's form, achieves coherence. The music in question is section IX, which Anhalt describes as, and no one could mistake for anything other than, a scherzo.[24] It is the third embedded movement of our single-movement symphonic genre. But before considering example 7.20, let us have a look at another of Anhalt's serial charts, given in example 7.19.

Here we have an asymmetrical partitioning of the aggregate into 4+5+3 tones, beginning as always with a form of the Ur-set-class, and dividing the eight-tone complement into a set of class (0,1,2,5,6) and one of class (0,1,4). For each form of the Ur-set-class there are four ways of partitioning the complement in this manner. The four resulting pairs of sets are labelled A, B, B′, and A′, with A and A′ being transpositionally related, as are B and B′. A is of course inversionally related to B, as is A′ to B′.

We may now turn to example 7.20, a particella reduction of section IX with analytical overlay and separate analytical notations above and below the music. On motivic grounds, the music groups itself into four subsections, with a short transition linking the first and second of these. (See table 7.3.) The first is eight measures long (mm. 366–73) and I have called it a "theme" because it is so closely patterned on a

Example 7.20 Symphony, section IX (scherzo): with analysis

Example 7.20 (continued)

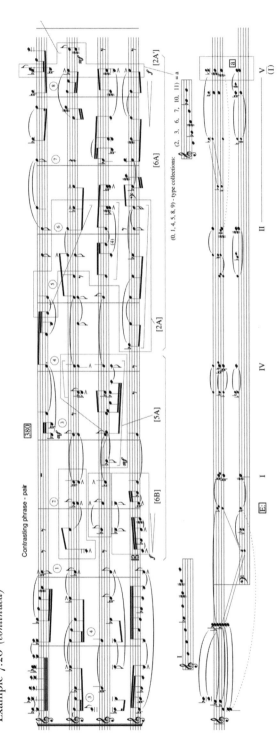

Example 7.20 (*continued*)

Three - phrase developmental group

Example 7.20 *(continued)*

Three - phrase developmental reprise - conclusion

classical model. The transition is five bars long (mm. 374–8) and uses motives from the theme in sequence.[25] This leads to a contrasting phrase-pair (B), which might be called a countertheme. It is seven bars long (mm. 379–85, with a long upbeat segment in m. 378), and is partitioned into 3+4 bars. While the odd-numbered lengths of the transition and the countertheme are significant as a disruption of the "quadratic" structure of the theme proper, the metric grouping of measures by twos and fours in fact continues, by virtue of accentuation, through to m. 385, so that the 5+7 is heard against a metric background of 4+4+4, and a refinement of rhythmic-metric interplay worthy of Chopin is evident. The next subsection is a developmental group (C) consisting of three phrases of decreasing length, 4+3+2. The bars of these phrases are shown with circled numbers in example 7.20. In the case of the last phrase of C (of two bars), there is a further subdivision by hemiola into three bars of 2/8 time. These three short bars are indicated, by means of circled numbers, below the music. There follows a final phrase group (A'), a reprise with development of the motivic material in the theme. Like the preceding developmental group, this is of nine measures, but here the lengths of component phrases increase incrementally, producing a 2+3+4 pattern. In effect, the progressive effect of the third phrase-group (C) is counterbalanced by a recessive effect here. The scherzo as a whole may be diagrammed, as in table 7.3.

As a twelve-tone structure, this movement draws mostly on the chart in example 7.19. The aggregate partitions used in the theme, at a rate of approximately one per measure, are indicated below the score in square brackets, with [1B], for example, designating the use of Ur-set-class 1, with its complement partitioned as in column B in ex. 7.19. Boxes are used on the score to indicate the deployment of relevant sets for the first few partitions. The motivic structure, in terms of pitch and rhythm, is very clearly that of a so-called sentence, consisting of a motive (2 bars), its quasi-sequential repetition (2 bars), a pair of compressed or truncated motive presentations (2 bars), and a cadential fragment (2 bars). Everything in the theme is thus very classical, with reference to both Viennese Schools.

The transition uses only forms of the Ur-set-class and various of their corresponding five-tone sets (see ex. 7.19), the (0,1,4) being left aside for the time being. In each measure, three forms of the five-note motive occur in close stretto. By glancing at the lowest staff in mm. 374–7 it will become readily apparent that this passage takes one measure's worth of material (m. 374) through a series of T_5 transformations, or, to put it in traditional terms, a descending circle of fifths. I will connect this observation with others of a tonal nature after completing this review of the music's motivic and set structure.

Table 7.3
Diagram of the scherzo's subsections in the Symphony

A		B	C	A′
Theme	*transition*	*Counter theme*	*Developmental group*	*Developmental reprise*
(2+2)+4	5	3+4	4+3+2	2+3+4

Moving on to the countertheme, we see that once again the partitions of example 7.19 are in use. For the first of these, in mm. 378–9, I have boxed each of the three component sets, with the partition name 6B appearing below in a square bracket. The next two aggregates in this section are boxed as wholes, but by referring to their square-bracketed partition names the reader should have no difficulty whatsoever in parsing them. Attention should be directed, however, to the use of an obbligato voice in this subsection. This begins in m. 380 and continues through to the end of subsection C, the developmental group. In subsection B this obbligato voice stands apart from the partition structure, dwelling instead on a single form of the Ur-set-class, $(4,5,10,11) = [6]$.

At the cadence point of B, on the second eighth of m. 385, a new formation is introduced. Creating a perfectly audible surprise, the voices converge on set $(2,3,6,7,10,11)$, a symmetrical hexachord of the $(0,1,4,5,8,9)$ type, which I will call the augmented hexachord. If we consider $(2,3,6,7,10,11)$ to be form "a," we may agree to call its complement (or T_2) "b" $= (4,5,8,9,0,1)$. Let "c" and "d" then designate, respectively, the two remaining forms of the hexachord, $(1,2,5,6,9,10)$ and $(3,4,7,8,11,0)$. Turning to subsection C, we see that the cadence chord of subsection B has in fact introduced a shift in the music's set-structure, the implications of which are immediately taken up. Subsection C is composed almost entirely of forms of the augmented hexachord, with only three notes in the obbligato part falling outside any of these forms. The boxes on the score in mm. 386–94 indicate the various sets used, from which it can be seen that the three phrases of subsection C consist in turn of (b,a,b,a), (c,d,c,d), and (d,c,a,b), the terminal "d" of phrase two doubling as the initial "d" of phrase three. The final phrase-group, or A', returns to the set-structure and motive forms used in A. Ur-set-class form [1] is heard very prominently in the tenor register in mm. 395–6, letting us know that we are into a reprise. And the reader should have little difficulty identifying the partitions used in this subsection, except perhaps in the last two or three bars, where the registral presentation of component sets becomes extremely fragmented. It should be noted that Anhalt uses the obbligato (also the highest) voice, which first emerged in subsection B, to effect pitch-structural continuity across the changing harmonic sound of the music. Thus, within C, notwithstanding the shift to contrasting harmonic terrain, the obbligato, using only a few extraneous tones, manages to move entirely in forms of the Ur-set-class. It is abandoned temporarily at the start of A', again in conformity with the music's intention of reprise, but when it is resumed, in m. 398, the obbligato once again restricts itself to Ur-set-class forms.

Finally, let us turn, as we have in other passages, to the genealogical counterpart of the motivic and set logic exposed thus far – its tonal substratum. We noted the suggestion of B as a tonic in the opening music of the Symphony. What was but a suggestion there is a bold assertion here, with strong implications of B as tonic present throughout and, in particular, at cadences and other points of rhythmic emphasis. This is not the case in the scherzo's first few bars, where the harmony, sketched in a reduction under the score, is seen to consist almost entirely of five- and six-tone octatonic subsets. The reference in mm. 366–72 is first to octatonic collection I = (B,C,D,E♭,F,F♯,G♯,A), then to octatonic collection II = T_1 of I (mm. 368–70), and back again to I (mm. 370–2). This is followed on the last eighth of m. 372 by a harmony rooted on E, which leads in turn, on the last eighth of m. 373, to another six-note chord found in II, which appears ordered in register as <A♯3,E4,A4,D♯5,G5,C6>. This is readily heard as a seven-tone chord of which the root F♯, which is also a member of II, is missing. In effect, the theme ends with a chord progression easily heard as IV–V, and therefore as a half-cadence, in B.

The transition (mm. 374–7), as noted above, takes us through a series of T_5 transformations. I have reduced its content to a series of four seven-tone harmonies. In mm. 374–6 these are polychords, consisting of a tetrachord of the dominant seventh or the diminished seventh type, on top of a different dominant-seventh-type trichord. The registral isolation of these subharmonies ensures that we hear the T_5 transformations. The transformation taking the music into m. 347 does not effect a further T_5 move; instead it restates the harmonic collection underlying the preceding measure with one change: the "root" G3 disappears and D4 is added. The result is a subset of octatonic collection I, a return to which makes sense in view of its referential status in subsection A.

With the countertheme, or B, a change in harmonic colour is effected despite the persistence of the same aggregate partition. In mm. 379 and 381, and again in m. 383, the three motives of the partition (see ex. 7.19) converge registrally and chromatically on accented chords. These are immediately perceived as triads with added notes –

the first an E major triad in 6-position, with added $A4$; the second an A minor triad in 6-position with added $B4$ and $F5$; and the third an F-sharp minor triad in 6-position with added $G^{\sharp}4$ and $F5$. The latter tone can also be understood as $E^{\sharp}5$, an added major seventh. A functional interpretation of these chords as I, IV, and II in the key of E (or IV of B) suggests itself, and this is confirmed when a final convergence of the same motives takes place on the second eighth of m. 385, a place already identified as the point of emergence of the augmented hexachord. Just before this point, during the preceding two eighths, another form of II in E is clearly audible – to wit, a root-position half-diminished-seventh chord (or minor-seventh chord, if $C^{\sharp}4$ is preferred as the chord tone over $C4$) on F-sharp. This then leads directly to the augmented hexachord, which I hear as a B major triad with added tones $B^{\flat}5$ and D6, and a subposed G, which I take as a mediant in E and as pointing toward tonic function.

The next phrase-group, C, treats the E-tonicity of subsection B as a subdominant expansion, and continues with II of B major, expressed first as a prolonged $D^{\flat}$ harmony in 6-position, then as a C-sharp-minor chord (with added $^{\sharp}7$), on the second eighth of m. 388. There follows, over the barline between mm. 388 and 389, a weak authentic cadence in B. The development of the harmony in the rest of subsection C is complicated. (The reader who prefers not to take my analysis on faith should test it repeatedly against the score, to confirm that salient features of the music are captured in the reduction.) In my interpretation, the second phrase of C is governed by a bass line rising in whole steps: $F^{\sharp}3$ (m. 389), $A^{\flat}3$ (m. 390), $B^{\flat}2$ (m. 391), and C3 (m. 392). Over these tones I hear a series of parallel sixths, then fifths, leading ultimately to the C-minor triad, a $^{\flat}$II in B, prolonged in m. 392. A succession of $\frac{6}{3}$ and $\frac{5}{3}$ chords is shown in the analysis of these measures, some as simultaneities and others using the standard diagonal beam to indicate an unfolded harmonic interval. The C-minor triad of m. 392 can be heard to pass through a V–I succession in m. 393, but the structural goal of this harmony is the cadence in m. 394. Here, the expected root $F^{\sharp}$ (V) is withheld, but the interval $C^{\sharp}5$–$A^{\sharp}5$ is unfolded in the top voices, along with $E4$, the seventh. The lowest tone of the cadence chord (generated by the prevailing augmented hexachord syntax), an $A^{\flat}3$, may be heard as a ninth (=$G^{\sharp}3$) substituting for the implied root.

Tonic function is now called for and we get it with aplomb at the start of A′, which begins with <B3,$F^{\sharp}4$> as part of Ur-set-class [1], while another voice supplies $D^{\sharp}3$, then D3. A smooth succession of triad forms is seen to flow from this B chord in the first two measures of A′, but an orgy of motives takes over this phrase-group as the movement rushes to its conclusion, and a clear sense of harmonic progression is lost. There is a clear E$\flat$ sonority of the $_{\sharp 3}^{7}$ type (including a $\flat$9) in m. 398, and I have designated this as a III, but the strongest reference to B as tonal centre comes at the final cadence point, where the lowest voices present Ur-set-class [1] in such a way as to give the unmistakable impression of a V–I bass motion. Coincident with this, there is a blurring motion in the upper voices, which clearly suggests an authentic cadence to C (shades of Strauss's *Zarathustra*). Finally, the reader will notice the dotted-line boxes in sub-sections C and A'. These isolate discrete segments of the analytical level that seem to me to reflect one another, specifically, the rising bass line motion departing from G$\sharp$3, and the rising upper-voice motion that terminates in <A4, A$\sharp$4> in the first case and <A5, B$\flat$5> in the second.

As a last comment on this movement, I would draw attention to its intensity curve, which once again is conceptually related to that of the Symphony as a whole. Subsection A begins at a fairly high pitch, and relaxes through the transition into B. The latter, at first maintaining a lower level of intensity, terminates at the crest of a small wave in m. 385. With the start of C, this wave recedes, only to begin to grow again after m. 390. This progression continues through the rest of C into A', which does not let up but progresses toward a terminal climax in the final measure. The overall result, then, is a sort of W-shape, a two-wave succession beginning and ending at a peak, with a smaller peak in the middle.

I have talked about the scherzo from many of the standpoints adopted in this study: its relationship to the traditional type, its motives and phraseology, its set structure, its tonality, and its energy curve. It is the most self-contained of the work's sections, and the only embedded movement that begins and ends with a palpable silence. And, to the extent that there is a work-spanning narrative in the Symphony (a question I shall take up below) the scherzo seems to stand to some extent outside the work as a whole, as if it were a pure gesture to the symphony as genre, and true to the spirit of its own subgenre, an ironic comment on the seriousness of the entire proceedings. But within the diadem that is the Symphony as a whole, it is surely of special resplendence.

SPARKSKRAPS (1987)[26]

The Source Materials and Their Implications of Critical Reception

While the Symphony took at least four years to compose, the piece to which I now turn, *SparkskrapS*, took less than seven months (May to December 1987), including the initial period of conscious precompositional planning. And, uncharacteristically for Anhalt, work on *SparkskrapS* began right on the heels of the completion of an equally complex and substantial orchestral work, *Simulacrum*. Commissions from major performing organizations were coming his way for the first time, in the wake of interest generated by the 1985 performance of *Winthrop*, and having the retired person's luxury of full-time creative work, Anhalt felt he had to accept them. Contrary to what one might imagine, however, the three orchestral works from the late 1980s were not dashed off – anything but. In fact, the volume of sketch and preliminary-draft material for *SparkskrapS*, all of which is in the Anhalt fonds of the National Library, is daunting, and exceeds by a factor of two or three that for the Symphony. It would seem that, able for the first time to devote himself entirely to composing and spurred on by spiritual impulses that had been developing within him for many years, Anhalt not only compressed his work schedule, but found more ready access to his musical imagination.

With respect to *SparkskrapS*, the fonds contain forty-three files of material.[27] Of particular interest are the following: (1) 183 pages of preliminary sketches in pencil (PS in the following); (2) 31 leaves of (verbal and numerical) notes, produced at various stages of the compositional process; (3) 10 leaves of music paper with pc-set structures; (4) a 54-page pencil holograph of an early (incomplete) draft of the work, written mostly on systems of two, three, or four staves, and cross-referenced to the pages of PS (a "concept score," or CS, in what follows); and (5) two drafts of the complete work, combined, by cutting and pasting, into one 76-page pencil holograph short score, with instrumental indications written more or less in full (SS in the following); also included among the 43 files are (6) a pencil holograph of the final score; and (7) photocopies of all the extracted parts. This considerable array of material repays close study, because its components are interrelated in ways that enable one to learn a good deal, not only about the process of composition, but about the composer's conception of the work, and his intentions for it as a field of expressive reference.

SparkskrapS appears to have developed in Anhalt's mind in a manner quite unlike that of the Symphony. Specifically, it is clear from the sources that it emerged as a series of musical reflections on a personal adventure, one of intellectual and spiritual dimensions. This much is clear from a perusal of the 31 leaves of notes, which begin not with sets or rhythmic ideas, not with sketches of motives or themes, not with formal plans, but with lists of words.[28] What appear to be five of the earliest leaves in this collection (on white, standard-size paper) are entitled, respectively, 1 Dimensions, 2 Ideas, 3 Procedures, 4 Forms, States, Situations, and 5 Symbols, hypostases, analogies.[29] Each of these categories contains one or more lists of terms and short phrases that, in Anhalt's mind, fit the subsuming category. These entries point to a peculiar array of sources and are somewhat baffling in their variety. For example, the fourth of these pages appears as follows:

4 *FORMS, STATES, SITUATIONS*

Unassimilability

Hardest, heaviest sparks (fall)

Brokenness, flawedness, unfinishedness

The abyss (into which the zaddik leaps)

The overturned lamp

Silences

The scintillating flame, flashing in lightning (of the 10 sefiroth)
Their end is as their beginning (Sparkscraps?)

Demonic captivity of the *Shekinah*

Psyche = sum of "Knots" (*Gnosticism*, 166)

Light ≅ consonance

It is clear that a rather special continuum of ideas is being invoked here – clear too that the ideas are of a religious nature, stemming, in large part from Jewish sources. The specific impetus to think creatively about them came from Anhalt's reading of Gershom Scholem, the foremost twentieth-century authority on Kabbalah, or Jewish mysticism, and the individual primarily responsible for restoring its doctrines to centrality and respectability in the modern Jewish world. I have little knowledge or understanding of these doctrines, and thus claim no capacity to clarify them for others. But a very few words of explanation seem necessary if we are to understand Anhalt's terms of reference, if only in the crudest way.[30] Kabbalah has a two-thousand-year history, its earliest texts and oral traditions having emerged around the period of the exile. Flourishing in the medieval world, these doctrines took a definitive form in key texts, most notably the thirteenth-century *Zohar*, a commentary on the Torah, or first five books of the Hebrew Bible. The basic question of Kabbalah concerns the relationship between the Divine – or the Eternal and Unlimited (*Ein Sof*) – which is not contained in space and time, and the whole of the material and energetic universe, which is finite. Light, as first created, is the key to this relationship. It emanates from the Divine as if from a prism, in ten stages, called the ten *sefiroth*. These are rather like Platonic forms (e.g., wisdom, understanding, judgment, kindness, majesty, force); they characterize the Divine and divine rule without limiting them. They are represented as contained in vessels, or bowls, symmetrically arrayed to form a tree the spatial arrangement of which conveys hierarchical relationships and oppositions (e.g., masculine/feminine). A particularly influential stream of kabbalistic thought emerged in the seventeenth century from the writings of Isaac Luria, who introduced a number of highly suggestive doctrines: *zimzum*, *shevirah*, and *tikkun*. *Zimzum*, or self-limitation, describes a process by which the Divine voluntarily limits its own infinitude to create room for the universe. *Shevirah*, or breaking of the vessels, refers to a tragic development at the start of creation: the vessels containing the harsher *sefiroth* (e.g., judgment) are too weak to bear their intensity; they break and the light they contain is scattered in the form of sparks throughout the space vacated by *zimzum*. As well, the Divine attempts creation more than once. Successive attempts are not to its liking and the debris of these attempts are called *kelippoth*, or husks. When the sparks resulting from the breaking of the vessels spread everywhere in the space that the *Ein Sof* has vacated, many find their way to the realm of *kelippoth*, which cover them and snuff out most (but not all) of them. This realm is also called the "other side," or *Sitra Ahra*. Other sparks remain free of this realm and continue to burn brightly. With these notions, Lurianic Kabbalism provides a metaphysical account of the appearance of evil – the *kelippoth*, or debris – and good – the still-shining sparks, including those obscured but not fully snuffed out by evil. *Tikkun*, then, is the task of restoration, of retrieving the sparks of light from their surrounding husks, and of gathering together all remaining sparks into the originally intended configuration of light. It is to be undertaken by the Divine, but also by the individual human, for whom the task may be conceptualized as freeing one's divine soul from one's bodily husk. Ultimately, the Divine decides when to reverse *zimzum* itself, and to nullify creation, which is not forever.

Three quotations from Scholem's *On the Kabbalah and Its Symbolism* grace the title page of *SparkskrapS,* and they seem to me to reveal the nature of Anhalt's preoccupation with these seemingly remote ideas. The first deals with *shevirah*, the second with the *Sitra Ahra* and the *kellipoth*, and the third with *tikkun*. Clearly, the dynamics of breakage and restoration, of the pulverization and reconstitution of what is holy, good, positive, or simply worthwhile, appeared to Anhalt as eminently worth thinking about. This is hardly surprising when one considers the lives he has based his dramatic compositions on, lives like that of Marie de l'Incarnation, who had to cut all ties to her past, even abandoning her only son, to pursue a divinely ordained mission in a New World. Nor is it surprising when we consider Anhalt's own life, in which a nascent creative impulse was very nearly snuffed out by evil in its most grotesquely concentrated form, and in which the struggle to create something beautiful and enduring in music has faced and continues to face so many obstacles: the dead weights of tradition, the grinding power of the market, the monodimensionality and ultimately destructive trend of triumphalist science and technology, the negative energies of politics. Out of his battle with all of these, Anhalt could not fail to respond to the Lurianic vision, and with his composer's ear and eye for patterns, he found a name for them: "scraps," the spiritually useless debris of our own and earlier eras, from which it is the good person's task to free the sparks of positive creativity and love of creation that animate us at our individual and collective bests. The title *SparkskrapS* concatenates the two focal and opposed notions of the divine spark and the human-historical scrap, suggesting at the same time the Lurianic ideas behind the work and the ongoing commitment Anhalt has to the underlying unity of music and language as expressive media. A "sparkskrap" denotes a husk containing a spark, and it is a portmanteau word that reflects the kind of patterning – of which the palindrome is a vivid instance – that is basic to the musical tradition in which Anhalt has been creating for more than fifty years, reminding us that, for all its formalism, this tradition, in his hands at least, has expression and the creation of meaning as its overriding purposes.

Form and Meaning in the Work as a Whole

As with the Symphony, I will consider the overall shape of *SparkskrapS* first, before moving on to treat particular passages in detail. It too is a work composed of many small sections that lacks an array of constants that might justify thinking of them as variations. Instead, these sections form a complex network in which each is related in a variety of ways to many (but not all) of the others. The search for a traditional archetype underlying the formal syntax of these sections – determining the order in which they occur – can also be soon and safely abandoned, as there is little in the character of most of these sections (especially when their order of statement is considered) that even remotely suggests the rhetoric of a traditional form.[31] But this is hardly surprising in a composer who, before composing the orchestral music of the late 1980s, had spent more than twenty-five years avoiding purely instrumental music and all the allegiances that composing such music would seem to entail. To be sure, none of this denies that many of the sections of *SparkskrapS* sound traditional, in ways that no passage of the Symphony quite does. For here are found singable melodies of vocal character (including one that emerges at the music's emotional high point), recurrent pitch-classes of emphasis that develop into tonics; undisguised references to tonal harmony; and evocations of a panoply of immediately recognizable musical styles: Hungarian folk song; the postromantic development to a climax via chromatic sequencing and motivic liquidation; the étude on a single pitch-class (as found in Berg, Carter, Ligeti, and Scelsi, among others); faux-vocal mystical homophony that recalls such contexts as Stravinsky's *Zvezhdoliki* (King of the Stars); Mahlerian Yiddishkeit; a plucked-and-struck ensemble à la Boulez; some almost baroque polyphony; and a dream of a class-piano session devoted to the Alberti bass.

I certainly do not intend this listing of stylistic references to sound like a hodgepodge, or to suggest incoherence. In fact, the scope of Anhalt's achievement lies nowhere more amply than in his ability to weave together these many kinds of music with no effect of pastiche, and with a result that is affectively and structurally seamless. But I am substantiating a claim that *SparkskrapS* is in no way classical in its orientation. Indeed, it might be described as antineoclassical, nothing could be further from the spirit or substance of this work than an intention to reinterpret baroque or classical forms, and *SparkskrapS* is in fact much more distant from such models than the Symphony.

This raises an obvious question: why refer to all these styles if not to recreate any of the genres in which they are found? Not that this question demands to be posed in Anhalt's case alone, since composing with shifting stylistic references is a hallmark of the postmodern in music. But in his case the intent is not what it often appears to be: familiar styles taken at face value and interpreted anew, as in George Rochberg; or seen through some fantastic-making lens, as in Alfred Schnittke; heard to have a special affect, as in Peter Maxwell Davies's use of foxtrots in grotesque parody, as an evocation of passion gone out of control; styles understood as recreating a cultural context, as in many an opera composed recently; or simply intended to delight by way of compositional virtuosity and humour, as in John Zorn. In Anhalt's case the intent is more far-reaching – namely, that passages in this or that style be understood as densely packed symbols that operate on many levels: European humanist high culture, with special attention to the concertgoer's frame of reference; mystical theory and practice, with a focus on Kabbalah; another, antithetically paired with the preceding, of modernism in its negation of the metaphysical; yet another of the experience of good and evil, with special reference to the Holocaust; and, among several others that could be cited, that of the body's experience of itself. Of course the sections in *SparkskrapS* and its companion works from the late 1980s are diverse: some evoke familiar styles and others do not; structural relationships of every kind cross the boundaries between the stylistically familiar and the "original"; and all sections of a work participate in its multiple referentiality, not just those that sound like other music. But those that do have a particular semiotic density; they stabilize a congeries of images that extends well beyond what music can do by way of standard topics, correlations with physical events and conditions, or conventional associations of tones and words. Specifically, these referential passages allow the intended hearer to import historical and cultural associations as surely as the quoted styles suggest structural descriptions, along with any more general (cross-cultural) associations they provoke. Of course, Anhalt is hardly alone in composing with music other than his own in this manner, and precedents stretch back at least to Mahler, but the intensity of his commitment to the approach and his skill in integrating the results are surely compelling.

All of this suggests that *SparkskrapS* and its companion works are a kind of program music, which designation raises far more questions than it answers. If there is a program, does it matter whether the composer has added it to the score or provided it to audiences in the form of notes? Can it be a secret program? Can an atemporal network of ideas and images constitute a program and, if so, can it be represented in musical terms? Can a succession of musical passages, however evocative, constitute a narrative? If there is an underlying narrative, in what temporal and physical dimensions does it unfold? The history of our time as we generally understand it? The times and spaces of different cultural stances juxtaposed? Fictional or mythic time and some corresponding world? Or the quasi-vertical and virtual time of the imagination, in which thoughts and sensations of all kinds must occur sequentially in actual experience, but are known by the experiencing subject to coexist at different levels of consciousness? Such questions have been formulated, of course, by many critics, and I have no illusions about avoiding the appearance of naïveté in broaching them.[32] However, *SparkskrapS*, when approached from a standpoint of familiarity with its sources and with other works by the composer, demands that the critic take a stand on these questions, and mocks any attempt to sidestep them. I have therefore chosen to consider the symbolic functions of the small sections (measure-groups) of *SparkskrapS* as constitutive attributes that are as essential to determining the meaning of these sections as anything about their notational or sonic structures. Table 7.4, which lists the sections of *SparkskrapS* and describes their symbolic as well as their formal functions, reflects this decision. (Because of its length, I have placed this table in an appendix, which immediately follows the main text of this essay. Before continuing with the main text, the reader may want to take some time to read carefully through this table, perhaps omitting the rightmost column, which needs some explanation. If a recording is at hand, one might read the table through again while listening to the music. Otherwise, the discussion which follows, of the table's structure and its symbolic and music-theoretical terms of reference, will be opaque.)

The hierarchical flatness and the very length of table 7.4 (see appendix) tell us that we are not dealing here with a traditional form or anything like one. My analysis distinguishes four parts, the first having two major subparts, but beyond this, no grouping of the thirty-six measure-groups (some of them subdivided) themselves. The length of table 7.4 is principally due to the fact that, with some exceptions, it is impossible to find standard, succinct syntactic names (theme, transition, development) for most of the measure-groups. These circumstances indicate that the music looks to something outside its own traditions as a model for succession and large-scale continuity or change. The fourth column in the table attempts to set down, in approximate terms, what that something might be. It is a kind of scenario, based entirely on the composer's notes and, specifically, on the descriptors he assigns to particular passages in the preliminary sketches (PS). The fifth column, then, shows the source of the relevant descriptive term. In most cases, the labels do not actually appear in the PS. They are, however, reliably assigned because Anhalt meticulously cross-referenced all the PS passages that he used in the final work (indicated by their PS page numbers) to a special list of descriptive terms included in his notes. (Some PS pages are assigned to only one descriptor in the list, others to several.) In these cases, the marker "list" is appended to the descriptor in column 5. In a few cases, however, he did write a label in the PS, and in these, the entry in column 5 is marked "PS." In a couple of instances, a label is found in a later source (CS or SS) and the entry is so marked. A number of measure-groups in *SparkskrapS* have no source passage in the PS and no label in any other source. Not being represented in the PS, they are not assigned to the list and cannot therefore be labelled. These are identified as "not present in PS."

How can one assemble a musical narrative out of these descriptors and such a nonconventional musical syntax? As Carolyn Abbate has pointed out, the problem with the concept of musical narrative is that music rarely, if ever, finds a way to distinguish between the teller and the tale, by constructing a narrator-subject.[33] Perusing the fourth column in table 7.4 makes this clear; in this instance, there is no narrator.

It is as if we were presented with a series of pictures, or film strips, and asked to make up our own story. But this is a kind of narration nonetheless, even if not determined or shaped by a narrator's personality. The story emerges only at the level of interpretation, and represents another dimension of the hermeneutic task, one no less integral to the music as a work of art than its interpreted musical structures.

Surveying the list of symbolic functions in table 7.4 (column 4), in conjunction with the second and third columns, leads me to two general thoughts. One is that the symbolism of the music rests on a number of basic but musically cogent oppositions – between high and low registers; between the labile and mellifluous and the rigid and heavily accented; between the augmented hexachord and the octatonic collection, a sort or reconceptualization of the major/minor dichotomy; between lavish melody in general (and rising melodic sequences in particular), and descending harmonic sequences more or less devoid of melodic content; between pc emphasis by tonal means, and by rhetorical means; and finally, between an emphasis on one or more members of the set (E♭,G♭,B♭) and a contrasting focus on the pcs of the D-minor triad (D,F,A). These are summarized in table 7.5.

As the table makes clear, all entries on the left refer to features connected to the Divine, to sparks, and to *tikkun* (restoration), while features on the right indicate distance from the Divine and proximity to the *Sitra Ahra* (the obscuring realm or underworld), scraps, darkness, and *shevira* (breakage). As is the case with all such schema, this one is an oversimplification, and the reader will doubtlessly recognize the following limitations. Melody can be found everywhere in the music, as can harmony; the functions of augmented hexachords and octatonic collections are sometimes exchanged; and the distinction between tonal and rhetorical emphasis may not always be clear. As well, there are a variety of harmonic formations, such as sets formed out of chromatically related tritones, that do not fit in the schema. Finally, when the music becomes tonal, the distinction between (E♭,G♭,B♭) and (D,F,A) – which pertains mainly to rhetorical emphasis – is obscured; for example, both B♭ minor and A minor, as *keys*, are implicated in the most gripping representations of spiritual longing, in measure-groups 24, 26b, and 26c. These points aside, table 7.5 will prove useful as a simple interpretive tool.

The second thought occasioned by reading down column 4 of table 7.4 is that, if there is a kind of story to be constructed by the sensitive listener in response to *SparkskrapS*, it is one that happens in at least three different kinds of time. Foremost among these, because it is constantly in effect, is what might be termed imaginative time, the time in which the music's constructed subject reflects. Is this not introducing a

Table 7.5
Oppositions of symbolic significance for *SparkskrapS*

Representing the Divine or the aspiration toward it	*Representing the* Sitra Ahra *(Evil) or a drift toward it*
higher-register events	lower-register events
flowing, labile textures, with arpeggios, tremolos, free rhythm	rigid textures, with accented, repeated pedal tones, metric rhythms
augmented-triad combinations, principally the augmented hexachord $(0,1,4,5,8,9)$, with increasing ambiguity as the work proceeds	$(0,3,6,9)$ combinations, especially octatonic collections, with increasing ambiguity as the work proceeds
stand-out melody, both traditional and newly invented; some rising sequences	harmonic sequences, descending, with little distinctive melodic content
quasi-traditional tonality, as an expression of human aspiration in this direction	rhetorical emphasis on a PC, as an expression of the pull of these forces
(D,F,A), emphasized individually or in combinations	(E♭,G♭,B♭), emphasized individually or in combinations

narrator through the back door? one might ask. No, because the listener constructs the subject, who can vary accordingly; it does not matter who he or she is and in what accents he or she speaks. The subject, in other words, is merely a vehicle or repository for the mental images depicted in the music. Imaginative time is constantly in effect because all the images represented in *SparkskrapS* can be construed as arising in a subject's imagination, in the order in which they appear in the music.[34] But in thinking, the subject refers to two additional lines of time. One might be described as mythic or Aggadic time, Aggadah being the Jewish tradition of commenting on the Torah in terms of legends and stories, of which the Kabbalah's account of Creation, given above, is a prime example. The other is biographical time, referred to as the subject remembers past events in his or her life and projects into a more or less certain future. Because *SparkskrapS* is a real-time imaginative episode, and corresponds to a particular train of thought and feeling, every measure-group in *SparkskrapS* has its place in imaginative time. The other two kinds of time described here are inconsistently represented. Therefore, some measure-groups happen in only one temporal dimension (the imaginative), while others happen in two or three. While a fourth line of time, that of world history, seems conspicuously to be missing, the following will make clear that it too is engaged, even if very sporadically.

With these thoughts in mind, one can write out a story – not *the* story of *SparkskrapS*, but one of a number of stories that could be written, equivalent with respect to the symbolic functions listed in table 7.4 and with regard to remaining within the time constraints discussed here. One might speak of a subject who imagines an ancient ceremony in which the Divine is invoked[35] and, at the same time, imagines the Divine projecting rays of light in Aggadic time (hereafter, AT). This is of course measure-group 1. In 2, an early state of the universe is imagined, one preceding the creation of light – the *tohu vavohu*[36] of Genesis 1:2. At the same time, the subject's own state of spiritual confusion is mirrored. The next group (3) might show matter (in AT) striving to unite with its creative source, to rise up, as it were, in spite of its heaviness, and depict a corresponding impulse in the subject, in imaginative time (hereafter, IT). Then, in group 4, the creation of consciousness is imagined and, given the priority of E♭ here, is perhaps thought of in terms of its tendency toward baser things. Unitary consciousness becomes a multiplicity in 4b, as AT advances toward IT, and this results in conflict, but spiritual impulses (the augmented hexachords) promote reconciliation in 5a, only to be undermined by something utterly contradictory, rather like a destructive force of nature (octatonic activity). Now, in 5b, the subject experiences foreboding as he or she imagines light – and by extension, the human soul – being trapped in the realm of the shells, the *Sitra Ahra* (in AT). This leads to 6, the end of the first half of part 1, in which the thought of group 3 is briefly returned to (in IT) but is cut short by an image and visceral sense of the power of the lower realm, represented by the cadence on an E-flat-minor triad.

The second half of part 1 begins on a different note. In group 7, something is remembered (in biographical time, hereafter, BT), reassuring but essentially drawn from the subject's mental scrap heap, represented by the emphasis on an E-flat-minor triad in a context that hints at B-flat-minor. This provokes a reaction (in IT), namely the vision of spiritual activity in group 8. This, in turn, generates (in 9) an extreme nervous reaction in the body (again in IT), which can also be seen as an image of matter revealing its nature as energy (in AT). By force of will, the mind overcomes this disturbance (in 10) and starts imagining abstract patterns. Thus, the patterns of 11a may be heard to represent themselves or their numerical equivalents (in IT). In 11b and 11c the mind begins to play with the data posited in 11a, and is aware of its own effort in doing so, but strength is lacking and the effort is abandoned, leading to a psychic treading of water. Finally, in 12, IT and AT are operative as the subject experiences an intimation of Divine radiance filling the world.

Part II begins with a reference to the tonal tradition, representing perhaps a memory (in IT) of success, or smooth sailing at some earlier time in BT. This activity, initiated in 13, continues apace in 14, but its flavour changes as the sequel to that time is remembered, in which its breezy confidence is undermined by disturbing currents. This takes us to 15b, in which the full, oppressive power of a time of intense suffering (in BT) is remembered. (Of course, an interpretation of these events in AT is also possible.) In 15b a strenuous effort to resist negative forces is recalled, as is its ultimate futility. The next group, 16, is squarely in IT, as the body reacts to these memories with profound sighs. But then (in 17a), quite unexpectedly, a new vision materializes, of a much earlier time in BT, a time of absolute simplicity and security, represented by the Alberti basses and the turn to (D,F,A). This engenders a spiritual recovery in IT, and another vision of a world replete with sparks (in AT) fills the mind. Now a strange image appears: is it a memory of childhood toys, now lost forever, or just another set of abstract objects? Somehow, this seemingly innocuous image calls forth another, in which the most terrible threats to one's security (in BT, past or future?) are envisaged (19). As a defence, the mind reverts back to its memories from groups 13 and 14 (in 20a and 20b, with their inevitable negative sequel in 20c), and closes this sub-episode with a final aborted retake of the same memories (in 20d). Suddenly, the mind finds a way to invert something in this memory to produce a new insight, an inspiration, which gives it a new confidence (21a). The power of the Divine is sensed (21b) and the feelings of inspiration confirmed (21c).

Part III seems to me, because of its suprapersonal tone, to clearly indicate a reference to BT, to a time when the subject felt him- or herself to have existed mainly as part of a mass of persons. In 22 this collectivity cries out on the tone F, appealing against its suffering. The causes of its pain are palpable in 23, but here an individual voice is heard to rise up over and against them. As the music touches on A minor, the crowd sallies in a song of supplication and propitiation (24). There is a flashback here, to a time before the suffering (in 25), when the surrounding social realm seemed friendly and accepting, at least superficially (the "folk song" in D). And then group 26, a return to the time of suffering, with the collectivity assembling around a project of salvation and beginning to drag itself, as if in ranks, toward the light. The mass begins a passionate song of deliverance, and pouring out its soul, brings its project to a climax, where it meets with a tragic reversal (26c, in B-flat-minor) and profound disappointment (the drop to A minor). A new catastrophe strikes and assumes whirlwind proportions, nullifying everything that the striving mass has built up (27a, b). One is tempted here to posit a fourth line of time, namely the recurrent historic experience of the Jewish people, a world-historical *leitmotif.* One could call this HJT. But at the same time, as table 7.4 indicates, an interpretation of the images of part III in AT is also possible.

Part IV continues in BT, as the crowd is remembered in prayer (28a). As this praying becomes increasingly repetitive and lacking in power (28b), the mind (in IT) imagines a pair of shocks being administered to the assembly, as if a Torah had fallen out of the open ark and a candelabra had been knocked over. Once again the self-protective powers of the mind intervene, as another shimmering passage, representing the restoration of divine light in AT, is sounded (30). But the prayer activity in BT resumes in 31, now with a more positive, energetic tone. The place of prayer now shrinks back to IT, as imagined congregants wait expectantly, sensing something is about to happen (32). Their expectations are met as an image crystallizes, of the *Shekhinah* (the Divine conceived as a feminine, protective presence) descending to protect the flock with her all-encompassing wings, one of the most beautiful places in the whole work (33). We return to AT (in IT) as the whole of Creation is imagined attempting to align itself in harmony with the *Shekhinah,* first its unconscious objects (34), then its conscious subjects (35).

The coda returns first to IT, as the mind tires of its imaginative efforts and begins to notice the body's basic activity (36a). This leads, with a certain inevitability, to thoughts of death (in BT, future) as the final sinking into the unknown is imagined, first in its purely physical aspect (36b and beginning of 36c), and then as spiritual fulfillment (end of 36c).

Detailed Analysis

While table 7.4 lists some basic pitch-structural features of each of the measure-groups of *SparkskrapS,* a more detailed analysis of selected passages, corresponding to what was provided for the Symphony, is clearly warranted. In this section of my essay, I will survey a number of passages, keeping my comments as brief as possible. Unlike with the Symphony, there is no way of presenting these passages in a simple-to-complex order, so I will proceed chronologically.

Example 7.21 presents a sketch of the opening passage of the work, measure-group 1. The opening chromatic gesture, occurring thirteen times in various forms, represents the projections of light or, as the example suggests, the trajectories of sparks. Of interest are the overlapping seven-tone octatonic subsets that accumulate toward the end of the example, while the emphasis on $<B^{\flat}1, D^{\flat}2>$ as the underlying dyad of the cadential sonority is of long-range significance.

Example 7.21 *SparkskrapS*, measure-group 1, mm. 1–13

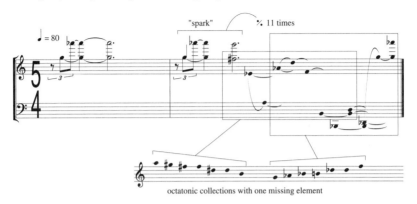

octatonic collections with one missing element

Measure-groups 2 and 3 are covered in example 7.22, a and b. In the first of these we see, in mm. 14–18, the chromatic pitch set from C4 to E4, which gives way to the chromatic pitch hexachord B♭3 to E♭4 in mm. 19 ff. The latter opens up into a harmony with pc content (10,11,2,3), which Anhalt refers to as a 1+3+1-type collection. This has a referential role in several passages to come and of course points the way to the augmented hexachord, which makes its appearance in mm. 24–35. In group 3, the single augmented hexachord (2,3,6,7,10,11) is prolonged by a series of transformations that take it to other forms of the same hexachord and lead them back to it (see the collections grouped in rounded boxes in ex. 7.22a, and by the lower beam of ex. 7.22b). Octatonic collections are also in evidence (grouped in straight-edged boxes in ex. 7.22a), first in the quasi-palindromically related melodies at mm. 26–7 and 29–31, and then in a chord at m. 32 and a series of chords in mm. 34–5. The chord at m. 32 is notable for its top note, E♭6, which interrupts a rising whole-tone scale from G♭5 to F♯6 in the structural upper voice of the passage (see upward-stemmed notes in ex. 7.22b, top staff), forming an arpeggiation of a diminished triad, <G♭5,C6,E♭6,F♯6> (open, stemmed notes in the same place). At mm. 32–3 (ex. 7.22a) a third interruption (after the two octatonic melodies) occurs, this one a more literal palindrome – again based on the 1+3+1 pattern. The use of an interval of 8 at the bottom of a widely spread chord, prevalent throughout group 3, is also a characteristic feature of the work.

The next example (7.23) concerns group 5a. Here, the augmented hexachord (1,2,5,6,9,10) dominates at first, but is polluted with the addition of C6 in mm. 49, producing a septachord that also contains a five-tone subset of octatonic I = (0,1,3,4,6,7,9,10). Its T_2

Example 7.22 *SparkskrapS*, measure-group 2, mm. 14–35

a. sketch

14 - 18, "moiré"   19 - 23, "vertigo, doubt"

1 + 3 + 1

24 - 35, canticle-like

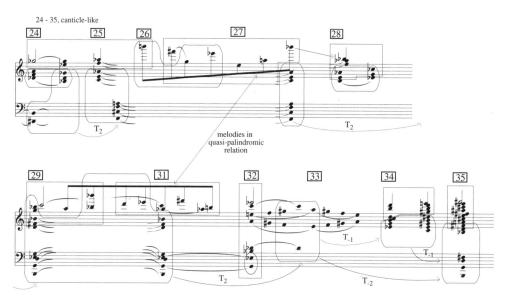

melodies in
quasi-palindromic
relation

b. reduction of mm. 24 - 35   prolongation of (0, 1, 3, 4, 6, 7, 9, 10)

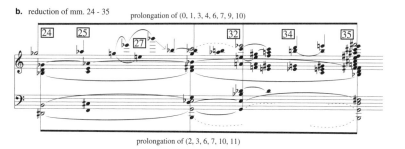

prolongation of (2, 3, 6, 7, 10, 11)

Example 7.23 *SparkskrapS*, measure-group 5a, mm. 47–55

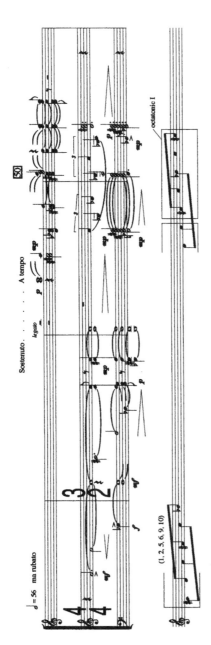

Example 7.23 *(continued)*

(3,4,7,8,11,0) takes over in mm. 51–3, but a sharply contrasting textural stream introduces octatonic I in scalar form (with F5 as a chromatic passing tone), and progresses to a quick alternation of octatonic collections I and II (T_1 of I), presented as a tremolo of six- and seven-part chords. Underneath this octatonic tremolo, I gains further expression in a thrice-stated and progressively expanded melodic motive.

The three measures of group 7, presented in example 7.24, contain a motive (m. 62) and two straightforward transformations (mm. 63–64). These are labelled "Scraps" by the composer in his sketches, and I have taken the label seriously, in its connotation of outworn hand-me-downs, interpreting the passage as traditionally tonal. This involves hearing some of the notes as harmonically functional for only parts of their time spans, a strategy indicated by representing harmonically functional events as filled-in note heads and their tied, nonfunctional anticipations or suspensions as Xs. The only exception occurs with the final chord, in which the top two pitches, notated as filled-in note heads, are nonharmonic, but function in the incomplete augmented hexachord presented at that point. The resulting harmonic progression, audible if one plays only the filled-in note heads, expresses B-flat minor in the most direct way, though it can also be heard in E-flat-minor. The first harmonic event, a B-flat-major triad, is obscured by anticipation of the E-flat-minor triad in the bass, but is not essential to the tonal argument in any case.

Example 7.25 (group 10) contains two melodic segments and a cadence. The melodic segments are loosely palindromic, the second also introducing imitation. The cadence is another alternation of two chords. The pitch basis of the palindromic melody, a 1+3+1 tetrachord (<F5,G♭5,A5,B♭5>) spills over to determine the structure of the passage as a whole, up to the cadence. What we have here is a registrally unfolded cycle of such tetrachords, in which the outer elements (e.g., F5 and B♭5 in the above) are mostly treated as harmonically primary, while the two inner pitches are mostly treated both as melodic passing tones and as sustained but secondary harmonic tones. The result is a primary harmony in which a B-flat-minor triad predominates, and a secondary harmony that takes the form <E2,G2,B3,D4,F♯4,A4,C♯6,E6>. The latter is pitch-symmetrical about E4 and pc-symmetrical around (4,10). The cadence of the passage moves to a quasi-pentatonic white-note collection (<B3,D4,F4,A4,B5,E5>), which obliterates the preceding harmonic field while retaining E6 as its top note and, conceivably, its root.

Most of group 14 is presented in example 7.26, a vivid instance of Anhalt's ability to compose expressively and with symbolic power while crafting a texture that places extreme demands on his skill as a poly-

Example 7.24 *SparkskrapS*, measure-group 7, mm. 62–4: "Scraps"

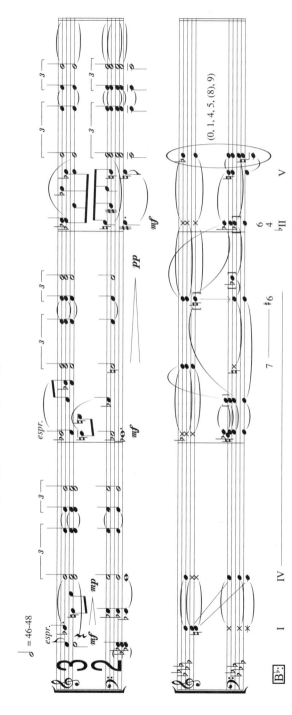

Example 7.25 *Sparkskrap̌S*, measure-group 10, mm. 75–81

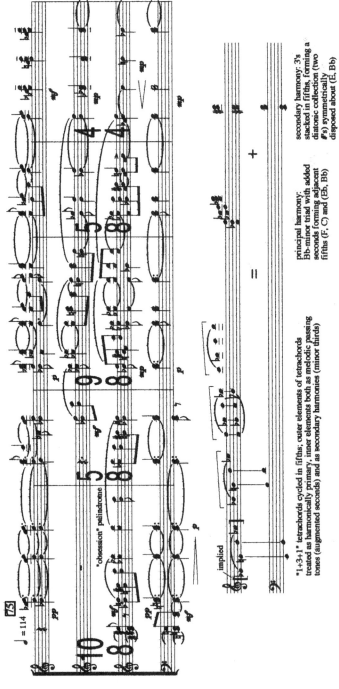

"1+3+1" tetrachords cycled in fifths; outer elements of tetrachords treated as harmonically primary, inner elements both as melodic passing tones (augmented seconds) and as secondary harmonies (minor thirds)

principal harmony:
B♭-minor triad with added seconds forming adjacent fifths (F, C) and (B♭, B♭)

secondary harmony: 3's stacked in fifths, forming a diatonic collection (two ♯'s) symmetrically disposed about (E, B♭)

Example 7.25 *(continued)*

white-note harmony, with
E sounding as possible root

phonist. The passage consists of up to eight voices engaged in a slowly accelerating descent, sometimes individually, often in groups of two or three. The example groups the voices on three staves. The lowest of these has a single voice descending, chromatically at first, then by 3s. The voices of *each* of the upper staves, after departing from pc E, group to execute in mm. 112–14 a succession of chromatically descending augmented hexachords, one per measure, with the middle staff's patterns a beat behind the top staff's. In mm. 115–16, the voices of the top staff thin out and become harmonically secondary to augmented hexachords formed jointly by the voices of the bottom two staves, and in the last three measures the harmonic colour changes, first as all voices coalesce on the downbeat of 117 in an extended tertian sonority, then as they enter an octatonic field in 117–18. In the final measure of ex. 7.26 a new split arises as the voices of the lower staff lead to an E-flat-major triad, while those of the upper staff perpetuate the opposition of thirds (4s and 3s), the former represented by $<G3,B3>$ in relation to $E\flat$ and the latter by $<C^\sharp4,E4>$ in relation to $(G,B\flat)$.

Example 7.26 also provides two increasingly simpler reductions of the passage. In the first, accented (long, on the beat) tones are retained and unaccented ones omitted. The result is quite enlightening.

Example 7.26 *SparkskrapS*, measure-group 14, mm. 111–19: cascading sequences

Example 7.26 *(continued)*

In mm. 112–14, the upper voices (all except the bass) are shown to arpeggiate one augmented hexachord per measure, with a T_{11} relation between successive measures, while the reduction of mm. 115–19 merely clarifies the observations made above about these measures. At the next level of reduction, arpeggiated harmonies are grouped into simultaneities in mm. 112–16, and some passing tones and repeated notes are eliminated from the later measures. Here we see, in mm. 112–14, a kind of multivoiced fourth-species counterpoint, with augmented hexachords functioning as off-the-beat consonances (not considering the bass), while whole-tone collections are produced by suspension of augmented triads on the downbeats. In mm. 115–17, the upper voices enter progressively into relations of relative consonance with the bass, which amounts to saying that the bass notes begin to sound like roots. And the change in harmonic colour noted above is fully palpable in this further reduction of the last three measures.

In this passage, E is significant as a starting point because, isolated as it is, it looks forward to group 28a, the opening segment of part IV, where its tritone counterpart (B^b) will be similarly focused upon as a point of departure, and it does so by way of group 22, the parallel place at the start of part III, in which an isolated F is gradually transformed into the dyad (F,B). Both the cadence on E^b in m. 119 (arrived at in the bass after a chromatic descent to A and arpeggiation through $F^\sharp$) and the overall shift from augmented hexachords to octatony are important symbols of the pull of the *Sitra Ahra*, as is the pervasive descent.

The oppressive power of the *Sitra Ahra* is fully evident in example 7.27 (15), in which octatonic collections prevail. Governing this whole passage are G^b in the upper voice and B^b in the bass. The former, as G^b3, serves as a pedal in mm. 123–31, but beginning in m. 128, overlapping voices trace an arpeggio ($<A3,D4,F4,A^b4,C^\sharp5>$) that leads to a climactic G^b5, in m. 136. B^b1, the bass pitch in m. 123, is immediately displaced by A^b1, which moves up to D2 in the first phrase of the passage (mm. 123–7). After a restatement of B^b1 (m. 128), the second phrase (128–31) takes the bass line from A^b1 through a rising arpeggio ($<C2, E^b2,G^b2,B^b2>$) to C^b3. In the third phrase (132–7) the tritone $<C^b2,F2=E^\sharp2>$ is unfolded in the bass (mm. 132–5), and the semitone-related tritone $<E2,B^b2>$ is then reached (m. 136) via a rising motion to G2, its bisector. This brings the bass line back to its pc starting point of B^b, now reinforced by its tritone associate E. This outer-voice framework is depicted in example 28.

Partitioning of the passage in example 7.27 by the three octatonic collections is indicated on the analytical staves by the use of vertical

Example 7.27 *Sparkskraps*, measure-group 15, mm. 123–37: the *Sitra Ahra*

Example 7.27 (*continued*)

Example 7.27 (continued)

Example 7.28 Outer-voice framework of example 7.27

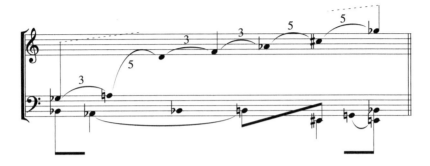

dotted lines. Once again, I = (C,C#,D#,E,F#,G,A,Bb), while II is its T₁ and III its T₂. There are two places in the passage where the harmony is based on (1,2,5,6,9,10), an augmented hexachord. The first is at the cadence of the second phrase, in m. 131, while the other, in m. 133, is fleeting and less important. More crucial in this second instance, and also in mm. 134–5, is the passing allusion to tonal centres. These produce little islands of light in the turbid atmosphere of thick octatonic harmony. In the first of these, in m. 133–4, there is a strikingly clear approach, from a seventh chord with added b6 on Bb2 via a whole-tone sonority on B2 (the latter functioning as an augmented-sixth chord) to a $^6_4$ chord with added ninth (and the sixth appearing in two forms) over C3 (m. 134, beat 2). The sense of F major is unmistakable. Considerably more obscure is the tonal allusion to F-sharp in mm. 134–5. This is produced by the simulation of a V $^6_5$ chord in the first part of m. 135, the bass E#2 of which is surrounded by F#s, and by the diatonic harmony on the last eighth of the bar, which I have read as simulating VI $^6_5$. Whether or not one hears this second tonal allusion, the harmonic-colour shift on the 3rd and 6th eighth notes of m. 135, with their pentatonic and diatonic chords respectively, is striking in context.

The music represented in example 7.29 (group 17a) is of unique character, and represents one of the high flights of compositional fancy – the "Gong" section of the Symphony comes to mind as another – that mark Anhalt's work and distinguish him from the general run of composers. In this example no reduced score is given, because the texture is essentially irreducible. It consists of many layers of undulating and arpeggiated figuration, coming under the descriptors "Alberti Pattern" and "Lyricism" in Anhalt's notes. "Vision of lost beauty and innocence" would be equally apt, as this passage clearly signals an aroused memory, veiled yet richly provided with sensible

Example 7.29 *SparkskrapS*, measure-group 17a, mm. 143–54: lyricism of
Alberti patterns, figured bass analysis

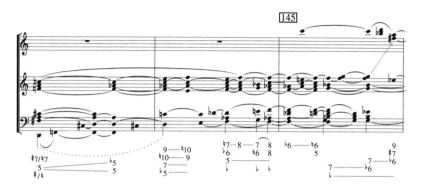

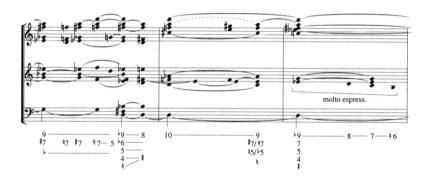

qualities, of treasured times and persons from the distant past. What is
utterly remarkable here is that in a texture of from eight to twelve
parts – the surface of which has an almost Ivesian appearance of layered disparity, and certainly of polychordal diffuseness – the overall
result is harmonically unified and, in fact controlled by the bass.
Struggling for a way to show this succinctly, I could find no better tool
than traditional figured-bass notation, because all immediate linear
activity (within the measure, that is) in this passage falls into standard,
or near-standard patterns of step-motion descent, the main difference
being that traditionally incompatible patterns are superimposed to
generate a surface in which rhythmic and accentual as well as harmonic frameworks are blurred. I will not give a detailed account of
surface linear activity in this passage, since the reader can easily grasp
it without assistance. All figured-bass patterns refer to the one or more
stemmed bass notes under which they are found. The bass begins on

Example 7.29 *(continued)*

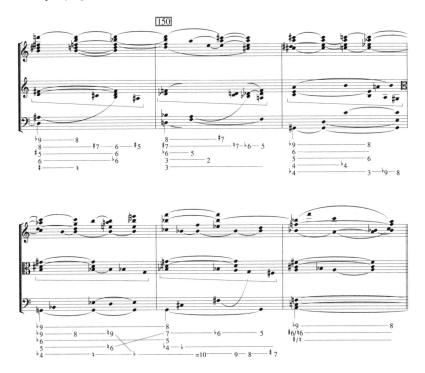

D2 and rises by step from D3 to G3 before dropping back down to D3 in m. 146. A shifting sense of tonality is engendered through these motions, beginning with D and moving through F (in 144–5) to G (146–8). Beginning in m. 148, a tenor-register voice intones a series of six measure-long sighing motives. In mm. 149 ff., the harmony takes on the aspect of parallel 6-chords, the bass taking the third of the prevailing harmony as the sighing motives trace such more-or-less standard patterns as 8–♯7–6–♯5, ♯7–7–♭6–5, ♭4–3–♭9–8, etc. Of course, the fauxbourdon is highly embellished and idiosyncratically stylized, but it is audible nonetheless. In m. 153 the bass, on G, sounds the harmonic root while a G-minor sonority (with F6 and a momentary C♯3, tritone associate of G) is unveiled in the upper voices; but in the next measure, as the bass reaches A3, we get, instead of the expected dominant harmony of D minor, a distorted from of F $^6_3$, with C5 and F5 contradicted by C♯4 and F♯4, and a dissonant B♭ resolving to A in two octaves but not the third. All the same, at the tonal level there is an implication, in the bass motion of mm. 150–4, of a reassertion of the prevailing D tonality. (D,F,A) in this passage may be heard to displace

263 Alternatives of Voice

($E^{\flat}$,$G^{\flat}$,$B^{\flat}$), from which most of the prominent tones in the music up to this point have been selected.

Example 7.30 contains an extract from group 18, one of the few passages labelled in the sketches themselves. It would appear that, as Anhalt composed page 91 of the sketches, he devised the name for the work as a whole, perhaps because the figures he was notating on that page (which appear in this example) capture the dual essence of "Sparkscraps,"[37] as things that can appear both incandescent and used up at the same time. As the entry in table 7.4 makes clear, the label "Scintillae" appears on this page along with "Sparkscraps," but it is clear that the latter is the better descriptor, capturing as it does not only the scintillating aspect of this music – evident perhaps most clearly in the bell-sound sextolets in mm. 161 and 163 – but its evocation of tales told too often, in the nursery-rhymelike eighth-note figures that begin each measure.

The pitch structures of this passage are based on the augmented hexachord, a form of which – (1,2,5,6,9,10) – occupies m. 160. The first bell complex, in m. 161, is a corrupted form of the same set, in which four of its elements are transformed by T_1, while the other two are held fixed. The basic hexachord returns in m. 162, while in the next bar a seventh pc (8) is added. Interestingly, this septachord contains a hexachordal subset (all the pitches except the low $B^{\flat}2$ in the first half of m. 163) that is T_{11} of the hexachord played by the bell-like instruments in m. 161 and repeated in m. 163. The passage is undergirded by pairs of pedal tones in two octaves. In the lowest octave are $B^{\flat}2$ and $G^{\flat}3$, which relate to the E-flat-minor triad that had played so important a role thus far, while in the next higher octave the pitch triad <$A3,F4,A4$> recalls the D-minor triad prolonged in the passage analyzed in example 7.29 as well as the As that undergird group 17b (see table 7.4).

A version of the refrain heard five times in various transformations in part II is given in example 7.31. This one is particularly straightforward since it consists of a simple and harmonically transparent sequence in which a pattern is stated and imitated twice at intervals of a descending semitone. The pitch material of each statement is taken from a hexachordal subset of one of the octatonic collections (all three are therefore represented), and the voices of each statement settle on a symmetrical six-tone chord (with some octave doubling) in which one diminished triad is superposed on another. It is hard to imagine a more direct translation, into Anhalt's musical language, of his notion of scraps.

If example 7.31 is suitably literal, the next example is appropriately subtle. It shows an interesting transformation of the refrain, its fifth

Example 7·30 *SparkskrapS*; germ material

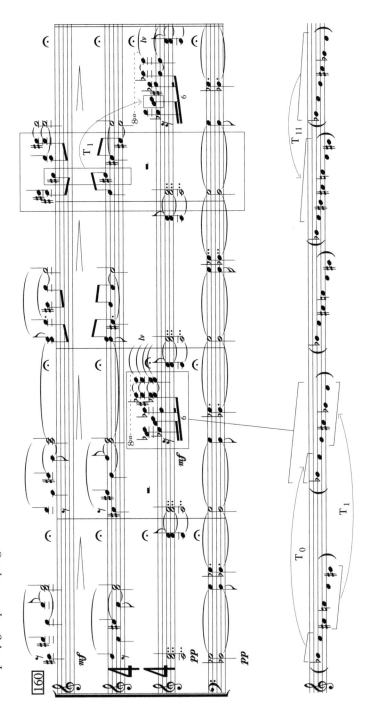

Example 7.31 *Sparkskraps*: threefold sequence of symmetrical octatonic chords

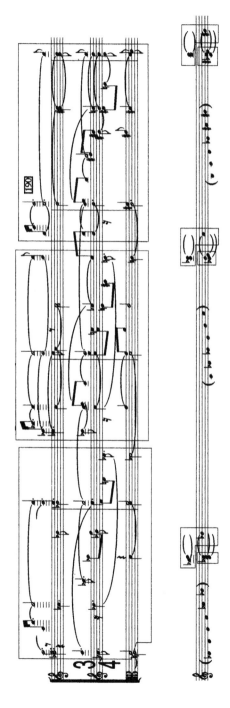

Example 7.32 *SparkskrapS*, measure-group 21c, mm. 201–14: harmonic and
aggregate structure

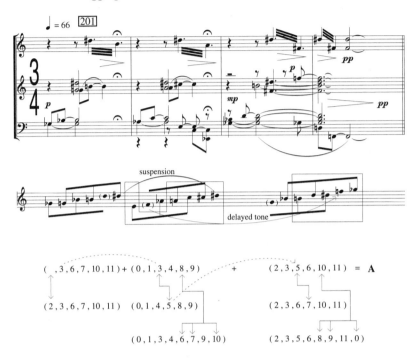

statement in part II. This transformation, which I have called *Refrain**,
has rising statements of a basic motive. The interval of transformation
is 2, and it may be regarded as the symbolic antithesis of the −1 in the
basic refrain. As well, refrain* is not a literal sequence, since one of its
voices is fixed, and each statement brings added pitch material. In fact,
the unambiguous but intricate set-structure of this passage makes it a
good representation of the *sephira* (emanation) called *hokhmah* (intellect or intelligence). The passage begins with an incomplete form of
the augmented hexachord (2,3,6,7,10,11), incomplete since 2 is missing. This is transformed by T_2 (and includes $4 = T_2(2)$) in the next
measure (202), except that the highest voice remains on D$\sharp$ (=E$\flat$),
which it will treat as a pedal, instead of rising by a whole tone to F.
Interestingly, the resulting hexachord – (0,1,3,4,8,9) – can also be
seen as a deformation of octatonic I, in which the subset (6,7,10) is replaced by 8. These relations are diagrammed in the example, below
the score. In the last two bars of the example (mm. 203–4), another
transformation by T_2 takes us to the hexachord (2,3,5,6,10,11). Like
its predecessor, this one can be seen as a deformation of either the

augmented hexachord or the octatonic collection. Moreover, the three hexachords presented in this passage complete the aggregate, as the last one gives us the D missing from the first and the F missing from the second.

The first three measure-groups of part III (22–4) are sketched in example 7.33. The first of these is the heterophonic treatment of F, which mutates into a similar treatment of (F,B), by way of the set $\{(E,B^\flat)+(F,B)\}$. This passage (205–24), sketched in only one measure in the example, recalls the Symphony by using the Ur-set-class of that work. Yet no musical utterance could be further from the Symphony's polyphonic spirit or from the tightness with which it reins in its emotional life. Here we have an outpouring that will not let itself be contained, the very force of which could not in the least abide the control necessary for polyphony to exist. The measure-group that follows, in mm. 225–31, is one of the most complex passages in *SparkskrapS*, and for the good reason that it effects a transition between two utterly different musical worlds – that just described, and the equally passionate but highly formal and stylized simulation of high baroque pathos (in mm. 232–6). In this transition, the tritone (F,B) is led first to $\{(5,11)+(0,6)\}$, then via T_{11} and T_9 to $\{(1,7)+(2,8)\}$, to which F (5), the bisector of (2,8), is added by being held through this transformational activity in the bass. What has consisted until this point in opposing tritones now thickens into opposed whole-tone subsets (2-partitions) organized in two streams. The top stream is organized in parallel five-pitch chords, the first of which – <$D^\flat 5,F5,A5,D^\flat 6,G6$> – is heard toward the end of m. 226. This is transposed by descending semitones through a minor third, and its top voice is abandoned, producing the chord <$B^\flat 4,D5,G^\flat 5,B^\flat 5$> at the end of m. 228. A further T_{11} lowers this augmented triad to <$A4,D^\flat 5,F5,A5$>, which is then voice led, at the end of m. 229, to the diminished triad <$A4,C5,E^\flat 5,A5$>. The bottom stream of whole-tone collections begins on <$G^\flat 3,C4,G^\flat 4$> at the end of m. 226. This is transposed as follows: T_3, T_9, T_9, leading to <$E^\flat 3,A3,E^\flat 4$> at the end of m. 228. This chord modulates from 2- to 3-partitioning as it becomes <$E^\flat 3,C4,E^\flat 4$>. In the meantime, a solo melody is introduced as a counterpoint to these chordal streams, beginning in m. 227. Composed mainly of 7s and 6s, this rising melody, once freely inverted, will turn into the beautiful "apotheosis theme" of 26b, to be discussed in connection with the next example. Intoned here by the baritone horn, it recalls that instrument's rising solo in group 4a. In terms of duplication or shared whole-tone collection membership, its principal tones associate first (in m. 228) to the chords of the lower of the two streams just described, then (in m. 229) to those of the upper stream, as if mediating

Example 7.33 *SparkskrapS*, measure-groups 22–4: "Appeal" mutating into "Hymn"

Example 7.33 (*continued*)

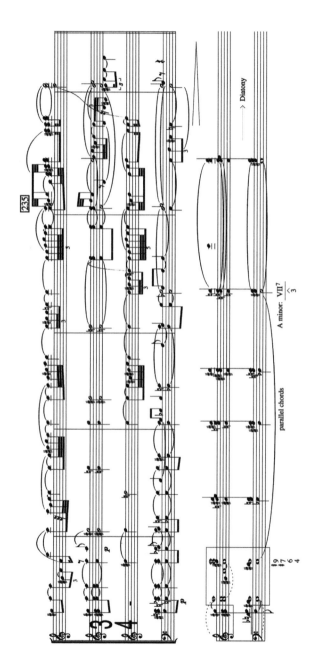

between them. At the end of m. 229 both chord streams and solo melody contribute to a unified sonority that is held through m. 230 and into m. 231, the chord <E3,C4,E♭4(=D♯4),A4,C5,E♭5(=D♯5),A5>. Neighbouring motion on the downbeat of m. 231 and further melodic activity in that measure make it clear that this chord should be heard as a modified A-minor triad in $\frac{6}{4}$ position, and as introducing the key of A minor. This brings us to m. 232 and group 24. Here a highly embellished upper voice rises stepwise – <C6,B5,C♯6,D♯6,D6,E6,F6> – while inner voices descend by step to form diminished-seventh chords underneath these top notes. The bass, meanwhile, drops chromatically from E3 to C3, adding a fifth pc to the diminished-seventh chords, the final one of which has the sound of vii°7 in A over 3. These technicalities do not, however, convey the impassioned atmosphere of this passage as it rises up out of the preceding transition and in which the sudden emergence of quasi-Bachian tonality carries with it a poignant, almost painful surge of longing for communion with the *Ein Sof*.

The next, very long example comprises group 26a–c. These groups are easily the most memorable in *SparkskrapS*. They contain melodic and harmonic substance of rarely paralleled richness and unfold a climax that is gripping in the attainment and shattering in the aftermath. The passage follows an eruption of pseudo-folk song in the Hungarian manner (group 25), in a transient but blatantly asserted D-major. This prepares one to hear its opening measures (243–5) as continuing a D-minor harmony with a melody of a Mahlerian cast in octatonic II (which contains D and F, but not A) grafted to it. The introduction of A3 in the melody, on the downbeat of m. 246, necessitates a harmonic shift, and the other voices oblige by arranging themselves to make the augmented hexachord (0,1,4,5,8,9), labelled A. As the melody fragments into short, imitatively related motives (246–8), the outer voices, in combination with key inner-voice pitches, express a harmonic progression in the key of D-flat, sketched and labelled on the analytical staff; at the same time, augmented hexachords are represented as prominent chords. Measures 249–50 turn towards the key of F major, which can be understood to link up with the earlier D minor. As thick, throbbing chords rise persistently, the upper voice moves <C5,D5,E5> while the bass descends from F2 to C2. Augmented hexachord A appears again on the third eighth of m. 250, but functions in context as a $\frac{6}{4}$ harmony on the dominant. Just preceding this chord, and now contributing to it, a new *espressivo* melody is initiated. With the addition of the modifier *molto* to this ascription, group 26b begins and the melody (in mm. 251–2) trumpets out a characteristic octatonic motive that will sound several times in the ensuing measures. I have called this eight-note motive (of seven pitches, since the penultimate one is immediately repeated) the "apotheosis theme," as it seems to me to represent all of humanity's aspirations, as a collective, for unification with the Divine. The harmony of mm. 251–2 makes reference to augmented hexachord C – (2,3,6,7,10,11), which as the complement of A has already occurred twice in the immediately preceding measures – and to two octatonic collections. At the same time, the first half of m. 252 contains another characteristic approach to a V $_4^6$ in F.

As the example shows, mm. 253–6 contain three statements of the apotheosis theme. The first, in mm. 253–4, is a half-step higher than the initial statement, while the next reverts to the original pitch level, but is answered in stretto by its T_3. The upper voice of the music (the top voice in the chords), instead of reaching an expected F5 after m. 251, reverses direction and begins to descend. This descent continues throughout mm. 253–6, over a bass that descends chromatically from C2 to G♭1, but no clear tonal affiliation is evident in these measures, in which a dense interweaving of the complementary augmented hexachords B and D with all three octatonic collections is discernible (see analytical staff, in which, as before, octatonic collections are enclosed in straight-edged boxes, and augmented hexachords in rounded ones). Beginning in m. 257 the music speeds up and the upper voice begins to rise once again, carrying all the inner voices with it. The bass moves from G♭1 to G1 and thence through a series of fifths to B♭1. The tones of this fifth-series – <G1,C2,F2> – sound harmonically functional because recognizably tertian sonorities are placed over them, though they are of tonally uncertain effect. But once on B♭1, the bass begins to rise chromatically to E♭2, breaking its pattern only once, to precede E♭2 with another reference to B♭1. This makes clear that E♭2 is an important goal, and looking back over the bass line in mm. 256–60, it is evident that it is to be understood as arpeggiating an E-flat-minor triad in 6-position – <G♭,B♭,E♭2> – in preparation for arriving on the massive F1 that underlies the triple *forte* B-flat-minor $_4^6$ chord in m. 262. As this tonal and emotional climax is approached (in mm. 258–61), the texture of the music becomes more nearly homophonic and the bass tones get to sound like roots, but all the verticals are more faithfully described in terms of augmented hexachords or octatonic collections than as tonal chords. It is only at a broader level that a careful preparation of the tonal eruption at m. 262 is discernible. (Example 7.34b summarizes the action of the bass line in mm. 243–65). One should also notice the appearance, at m. 257, of a new motive of chromatically descending tritones in a characteristic

Example 7.34a *SparkskrapS*, measure-group 26: emotional climax; the apotheosis and tragedy of idealism

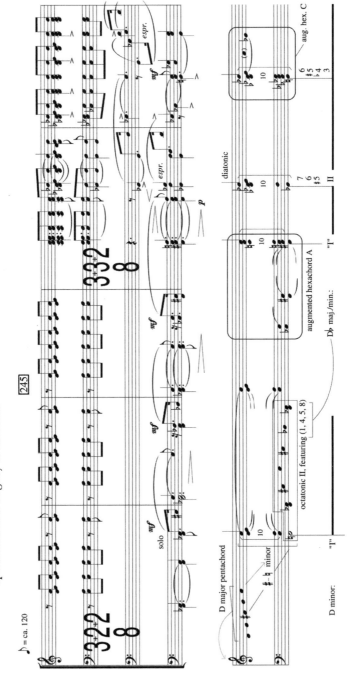

Example 7.34a (*continued*)

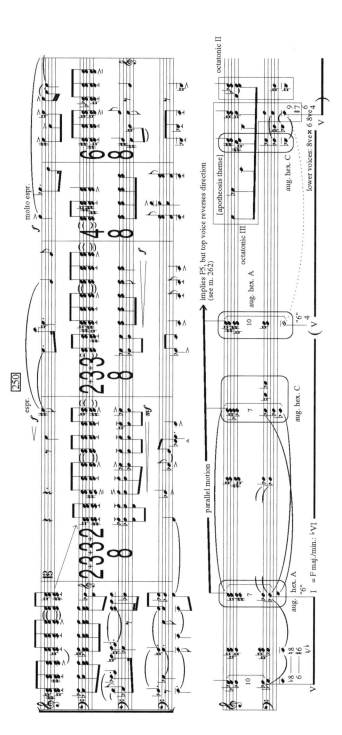

Example 7.34a *(continued)*

Example 7.34a (*continued*)

Example 7.34a *(continued)*

dactylic rhythm, labelled *Davenen*, a characteristic style of Jewish prayer.[38] This plays a central role in groups 28a and b, and 29, and will be discussed in connection with example 7.35.

The last six bars of the example (group 26c) represent the tragic reversal experienced just as the intense aspirations expressed in the preceding passage seem about to reach their intended goal. Here we have two statements of a threefold sequence that descends by whole steps, and thus another transformation (the first in part III) of the refrain. The first statement departs from the B-flat-minor chord mentioned

Example 7.34b *SparkskrapS*: bass line summary of ex. 7.34a

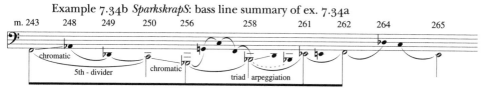

above, while the second drops a half-step to an A-minor chord in a representation of crushing disappointment. Both statements contain the apotheosis theme, the tonal potential of which is overwhelmed as the surrounding tonal harmony of each dissolves into grizzled octatony, and any hint of the more open-sounding augmented hexachord is eschewed. It can only be significant that just as this whole passage emerged from the "Hungarian" music of group 25, it ends with the snapped Hungarian rhythmic motive from the end of the apotheosis theme, repeated six times within the two sequences. This is perhaps the single section of the work where an invocation of biographical time seems most pressing, and where a sense that it is indeed autobiographical time is most vivid.

Example 7.35 shows the beginning of part IV, which parallels that of part III and puts these parts into an antecedent-consequent relationship. We return here to tritone-based harmony, which is a dominating element in this last large section of the work, and comes especially to the fore in the coda, which represents the gradual closing down of the mind-body. While closely related to octatonic harmony, the tritone-based passages of part IV sound like something new because they are essentially chromatic. One might describe them, in relation to the rest of the work's harmony, as antitriadic, since both augmented-hexachordal and octatonic harmony are exploited for their triadic potential in *SparkskrapS*. In example 7.35, tritone harmony is introduced by way of the *Davenen* (praying) motive, which is meant to be an iconic symbol that conflates the sound and gestural quality of traditional Jewish prayer. This motive is seen in its canonical form in mm. 300–2, in the second staff from the top. It consists of a chromatic motion from the tritone <E5,Bb5> to the tritone <Db5,G5>, in which the lower neighbour <C5,Gb5> is also touched upon. The passage as a whole begins on a multi-octave Bb, and this pc dominates throughout. The analytical staves show various motions by means of which other pcs are made prominent. For the most part these are motions through a rising or falling minor third, the termini of which are therefore related as members of the same (0,3,6,9)-type set. In mm. 297–304, all the important (terminal) pcs are members of (1,4,7,10), but in mm. 305–7 there is an expansion of structural pc content, as one motive (in the highest octave)

Example 7.35 *SparkskrapS*, measure-group 28a

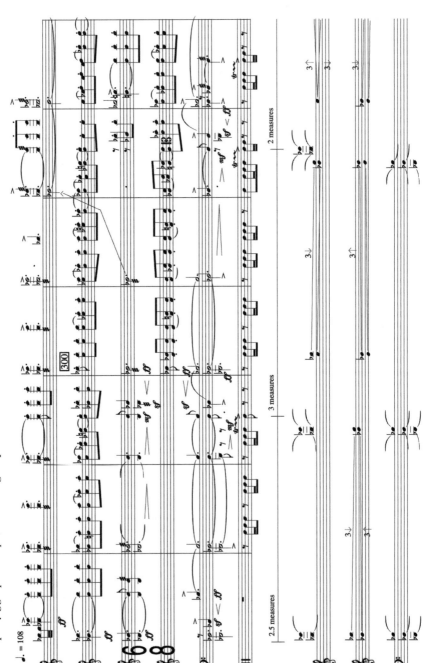

Example 7·35 (continued)

Example 7.35 (continued)

descends from <F,B> to <D,G$\sharp$> and another, in the next-lower octave, descends – by an atypical 2 – from (B,F) to (A,E$\flat$). But the goal of the passage is not aggregate completion. Instead, in the last three segments of the passage (mm. 308–15), each of the three (0,3,6,9)-type collections is assigned a different structural weight. In the first two of these segments (mm. 308–12), motivic motions outline the complete (1,4,7,10) set, two members (2,8) from the (2,5,8,11) set, and a single member (3) from (0,3,6,9), the latter serving as the pedal E$\flat$5. In the final segment (mm. 313–15), the complete (2,5,8,11) set is made structural, as are (4,10) and, once again, (3). The net result is that the seven structural pcs in mm. 313–15 form a set that is inversionally related about (A,E$\flat$) to the set formed by the structural pitches of mm. 308–12. The only pcs that have no structural role at all in this passage as a whole are C and F$\sharp$. Interestingly and, I believe, significantly, C gets used as the stable root underlying the extravagant harmonic assembly at group 30 (Ecstasy), mm. 326–31 and F$\sharp$ (=G$\flat$!) serves as the pedal tone under which the greater part of the coda (mm. 366–79, groups 36a, b) unfolds. Finally, the last melodic gesture of the piece, which represents the etherialization of consciousness, ends by arpeggiating the dyad <C6,G$\flat$6> in m. 387.

My last example (7.36) presents and simplifies another of the singular passages (group 33) in this magnificent work, in which the descent of the *Shekhinah* (the Divine as feminine protector) is depicted. The *Shekhinah* is always imaged in classical Jewish sources as having wings, under which the spiritual aspirant is portrayed as finding peace and security. To translate the act of descent and the gradual settling of immaterial "wings" Anhalt uses a form of his refrain, (i.e., a chromatically descending sequence with three statements of a pattern), but emphasizes its melodic rather than its harmonic dimension. The texture is composed of seven melodic parts on top of a bass line. The seven melodic parts are in a very complex relationship that is part contrapuntal and part heterophonic. Collectively, they outline a series of harmonic triads drawn from the set-classes (0,1,3) and (0,2,4) (see the top analytical system, top staff), which can be reduced, on the basis of registral and rhythmic considerations, to dyads of the form (0,3) and (0,2), with (0,4) in a secondary (neighbouring) role (see the middle analytical system, top staff). When the resulting dyads are heard in combination with the bass, a new series of triads is formed (see the second analytical system), this time with (0,1,4)- and (0,1,3)-types assuming the key (terminal) roles in each pattern of the sequence. Invoking a traditional interpretation of the intervallic patterns shown at this level, one can further reduce them to a chain of imperfect consonances, in which each pattern of the sequence is reduced to a minor sixth that

Example 7.36 *Sparkskraps*, measure-group 33: the *Shekhinah* descends

expands, by half-step descent of its lower pitch, to a major sixth. In my
estimation, Anhalt creates, in this brief passage, a marvellous image of
incorporeality by transforming a commonplace two-dimensional pattern into an action that seems endlessly multi-faceted. This passage

eludes easy description except by way of a reduction, the simplicity of which is illusory compared to the musical experience to which it corresponds but does not pretend to capture.

The best teachers are not above hortatory use of the occasional cliché, and Anhalt was no exception. "You must find your own voice," he would exhort a favoured student. Being one, I was forced to cover inward resentment of these well-intentioned urgings with respectful silence, duly suspicious as I was of the modernist credo of the heroic artist pushing against tradition; what spoiled the joy of learning to compose, for me and many others, was the notorious pressure of the time (it was the 1960s) to conform to the pointless agendas of the newly self-anointed masters of the "international," but basically European, new-music establishment. Ironically, twenty years later the call to find one's voice would have meant something, because for most composers music had stopped being about style and had become a matter of expression, but in the strange art-music vacuum that we as students inhabited in the '60s, finding one's voice meant inventing one's own style – a contradiction in terms if ever there was one.

A few words of explanation are in order. By musical style I mean an accepted body of ideas about the sound and structure of music, derived from a body of works. It is obvious that, for all of the nineteenth century and well into the twentieth, becoming a composer meant mastering a style or group of styles, and then personalizing it, moving beyond what one had mastered by rethinking it in significant ways. As is well known, the tempo and extent of personalization sped up in this period, so that in the 1930s and 1940s one could speak of the terrain of art music as divided into provinces, each of which was governed by the personalized style of one of the great emigré composers – Bartók, Stravinsky, and Schoenberg – as practised by him and his epigones. Of course, throughout the approximately 150 years that I am talking about, art music was also understood to be a vehicle for personal expression, which in exceptional cases – late Beethoven, Wagner from the 1850s on, Debussy – seemed to overwhelm musical style. By personal expression I mean the creation, by the composer, of bits of music as personal symbols of feelings, perceptions, imaginings, or abstract thoughts, and a conception of composition as the act of assembling such bits so as to make a coherent statement about the world. Composition as personal expression may have taken centre stage in the shadow of Wagner and Debussy, but after the First World War the balance shifted decisively to composition as style mastery, so that by 1940 to compose seriously meant to master the style of one or more of great moderns and, by way of such mastery, to inherit the whole of the central European music tradition of the eighteenth and nineteenth centuries.

For Anhalt, working as an academic in the cultural backwater of 1950s Montreal, there were other avenues to a kind of mastery. There was the French Conservatoire tradition, still being pursued by Québécois composers of the older generation, and the neomodality derived from British sources. Anhalt had had considerable exposure to the first and more than a passing interest in the second, but as a central European emigré himself, and someone who was rare, if not unique, among ambitious Canadian composers of that time in having made a deep study of each of the three great emigré figures, his only real option was to attempt a synthesis and thorough personalization of their styles. He had the equipment for this daunting task and, in my estimation, is the Canadian composer who has managed it best. The Symphony is the fruit of these labours, and offers ample support for the claim I have just made.

Sadly for many composers of the 1940s and 1950s, and also for the Symphony, the idea of composition as style mastery was fast being played out. Why? Because a style never takes hold entirely for its own merits. Underlying each style is a master narrative or set of narratives that listeners find important and fascinating. In due course, however, these stories become uninteresting, old hat, even offensive, as feminist scholars have been pointing out; once this happens, the stylistic means lose their raison d'être. While the foregoing discussion has stressed the Symphony's formal attributes and its structural detail, it is clear that it also serves as the vehicle of a narrative: a story of an individual voice that emerges into the world against a background of conflict, that struggles against odds, endures disappointment, retreats into an inner world, re-emerges with redoubled determination, and, by tapping into the energies of the community, achieves victory. At the same time, it is clear that this is also the story, with this or that detail changed, of many a symphony from Beethoven on.

When a style gets played out because no one wants to hear the stories it can tell, a new style should by rights emerge to replace it. But this is a cultural project requiring time and the relatively slow development of new musical resources, particularly in the absolutely crucial dimensions of pitch and surface rhythm. For a complex of reasons that have yet to be fully understood, such development was not possible in the decades after the Second World War, and has not really become possible since.[39] Instead, some young composers achieved power and influence by successfully posing as creators of personal styles from scratch, on the one hand, and as sole legitimate heirs to the tradition of Beethoven, Wagner, and Debussy, on the other. This bizarre distortion of the romantic idea of the artist was in fact a bogus grafting of the idea of personal expression on to that of style. Style created from scratch, style without mastery of anything or responsibility toward anything except the constraints one has cooked up, is an oxymoron. Yet this is what was being propounded by leading composers of the 1950s and 1960s, some of whom have scarcely changed their tune since then.

For Anhalt, the temptation to go along with this way of thinking was not small, since he shared in the then common, if now self-evidently silly, belief in musical progress. But he did not end up going along – mainly, I think, because he could not betray the mastery he had so painstakingly but fully achieved. In practical terms, this came down, and continues to come down, to a matter of being true to one's ear, to demanding that one pass judgment on every detail, using all of one's musical experience to reach a verdict. For Anhalt, the store of such experience was great and deeply lived; hence the judgments were invariably harsh. It was therefore impossible for him to compose avant-garde or academic music in the manner of those times, or to resort to chance, that last refuge of nonmastery.

Instead, Anhalt became one of the earlier North American composers to see that style (personalized or self-initiated) was no longer a viable option, and that one would have to turn to personal expression to make headway as a musical artist. This is all the more remarkable because he was able to take this turn while well into his fifties, after giving up on devoting himself to electronic music and in the wake of some only partially successful efforts at language-based and multimedia composition. The challenge for him was to hold on to the mastery he had attained, but to refashion the craft in which it consists for the new task of personal expression – to make over the tools he had learned to use with such virtuosity in polyphonic composition in the European tradition, to create the more homophonic and heterophonic and more timbrally conceived musical symbols that he now needed. In my view he fully managed this for the first time with *Winthrop*, and in a musically purer (because linguistically unencumbered) form, in the orchestral music of the late 1980s.

The distance between the Symphony and *SparkskrapS* can now be measured. It is not that the latter is tonal where the former is not, because as I have shown the Symphony is in fact more tonal in the traditional sense than is *SparkskrapS*. The difference is that the Symphony is tonal because it derives from styles which derive, in turn, from tonal styles. Its tonality is therefore immanent, or to use a metaphor Anhalt used in class with respect to Schoenberg's op. 11, no. 1, many of its passages are "drenched in tonality." With *SparkskrapS*, tonality is symbolic, and it comes and goes according to what is being symbolically represented. It can be described, contrastingly, as emergent tonality, since what emerges can also recede from view, and the manner of emergence, whether traditional or not, will vary according to the demands posed by the representational task. The same considerations explain the differences between the two works with respect to surface rhythm, texture, and density of content. The Symphony is thoroughly metric, usually polymetric in fact, and is constructed entirely in waves of intensity, always progressing to and receding from climaxes. The only exceptions to this prevailing character are in some of the passages of the slow movement, which, significantly, are closer in spirit to *SparkskrapS* than anything else in the earlier work. The textures of the Symphony are almost all polyphonic, with much use of disguised canonic procedures. The flow of ideas is rapid, the individual variations are packed with content, and literal repetition is avoided at all levels. All these attributes have one and only one source, which is the style (or styles) that Anhalt had personalized to be able to write this exceptional work. Apart from some variations in the slow movement, there is one section that stands apart from the rest of the work. This is section VI, or intermezzo II in part 1 of the development of movement 1, the so-called "Gong." Here, it is as if Anhalt stepped outside the stylistic confines of the work to attempt to convey a vision that occurred to him while composing it. This discrepancy could be counted against the Symphony as a flaw, but the result is among the most remarkable moments in the music of those years.

SparkskrapS, by contrast, is rarely metric in any sustained way (its meters, too, are emergent and evanescent) and makes much use of complex, free-floating rhythmic surfaces. The textures are normally unitary in some way: either basically homophonic, variously heterophonic, or assembled into supervenient unities out of many contributing elements that lose their individual identities in the ensemble. There are exceptions, to be sure, for example, the canonic treatment of the palindromic melody in measure-group 10, or that of the "apotheosis theme" in 26b. But these are utterly obvious; far from making any attempt to disguise these contrapuntal devices, as he does in the Symphony, Anhalt here makes a point of them. The same applies to the use of sequence, which in an underlying structural sense is virtually pervasive in Symphony, in that so many of its passages are made up by taking a small fragment of material through a transpositional cycle. But whereas in the Symphony the sequences usually become evident only through analysis, and are heard only indirectly, by attending to certain pitch or pitch-class lines in isolation, in *SparkskrapS* they are again completely obvious. Finally, *SparkskrapS* moves slowly through its material, giving the listener time to experience details fully. It has only one clear intensity wave – the approach to the climax in groups 26a and b – and it is replete with (and unabashed in its use of) repetition, from the thirteen projectile motions of group 1 to the slow breathing of the coda. All the features of *SparkskrapS* are attributable, of course, to its status as personal expression. The repetitiveness, the slow evolution of ideas, the unified textures, the emblematic use of devices such as canon and sequence, and the lack of a pervasive beat are all indicators of what is being represented, a real time episode in the life of a mind.

The basic difference between personalized style and personal expression also explains another important point of contrast between the two works, which is that the musical language of the Symphony is itself unitary, while that of *SparkskrapS* is essentially dualistic. The Symphony proceeds from an Ur-motive; every other object in the work can be traced back to it and finds a place in some constellation revolving around it. In *SparkskrapS*, each object (pc, collection, motive) is situated between the poles that represent the Divine and the *Sitra Ahra*, and that are marked by the features listed in table 7.4. Nor could things be otherwise with the two works, since style, as a means of coordinating a profusion of material under the aegis of a guiding concept, is unitary by definition, while what *SparkskrapS* is about is the inherent duality of our moral existence.

Finally, one must deal with the story that *SparkskrapS* tells, in contrast to that which underlies the styles upon which the Symphony draws. The latter is impersonal by definition, a sort of deeply imprinted cultural trace that can well be safely overlooked by the listener, and that the composer can abandon and take up at will, inserting passages (like the scherzo) that are essentially games, unconnected to any symbolic purpose, and that make the story intermittent. In the end, the story of *SparkskrapS* is, at one level, a personal story, and therefore cannot be casually left off and taken up. This is hardly surprising, when biographical circumstances are considered, for the Symphony is the music of a recent immigrant, who brings to a young, unformed society all the wealth of an ancient, but used-up civilization. It is a music of anonymity, of wanting painfully to contribute, but also to fit in and not be noticed. *SparkskrapS*, on the other hand, is the music of an individual at peace with what he is and where he comes from, and who wants these to be recognized for what they are. It is a music of heritage and identity, critically but lovingly embraced. Its story is therefore gripping, one that must be told and acknowledged.

SparkskrapS and its companion works (*Simulacrum* and *Sonance•Resonance (Welche Töne?)*) are of special cultural importance because they preserve mastery in the aftermath of style. This is evident in *SparkskrapS* from the fact that the basic pc-combinational techniques worked out in the Symphony continue to structure discourse in the later work, although to very different effect. For example, the opposition of augmented hexachords to octatonic collections can be found in the Symphony, though in a large-scale form-creating role, and not as a means of re-creating the symbolic power of the major-minor duality. Finally, though, these works will last not just because they are well made and resonant of the stylistic traditions they have moved beyond, but because they manifest another kind of transcendence, that of the self. One of the dangers of a focus on the symbolic powers of music and on the composer as the architect of structures founded on them is that of hermetic absorption in a world of purely personal symbols. One thinks here of a composer like George Crumb, whose powers of self-expression are undeniable, but whose music fails to sustain interest because listening to it is like listening to someone lost in his private world.[40] The major composers of our time are those who have been able to devise a musical symbolism that works suprapersonally – composers like Luciano Berio, György Ligeti, and Peter Maxwell Davies in their best moments, and Anhalt in these later orchestral works. Of course, there is nothing new in this: the power of Wagner's music lies in the enormous force of its musical symbolism, embodied in its leitmotifs, which are so often undervalued by modern critics. But with the disappearance of style as an option, for the foreseeable future at least, the ability to compose with symbols that function suprapersonally is probably the main determinant of compositional relevance. By this I mean not only that the symbols are open to shared apprehension by members of a cultivated audience, but that they speak to listeners in a manner that moves them deeply, by capturing the dynamics of thought and feeling, individual and collective, that give meaning to their lives.

I began by pointing out that criticism has a role to play in ensuring that significant art is not buried under everything else that is excreted in life around us, particularly today. Ultimately though, art must rely on itself. The art that hits us where we live will survive. As highly as I have come to regard the Symphony by studying it over a period of three years, I am not sure it will receive the performances it deserves. But Anhalt's later orchestral work should find its place in the repertoire when the present century digs itself out from under the debris of the previous one. This work is a testimony to one man's ability to grow into the artist he was meant to be, and with auspicious if improbable timing, since who would have imagined a man of sixty-five finding the voice we wanted to hear among the jangling alternatives of recent musical life? And it will serve, for this reason, as a testimony to who we were – more telling, I dare say, than all the literal images stored in today's proliferating data banks. In the end, I think the intention behind Anhalt's music is that of much of the finest art in general: *tikkun*, the restoration of the world as it was meant to be. This is what informs the music above all else, and what must surely command our deepest interest and that of our successors.

APPENDIX

Table 7.4
An overview of the sections of *SparkskrapS*: formal and symbolic functions

Measure-group (measures)	Form-syntactic functions (rhythmic, textural, and dynamic attributes)	Pitch-structural features	Symbolic functions[1]	Composer-generated descriptors[2]
	PART 1: (THE) CREATION (OF DIFFERENCE)			
1 (1–13)	*introduction*; repetitive and static, harmonically and registrally accumulative; loud at first, decreasing	aggregate minus (C,E); octatonic collections suggested	invocation of a transcendent reality; projectile motions into a gradually filling void	embellished unison Lines (PS, 20); Sparks (CS, 12)
2 (14–23)	*exposition* of an initial state; repetitive; narrow middle register gradually extended downward; octave doubling applied to chromatic fields generates subtle shifts in pc priority; soft, then louder	chromatic heptachord (10,11,0,1,2,3,4); (C,E) emphasized first, then (B, E♭)	indistinct, inchoate forms; blurred and confusing; a state of being unable to discriminate	Moiré (PS, 23); Vertigo (Doubt?) (PS, 177); "live" Cluster with bass support (PS, 17)
3 (24–35)	*slow, directed motion*; complex chords thicken with top voice rising, interrupted three times by (1) melodic antecedent phrase, (2) melodic consequent phrase, (3) melodic palindrome; dynamic contrast, getting loud overall, with terminal decay	prolongation of an octatonic collection above that of an augmented hexachord (=(0,1,4,5,8,9)-type); top voice of chords rises in whole tones; third interruption = palindrome based on (0,1,4,5)	homophonic canticle, without words; murky attempt to reach upwards; interruptions represent majesty or power as if viewed in a clearing of perception	*Gevura* (Power) (PS, 29a and b) [refers to third interruption only]
4a (36–44)	further *development* of 2, with a solo melody emerging to dominate texture; medium to loud	E♭3 has priority, soon undermined by linkage with E2; augmented hexachord (11,0,3,4,7,8)	an individual consciousness appears out of the formlessness	[not present in PS]

1 This column is based on the composer's notes and sources for *SparkskrapS*.
2 All Hebrew terms in this list are italicized, whether underlined in the composer's materials or not. All descriptive nouns begin with an upper-case letter, irrespective of how they appear in the sources. Abbreviations: preliminary sketches (PS), concept score (CS), and short score (SS).

Table 7.4
(*continued*)

4b (45–6)	*outgrowth of and cadence to 4a*; activated 3-tone scale fragments in close imitation; upward proliferation; medium dynamic with decresc. of lower elements	column of 11s=<F2,E4, D$\sharp$5,D6>, ornamented with scalar activity	consciousness develops into argument as different voices are heard	*Gevura* (Obsession) (list); Argument (*Pilpul*) (list)
5a (47–55)	*transparent form of 2* (and 4a); individual tones form harmonies; feverish high-register linear activity superposed starting in m. 51; medium-loud, then increasing	harmonies are augmented hexachords; superposed activity is octatonic	order established, then contradicted by highly contrasting (destructive) element	harmonic Assembly (list) [initial measures]
5b (56–7)	*sequel and cadence to 5a*; slow low-registral linear activity with mirror inversions; loud, intense	(0,1,4,5)-type lines fill in a harmonic space =<A$\flat$2,D3,G3>	a suddenly dark, almost menacing reaction; the lower realm resounds	*Sitra Ahra* (PS, 83); Sparkscraps (list) [linear counterpoints of (0,1,4,5) motives] (PS, 79)
6 (58–61)	*continuation of 3*, rising quickly, cut off and led to a major cadence point in low register END OF THE FIRST LARGE SECTION IN PART I (at Golden Section?); decreasing dynamic	complex chords = minor triads with added tones; in 60–1 augmented-hexachord linear activity leads to an octatonic cadence chord, E$\flat$ root (?)	a spiritual quest is cut short, contradicted by opposing force; but feeling at end is of relaxation	sparks Assembly [high added tones in 58–9?] (PS, 50); heterogeneous pattern Assembly (list)
7 (62–4)	*new beginning*, the same motive three times; melodic upbeat to repeated, sustained chords; start-stop; medium dynamic	vague sense of B$\flat$ minor, with harmonic progression IV to V; the latter, an augmented hexachord	a memory; something traditional, reassuring	Scraps (PS, 53)
8 (65–7)	shimmering, high-register *tremolando over a low chord*; free rhythm; soft, increasing	octatonic collection, as in end of 6	a mental window is opened to some upper realm and the activity therein	spiralling Ascent (list)

Table 7.4
(continued)

9 (68–74)	*explosion of activity*; multi-tracking of fast, repeated-pitch figures in various registers; loud	chromatic 8-tone set from E♭ to B♭, with E in bass and rhetorical emphasis on E♭; major and minor thirds separated by 11 or 13	a frenetic reaction is precipitated; a multilevelled pulsation of energy at various frequencies	interval Pillar (PS, 57); broadly, but with vigorous Excitement (SS); Assembly (list)
10 (75–81)	*palindromic melodies* in canon with sustained filler, related to third interruption in 3; activity ends in stasis; wide register, but bottom soon drops out; soft, cresc.	(0,1,4,5)-type sets are cycled in 7s; overall harmonic result emphasizes (E,B♭) as centre of symmetry and as chord roots; A♭ missing from aggregate	a sense of control is reasserted, or else the determination to achieve it; tenacity	*Gevura* (Obsession) (PC, 59)
11a (82–5)	exposition of high-register *plucked-and-struck ensemble* (bell) sounds; rhythmically free; medium loud	two augmented hexachords combined, generating aggregate with A♭ missing	gnomic utterances or thoughts; glittering gems, or the tintinnabulations of rejected metal objects?	SparkscrapS (list); Patterns, Mixtures, Textures (list)
11b (86–92)	*continuation of 11a*; lower-register string chords are subposed; chords softer than bell sounds	symmetrical 8-pc collection =(2,3,4,7,8,11,0,1), with emphasis on the six central pcs = augmented hexachord	the items in 11a are conceived as acted upon by human or other active agents	heterogeneous pattern Mixtures (list)
11c (92–100)	*further continuation*, with metric regularization and overall intensification; chords rise beneath counterpointed bell-ensemble sounds; pattern falls apart at end; medium dynamic with terminal decresc.	complementary augmented hexachords, transposed in sequence	a sense of effort resulting in psychic motion; determination, but ending in dissipation and hesitancy	Doubt (list) [last two bars only?]; floating Bodies (list)
12 (101–2)	*further development of 8*, another assembly of undulating patterns, arpeggiations, and tremolos; wide medium register; soft, dynamic hairpin	9-tone collection, three augmented triads; complement of (F,A,C♯)	something beautiful and radiant is perceived to fill the world	sparks Assembly (list)

Table 7.4
(continued)

PART II: EXPERIENCE AND INNOCENCE			
13 (103–10)	*introduction,* later proves to be *refrain:* a threefold sequence (model and two imitations) that provides much harmonic, motivic, and gestural material for part II; each pattern reaches a terminal chord via a descending melody and quasi mirror-related ascending inner voice; moderato; medium soft with decresc.	terminal chords of first two patterns are chromatic accumulations of thirds; last pattern ends in minor triad with added major 7th and 9th, effecting sense of resolution	a return to tradition, this time in a more explicit way than at 7	laborious Descent (list); pseudo-Tradition (list)
14 (111–22)	*exposition of a lengthy cascading descent* in seven to nine canonic, registrally overlapping parts; quite fast but slowing down a lot as lower register is reached	begins with multi-octave E; two streams of augmented triads descend chromatically, out of sync, over a chromatically descending bass; at 115–16, chord roots are heard in bass; 117–18, octatonic; weak tonicization of E♭ in 119	descending motions, breezy and graceful at first, seem to get caught in something viscous and turbid as they proceed; a gradual sense of entering a kind of underworld	*Sitra Ahra* (PS, 83) [concluding measures]
15a (123–31)	*countertheme,* metric; highly accented (with syncopation), slowly rising lines under a pedal; loud	top-voice pedal G♭3, with bass departing from B♭1 arpeggiating its way to B♭2; uses two octatonic collections in series, but cadencing in m. 131 on 5-tone subset of augmented hexachord	an oppressed mood; harsh and pitiless; also, an attempt to resist oppression, to rise out of the mire	*Sitra Ahra* (PS, 107)

Table 7.4
(continued)

15b (132–7)	*continuation of the preceding*, dense harmonies composed of rising lines, with upper voice rising through minor 9th; begins *mf* rising to *f* and decays at end	octatonic harmonies temporally frame more consonant chords with passing tonal implications; top voice rises from F4 to G♭5, as bass moves down from B2 to (B♭2, E2) dyad	a more concerted effort building on the preceding, achieving passing success but ending in the same place seen from a different standpoint: failure	[not present in PS]
16 (138–42)	*fragmentary reworking of material of 14*, but slower, with lines descending at different rates, and threefold gestural plan of 13, hence acting as *refrain*; three decresc. patterns	augmented hexachords; nonsystematic octave doubling in harmony	*espressivo*; massive sighing exhalations; tragic character, as if realizing the implications of resort to scraps	[not present in PS]
17a (143–54)	*Alberti basses and other undulating patterns*, moving at various rates, fill total registral space; melodic sequence begins at m. 148; pattern descends chromatically bar by bar; slow, soft	dense harmony, up to 9 real parts; bass roots are dimly heard throughout, governing figured-bass patterns in all upper voices; bass emphasizes D3, ends on A2	a phantasmagoria, or dreamlike vision, perhaps of something remembered as beautiful; a continuation (from 16) of sighing, now more like rocking; *espressivo*	Alberti Pattern (list); Lyricism (list)
17b (155–8)	*fast arpeggiations* activate and expand chord at end of 17a, as if improvising on whole orchestra as one instrument	sonority of 10 pcs, with partly cyclic internal structure of diminished triads over an augmented triad; A1, A2, and A3 undergird sonority; no D or E♭	the vision of 17a becomes incandescent, producing sparks	homogeneous pattern Assembly (list); chord Pillar (list)

Table 7.4
(continued)

18 (159–67)	*static presentation of core harmonic material*; simple, four-note patterns recur repeatedly, with component notes in changing order; responded to by faster, ringing echoes; soft	augmented hexachords, some embellished, with (1,2,5,6,9,10) functioning referentially; D6 emphasized, with sustained G♭3, B♭2 in bass; no C	a collection of objects, rather like toys that belong together – sparkling but also likely discards	Scintillae, Spark-scrapS (PS, 91); [this could have been the first material composed]
19 (168–84)	*related to 15a*; repetition of a rhythmic motive brings about a gradual and deliberate piling up of harmony with no harmonic shift until the end of the passage; processional tempo; loud and strongly accented, with cresc., but fading out at end	G♭1, G♭2, and B♭2 serve as foundation for enormous piling up of major and minor thirds with octave doubling; the bass drops to F and harmony shifts at end of passage	a horrific vision; something grotesque rears its awful head; a terrible obsession; obviously part of the *Sitra Ahra*	[not present in PS]
20a (185-6)	a *short link*, light and transparent; *dolce*	melodic arpeggiations of C- and A-major triads terminate in a 6-pitch chord (A3,D4,A♭4,D♭5, F5,B5), which is symmetrical about (F,B), the tritone of C major	innocence recovered, remembered, clung to	*Espressivo*, Lyrical (list)
20b (187–90)	*refrain* (based on 13): three-fold sequence, each pattern of descending melodic voices terminating in a registrally extended chord; soft and transparent	chord resultants are symmetrical octatonic subsets; they descend chromatically	another attempt to start out from a traditional basis; somewhat lighter and less burdened here	[not present in PS]
20c (191-2)	*pattern used in sequence of 20b is transformed*: longer, lower, thicker; loud, with terminal decresc.	(2,3,6,7,10,11) with octave doubling	once again: the *Sitra Ahra* attracts like a black hole	[not present in PS]

Table 7.4
(continued)

20d (193–5)	*partial retake* (2 statements only) of 20b; very soft	similar to 20b	traditional means reveal their futility; they lead nowhere and are abandoned	[not present in PS]
21a (196–8)	transformation of *refrain* into rising movement = *refrain**; upper voices have sequential activity over static harmony; very soft	melodic intervals of 13 rise in whole steps over a static (F,A,C$^\sharp$) harmony	a sudden transformation of a device yields a new insight, a positive inspiration from above	*Hokhmah* (intellect as an emanation of Divine) (PS, 117)
21b (199–200)	*interruption of preceding*; brass chorale fragment, as if from a distance; quasi palindrome; soft	parallel melodic line-pairs, separated by 8s and 3s, under pedal E$\flat$5; begins and ends with <G3,E$\flat$4,A$\flat$4,B4, E$\flat$5>	the power of the Divine is glimpsed from afar, as if obscured by intervening partitions	*Gevura* (virility, as emanation of Divine) (list)
21c (201–4)	*refrain**; a more elaborate version of 21a; harmonic as well as melodic sequence	deformations of augmented hexachords, transformed by T$_2$; most voices ascend by 2s	the inspiration in 21a is confirmed	*Hokhmah* (list)

PART III: TRAGEDY

22 (205–24)	massive *heterophonic treatment of a pitch-class*, which is activated by diminutions in all registers and is subtly transformed into a dyad consisting of itself and its T$_6$; very loud	F emerges as paramount for the first time, becomes transformed into B (with F) by way of (4,5,10,11), as if B and F were alternate forms of the same pc phenomenon	the collectivity of consciousnesses cries out, as if in a massive appeal against its suffering; tritone transformation could indicate the moral ambiguity of consciousness	Appeal (PS 165); quasi Homophony, Heterophony (list)

Table 7.4
(continued)

23 (225–31)	*transition* (scene change) of extreme complexity; the dyad becomes rich harmony that slowly descends cyclically in several layers; this is counterpointed by a solo *express.* melody that rises through two octaves; melody connected to that in 4a; *f* decresc. to *p*	modulation from dyadic harmony to harmonies of 6 and 7 pcs, organized in two whole-tone streams; bass gradually moves down from F3 to E3 as upper voice gets to A5 via chromatic descent, at which point an A-minor 6/4 chord with added tones is heard	the now-familiar power of the *Sitra Ahra* once again palpable, but an individual consciousness manifests the power to resist it	[not clearly labelled in sources, though present in an early form in PS]
24 (232–6)	*concerted lyrical passage*; highly embellished obbligato melody rises in step motion, with some octave doubling and heterophonic treatment, against a bass and inner voices moving down chromatically; soft	melodic line and structural notes in lower voices give sense of A-minor tonality; use of (0,3,6,9)-type sonorities in chromatic parallel motion also has a traditional quality	quasi-baroque feeling; a religious quality, as if from one of the Bach Passions; a mood of supplication and generally of profound feeling	Supplication, Offering, Propitiation, Hymn (list)
25 (237–42)	sudden eruption of *simple melody against drones*; *espress.*; melody descends sequentially as accomp. fades texturally and dynamically; clear beat in accomp., with metric freedom	diatonic melody (D major) that fades away into octatonic motives	Hungarian-sounding, like a Bartók folk song arrangement; the Divine responds; a feeling of warmth and connectedness; alternatively, the human world is experiences as warm and accepting	*Hod-Hesed* (splendour-a charity) (list)

Table 7.4
(*continued*)

26a (243–50)	*processional begins*, with a melody under strummed chords; using dotted-rhythm motives and enlarged intervals, melody stretches upwards as repeated eighth-note chordal accompaniment thickens; very *espress.*; overall cresc.	initial D tonality shifts down to D♭, with varied harmony, mostly augmented-hexachordal; shift to F tonality; clear step motion pattern in all upper voices over root progressions in bass	initial Jewish-sounding melody gives way to thickening pulsations of motivic harmony, as if the Divine is drawn by human supplication to fill the void; alternatively, a collectivity begins to assemble around an idea and to move, in ranks, out of spiritual exile = an exodus, under Divine protection	*Hod-Hesed* (list)
26b (251–61)	processional continues, with emergence of distinctive melodic idea (= *apotheosis theme*) over the pulsating harmonies; idea repeated in numerous transformations and treated canonically; a little faster and more legato in last 5 bars, with new motive of chromatically descending tritones in inner voice at m. 257; eight-part texture, rising overall; cresc. to *ff molto espress.*	melodic idea is octatonic; chords shift between melody-determined harmony and augmented hexachords, the latter dominating in the end; implied tonality of F minor (see 26a) dissolves in tonally neutral passage, which gives way to an emergent B♭ minor, as outer voices ascend in quasi-parallel motion to F	the emanations of the Divine fill the void; alternatively, the collectivity dominated by idea of the Divine and, pouring out its soul in song, brings this idea to apotheosis; the emotional climax of the music reached	[as for 24, with emphasis on Hymn] (list)

Table 7.4
(continued)

26c (262–7)	*form of refrain* in two short phrases begins at point of climax; each phrase of three "Hungarian" motives (short-long) in successive whole-step descent; phrases begin very loud, *molto espress.*, decay at their ends	climax is also clearest tonal moment = V of B♭ minor, but first phrase then shifts into octatonic collections; second phrase begins similarly, but on V of A minor; also dissolves into octatony	the light of the Divine fills the void with its emanations and there is a sense of imminent perfection, but the created entities cannot sustain the fullness of the Divine; alternatively, the idealism of the collectivity runs into a barrier at the point of seeming to reach its goal and experiences tragic reversal	[treated as continuation of preceding in list]
27a (268–76)	*fast, developmental passage,* made up of three 3-bar segments, each a rising sequence; melodic material is that of 26b (= *apotheosis theme*), but here this idea is progressively liquidated; obviously, a development of *refrain** as well as of melodic idea; a crescendo in each segment; overall accelerando	first sequence rises in whole steps (2s), the second in minor thirds (3s), the third in major thirds (4s)	postromantic; a whirlwind; some catastrophe has struck and what has been achieved is being destroyed	[not present in PS]
27b (277–96)	*preceding continues*, reaching a feverish pitch; motives are further neutralized and repeated many times with small alterations; tempo more than doubles; all instruments move to their upper registers	harmony fully chromatic with registral and/or instrumental partitioning into (0,3,6,9) types in evidence; no tonality	the whirlwind reaches its most ferocious intensity; things come to a total breaking point	[not present in PS]

Table 7.4
(continued)

	PART IV: *TIKKUN* AND DEATH			
28a (297–315)	begins as another *invention on a pc*, hence a modified parallel to 22; texture rapidly becomes polyphonic, based on streams of chromatically descending tritones, first sounded at 26b; highly accented, repetitive material, with changing group lengths; moderate allegro, loud	the B♭ here is tonally related to the F at 22; various streams appear, each consisting of a tritone that moves chromatically through an interval of 3; modulation from pc monad to 7-tone sets of type (0,1,2,3,6,7,9); B♭ and E dominate throughout	the collectivity responds with another appeal, this time in the form of prayer; individuals recite the same phrases at differing times and in various tessituras; activity has a desperate, oppressed, compulsive quality	*Davenen* (list) [motive of descending tritones]
28b (316–19)	more static *continuation of the preceding*	(E,B♭) continue to dominate within (4,5,10,11) and (3,4,9,10) sets	prayer reaches a point of repetitive stasis, as if exhausted and waiting for something to happen	[as in preceding]
29 (320–5)	*activity of two preceding groups continues* in a reduced form in lower registers, punctuated by two end-accented descending riffs on drums; slower, loud	descent through sets (2,3,8,9), (1,2,7,8), and (0,1,6,7) complete the aggregate together with sets of the same type in 28b.	stultified prayer continues as a twofold shock is administered; something is broken	Overturning of the Lamp[3] (list)
30 (326–31)	*interruption* of surrounding material; another shimmering passage unfolds, related to those in 8 and 12; several streams of arpeggiated figures against the background of a widely spaced chord	arpeggiated figures are mostly augmented hexachords; the chord contains two chromatic tetrachords a tritone apart = (5,6,7,8,11,0,1,2), but has consonant (0,7) undulating in bass	as if out of nowhere, a sudden brightening; a restoration of light; the higher realm is envisioned as in a delirium	Ecstasy (list)

3 Presumably "overturning of the lamp" is a kabbalistic metaphor for the elimination of light from some realm. I have not found a reference to it elsewhere.

Table 7.4
(continued)

31 (334–9)	*activity of 29 returns*, with some overlap by 30, and is taken up by whole orchestra, but moving by motive super-position into a high register as the lowest tones are abandoned	pitch structures composed of chromatically adjacent tritones, as in 28b, 29, and sustained chord of 30; cadential sonority $=<F2,B2,F3,C4, G^\flat4,C5,E5,B^\flat5,E6>$	the prayer activity resumes but as if enlightened by the preceding	*Davenen* (list)
32 (340–6)	*music slows and settles*; slow arpeggiated figures lead to a series of four minimally changing chords, each with a fermata; a fifth bar, harmonically similar to the fourth, with new step-motion lines emerging from the chord (a preparation for the following)	octatonic; basic harmony is $<A^\flat,E^\flat,A,B,D>$, in registral order, with octave doubling	something has entered the place of prayer and all wait expectantly to discover its nature	[added only in the final score]
33 (347–52)	totally new variant of the refrain idea = *refrain§*: another sequence, here descending by half-steps; a richly textured heterophony expressing four underlying parts; very slow and quiet	simple 6(min.)– 5–6(maj.) intervallic pattern over a bass falling by a semitone; $^\flat8$–$^\sharp7$ motion is superimposed to coincide with the 6s	a sense of profound peace and safety takes over as something magnificent descends and hovers over the scene	*Shekhinah* (list)
34 (353–8)	response to the preceding = *refrain†*: succession of three chords, each arpeggiated as a series of dyads, from bottom to top; *mf* to *p* twice, then *f* to *p*	each chord a hexachord (augmented hexachord with one tone replaced by its tritone) presented registrally as 3s and 4s with octave doubling; pitch content changes subtly from chord to chord, with top voice holding to $B^\flat6$ and bass moving $<C2,B1,B^\flat1>$	the created universe strives for a sort of harmonic alignment in the presence of the *Shekhinah*; an attempt at *tikkun* on the part of things in themselves	interval Pillars (list)

Table 7.4
(continued)

35 (359–65)	*phrase in five motivic segments*; a melody of dyads is sounded over a pedal dyad in the bass; between segments 4 and 5 an interruption, harking back to 34; cadence on a widely spread chord	drawn from alternating octatonic collections, except for interruption, which relates to 34; bass pedal is <B♭1,D♭2>; in cadence chord top dyad is <E♭6,G♭6>	humanity tries, individually and collectively, to restore itself, making an effort to subordinate evil to good impulses	[not present in PS]
36a (366–72)	*coda begins*: two very similar sequences, one of four statements, each 1 m. long, a second of three statements, each 1 m. long; simple, regular gestures, sparse texture, mid-to-low register; medium dynamic	under a pedal F♯5, four chromatic trichords, and then, three (0,1,6,7)-type tetrachords are arpeggiated	a winding down; gestures are minimal, almost mechanical	[not present in PS]
36b (373–9)	*continuation of preceding*, but more reduced in scope, with more repetition, less movement across section; getting slower and softer	under pedal G♭4, two pairs of tritones move up and down by semitone in each bar, at first exchanging pcs within a single (0,1,6,7)-type tetrachord, later forming a succession of two such tetrachords	a rocking or alternating motion in a moderate tempo, like quiet breathing; the body is conscious of itself as its spirit departs	[not present in PS]
36c (380–9)	*further continuation*; a series of six statements of the same measure of material, arriving at a final mid-to-low-register sonority; *completion* achieved with a rising melodic gesture in the high register; soft, with final hairpin	under a pedal B3, two (0,1,6,7)-type chords alternate, once per measure; final bass motion is <A1,A♭1> a descent from earlier B♭1 (35); upper-register melodic completion shows registral symmetry, relates octatonically to final sonority, and has <E♭6,G♭6> as its top notes	as the spirit departs there is a sense of integration with a universe that is at least partially restored	[not present in PS]

NOTES

Preliminary research for this essay was undertaken at the National Library of Canada in May 1995, with the assistance of a grant from the Humanities and Social Sciences Grants Committee of the Faculty of Arts, University of British Columbia. I am grateful for this assistance, which also helped to defray part of the cost of preparing camera-ready musical examples. Ms Maureen Nevins, of the Manuscript Section of the National Library's Music Division, was most gracious and expedited my work considerably; and I would also like to thank the acting head of the section at the time, Ms Jeannine Barriault. Mr Tom Borugian, a composition student at U.B.C., did an excellent job of turning my pencilled examples into computer-notated copy.

I have much to thank Istvan Anhalt himself for, in his capacities as teacher, mentor, and friend, but perhaps this comes through in the previous pages. Let me here add only my thanks for some valuable insights he communicated during two extended visits we had over the last three years, and for his enthusiastic response upon viewing some of my early results. Finally, I would like to express warmest thanks to my wife Carol for moral support in the form of unflagging expressions of confidence which saw me through what turned out to be a much more demanding project that I had anticipated.

1 The biographical note on Anhalt, by Udo Kasemets and Louis Applebaum, in the Canadian Music Centre's Directory of Associate Composers (which I perused on-line), also describes his compositional career as falling into four phases, as I do, but does not identify the same points of division between the first and second, and between the second and third. They regard phase one as extending up to 1958, and phase two as only four years in duration (1959–63), and therefore coinciding with Anhalt's involvement in electronic composition. The reader will notice that I regard 1954–58 as a distinct phase, while grouping 1959–63 with the third phase, 1959– ca 1974.

2 The second of the *Chansons d'aurore* has a particularly strong connection with the first part of section XI of the Symphony (mm. 450–61). I am indebted to Anhalt for drawing my attention to this relationship.

3 The passage in example 7.1, at letter x of the first movement is to me quite specifically reminiscent of the development section of the first movement of Brahms's first violin sonata, op. 78. The principal motive of this passage is the same as one that first appears in m. 5 of Brahms's movement, in which it plays a signal role.

4 The first movement of the Piano Trio ends with a strange repetitive passage, sounding, as Anhalt puts it in the notes he prepared for the Radio Canada International recording of this work (in *Anthology of Canadian Music*, vol. 22), "as if the needle would have got stuck on a turning disc." In this passage, a one-measure segment is repeated eleven times, before a

final cadential gesture. The parallel with the closing passage of *SparkskrapS*
is uncanny. In the latter work, the final gesture is preceded by two such
repetitive passages, one following immediately upon the other, each of
which contains six statements of a one-measure segment. Needless to say,
the effect in *SparkskrapS* has nothing to do with stuck needles.

5 This judgment does not extend to the *Symphony of Modules* (1967), which I
do not know and is as yet still unperformed. This work involves only instrumental and electroacoustic media. It contains the first important instances,
in Anhalt's oeuvre, of quotations from earlier music.

6 Schoenberg's String Trio and the Fantasy for violin and piano come to
mind.

7 Anhalt's Symphony was published by BMI Canada (Toronto, 1963), and
dedicated to the bicentenary of Canadian Jewry. The publication rights
were later transferred to Berandol. Unfortunately, no commercial recording of the work exists. The tape in my possession, a remote descendant of a
master tape of a 1960 performance by the Toronto Symphony under
Walter Susskind, was not well recorded, and the playing is competent but
perfunctory. I do not know whether a more satisfactory recording of this or
any other performance exists. [But see pp. 56–8. *Eds.*]

8 All of Anhalt's written comments and descriptions cited here are taken
from program notes he wrote for the Symphony, probably in 1959 (hereafter cited as Symphony program notes). He drafted these notes in several
versions. All are found in the Anhalt fonds, National Library of Canada,
Ottawa, specifically in folders 9.1.3 through 9.1.8 and folders B2.14–17.
The most definitive version of the notes, from which this quotation is
taken, is found in folder B2.15.

9 Carl Morey describes the Symphony as "a set of variations in 13 sections."
"Anhalt, Istvan," *Encyclopedia of Music in Canada*, 2nd ed., 27.

10 Anhalt, Symphony program notes.

11 Graphs are found in the Anhalt fonds, folders 1.1.73 and 1.1.74. See
note 15, below, for an account of the materials for the Symphony in the
fonds.

12 For an excellent analysis of one of these works along these lines see Lynn
M. Cavanagh, "Tonal Multiplicity in Schoenberg's First String Quartet,
Op. 7" (Ph.D. diss., University of British Columbia, 1996).

13 To this extent, the passage refers very obliquely to the use of "learned"
counterpoint in the development sections of classical and romantic
symphonies.

14 An obvious example in the case of common practice tonal music is pitch-
class (pc) interval 2 (semitone). In later tonal and early posttonal music,
pc interval 11 and its larger octave equivalents can be either consonances
or dissonances (see note 17). In taking the position that such ambivalence
is normal, I am positioning myself in opposition to those who say that

prolongation should only be asserted where pc sets can be rigorously parti-
tioned into consonant and dissonant types. See, for example, Joseph N.
Straus, "The Problem of Prolongation in Post-Tonal Music," *Journal of
Music Theory* 31, 1 (1987): 1–21.

15 The material in the fonds is contained in boxes 7–9 and box 52. Box 7 contains serial charts (folders 1.1.71, 72, and 75), graphs (folders 1.1.73 and
74), and preliminary sketches (folders 1.1.76–81). The sketch material is
not comprehensive; much of it deals with section VII. The last folder
(1.1.82) in box 7 and the first five (1.1.83–7) in box 8 contain the meat
of what is useful for the analyst and student of compositional process: a
pencil holograph of a first draft of much of the work, with various sections
appearing in various short-score formats. This is of great interest not only
because it is different in many respects from the final version, but because
where it does conform to the latter in content, its format is often more
revealing of linear structure. The rest of box 8 (folders 1.1.88–93) contains
a pencil holograph of a second draft of most of the work, in fully orchestrated format. Box 9 contains ink and ozalid holographs of the complete,
final score (folders 1.1.94 and 95), and a miscellany of materials, including
edited portions of the ozalid holograph, some abandoned drafts of pages
of the final ink score, a single sketch, and a list of corrections.

16 Readers who are familiar with pitch techniques used in Elliott Carter's
music from the years just after composition of the Symphony (1958) will be
struck by their similarity to Anhalt's. Carter's Second String Quartet (1959)
and his Double Concerto (1961) provide clear examples of such usage. Of
course, this circumstance implies no historical relationship between the
two men. For an elementary but useful exposition of Carter's approach to
pitch in these works, see David Schiff, *The Music of Elliott Carter* (London:
Eulenberg, 1983), 60–9.

17 The idea of major sevenths above primary and secondary chord tones
(secondary chord tones are sevenths, ninths, etc.) as tertiary harmonic elements is not generally recognized, but it seems to me of general validity
and usefulness for much early-twentieth-century music. I wrote about this
at some length in "Harmony in Radical European Music (1905–14)"
(paper presented at the national meeting of the Society for Music Theory,
Philadelphia, 1984).

18 Anhalt of course studied with Boulanger after the war, and the music of his
first period intermittently reveals a fascination with Gallic idioms that she
would have championed. In one sense, German harmony leading up to Expressionism is a massive development of the resources of the diminished-
seventh chord, and its counterpart in France, leading up to and including
Impressionism, is a parallel development of the resources of the augmented triad. This is of course a gross oversimplification, but it is a useful
one. As we shall see, the two streams are brought into a dialectical relationship in *SparkskrapS*.

19 Freud uses this analogy as a way of talking about the relationship between the infantile psyche and that of the adult, with specific reference to ancient and modern Rome, in *Civilization and Its Discontents*, trans. and ed. James Strachey (New York: Norton, 1961), 17–19.

20 Edward T. Cone's illuminating discussion of Schoenberg's approaches to this problem in his early music is relevant here. See his "Sound and Syntax: An Introduction to Schoenberg's Harmony," *Perspectives of New Music* 13, 1 (1974): 21–40.

21 Anhalt makes reference to an early interest in jazz in "What Tack to Take?" a spoken autobiographical sketch recorded as part of ACM 22 (see note 4). In the liner notes for the works in this recording he refers to a "certain jazz style in at least one place" in the second movement of the Piano Trio (1953). But the most sustained and most blatant reference to music from outside the concert hall is the evocation of the pop singer in *Traces (Tikkun)*, his 1995 "pluri-drama."

22 See note 15, above.

23 The peaks in the Symphony as a whole are (1) mm. 1 ff. and 64 (2) mm. 180 ff.; (3) mm. 486 ff.; and (4) the final measure.

24 Anhalt, Symphony program notes.

25 In identifying a phrase as being of x bars, I means that it traverses x downbeats in some projected metre.

26 *SparkskrapS* remains unpublished. It is available through the Canadian Music Centre under the call number MI 100 A596sp. A CBC recording of the work, by the Esprit Orchestra under Alex Pauk, has been issued. The number is SMCD 5132.

27 These materials boxed and filed as follows: preliminary sketch (PS) in box 4, folders 1.1.30–3; notes in box 4, folder 1.1.34, and box 5, folder 1.1.42; pc-set-structure, in box 4, folder 1.1.35; concept score (CS) in box 4, folder 1.1.36 and box 5, folder 1.1.37; short score (SS) in box 5, folders 1.1.38–41; final score in box 5, folders 1.1.43–8; and parts in box 6 and the first folders of box 7. There is also one *SparkskrapS* file in box 1 and another in box 52, both containing brief explanatory notes relating to the work's points of ideological and symbolic reference.

28 Along with such lists, the 31 leaves include (1) lists of numbers that refer to the page numbers in PS, and thus to the musical fragments on those pages, grouped in various conceptual categories, such as Precipitous descent, Spiraling ascent, "Alberti" pattern, *Espressivo*, Obsession … (*Gevura*); (2) a listing of all pc-set classes using a nomenclature peculiar to the composer; (3) an ordering of fragments from the PS (identified by their page numbers in PS) as they appear in CS; and (4) a listing of all the fragments in PS according to their employment of various set-classes.

29 It seems clear that these are of early provenance, and almost certain that they predate composition proper, because they contain terms that relate directly to the work, and others that are only peripherally related to it.

Directly related are the names of various fragments from PS, but in the lists on these putatively early pages these names are listed alongside various other phrases, abstract terms, obscure references, etc. It hardly seems likely that Anhalt would have compiled such heterogeneous lists while composing. On the other hand, the items listed in note 28 are clearly mnemonic devices intended as aids to composition of a work in progress.

30 Readers with an interest in these matters should consult Gershom Scholem's books.

31 Of course, those sections that evoke traditional European art music styles could tend to evoke the forms in which these styles are expressed, but only if their placement in the work made sense of this evocation, which is not the case. One exception is the great chromatic sequential passage at m. 268 ff., which sounds like the climax of a development section and happens at the point in the piece where such a climax might traditionally occur. Usually, of course, such a developmental climax prepares a recapitulation, but this is not what happens in *SparkskrapS*.

32 My awareness of the considerable literature on these questions has come from reading some recent papers of my colleague at the University of British Columbia, Prof. Vera Micznik. Two of these are "Music and Narrative Revisited," *Journal of the Royal Music Association* (forthcoming), and "The Absolute Limitations of Program Music: The Case of Liszt's 'Die Ideale,'" *Music and Letters* 80, 2 (1999): 207–40. The notion of musical narrative has come under attack or qualification from many sources. See, in particular, Jean-Jacques Nattiez, "Peut-on parler de narrativité en musique?" *Canadian University Music Review* 10, 2 (1990): 68–91.

33 Carolyn Abbate, *Unsung Voices: Opera and Musical Narrative in the Nineteenth Century* (Princeton: Princeton University Press, 1991), 10–29.

34 This is not an empty characterization, in that it might be made of any piece deemed to be in some way representational. There is a difference between depicting a context and depicting the flow of mental representations in which that context is among the things represented; also some pieces are representational only intermittently, while *SparkskrapS* is so throughout. A phenomenological account of those qualities of the music, principally rhythmic and textural, that lend it this quality of depicting a reflecting consciousness would be a worthwhile project, but it is not one I shall undertake here. The composer has spoken publicly about another of his late orchestral works as a representation of mind-body consciousness. The occasion was a radio interview at the time of the premiere of *Simulacrum*, in 1987.

35 Already here, one might speak of a reference to world history, or prehistory.

36 Usually translated as "formless and void" or "waste and void." But these are confusing, since the opening sentences of Genesis make it clear that matter

was created before light, that first there was earth and water and wind. "Formlessness in what had been the void" would make sense, but would not preserve the idiomatic quality of the original, which is really a sort of Hebrew gibberish, rather like the English "hurly-burly," though not, of course, meaning the same thing. "Chaos and confusion" is a better translation.

37 Anhalt hesitated about using the artificial form *SparkskrapS*, which is strictly palindromic, but eventually decided upon it in preference to the more natural *Sparkscraps*, which appears in the sketches and notes.

38 I imagine that the dactyl occurred to Anhalt as much through saying "*davenen*" over and over again as in the attempt to picture the activity itself.

39 It is probably true that American minimalism is the one exception that represents successful defiance in the face of this apparent impossibility. It produced a true style, but at the expense of considerable self-impoverishment. What aspects of our life experience, what aspirations of ours do minimalist compositions reflect?

40 Brian Ferneyhough seems to me another, if very different, example. A composer as gifted as Elliott Carter, on the other hand, is caught, in my view, between an approach to symbolism that is narrow (he uses music to symbolize natural and social processes, but not feelings or perceptions) and a continuing obsession with the hopeless modernist illusion of a personal style (his harmonic and rhythmic systems).

PART THREE

Writings

8 Words for Music: The Composer as Poet

CARL MOREY

I guess I am an oral person at heart, not a print oriented one.
Istvan Anhalt, letter to John Beckwith, 1988

Anhalt is a poetic composer, one who values words for both sound and meaning. Moreover, he is intrigued by the ways in which words and music meet, and in his book *Alternative Voices*[1] he offers original and penetrating discussions of the changing treatment of text in conjunction with music. What distinguishes *Alternative Voices* is the way in which Anhalt examines texted musical compositions from the verbal side of things, rather than more conventionally from the musical side, and it is this approach that serves as a model for the following consideration of Anhalt's compositions that use texts.[2]

About half of Anhalt's list of works consists of vocal music, the texts of which fall into two simple categories: texts by various poets, and texts assembled or written by Anhalt. The first half-dozen works utilize poems by other authors and cover the period from 1941 to about 1955. In 1954, however, Anhalt abandoned ready-made texts (with the single exception of *A Little Wedding Music*,[3] composed in 1983 to a text by Gerard Manley Hopkins) and turned to other sources.

His first acknowledged composition is *Six Songs from Na Conxy Pan*, to poems by Sándor Weöres, composed 1941–47 in Budapest and Paris. The songs meant enough to the composer that he made an English version of them in 1984. Not surprisingly, given the time and the youthfulness of the composer, the setting of the texts is straightforward in a clear and orderly presentation, varied in musical response, but not in any way radical in the musical treatment or in the disposition of the text within the musical framework. Care is taken to expose the voice, unobscured by distracting musical material. But there are perhaps

adumbrations of things to come. The poems do not readily yield up
their inner meanings, although syntactically they are clear and understandable. There is a melancholy in them, and in one of them, about a
caged ape, there is gruesome violence that has an unsettling effect
without obvious reason. The sense of drama that becomes so strong in
Anhalt's works is already evident in the instruction for the performance of the first song: "Reciting fluently, flexibly, and unhurriedly,
but with a sense of solicitousness and urgency." And the poem about
the ape includes a refrain of sound rather than syntactical sense: "Dan-
dandan darandan darandan / daria harridan dari dandan."

Subsequent works, all of them now to English texts, draw on the
richness of English lyric poetry (by Walter de la Mare, Robert Herrick,
William Davenant) and traditional ballads for *Three Songs of Love* (SSA;
1951) and *Three Songs of Death* (SATBB; 1954). Over both sets, despite
their contrasting subjects, is a darkness that is not pessimism or despair
so much as quietude and sad reflection. Between these two sets is *Journey of the Magi* (1952) for voice and piano on the poem by T.S. Eliot.
Eliot's telling of the story is unromantic, devoid of the soft religious
light that customarily glows around the Magi. Anhalt marks both voice
and piano parts *parlando*, and sets the text in a plain quasi-recitative
style as a narrative almost bardic in its declamatory style. These songs
of the 1950s draw on an established body of poetry, but poetry that is
rich in the interplay of sound and meaning, poetry that recalls Eliot's
observation "that the music of poetry is not something which exists
apart from the meaning."[4] There is the nursery-rhyme manner of
Walter de la Mare's "The Song of the Mad Prince" (*Three Songs of Love*):

Who said, "Peacock Pie"?
  The old King to the sparrow;
Who said, "Crops are ripe"?
  Rust to the harrow.

In the same set, there is the verbal interplay of the anonymous ballad,
"The Maid of the Moor":

Maiden in the moor lay,
  In the moor lay,
Seven nights full, seven nights full,
Maiden in the moor lay,
  In the moor lay,
Seven nights full and a day.

All of Anhalt's settings of poetry in this period respect the syntax and
the ordering of lines and phrases. There is little repetition, little to

obscure the direct understanding of the poems, which are supported on the unobtrusive foundation of the music. At this point, though, Anhalt moved away from using established texts and engaged the question of meaning and the utilization of poetic sound at a level of expression that was to affect all his subsequent vocal writing.

The three songs of *Comments* (1954) have as texts clippings from a newspaper. The setting, for voice, violin, cello, and piano, is conventional enough in the presentation of the texts, not dissimilar from the settings of the earlier poems. But what is to be made of this arbitrary choice of mundane texts? What do they "mean"? Meaning in poetry is a vexed and vexing question and not one that is about to be resolved here, but it cannot be set aside without some consideration. While ordinary sense may be an element of poetry, it is commonly understood that it is the meaning beyond the obvious surface of the words that gives poetry its distinction. The special power of poetry lies in its ability to express undefinable feeling without specifying that feeling. In talking about poetic drama, T.S. Eliot describes the advantage of poetry over prose:

> It seems to me that beyond the nameable,
> classifiable emotions and motives of our
> conscious life when directed towards action ...
> there is a fringe of indefinite extent, of
> feeling which we can only detect, so to speak,
> out of the corner of the eye and can never
> completely focus; of feeling of which we are
> only aware in a kind of temporary detachment
> from action ... This peculiar range of
> sensibility can be expressed by dramatic
> poetry, at its moments of greatest intensity.
> At such moments, we touch the border of those
> feelings which only music can express.[5]

The motion of poetry towards music becomes most palpable in the musical realization of a text, perhaps most of all where text and music arise from a single creative imagination. Scraps of newspaper reports hardly seem to fit any traditional definition of poetry, but the temporal or spatial isolation of commonplace materials and their recombination have been shown to have powerful poetic force, whether in Picasso's transformation of a bicycle seat into the head of a bull,[6] or John Cage's framing of whatever sounds occur during a performance of $4'33''$ (1952).[7] The use of newspaper texts even appeared in a popular motion picture, *A Song is Born* (1948). To liven up a group of "longhair" musicians, the leading lady tears some random items from a racing journal and gives them to her musicians to use as texts for a jazzed-up version of the quartet from *Rigoletto*.

Comments is built of three items: (1) the death in 1952 of a noted Balinese dancer, who had brought a gamelan to Great Britain and the United States; (2) a trapeze artist who suffered a paralysis in his arm while performing before a crowd of spectators and who was rescued by his wife; and (3) a report of weather conditions in Ontario and Quebec. A glance at the score reveals nothing unusual to match the way in which the texts are unusual. There is, though, a tension between the apparent triviality of the texts and the seriousness of their setting, for there is a serious undertow to all the texts. In the first song there is a violent death, and the implied division between East and West. In the second a near tragedy takes place before 6,500 spectators, in a forum where potential death is implicit in the thrill of the show. And the innocence of the weather report can, as Gordon Smith has demonstrated, be read as an early indicator of the coming storm between Quebec and Canada.[8] By containing the texts in a formally conventional piece of chamber music, Anhalt draws attention to that peripheral meaning of which Eliot spoke – a meaning, along with the feelings it evokes, that lies below the evident surface meaning of the words.

More than a decade elapsed before Anhalt returned to music with text, but when he did so, he carried his imaginative experience with the voice further along his creative path. It was with *Cento* (1967)[9] that Anhalt realized the many facets that lay within the potential of a voice, and more importantly, how inextricably those facets are bound to equally varied potentials within a text. A voice, after all, only exists when it utters something, and in *Cento* the utterances, both vocal and textual, are released from the confinement of strictly syntactical sense. For twelve-part choir and two-channel tape, *Cento* is built on a text chosen by Anhalt from a pre-existing poem, but chosen with far greater personal intervention than had been the case with *Comments*, and treated far more radically. "*Cento*" is a Latin word for patchwork, or a cloth of diverse colours, and came to be applied in the seventeenth century to literary pieces that were formed by using scraps from various authors. As a technique of musical composition, it was applied much earlier in some Gregorian chant repertoire.[10] Anhalt's application of centonization is literary, although the piece is not without an element of aural patchwork as well. The basis for the text is a poem by Eldon Grier, *An Ecstasy*.[11] Around the image of the city, Grier constructed a series of twenty poems that range through sadness, optimism, reminiscence, the richness of urbanity. From this long piece, Anhalt chose a scant twenty-five disparate lines, five of which, indeed, are not even Grier's lines but compilations of words quite distant from one another in the original text.[12] The result is a kind of telegraphic version of the Grier poem, but where the poem speaks of life in the context of the modern city, Anhalt expunges all obvious urban reference and creates a new poem of personal, internalized wondering. At the same time, his realization of the crowded simultaneity of speech is characteristic of many situations that are typically urban. The musical setting is not sung but spoken – both on the tape and by the active choir – in a carefully regulated framework of inflection and rhythmic positioning of performance details. The text is never heard in its grammatical entirety; it bubbles up through the conflicting din of live and taped voices, grasped only in flashes. The manner has been likened by the composer to a cocktail party where snatches of conversation come and go,[13] and ordinary understanding is replaced by a personal reconstruction of whatever can be caught from moment to moment. Another analogy might be with the busy check-in area of an airline terminal. The taped voices of *Cento* have that depersonalized character of publicly amplified voices, where an electronic framework surrounds the text and at once isolates it, emphasizes it, and distances it; in the terminal, the half-intelligible public address announcements mix with the same-subject babble of the travellers. If the cocktail-party syndrome is a kind of aesthetic for the musical construction of the piece, the extraction of lines and words from Grier's poems is a literary complement. Furthermore, the manipulation of this already fractured text results in new combinations. For example, "without regrets … a clean blackness" becomes "lean of clean" or "lean without black." At the extreme, the text vanishes into pure sound – "tra rage dje dim ding."

The unintelligibility of much of the text and the disintegration into nonverbal units of already disjunct material beg the question as to why bother with a text at all. Unquestionably the human association with uttered sound is so fundamental and universal that we all carry unsuspected associations and interpretations of sung and spoken sounds. In an essay, Anhalt says that his subject "will be the thought and feelings which the musical voice makes audible and potentially comprehensible."[14] "Thoughts" can to a great extent be articulated with words, but what of "feelings"? For Liszt, the power of music lay in the fact that it "embodies *feeling* without forcing it – as it is forced in its other manifestations, in most arts and especially in the art of words – to contend and combine with *thought*. If music has one advantage over the other means through which man can reproduce the impressions of his soul, it owes it to its supreme capacity to make each inner impulse audible without the assistance of reason."[15] But Liszt, in his nineteenth-century romantic vision of music, was too quick to discount the possibility of a similar attribute in words. Language is notoriously limited in articulating more than the superficialities of feelings, although, as Eliot has pointed out, collections of words in the shape of poetry may impart a meaning beyond the evident meaning of the text. The concision of poetic statement has always produced a density of meaning greater than ordinary speech, and "sense" is not even a necessary part of poetry. The lasting interest of Edward Lear's poems, beginning with *A Book of Nonsense* (1864), is ample demonstration of "non-sense" becoming a kind of mysterious and nonrational sense that is nevertheless understood. Edith Sitwell's poems in *Façade* (1923) make grammatical sense, but only intermittently do they make syntactical sense; "meaning," at various levels, flashes in and out. The development of scat singing in American jazz in the 1920s moved sung language away from words to the free association of melodies and syllables, from which it has been a short step, throughout the field of modern linguistics, to the utilization of phonemes to weld together voice and music. Closely related is the drawing into textual material those expressive sounds that are as common as language and sometimes as expressive, but which are well outside the category of verbalization. In Anhalt's phrase, "we all are experienced at 'reading' the voice."[16] We may "read" sounds in ordinary language, but also in the inflections of language, and in nonverbal interjections and additions. A common example unconsciously employed but effective in its usage is the ubiquitous and endlessly varied "eh" of English-Canadian speech. As for "understanding" a text, it is a common phenomenon, especially with the twentieth century's cult of "original performance," for audiences to sit though opera performances and song recitals where they comprehend little or nothing in terms of literal interpretation of the language being sung; yet those same spectators would likely insist that they "understood" what was happening. Further, they would likely insist that they respond to that understanding at some level of internalized feeling. "Comprehension" at an intellectual level is something different from "understanding" at many possible levels. If in his earlier vocal settings Anhalt sought the subtext beneath the surface of the poem, tentatively with *Comments* and assuredly with *Cento* it seems that he first understood the subtext, and constructed the text upward from it. In other words, he became a poet.

Foci (1969)[17] requires greater forces than *Cento* and draws on more resources within the listener. The ensemble consists of ten instrumentalists, soprano, four operators of electronic equipment, and the "hammer man." The texts are assembled from many sources in many languages and, except for the extended vocal solo in section 9, all the text material is heard though the medium of prerecorded tape. The most directly coherent parts of the texts are four definitions drawn from a dictionary of psychological and psychoanalytical terms – coping behaviour, the soul, interaction, lying.[18] Additional text was "found" among a range of sources from voodoo texts to newspapers, Greek words, and invented phrases. The sources of the materials, however, are of no more importance than the origins of items assembled by an artist into a collage. What matters, and what is ultimately undiscoverable, is what these objects of words evoke in the mind and memory of each individual beholder. The fractured, macaronic text has some similarity to the text and its treatment in *Cento*, but in *Foci* the scope is much greater. The sporadic texts, phrases, words and sounds, which are always spoken and always emerge from the electronic source, finally coalesce in the actual voice of the soprano, whose solo is presented in a fully lyrical style, only to dissolve at the end through a diminishing vocalise, through nonverbal sounds, and to vanish finally in a gentle, oscillating moan that slips into the void of primordial silence. In some obvious ways, *Foci* stimulates memory and association to a greater extent than previous vocal works by Anhalt. The "hammerman," with his mallet blows, exists outside the sections of the piece and serves to announce and to define them. His invisible offstage presence recalls the French theatrical tradition of announcing the beginning of a performance by striking the stage floor with a heavy stock, a tradition that continues to the present day. "Measures," the first extended section following the opening "Preamble," is built entirely around the pitch A, while speaking voices emit disjointed words and numbers, clearly reminiscent of the tuning up and testing at the beginning of a performance. The final exit of the players one by one cannot help but recall the finale of Haydn's "Farewell" Symphony. The withdrawal of the musicians at the end is paralleled by their appearance at the beginning of the work, where they march on one by one, again reminding the audience of a conventional concert, but with the unorthodox accompaniment of a text in English, German, and French (the first of the "definitions"), which is coherent and precipitates the musical and dramatic action: "Action that enables one to adjust to the environmental circumstances; to get something done." The visual control of the opening and closing of the work is brought close to ritual in the appearance of the soprano, who approaches the stage through the audience during the lengthy "Preparation" that precedes her solo. The visual element in concert music has been a consideration for composers other than Anhalt. One thinks, for example, of the masked players in George Crumb's *Black Angels*, or any number of incidents in the works of R. Murray Schafer. Such visual details touch on the ritual aspect of theatre and, in combination with words, excite a myriad of responses in the spectator. *Foci* reminds us of the common experience of concert going, it recalls some vague theatrical tradition for announcing a beginning, and it conjures up the varicoloured world of language that is discovered in turning the dial on a short-wave radio. Beyond all this, it disturbs thought that is not yet articulated.

Recollection is one of the levers of the mind that is operated by *Cento* or *Foci*, and it is an element that begins to take on increasing importance in Anhalt's own writing – recollection that is personal, recollection that stirs within the listener. Even the later orchestral pieces *Simulacrum* (1986–87) and *SparkskrapS* (1987) contain elements of retrospection – not in a programmatic way, but in the utilization of material that originates in shadows across the composer's own memory. In a work for string quartet in memory of Glenn Gould, *Doors … shadows* (1992), Anhalt's note concludes: "What does the piece add up to in the end? … memories … blurred shadows behind half-open doors."[19] Memory, so urgent a concern of Anhalt's, is at the very root of Wordsworth's famous definition of poetry in the preface to *Lyrical Ballads* (1800): "I have said that poetry is the spontaneous overflow of powerful feelings: it takes its origin from emotion recollected in tranquility."

As with *Foci*, the text of Anhalt's first large dramatic piece, *La Tourangelle* (1975),[20] is drawn from many varied sources; most of them are directly related to Marie de l'Incarnation, the Woman of Tours, although some of them are peripheral. That the texts are in both French and English clearly has symbolic value within the extended historical framework of the the country in which Marie and her successors will do their work. Marie, who is always represented by a trio of sopranos, sings only in French until the final scene of arrival in Quebec, when the achievement of the spiritual and physical destination of Quebec is distinctively celebrated in Latin. As in *Cento* the taped voices and the performing singers may overlap, move in parallel, or alternate, and their texts may be shared, may be closely related, or may represent quite independent streams of thought. But whereas in the choral piece the text was compressed, here the multiple texts cover a range of information and expression, and it is the fusion of differing levels of expression through their sharing of a single subject that produces the poetic character of the piece. The drama – for it is a drama, even if it is not scenic in a theatrical way – consists of five initial episodes that provide the factual and spiritual history of Marie de l'Incarnation, and that lead to the arrival of Marie in Quebec as the climax, so that most of the work is preparation towards that event. The work is about two voyages: one is spiritual, from secular wife and mother to Ursuline sister; and the other is physical, from Old World to New France. This is the art of history, where the aim is not objectivity, but a subjective recovery of past events and their reverberation in present memory. Verdi, Meyerbeer, Donizetti, among many others, wrote historical operas in which history is modified to serve musical and dramatic ends. In *La Tourangelle* factual account and personal reflection run parallel. What is true for the origins of poetry, at least as Wordsworth saw it, might be said to be equally true for one's reaction to it. Although the musical and dramatic situations may be anything but tranquil, the spectator to the musical/textual work is nonetheless drawn to the still centre of interior emotion.

The canvas on which *Winthrop* (1983) is drawn is much larger than the one for *La Tourangelle,* but the approach is similar. This "Musical Pageant in Two Parts" is a nontheatrical dramatic work in which the "action" advances by a series of discrete episodes which, cumulatively, relay to us the external facts and the interior existence of John Winthrop, first governor of Boston. Again, Anhalt drew his text from a myriad of sources ranging from the papers of Winthrop himself, to religious tracts and books, and the works of such authors as John Bunyan and Christina Rossetti. In parallel texts, phonetic texts, dramatic dialogues, and lyrical episodes, the story unfolds at multiple levels from the plainly factual to the abstractly spiritual. Anhalt has commented on the crucial scene where the Puritan settlers first see the land after so long at sea and their mixed relief and terror when "the virgin forest, reaching down right to the shore line, comes into view, astonishment, confusion, fear chokes off the voices, so jubilant just a short while ago. This changes within minutes into short bursts of exclamations, interspersed with silence (holding one's breath), conveying the effects of disorientation, indignation, fear and outrage."[21] More personally, the composer has related this scene to the experience of his arrival in Canada in 1949 and his impression of the vastness of space and the forests as he travelled from Halifax to Montreal.[22] Forty years later, the memory of this experience was written into the journey and arrival of John Winthrop. During the Puritan voyage, the temporal aspect in the weather report – "Fair, clear weather, in the morning and wind west and north" – contrasts with the spiritual aspect – "A Citty upon a Hill we shall be, the eyes of all the people upon us." The sight of land calls up pleasant observations – "many small islands ... Warm pleasant air," but the arrival projects both the dismay of the settlers as well as the future of the city: "A Citty, Boston ... We all die in Boston. It is wet and cold in Boston. Bitter frost and snow, we know fear, death in the woods, death in the dark, the scurvy ... no hope ... Boston a Bust-ton, a Sub-ton, a Frost-ton ... a Snow-ton ... a No-ton." The text becomes cross-currents of phonetic outbursts, plays around the word "Boston," recitations of the prosaic business of building a city of law and authority, punishment, taxes, and treachery.

Soon after composing *Winthrop*, Anhalt completed *Thisness* (1985), for soprano and accompanist. *Thisness* and *A Wedding Carol*, from the same year, are the first works with texts written entirely by Anhalt, as distinguished from those texts that are his original collages. The text of the *Carol* is simple and direct, its setting a controlled declamation over sustained chords. By contrast, *Thisness* is a large work in ten sections and, like *Winthrop* and *La Tourangelle*, it is a dramatic piece, described in the subtitle as "a duo-drama cycle for mezzo-soprano and accompanist." Anhalt has written that *Winthrop*, *La Tourangelle*, and *Thisness* "have a common *locus*. It is not a place, nor is it an area, but rather a 'state,' both in the physical and psychic sense: 'the state' of being in 'transit,' going from one place to another ... On second thought, ... it is rather the memory of being 'in transit' that I was composing in these works."[23] Lines from the opening poem could be a motto for all of Anhalt's vocal works, especially the later ones:[24]

Listen first
 and then listen some more
 to the voices that come along.

And towards the end of the piece, lines refer again to memory:

Silence only
 remains ...
  wrapped in recall ...

Between the beginning and the end of *Thisness* are phrases that catch at the prevailing sense of the piece: "that distant land," "questions," "a voice speaking in silence," "the journey back home," "where is my home?" "the voice across the din," "thinking of days yet to come / and of those that one ought not to forget," "the voice, also, will go away ... / in time," "a long time ago."

The climactic midpoint, "Vertigo," spins its words into segments, until phonemic material itself (written with the international phonetic symbols) replaces verbal formulations.[25] "Theatre pieces" became a commonplace in the late-twentieth century, whether in theatres, performance spaces, or even concert halls, and *Thisness* belongs to the genre. The visual activity of both performers is an integral part of the piece, so that action is one with text and music. The unity of text and music, the manners of delivery, movement, costume change, the visual/musical/textual involvement of the singer and accompanist – all of it focused around the singer, who is the vehicle, the voice of the work. To paraphrase Yeats, can one tell the singer from the song?[26]

The nonscenic dramas, dramas of the voice, that began with *Cento* all lead to *Traces (Tikkun)* (1995), "a Pluri-drama in One Act for Lyric Baritone and Orchestra." The solo singer, according to the composer/poet, may represent a number of persons, incidents within the mind of a single person, or an ambiguous combination.[27] The work is preceded by a set of quotations, two of which give clues to the title. One is from Plotinus, *Enneads* (book 6.7.17): "Whenever intellectual Principle becomes the determinant of soul, it shapes it into Reasoning Soul, by communicating a trace of what itself has come to possess."[28] The other is from Gershom Scholem's *Kabbalah*: "*tikkun* ... the restoration of the universe to its original design."[29] Whatever Anhalt may say about the various possibilities for interpreting the identity of the soloist, it is not difficult to perceive the author in the ten sections of the text, as he sets out traces of his own existence and seeks the original design of his own universe. The lines that are traced out are not always pleasant – the tortured and terrifying passage through the labyrinth, the cruelty of modern life, the repression of life forces – images that are cast out of a darkness that threatens but does not overtake Anhalt's earlier works. We are taken back fifty years to the caged ape of *Na Conxy Pan* with the brutality of the images. But here there is "The Answer," as the last section is entitled, in a resolution of the tensions of existence, which becomes an apotheosis towards a lightness of being as text dissolves into sound and into silence:

The Voice now points to an incline that I haven't noticed before.
I obey and move along
feeling extremely light, with things melting into a blur of grey
I seem to be floating now
shifting into the weight of light
a self-free thought
a free-from-all-thought self
a thingless spark amidst other sparks
in a no-where and everywhen
the ONE-NO-END
father, fader, athir
mētēr, muotar, mathir
abba, imma
to all
pulsing, pulse
/pal//pal//pal//pa//pa//pa//p//p//p//p/

The centripetal motion of Anhalt's art repudiates the centrifugal movement of modern life in the twentieth century, and the guide on the inward journey is the voice, in which music and poetry meet.

NOTES

1 Istvan Anhalt, *Alternative Voices: Essays on Contemporary Vocal and Choral Composition* (Toronto: University of Toronto Press, 1984).

2 The scores of all works by Anhalt mentioned in this article are available at the Canadian Music Centre. Where a composition has been published, the details are given in a note at the first mention of the piece.

3 Istvan Anhalt, *A Little Wedding Music* (Toronto: Berandol Music, 1985).

4 T.S. Eliot, "The Music of Poetry," in his *On Poetry and Poets* (London: Faber & Faber, 1957), 29.

5 T.S. Eliot, "Poetry and Drama," in *On Poetry and Poets*, 86–7; ellipsis added.

6 Pablo Picasso, *Bull's Head* (1943). The work is formed from the juxtaposition of a bicycle seat and handlebars.

7 The piece is defined visually by the opening and closing of the fall-board over the keys of a piano. The only sound is what occurs naturally within the visually defined time frame.

8 Gordon E. Smith, " 'Deep Themes' Not So Hidden in the Music of István Anhalt," *Queen's Quarterly* 98, 1 (spring 1991): 103–4.

9 Istvan Anhalt, *Cento* (Don Mills, Ont.: BMI Canada, 1968).

10 See Willi Apel, *Gregorian Chant* (Bloomington: Indiana University Press, 1958), 316, 340.

11 In Eldon Grier, *Selected Poems 1955–1970* (Montreal: Delta Canada, 1971), 34–55.

12 Anhalt's text is printed in Istvan Anhalt, "The Making of *Cento*," *Canada Music Book* 1 (spring-summer 1970): 82.

13 Anhalt, "The Making of *Cento*," 83.

14 Istvan Anhalt, "Pst ... Pst ... Are You Listening? Hearing Voices from Yesterday," *Queen's Quarterly* 93, 1 (spring 1986): 71.

15 Franz Liszt, "Berlioz and his 'Harold' Symphony" (1855; reprint, Oliver Strunk, ed. and trans., *Source Readings in Music History*, New York: W.W. Norton, 1950), 849.

16 Anhalt, "Pst ... Pst ... Are You Listening?" 71.

17 Istvan Anhalt, *Foci* (Toronto, Ont.: Berandol Music, 1972).

18 Horace B. English and Ava Champney English, *A Comprehensive Dictionary of Psychological and Psychoanalytical Terms: A Guide to Usage* (New York: David McKay Co., 1958). The definitions are coping behaviour, the soul, interaction, lying.

19 Program book for the opening of the Glenn Gould Studio (CBC Broadcast Centre, Toronto, September 1992), 133; ellipses in original.
20 Istvan Anhalt, *La Tourangelle* (Toronto: Berandol Music, 1982).
21 Istvan Anhalt, "Music: Context, Text, Counter-text," *Contemporary Music Review* 5 (1989): 129.
22 Smith, "Deep Themes," 99.
23 Anhalt, "Music: Context, Text, Counter-text," 113; ellipses in original.
24 The text for *Thisness* is printed in Istvan Anhalt, "*Thisness*: Marks and Remarks," in *Musical Canada: Words and Music Honouring Helmut Kallmann*, ed. John Beckwith and Frederick A. Hall (Toronto: University of Toronto Press, 1988), 215–24; ellipses in original.
25 The text of "Vertigo" is printed in Istvan Anhalt, "Text, Context, Music," *Canadian University Music Review*, 9, 2 (1988): 15. See also, Anhalt "*Thisness*," 219.
26 O chestnut-tree, great-rooted blossomer,
    Are you the leaf, the blossom or the bole?
    O body swayed to music, O brightening glance,
    How can we know the dancer from the dance?
        (W.B. Yeats, "Among School Children")
27 Composer's note at the end of the unpublished libretto.
28 Plotinus, *The Enneads*, trans. Stephen McKenna (London: Faber & Faber, 1969), 575.
29 Gershom Scholem, *Kabbalah* (New York: Quadrangle, 1974), 140; ellipses in original.

9 Between the Keys:
Istvan Anhalt Writing on Music

AUSTIN CLARKSON

In memory of Alan Lessem •

How delicately
The silver threads of rain
Sew sky to earth

Basho[1]

Words about music enliven the distances that separate the musical idea from the experience of music like the threads of rain that, in the lines of the haiku, sew sky to earth. When composers who are drawn to express themselves in language as well as in music also devise their own verbal texts for vocal compositions, there is a reciprocal effect – as though the rain threads upwards as well as down.

There is a dynamic engagement between speech about music and music itself, between reflection on music and musical thought, that differs greatly from one composer to another. For some, language is a means of objectifying and transcending music, while for others language subjectifies and embodies the sounding image. For composers like Istvan Anhalt, music and language are mutual fields for creative thought. A new idea in one has implications for a new idea in the other. At any given time one may find Anhalt constructing typologies to describe the range of effects of a vocal composition, immersing himself in a hermeneutic approach to the deep structure, or composing his own dramatic or poetic text to set to music. Since 1967 most of Anhalt's compositions have been formed around verbal texts and vocal behaviour in general, and his writings focus on his own works and pieces by contemporaries who are similarly engaged. In Anhalt's work, speech about music, music about speech, and the music *of* speech flow together. Though it is not easy to separate these activities, this essay mainly addresses Anhalt's speech *about* music.

The first impression one has when reading Anhalt's prose is of being told a story. Anhalt guides the reader across expanses of intellectual terrain and into thickets of sometimes abstruse ideas as though it were some kind of adventure. He avoids the hortatory style in which strings of propositions and networks of syllogisms are unrelieved by a pause to take stock, pose a question, or appeal to the feelings and imagination. Anhalt blends assertions and questions, images and demonstrations, abstractions and concrete descriptions in a way that leaves room for wondering and perhaps asking one's own questions. Which is not to say that he does not set out to make a point, but he does so circuitously, or better spirally, burrowing in masses of detail until a larger picture eventually becomes clear. Topics succeed each other rather like ideas in his music, with an inner necessity that depends on the powers of intuitive association rather than linearly directed thinking. The straight lines of the warp and woof are often hidden by the figures in the fabric, and sometimes they are strained to the breaking point by the wealth of ideas and images attached to the matter in question. But this is the *felix culpa* of one whose curiosity knows few bounds and who takes pleasure in sharing the lore he has gathered. In an autobiographical sketch Anhalt tells of a four-year-old boy who poked a penknife blade between the keys of the upright piano in his living room to discover what sounds were hiding in the thin dark spaces between the keys.[2] It is just such rummaging about in the in-betweenness of things that gives Anhalt's writing its interest and value as a contribution to the theory of new vocal music.

In the 1970s Anhalt published essays on his own musical compositions and Berio's *Sequenza III* (see appendix for Anhalt bibliography). Then in 1984 the University of Toronto Press brought out *Alternative Voices: Essays on Contemporary Vocal and Choral Composition*.[3] After *Alternative Voices* Anhalt wrote further essays on his new compositions and continued to theorize about new music for the voice. In "Text, Context, Music"[4] Anhalt proceeds from the text outward to particulars of musical setting, while in "Music: Context, Text, Counter-text"[5] he constructs a typology of contexts and moves from there to the notion of genres of new vocal music.

Alternative Voices marks the first book-length theoretical treatment of music from the 1960s and '70s that employs extended vocal techniques. Even to this day that repertoire is hardly mentioned in texts on the theory of twentieth-century music. On the threshold of the twenty-first century, music that does not prescribe tempered pitch classes and metred durations still arouses little interest among music theorists. The first half of this pioneering book consists of analyses of three vocal compositions – Luciano Berio's *Sequenza III*, György Ligeti's *Nouvelles Aventures*, and Witold Lutoslawski's *Trois Poèmes d'Henri Michaux* – while the second half comprises four essays that treat a broad repertoire according to topics that were raised in the course of the analyses. The subject is vast – new music for voice from the mid-1950s through the 1970s – and Anhalt does not take the task lightly. Although he casts his net very wide – the list of compositions mentioned numbers an astonishing 265 titles by 109 composers – the approach is not that of the usual survey. The focus constantly shifts from a few works examined in depth to overviews of broader swaths of the repertoire. In addition to the three composers mentioned above Anhalt shows special interest in John Beckwith, John Cage, Peter Maxwell Davies, Mauricio Kagel, Luigi Nono, R. Murray Schafer, Dieter Schnebel, and Karlheinz Stockhausen. (He mentions four of his own pieces, but does not give them an extended treatment in the book.) No less extensive than the number of compositions mentioned is a bibliography of more than 350 authors in fields as far-flung as anthropology, ethnomusicology, linguistics (phonetics and psycholinguistics), literature (narratology and prosody), mythology, philosophy (epistemology, semantics, and semiotics), physiology of the voice, depth psychology, religion (esoteric traditions and shamanism), sociology and sociolinguistics, and visual art.

The book is the record of a search through the intellectual highways and artistic byways of the last thirty years for a context for musical ideas that for the most part have been ignored by music theorists. It is unusual to be conducted on such a tour by a writer whose primary medium of communication is organized sound. Many composers commit their thoughts to the printed page with essays on their own music, their formative influences, and their life and times, but few contemporary composers have made the effort to analyze in depth the music of their immediate contemporaries. Stockhausen, for one, admits that he writes prose only about his own music, introducing a recent collection of his writings this way: "The fundamental purpose of this selection of texts is to make the reader aware that Stockhausen is a composer who has also from time to time expressed himself in words, and that his music expresses what is beyond words in a purer and more universal language."[6] Anhalt, by contrast, strives to convey what is beyond words in both language *and* music, preferably in tandem. And so his words about new vocal music serve not only his own compositions, but those of his contemporaries as well. His approach might be compared to that of George Rochberg, who is one year senior to Anhalt and whose book *The Aesthetics of Survival: A Composer's View of Twentieth-Century Music*, a collection of essays on many different topics, appeared in the same year as *Alternative Voices*. But Anhalt's book treats at length a subject that emerges from the composer's own workshop and so is more closely related to Harry Partch's *Genesis of a Music* (1974), R. Murray Shafer's *The Tuning of the World* (1977), or Iannis Xenakis' *Formalized Music* (1971). In *Alternative Voices* Anhalt develops his interest in new vocal music, especially opera, into a comprehensive study of the genre. His approach to building a theory for this music is of necessity eclectic, as there are few precedents for analyzing extended vocal techniques and few studies of contemporary opera. But there is an overarching objective, and that is to discover the broad commonalities and the deep structures of this music. The book documents a composer's journey as he seeks to understand his own creative process in the context of his contemporaries.

The introductory chapter is a synopsis of the trends in vocal practice that depart from the tradition of *bel canto* singing in the first half of the twentieth century – the cabaret *diseur/diseuse*, the operatic melodrama, the Dada sound poem, automatic writing of the surrealists, the agit-prop speech choir, the theatre of Alfred Jarry and Antonin Artaud, the novels of James Joyce, and so on. Anhalt's leading question is whether extended vocal techniques and nonlexical texts are merely a passing phase. That these new developments are here to stay is affirmed by the scope of the survey and the depth of the essays that discuss outstanding compositions in the genre.

Anhalt does not set out a fully articulated theory exemplified by excerpts from a variety of pieces of music. His method is inductive rather than deductive. Rather than worrying about semantics and terminology, he gives pride of place to the complete work and begins with the three signature essays on pieces by Berio, Ligeti, and Lutoslawski, arranged in order of increasing size of performing group. The theory accumulates in stages in the course of analyzing these pieces, as the nature of each piece poses a different theoretical issue. The Berio work is for solo voice, the Ligeti piece is for three solo voices and a small instrumental ensemble, while the Lutoslawski composition is for two large ensembles – a mixed chorus in twenty parts (one to three on a part) and a chamber orchestra of twenty-three musicians, with a conductor for each ensemble. Furthermore, Berio treats a short text to multiple degrees of dissociation, the text of the Ligeti is constructed from a kind of artificial language, and Lutoslawski sets three extensive poems, one for each of the three movements. The three essays taken together approach many of the most difficult issues of analyzing and interpreting new music for voices; nevertheless, they are linked by assumptions fundamental to Anhalt's method, which can be inferred from the opening paragraphs of each essay, reproduced as follows.

Berio's Sequenza III *: A portrait*

In *Sequenza III* Luciano Berio has created a vocal portrait of a woman, probably North American, who goes through a series of puzzling and disturbing vocal behaviours, making us wonder why she expresses herself in this manner and what she wants to convey to us. It seems that she is in no mood to address us through a coherent discourse, spoken or sung, and perhaps she is incapable of doing so. She seems, during much of her delivery, to be oblivious to our presence and to her environment. The thought may occur to us that she is acting in a dream. She reveals what might appear to one as a great variety of feelings, highly unstable moods, anxieties, neurosis, psychosis, and she is quite unconcerned with these and possibly unable to conceal them. In some ways she acts like a young child, or like an adult who has regressed to childhood, and her account gushes forth with great intensity. We sense that she may be a person whose thinking and perceiving are regulated more by irrepressible desires or needs, than by an awareness of any objective reality around her. Her changes of mood occur erratically and, at times, rapidly. We have no clues as to the psychic triggers that set off her vocal actions, and she seems to relate to no outside trigger at all. The impression that she exists in, and speak-sings from, a dream world persists, but on occasion we may discern an inflection of appeal in her voice, as if she is calling out of the dream, addressing people "on the outside." These appeals do not last long, though, and she soon relapses into her dreamlike world.

As contrast follows contrast in her delivery we wonder what is taking place in her mind. What are the sources of her anxiety? Whom is she fighting? From whom is she fleeing?[7]

Ligeti's Nouvelles Aventures *: A small group as a model for composition*

György Ligeti's *Nouvelles Aventures* is a story in music, vocal and instrumental, about three people. The language used is artificial, invented by the composer himself. Far from sounding like gibberish, it appears as a pseudo-language possessing clearly observable properties such as a limited phonemic repertoire, restricted assemblies of phonemic dyads and longer chains providing structure and order, as if it were the language of a newly discovered tribe or perhaps an enactment of the linguistic evolution of such a group. Such a supposition may suggest certain Jungian echoes, resonances from a shared phylogenetic past or from the early history of the species. This strange-sounding language, complemented with facial and other gestures, seems to tell us about certain basic situations in a social setting as old, if not older, than the ochre bulls on the walls of the caves of Lascaux, yet also as fresh and topical as yesterday's context among rivals for power and as timeless as a courtship ritual or family scene.

Ligeti seems to have two concerns here. As the piece unfolds we are learning about the personalities of the three protagonists, and about the syntality[8]

of the group. Of the three vocalists, two sustain at times what one is led to identify as roles. In the first of the two parts of the work the baritone appears as an
initiator of actions that reinforce the cohesive tendencies of the group. The
other role-player, the soprano, assumes the character of a person with a disrup-
tive influence (this emerges in the second part of the piece). Apart from these
relatively stable character traits, the moods of the three protagonists shift frequently, and often surprisingly. There is no plot. The composer suggests that
we observe the unfolding of emotive curves, surges of affects and energies, that
engage us in empathy or aversion. As the piece begins we are trying to guess
the nature of the affective states portrayed and their causes, the changes of
moods, the patterns of interaction, and the environment. Despite, or perhaps
because of, the largely a-semantic pseudo-speech, we find it possible to identify
group attitudes, such as agreement, disagreement, dominance, submissiveness,
sincerity, lying, persistence, hesitation, fatigue. Certain sustained group attitudes and tendencies can also be sensed. These emerge in the course of the
work and indicate the macro-structure of the composition. This structure depends on the energy generated by the group and on the succession of such
patterns of energy. These energy packages are divided between those that are
aimed at the formation and maintenance of the group itself and those that
constitute action directed towards the external world. The various ways of ap-
portioning the available group energy constitute one of the deepest strata of
the work. Ultimately the work appears as an enactment of the emergence of a
small society, its evolution, and its eventual decay.[9]

Lutoslawski's Trois Poèmes d'Henri Michaux: *Voices of a multitude*

At first impression this work appears as a statement of the collective soul of a
community, an utterance pensive, aggressive, and distant in turn, supported by
instrumental sounds of considerable complexity and of many hues. Repeated
hearings, and a study of the score, bring out numerous details of such ordered
intricacy that one's attention slips away from the broad expressive contours of
the work, and one becomes occupied with the special nature of the component structures, with the composer's methods of work, and with the fascinating
strategy required for the performance. However, as soon as a clear enough understanding of the details is achieved, all the elements come together again,
and the original perception reasserts itself with force. All the techniques, material, and strategies are then understood to be serving a unified affective whole,
without losing their identity in the multi-faceted hierarchy of the work. There
is a complementary relationship between the sharply etched contour and
sculpted surface on the one hand and the richly diverse, and always appropriately crafted, detail on the other. This balance makes the work a statement that
sounds right, is to the point, and is credible, articulate, timely, and timeless. It
is composed so well that it appears spontaneous, easy, almost an improvisation

in places. It is a work of grandeur, of bold strokes and large gestures, and may remind one of the allure of the murals of an Orozco or a Siqueiros, in as much as it exhibits a combination of raw strength and broadness of grasp with a capability for tenderness and subtlety. Lutoslawski speaks in terms of sound-masses, and not in terms of individual melodies, polyphonies, or harmonic structures in which individual lines maintain their identity. His vehicles here are almost exclusively, vibrant, multi-voiced choral declamation; heterorhythmic structures, using from one to twelve pitch-classes, and their variants; and compound constructs consisting of combinations of these structures in a considerable variety of relationships. Even when the piece speaks in hushed tones, it implies large spaces of the depths of a collective subconscious. The entire work lives in a non-pulsing sound-time, a feature that contributes its seeming spontaneity and elemental strength. Groups, and their individual constituents (which almost always remain submerged in the whole, except at the work's seams – the beginnings and the endings of certain substructures), have just the right length. How is this flexibility achieved? A glance at the score shows that Lutoslawski not only had a clear conception of the total character of the piece, but also engineered an ingenious and economical notational scheme and a matching performance strategy to bring the work to life.[10]

Some general observations about these passages follow:

1 The analysis proceeds from a holistic image of the deep structure to the analysis of parts. Priority is given to an imaginative engagement with the music as a whole conveyed in language rich in affects and synaesthetic images. It is a hermeneutic in which musical elements have both a metaphorical and a structural function. Synthetic statements are balanced by analytic statements, for attention shifts readily from parts to the whole and from deep structure to surface details.

2 Music for voice is contingent on the form and expression of the literary content. The deep structure of a vocal composition can thus be represented by a plot, story, or dramatic narrative that is usually directed toward a catharsis.

3 The elements of conscious vocal behaviour (phonemes, morphemes, lexemes, whether linguistic or paralinguistic) embody postures, gestures, and psychosocial interactions that link an utterance to instinctual, unconscious, archaic levels of culture. Speech sounds thus have symbolic (connotative) as well as denotative meanings so that the surface features of a vocal event embody archetypal images of psyche and society.

4 Each verbal/musical image carries an affect, and each affect-image carries a charge or quantum of energy. The flow of energy quanta can be described by concepts and nomenclature from psycho- and

sociolinguistics (e.g., syntality). The deep structure of a vocal composition can be formulated as a pattern of affect-images and social interaction marked by such terms as "agreement," "dominance," "sincerity," "persistence," and their opposites.

5 Synaesthesia is an essential modality of imaginative perception and cognition; hence synaesthetic correspondences are a valid means of interpreting musical images. Music may be associated with visual art, film, dance, or poetry; and visual imagery and gestures can evoke musical sounds.

6 The listener has an intuitive capacity to evaluate music as successful or "just right." An important criterion of success is whether the work gives the impression of improvisation and spontaneity. Listeners are thereby invited to trust their innate formal sense as to what is "just right" (or "just wrong").

These points indicate that Anhalt's theoretical position presents a challenge to mainstream music theory, which is concerned for the most part with nontexted music. In fact, we might conclude that a theorist's position is contingent on the musical genre of choice, and that Anhalt's "alternative voices" are raised in support of an alternative music theory.

It is fitting that Anhalt should give pride of place to the music of Berio, the grand master of the new music for the voice, who is as accomplished with *bel canto* as with radical digressions from it. For *Sequenza III* Anhalt must devise a system for the analysis of vocal music which is indeterminate with respect to pitch and duration. He first distinguishes five classes of oral expression, namely (1) rapid, well-articulated, periodic utterances; (2) pauses; (3) vocal tics and other interjections; (4) sustained singing; and (5) timbre modification. Each of these classes is then described in terms of such features as affect, range, register, directionality, intensity (degrees of loudness), duration, text use, and psycholinguistic analogies. This produces a sufficiently detailed matrix to cover the techniques employed, and the essay concludes with a summary table in which the piece is described section by section with respect to this matrix. In this way an extensive array of types of vocal utterance is construed as a structure of affect-images. At a deeper level the analysis demonstrates that Berio's composition is a play of psychosocial processes.

Ligeti's *Nouvelles Aventures* employs tempered pitches and metrical durations in addition to extended vocal techniques, and so Anhalt adds more familiar analytic techniques to the schema of affect-images of vocal behaviour. The new dimension in this analysis is the sociolinguistic process that arises from the interactions among the three singers. At the outset Anhalt sets up the hypothesis that phonemes are associated cross-culturally with particular affects. It is a hypothesis that is, of course, disputed by relativists, but is consonant with the view that at least some universals prevail in human biology, physiology, psychology, and sociology, as well as language. Where relevant, Anhalt discusses tone-rows and their manipulation in terms of serial schemata and feeds the pitch and duration structures back into the deep structural process of the underlying drama of interactions. For example, when the alto and baritone sing a few phrases in a pseudo-chorale style, he points out that "it is a rigorous construct derived from the basic row, using the unordered hexachords of the 2P [prime] and 5I [inverted] [12-tone row forms] in the two voices ... Harmonically the two phrases show identical interval distribution ...

The overall affect is of a liturgical ceremony, all trappings and no substance. It is a rough caricature, abrasive by design. It suggests that a pseudo-harmony and an over-simple mode of synchronization have been substituted for the co-operation that prevailed during part I."[11] Anhalt fleshes out the scenario with detailed descriptions of the vocal sounds and phonemes uttered by the singers and interprets these as affect states and, at a higher level of organization, as patterns of psychosocial interactions between the singers. The first scene "begins with a short but mighty yell emitted by the baritone ... Its characteristics are as follows: high-pitched, loud, short, emphatic, on the vowel /a/, a typically male open-mouthed sound ... This sound, the result of a brief burst of powerful sound energy, is an optimal signal for relatively long-distance communication. It may be a command message, or an appeal perhaps ... Whenever it appears, it is a signal for some action aimed at strengthening the bond among the three participants."[12]

For Anhalt the musical content is the outer manifestation of a deep structure, which is a plot that he introduces in the opening paragraphs of his discussion of Ligeti's *Nouvelles Aventures*, given above, and then synopsizes as follows: "This drama has two parts of approximately the same duration. The first part begins with what appears to be a chance encounter of the three individuals [soprano, alto, baritone] and shows the group's evolution from a less to a more complex state. The second part depicts the group as it destroys itself through aggression conveyed through speech acts and kinesics. (It is a progression from a more complex to a less complex state.) Increasingly strong centrifugal tendencies come to dominate and gradually outmatch the dwindling residue of the energy that earlier provided cohesion. Ligeti tells this intricate tale in about twelve and a half minutes, a remarkably short duration, given its content and impact."[13] The translation of the music into the plot of a psychodrama is persuasive and arresting, but one understands that he is inviting us to confirm or disprove his interpretation by listening to the music for ourselves. In the closing summary he states his conclusions with unmistakable finality, and yet poses questions that cut through to fundamental issues of ethical social aspirations: "The meaning of the conclusion of *Nouvelles Aventures* is all too clear in its terrifying pessimism. Ligeti, after offering us a compressed model for socio-genesis, ends with a show of social disintegration. Are the causes for the extinction of the group to be looked for outside or inside itself, or both? Is there an inherent conflict between personality and syntality, between personal freedom and group organization? Are there irresistible destructive forces embedded in the human brain, co-existing with the constructive ones? What are our chances of making the constructive forces prevail over the destructive ones?"[14]

After finishing this essay Anhalt came upon a description that Ligeti himself had written of the composition. For the most part Ligeti's remarks confirm, sometimes uncannily, the general tenor of Anhalt's interpretation. For instance, Ligeti wrote, "Through the affective stratum of the text-sound composition, as well as through the gestures and mime that derive from it, the purely musical layer suggests the direction towards an emotively exactly defined imaginary scenic disposition that is yet undefined as to content. By listening to a performance of the concert version of the piece one experiences a kind of 'opera' with fantastic imaginary adventures of imaginary persons on an imaginary stage."[15] But Ligeti maintained that there is no "deeper meaning" hidden beyond the performed events and so there is no need to construct a deep plot: "Despite the seeming absurdity and enigmatic character, the protagonists and the emotional and social situations are directly intelligible, and transparent. We don't find out what the story is about – and, in a deeper sense there is, of course, no story, yet we quite precisely find out how the persons behave and in what relationship towards each other they stand."[16] Ligeti prefers to leave the drama ambiguous, as though it were an abstractionist play of dramatic elements. Anhalt's interpretation is thus an intervention, the creative product of his imaginal bonding with the piece, which embodies his own projections on the work. While Anhalt endows the music with a sociopsychological program, Ligeti would have it that his music is devoid of such tendentious messages: "The alienated presentation of human behaviour does not mean by itself a criticism of society. When aspects of 'society' are treated ironically, are caricatured or daemonized, through the process of being recomposed, this takes place without any bias. Precisely, the aversion to 'deeper meaning' and to ideology makes for me any form of 'committed art' impossible. The behavioural clichés of society are for my compositional work merely material for realistic formation and transformation; to project the work back onto society might take place unintentionally but it was never the object of my artistic reflections."[17] Of course composers have written music to programs that they have then declined to publish, or, once published, have later withdrawn – Ligeti appears to rule that out. Anhalt does not confront the differences between Ligeti's paradigm of meaning and his own, but closes off the essay by saying simply that the piece is open to a variety of personal assessments of its meaning. Later, he would take up the question of multiple interpretations that listeners bring to the work of art in "Music: Context, Text, Counter-text."

Lutoslawski's *Trois Poèmes d'Henri Michaux* at first glance appears to be a more familiar type of vocal music in which the composer selects a set of poems and then proceeds to write a musical setting. But the situation is more complex. Lutoslawski stated that he selected the poems by Michaux after and not before he had made a general outline of the entire work. He stated, nevertheless, that "the verse, its sense and construction, and even particular words had to exert an influence on the music of my composition."[18] Anhalt discusses stylistic and thematic parallels between Michaux's poetry and Lutoslawski's music in considerable depth. In describing the music Anhalt comes to terms with the analysis of Lutoslawski's characteristic mass structures and mass events in which individual voice parts are submerged in a vast panorama of collective activities. Here Anhalt's background in electronic music comes to the fore as he coins terms and concepts for handling these musical processes economically but evocatively, supplying a valuable glossary of definitions of the terms he has invented or borrowed – for example, accumulation, bundle, double pump, fan, interlock, and sweep. Rather than a section-by-section description of the piece, the emphasis is on topics – the element of chance, and how problems of notation and performance are solved, for example. The essay is a fascinating introduction to the composer's workshop by someone who so genuinely admires his colleague's work. The essay closes with a formulation about the structure of *Trois Poèmes* that highlights the importance for Anhalt of the archetypal and depth-psychological dimension of vocal music: "Lutoslawski has composed the details of this work in a manner congenial to the individual performer; by massing many such performer-individuals into groups, he has created a work that gives voice to the group as a whole. This voice has many shades of expression. At times it may even sound as the expression of the subconscious of a larger-than-life-size individual. Through this illusion the group and the individual merge into each other. The implication of this symmetrical relationship, which exists between a person and the groups to which he or she belongs, brings one to a deep stratum of the work, beyond notes and beyond other surface features. This is the level where the listener finds himself, face to face, in the most intimate contact with the composer."[19]

By representing the deep structure of the work as the internal process of a single psyche, Anhalt is proposing a hermeneutic reading of psychological dynamics both inter- and intrapersonal.

In the course of these three chapters Anhalt builds up a comprehensive set of analytical procedures on the frameworks of concepts and terminology supplied by the psychology of linguistic and social behaviour and the composition of electroacoustic music. It is a comprehensive framework for the theory and practice of this repertoire. The remaining chapters of *Alternative Voices* take broader perspectives of the repertoire. "Blurred Boundaries" sets out from the observation that the concepts of "a composer," "a composition," "a poem," and so on, are loosening and blurring as Eurocentric culture is infused with musical practices from around the world. The essay then focuses on voice quality and surveys the many varieties that are called for in different performance traditions.

In "Deep Themes, Not So Hidden" Anhalt investigates pieces from the repertoire as "hierophanies," that is, as ritual or ceremonial forms. He surveys a number of works that employ sacred names, mantra-like repetition of words, texts taken from magical incantation, ceremonial evocations of childhood, rituals of sacrifice and scapegoating – compositions which are theatre as much as music. Anhalt concludes that these tendencies may arise on the one hand from a desire for more universal, "cosmic" forms of expression, and on the other from an atavistic longing for a paradisal past in which society is ordered and given purpose by ritual and ceremonial forms.

The next chapter, "Orpheus Resurgent ... Perhaps," invokes the name of the shamanic musician with the power to infuse matter with spirit. Anhalt surveys vocal practices from diverse traditions – Kabbalah, Sufi, Hindu, Buddhist – that accompany ecstatic prayer. He then surveys compositions from the repertoire that specify similar ways of making vocal sounds: breathing sounds, unvoiced and paralinguistic sounds, unusual phonemic and phonetic constructs, sounds of vocal-tract behaviour, and so on. Many composers are reviewed, but Berio again receives special attention, particularly for *Coro*. Of interest to Anhalt here is the musicalization of speech or of speechlike events by composing with purely phonetic sounds. He pursues the notion that the speech act is an utterance in which word and world are united. This leads to the final essay, "Alternative Voices," in which he discusses three compositions – *Gas!* by John Beckwith, *In Search of Zoroaster* by Schafer, and *Coro* by Berio. These analyses draw the book to a close by applying approaches developed earlier. The culminating full-length discussion of *Coro* is an impressive synthesis of Anhalt's approach to analysis of vocal music as he takes up its form, the texts, the usage of voices and instruments, and ultimately its deep structure. Anhalt suggests a possible mythologem: the renewal of communal life through a tragic-heroic death. He does not shrink from speculating: "The key to *Coro* seems to be the text of the refrain, telling about some gruesome events (murders, most likely), the evidences of which still are visible in the streets. Or are they? Is it not conceivable that the fragments of the refrain refer to past events, possibly to ones that took place a long time ago? The group (or groups) of people cannot, do not want to, and/or are not allowed to forget the tragedy. The showing of the blood in the streets is in the process of becoming, or has already become, a ritualistic (i.e. sacred) event in the lives of the people concerned. If so, we are witnessing either a myth in the making (mythopoesis), or the re-enactment of the genesis of a myth, intertwined with all sorts of other details from the lives of the people."[20]

Anhalt concludes this richly worked treatise on the avant-garde vocal repertoire of the postwar period with an epilogue in which he sets forth the intent that underlies the project. It is here that he articulates the ethical program of his Orphic aesthetic theology of music. For Anhalt the arts have a role to play in alleviating the ills and suffering of humanity, and music that employs the human voice has a particularly important part in this because the voice is the "most intimate musical means for expression."[21] And thus Anhalt sees that *alternative* approaches to music for the voice are a means of reviving for music its *unitive* function as a means of healing mind, body, and the common weal. The ethos that has sounded in the background of Anhalt's project steadily, like a pedal point, is here recognized and resolved. It suggests that Anhalt's approach to music as a subset of expressive behaviour in general is intended to counter the formalist mainstream that would prefer not to deal with a composer's ethical intent.

The later essays – "Text, Context, Music" and "Music: Context, Text, Counter-text" – are sequels to *Alternative Voices*. The titles declare that the concern is now with the threshold situations that obtain between the verbal/vocal text and the context that interacts with it. The text is not a static entity, but an elusive presence that emanates from the idea to the manifest work. Here one is reminded of Schoenberg's aesthetic theology, although Schoenberg's sources lay in Swedenborgian theosophy rather than the ancient tradition of Jewish mysticism. Anhalt finds an analogy in kabbalistic thought and quotes the thirteenth-century mystic Isaac the Blind, who proposed three degrees of manifestation of the Torah: primordial Torah (in the mind of God), written Torah (potential), and oral Torah (in embodied form). In Anhalt's aesthetic theology the arbiter of interpretation is not invested in the supreme authority of the composer, but is distributed among the listening faithful, so to speak.

After an interlude on the etymology and semantic fields of the word "text" (Latin, *texo* – texture, cloth, weaving) Anhalt quotes the linguist. Hjelmslev[22] for a sweeping pronouncement on language as "the instrument with which man forms thoughts and feeling, mood, aspiration, will and act, the instrument by whose means he influences and is influenced, the ultimate and deepest foundations of human society."[23] It is a measure of Anhalt's investment in the supremacy of language that he does not contest Hjelmslev's sweeping claim with the objection that music shares in at least some of these powers.

Anhalt constructs a typology of texts according to purpose, theme, genre, authorship, and language,[24] and discusses works by Berio, Schafer, and especially Trevor Wishart in these terms. The categories are exceedingly variable, including such items as stories, creeds, dreams, myths, histories, magical texts, cross-cultural borrowings, tropes, etc. To find a precedent for Wishart's radical dissociation of linguistic sounds into primordial phonemes and morphemes, he refers again to the Jewish mystical tradition, this time to the Hassidic teacher Pinhas of Koretz. Such notions become increasingly important for Anhalt as he finds parallels for his own aesthetic theology in the practises of contemporary vocal music and in kabbalistic doctrines of language mysticism. (Four of Gershom Scholem's books on Jewish mysticism are cited in this essay.) In these respects, Anhalt's project has similarities to that of the Romanian-American composer Mordecai Sandberg (1897–73), whose life's work of setting large portions of the Hebrew Bible was a nonsectarian but deeply religious undertaking. For Sandberg, "music is sounding Kabbalah. A real composer is an initiate, and if a measure of greatness exists it is but the degree of initiation attained. The technic of creative thinking in music has been derived from the technic of cabbalistic meditation."[25] Anhalt thus appears to stand with such figures as Sandberg who are close to Martin Buber, whose humanistic Hassidism harmonizes the sacred and the profane through the anecdote or, in Anhalt's case, the musical word.

For Anhalt, the relation between a text selected by the composer and the context the composer creates for that text, whether with other texts or with music, is an issue of great subtlety and scope. The dynamic relationship between a text and its context gives rise to a potentially infinite regress as one moves from the idea of the text to the actual words and vocal sounds, and from these to the context the composer makes for the texts he or she has selected for a work. For Anhalt, "what matters here is the process that changes text and its context into a compound new text, which, in turn, is 'read' in one, or another, still broader context, and so on, seemingly without end."[26] The text-context couple is an ever-widening sphere of nested relations that radiate outwards from the core idea or intent of the utterance. Thus the context can expand enormously to include the architectural space in which the piece is to be performed – as, for instance, when the Ontario Science Centre became the context for a performance of Schafer's *Ra*. Quoting Paul Ricoeur, Anhalt then touches on how multiple interpretations decontextualize a given text sociologically and psychologically, but how a particular act of reading or listening may recontextualize it.[27] Anhalt has raised the issue of how the meaning of a text is distributed in multiple readings but does not enquire further into the shared intersubjective field in which the audience creates multiple readings of a piece of music. Anhalt closes by noting that the missing link is "the one who listens and responds," citing the kabbalist Isaac Luria on the primacy of revelation and Michael Polanyi's tacit knowing: "every word of the Torah has six hundred thousand 'faces,' that is, layers of meaning or entrances, one for each of the children of Israel who stood at the foot of Mount Sinai. Each face is turned toward only one of them; he alone can decipher it. Each man has his unique access to Revelation."[28] By appealing ultimately to personal knowledge, Anhalt opens his aesthetic theory to include the infinite variety of personal experience. By valuing the contribution each listener makes to the interpretation of a composition, and thus distributing the task of making meaning, his hermeneutic system becomes radically open. He does not propose a methodology for incorporating multiple individual responses to the music, but he infers that the work thereby becomes a conduit for bringing prophetic knowledge of what needs to be known into the conscious awareness of the community. Admitting personal revelation into the hermeneutic process assumes that the experience of the ordinary listener is not an imperfect approximation of what experts do much better, but is a valid interpretation that may produce new insights. Anhalt seems to be asserting that each listener has a part to play in the history of reception of a given composition and in the discovery of its truth values.

The last essay we shall consider here, "Music: Context, Text, Counter-text," picks up the topic of revelation where "Text, Context, Music" leaves off, with a quote from C.G. Jung on the topic of projection: "Projections change the world into the replica of one's unknown face ... What, then, is this projection-making factor? The East calls it the 'Spinning Woman' – Maya, who creates illusion by her dancing."[29] The concept of projection opens up the enquiry to the realm of intersubjective phenomena.[30] If personal revelation is admitted into the hermeneutic arena, then both conscious and unconscious contents enter into the picture, and projections inevitably become a factor. But the question arises as to whether the qualities or contents found in the object are revelations about the object or are only projections of what the subject does not know about him or herself. Projection is a double-edged sword – it is the process by which we become conscious of our unknown face, but at the same time it may contaminate the object with an excess of personal material. This is why subjective methods of interpretation, which are referred to disparagingly as mentalistic or impressionistic, are treated with such suspicion by the "scientific" mind.

Anhalt approaches the liminal space between the artwork and its context as an energic field of reciprocal effects, where meanings are generated through the mutual influence of the context on the artwork and the artwork on the context. As an example Anhalt relates an experience he had while viewing a Velázquez painting in the Prado (a full-page reproduction is supplied), which brought him a flash of insight into the multiple levels that obtain between a text and its contexts. After a lengthy discussion of the subtle interactions between texts and contexts, he proposes an ordered categorization of contexts that proceeds from the general to the particular: (1) the world view; (2) the milieu; (3) the immediate context; (4) the situation (an element of the context having to do with time, place, and actants); (5) the moment; and (6) the gesture. This leads to discussion of a vast repertoire of operas in these terms, the most frequently cited composers being Berio, Harrison Birtwistle, Benjamin Britten, Peter Maxwell Davies, Schafer, Stockhausen, Michael Tippett. The next major topic is that of the genre, and here Anhalt attempts to create a classification system that provides a place for any contemporary composition with text. It is a daunting undertaking, and the categories suffer from an excess of generality. An extended discussion of the repertoire in terms of these genre categories follows. Many works seem to find a place in several categories of the typology, so it is not altogether clear that the question of genre has been resolved.

Anhalt does not describe his own music in these essays, but one senses that the writings are as much for his own delectation and instruction as they are contributions to a general theory of contemporary vocal music. By revealing the unfolding purpose of his own life's work, Anhalt enlightens us about the global context – social, intellectual, technical, personal, and transpersonal – of the music of his contemporaries. Anhalt's writings provide a coherent, original, and multifaceted approach to a well-defined but diverse repertoire of contemporary vocal music. By siting the approach in a broad intellectual and spiritual environment, he explores a wider range of issues than are considered in most analyses of such music. The interpretations of particular works are unfailingly stimulating and challenging, and richly nuanced through relating deep structures and surface phenomena. For me, Anhalt's ultimate contribution is his flair for bringing particular works to imaginative life and so preparing me to listen to them and his own music with fresh ears.

NOTES

1 Quoted in R.H. Blyth, *Haiku*, vol. 3 (Tokyo: Hokuseido Press, 1981), 722.
2 Istvan Anhalt, "What Tack to Take? An Autobiographical Sketch (Life in Progress ...)," *Queen's Quarterly* 92, 1 (spring 1985): 97.
3 Istvan Anhalt, *Alternative Voices: Essays on Contemporary Vocal and Choral Composition* (Toronto: University of Toronto Press, 1984).
4 Istvan Anhalt,"Text, Context, Music," *Canadian University Music Review*, 9, 2 (1989): 1–21.
5 Istvan Anhalt, "Music: Context, Text, Counter-text," *Contemporary Music Review* 5 (1989): 101–35.
6 Karlheinz Stockhausen, *Towards a Cosmic Music: Texts by Karlheinz Stockhausen*, selected and trans. Tim Nevill (London: Element Books 1989), xi.
7 Anhalt, *Alternative Voices*, 25.
8 Note in original: "The nature of a social group as revealed by consistent behaviour of the group as such ... " Horace B. English and Ava Champney English, *A Comprehensive Dictionary of Psychological and Psychoanalytical Terms: A Guide to Usage* (New York: David McKay Co., 1958), 540–1.
9 Anhalt, *Alternative Voices*, 41–2.
10 Ibid., 93–4.
11 Ibid., 87–8; ellipses added.
12 Ibid., 45, 55; ellipses added.
13 Ibid., 42.
14 Ibid., 90.
15 Quoted in ibid., 91.
16 Quoted in ibid., 92.
17 Quoted in ibid., 92.
18 Quoted in ibid., 98.
19 Ibid., 143.
20 Ibid., 264.
21 Ibid., 267.
22 L. Hjelmslev, *Prolegomena to a Theory of Language* (Madison, Milwaukee, and London: University of Wisconsin Press, 1969).
23 Anhalt, "Text, Context, Music," 4–5.

24 Ibid., 5–6.

25 See A. Clarkson, K. Pegley, and J. Rahn, "Mordecai Sandberg: A Catalogue of His Music," *Musica Judaica* 13 (1993–94): 39.

26 Anhalt, "Text, Context, Music," 11.

27 Ibid., 14.

28 Ibid., 18.

29 Anhalt, "Music: Context, Text, Counter-text," 101.

30 Anhalt does not define projection. In Jungian terms, it is the process whereby an unconscious quality or content of the subject is thrown out onto an outer object and perceived and reacted to by the subject as though that quality or content belongs to the object. What Jung means by the first rather gnomic sentence is that it is through projections that the ego gradually learns of those aspects of the personality of which it is unconscious. Our unknown face gradually becomes known as we recognize projections as elements of our own personalities. See Andrew Samuels, Bani Shorter, and Fred Plaut, *A Critical Dictionary of Jungian Analysis* (London: Routledge and Kegan Paul, 1986), 113–14.

10 The Istvan Anhalt Fonds at the National Library of Canada

HELMUT KALLMANN

The Istvan Anhalt fonds comprises one of the largest and most detail-intensive units among the over 300 fonds and collections housed in perpetuity in the Manuscript Section of the Music Division of the National Library of Canada.[1] The Anhalt fonds remains in a state of growth as the composer continues to compose, lecture, and write. It remains Anhalt's intention to offer the library further blocks of material as he is ready to part with them. This essay examines the Anhalt fonds with a view to determining what it contains, how one gains access to it, and for what ends one might consult it.

SIZE AND ACQUISITION

In 1994 the *Catalogue of the Archival Fonds and Collections of the Music Division* recorded the Anhalt fonds as consisting of 24 linear metres of textual records, 1,562 photographs, 117 slides, 44 negatives, and 113 audio tape reels.[2] "Linear metres" are counted by placing (in theory) all papers on top of one another, forming a tower, or by measuring the horizontal shelf space. By 2000 another 1.35 metres of textual records and 187 photos had been added. The Anhalt fonds vies in size and richness with those of Sir Ernest MacMillan, Percival Price, R. Murray Schafer, and Glenn Gould. Richness, as used here, denotes not only size or completeness but biographical documentation and intellectual content.

Negotiations for the acquisition began in 1984 when Anhalt invited the author, then chief of the Music Division, to inspect and consider acquiring the musician's archives. After negotiations with the library's Collections Development Branch, the first – and so far largest – transfer of materials occurred in March 1985. The original acquisition has been followed by a number of further installments, each containing a broad variety of material, such as correspondence, scores, sketches, tape recordings, lecture notes, publicity material, photos, and various memorabilia. One installment, arriving in 1988, consisted of five recent compositions – *Winthrop, Thisness, Simulacrum, SparkskrapS,* and *A Wedding Carol* – for a total of 1,087 pages. Another, transferred in 1993, included the abundant resource material for the proposed operatic work *Oppenheimer* for which Anhalt wrote the text (the composition material is limited to a number of sketches). Sketches and manuscripts of *Millenial Mall* were added to the Anhalt fonds in the spring of 2000.

CONTENTS AND ORGANIZATION

While the following brief tour through the Anhalt fonds is largely concerned with numbers and names, I hope that it will at the same time facilitate the appreciation of Anhalt's ideas and creativity. It is the job of the archivist to safeguard, arrange, and inventorize the papers so that efficient and creative use can be made of them. The Music Division staff integrated the papers in the Manuscript Section under the number MUS 164 and grouped them in the following series:

A Compositional activities
B Notes on compositions
C Biographical information
D Teaching activities at McGill University
E Teaching activities at Queen's University
F Literary activities
G Associations and interests
H Correspondence
I Financial documents
J Miscellaneous
K Recordings
L Photographs

A detailed inventory of the Anhalt fonds was prepared in 1994; it runs to 286 pages.[3]

Let me now guide you through the files, stopping here and there in that vast treasure trove. Most materials arrived carefully bundled together in boxes or files that corresponded to cabinets, shelves, and desks in the composer's Kingston home. Thus a basic order had already been established. The task of the archivist is to respect to the greatest extent possible the order established by the donor or vendor, but at the same time to consider also the logical grouping of similar materials and, within the major groups, the most suitable arrangement – physical, chronological, or alphabetical. For example, scores usually require larger storage containers than correspondence, and photos require protective envelopes. Furthermore, duplicates beyond a handful of printed programs or announcements have to be weeded out. For practical reasons, each installment arriving at the library is filed in a separate sequence, each with its own sequence for scores, correspondence, or photos. I will now describe sections A, F, H and L in some detail.

A: Compositional activities

Table 10.1
Holographs in the Anhalt fonds

Series	1	orchestra	1,849 pages
	2	opera	2,855 pp.
	3	chamber	398 pp.
	4	solo voice	81 pp.
	5	choir	182 pp.
	6	keyboard	91 pp.
	7	sketches	657 pp.
	8	electronic	–
	9	notes	not counted
	10	miscellaneous	6 pp.

Note: this count of 6,119 pages was made in August 1989

How completely does this represent Anhalt's output to date? Were some works lost, or destroyed by the composer, and do some still rest in his home? Of Anhalt's pre-Canada works, relatively few survive. The student period is represented by the a cappella choral work *Ünnepek (Feasts)* (1942) and some sketches. From the Paris period date a string quartet, a piano sonata, and *Concerto in stilo di Handel*, all written 1946–48. Among the lost works are some chamber music pieces written in the early 1940s (see the Anhalt works list in this volume). In short, what is not in the Music Division may be presumed to have been lost.

Anhalt's compositions typically go through a long process from idea to fulfillment. The composer notes that his customary working procedure goes from "more to less" by elimination and reduction, rather than through accumulation and addition.[4] He adds that at certain stages of composition or writing, other more complex procedures may come into play. What makes the collection of compositions interesting is precisely this complexity with its multitude of sketches, drafts, variants, discards, preliminary notes, tables of twelve-tone rows (where used), and graphics (especially for the *Symphony of Modules*). In some cases there are lists of corrections or changes – what Anhalt calls "fine tuning" – after the score has been finished.

F: Literary Activities

A similar variety of documents exists for Anhalt's literary works. There are research notes, drafts, or outtakes for the book *Alternative Voices*, for various articles and speeches, and for the text for *Oppenheimer* (originally intended as an operatic work, this became a three-act drama with some 200 pages of musical sketches). *Oppenheimer* and the libretto for *Traces (Tikkun)* went through at least seven versions each.

H: Correspondence

The correspondence – some of it in Hungarian – includes more letters *to* than *from* Anhalt. When photocopying became commonly used, he began keeping copies of all outgoing letters (most of which are handwritten) in his possession for quick reference. Letters written by Anhalt on professional business are usually typewritten.

In Anhalt's estimation there are more than 150 correspondents of significance, and this exchange of letters would go a long way to providing a biographical account. "I would imagine that *much* of my life can be (in some measure) traced in these correspondences." "With care and imagination, *and* patience, bits and pieces from the bulk of correspondence (which still grows …) can (could) be pieced together as bits of a jigsaw puzzle. – And as long as I live I am quite ready to provide some of the 'missing pieces,' subject only to my capacity for recall and discretion wherever applicable."[5]

The subject matter of the musical correspondence ranges from administrative details, evaluations, introductions, appointments and references to statements of aesthetic viewpoints and judgments of compositions. Some exchanges remained on a formal basis (e.g., that with Arnold Walter) and were limited to specific matters; others initiated a lasting friendship. Thus the appellation "Mr Beckwith" soon blossomed into "Dear John." The long chains of letters with fellow musicians such as John Beckwith and George Rochberg are "repositories of 'stations' in one's life, accounts of 'development,' of all kinds of processes over time."[6] But even some brief exchanges can be of interest; for instance, in one letter Witold Lutoslawski submits an alternative to Anhalt's interpretation of his work in chapter 4 of *Alternative Voices.*

To provide an idea of the scope of Anhalt's correspondence I have arranged the correspondents in three categories below. Selective notes relating to quantity, span of years, or subject matter are indicated in the following.

H: Correspondence (Family)
This group includes more than 80 postcards sent by Anhalt from labour camp (1942–44) and later letters from Paris and Canada as well as mail from the parents.

H: Correspondence (International)
Nadia Boulanger (17 items), Anhalt's composition teacher in Paris
John Cage (12 items)
Lajós Heller (13 items), an important mentor
George Rochberg, whom Anhalt first met at the 1960 Stratford International Conference of Composers; several hundred letters "cover a broad thematic area"[7]
Edgard Varèse (3 items), whom Anhalt met at the 1960 Stratford conference and later visited in New York City
Theresa de Kerpely, a friend since the 1930s who died in 1993; an extensive exchange of letters with Anhalt, which he considers "an island in the totality of the life-experience"[8]
Gottfried Michael Koenig ($\frac{1}{2}$ cm of items), Karlheinz Stockhausen (12 items), and Hans Helms (13 items), in part concerned with Anhalt's 1958 visit to the electronic music studio in Cologne
Milton Babbit (15 items)
Other correspondents include Cathy Berberian, Luciano Berio, George Crumb, Lukas Foss, Zoltán Kodály (a letter of recommendation, 1947–48), György Ligeti (1958–64), Witold Lutoslawski, Soulima Stravinsky (1945), and Josef Tal.

H: Correspondence (Canadian)
John Beckwith; the years 1955–70 have been deposited, with over 100 letters each way
Graham George (16 items)

Alan Gillmor, including some that are of quite extended length
Glenn Gould (10 items)
Eldon Grier and Sylvia Tait in West Vancouver, a wide-ranging corre-
    spondence
Udo Kasemets (1956–68)
Pierre Mercure (23 items)
Jean Papineau-Couture (20 items, mainly before 1970)
R. Murray Schafer (1961–67 and later)
There is also correspondence with colleagues and former pupils,
    including, among others, Kevin Austin, Claude Champagne, Bengt
    Hambraeus, Keith Hamel, Hugh Hartwell, John Hawkins, Alan
    Heard, Sydney Hodkinson, David Jaeger, Bruce Mather, Jean-
    Jacques Nattiez, Paul Pedersen, Clermont Pépin, Harry Somers,
    Arnold Walter, and John Weinzweig.

L: *Photographs*

The bulk of the photos are of people. Family members, from Anhalt's
grandparents in Hungary to his grandchildren in Canada, are richly
represented. The composer is shown at all stages in his life. Many pictures focus on specific places and events. One album (box 14) depicts
the Anhalt residence at 274 Johnson St, Kingston. Other files document the 1982 McGill convocation where Anhalt got an honorary
D. Mus. degree and the launching party for the book *Musical Canada*[9]
in Toronto, showing many friends and colleagues, among them John
Beckwith, John Weinzweig, Carl Morey, Mary Morrison, William Aide,
Keith MacMillan, William Littler, Gilles Potvin, and myself.

Rehearsals for Anhalt's *SparkskrapS* under Alex Pauk are among the
performance shots. An album (box 15) for *Winthrop* includes photos
of Elmer Iseler, Louis Applebaum, Raffi Armenian, Maureen Forrester,
Gilles Potvin, John P.L. Roberts, John Meisel, and others. Box 16 documents the performances of *Simulacrum* and *Sonance•Resonance (Welche
Töne?)* with shots of the respective conductors, Gabriel Chmura and
Günther Herbig. There are some large prints of Glenn Gould, issued
by the CBC.

Boxes 23 and 24 from the first shipment include 963 prints (or picture postcards), 117 slides, and 17 negatives. In box 23 approximately
100 photos are pasted on large index cards with Anhalt's handwritten
commentary on the back. Where necessary, the commentary is continued on another card. Boxes 45 and 46 contain 599 prints and 27 negatives. Of special interest in box 46 are photographs of Jean Papineau-
Couture, André Prévost, Robert Silverman, William Benjamin, John
Beckwith, Gilles Tremblay, George Rochberg, and R. Murray Schafer.

Other Series

There is no room to describe the other series in any detail. Note should be taken, however, of the close association that Anhalt has had as an educator and administrator with McGill University and later with Queen's University, and of the vast amount of preparation and writing that went into his book *Alternative Voices*. There are sound recordings of some 150 concerts, including master tapes of Anhalt's electroacoustic compositions. There are also many concert programs, program notes, and reviews.

Vertical Files

For quick consultation the Music Division's biography files are open to all visitors. Like all vertical files, they were assembled over the years, piece by piece, independently of and preceding the acquisition of the Anhalt papers. In 1995 there were close to 100 items in the Anhalt folders, including lists of compositions, program notes for specific works, *curriculum vitae*, announcements, articles by or about the composer, and reviews. Rare items include the original copy of the questionnaire that Anhalt filled in for the revised *Catalogue of Canadian Composers* issued by the CBC in 1952, the text of the poem "Mirage in Elöpatak," a CBC press kit with some forty newspaper articles about *Winthrop*, and scripts of several lectures.

CREATIVE POTENTIAL

The value of a musical fonds is twofold: it lies in the information yielded by the contents and in the insights to be gleaned from the form. The contents of the fonds reveal the creative path from first sketches, abandoned passages, and variants to the final version of a composition, and provide the material evidence that performers, editors, and theorists may wish to consult. Doubtful dates and sequences of events may be settled, authentic readings established, and anecdotes proven or disproven.

By the "form" of a fonds I mean the many incidental characteristics that project an image of the composer's mind and personality. They tell of such habits as orderliness, neatness, calligraphy (in which Anhalt excels), promptness of replies to correspondents, labelling of sketches, habits and rationales for preserving or discarding all manner of notes, drafts, and incoming mail. What was preserved, how much or how little, and how carefully or haphazardly was it filed? Does the writing show signs of speed, or deliberation? How well are sketches and letters identified (by date, name of correspondent, or the name of a composition to which the sketch belongs)? The attitude towards the documentation of one's own life reveals respect for one's self as well as concern for future researchers and performers and their task of consultation. All these traits shed light on the individual.

The preservation of the documents of his life and work was not a deliberate initiative of Anhalt's. Preserving so many records began passively as "nothing but an instinctive act on my part."[10] Eventually Anhalt felt that some experiences he participated in might one day become of interest to some others as well.[11] The thoroughness of Anhalt's documentation will surely earn the gratitude of its users; indeed, Anhalt himself has already been creatively inspired by the fonds.

Visiting the National Library of Canada after the initial deposits and seeing his life's activities graphically spread out in front of his eyes had a startling effect on Anhalt. He saw his material as "a 'land,' a vast terrain, a 'country,' a repository of much evidence that documents the sundry details of a life."[12] In the same letter he refers to the papers as "a sizeable 'memory hill' which can be 'dug-up' and explored, stratum by stratum, and which keeps on growing, sediment by sediment, as life still goes on."[13] Elsewhere he writes, "I am even more ready to regard the *Fonds* ... as being also a special kind of open-ended *composition* which will end, abruptly I expect, only with the moment of my death ... it suggested elucidatory comments from me soon after ... This gut-reaction resulted in *A Weave of Life Lines*, which I wrote in a very short spurt, and only re-read in parts, hence its very raw, unedited state. Subsequently came the 'inserts,' the 'addenda' to date, and as I regard this as an 'open'-ended text, I'm adding to it as the need for this arises. – This *Weave subsequently* appeared to me as a possibly useful 'guide' to some parts of the entire *Fonds* itself."[14] This passage exemplifies the creative role of archives, which are more than data banks and mausoleums for work accomplished. They are birthplaces of new thoughts, new inspirations, new combinations forged from old ideas. Archives live and breathe! One must approach them without fear of dust and brittle paper, with a good dose of curiosity – and a lot of time at one's disposal.

BIOGRAPHICAL ASPECTS

Much of Anhalt's work is autobiographical and introspective. What happened? Where do I belong? The composer's flight from a painful experience in his home country, his identity as a Jew and a Hungarian, his adjustment as a European to North American society – these continuing ties to the past have been and remain pre-eminent themes. Anhalt's preoccupation with his roots, with the fact of not having been quite accepted as Hungarian even before the war, have made him see "with a measure of clarity the nature of this 'belonging' to a Jewish continuity."[15] Even as a teenager he observed that he was regarded as not quite as Hungarian as his Christian school chums, a stateless person in his native land. Reinforced by the gruesome experiences of the war, his feelings toward his native land have remained ambivalent and largely negative[16] and have conditioned his "emotional self." Yet he has always been willing to seek peace and reconciliation wherever possible.

Even as a young man, Anhalt already had a life full of cataclysmic experiences – the loss of his homeland and the prospect of contributing to its culture, the delay of his advanced education, the experience of fascist inhumanity, the loss of relatives and friends, the need at war's end to search for and adapt to a new homeland. After settling in Canada in 1949, he carved out a very special niche among musicians as an explorer of new musical terrain, as a "composer's composer," but also as a music educator and theorist. It appears, as in so many people, that the search for roots and identity has grown stronger, not weaker, with the advance of years. Anhalt's identity search hearkens back to his upbringing in Hungary and the questioning of his Hungarian identity by the fascists. Further back still is the intriguing history of those ancestors who were not Hungarian, bearing the name of a German duchy, Anhalt.

If the question of identity looms large, it hardly concerns Anhalt's status as a Canadian, for his assimilation has gone smoothly. Being part Canadian and part European has not resulted in a spiritual or emotional conflict. As a result of his history, Anhalt considers himself a "bridge figure ... someone who came from turbulent central Europe ... a survivor, a survivor son of survivor parents, they, in turn, being survivors, children of even earlier survivors, struggling folks ... This I.A. finally lands in Halifax in January '49, with all that baggage on his back, and *he himself* is only dimly and partially aware at the time of the baggage which he carries, or to put it differently, the *baggage which carries him.*"[17] Then comes the experience of the vast new land – assimilating, finding room for his own voice, contributing.

Anhalt's later compositions, especially *Simulacrum, SparkskrapS*, and *Sonance•Resonance (Welche Töne)*, thrive on "plumbing the past." *Simulacrum*, for instance, has an element of retrospection in which tunes of importance in his earlier years are recalled. The "bridge figure" is easy to trace, but he is represented through other figures (alter egos might be too strong a term) as well. Thus Anhalt's opera triptych[18] deals with the Old World New World question – in *La Tourangelle* with its Roman Catholic manifestation, in *Winthrop* with Protestant Puritanism; and in *Traces (Tikkun)* with Judaism. In Anhalt's words "these all deal with persons who 'move' to a new place in search of peace, opportunity 'to be' ... or rather, to 'become.'"[19]

RESEARCH POTENTIAL

It is plain from the previous pages that the Anhalt fonds is a stimulus to future research. Several contributors to the present volume have already explored the fonds in depth for their essays. The following paragraphs suggest a few areas for further exploration.

Anhalt Studies

Work might be done in two main areas: correspondence and process of composition, the former necessarily by someone with a knowledge of Hungarian. The possibility to develop one's work through contact with a living person should be a great incentive for the researcher. The devoted listener rarely is satisfied knowing a composer's music by his music alone. Human curiosity extends to the communicator behind the communication, the individual behind the message, the artist in the context of personality, environment, and times. An honest autobiography can save speculation and guesswork, but only an outsider can provide an objective assessment and see through possible self-deceptions. A certain amount of autobiographical writing has already been done in several articles and commentaries and in Anhalt's genealogical sketch of his family,[20] which he feels is "a kind of road-map"[21] to set the stage. The scarcity of documents pertaining to his early childhood is made up to some extent by "A Weave of Life Lines," already mentioned.[22] Another important source is a photocopy of Dr George Webber's Autobiography in the fonds, an eyewitness account of shared labour camp experience, 1943–44. Anhalt's letters to a cousin, Mrs Z. Gács, and those to and from a schoolmate, T. Földesi, should also cast light on his childhood.

Profitable work could derive also from an examination of composition processes and methods, through analysis of sketches and alterations. Anhalt himself suggests a thesis topic on his involvement with "synthetic music."[23] Like any writer or composer, he has wisely kept sketches and drafts. For indeed, at the stage of revising a composition or conceiving a new one, the composer may wish to return to earlier versions and discarded ideas. Anhalt himself is attracted to the sketches of the "great" composers and the mystery of their writing processes.[24]

Anhalt the teacher, as seen by his students, would make a fascinating topic for a former student. The raw materials in this case are unsorted notes and examples, because much of his teaching was improvised to suit the standard of his students, which changed from year to year. This is one activity where methodical preservation did not apply. Anhalt enjoyed teaching, but his notes, examples, and other course materials hardly can be sorted to cover any one particular course he gave. Anhalt the writer: a study of *Alternative Voices*, or "papers which complement it,"[25] and of points brought up in its reviews could be undertaken by someone with an interest in vocal music. The fonds documents ten years of plans, drafts, and lists for Anhalt's book on contemporary composition for the voice.

Tangents

To the history specialist the material relating to Hungarian and Second World War history – labour camps, persecution of Hungarian Jews, postwar conditions, emigration – would yield much of political and human interest. In this investigation the biographer or researcher would need to have a reading knowledge of Hungarian and French.

To a certain extent the Anhalt and other National Library music fonds supplement each other. The study of the development of composition in any society is not only a matter of writing up so many individual biographies and oeuvres, but also of tracing the person-to-person relationships, shared experiences, mutual suggestions, inspirations and criticisms *between* composers. Thus the Anhalt correspondence is important not only for what it says about Anhalt but what it reveals about his colleagues. Students of the life and work of Graham George, Glenn Gould, Hugh Le Caine, R. Murray Schafer, and John Weinzweig may find relevant research material of value (beyond correspondence) in the Anhalt fonds. Others may make use of the material on John Beckwith (including tapes of seven compositions), Zoltán Kodály, Otto Laske (a "composer-philosopher"), László Gyopár,[26] George Rochberg (3 tapes), Harry Somers, and others. The fonds also casts light on a number of musical events including the Stratford International Conference of Composers in 1960, World Music Week 1975, and the opening of the Harrison-Le Caine Hall at Queen's University in 1974.

THE LIVING COMPOSITION

Archive, person, composition – these elements form a trinity in Anhalt's case. A composition is a mirror of an eventful, ongoing life, an archive of life lived until the present moment, a life documented with the instinct of an archivist. An archive perpetuates a person and his or her compositions; it is itself a composition in its juxtaposition of subdivisions, like the movements of an orderly symphony, an organization in which all parts contribute to the whole. In the case of the Anhalt fonds, a person creates compositions that are deposited in an archive, and the archive redounds on the person, inspiring him to write an autobiographical guide to the archive. Although one cannot easily separate the strands of such a trinity, one may trace relationships and mutual enhancements. That should be a biographer's dream come true. The truth is, Anhalt's archive is a life and a composition.

NOTES

1 Since the term *fonds* (singular and plural) is not a traditional part of the English vocabulary, I should explain that it has been adopted by the Canadian archival community (replacing the traditional *papers*) to designate "the whole of the records, regardless of form of medium, automatically and organically created and/or accumulated and used by a particular individual, family, or corporate body in the course of that creator's activities and functions." In distinction, a *collection* is an "artificial construct, an arbitrary creation, often the work of choice." Bureau of Canadian Archivists, *The Archival Fonds: From Theory to Practice* (Ottawa, 1992), 40, 41. Although one may speak of a person's *archives* in their own possession, that term normally refers to the institution housing the material.

2 Jeannine Barriault and Stéphane Jean, *Catalogue of the Archival Fonds and Collections of the Music Division / Catalogue des fonds et collections d'archives de la division de la musique* (Ottawa: National Library of Canada, 1994), 7–8.

3 "Istvan Anhalt: An Inventory of Archival Fonds Held in the Music Division of the National Library of Canada" (Ottawa: National Library of Canada, 1994, typescript).

4 Istvan Anhalt, letter to the author, 11 September 1995, 5.

5 Ibid., 13, 25; ellipsis in original.

6 Istvan Anhalt, letter to the author, 23 August 1995, 5.

7 Istvan Anhalt, letter to the author, 11 September 1995, 13.

8 Istvan Anhalt, letter to the author, 23 August 1995, 5.

9 *Musical Canada: Words and Music Honouring Helmut Kallmann*, ed. John Beckwith and Frederick A. Hall (Toronto: University of Toronto Press, 1988) includes Anhalt's article "*Thisness*: Marks and Remarks," pp. 211–31.

10 Istvan Anhalt, letter to the author, 23 August 1995, 4.

11 Ibid.

12 Ibid., 9.

13 Ibid., 10.

14 Ibid., 7; ellipses in original. The document Anhalt refers to is "A Weave of Life Lines" (Kingston, 1992, manuscript).

15 Ibid., 14.

16 Ibid., 12.

17 Istvan Anhalt, letter to the author, 11 September 1995, 17; ellipses and emphases in original.

18 Ibid., 10–11.

19 Ibid., 20; ellipsis in original.
20 Istvan Anhalt, "An Interim Account of My Search for Genealogical Information Pertaining to My Family's Background" (Kingston, 1995, manuscript).
21 Istvan Anhalt, letter to the author, 11 September 1995, 17.
22 See note 14.
23 Istvan Anhalt, letter to the author, 11 September 1995, 9.
24 Istvan Anhalt, letter to the author, 23 August 1995, 4.
25 Istvan Anhalt, letter to the author, 11 September 1995, 19.
26 László Gyopár was a Hungarian composer whom Anhalt befriended first as a fellow student under Kodály, then in the forced labour brigade for young Jewish men, in which Gyopár was shot in 1944. Anhalt obtained in the early 1950s a handwritten copy of the score of Gyopár's *Missa*, which is now part of the fonds, and thanks to Anhalt the work had its world premiere at the Budapest Spring Festival in 1994. Correspondence with notable Hungarians, and especially with the composer-musicologist Dr András Szöllösy, a fellow student of Kodály who helped to arrange this performance, is in the fonds, as is a video/audio cassette documentation of this performance.

11 Reflections on a Colleague and Friend

GEORGE ROCHBERG

These are reflections and ruminations, thoughts and feelings about my friend Istvan Anhalt and our long friendship of over forty years.[1] We first met at the International Conference of Composers held at Stratford, Ontario, in the summer of 1960. It's hard to pinpoint precisely what drew us together. Surely our initial responses to each other's music, but beyond that, those human places from which music itself arises. One of William Blake's proverbs comes to mind: "the bird a nest, the spider a web, man friendship." Genuine friendship is not possible without the kinship of shared attitudes, tastes, interests. But too there must be a deeper, indefinable sense that, despite and whatever differences might characterize the individuals involved, there is an unspoken sympathy that flows between them which accounts for the pleasure they take in each other's company and thoughts. Surely there is no guile of ulterior motive – otherwise it would not be friendship.

I still retain a sense, not of the actual sound of Istvan's music that I first heard – its ideas, textures, and colours – but, after all these years and only one hearing, a sense of the absolute seriousness of the composer, his solidity of craftsmanship, his sure control of orchestral means and compositional design and structure, and his imagination, especially in the handling of timbral groups. What I admired most was his sense of what a symphony composed in midcentury should and could be like after Schoenberg and Berg and Webern, Stravinsky and Bartók. Clearly there was a large talent at work behind the music. That is what drew me.

And so the friendship took hold. Being addicted to words and verbal expression as we both are, we started writing letters to each other – so many I've lost track by now, though I suspect Istvan, who is better organized than I am, has at least a rough idea, where I literally have none.[2] Often I would vent, pour out in my disheveled stream-of-consciousness way of writing personal letters angers and rages and despairs at life's offences against me and mine. After a while would arrive a long, thoughtful, slow-paced, calming response from my friend. Beautifully and thoughtfully phrased, always deeply meant, always heartfelt. You might say Istvan's letters were often the calm *after* the storm of my letters. But of course there's more to it than that. There's the exchange of experiences, work, travels; the exchange of thoughts and feelings about ideas – call them intellectual matters, including of course things going on in music, which were always of prime importance to both of us.

Often enough politics was the subject. Living in the United States, as I do, and Istvan having settled in Canada after the bloody Second World War provides two distinctly different political experiences. America is brash, vulgar, and loud, where Canada seems quiet, almost sedate, except now for the French-Canadian separatists. (Where do the French – in Europe and in Canada – get their mad passion for so-called "purity" of language, of culture, of blood? Totally illusory as far as I'm concerned.) Since the days of Nixon, American politics have turned nasty and vicious. I don't know about Canada – I wouldn't like to think that anything like the plague of Republican mean-heartedness and mean-spiritedness let loose in the November 1994 U.S. elections would ever threaten Canadian politics.

Istvan's roots are entirely and deeply European. That shapes a person in a certain way, gives them a certain texture, even flavour of persona and personality. I've seen it in more than one friend of European origins, especially those whose destinies were shaped by the terrible pressures and events of the Second World War. I was born in the States of immigrant parents. Inevitably this produced all kinds of fantasies in my young head about who and what I was. My mother and father came from Uman, a largish city in the Ukraine which, according to the Jewish Encyclopedia, was famous for two things: pogroms (a bad Czarist Russian habit of trying to exterminate Jews) and *klezmerim* (the Yiddish term for musicians who played fiddle, clarinet, and other instruments for social occasions mostly). I grew up half thinking of myself as Russian – a quasi-cultural fantasy fed by reading Tolstoy, Dostoyevsky, and Chekhov. Not entirely untrue either. So the European connection runs deep in Istvan, who actually grew up in Hungary, the land of Magyars, Gypsies, the czardas, Bartók, and Kodály. Some of

Istvan's dreams, perhaps even to this day, are about his early years in Budapest, or whatever town he was born and grew up in. I was born in a town in northern New Jersey, an industrial town famous for its waterfalls, which the American poet William Carlos Williams celebrated in his poem about Paterson. As I boy I remember my mother telling about rats that she and my father had to battle in the house in which I was born along the industrially polluted Passaic River, which empties into Newark Bay. I still dream of the places of my childhood. Strangely discomfiting, painfully sweet, never quite happy dreams. (Something odd suddenly strikes me. I have a Japanese pianist friend who plays Schubert sonatas as though born to them – she says she's not sure whether I'm American-European or European-American.)

One day I received a long letter from Istvan (we both wrote long letters by hand, the old-fashioned way) in which he described meticulously, as only he can – detailed circumstances, surrounded with the colour and atmosphere and texture of the time of the occurrence itself – how he had escaped from the brutal labour battalion into which the Hungarian Fascists/Nazis had forced all able-bodied Jewish men. It's a hair-raising story. I can hardly believe it happened to my gentle friend, but it did. These are not the sorts of things people who survived the Holocaust invent to dramatize themselves. It is utterly inconceivable to me that there are people in the world who claim that the Holocaust never happened, that it's a hoax. Just as inconceivable is the continued bitter hatred of Jews, especially in those same European countries where virtually entire populations of Jews were exterminated. Yet anti-Semitism continues unabated in these very places because people refuse responsibility for what they themselves have allowed to happen or made happen. They are simply incapable of self-examination and the frank admission of flaws and faults which must come with honest self-reflection.

This harrowing labour camp experience happened to Istvan because he was a Jew in Hungary caught in the gears of a fiendish plan to destroy intelligence and sensitivity, a plan that spread from Germany to western and southwestern Europe across eastern and into central Europe. I have long maintained that Europe has been suffering a deadly pathological sickness of soul and spirit for centuries, not just in the twentieth. Nor am I dissuaded from this view by the self-congratulatory blandishments of intellectuals who read Western history through the curious lens of self- and species-glorification. Evil is always what others do, never what *we* do. So the litany goes.

The war years were totally different for me. They followed a wholly different scenario, which took me to England, Germany, Belgium, and Luxembourg as a second lieutenant in the U.S. army infantry. I suppose it was inevitable that I ended up as foot soldier. From boyhood I'd been a great walker, but the army couldn't have known that. No, they put me in the infantry because that's where they needed able-bodied young men, and my still undeveloped talents as a composer were of no particular use to them. I'm not sure of dates, but it is entirely possible that while Istvan was walking around Budapest disguised as a priest (after he'd made his escape, he'd been taken under the protective wing of a Catholic order of priests who quite literally saved his life), I was probably in one of my first battles in August-September 1944. Years later I found out that where I'd been wounded in a heavy encounter with the German *Wehrmacht* was close by the town of Mons (not far from Verdun, site of one of the major killing fields of the First World War), the birth place of the great Josquin des Prez. I remember with that special warmth and glow of one of those *good* memories that the night before the fight, my platoon sergeant, platoon runner, and I were invited to sit down to what seemed then an unbelievable feast of chicken, potatoes, country bread, and wine by the French farmer and his family whose barn we'd requisitioned as temporary quarters. Anyway, I can almost see Istvan in his priest's cassock, even though it seems so unlikely, and I smile at the inner image. Because he always has had – and still retains – that unaccountably innocent look of the good person: sympathetic, compassionate, open, honest to a fault. Just the right look for a priest. Someone to whom (if he were in fact what he appeared), you would quickly tell your worldly and spiritual troubles. The anomalies of life grow thicker with such images and only add to the puzzlements and bafflements that increasingly cloud my understanding of existence. So there is one set of images – Istvan in the Hungarian labour battalion and later in a priest's disguise walking Budapest. And then another – me walking Europe as a soldier, fighting, getting wounded, recuperating for three months in France and England, going back just in time for the Battle of the Bulge, Christmas-New Year, 1944–45, snow up to my thighs, brutally cold, nothing hot to eat, just chocolate к-ration and snow. I'm sure Istvan must marvel at times – especially now, looking back through the decades – that he's still alive, still here. I find myself more and more amazed that I've made it this far, still here, still struggling to comprehend what we humans call "life."

Did these experiences shape Istvan's psyche, his music? Of course. They had to – how could it be otherwise? I know in my own case the war years had a profound effect on me and determined directly that I should take up the language of atonality, of musical modernism in order to give voice to the growing sense in me that life in the twentieth century was being lived under a dark "cloud of unknowing" in more ways than only the religious. I've always felt that modernism in any and all of the arts – if taken up as an exercise in abstract detachment from the harsh realities, or if taken up as pseudomathematical/scientific thought experiments to see how far sound or texture or colour or structure could be pushed before music and painting and literature devolved into cold, sterile meaninglessness – was wholly spurious, totally unreal. In any case, our experience – my friend's and mine – in no way fits the comfortable, safe, academic image of composers' lives retailed in the passionless history of music books.

As time went on it became apparent that both Istvan and I had become, with advancing years, deeply preoccupied with tracing our respective family backgrounds. Pure coincidence perhaps, but we were both driven by strong needs to find deeper biological connections to ancestral pasts. Inevitably, I'm convinced that led to talking about our being Jewish and pondering what that meant. The question of being Jewish is not quite the same as the question of being Christian. The latter seems to rest fundamentally on the presence and strength of faith, on belief in the divinity of Jesus Christ, more than by degrees of adherence to matters of doctrine, whether Catholic, Protestant, Eastern Orthodox, or the many other varieties of Christianity that have developed. It seems that Jews themselves are forever attempting to define or describe what it means to be Jewish – without much success, I might add. All by itself it is one of those unending bafflements. No Jew I've ever asked the question of, including my own father, could say what he or she thought it *really* meant. Although it seems all Jews talk about it, and some claim (usually in narrow theological terms, sometimes in historical terms, sometimes in purely sociocultural terms) to know what it means, most don't really seem to know or have anything resembling a rational answer. Truth is, I suspect there's no "answer," certainly not a rational one.

I know a Frenchman who can trace both sides of his family (his is a hyphenated name) back to the middle 1600s to the city of Lyons. This is rare indeed, although in this country there are the Daughters of the American Revolution, and some individuals know for certain (I know one or two personally) that they are descendants of pilgrims who landed at Plymouth Rock, and so forth. But for most of us mortals, we're lucky if we can trace our family background further than two, at most three generations. For all our prating about education and culture, certainly in the States, the living sense of history, personal or national, has evaporated, and all that seems to be left is the lurid present lit up by the light of TV screens.

Istvan has written me often and at great length about his researches into his family history. For one thing, he has been trying to locate the source of his family name. If I remember rightly, he's discovered some male ancestors going back to the 1800s, maybe earlier. He's also located a town in Germany with a double name, one of which is Anhalt. The need to connect with the past is part of the need too – to know that, ephemeral though we all are as individuals, we belong to an ongoing stream of life that stretches back and hopefully will stretch ahead, far ahead. We can't accept that life ends, that there was nothing before us and there will be nothing after us. In some way that is hard to pin down, the urge for biological legacy before and after our brief appearance on the world stage, however large or small our individual roles, is built into our genes and neurological makeup, and therefore into our psychic (thinking and feeling) life. I also believe it's intensely related to historical ideas of what the ancients called "fame," to ideas of posterity, to the wish for either personal immortality or for the immortality attaching to intellectual and artistic work. The ancient Greeks and Romans certainly built such notions into the fabric of their cultures. Hermann Broch, the Austrian novelist, has written a long, slow-paced, beautiful novel, about this – *The Death of Virgil,* in which the dying Virgil is trying to convince his friend and protector, Emperor Augustus Caesar, that the creation of the Roman Empire is a greater work than Virgil's poetry and will earn the emperor his fame to the end of days. Augustus, denying the poet's claim, tells him that he, Virgil, the soul and voice of the people of Rome, will live forever in the memory of mankind. Add to this such statements as William Wordsworth's telling us that he chose as his poetic, spiritual forebears the writers of the Bible, Shakespeare, Spenser, and Milton. The need to feel deeply connected and to live in ongoing memory runs deep in the human soul.

Istvan's searches began, as did mine, in advanced age, say mid-to-late sixties. Beyond my grandfather on my father's side, my biological line remains obscured. Only in another sense do I have a clue. My father once said we were Levites. These were the men of a priestly caste who in the Biblical days of the temple in Jerusalem tended the liturgy, probably sang prayers in the services, perhaps played instruments, for tradition tells us that Levites were musicians devoted to the worship of Jehovah. I connect with this the fact that my father, hardly a religious man in the strict sense, had a beautiful clear high baritone voice. When I was a boy, I remember him singing when he was home from work – Russian songs, Yiddish songs, American songs. I can't go back much further on my mother's side. The Hoffman family boasted several musicians, one a pianist who studied at the conservatory in St Petersburg. The most interesting (to me) relative on my mother's side was an uncle who was in the Czar's Guard – which czar I don't know. He was a large man, a prerequisite for being in the Czar's Guard. Although a Jew, he was permitted by special dispensation to live in St Petersburg with his family – a rarity, I gather, in those days. Beyond that generation, again I draw a complete blank. Often I have wondered how long my people, whoever they were, were in Russia, in the Ukraine, and where did they come from? Did the line on my father's side, expelled from England in 1190 along with all the other Jews of Great Britain, take its name from the city of Roxburgh in the borderlands between England and Scotland? Was the name Germanized as my ancestors moved eastward across Europe? Perhaps this is another of my fantasies. (A delightful man whom I met three years ago in England, a retired bishop of the Anglican Church, thinks it's entirely unlikely we are related in any way. His name is Roxburgh, which he pronounces "Rocksburra," which I gather is the way the Scottish say it.) In any case, the longing for biological connection goes on in Istvan and myself but remains, at least so far, unsatisfied.

In a recent fracas in the Israeli Parliament over King David's questionable behaviour in regard to Bathsheba, Shimon Peres felt it incumbent on himself to defend his very sense of being Jewish against members of the Orthodox party who were attacking him. It's hard to believe that the foreign minister of Israel would find it necessary under the circumstances to go so far as to *define* his personal view of Judaism. This, it occurs to me, is one of the strangely uncharacteristic things about Jews: they are always trying to understand and define what Judaism means. In his last ten years or so Istvan has been very concerned – as I have – with the question of being Jewish. It's very easy to understand why this would be so in his case: to have been condemned to hard labour just because one was born a Jew is hardly something easily sloughed off simply as vicious, insane politics. If this has been your fate, how can you ever reconcile yourself to the flood of hatred let loose against the Jews of Europe? The pathology of it is mind-shattering. Even those of us who were not directly affected because we were physically far from the epicenter of this unbelievable madness have difficulty dealing with it. How much more difficult must it be, then, for those who, like my friend, went through it somehow and survived. Inevitably you want to understand something – at least, if at all possible, though I don't really believe it is. So, you settle for trying to understand what it means to be Jewish, to try to encompass the history of the Jews from Biblical times on and their religious evolution within that history. Along the way you discover high moments that captivate you, that draw you in. In Istvan's case, the Kabbalah – its mysticism, its esoteric religious symbolism, and rich verbal imagery. In my case, the destruction of the temple by the Romans, a major chapter not only in Jewish history but in the history of the Roman Empire.

I have been wrestling with all these questions – but under totally different circumstances – since I was fifteen. The supreme philosophical, metaphysical question for me remains the problem of untying the knot of being Jewish and human all at the same time. One is always human, our neurological systems see to that. One is always human no matter what genetic and cultural legacies imprint themselves on us. Yet what Jewishness is as a condition of being human, all too human, eludes me. Still, in the very nature of things I know I am Jewish. But certainly not for religious reasons, not for reasons of race. They strike me as wholly lacking in any kind of convincing evidence. I have always been intrigued by Freud's wanting to be "Egyptian," following his notion that Moses, who created monotheistic Judaism, was himself an "Egyptian" aristocrat. I have been equally fascinated by Arthur Koestler's story of the pagan Turkic tribe of the Khazars (related by culture to Bulgars, Magyars and others) who converted to Judaism around A.D. 700–800 in order not to be swallowed up by the Arab Muslims, who were constantly raiding the Caucasus region when they weren't just trading, or by the Christians of the Byzantine Empire. Koestler was convinced that the Jews of Russia, Ukraine, Poland, and the Baltics, who comprised the great mass of Jews slaughtered by the Nazis, were the descendants of these very same Khazars.

There is no way of knowing if Koestler was right; mysteries abound on all sides. It is really wonderful, though, the things people will and do believe. I've come to the conclusion that it is essential for their psychic health to believe in something. The issue is not *what* they believe but *that* they believe, the act of believing itself discharging enormous amounts of emotional energy that are displaced into the objects of belief. Which explains to me in a rough sort of way why the passions of people over matters of disputed difference in religious and political doctrines and symbols can catch fire and flame out in bitter hatred, violence, and war.

Istvan and I have written and talked much to each other about these matters. Like virtually all of the most important things that preoccupy human minds and hearts, these are largely, if not entirely, unresolvable – mysterious because unknowable, refractory because fraught with knots and tangles which do not untie readily, impossible to set aside because they are part of existence itself, particularly this strange time in which we lead our daily lives.

Finally, a word about music, because we have both lived and worked as musicians and composers – not to mention as teachers – for most of our lives. Music, I'm convinced, has been the source of our sanity, balance, and maybe even our longevity. Of course genetics are involved; nevertheless, I believe that the spiritual energies which music generates for the dedicated (even obsessed) human soul, heart, and mind has profound effects upon our neurology, and therefore our bodies and minds, which are unitary entities, inseparably interwoven. The intensities music embodies shape those who make music. These intensities are not abstract. They must be lived and experienced to be real in their projection, felt as forms of reality by those who make them and those who receive them. Our job is to put a little beauty out there in the world. Istvan Anhalt is one of our generation who has made music such a living reality, who has put some beauty into the world.

I salute my friend and wish him long years in good health, joy in his family, and continued good work whether in music or in words. *Tante auguri*, Isty, and *sempre avanti* – if not in Tempo Allegro, at least in Tempo Andante Comodo.

NOTES

1 This text was written in December 1994, when the idea of this book was first conceived.
2 Dating from 1961, the voluminous (and ongoing) Anhalt-Rochberg correspondence is the current subject of a study by Alan Gillmor.

PART FOUR

In Anhalt's Voice

Introduction

Throughout his career in Canada, Istvan Anhalt has demonstrated a stimulating talent not only for composing but also for writing about music. For all of his own major compositions he has provided at least one and in some instances several essays explaining the work's aesthetic and musical qualities. His major contribution as an engaged and profound thinker about music is his book *Alternative Voices*, in which he brings his wide learning to bear on the subject of contemporary vocal and choral composition. It seems fitting, then, to include Anhalt's voice here, in a number of essays that deal with his own vocal and choral compositions.

The opening texts (grouped together as "An Operatic Triptych in Multiple Texts") are about Anhalt's first three operas, *La Tourangelle*, *Winthrop*, and *Traces (Tikkun)*. They include genesis, narrative, and analytical commentaries, as well as thoughts on the voices and choral writing in the operas, a topic of continuing interest to Anhalt. This is followed by a talk Anhalt gave at both Queen's University and the University of Toronto in the spring of 1996, a few months before *Traces (Tikkun)* received its premiere at the Glenn Gould Studio in Toronto. Constructed as a dialogue between the composer/author and an interlocutor – a kind of performance piece – this text is particularly engaging as well as informative.

Anhalt's opera writings are followed by a paper he presented at the University of Toronto in January 1988 on the contexts of one of his orchestral compositions, *Simulacrum* (1986–87). In "From 'Mirage' to *Simulacrum* and 'Afterthought'," Anhalt describes the various memory levels at work in this composition, references to earlier musical compositions in the piece, and their relationship to different sites from his past. As Anhalt continues his search for past connections, an essay on *Three Songs of Love* discusses the multilayered compositional contexts of a work the genesis of which dates back more than fifty years. This theme is explored further in relation to a number of Anhalt's seminal compositions from the 1950s forward (*Comments, Cento, Foci, La Tourangelle*) in his essay "A Continuing Thread? Perhaps." The final text in this section of the book is the libretto of Anhalt's most recent opera, *Millennial Mall (Lady Diotima's Walk)*, followed by the composer's commentary.

Throughout these writings we see the importance Anhalt has attached and continues to attach to *memory* in all of his creative activity. As Anhalt reflects now more deeply than ever, this theme emerges as a central metaphoric pathway through his life and work.

G.E.S.

12 An Operatic Triptych[1] in Multiple Texts

In remembrance of Felix Letemendia, a friend

THE BRIEF HISTORY OF AN OPERATIC TRIPTYCH

The first work in this triptych, *La Tourangelle,* was the outcome of a CBC Radio commission. Its story is told elsewhere on these pages. The composition took place during the years 1970–75, and the premiere in the summer of 1975. It was followed by *Winthrop,* which I began in the fall of 1975 and completed in 1983. During the early 1980s, while still at work on *Winthrop,* I began to think that eventually I should consider adding a third work, one based on the story of a Jewish figure, thus endeavouring to tell about the group with which I share traits due to family history as well as life experience. In this intent I was strongly encouraged by John Beckwith, a friend of many years. As it turned out, this piece proved to be the most elusive to get into focus. It was clear that the chronotope (time and place) shared by both Marie de l'Incarnation and John Winthrop – early seventeenth-century North America – would not yield a suitable personage. Thus the place-time angle became a matter of free choice. After several years elapsed – taken up by other projects – in 1990 I came to focus on Robert J. Oppenheimer, the great physicist and the director of the Los Alamos laboratories during the Second World War. After considerable work on a would-be libretto, and some of the music itself, and negotiations with an opera company over several years, the project came to naught. What I had at the end (and to this day) is a three-act play, entitled *Oppenheimer,* unperformed.

Subsequently, spurred on by a sudden idea, I wrote the first draft of a text, entitled *Traces (Tikkun)*, in 1993. This was followed by numerous revisions, as usual. In the libretto, as will be described shortly in some detail, one reads of some of the life experiences of an unnamed man, details of the kind I myself was personally familiar with, or could imagine, and which, I strongly felt, were also shared by many of those who, after certain experiences, were compelled to seek admittance into a new community where they hoped they could find conditions that would be conducive to a more peaceable existence than the one which was their lot before. Simply put, *Traces (Tikkun)* is, once again, the tale of an emigrant-immigrant, like Marie de l'Incarnation and John Winthrop. It might be worth noting that the word "Jew" does not appear in this text, thus allowing for a greater generality, a greater amplitude of relevance based on the shared motive of displacement in the search for a new homeland. The new piece came to take the character of a "pluri-drama," in as much as its story is told/sung by a single (male) vocalist who, by suitably modulating his voice, has the task of giving an impression of a considerable number of "others," whose personae he has encountered during his life and who have made a lasting impression on him, in a series of dramatic situations. The way I undertook to portray this will be recounted in some detail elsewhere in the course of this narrative. This work was completed in 1994 and premiered in May 1996, almost ten years after the premiere of *Winthrop*, which took place in September 1986.

The idea and plan for this cycle developed in the course of composition, during the years 1970 to 1994. As it now stands, a few unifying features can be discerned in it. Firstly, each work is based on and expresses what one might call – with some trepidation these days – a certain specific spiritual attitude. In *La Tourangelle* it is that of seventeenth-century mystical French Catholicism. In *Winthrop* we encounter a Puritan world view, anchored also in the mid seventeenth century, as practised in England, and subsequently New England. The place-time "home" (Mikhail Bakhtin might have called it "chronotope") of *Traces (Tikkun)* is somewhat resistant to clear localization. But we might not stray far from the truth if we declared late-twentieth-century central Canada to be its principal "acting terrain" and period, with numerous flashbacks to other places and times.

Secondly, as to focus, each of the three works features a "hero." In the first two these are historical personages: Marie de l'Incarnation, the strong-willed superior of the Ursuline order in Quebec City, and John Winthrop, the powerful governor of the Massachusetts Bay Colony. The protagonist-hero of *Traces (Tikkun)* has no name. He is probably a much-travelled European-born Jew who settled and set down roots in Canada after his experience in, and survival of the years between, say, 1920 and 1950 in Europe. While he is an eager learner of things North American, he is also hanging on to his European memories, which slowly, ever so slowly, he begins to understand. In reality, he swings back and forth between an involvement in the late-twentieth-century scene in Canada and the rich storehouse of his memories. Slowly these two strands start making sense to him *in relation to each other.*

Thirdly, the "fashioning" of the leading characters in these works is somewhat peculiar. In *La Tourangelle* a trio of sopranos portrays a single "larger-than-life" figure. In *Winthrop* three vocalists come to play the three ages of John Winthrop (tenor, baritone, and bass, in this order) in the form of solos, duets, and lastly as a trio, shortly before he dies. The protagonist in the pluri-drama *Traces (Tikkun)* is a person who displays in his character the tell-tale signs of numerous influences acquired during a long life, thanks to the events lived through, a talent for observation, a good memory, and an interest in people. This person learned from Martin Buber (*I and Thou*) and also from Mikhail Bakhtin. This role requires that the soloist impersonate, in soliloquies and in pseudodialogues, the minds and voices of about a dozen persons.

Fourthly, the three layers, components, or foundations of this triptych, each rooted in one of three monotheistic faiths, could be taken as an attempt by the librettist/composer to explore these "deep" layers one by one, and now, as the triptych is complete, in totality. However, much of the work of integration (should this prove to be achievable) is left to present and future listeners to puzzle out.

Fifthly, the librettos of *La Tourangelle* and *Winthrop* are, in large measure, assembled from pre-existing texts, predominantly from documents contemporary with the periods concerned. The text of the third opera is an original work written by the composer.

LA TOURANGELLE[2]

The impetus for this work came from John P.L. Roberts, then Head of CBC Radio Music, who in 1970 asked me to compose a work expressing "the search for order and meaning in life through the focus of religion – the search for God in other words." In response, I immediately thought of centring the work on a historical figure whose life could be seen as embodying this objective. Living in Montreal at the time and needing advice in the identification of a suitable personage, I turned to the historian Laurier La Pierre, who was then a colleague at McGill

University. He suggested only two names, one of whom was Marie de l'Incarnation, the early seventeeth-century Ursuline nun who made a lasting mark on the history of La Nouvelle France. Reading, subsequently, both her writings, as well as works about the historical milieu in which she lived, I became convinced that Marie would be an excellent heroine of an opera. In the source materials she came alive to me as an extraordinary and powerful individual whose character included sound practical sense for worldly matters alongside a secret propensity for mysticism. Her life is full of dramatic detail both in interpersonal relationships and in public situations. The substance and diversity, as well as the depth, of the known details of Marie's life promised a rich domain for the work. I began to hear a complex and expressive "symphony" of voices swirling around her and, in response, also emanating from her. I was ready to begin work on the piece.

The "woman from Tours," Marie de l'Incarnation came to Quebec in 1639 at the age of forty and spent more than three decades there doing God's work. From relatively humble beginnings she rose to preeminence through an extraordinary combination of intelligence, perseverance, religious fervour (reaching into mysticism in certain moments in her life), vision, allied to a remarkable practical sense and business acumen. Obeying her parents' wishes, even at the cost of suppressing her own preferences, she married young, and in rapid succession became a mother and widow. Faced with the necessity of providing for herself and her son, she took employment in the house and business of her brother-in-law, first as a common servant, but soon rising to the post of manager. During all this she was continuing her spiritual apprenticeship under the guidance of a father confessor. The next momentous event in her life was being accepted – against severe odds, prevailing societal norms, and religious doctrine – into the Ursuline order, creating thereby a difficult situation for herself, her son, her family, and for her order, and sorely testing the threshold of tolerance of the community at large. She managed to overcome the crisis that resulted from this and soon regained a measure of inner peace. This made it possible for her to heed a message that came to her in a dream (likely prompted by letters written by Jesuit missionaries from Canada), to undertake missionary work in that distant and unknown land. She obeyed the call and, leaving behind all persons and ties dear to her in her native country, was soon on the way to her "promised land." Her crossing, in the company of a handful of other nuns and priests, was, according to the record, a harrowing experience. The reception she and her companions received in the harbour of the small village that was Quebec at the time could not have been a greater contrast: it was filled with joy both on the part of the weary travellers and those who received them on shore. *La Tourangelle* concludes with this moment in the life of Marie de l'Incarnation.

In calling *La Tourangelle* a tableau, I am suggesting that it be thought of as a dramatic work that is staged in a somewhat stylized manner, showing, instead of a realistically enacted plot, a succession of almost static situations, characteristic attitudes, frames of mind, emotional states, decisive moments, and crises, in the lives of individuals and groups, representations of societal norms, institutional attitudes, and even etiquette, in a series of *tableaux vivants*. To underscore this, the work includes, besides the historical narrative which is its core, a "frame" also, that contains the voices of chroniclers, commentators, teachers with their pupils, who first introduce the story and then participate in its enactment. The work is meant to be approached primarily through the ear. It invites the listener to imagine the scene: the looks of the protagonists, their attire, and all other features of the visual environment that are deemed to be relevant.

The work is composed for five solo voices, of which the three sopranos together create the persona of Marie de l'Incarnation. The two male soloists assume various roles: father confessor, the voice of a saint, priests, townsfolk spreading calumny, and habitants in the settlement of Quebec.

The orchestra consists of sixteen musicians. In addition there is a considerable amount of material (mainly vocal and choral) stored on tape, which, in the form of playback, is an integral part of the music. On these tapes there are many individual voices, as well as two boys' choirs, one in French and the other in English. This bilingualism is an important feature of the entire work. Marie de l'Incarnation always sings or speaks in French. The remaining materials are in either one, or both, of these languages.

La Tourangelle is dedicated to the memory of Pater János Antal, superior of the Salesian order of St John Bosco in Budapest, in 1944, who had shown great compassion and rare courage during the final months of World War II.

Synopsis

1. *Panegyric.* Devoted, solemn and somewhat stilted voices are praising Marie de l'Incarnation. A real or imaginary assembly of nuns, churchmen, and schoolboys with their masters evoke her memory. A protesting voice from the past (her own) twice interrupts this recitation. Suddenly, Marie's terrifying vision of 1620, in which she felt her soul

being immersed in the blood of Christ, and thus purified, is evoked. A prayer sung by nuns follows, leading into the story of her life, as it may indeed have happened.

2. *Disciple.* Servitude and obedience; an account of her difficult spiritual apprenticeship under the guidance of Dom François de Saint Bernard, her director, in search of humility, docility and purity of soul. Aiming at becoming "nothing" in order to be able to be dissolved in the "big sea of purity" that is God.

3. *Communion.* Her soul having "sunk into a sweet labyrinth," Marie speaks of, and to, God: "Oh Breadth, Oh Height, Oh Depth ... You are not fire, nor water, nothing that we can utter in words ... You are what You are ... You are life ... I was made for You ... I know that You want what I want ... Come, come and take me to be Yours ... Oh forgive my boldness, my sweet love ... I cannot speak on this earth ... take me away from here ... I know who I am ... the nothing worthy of all disdain ... nevertheless ... You are my love ..."

4. *Isaac.* A scene of scandal and confusion in Tours. Adults' and children's voices of cruelty, pain, complaint, trial and condemnation: "her own son was an Isaac ... an only one ... given to her ... to test her ... she decided to sacrifice him ..." Words from an ancient edict are invoked: "If someone abandons his children ... if he is doing this for the love of God ... if he believes that to abandon them and to enter into monastic life is more important that the task of raising his children ... he should be anathema." Fight ... flight ... A sense of despair and utter exhaustion.

5. *Mission.* A distant and anonymous voice pleads for understanding and help, from a faraway land in distress – Canada: "France, my dearest Cousin. Nature does not want me to take my complaints to anyone else but yourself ..." The King's and the chancellor's points of view in response. Marie's dream of Canada: a vast country of mountains, valleys, heavy mists ... and in it a house of white marble ... with the smiling Blessed Virgin seated in it. She knows that the dream is a call for her to go and build a house for God there. The dream becomes a reality with miraculous speed and she is on her way, with a few companions, to her "Paradise," the New France.

6. *Interlude (Voyage).* An impression of a long and perilous voyage, of fear and prayer.

7. *Destination.* A fantasy upon her and her companions' arrival in the tiny settlement of Quebec of 1639. Voices of relief, joy, welcome, dedication and thanksgiving. *Te Deum Laudamus* is sung. Then the scene gets blurred: the picture and sound recede and only echoes of what one just took part in remain ...

WINTHROP

The dominant thought behind this work was to focus on a figure that could be seen as representing the North American Protestant English tradition, paralleling the way Marie de l'Incarnation stands for the French-Catholic world view. I thought about a male figure of historical importance who was also an immigrant at about the time Marie made the crossing to North America. It soon became evident that for a person with these attributes I would have to look into the history of New England. The late George Rawlyk, a colleague at Queen's University, made this clear to me. He mentioned only one name: John Winthrop, the founding governor of the Massachusetts Bay Colony and builder of the city of Boston. A few hours of reading about him persuaded me of the rightness of Rawlyk's advice. This was further strengthened by the realization that Winthrop can, with justification, be seen as a person who, through his historical role, has had important bearing also on the history of English Canada. Having made the choice of John Winthrop as the central personage of the new work, I began the usual preparatory work (mainly reading about the subject figures and the historical context). It took little time after this to realize that I had chanced on a story that at least matched the drama of the "life and times" of Marie de l'Incarnation. In the course of this phase I began to hear "voices" – those of political personages, preachers, propagandists, messengers, those of individual commoners expressing various views relating to social or economic conditions, or other burning topics. In addition to these I began to imagine the great variety of the voices of the collective in numerous situations. The outcome of this, after the necessary work, was *Winthrop*, the opera.

Winthrop: The Work, the Theme, the Story [3]

The Work [4]

Winthrop is an opera (in the manner of an historical pageant) in two parts, with a total duration of about two and one-half hours. Completed in March 1983, it is scored for six solo singers, a mixed choir of at least twenty-four voices, a small boys' choir, and an instrumental ensemble of at least thirty players. I assembled the text myself, relying principally on original sources from the first half of the seventeenth century, but borrowing also from others that date from earlier and from more recent periods. I completed the libretto by adding, here and there, a few passages, as the need for these arose, and whenever no suitable "authentic" text was at hand.

The Theme

The central figure of the piece is John Winthrop, governor of the Massachusetts Bay Company, the founder of Boston, the most commanding figure in the history of New England from 1630 to 1649. Winthrop was born in England, lived and died an Englishman, yet he was also a major contributor to the evolution of what might be called the "New England mind," and, by extension, also the "English-Canadian mind." (A claim that John Winthrop might be considered a founding father of Canada also would have to – and I think does – rest on the evidence of the vital role Massachusetts, and other parts of New England, played in the history of Nova Scotia and Lower and Upper Canada before, during, and after the American Revolution.)

In addition to the genetic legacy, Winthrop, members of his original group, and their descendants left also a spiritual one, which is shared to this very day by large segments of the English-speaking societies in the United States and Canada: it is what one may call the Puritan ethic, or world view. This inheritance is a recognizable component in the lives of many men and women who have significantly contributed to the evolving North American experience as individuals, and at times also as members of diverse institutions, in an uninterrupted flow ever since John Winthrop's time.

But John Winthrop is still more than an outstanding historical personage, a founding father, and a paradigm for an ethical-philosophical outlook. He is remembered also, and foremostly, as a human being, somewhat larger in certain dimensions than most, yet identifiable as such in his passions, striving, gropings, doubts, triumphs, failures, and his compromises. Only when one is able to regard him from this viewpoint, can one begin to understand him in his public roles and feel with him in his actions. When coming to know him in this manner, one begins to sense that through the life of this man one might also have gained a glimpse into the universal human condition. It is the aim of *Winthrop* to bring about a synthesis of representations of private and public worlds, of times past and present, of historical events, and of some of the complex currents of ideas and feelings underlying them, for the purpose of creating a framework for such a kind of understanding.

The Story (A Synopsis)

Part One

1 *Pilgrimage and Discovery.* A pastoral scene near Groton, in Suffolk, England. It is a beautiful summer afternoon, in the present. One hears the sounds of distant bells. A man and woman are heard talking:

inward monologues ... and an elliptical conversation. The pull of the past is felt and is constantly increasing. Memory images float by ... A dreamy state of mind, a feeling of *déjà vu*, takes hold ... The attraction of "roots" is becoming irresistible ... Memory layers long dormant, or perhaps never tapped before, come to life gradually, activated by sights, sounds, and by other aspects of the general ambience. Hardly legible inscriptions on tombstones draw attention to the Winthrop family, members of a clan of strivers from the North. Their upward struggle is remembered and briefly, but vividly, re-enacted, culminating in the sudden appearance of a royal messenger conferring rights and privileges on an Adam Winthrop for services rendered to the King. The past and present constantly and simultaneously tug and pull the hearer/viewer ... One is uncertain whether one is awake, dreams, imagines, or is actually transported back into a living past ... The latter wins out ... The present fades away and one hears the announcement of the birth of a John Winthrop; the year is 1587.

2 *Young John.* This is an aria that shows the transformation of a confused adolescent into a young adult who has managed to achieve a certain measure of control over himself.

One first sees/hears the young John Winthrop (a lyric tenor) as an early seventeenth-century type of rock singer, overflowing with energy and passion. The music is powerful, athletic, expressed through large gestures, and is indicative of a strong inner drive that pushes him onwards, close to the edge of seeming insanity. He first sings using a kind of scat language (vintage, say, of anno 1603). One senses in his delivery very considerable physical and mental powers, which are, as yet, incapable of being manifested in a rational way. When the first intelligible words are formed they speak of a sense of guilt felt over sexual urges.

Two groups of singers comment on this scene (they gradually emerge from a dark background): the first is that of nine to fifteen younger boys who comment with empathy in a counterpoint imitating psalmody; the other group consists of women who are horrified by, yet attracted to, the tribulations of the young Winthrop. They utter, in brief bursts, various prayer formulas, as well as other kinds of complementary material.

Very gradually young John gains understanding and a degree of maturity. The aria ends with an impassioned pledge.

3 *John and Margaret.* This is an intimate dialogue between Winthrop and his young wife: a love duet. It is alternately tender, affectionately passionate, and tender again. It depicts the two in a clearly expressed relationship that acknowledges roles, reciprocal responsibility, and a high level of mutual support.

The scene is witnessed from a distance by small groups of men and women, who, in places, echo what John and Margaret are conveying to each other.

4 *Famous Brittany*. This section depicts the turbulent socio-political situation in Britain that led to Winthrop's emigration to America and to the revolution that caused the demise of Charles I and Cromwell's ascent to power. At another level, it is a paradigm of any struggle for socio-political power, and related human group behaviour, that causes events to occur, *and* is being buffeted by them.

The scene could be that of a fairground, a kaleidoscopic representation of society. A brief orchestral introduction depicts turmoil, dissatisfaction, suppressed hostility, passion and brutality, engendered by conflicting forces and feelings.

This is interrupted by the first vocal sounds: "Call to mind!" This alarm signal refers to certain dangers menacing church and state. In response a frantic action erupts. Contending groups sing and shout words at each other indicative of various and opposing attitudes and beliefs; a choral battle takes place. This gradually degenerates into a frightened, forced half-whisper, broken by silences. Fear takes hold of all, subsequently giving way to growing anger. The next attitude broadcasts, at an always more and more excited level, prejudices in the form of political/moral slogans. After these the centre of attention shifts to a group of women who utter a series of curses, culminating in hate-filled sneers. A group of urchins laugh at the goings-on. Some men begin to intone what sounds like a patriotic hymn, which they belt out, drawing others along with them. One is uncertain how much of this is an expression of conviction, how much mockery, or perhaps both, simultaneously. The boys, for certain, are having a good time of it: they repeatedly punctuate the proceedings with bursts of loud laughter.

A sudden break occurs: one hears the music of a village band, a kind of quick polka. To its tune a small group of women recite/intone the words of a ballad, which in their interpretation takes on the character of a bawdy song.

The stern voice of a preacher is heard next, warning of religious deviation. He is sustained by responses of a group of frightened faithful. The spectre of Judgment Day is evoked ...

But there is hope in all this confusion and gloom. It is offered by another voice: that of a herald, who speaks of a haven and of a new life to be found overseas, in America. He is really a promoter of emigration, a proto-adman, who seems to believe in what he advocates. He speaks and sings with rising passion, describing the alleged riches as well as the spiritual salvation a New England holds in store for all. His delivery is infectious and he carries the crowd with him into an enthusiastic outburst of agreement and pledge.

The scene accelerates musically and is accompanied by a rapid visual fade-out, preparing the way for the next section and scene.

5 *Call and Response.* This section enacts events that took place during the period 1628–30.

At the outset, Margaret, in her study (or parlor), reads (sings) aloud passages from a letter of John Winthrop, written from London. We hear the description (eyewitness or close approximation thereof) of one of the most significant and dramatic scenes in seventeenth-century British parliamentary history. We imagine, or may actually see, through projections on a backdrop, the fateful events that set into motion momentous political changes in Britain as well as in America.

The next sub-scene shows Winthrop in deep thought debating the pros and cons of emigrating to the New World. The leading voice now is that of the middle-aged Winthrop (a baritone), but during this interior debate the young Winthrop (a tenor) takes the other part. As the decision to go to America appears to become the preferred one, groups of men and women join in, supporting this choice. They reach a certain point of enthusiasm, which suddenly gives way to the next sub-scene.

This is the oath-ceremony. Winthrop is, in short order, elected governor of the newly formed Massachusetts Bay Company, and takes the governor's oath in the course of which one sees/hears him transformed into a forceful leader, who has no more doubts about his mission.

The next sub-scene depicts the busy goings-on (there is so little time left before the designated departure date) during the preparations for the voyage and emigration of about one thousand persons. Men and women rush around storing and packing various goods and provisions ...

The preceding activity comes to an abrupt end: a new sub-scene begins. We are in a port, ships are seen, and farewells are being said. The atmosphere is solemn, and quietly emotional. Promises are being made; support and forgiveness are sought. The three ships glide out of the harbour ... the wind gets into the sails ... echoes of the farewell mix with sounds of the sea ... the sounds fade out as the ships disappear from sight.

Part Two

6 *Covenant and Lesson (The Voyage).* The scene: on board Winthrop's flagship, the *Arbella*, on the high seas, on the way to America.

The protagonists: a look-out, who is the "eye" of the ship, high on a mast (sung by the young Winthrop) and the governor (the middle-aged Winthrop) who is the "brains" of the group, the leader. They are complemented by a group of boys who are given instruction in catechism and by groups of men and women in various roles.

The first vocal sound we hear is the first announcement of the look-out; focus on the environment.

This is followed by a dialogue between governor Winthrop and a group of men as they outline the terms of a covenant. Inward focussing: "A Citty upon a Hill we shall be."

The second announcement of the lookout.

Antiphonal exchange between Winthrop and the boys: the catechism.

Women join in with a pledge: "I do believe with my heart … etc." "A Citty upon a Hill we shall be."

Boys begin a dream-like description of this "Citty." Their fantasy carries along the entire group whose communal song reaches an ecstatic level.

The third, excited intervention of the lookout announces the sighting of land. This breaks the spell of the preceding fantasy, and engages every person on board in a free-for-all outburst. Slowly the shores of the "New World" come into sight. A great sense of expectation descends upon the group as men probe the depths for a landing … A final promise is voiced about co-operation … The land nears … the voices on the ship fall silent … From the distance one faintly hears the steady throbbing of a deep drum … the heart-beat, or voice, of an unknown world perhaps … The ending of the section is tinged with a sense of foreboding that contrasts with the series of moods experienced during the voyage.

7 *Boston … a Citty.* There is no break between the preceding section and this one. The distant drumming continues … a great hush and immobility persist on the ship as reality sinks in: America appears, from this vantage point at least, as an immense jungle, containing little promise, but much threat. The mood swings to instant despair, expressed in the words: "We all die in Boston," and other similar expressions.

This section spans about six years and tells of various episodes that highlighted the history of Boston during the years 1630–36. From the first hours of landing the story leads to the political crisis caused by Mrs Anne Hutchinson, who challenged Winthrop and the ruling group for power in 1636.

The initial sub-scene develops into near mutiny on the very shores of the unknown territory. This mood of defeatism, engendered by fear, is successfully challenged by another attitude, calling everyone to work. We indeed see the community exerting a great effort in building the new town, Boston.

Interruption: sudden announcement of a harsh punishment, the first indication of certain judicial standards and practices in the community.

Work resumes: another interruption tells of further punishments.

Focus on the Court, and the way "law and order" is maintained in this frontier town. One senses the clash between those in power and those who do not benefit of the same in equal measure. A considerable degree of tension is building up through choral and scenic action.

The tension rapidly dissipates, giving place to a call (by Winthrop) for public thanksgiving. Winthrop reveals a personally compassionate attitude in socio-economic matters.

Interruption by the cries: "Fire," "A house on fire." An accident? Or arson, perhaps? Both are possible. The tension returns.

The distant drumming (which faintly persisted in the background during all the preceding sub-events) now comes into the foreground. We see the arrival of a group of Indian visitors to Boston. Their attire and their music have little that is authentic to them. They appear as presumably seen/heard by the Bostonians of the time: either as noble savages, or as children, or as incomprehensible beings, to be feared, to be mistrusted, and perhaps also ridiculed.

The next sub-scene takes over from the preceding one: the colony's soldiers train in the distance, in the dusk ... One hears faintly the sound of military drums, trumpets, and pounding feet ... fade-out.

Someone (it turns out to be Anne Hutchinson) asks a key (and fateful) question, "What is the nature of grace?" which within a short time-span will come close to tearing apart the colony. A group responds to it by citing names of ships, implying that the answer lies in the direction of "good works." This causes the eruption of an impassioned choral debate between groups holding contrary opinions about the issue.

A sudden break follows, caused by the announcement of the violent death of a white man (John Oldham), allegedly killed by some Indians. The focus of passions abruptly changes. Calls for revenge are shouted.

More bad news: the plague has hit Boston. Chant: "We fear the plague in Boston."

Return to the concern of revenge for the death of John Oldham. The bloody deeds of a punitive expedition, the massacre of an entire Indian settlement, are enacted. We hear the sounds of dying women and men ...

Back to the interior concerns of Boston: an account of harsh punishment meted out for an assortment of unlawful behaviour. The level of repression and tension reaches a high pitch ... One feels the need for some kind of remedial action in the colony. But what we hear now is the voice of a young town crier announcing three times (at various locations, backstage): "The twelfth day of the month a day of humiliation, to entreat the help of God." A mood of foreboding, marking for time ... a sense of crisis hangs in the air ... Without a break an orchestral ostinato leads to the next section.

8 *A Crisis.* One finds Winthrop (baritone) alone, thinking of the grave situation in which his colony finds itself, as a result of the political polarization caused by the activities of Anne Hutchinson and her followers. He realizes that to safeguard the very existence of his community *as he sees it,* he must confront and politically destroy the woman unless she agrees to recant. A trial is unavoidable, even necessary. His thoughts (expressed in the form of an aria) are counterpointed by choral sounds.

The stage opens up and we see a court scene, with Winthrop as the presiding judge, a court clerk, witnesses (a group of six ministers), men, women, and children of the community, and the soon to be accused: Anne Hutchinson.

Winthrop ends his soliloquy by instructing the clerk to call Anne Hutchinson before the court. This is done.

Here begins a series of exchanges between Winthrop and Anne Hutchinson. First the latter says little and her clever and effective evasive actions gradually frustrate Winthrop. He comes close to losing his temper. These exchanges function as bouts between two skilled fencers who duel in the awareness that only one will leave the ground alive … From time to time the audience (women and children) provides a background commentary. Their sung interventions, in their naiveté, contrast the life-death struggle of the protagonists.

Winthrop, feeling exasperated on account of his adversary, finally tries a new approach: he calls the ministers to testify. (They were, allegedly, berated by Anne Hutchinson on the ground of theological differences between her and them.) They voice their accusations in three closely co-ordinated interventions, which are, each time, denied by Anne Hutchinson, yet are approvingly echoed by the community, whose sung commentaries contribute to the constantly rising tension of the scene, leading to a powerful climax. This is abruptly cut short by the presiding judge, Winthrop, who came to realize that the testimony has produced no conclusive evidence that would prove guilt on Anne Hutchinson's part.

Silence, heavy with meaning. It begins to be filled with children starting to sing timidly slogans of common wisdom learned in school, in absurd contrast with the tense situation at hand. Parents interrupt the children by uttering hushing sounds. Another pause, this time filled with excited, whispered gossip of adults … The stalemate continues …

Suddenly Anne Hutchinson, sensing victory, rises and begins, unasked, a statement (an impassioned aria), telling about her feelings, her motivation, and the thoughts that in her mind fully justify her activities, despite the censure of Winthrop and his group. In the end she makes a revelation that will prove to be her undoing. With this she gives the means by which she will be found guilty of unpardonable unorthodoxy by her adversaries and prosecutors.

Her testimony gives rise to an immense outburst of public indignation, which grows into the very climax of the entire composition. Her ensuing feverish self-defense and subsequent threats are of no avail. Winthrop is ready, and delivers the verdict, which is banishment from the colony. Crushed by the weight of the punishment (and by the concomitant perils it entails), Anne Hutchinson tries to utter a final plea, but receives no charity in response. She is destroyed, politically and socially, as well as being afflicted physically: she can hardly remain standing before her judge.

Winthrop, on his part, is paying a heavy price for committing this judicial act of destruction. He has to face up to the fact that, to defend a utopia, or at least a status quo *resembling in part a utopia that was*, he lost a great deal of moral strength in the eyes of some of his contemporaries, in the perspective of history, and, what is most important, probably in his own view of himself. The price of defending Boston, as he conceived it, was to destroy a person with equally strong, but conflicting, views. In the course of the trial Winthrop aged much. This is conveyed by the addition of the "third Winthrop" (a bass) to the "second Winthrop" (a baritone) as he reads the verdict. The "first Winthrop" also joins them, to show the indivisibility of the "three ages" of the man.

As Anne Hutchinson hobbles out of the Meeting Hall one sense waves of compassion flowing toward her, timidly expressed, by parts of the chorus. Snatches of a psalm are sung softly ... then she takes a few more steps ... halts ... another psalm fragment ... another step or two ... and, finally, she disappears from sight ...

Rapid fade-out of light.

9 *Interlude (Orchestra only)*. This section serves several purposes: first, to give a respite to the audience after the tension of the past forty-five minutes or so (Sections 7 and 8); second, to allow for a possible change of scenery; but, foremost, it represents both a nightmare of Winthrop's following the trial and the lapse of a dozen years.

The music is "seamless." Swirling clusters, in which faint, isolated sounds appear and disappear, persist throughout. All is very soft, restless, speaking of inner turmoil ... After approximately three and one-half minutes this gradually clears away and without a break the next (final) section begins.

10 *Stocktaking*. The year is 1649. The old Winthrop, sung principally by the bass, but also by the two earlier Winthrops (tenor and baritone), is ready to make an accounting (in part private, in part public) of his life and deeds. He appears to be, and is in reality, at peace with

himself: a man who is aware of his accomplishments, as well as of his failures. The record he sees and tells about is a mixed and human one, and the three Winthrops, with a unified voice, show genuine humility and acknowledgment of frailty. As he reminisces about times of old, including those of danger, he is being echoed by "unseen" voices of the chorus. He reveals a strong religious feeling. Memories of personal battles come to mind. One senses that Winthrop still feels the scars of some of the fights of yesteryears. He is relieved that all those crises are over now ... He reveals a need for self-justification and gives a brief testimony to his beliefs concerning the nature of liberty and personal freedom ...

One hears the first of several paeans sung in his honour. This is followed by others. The praises appear as farewells to an aging leader who is held in high esteem by the community. The last few snatches of trivial remembrances by Winthrop are heard, accompanied by a gently supporting chorus. One senses that Winthrop's life nears its end. A final sigh of relief from his threefold self before he dies ... A final paean, as if sung by angels, is heard ... and the scene dissolves. The only instrumental sound remaining is that of a solo violin, playing an indifferent sequence. It accompanies the businesslike speaking voices of two auctioneers who, unseen, in the fading light, take stock of the modest estate Winthrop left behind, listing furniture, tools, old clothing, and other personal effects, together with such worthless items as glue ... The final stages of the fade-out of light and sound ...

Complete darkness and silence.

TRACES (TIKKUN)

About Traces (Tikkun)

Persons
The person behind the single voice of this "pluri-drama" has no name. This enables him to assume a number of different yet interacting identities. He and his "doubles" pass through a series of "life situations" in which strangers also appear. In these encounters we are presented with various "I and Thou" kinds of mutual influences that leave no one involved unchanged.

Places
The most likely location of the drama is the mind, as one revisits memories of events and situations lived through in the course of one's life. Some of these recollections are evoked with such vividness that at

times it is difficult to believe that the actions are not happening in our presence.

Times
Past and present are made to merge here. Some of the implied moments are easy enough to place in time, especially if they bear unmistakable marks of the present. In contrast with these, other kinds of times float by uncertainly, due perhaps to the greater generality or enigmatic character of content.

Signposts
The following series of "clue words" will point to further details in the piece: Arrival, Questions, Labyrinth, Oasis, Desert Town, Metropolis, In the Highdome, After the Show, Visitors, and The Answer. The dramatic actions represented by these merge into each other, in the given order, seamlessly.

Questions
When – after a shorter or longer life span – does one become aware of having left numerous marks, "traces," behind? What can we know about the pattern these might be seen as adding up to? Could this also be seen as mirroring on the human plane the kabbalistic notion of *tikkun*, that of reintegration?

The Title
The word *traces* stands for some or all of the actions a person undertakes in his/her life, for all of the steps and decisions that cause these actions, steps, "traces" to happen. *Tikkun* denotes a concept borrowed from kabbalistic thought. It represents a "making into a whole" from fragments something that may have been a whole before, but subsequently has fallen apart. Here it more narrowly refers to a process in which seemingly unrelated actions may be seen as forming an integrated whole as the series moves towards its conclusion. The word may also suggest questions about freedom of choice, about determinism, about the relationship between individuals and between an individual and the society of which he/she is a member.

The Voice
The text of the pluri-drama is performed by a single lyric baritone voice who enacts a series of actions by a number of people in implied situations. He engages in a variety of dialogic exchanges with implied "others." The idea behind this is the thought that a person is continuously

influenced by the actions and thoughts of other persons. One might come to think that this interactive process is the key to the unfolding of an individual's normal evolutionary development. To put it simply: a person grows into who he or she is through such "I-Thou" dialogic processes.

Synopsis
1 *Arrival.* The singer enters and expresses the belief that someone – unseen, but present – is about to address him. He reveals a readiness to listen.

2 *Questions.* The "unseen" voice places the "other" in the expectation that life's end might be not far away, and when it comes it will have to be faced in solitude. A brief respite is allowed, though. Its purpose is to allow time for facing up to fundamental questions, such as when, where, and why?

3 *Labyrinth.* The would-be answers turn into an account, developing into an enactment, of a series of nightmares, of recurring dreams. Terrible images follow in close, relentless succession: narrow, suffocating passageways, underground tunnels, foiled attempts at escaping, a sense of disorientation in the dark, threatening loud noises, surging water, the fear of drowning, etc. Then comes a sudden relief: one awakes; there is light again and fresh air. This scene of fear stands for any and all threatening situation(s) a person might have encountered in life. It symbolizes extreme danger, as well as a sudden liberation from it.

4 *Oasis.* The word stands for a place of relief, a metaphor turning into the depicting of a symbolic environment of rescue, hope, freedom, exultation, and exuberance. There are two voices here. One is euphoric, the other tries hard to bring the first "down to earth," to "sanity."

5 *Desert Town.* The implied scene is given in the title of this section. The period in which the action takes place is left uncertain. Are we in a Biblical period/scene, or in a contemporary frontier town? It could be either one. The situations and the dialogues seem to be timeless. There are two dominant voices here: the one who is within the walls is an insider; the other is an outsider who wants to "come in." The issues of concern soon become clear; they are those of order and power. The first voice gives a glimpse of the nature of the society within the walls and extends a welcome to the other. Moreover, he reveals that the rich opportunities of the place have been beset lately with certain problems, as can be expected. Also, behind this individual's concern with public affairs emerge the same person's thoughts about intimate matters, such as sexual attraction.

6 *Metropolis.* An incident on a busy street of a modern city has almost taken place. A passerby berates another who barely avoided becoming a traffic fatality. The latter is obviously still distracted, while the former is alert, very much a part of the environment and the given "scene." Suddenly voices are heard from a distance, a sort of rhythmic chanting by young people. They voice slogans about "belonging," "sharing," etc. Their message is a mixture of righteousness tinged with a degree of naïveté perhaps. The responding voice is firm, matter-of-fact, unsentimental, and somewhat short of empathy, all expressed in a kind of contemporary idiom. The little band of young demonstrators suddenly abandons the dialogue and announces the intent to attend a rock concert, which is about to take place in the nearby Highdome.

7 *In the Highdome.* An enactment of a rock concert, which eventually turns into a semblance of a bacchanalia, all of it seen and heard through the sympathetic eyes and ears of a somewhat older person present, who watches the goings-on with fascination and perhaps also with a yearning to participate fully, in person, in all of this.

8 *After the Show.* Suddenly the persona of the concert's promoter appears. He is the man behind it all. He made it "happen." He is the proud entrepreneur, the one who knows the ropes, who put up the money and is aware of the financial risks involved in the enterprise. He has courage in relation to this business, and understands the relationship between risk and profit. He has little patience for (and perhaps little understanding of) "dreamers," and not too much personal concern for the patrons of the show. But he reserves his strongest disdain for an older person who happens to pass by. Is he abusive to him because he understands him so little and, consequently, perhaps fears him? One senses here a clash not only of generations, but also of world views and related values as well.

9 *Visitors.* The previous noise and commotion have died down by now. The implied performance/acting space narrows. We are presently in the visitors' room of a comfortable up-scale nursing home. The voice now is that of a resident in that home. We get a glimpse of the surroundings. The resident's mental world is now often located in memory-space. Suddenly visitors arrive … the family. A brief intimate interplay takes place. After the visitors have left, the resident reverts to his customary "inner space." Memory images float by and then disappear. Suddenly a child's voice is remembered with great affection – obviously a cherished memory. And now suddenly a vision appears. A silent, immobile figure is noticed standing by the door. Who is he?

10 *The Answer.* Without doubt the identity and purpose of the visitor becomes clear. He is the one who signals "the end," the fact that

one's time is up. It is time to prepare for the final departure. The next few words depict a dissolution of the "reality of things." Everything becomes indistinct; things lose their firm outline, colours wash into each other and the process of dissolution into elementary particles is gathering speed. An otherworldly state of stillness and repose is implied at the end.

More about Traces (Of Selves, Others, and Mirrors)

There seems to be a reciprocity linking the knowledge of oneself to the knowledge of others. There might also be a causal connection between the two: the better I understand myself, the greater is the likelihood that I will understand others. Or conversely, the better one understands others, the greater the likelihood that one will come to understand oneself. Such insights may be acquired in either order, over time. Insight is likely to appear spontaneously, provided that the ground for this has been prepared beforehand.

The foregoing thoughts came to me after reading this quotation from Novalis: "The supreme problem of culture is that of gaining possession of one's transcendental self, of being at one and the same time the self of oneself. Thus it should not surprise us that there is an absence of feeling or complete understanding of others. Lacking a perfect comprehension of ourselves, we can never really hope to know others."[5]

This process, from the self to the other, or in the reverse order, is being played out as long as the thinking person lives. This knowledge acquisition, retention, erosion, mutation, and so on, persists to the end of one's life. Its "acting-out space" might be called situations that amount to "scenes in a life." Such scenes in all their complexity create the frame within which learning, the development of self, and the decipherment of others take place. As one lives one's moments, days, years, one receives signals from many "others" and, in turn, signals back to some of these others. Such actions and interactions leave traces in one's memory. The overall pattern of such traces is tantamount to the playing out of one's life, as one proceeds from action to action, from trace to trace, all in a giant exchange of great complexity. Over history many have reflected on this vast generation of interaction. Yet it must be taken as given that the overall pattern will remain hidden even from the best minds, although partial discoveries occur repeatedly. Among other manifestations of the human intellect, a great novel, a poem, a composition, or a painting – each and all testify to this. A series of works by an author (composer, painter, etc.) might be seen as linking up to demonstrate this with particular emphasis. Some ancients called such a connected narrative of several works a *carmen perpetuum*. This might come about, at times, only instinctually.

In the course of creative work the doer gives public evidence of the process of self-discovery. At times the creator might come to feel that s/he is working not unlike a sleepwalker, in a quasi-dream state. Under such conditions s/he might come to feel engaged by the work-in-progress in a sort of sustained dialogue. The work serves as a mirror image, an echo, telling the maker about the appositeness of a preceding act. It talks to him/her as an "other." In such moments the identity or primacy of a creator (or conversely a thing in the process of being created) is likely to become blurred. Who is the writer? "Who" is the text? Did the former create the latter? (I think it was Mahler who said that the work composes the composer, and not the other way around.) But perhaps the more accurate (albeit less poetic) way to put this would be to say that a kind of mirror-play might be at work here. The writer interacts with the reflections that the work in the making sends back, as a sort of mirror. Through this creators become their own re-flected "other." This reflected (and re-reflected) other is the *simulacrum* that helps writers to make a new "trace" – a new work, a new phase in their ongoing *carmen perpetuum*.

The fundamental idea underlying *Traces (Tikkun)* is derived, in large measure, from the foregoing. That is why the work was conceived for a single vocalist. In this single voice, a self and numerous others are made to coexist, hence the appellation of the work as a "pluri-drama." Through this I aimed to portray the reciprocal interactions of two existential dimensions, those of a self and its "others," in a single mind, through a single voice. The compositional aim, which amounts also to a challenge to the audience, was to create a succession of implied scenes/situations that would stimulate the listeners to try to "track" the voice and to endeavour to decipher the identity (or the "type") of the implied others, as well as the time and place (the chronotope) of the action. Through this device of the "many in one" I aimed at placing the entire chain of events (the traces) in the mind of a single person (and in a single voice). From the angle of this objective the number of actual protagonist-singers had to be one. The textures of the orchestral layer aim at mirroring the multifaceted work of the mental process and the many features of "situations."

What is the role of the composer-librettist in all this? He is a participant, a witness, a chronicler, and the one who turns an experience of life into an abstraction, a piece of music.

VOCAL AND CHORAL QUALITIES IN
LA TOURANGELLE, WINTHROP,
AND *TRACES (TIKKUN)*

*A Few Remarks about the Character of
the Individual Voice and That of the "Choral Tone"*

To think about the character of an individual speaking or singing voice is more or less analogous to perceiving "indexical information."[6] This pertains to the information embedded in and communicated through the voice. It tells about gender, age, state of health, vocal physiology and its multifaceted deployment, mood, feelings, and other features. The richness of indexical information makes a good case (at times, to some observers) for the (near) uniqueness of each person's voice, although the perception of this uniqueness is curtailed by certain factors.

In contrast with this, a choral tone (voice) produced by a group (speaking and/or singing) is characterized by the *absence* of the idiosyncratic bundle of characteristics that constitutes individual indexical information. This absence imparts a certain generality, or neutrality, to this collective tone. Instead of idiosyncratic features, the "choral tone" is able to convey a sense of stability instead of the microvariability of the individual voice.

The following connotations suggest themselves here: the voice of a unique individual announces his/her presence as well as a unique message. In contrast, the choral tone bespeaks a group, a community (whether harmonious, or rent by conflict) and cannot help but speak on behalf of that community – of its culture, codes, societal structure, synergy (or the lack of it), power distribution, and the like. The realms of competence of these two kinds of voices (the individual and the group) are thus essentially different from each other.

However, the notion of indexical information is not entirely incompatible with the choral voice, which can convey information about gender, age, affect, and possibly other features as well, but in a manner that is different from that of an individual voice. Massed choral voices are, in contrast, rich in connotations that are beyond the expressive limits of a solo voice, which is only able to portray *in a sequential manner* (as *Traces* endeavours to enact) numerous individual voices that differ from each other in indexical information. (One could even allege that the voices of all speakers can and do undergo significant modulation as they endeavour to convey or, conversely, disguise information. A special instance is that when a hearer correctly identifies a dissembling voice.) The expressive domain of the choral voice offers the possibility for portraying social structure, process, transformation, mass mood, harmony, or dissent – all these in many shades and at many levels of intensity. The subtle information content and depth of an individual voice is here supplanted by the intricacies of polyphony, heterophony alternating with other structural/textural types. The choral voice is in essence the articulator of cultural codes and the vehicle of showing cultural action.

Thus it can be understood how the domains of the solo voice and the choral voice are essentially different from each other: the one has a limitless richness and depth as it "reflects" individual character (or a series of such), and the other a similarly near-infinite variety in depicting cultural "states" and group action. The two dimensions also share features: the individual voice can convey information about the person's role as a societal member; and the choral voice can inform about "gross" indexical features, like gender and age.

> *The Solo Voices in* La Tourangelle, Winthrop,
> *and* Traces (Tikkun)

La Tourangelle

The part of Marie de l'Incarnation is realized through three sopranos singing together, almost through the entire work, in various ways – unison, homophony, or polyphony, as well as in heterophony. Behind the idea of "giving voice" to her in this manner was the intent to portray the complex process of a thinking, feeling mind – in other words, the indescribable intricacy of the activity of a human brain, especially that of an extraordinarily subtle person such as Marie. In this way the three sopranos (as one) are able to conserve their indexical uniqueness while adding a polyphonic dimension as well. The three represent the feelings of a single individual, including ambivalence, doubt, inner struggles between alternative courses of action.

The two male solo voices take on a variety of roles: Marie's "spiritual director," townsfolk in Tours in a crisis situation, fellow passengers (Jesuit priests) on the tiny vessel sailing from Dieppe to La Nouvelle France, and, at the end, habitants in the small settlement of Quebec welcoming joyously the weary passengers at the hour of their arrival.

In addition, the work also contains about ten solo voices recorded on tape. These voices were selected for "suitability," considering the roles they were to represent, and were rehearsed before recording. Through them the work gains additional depth of characterization, and of context also. (Four operators control the output of these tapes under the overall direction of the conductor.)

Winthrop

The role of John Winthrop is also realized by three vocalists (tenor, baritone, bass) who represent his three "ages": youth, middle life, and the years of old age. The young Winthrop appears first in an extended aria. The mature Winthrop carries the role, either alone or in conjunction with his youthful alter ego (suggesting memory and recall). The old Winthrop appears first in section 8 ("A Crisis"), indicating aging as the result of a particularly stressful experience. The old Winthrop is prominent in the final section ("Stocktaking"), where he sings together with his two younger selves, suggesting the indivisibility of the man as he recalls past experiences while approaching the end of life.

The two female solo voices are those of Margaret, Winthrop's wife and devoted companion, and Anne Hutchinson, his antagonist, whom he had to bring before a court of justice where he performed the roles of both accuser and the presiding judge.

The Herauld is a Hermes-like figure: a messenger, whose appearances indicate a peripeteia. He also contains elements of the trickster, the persuader/propagandist, like a Peitho incarnation. At times, he is an inciter of a multitude ready to be swayed to action for whatever purpose. Yet he is also capable of leading a paean for a good man.

Traces (Tikkun)

As distinct from the "one through three" representations in the two earlier operas, here the portrayal is "many through one," hence the genre appellation "pluri-drama." These voices imply the following cast of characters:

1 A senses the presence of B. He tells B that he is ready to listen to him.
2 B speaks to A.
3 B describes a harrowing ordeal, which might have been a past nightmare of A's. It ends with A's escape from it. The distinctness of A and B is now blurred.
4 B is now merged with A. The composite A/B is exuberant to the degree of euphoria. C tries to calm him down.
5 Either an earlier person, or a new one, D, announces new arrivals. E provides more up-to-date information. D/E is an "insider," an upholder of the rules of that walled-in town. F is a spokesman of the "outsiders" who want to come in. They are admitted under certain conditions spelled out by D/E. The latter becomes loquacious. He reveals some problems besetting the community. He is unable to

stop speaking and we hear him revealing intimate thoughts about women. He is carried away, forgetting completely where he is, and that he has an audience.

6   A traffic accident is barely averted. D/E has lost his composure, his control, and nearly his life. He is scathingly belaboured by G, a bystander. D/E tries to defend himself, but without success. Suddenly a group of young demonstrators, H/I/J, appears. They demand consideration; G takes them on. An argument ensues between them. This is broken off by the group, which announces its intent to go to attend a rock concert.

7   An older spectator, D/E or K, watches the concert in fascination and is almost carried away by it. The act, as if mirrored in the mind of this spectator, is performed by a group, L/M/N. There is an obvious identification between performers and spectator.

8   O, a rock impresario, appears. He speaks with pride about the intricacies of the business. Later he notices an older spectator, P. He expresses hostility towards P, who refrains from responding to this; O leaves.

9   P (is he the earlier B, or D/E, or K?) is now a still older man, a resident in a nursing home. He has an intense interior life, focused on a rich past and a sensitivity to his surroundings. A group of relatives comes for a brief visit. They remain silent, with the exception of a small child who addresses the resident with a few tender, affectionate, and surprising words, which startle the old man. The visitors/relatives leave. The resident now notices yet another visitor, Q.

10   Q utters a short phrase, the meaning of which is instantly clear. P responds without hesitation as he is expected to do. Q leads P, gently, to the predictable end.

Notes on Two Primarily Choral Scenes in Winthrop

There are two choirs in *Winthrop*: a mixed adult ensemble (soprano, mezzo-soprano, alto, tenor, baritone, and bass) and a children's choir (soprano, alto). They have a role of first importance in the work – they speak for society. The adult voices enact a number of events and also appear as "voices from history." They provide the historical-social foundation upon which the key individual protagonists act, or to which they react. In section 1, for example, the main choir sings (or declaims in a dramatic theatrical manner) as voices from history. In section 2 they watch the young Winthrop and comment upon his efforts as he struggles to become a man. (Mainly women's and children's voices are employed here.) In the love duet that is section 3, a mixed group (men and women) echoes the feelings John and his beloved

Margaret convey to each other. In section 4 ("Famous Brittany") the choir is the principal protagonist. The imaginary locale of the action here is a marketplace and a fairground. People are milling around and we hear them giving evidence of great social and political turmoil, which they react to with a great intensity that reaches the level of vehemence. (A more detailed account of section 4 follows later in the appendix to this chapter.) In section 5 members of this community are preparing for departure for America. This section (and Act One) ends with voices imitating a sea breeze as the vessels leave the harbour for the open sea.

Act Two begins with the voyage; we are on board ship. The time is spent with John Winthrop, the future governor, who interacts with his fellow emigrants, segregated as to gender or age. He sets the terms of a covenant with the men, instructs the women, and teaches catechism to the children. Through these interchanges the audience learns about the social-ethical values of the group and of the manner in which they are articulated and transmitted from a person of authority to others. The next section (no. 7, entitled "Boston ... a Citty") is also a primarily choral movement. A considerable number of sub-scenes articulate what takes place here. In fact, this section covers approximately five to six years in the early history of that frontier town. At the outset there is stupefaction at the reality awaiting the settlers as they view the shoreline from their ships. This gives way to expressions of despondency and defeatism that threaten to turn into an open mutiny. However, some resolute voices succeed in turning this dark mood into an attitude of constructive action – as if saying, or actually decreeing, "Let's get down to work!" The whole community now feverishly applies itself to the task of building their "dream city," a "citty upon the hill"; that is, a New Jerusalem.

But problems remain ... There are many "miscreants" amidst the workers (or so they *seem* to many). They must be (and are) punished, with considerable severity, as it turns out. Indeed, Boston is a place where harsh justice is the rule for those who are unwilling to conform to the written and unwritten laws. And so this community evolves and we witness its struggles, as will be shown in a more detailed account (see appendix). The section ends on a tone of crisis. Something has to be done and is going to be done: the person who is regarded as being the chief inciter of dissent, Anne Hutchinson, will be submitted to the scrutiny of a trial.

This trial scene constitutes the entire section 8. The action takes place, most probably, in a meeting hall. Winthrop is the presiding figure here and he is soon embroiled in a ferocious mental/verbal duel with his antagonist. The chorus members are "spectators," the townsfolk who express a range of feelings and attitudes upon witnessing the procedure. The children also "pipe up" from time to time, and when they do this in a particularly tense moment, the grown-ups quickly hush them. (Actually both adults and children sense that a moment of peripeteia is likely to occur soon.) Pandemonium breaks out as Anne Hutchinson stumbles in her self-defence. After the verdict is announced (she is found guilty), waves of compassion wash over the community and they are led to express sympathy for Anne, as she hobbles, stricken, out of the courtroom. In the tenth and final section the choir contributes to the reminiscences of the three Winthrops, taking stock of past difficulties and the consequences of having lived through and coped with these difficulties. In its last contribution the choir sings a paean to John Winthrop, who, at some cost, managed to achieve, with the help of others, the survival of his community.

The appendix gives a more detailed account of some of the preceding comments.

APPENDIX

Table 12.1
Choral scenes in *Winthrop*

Bars	Text	Choral type – affect
Section 4: Famous Brittany		
43 –	"Call to mind"	A choral fanfare; public exhortation. Aim: to whip up excitement. Evidence of action by inciters
58 –	"Forces of fire!" "Fire of division!" (a surfeit of *f* sounds).	Rhythmic theatrical declamation aimed at igniting crowd response; psychic "contagion" through quasi-magical, incantational recitation; autohypnosis
82–8		Dissolution of the former group
94 –	"That … what … we … then … feared"	Hocketlike sung polyphony. Character: a fear-ridden group; hesitation induced by uncertainty and fear. (The preceding aggression is replaced by an expression of fright.)
118–21	"Fear … A plague"	Polyphonic saturation (sung). A cry of anguish
123 –	"A fire of division" "A doctrine established"	Antiphonal pseudofanfares (sung). Religious fervour: church militant in action; a series of utterances of dogmatic opinions

Table 12.1
(continued)

136 –	"May God forsake ye" (women) "Blasphemy and bedlam" (men)	Women cursing doctrinal opponents; sung incantational as if at a witches' session; inexorably rising register. The men in highly inflected dramatic declamation. Two contrasting expressions (delivered through two autonomous polyphonies, superimposed)
143–9	Same as above	Six-part polyphonic declamation; the utmost in cursing and desperation; merging of opposing groups
150–95	"Famous Brittany"	An expression of patriotism and/or mocking the same. The style is a blend of hymn and popular march; strict five-part polyphony. The flag, the church ("standing at attention," "saluting the flag") implied. Bursts of mocking laughter from groups of children, all moving to a climax, but instead of it the scene suddenly shifts into …
197–213	"When Adam was deceived" (women) Laughter (street urchins)	a fast polka, played on two out-of-tune tavern pianos … a bawdy song declaimed in a mocking tone by market women; hilarity, merriment
217–37	"From every religion"	Exaggerated (solo) voices of two preachers propounding an apocalyptic vision
238 –	"Feel God shaking the Heavens and the Earth"	An apocalyptic vision announced by massed voices
253 –	"In this very time" (the Herauld, a con-man, propagandist)	Herauld incites the crowd and offers a solution to problems by advocating (shades of Peitho) emigration to New England, a "land of milk and honey." He advocates joining a crusading army. A march takes place in song as people respond to his exhortations. The propagandist's work is most effective.
279 –	"lime – stone" "Go in the name of God!"	Details of the riches to be found in the colony. A new marching tune; people falling into line and joining the march
290–337	"Oh, yes!"	The mass hysteria reaches a new level of intensity; paroxysm of mass hypnosis at work
238 –	"As you shall be shipped for his service"	The mesmerized crowd is by now reduced to a barely articulated overrapid mumbling … All individuality is drained from these people; they have become near-automatons, uttering indiscernible words.

Table 12.1
(continued)

Section 7: Boston ... A Citty

4–34	"A Citty ... It is wet ... frost and snow ... Death in the dark ... The scurvy ... No hope ... Boston a Bust-ton"	The text is "sputtered" through tense voices in bitter, rapid declamation, interspersed with silences. The voices convey stupefaction and fear, also expressions of sarcasm and anger.
35–40		Exhortation by the Herauld; he calls the people to work.
41–63	"We work in Boston"	A polyphonic construction, as if imitating the work of building crews; dense, euphonious
63–5	"Whipped for running away"	Sudden interruption/distraction: harsh justice is meted out to a disobedient worker, the first taste of the code of punishment in Boston.
66–8	As in 41–63	As in 41–63
69–74	As in 63–5	As in 63–65
81 –	"There's a court in Boston ...	Enactment and observance of instances
104 –	of order and conformity ... the court is power"	of judicial practice in Boston; power and obedience enacted. The social fabric reveals itself further: an oath of
105 –	"The court is power"	allegiance, agreements announced, etc.
125 –	"Fair wages, fair prices ... For uttering scandalous speeches against the government"	Tense, rapid declamation ... polyphony
127 –	"Phillip Ratcliffe shall be whipped"	Savage retribution
146 –	"None but the General Court"	Inflexible rhythmic monotone, conveying rigidity; oligarchic control in evidence
154–69	Laughter and other expressions of dissent	Contest between the societal "ins" and "outs"
170–193		Expression of a sense of fairness and social conscience by Winthrop (sung)
194–200	"Fire! We fight the fire!" "Or the laws!"	Ambiguity. Was the fire caused accidentally, or by arson?

Table 12.1
(continued)

201–25	Distant drumming (drum language)	A visit by Indians. Solo spoken utterances, informing about the uneasy relationship between the settlers and the natives
226–38	"The captains train their bands every week"	Militia drill. Unison singing on a monotone (implications of military discipline); trumpet talk
239–48	"What is the nature of grace?"	A doctrinal question asked by Anne Hutchinson (her first appearance)
249–67	Answers: *Success, Friendship, The Jewel, The Gift,* all names of ships	Optimistic answers, through metonymy. Unidirectionally rising and descending sung lines; Polyphony.
269–72	[Orchestral transition into a new sub-scene]	
272–83	"A doctrine of works" "Blasphemy, travesty, heresy" "Sanctification no evidence of justification"	A spirited, even aggressive, doctrinal debate, proving the inadequacy of ships' names as an answer to Anne Hutchinson's probing question. "Formulaic" (difficult to sing) melodic designs indicate mental effort and committedness of opinions. This polyphonic ensemble mimics conditions of "set battles" of earlier periods. All this occurs within an iterative formal musical plan, suggesting that the opposing groups debate about details within a shared religious belief system, implying thesis-anti-thesis-synthesis" (solo voices)
278–93	As above; debate expanded to include the full choir	Psycho-societal expansion of conflict
294 –	The Herauld brings the news of John Oldham's murder: "The Pequots!" "Revenge!"	Peripeteia; the Pequot tribe is immediately accused as the perpetrator(s) of the deed. Furious declaimed expressions of hatred, calls for revenge
296–8	"Contempt and shame!" "Justice and revenge!"	Several problems call for resolute action.
300–11	"We fear the plague!" "Revenge! Death to the Pequots!"	A new problem! Expressions of terror; problems pile upon earlier problems. Structure: simple, rigid, syncopated (up/down) cascades of augmented 4th chords; expression of "rigidity." Another instance of "psychic" epidemic (differing degrees and modes of coordination)
320–7	Sounds of dying men and women: "Punished"	Extreme paralinguistic expressions of people near death: the perpetrators of the mass slaughter utter a final word.

Table 12.1
(continued)

329–58	Expressions (utterances) of cruelty; crime and severe punishment, ending in a collective howl	The climate of cruelty in Boston rises, showing a society of oppression.
359–66.1	Idling instrumental "machine" at a loss for direction	A metaphor for a community not knowing which way to turn
367	"Boston ... a Lost-ton ... A No-ton"	Lonely (solo) utterances expressing helplessness and "rudderlessness"
368–80	"The twelfth day of the month a day of humiliation"	A drummer boy makes his rounds (backstage), announcing his message repeatedly on gradually rising pitch levels; palpable air of crisis

An aria by Winthrop leads to the trial scene (section 8), which has the objective of re-establishing viable societal conditions in Boston.

NOTES

1 [This text was written before Anhalt completed his fourth opera, *Millennial Mall (Lady Diotima's Walk)*, hence the idea of an operatic *triptych*. Eds.]

2 [The text regarding *La Tourangelle* was first published in the liner notes for *Anthology of Canadian Music*, vol. 22, Radio Canada International, 1985, sound recording. It is published here with permission from RCI. Eds.]

3 [This text was first published in the *Canadian University Music Review* 4 (1983): 184–95. It is published here with permission from the *Canadian University Music Review*. Eds.]

4 This account does not aim at reflecting on the various stages of the compositional process, but wishes only to give an idea of certain aspects and details of the final result.

5 Novalis, *Werke, Briefe, Dokumente*, vol. 1, *Die Dichtungen*, ed. Ewald Wasmuth (Heidelberg: Schneider, 1953), 315. (My thanks to my friend Anthony W. Riley for locating this source.)

6 On "indexical information," see D. Abercrombie, *Elements of General Phonetics* (Edinburgh: Edinburgh University Press, 1967).

13 On the Way to *Traces*:
A Dialogue with the Self[1]

Q: Would you play some music from your new opera *Traces (Tikkun)* which, I hear, will soon receive its premiere?

A: I would do it gladly but I cannot because no part of it has been recorded as yet.

Q: Play it on the piano, then.

A: You would not want me to make a hash of it this way, with or without attempting to add some of the vocal part. I am not much of a singer, and the piece demands a fairly high level of vocal agility, besides.

Q: That's a pity. Are we to be left then only with a conversation between the two of us, and not a single musical sound?

A: I see your point. Let me think ... Perhaps we can find a way. What if I played for you, instead of something from the opera, an excerpt from *SparkskrapS*, a fairly recent orchestral piece of mine, which was premiered in 1988? Come to think of it, it has a "sound climate" that is, in part, not far from that which you can expect to find also in *Traces*.

Q: Good idea. Let us hear a few minutes from *SparkskrapS* then.

[An excerpt from *SparkskrapS* was played for the audience.]

Q: An intriguing sample ... One day I would like to hear the piece in its entirety. But for now, let us turn to the opera. After all, this is the purpose for our meeting here, is it not?

A: Indeed.

Q: My first question, then, is regarding the meaning of the word "pluri-drama" by which you characterize the nature of the work. I do not recall having encountered this term before.

A: Neither had I, before thinking of using it for *Traces*, that is.

Q: A new expression then? What does it stand for?

A: I was hesitating to adopt it here, and would have preferred to use a more traditional word, provided I could have found one that would have conveyed the same idea equally well and as concisely.

Q: What idea?

A: That of a dramatic piece for a single vocalist who is to enact, all by himself, the character and utterances of more than ten persons.

Q: Did you do this for the sake of economy?

A: This was not the reason for it. Rather, I wanted to draw attention to the commonplace fact that every individual, each of us, internalizes within him/herself the personae of many others with whom he/she comes in contact.

Q: True enough ...

A: Moreover, these interactions, frequently through acts of dialogue, play a formative role in how a person becomes the individual he or she is.

Q: You seem to be voicing some ideas of Martin Buber here, if I am not mistaken.

A: You are right in thinking about him in this regard. I gladly admit to having learned from Buber.

Q: Let me make sure that I understand this. A single performer on stage in your work impersonates over ten characters in the course of the opera. And by making him do this you expect to demonstrate the strength of the idea that, in large measure, we become who we are through a multitude of such dialogic exchanges. I see good dramatic potential in this, I must admit.

A: I appreciate your positive view about this.

Q: Not that I am entirely free of doubt in this regard ... Are you certain that the audience will be able to make the right connections about who is who in a given moment and situation?

A: While composing the piece I was aiming to achieve this. You are absolutely right, this had to be a central objective. Without it the piece would dissolve into a heap of confusion. But if I succeed in keeping good control of this, the overall result will be an entirely different story.

Q: I want to latch onto the word "story" here. Does this opera have a story line? I mean, does it go from point A to point B?

A: This is a difficult question to answer with an unequivocal yes or no at this point. But, since I do not want to leave you with the suspicion that I am evasive in this respect, let us say yes; it does have a story line, but one of a special character.

Q: And the nature of this character?

A: One finds out about this in the course of the work. And, I would expect that something more will also surface in the course of our conversation.

Q: Do you intend to make your audience work hard while following the action?

A: If this were the whole story I would court disaster, no. Of course, there will be some puzzling questions, but all this will be supported by strong hints and much revealing detail, both on the part of this virtuoso vocalist and in the nimble orchestral layer, which will have the role of suggesting place, time, emotional content, and more besides.

Q: Let me turn to something else now. Somewhere, you have made reference to the period aspects of the work, how it fits into the flow of time. Can you repeat here what you said?

A: Gladly. *Traces (Tikkun)*, to cite the full title of the piece, is neither exclusively in the "here and now," nor is it entirely located in a past. It finds its habitat, if I may put it so, in both. Furthermore, there are two pasts involved here: a personal past – that of the protagonist, who represents "someone" – and also a distant past that preceded his lifespan, but which nevertheless succeeded in entering the mind and soul of this man through exposures of various kinds.

Q: Are you pointing to the time to which the word *tikkun* refers?

A: Yes, but let us leave this for the moment. We might return to it later.

Q: Why not begin with the "here and now" aspects of the piece then?

A: For starters, I should perhaps draw attention to the fact that the text is full of allusions to situations, verbal usages, and the like, which are familiar to us from routine exchanges, as well as from exposure to the local daily press: the *Globe and Mail*, the *Toronto Star,* etc. The text is entirely in English and the singsong of the vocalist is full of recognizable intonation types. In all this there is a strong degree of recognition potential.

Q: What do you mean?

A: At all times the listener can expect to guess, without undue effort, where the action takes place, what social role is implied by what is being said, the character, and at times also the socioeconomic position, of the implied figure.

Q: Are you ready to give a concrete example?

A: Yes. About one-third of the way through the piece, following some high voltage passages, the "climate" of the work calms down somewhat. When the new section begins, and the vocalist "reappears," we immediately realize that a change of place has occurred. We are now located at the perimeter of a walled-in town. There are people inside the walls and others, approaching from a distance, on the outside. The "insiders" talk to each other first, and then we hear, a short distance away, the approaching "outsiders." The topic is the condition of admitting the outsiders into this fortified place, which we are later able to place in a desert location, because of references to palm trees, the importance of the water supply, and the rather strong fear of giant snakes infesting the community. Despite all of these conditions, the community appears to be prospering. In negotiating admission, there is talk about a toll fee, restricted access, and the necessity for pledges to be made to the effect that, once inside, the newcomers will obey the laws and observe the conditions of good order. A figure of authority, or perhaps of a loose tongue, quite candidly spills information concerning some difficulties that his community has recently faced.

Q: What difficulties?

A: Pertaining to the young, to trade, and, last but not least, to women.

Q: Ah ...

A: Yes, feminine issues – head covering, dress codes, and the like. And a somewhat timid voyeur also appears at one point.

Q: A voyeur? Interesting ... go on please.

A: A surprising event happens at this moment.

Q: Yes? What?

A: The voyeur is almost run over by a car.

Q: A traffic accident? Screeching brakes and all that ...

A: Correct.

Q: Does he get killed?

A: No, but it was a near miss. The one who speaks to him now is pretty mad at him.

Q: Wait a minute. I am losing track of the story line. The one who nearly gets killed here is the voyeur, true?

A: Yes.

Q: Was he also the official at the gate?

A: Most likely.

Q: Are we still in the same place? A town in the desert? And now a car accident nearly averted, implying perhaps heavy traffic ... I don't understand.

A: Simple. The preceding scene was also a quasi time machine, if you allow me to put a simple thing in a fancy way. Since it is possible, *even necessary*, to regard the true locale of the opera as being what you could call *memory space*, you are free to roam forward and backward in time at will.

Q: Your audience ought to be empathized with if they feel you have taken them on a roller coaster ride.

A: Perhaps so. Do you want me to plead guilty of causing vertigo?

Q: You are joking. OK. But to return to the story line, may I ask you to read the text of this desert town scene?

A: This might be a good idea, indeed. Here is a passage from "Desert Town."

Have you heard? The traders are coming. Yes, they're already here, by the east gate, shouting: "Let us enter!" "Let us come in!" Man the guard posts! Man the gates! Order! Order! Entry by the toll gate! Only by the tollgate! "Is life plentiful here? Are we allowed to stay?" You'll have enough to eat; and you'll multiply with ease, thanks to the fruits of our trees, and to your own efforts; and thanks to our saintly ones' prayers and chants that unleash the rains, tame sand storms, and keep the giant snakes at bay during the night ...

Order! Order! We prize order here. Disorder threatens our ways and our beliefs; it is the enemy. Yes, yes! We know ... things are less simple now. Our trade and the young cause concern ... and yes, our women, too ... Yes, yes! The women ... surely a fountain of bliss, but of trouble, too; they are restless, restless ... The preachers have a point, but some went too far. Imagine: some would impose baldness on our wives; shapeless tents of cloth, bulging balloons, hiding – you have guessed it – the charms of young girls, and the ripe curves of our mature womenfolk. Why? Why? To keep your mind on your work. A phallic ... I mean, a fallacy ... It excites us more, drives us to distraction. We fantasize about beauteous lines, alabaster skin, firm flesh like a rubber ball; ankles and wrists, the fullness of buttocks, and the smoothest of thighs ... Oh! Oh! But that's not all ... Oh! those scents; perfumes, secretions, those fumes trailing behind, to our torment and despair.

Q: And now comes the near miss of that traffic accident, if I am not mistaken.

A: Yes, and a passerby berates the one who nearly was run over.

Q: What happens then?

A: One gets a demonstration of inflated civic pride and then some.

Q: And?

A: This gets interrupted by the arrival on the scene of a small group of young demonstrators.

Q: What is their complaint?

A: They protest against what they regard as their social marginalization. Being out of work, having lost hope, and the like. The older man has little sympathy for them, and that rankles.

Q: What does he tell them?

A: The usual prescriptions: their skills need upgrading and society needs human resources that are "up to scratch." Now, these last few words really seem to bother them.

Q: What do they say in reply? Tell me the actual words.

A: "Human resources? You said, *resources*? Strange, I thought I'm a person ... a sweating, panting, making-out person."

Q: I see, some of them must have been stung by being called "resources." ... Come to think of it, this appears to be a recent accretion to the semantic field of the noun "resources." Do you have an opinion about this?

A: In fact, I do have ... otherwise I would not have included this dialogue – after considerable soul-searching, I do not mind admitting ... I felt this use of the word carries special meaning.

Q: Have you checked it out in a dictionary?

A: The *Oxford English Dictionary*, second edition, from 1989, suggests some sources for this semantic change. These are related to network analysis, also to critical path studies and resource allocation questions. All this seems to have occurred in the course of the preceding twenty to twenty-five years. Its use still seems to be expanding.

Q: I see, but let us move on ...

A: That is exactly what that small band of youngsters decided to do.

Q: What do you mean?

A: They took off in the direction of the nearby Highdome, because there a concert was about to begin. They were after some fun.

Q: Following the old saying, if bread is scarce let us have entertainment instead, I guess.

A: Possibly, or should I say, probably? They went to a rock concert.

Q: Don't tell me: you got yourself in the predicament of having to compose a rock scene.

A: One thing followed another ... It was, at this juncture, absolutely unavoidable.

Q: Have you ever composed in this vein before?

A: Never, which made it all the more interesting. It was a question of trying to avoid falling on one's face.

Q: As you composed this scene, did you rely on the ability of your vocalist to improvise in a particular style?

A: No. I knew that here also I had to put down on paper pretty well everything I wanted to hear. And this applied to the orchestra, as well, which starts with the usual electric guitar, synthesizer, and drum set, but which undergoes significant changes as the section progresses.

Q: Progresses towards what?

A: Towards a Woodstock-like scene, which might not have been unlike a bacchanalia. At least that was my aim here, on a smaller scale, of course.

Q: This must have been fun to write.

A: It was.

Q: The young rock crooner gyrating on stage and the rest …

A: This is surely a part of it, but not the whole story.

Q: Another surprise up your sleeve?

A: Will you allow me to put this in a slightly different way?

Q: Go ahead.

A: The character that the vocalist represents here is, simultaneously, two characters in one.

Q: What are you aiming at here?

A: Once again, we are in a situation where a compelling statement, here the singer's, induces another, a listener, to absorb it into his or her memory. Intense empathy, and internalization, once again. In other words, performer and spectator unite in a single figure. Now, as to the means … to describe it in words would take us afar. Musical performance, a "showing," some would call it, is so much more concise and telling. May I ask you to wait for an answer, which you may get during the performance?

Q: Sounds reasonable enough. Let us go on then. What happens next?

A: The show is over and its resonances are still felt as the audience leaves the place. Then a meeting takes place.

Q: Who is meeting whom?

A: An older spectator, the one who was so taken by the rock vocalist, sees a happy-looking man standing by one of the gates.

Q: An official? Connected, perhaps, with the spectacle just ended?

A: Yes. It turns out that he is the one who organized the whole show. He is the rock impresario and entrepreneur rolled into one, a prototype of the promoter of the popular arts.

Q: I am curious to find out how you have portrayed him. I am somewhat suspicious though. With your known preference for highbrow – not to say elitist – art, even with the best of intentions you might have found it irresistible to portray him as an ogre.

A: I am nearly speechless and reeling on the ropes … You are anticipating here with an almost uncanny insight, I must say. What could I say in my defence for what I have done? But first, let us be clear about a few basic premises. To start with, this is not a defenceless creature. Just the contrary. He is a most vigorous, even aggressive individual who knows the ins and outs of his rather tough business thoroughly. He is an expert risk taker, and is mainly influenced by money, and a lot of it, in his dealings.

Q: Is this a punishable offence in law?

A: We both know that it is not. And a single well-done rock concert is also an "artistic event" of sorts. But there are at least two more aspects to consider.

Q: And these are?

A: The frequently destructive content – understandably attractive for immature minds, and there to excite and titillate with the usual exclusion of other more thoughtful responses – is one. The other feature is the vast proliferation of the genre and the exploitation of young performers and young patrons alike by giant entertainment conglomerates; and all this taking place on a global scale. As a by-product, the noise, the hoopla it generates, seems to cast doubt on the very viability of serious art, as many of its groups struggle under increasing financial hardships, and are seen as fighting for their very survival. But forgive me, I am sounding like someone on a soapbox. I regret to leave you with this impression. Besides, it is counterproductive. Let me assure you, here; above all, I was interested in creating character and action, but as you have seen already, sometimes I had to engage my silent self and my characters in a heated argument. That is how the opera grew.

Q: The description of your creative process, well … I don't know what I should say about it, for now at least … But let us return to the story line. I refrained from asking you to read the text of the rock scene. But would you now introduce to us the rock promoter, by reading the words you gave him?

A: Gladly. But first, it needs to be pointed out that this is a soliloquy. We are made to look into the mind of that person as he stands by that exit gate. As an introduction to this scene, that of the rock promoter, let me read to you the concluding lines from the rock scene. These will lead into the text of the next scene, that of the promoter.

The frenzy mounts! Amplify! Amplify! Spin on the spell now! Selah! Selah! Refeed the earth! Plow in the seed! Let's climb the hills now! Come! Come into my cave! I'll be nice to you … Osanna! Osanna! This is the truth. The only truth, Youth truth, Freedom truth. Magna Charta and Gypsy rhapsody …

And after a short orchestral interlude, one hears the promoter's voice:

Yes … Yes … Why not! Truth to live … and truth to die … Balkan wars rerun truth, *Aïda* in the Highdome truth … Hear Amonasro's rage on super-giant video screens! You can sell elephants if you know how. But keep out the wrong dinosaurs, like you! Who are you, anyway? Standing there like a pile of woe … 'Scuse me, but the world has passed you by … Sorry, but we have no use for you anymore. Get yourself a wheel-chair, or whatever. Just don't waste our time with useless blabbering. What was it again? Tunnels? A flood? You surely must have had a nightmare, or something … Who cares anyways. Just keep that crap to yourself.

Q: You gave this man some pretty powerful lines. And your reading
might have given an inkling of his character. Did this mimic the
vocal part in the opera?

A: It is much more dramatic in the opera. And it is reinforced also by
the orchestra, which is strong, masculine, direct, and suggestive of
power, not necessarily of a benevolent kind.

Q: Hmm ... there is another question, which churns in my mind about
some things you said regarding this scene. But, I am not sure I
should ask it.

A: Obviously, you must ask it.

Q: In your own youth, say between ages thirteen and fifteen, were you
immune to the lure of popular music of your time, which I would
locate in the 1930s, if I am not mistaken?

A: Immune? Anything but! I also admired and was in love with stars
like Fred Astaire, Ginger Rogers, Eleanor Powell and the rest, of
"Broadway Melodies" fame. But here is a "surface" difference: they
were seen by audiences (including my fifteen-year-old self) as
clean, inoffensive types. Typical upper-middle-class figures, top
hats and all, and ruffled skirts on the women. Elegance in clothing
matched by effortless elegance in song and dance. No violence, no
drugs on the screen. Illusion all the way – one type of illusion, one
could interject – and *that* in the Depression years to boot. Today,
one gets *cinéma-vérité*, near-explicit sex, and not infrequently also
hints of raw violence upon the stage. And now I hear a voice saying,
"You are still talking out of prejudice!" The voice continues by
asserting that today's portrayal of life by and through popular performance art, via song and dance, is more "down to earth," more
"honest," according to some unspecified criteria, than that of the
1930s. Perhaps so ... perhaps not ... Perhaps both are most truth-
fully seen as being, above all, only entertainment, distraction, and
commercial enterprise, with few holds barred ... in the words of a
very recent report of a 1970s rock festival, "spaced out hippies
dancing naked, flashing peace signs, smoking pot, frolicking, playing frisbee and basically grooving to the pop aristocracy performing on stage."[2] Do these responses in me add up to a persisting
ambivalence? It is possible ... and if so, it is likely that listeners will
be able to spot this ambivalence, mixed in with other sentiments,
in certain moments of *Traces*.

Q: I see ... you are still debating these matters in an interior way.
But let us leave this detail behind, for now. You spoke earlier
about a time layer, which you have located in one's "personal
past." Does it pertain to some memorable, even momentous experiences remembered?

A: Yes. I would go so far as to characterize some of these as personal myths.

Q: What do you mean by "myth" here?

A: A periodic recall, remembrance, a celebration of an event that a person or a group experienced and survived; subsequently it was turned into a sacred object through the act of recurring tellings, the individual or group expecting to derive renewed strength from them ...

Q: Like from the story of Easter? Or that of the Exodus of Jews from Egypt ... the remembrance ceremony of Passover, that is?

A: Yes, these are among the most potent myths, told and retold according to the annual calendars. But there are involuntary myths also, often private ones, that could and do "surface" at irregular intervals, uninvited, so to say, and often in dreams, like nightmares, and for all this they have a special potency.

Q: I take it that you have made one such dream sequence appear in *Traces*?

A: Yes. It is a recall turning into a frightening daydream. It forms section 3 of the opera. It is entitled "Labyrinth."

Q: Is your intent, here, to portray horror, if not a sense of fear?

A: Yes. You have it right. The sense of danger is present. But for some reason or other, the sense of fear, perhaps on account of the abstraction, is expected to be absent. I want to be clear about this thing – of not having wanted to portray horrors like the Holocaust, or recent events in Rwanda, or Bosnia, or ... well, we could go on reciting the list of contemporary horror spots that stand as testimonial to what can occur in a climate of intense and protracted hatred ...

Q: Hold it! Is there a hidden rationale at work here? Your shunning of extreme forms of hate ... It appears to me not wholly incompatible with hating "in the Canadian way," if I may put it this way ... Was this a conscious exclusion?

A: You are probing deeply here ... No ... it was certainly not conscious, yet it is there ... who knows ... I cannot claim a consciously thought-out purpose here. Just one more act of the sleepwalker, perhaps you could say ... Can we leave it as that?

Q: I am ready to go along, provided we have a trade-off: you agree to read now some part of the text related to this.

A: Very well, here is an excerpt from the section called "Labyrinth."

And have no illusion. Your answers: a dreamer's gropings along twisting, airless corridors, as you keep running through tunnels, passageways, trying to escape from revolving doors, tapping, tapping the walls, stumbling on shadows, doubles, ancient refuse, all your own. Then more and more turns, still more bends, countless loops in that crawl space. Now an enormous blast … In its wake a long, low rumble bouncing all around … a tattoo of echoes … zigzag cracks in the mirror-screens appear … Now surging water sounds … Jets of water spurt from all sides. More water … Hot, stinking streams push up from volcanic lakes below … boiling whirlpools, torrents of foam … wave after wave slamming against crumbling clay, fissured rock, exploding quartz, melting sediment … until you burst free in the air, in the light, into life!

To perform this is a very stressful experience, for both the performers *and* the audience. Following it, the piece erupts into the fresh air and blinding light of an oasis.

Q: I see dramatic potential in all this. Now, let us see where we are in your presentation. We now know your reasons for calling the piece a "pluri-drama." We had numerous demonstrations of the here-there-and-now time layer, and with the section you call "Labyrinth" we had an illustration of a recurring recall, perhaps one of yours …

A: Perhaps one of mine … Yes, but please tell me: do you believe that there are people who go through life without having acquired in the process such recurring memories – happy ones, sad ones, and even frightening kinds?

Q: I take it that you have asked a rhetorical question. Let us leave it, then, at that. But have we not one additional time layer to visit?

A: Yes. The ancient one, the one that is located beyond the boundaries of one's personal past. It is a past which one learns from legends, oral and/or written history, literature, and other like sources.

Q: I am afraid you are going to take us now for yet another dizzying ride. Please keep in mind that the hour is getting late and that you have exacted much attention from your audience to what you had to say already.

A: I am sincerely grateful for your reminder. I shall keep this as brief as possible, yet without running the risk of leaving you shaking your head, up in the air. So, a compromise … Can you bear with me for a few more minutes?

Q: Go on, please.

A: An ancient lore, called the Kabbalah, teaches that "the process of creation involves the departure of all from the One and the (eventual) return to the One." Moreover, it says, applying this to each and every human being, that the "crucial turning point in this cycle (of fragmentation and re-integration) takes place within man the moment he begins to develop an awareness of his true essence and yearns to retrace [note the word 'trace' here] the path from the multiplicity of his nature to the Oneness from which he originated."[3] You could say that with this the moment for *tikkun* has arrived.

Q: Could you relate this idea to *Traces* unequivocally?

A: Yes. In *Traces* we follow the protagonist as he revisits or, better, re-lives a number of formative episodes from his past. Through these he hopes to find a pattern, a "line," into which all these smaller or larger traces unite. This pattern might prove to be the key to his life.

Q: Is there a guarantee that everyone, all of us, will find this line, this overarching, connected pattern?

A: Your question appears to lead into the heart of kabbalistic teaching, as much as I, a casual reader about it, can say. The best thing would be to leave it at that. But I cannot resist thinking that, perhaps, the essence here might not be looked for so much in the "finding," but, instead, in the frame of mind of never giving up searching for it, yearning after it. Eventually, at the end, we can expect to find ourselves at a spot closer to or further from this elusive, almost im-possible-to-attain goal, but as long as one keeps on trying ...

Q: You almost sound like a preacher.

A: You are right in yanking me back from this pretense. Excuse me, I got carried away ... But this might give you an idea about the swirl of ideas that rumble through the head of a composer at times.

Q: You are being unnecessarily self-deprecatory. You have obviously read into the lore of the Kabbalah. Is this also a kind of early form of psychology?

A: One of its greatest twentieth-century proponents, the scholar Ger-shom Scholem, of the Hebrew University of Jerusalem, thought so. Moreover, he believed it is also an early theory of anthropology. Many of his reconstructions and interpretations follow the doc-trines of the legendary rabbi of Safed, Isaac Luria, who lived and taught there in the course of the sixteenth century.

Q: Which concepts did Luria use to teach the Kabbalah?

A: Using metaphors, he taught in terms of the "divine sparks," which were captured by the "shards." That is one idea; the necessity of pu-rifying the "sparks" and reuniting them through a process he called *tikkun* is another. At this point my story comes to a temporary close, but perhaps you are left with some more questions ...

NOTES

1 This is the text of a talk delivered at Harrison-LeCaine Hall, Queen's University, Kingston, Ontario on 20 March, 1996 at 8:00 P.M.

2 Betsy Powell, *The Globe and Mail* (19 March 1996): C3.

3 Gershom Scholem, *Kabbalah* (New York: Quadrangle, 1974), 152.

14 From "Mirage" to *Simulacrum* and "Afterthought"[1]

I am here to speak about *Simulacrum*, which I shall do. Alongside this, I shall also have things to say about memory, recall, and about certain specific things I remember that, in one way or another, found their way into *Simulacrum* as I was composing the piece.

But first, the question of where to start. Where should the story begin? Where does *anything* begin? Now, the answer that comes to mind to the last question is that it depends, of course, on the perspective. It hinges on how far one is prepared to go back in time, which in turn will depend on the context in which the question is being asked. So, as we shall see, there is a measure of arbitrariness in this, but at the same time it is not wholly arbitrary. The reconfirmation of this, as it applies to *Simulacrum*, came to me only two days ago, to my great surprise. It elicited the typical "aha!" effect, and when I get around to telling you about it later, I hope you will be able to share in it with me. For the time being, to get started, we do not need to go back into the past beyond the year 1984 when the traceable "surface" history of *Simulacrum* can be considered to have begun.

The year 1984 was busy for me. It saw the completion of the score of *Winthrop* and the public appearance of *Alternative Voices*, the nonidentical twins that gestated together during the preceding eight years. Now I had to undertake the job of writing out the piano-vocal score of the opera just in case an urgent request would one day materialize from the Met, or from the Canadian Opera Company. Also, in the summer of that year I was writing an extended autobiographical sketch for Radio-Canada International (RCI), which is not my favourite literary genre, I confess. (It resembles too much a c.v. which I always looked upon as an invitation to justify one's existence.) But this time it was different. First of all, RCI gave me space quite generously, and the moment for "looking back" seemed also timely, because I was on the verge of retiring from active university teaching, having reached the statutory retirement age of sixty-five. Consequently, the title of this sketch, "What Tack to Take?" not only indicated the presence of a temporary, brief "writer's cramp" in facing a blank first page, but was also an allusion to, and an acknowledgment of, a milestone in my life. From the latter perspective, "What tack to take?" came to mean, in effect, "Where do I go from here?"

Well, for one, there was the task of the piano-vocal score of *Winthrop*. This kept me busy well into 1985. During the summer of that year, a request suddenly came from Phyllis Mailing, a friend and close colleague of long standing, asking me for a new piece to be premiered early in 1986. I should add that, by that time arrangements were in place for the premiere of *Winthrop* in 1986 under the auspices of CBC Radio-Music and the Kitchener-Waterloo Symphony Orchestra, which gave an added degree of urgency to the completion of the rehearsal score of *Winthrop*. Still, I felt that I could not say no to Phyllis, so work on *Winthrop* had to be interrupted for the time it took to compose *Thisness*, a fairly extended duodrama for her. I mention this work because, in a way, it also deals with retrospection, with the theme of a personal journey, the topic (or genie out of the bottle) that emerged with "What Tack to Take?" As I thought of it, I realized that *Winthrop* also belongs to that theme-idea – a personal journey, a quest by a man who also decided to take the Atlantic route, like so many others have done since. So when I wrote the text of *Thisness*, I felt I was tending the same garden – a personal search for answers to questions such as, Why there? Why then? Why did I come? Where shall I be going now?

The premiere of *Winthrop* took place in the fall of 1986 with the help of a few who lent to it enormous effort, goodwill, and talent. I found myself on "cloud nine" after hearing it, and Bea and I took a brief vacation, which took us to Devon and Yorkshire and on the way back to London through "Winthrop country." I felt as if reporting to my eponymous hero what transpired in the Centre in the Square in Kitchener on the preceding September 6. Back at home I was looking forward to some leisurely "looking around" until something would induce me to pick up the pen again. But the expected tranquility of those weeks was broken by two phone calls: the first was from Alex Pauk, who asked me to write a piece for his ensemble, the Esprit Orchestra (I said yes to that); and the second, soon after, was an invitation from Gabriel Chmura, the new music director elect of the

National Arts Centre Orchestra (NACO), to attend a concert of his in Ottawa. "Aha, a commission", something in my head told me. And soon after, the same voice said, "I don't want a second commission. I don't like the idea of working under such pressure." Nevertheless, I did go to Ottawa, and I was glad that I did, because the concert was beautiful. A fine program (Fauré, Martin, Dvořák), an extraordinarily gifted musician as conductor, and a remarkably polished, sensitive orchestra. So when on the next morning Chmura did ask me for a new piece with which he would begin his inaugural concert as music director in the following season, I said a tentative yes, to be confirmed within a day. (Another thing that impressed me was his courtesy in saying that if the piece was not to be ready, he would do it at a later date, and the commission would still stand.) As it happened, while I was driving home from Ottawa, the first ideas of the music began to churn in my head. I decided to compose the piece for Chmura and NACO first, and the one for Pauk and the Esprit Orchestra after it. Things went very fast. In three months' time I had the score ready for Ottawa, and this is the work which I decided to call *Simulacrum* shortly after beginning to compose it.

Now, what is a "simulacrum"? It is an image, a portrait, a reflection in a mirror, in water, a shadow, something imagined, the recollection of a thing (and this aspect of it intrigued me greatly), an imitation, a mirage, perhaps, and other things besides. In short, working on the piece, once again, meant looking back into the past to ask questions, to look for connections, correspondences, and the like. And when one does this, one almost inevitably finds a child standing somewhere way down the corridor of memory who, as John Updike wrote a while ago, from time to time takes the adult self to task, asking whether one was faithful enough to that child's dreams, whether or not the compromises that were made were truly unavoidable. Yes, a "simulacrum" is what the piece is going to be, an amalgam of the present and the past; not only my own, but, as was the case with *Thisness* – which dealt with myself *and* with Phyllis Mailing – *Simulacrum* would have to have a relevance to Chmura's past also. I knew that he was born to Jewish parents in Poland in 1946. Were his parents survivors of a concentration camp? As it turned out, they escaped that experience, because they spent the war years in Russia. Then I found out that his father was an opera singer. Suddenly the thought occurred to me that I could be the father of Gabriel Chmura; I share some of the same experiences his parents had. Should he be my son, he who now conducts opera, I could also tell him about my brief stint at the Hungarian Opera as a *répétiteur* (and not a very successful one, as it turned out) during the months following the cessation of hostilities in Budapest in 1945.

(Should I have been a more proficient *répétiteur,* I probably would not be standing here now relating this story.) And I could also tell him about other things in the past.

What is this threefold something that we call the past, the present, and the future? Increasingly (and I came to feel it stronger and stronger as I composed *Simulacrum*), I had to think of it as a pluridimensional maze. Normally, when we say "past," it is really the current act of "remembering" whatever we are referring to. And when we envisage the "future" it is also an act, a projection, undertaken in this terribly narrow sliver of an existential moment to which we give the name "present". And the present? It may be, from one angle at least, an awareness of the process of living, of existing in all the dimensions and at all the levels that are perceived as being "active", as a result of having become energized by outside or inside stimuli, or by both. But are the time-indexes of the past and future so unequivocally determined as this description would have it? Far from it. Because I can remember past moments that consisted of projections into indeterminate future moments (and this holds the key to the suspenseful "secret" to which I alluded a while earlier), and I also know of projections into the future that deal with the past events or ideas. (A case in point is the work that I was to write for Alex Pauk, for which I had no name as yet, but which subsequently I came to call *SparkskrapS.*) So you see, past, present, and future are intertwined, one melting into the other in organic tangles, so many interlocking chains of memory cells interacting with each other in a manner never to be unraveled.

In composing *Simulacrum* an early task was to keep track of the material that was rapidly accumulating and that wanted to be included. Most of it was what one could call "original" stuff, but there were also fragments from other works that demanded inclusion. Soon, all these added up to a "pile" of considerable bulk that contained all sorts of references, some of which pointed to past situations, others to affects, the memories of affects, or affects felt as a result of remembering. At that early point I also knew that the piece would also begin "low" – that is, low in register, soft in dynamics – and "loose" in texture – tentative, groping, as if listening intently to a faint voice inside, not unlike the psycho-physiological awareness of a beating heart. There would be many ups and downs, slopes, curves, broken lines, sustained lines, until, at a later point, the piece would be so charged with energy that it would drive ahead steadily for longer stretches.

At one point I had to return to the fragments from other works that stubbornly waited for a place to be assigned to them in the emerging work. Perhaps I should say a few words about them in the order in which they actually appear in the piece. The first of these (bars 78–81) is from Bach's *St Matthew Passion*. It is the passage when the crowd bellows: "Let him be crucified." It is preceded, as you know, by the Evangelist relating how the high priests and the elders undertook to persuade the multitude to choose Barrabas over Jesus. They succeeded only too well in this. When Pontius Pilate asked them who should be pardoned, the well-rehearsed answer came promptly in the shape of a terrible shout (in Bach's musical language, a diminished-seventh 7 chord): "Barrabam." Then came Pilate's second question: "What is to be the fate of the other one"? For *this* question, the mob was not prepared. So there was a moment of hesitation – a musically marvellous pause that should last a second, or so. This pause is then interrupted by an *agent provocateur* (or a few of them) – the basses in the choir – who intone brutally, *"Lasst ihn kreuzigen"* (Let him be crucified). Others – the tenors, the altos, and finally the sopranos – thinking this is a fitting idea, echo the dreadful suggestion in that confusing, complex ensemble which Bach composed as a fugato, portraying what we might call today a psychic epidemic taking hold of an excitable crowd of people. The fugato, having reached a peak, is suddenly broken off, and the resonance of its last dissonant chord hangs in the air. From this, a chorale emerges in a marvellous compositional gesture of modulating, simultaneously, in time, space, and affect. Now, the way this quotation appears in *Simulacrum* is determined by the material that precedes it, in relation to which it represents a surprise. Moreover the furious character of the original has been tempered by a slower tempo, very soft dynamics, overlays of additional contrapuntal lines, all aimed at giving the impression that it is but a "recall of a thing", a memory image, which is being cited here more for its connotative value or symbolic potential than for its literal reference to a peak work, to an icon in the repertoire.

Out of this quotation grows an "original" passage for solo woodwinds and a solo violin, the latter dominating the ensemble more and more as the music continues. This single violin line gradually acquires unison companions, which eventually split off into independent lines, constituting a transparent tissue of figuration. Emerging from this, as if from a mist, comes the second quotation (bars 136–49) – the beginning of a well-known little tune from Richard Strauss's *Der Rosenkavalier*. In giving you the reasons for the inclusion of this quotation I have to, I am afraid, become a little personal. The matter has to do with my father's love of this tune, which he tried to "find" – that is, to play by ear with the proper harmonies – on our piano. I remember him sitting, on numerous occasions, in front of the keyboard trying to play the elusive melody with its even more elusive accompaniment. The scene somehow became indelibly fused in my mind with my father, of whom I was very fond. He also played the violin – not very well, but that did not seem to bother him greatly, because it gave him so much pleasure over the years. My father and his violin remain a permanent image in my memory, a recollection that includes much sweetness, despite the tenseness and the harshness of the 1930s and 1940s we shared in Budapest. The brief appearance of the *Der Rosenkavalier* theme, as if in a dream, gives way to related sentiment and concern. But as of bar 235, we seem to be moving towards another memory event; this time it comes (starting in bar 237 in the violin 1 and horn 2) in the shape of two traditional Sephardic tunes, taken from volume IV of Abraham Zvi Idelsohn's *Thesaurus of Hebrew Oriental Melodies* (nos. 253 and 246). These tunes are to be played passionately, as if two orthodox *chazzans* were trying to out-sing each other, with their individual, independent cantilenas. Other instruments join them and before long the whole orchestra is aglow with this assembly of competing lines, which somehow, as if for a "superior" reason, do not cancel out but instead reinforce each other with an implied common purpose, which asserts itself despite the seeming free-for-all. Perhaps a similar idea or situation, not unlike the one I was composing here, was in Isaac Luria's mind when, sometime in the sixteenth century, he wrote that "every word of the Torah has six hundred thousand 'faces,' that is, layers of meaning or entrances, one for each of the children of Israel who stood at the foot of Mount Sinai. Each face is turned toward only one of them; he alone can see it and decipher it."[2]

Yet, when I was composing the passage with the Sephardic tunes (bars 237–58), I did not think of Isaac Luria but of my paternal grandfather, who was a practising orthodox Jew, a taciturn, kindly man, whom I did not see very frequently, but whom I always "visited" with my father on the Day of Atonement, in his very small synagogue in the Jewish Quarter of Budapest. He was, according to custom, clad in his all-white death shroud (if I am not mistaken), with the black boxes of *tephillin* securely fastened with leather straps onto his forehead, and he stood while rhythmically bowing and straightening up as he was reciting his prayers and texts from the Scriptures, together with all the fellow worshippers. He did this, more often than not, at his own pace, as all the other men there did. I recall that this procedure added up to quite a din, over which, from time to time, floated the *chazzan's* ornamental song. I recall the place was hot, smelly, intense, and despite the occasional silent smiles my grandfather gave me, I was glad when the moment to leave came. For over six decades this was but a faint memory – until *Simulacrum* came along, that is, and demanded that I send a much belated message to my grandfather, a kind of reciprocal gesture for his gentle smile that would say: now, after much delay, I am beginning to understand you ...

This memory image is suddenly broken off, and when its echo attenuates almost to silence, another somewhat related tune appears – one from Verdi's *Aïda*. It is the melody the high priestess of Phtha sings in the temple of Vulcan, asking the god, in the eerie quiet of that sanctuary, to bestow his support on the newly elected commander of the Egyptian army, Radames. Elsewhere I described this scene (as well as some of the other quotes in *Simulacrum*) in words that try to explain my interest in it.[3] To this I probably ought to add that I was quite taken by the mutual affinity, if not overt resemblance, between the two Jewish melodies and Verdi's inspiration of this "Egyptian" tune. I need only add that I am a regular reader of news reports from the Near East, and this momentary harmony between Jewish and "Egyptian" melodies appealed to me to the extent that I felt I ought to put them side by side.

After this Verdi quote is left hanging in mid-air, the piece is finally launched into that "energized" section which I referred to earlier. Now there are but two more quotes to account for. The first of these arrives at a peak moment. It is borrowed from scene 1 of Verdi's *Otello* (bars 367–71 here). It is the moment when men and women, assembled at the edge of the sea in the Cypriot port city, turn their voices heavenward to implore God, in an almost propitiatory act, to spare the hero and his companions as they battle the waves in their effort to reach the safety of the port. It is a moment of supreme danger to the lives of many a dear one, and the prayer is full of passion and despair. This quote is suddenly interrupted in *Simulacrum*; but instead of a contrast, we hear an even more chilling series of sounds, as if another source of danger had been sighted, with the realization that this time hope for a rescue is nonexistent. The passage conveys the impression of piercing shrieks of fear and laments. Probably few persons among those who have heard the work realized that this passage (bars 372–88) is a slightly modified fragment from the duodrama *Thisness*, about which I spoke earlier. The passage occurs in the accompaniment of *Thisness*, section 7, entitled "Unreason." Here is its entire text.

Unreason

Is this the end of your speech, foreigner?
How strangely you speak.

I hate you for it.
I hate you, pharmakos.

They claim: you know all
that I don't understand …

I fear you, *pharmakos,*
wizard and poisoner.

You stir up my life,
sacred and accursed soul.

You must be exorcised!

And what's the worst,
you dweller upon the boundary line,
you bring what I've come to need.

I hate you the more for it.

Strain, stress, strife ...
the going gets rougher now.

You, Ishmael, you are at hand to blame.

  "The plague's upon us!
  Bring out the *pharmakoi!*"

You are handy to strike.

  "Blow, *pharma,* blow, *pharma,*
  pharma, blow!"

More yet to come!

  "Attack between the legs!"
  "Aim at the head!"
  "Blow out their lights!"
  "Destroy the forms!"
  "Erase their formulas!"
  "Kill to clear!"
  "Kill to clean!"
  "Kill to cure!"

The boil is lanced ...
the air is heavy ...

Trace and retrace ...
... try to forget ...

peace will now return
with the settling dust ...

And now a warning:

You mustn't ever, ever bring it up again.
It never even took place.
Then ... perhaps ...
the voice, also, will go away ...
in time ...

For me this passage enacts an unspeakable deed of cruelty, a specific one. But it also could apply to any and all acts of cruelty perpetrated by some to the irrevocable detriment of others. This brief
passage can only lead to one sentiment and act: great sadness, and
mourning, hence the "Quasi una marcia funebre" section that begins
in bar 395.

The piece cannot end here, as life continues for those who are the
survivors. Other memories take over; there is time now for other gestures, however fragmentary they might be. Towards the close there is
an attempt to achieve a gesture of apotheosis, but perhaps it is not
"full" enough; it cannot, or doesn't want to, sustain itself, and afterwards, the piece returns to the vicinity of the same affective terrain
from which it emerged at the outset.

[At this point an extended section from performance of the work recorded by the National Arts Centre Orchestra under Gabriel Chmura,
the artists to whom the work is dedicated, was played.]

I now hear some of you reminding me about the promise I made
earlier to tell about a discovery I made a day or so ago. Yes, now is perhaps a good moment to speak about this. It takes me back once again
to the title of the work, *Simulacrum*, which means a number of things,
as we know, including the notion of "mirage". All the remembrances
that I included in this piece, all the glances to the past, as it were, can
be seen as conversations, however fleeting they may be, with persons
who are no longer here, with situations (can one "converse" with a
past situation? It seems far-fetched ... but perhaps as a figure of
speech it might be allowed to stand), and so on – all these being integrally woven into the tissue of one's present. This much we know of
the work, but the *new* information is this: forty-five years ago, while
serving in a labour battalion of the Hungarian army, a unit especially
created for young Jewish men, and being stationed in a dusty little village in Transylvania, called Elöpatak, on a very hot Sunday afternoon
in the month of August, I wrote a poem, my first poem ever, entitled

"Mirage in Elöpatak". That "mirage" was, actually, what I felt must be done in that distant moment – namely, to take a look into a future in which, so I wanted to convince myself, resided hope for good things to come, in contrast with the severely restricted horizon that was available to me and to my comrades at that point in time. Yes, it was a kind of wishful thinking that helped to sustain me, and it did precisely that.

Mirage in Elöpatak

Strolling happy friends with wit abounding,
Thoughtfully smiling, invite you to join:
Come along, pal, if it suits you;
Surely you know us – forever calling,
Yet also keeping you at a distance …
Familiar? Of course. You also play by the same rule.

Look: the sage is resting in the shady gardens,
Streams of flushed-faced young
Press towards him – the hub –
Along the spokes of the wheel,
With thirsty lips gently curving,
Spirits alight
To await word of the coming dawn.

Ideas flow following idea
Trust from the past welding onto offspring;
An unringed migrating crane – leading
At the apex of a swift winging v …
Oh, what a splendid morning!

Lo: safely nesting in his roomy basket
Contentedly the just-fed infant coos,
Delighting all with the primeval song.
Soup on the stove; the bubbles are bursting,
Tiny pea-balls dance in the sweet-smelling stream
Tender shoots blending into flavour,
Surrendering self to form a whole
For the mid-day meal of a scorching day.
So the soul fuses all that is worthwhile to keep.

Reflecting the pane, by the window, a brother is speaking:
Do you accept this? Something in which you could share?
A magical call: to excel by doing well

The job at hand, yearning for mastery,
As the distant spires of shape
Urge you on to find the right place.

You uncatchable slippery buddy of mine
Time, all cartwheels, tumbles and twirls;
You are full of tricks.
You make me dizzy
As you turn the "now" into "past"
What will you do to the moment about to arrive?

The minute-hours roll by on the wheels of substance.
The view is rewarding, never twice the same.
On and onward towards the Crystal City
Until, in a well-guarded courtyard – we hear it –
The great bell is sounding;
The word of the king, the voice of the sun.
Noon!

If that's what you need: well ... then rest.
Stretch out your limbs in the hollows of hills
By the edge of the darkly-pensive woods
Where you just might catch, unexpectedly,
A few words resounding from a generous spring:

"On the grassy plains you feed me, my Lord,
And even by the rim of the abyss you are my shepherd ... "
Comes from a distance.
Then ... silence
The voiceless word echoes as long as you hear the thought.

The heat of the hour wets palm and fingers.
For a while it is an effort to move.
But slowly the disc descends along its arc
And life returns to the squares and streets.
The multitude moves ... each looking for something,
Peeking, peering as far as the eye can see.

The afternoon gardens prepare for the evening,
Distilling scents for the feast ahead
To please the dearest ones:
You, darling Ágicám.

In the waning warmth of the dusk
Your firm back trustingly fills the bay of my caress
And your peach-tasting lips chase
The last specks of dust from our content and joy.[4]

And now the revelation that I had yesterday. The *new* "mirage", *Simulacrum*, which peers into the *past*, and questions it for meaning, meets another "mirage", the text of an *old* poem, which looked into the *future*. Somewhere in mental space, unexpectedly, like two brothers, like two faces of the same person forty-five years apart, they meet, smile at each other, recognize numerous features that have not changed at all, and acknowledge the few, not very consequential ones that did. In mutual agreement they declare the indivisibility of the person over a large span of time – a truly rare and festive moment, worth at least a deep breath and the uttering of a soft "aha!" I could stop right now, but somehow an ending here would be just that – an ending – and, so far, things have never "ended" for me. So I will go on for just a little longer and tell you what has happened after *Simulacrum*.

For one thing, I immediately turned to *SparkskrapS*. This work, in its turn, may be regarded as trying to portray a *very* old timeless theme: the struggle between conflicting urges within us – urges that we have come to label over time as the good and the evil. Now, there are many vantage points from which this has been treated in the past in word, music, art. My angle was to be a special one, one that was propounded by some of the Jewish kabbalistic sages, among whom belongs also Isaac Luria, the rabbi of Safed, whom I have alluded to earlier. I learned of him through the fascinating accounts of Gershom Scholem, the late, great scholar of Jewish mysticism. You have before you two short quotations from works by Scholem, which might shed some light on the meaning of the strange title of my piece for the Esprit Orchestra:

> In the symbolism of the Zohar concerning the *sitra*
> *ahra* (the "other side") … the *kelippoth* ("shells" or
> "husks" of evil) are sometimes understood … as
> the last links of the chain of emanation where all
> turns to darkness … there is a spark
> of holiness even in the domain of "the other side"
> … The realms of good and evil are to an extent
> commingled and man's mission is to separate them.[5]

> Every man who acts in accordance with this law,
> that of the *tikkun* – "restoration," or "reintegration" –

brings home the fallen sparks of the *Shekhinah* and
his soul as well.[6]

But true to "normal" practice, work on *SparkskrapS* had to be briefly
interrupted. Elizabeth Whalley called and asked me to write a few
words for a volume that would honour the memory of her late husband, the great English scholar and poet George Whalley, a close colleague and friend of mine at Queen's for many years. After having
finished this text of remembrance, my pen just kept on moving and I
found myself wanting to add an afterthought to it … an "afterthought"? Yes, this is very familiar. There is always an afterthought to
add following an "ending" … any ending, probably all endings but one.
Yes, perhaps here also I should leave you with an "afterthought" instead
of pretending that there is an ending, to anything, ever …

Afterthought

Where does one go from here?
   There.
But where is "there"?
   It depends on the way "where" is put.
Are "where" and "there" the same?
   Almost so and they both hinge on the "way."
How to look for the "way"?
   Begin with the "here."
Have I not begun already?
   The question is your answer.
Is the line circular then?
   No, more like a spiral it is.
Do you see its direction?
   I cannot say, we both are spinning with it.
The push that started it to move, then?
   This question, too, comes out of the same spin.
Is there anything more to add?
   Probably not, but if you wish, you may
   continue to speak.
May I sing instead?
   If you can, it might be better still.
Do you want to sing along? A duet perhaps?
   Let us begin, then, without delay.
Would you give the first tone?
   Where shall we go from here?

NOTES

1 Talk presented at the University of Toronto, Faculty of Music, 5 January 1988.

2 In Gershom Scholem, *On the Kabbalah and Its Symbolism* (London: Routledge and Kegan Paul, 1965).

3 "Pst ... Pst ... Are You Listening? Hearing Voices from Yesterday," *Queen's Quarterly* 93, 1 (spring 1986): 71–84.

4 This poem, originally written in Hungarian, was translated by the author in the 1980s.

5 Gershom Scholem, *Kabbalah* (New York: Quadrangle, 1974), 125.

6 Scholem, *On the Kabbalah*, 116.

15 *Three Songs of Love*
(The Story Behind)

There are two versions of this piece for women's choir: the first was written as an a cappella work, in 1951 in Montreal; the other, with two added wind instruments (flute, clarinet), in 1997 in Kingston. The sentiment and thought behind it, however, go back to the year 1941. Its contents were also influenced by events and conditions that occurred in my life in 1951–52, and after a long hiatus, in the mid-1990s.

The terrain of these pieces is that of private lives in which fundamental intimate relationships take shape and are enacted. These appear to be universal and time-independent. Central concerns brought to the fore here are about being alive, courting, mating, procreating, the shadow of dying, man's place in nature, and so on, all expressed here in a poetic language of text that is rich in allusion to myth, symbol, metaphor, dream like experience, and other related modes of expression. The actors of these private domains seem to be preoccupied with themselves and with each other, ostensibly without feeling a need to relate themselves to the outside world and to the spirit of the times. The urge of the being-in-itself orders and sustains this inward glance.

Yet the moment in time might not be far away when the individual begins to see, at first dimly, the outlines of an outside world which infringes unavoidably on his/her life in the present, or in memory. This new vision might even compel a new appreciation of the "old" picture, an experience that was. Sentiments then may acquire new resonance; doubt, ambivalence might creep into memory, calling to new life a blurred story, giving it the light of a new insight. Somewhat attenuated old sentiments may acquire, then, a fresh intensity and invite review, even re-enactment. This happened when I came to feel the need to compose *Three Songs of Love*.

As the title intimates, the central theme of these pieces is love. More specifically, the first and third pieces tell of autobiographical love stories. The first of these ends tragically: after a brief love experience, the pair is separated in a terrible war. The young man survives, goes home, and looks for the girl. She is nowhere to be found. Reluctantly, and in sorrow, he concludes that she probably did not survive those years (1939–45), but he has no *proof* of this. He leaves the country, the continent even, with this unresolved enigma. In his new home (Montreal) he tries to come to terms with his past (in Hungary) and decides to compose a piece in the (inconclusive) memory of the girl. By that time hope, new friendships, and a new, even deeper love for another girl are part of his life. Two other compositions are added to make a triptych, with a symmetrical structure:

Table 15.1
Structure of *Three Songs of Love*

No. 1	No. 2	No. 3
Past, tragically (?) ended love	Friendship and love for a young couple who helped the composer to bridge the two phases of his life: then / there and now / here.	A wonderful young woman appears who, after some hesitation, joins the composer in marriage. The two live happily ever after.

UNEXPECTED EPISODE

In 1995 (or was it in 1996?) I was in the stacks of the Robarts Library in Toronto. There I found, half by chance, a so-called "memorial book" (recently published in Hungary) on the fate of the Jews of Debrecen (a larger city in the eastern region of Hungary) in the Second World War. The book contained many pages filled with the names of persons who were deported in the summer of 1944 to the concentration camp in Auschwitz (Poland), where they were killed and burned in what came to be known as the Holocaust. I took the book to a table and pulled up a chair … I did not have to read on very long to find the name of Ágnes Berkovics (one of twenty-four persons with that surname) listed among those who were deported from Debrecen, and who never returned. Here was an answer to the concern, turning later into an enigma, regarding the fate of "Ági," which was on my mind ever since I last saw her (on a furlough) in 1943.

The poems I was fortunate to find evoked for me the memories sketched here. Moreover, they turned what originally was personal into what might be seen as commonly shared, by the use of metaphor, symbol, and even a hint of magic in places. In this collective ambience the words of Walter de la Mare combine readily with the contents and the expressions of two folk texts. His poetry is often in the nature of a fairy tale and, in places, has an incantational quality, which is also to be found in some nursery rhymes. "The Song of the Mad Prince" also appealed to me forcefully because of some memories I still hold of my early childhood. (I am here suggesting that the inspiration – some of it at least – may have its roots in those distant days and moments in, say, the years 1922–25.) What does this poem say that evoked "Ági" for me in 1951? What else does it speak of? (For texts of all three poems, see appendix.)

Ági Berkovics was a beautiful ash-blond girl of sixteen or seventeen when I first saw her, at a distance. She immediately reminded me of Botticelli's famous painting *The Birth of Venus*. She looked pure, innocent, yet sensual, an "incarnation" of a youthful Venus, or Aphrodite, her Greek equivalent.

The figure of the peacock is a powerful reminder of childhood memories for me. The wild shrieks of peacocks were part of the "scene" in that magical park in the Danube River, in Budapest, called St Margaret's Island, an expanse of flowers, lawns, historic buildings, ruins, playgrounds, places for refreshments, and more. I now know that the peacock is also a symbol of the apotheosis (deification, glorification) of princesses. In Christian art it is a symbol for immortality. The questions in "The Song of the Mod Prince" – Where sleeps she now? Where rests she now her head?" – I read as near echoes of the pained doubt I felt about Ági's fate in 1951. Sleep (Sleeping Beauty?) again evokes memories ... is it "sleep," or is it no longer being alive? "Mum's the word" suggests the enigma: the past will not speak, the secret remains. "Green dusk for dreams, / Moss for a pillow" can be heard as strong implications that she might be dead. "Sexton" and "willow" (weeping willow?) evoke the churchyard as a burial ground. This is reinforced by the words "narrow bed." Is this a coffin ... a grave, perhaps? Finally we hear the powerful words "life's troubled bubble broken" and we experience (nay, "perform", by uttering all these *b* plosives), the distant sobs (another *b* in the middle) that give expression to mourning. The music underlies, tries to express, this tale of love, pain, enigma – all seen through the opaque glass of recall of memories from more or less distant moments in the past.

The anonymous (folk?) text of the second song represents in its imagery a healing, transitory phase in existence. The past (so strongly alluded to, for me, by the de la Mare poem) doesn't yet give up its hold on the mind in this poem. Elements, places, and the figure of a maiden lying in the moor (is she alive? or is she dead?) create here an atmosphere, a mood, which spins forth from where the first song left off. The moor, an extensive area of wet waste ground, the bower, a tiny shelter made of twigs and leaves, suggest exposure to raw nature. This is reinforced by the complex symbol of the well: a deep hole in the ground. It could be seen as a symbol for "deep" memory, a place from which one could draw up half-forgotten recollections. This act has also been interpreted in the past as an attitude of deep contemplation, thought. Also the hope is implied that from the deep well one just might obtain refreshing and purifying water, which might have a cleansing, healing quality.

The symbol of flowers could, once again, remind one forcefully of Aphrodite, the goddess of love. In her cult the rose signified completion, consummate achievement, perfection. The lily, in relation to her, was an emblem of purity, virginality – one of the possible attributes of the girl who dreams of the love goddess.) (I hold an image of Ági Berkovics that is very close to this.)

"The Maid of the Moor" is dedicated to Isabelle and Jean Papineau-Couture, the Quebec composer of high renown and his late wife, Isabelle, who offered lasting friendship to me just days after my arrival in Montreal in January 1949, almost fifty years ago. They made my life in those early days in this land so much easier and hopeful than it would have been without them. They truly helped me in the far from easy task of "bridging" a past that still had (not surprisingly) a strong hold on me, and a future which I only began to see, in dim outlines, ever so slowly as the weeks and months rolled by. So it is right to record here that the dedication of this song to Isabelle and Jean was, and remains, a "thank you, friends" for what they gave me then.

The third song, "The Two Magicians" (on a folk text), enacts on a small scale, and in symbolic language, the drama of a courtship, which takes the shape of a chase made even more exciting, alluring, enticing, through a series of transformations or metamorphoses. The one courted, the girl, flees the suitor: a "coal black smith," a figure that resembles the Greek god Hephaestus, the keeper of fire, the husband of Aphrodite. Here he enacts the role of male power, aiming to conquer, to possess, to "get" the girl. One might even state that while this "coal black one" is almost genetically programmed to initiate and carry out the pursuit, the girl might also be enjoying this timeless re-enactment of the mating game, which is her inheritance, too. The element of (slight) uncertainty about the outcome intensifies this small yet vitally essential drama between the female and the male – told here through the women's voices, which assume *both* roles.

There is little need for belabouring the simple yet exciting scenario of dissembling, chase, more dissembling, and further chase. She turns into a duck fleeing on water, later into a hare on a plain, finally into a nimble, difficult-to-catch fly. But he is also resourceful, and transforms himself into a water dog, subsequently into a greyhound, and finally into a spider. The music, both the choral and the instrumental layers, undertakes to enact this small drama, which is punctuated by a telling refrain of resistance and unwillingness to yield on the part of the girl. A surprising softening at the very end implies that she is finally ready to give in to his insistent urgings, expressed in the three pursuits, and is ready to join him in a lifelong union of love and procreation.

This piece is dedicated to a beautiful chestnut-brown-haired girl in her twenties, in 1951 in Montreal, by the name of Beate Frankenberg. Since early 1952 she has been known as Beate Anhalt, my dear wife. We got married after a courtship that lasted almost two years.

APPENDIX:
TEXTS OF *THREE SONGS OF LOVE*

1 The Song of the Mad Prince

Who said, "Peacock Pie"?
    The old King to the sparrow;
Who said, "Crops are ripe"?
    Rust to the harrow:

Who said, "Where sleeps she now?
    Where rests she now her head,
Bathed in eve's loveliness – ?"
    That's what I said.

Who said, "Ay, mum's the word";
    Sexton to willow;
Who said, "Green dusk for dreams,
    Moss for a pillow"?

Who said, "All Times delight
    Hath she for narrow bed;
Life's troubled bubble broken"? –
    That's what I said.
                    (Walter de la Mare)

2 The Maid of the Moor

Maiden in the moor lay,
  In the moor lay,
Seven nights full, seven nights full,
  Maiden in the moor lay,
  In the moor lay,
Seven nights full and a day.

Well was her meat;
What was her meat?
  The primrose and the, –
Well was her meat;
What was her meat?
  The primrose and the violet.

Well was her drink;
What was her drink?
  The cold water of, –
  The cold water of, –
Well was her drink;
What was her drink?
  The cold water of the well-spring.

Well was her bower;
What was her bower?
  The red rose and the, –
  The red rose and the, –
Well was her bower;
What was her bower?
  The red rose and the lily flower.
                    (anonymous)

3 The Two Magicians

O she looked out of the window,
  As white as any milk;
But he looked into the window,
  As black as any silk.

Hulloa, hulloa, hulloa, hulloa,
  you coal black smith!
O what is your silly song?

You never shall change my maiden name
That I have kept so long;
I'd rather die a maid, yes but then she said,
And be buried all in my grave,
Than I'd have such a nasty,
   husky, dusky, musty, fusky,
Coal black smith.
A maiden I will die.

Then she became a duck,
   A duck all on the stream;
And He became a water dog,
   And fetched her back again.

Hulloa, etc.

Then she became a hare,
   A hare all on the plain;
And He became a greyhound dog,
   And fetched her back again.

Hulloa, etc.

Then she became a fly,
   A fly all in the air;
And he became a spider,
And fetched her to his lair.

Hulloa, etc.
                      (folk song)

16 A Continuing Thread? Perhaps

I am writing this in December 1997, about a year and a half after the premiere of *Traces* (*Tikkun*). I am now in the midst of composing a new work for voices and orchestra which I am calling "A Voice-Drama for the Imagination." As on earlier occasions, the thought that these works might be related, in some way, to my earlier works for voices (*Comments, Cento, Foci, Thisness*, and others) keeps coming back to mind. I now believe that there is a connection linking these pieces together; as a result, they could be, or perhaps even ought to be, regarded in their association to each other as a "continuing thread" that expresses a single superordinate theme which they give voice to in their individual ways. I shall try here to identify that supposedly shared theme, that core idea, and will comment on how the different works express that common topic in their individual ways.

What might that shared theme be? Let us begin with (and test) the assumption that all these works aim at expressing some kind of insight into the relationship between an individual and other individuals (or groups in society) in various situations or "contexts of situations."[1] Another relevant concept in this respect is Mikhail Bakhtin's chronotope,[2] which expresses relationships of time and location. The notion of time here might be synchronic, or diachronic, or both, in relation to each other. The latter orientation in time is unavoidably at hand whenever reference to memory occurs.

Society, in turn, is defined by its institutions, values, norms, customs, history, its exercise of power, its attitudes to change, its key individuals and groups, its languages (dialects included), and other features too numerous to mention here. What matters to the writer/composer is that, to depict (enact) a societal "event," the choice of modalities are very numerous indeed. And if one combines this complexity in the imagination with the multifacetedness of an individual (no less complex, but different in nature), one is faced with a "double system" of complexity of complexities. One can cope with such a "field" only through imposing on it limitations in one manner or another. But such a circumscribed enactment always takes place in a field of surrounding darkness formed by the neighbouring material or environment that one decides not to include. This "black halo" might prove to contain essentially relevant detail to the core idea at hand. If so, an adjustment might be called for.

In the light of the foregoing, the nature of a musical portrayal – a "showing," more or less abstracted – would seem to demand the setting up of contexts, relationships, the selection of modalities of expressions, roles, within which individuals and groups within an implied society might reciprocally define each other. Another feature to consider is the degree of (relative) stability/instability of that society. All these invite – even depend on – the composer's concern with an imaginary audience. What degree of "decoding" experience on the part of an audience does he/she decide to count on? How will he/she endeavour to lead the audience toward a new aural insight? What risks are acceptable in this regard? These matters I have often weighed, more-or-less consciously.

Now let us turn to the consideration of specific works to see how they might be seen as exemplifying the assumed common theme.

COMMENTS[3]

This is a relatively early work (1954), composed in Montreal. I regard it as my first truly "Canadian" piece in the sense that, in some way or other, in having conceived and written it in the way that I did, I was responding to the character and concerns of a chronotope. But I also knew that this was not all that was contained in the piece. As will become clear shortly, I also responded to the recall of experiences lived through, or events learned about, before coming to Canada in January 1949.

The piece is a series of songs for contralto voice with an accompanying trio of piano, violin, and violoncello. The composition of the work was occasioned by the reading of three short report items in an edition of the daily newspaper, the *Montreal Star*. At the time I was only instinctively aware of the reasons for selecting these texts, rather than others. From the perspective of these forty-three years I see more clearly the underlying reasons for this selection. I shall come to this shortly, but first I shall indicate the events these texts report on.

The first report is about the murder of Sampih, a famous dancer of the island of Bali. The second report is about a tense episode in the course of a circus act, which could have ended in tragedy, but did not. The third text is part of the daily weather report pertaining to the border region between the provinces of Quebec and Ontario. It is clear now that each of these accounts relates to some kind of conflict and a resulting tension leading to a real (or at least potential) clash of attitudes that could – and, in the third case, did – result in a tragic outcome. In the year 1954 I was, for personal reasons, "open" and responsive to this particular overarching theme of conflict, strife, and a potential for a tragic outcome.

In the first of these songs, about the famous dancer Sampih, of Sayan, I tried to express the colour of a Balinese gamelan orchestra, an interesting endeavour considering the nature of the instrumental forces at hand. I had better mention at this point that I was drawn to Balinese music ever since I obtained a few discs of gamelan pieces from Bali, recorded by the Austrian ethnomusicologist E.M. von Hornbostel in the 1930s. The period when I heard these was, I think, between 1937 and 1939, when I still lived in Budapest and was a student at the Academy of Music there. The deep impression these recordings made on me (inspiring me to improvise gamelanlike sounds on the piano) was reinforced by a concert held in the Great Hall of the Academy (in the late 1930s). The program consisted of a number of pieces transcribed from these very same Hornbostel recordings for an ensemble of Western instruments. (I recall a vocal piece sung by a young girl with an "uncertain" voice was assigned to a double bass player (!), playing in a very high position on the G string, with a comic effect.) Several of these transcriptions were very effective, even beautiful. Here was a precedent for me as I set out to compose this movement.

In reality, this was only the surface inspiration for this piece. The essential component of the impetus to write this piece must be looked for elsewhere – in the cultural-societal situation the news item reported on. What were the issues at play? Who were the "actors?" What value system, or systems, provided the "context of situation"? What did Sampih do to "deserve" and receive the ultimate punishment of execution by murder? According to what code of laws was he condemned to pay this price? These remarks on *Comments*, it is useful to point out, are made from the vantage point of the present; they relate to the conception and the composition of the work in a manner that constitutes yet another topic: How to determine the work's "context of situation" from today's perspective? I see this as forming a concentric pattern of contexts of situations consisting of the following: 1) that of the reader of a newspaper report in Montreal in 1954; 2) that of a touring Balinese performing ensemble (singers, dancers, instrumentalists, escorts) in London, where they performed, through the managerial activities of a local impresario, and the local people with whom they might have come in contact there; 3) the society of the village of Sayan, where Sampih was born, grew up, was "discovered" for his talent as a dancer; and, finally, 4) Sampih's family and within it Sampih, the person himself, the very centre of these concentric circles of contexts of situations. The piece appears to pose a question: is it reasonable to believe that Sampih's tragic end could have been caused by a conflict of cultures and some operative incompatibilities resulting from this? (The consideration of this has a strong degree of topicality in the present in view of the migrations of millions of persons in search of new homes that would hold out a hope of a better life. Often these displacements take place across cultural boundaries.)

The song begins with a street scene. Amidst urban noise (traffic, etc.) the voice of a newspaper vendor is heard, hawking the paper by intoning a headline in a singsong voice: "Bali's Leading Dancer Slain ... Bali's Leading Dancer Slain." After we have heard him sing this, typical Balinese melodic and rhythmic elements begin to appear, both in the voice part and in the instrumental complement. The allusion here is to a context of situation centred on Bali. The music takes on a somewhat "manic" character (alongside the Balinese allusion) as the words tell the hearer that the Balinese ensemble was "brought to the outside world ... for the first time in a generation" by an impresario from London. The name of this impresario, a part of the report, is also a part of the text set here. The character of the music also changes: a sense of foreboding is suggested. And then comes the awful news of what happened to Sampih. The character of the instrumental layer changes drastically to jagged attacks, *sul ponticello* tremolos to accompany the quasi-frozen monotone recitation of the voice. This gradually turns into an extended keening, over the persistence of jabbing and "trembling" sounds in the instruments. This is already part of an allusion to fellow villagers and family members mourning Sampih in the village of Sayan. This phase brings back the traditional intonation cells heard before, but here they have an almost ritualistic, culture-determining character and function. They seem to say, this is who we are ... our custom decides what is right ... we accept the consequences of punishment meted out to those of us who have been found to transgress our societal boundaries. This apperception would suggest that the given environment of customs and unwritten laws constitutes yet another invisible "context of situation." The final "gesture" of the song is the slow, pain-suggesting descending octave glissando in the cello.

In the second song the ensemble suggests a light waltz of the "salon music" type. Over this, which one might call the antidramatic instrumental layer, with its ostensible function to entertain, to make people feel comfortable and secure, we are to hear the story of a barely averted fatal accident taking place before the unsuspecting spectators at a circus. The spectators expect to witness an assortment of acts, including some that demand the display of great skill in the execution of daredevil action. The contrast here is posited between a paying audience, who waits to be titillated and takes for granted the successful performance of a dangerous maneuver, and the performers, who are aware of the risks involved each time a difficult act is executed. But on the specific occasion the news item comments on, the high wire act does not take place. The reason for this is that "a woman trapeze performer suffered a sudden paralysis of her left arm, while doing an act seventy-five feet in the air ... but was saved by her husband before she could fall." This occurred before the eyes of "six thousand five hundred persons," who watched the rescue while the orchestra (at least in this setting) continued to play ... with the implication that "there is nothing to worry about, keep calm, this is part of the show," or something to this effect. The text (and the vocal part) then turns to a more detailed description of this event. The voice conveys here the mounting anxiety of the pair high above the heads of the spectators. The orchestra keeps on playing the waltz, but it takes on a frantic character for a brief while, and we can assume that many in the audience have become aware by now that something unscheduled is taking place, and consequently join in the tenseness and fear that characterizes this context of situation. Yet the audience appears to be absent from the musical fabric here. How could one surmise, then, that the audience is part of the totality of this situation? There are two signifiers for this: the one is the *absence* of vocality of those "thousands" (inherent in the chamber ensemble itself); the other is the telltale changes in the accompaniment (as if the change in the character of the waltz were also mirroring a change in the collective emotional state of the spectators). Concurrently with the rescue by the husband, the waltz returns to its initial character.

The third song begins with a long instrumental introduction. This could be understood as having two functions: to allow for the dissolution of the tension remaining from the two preceding songs, and to suggest a slow drifting of clouds in the sky, in preparation for hearing the text of a weather report, of all things. Why a weather report, one may ask? First, consideration of the weather is an important enough topic in the country. Secondly, "weather talk" is a safe vehicle for phatic communion in typical exchanges of the prevailing contexts of situations here; it is a safe time filler when one senses the need to avoid a controversial (political?) topic. Following this, the entering voice is calm, displaying only two pitch-classes (C and E), over a thinned-out instrumental texture, implying perhaps a *plein-air* environment of broad vistas of sky, with clouds floating by at a slow, steady pace. Over this near-idyllic scene the words "Quebec," "Ontario" come up. They are not only geographical locating words, but also terms denoting complex packages of historical, political, social, economic, and cultural differences, tensions, and struggles in the present day chronotope; hence they possess deep metaphorical baggage, especially for the inhabitants of this land, who can readily recognize the depth of this implication and interpret it from their own points of view. This became clear to me, a resident of Montreal, by the year 1954. Consequently, expressions like "the storm which gave heavy rain across Ontario and western Quebec has become stationary over the eastern portion of the province" suddenly acquired a near metaphorical potential. But change is in the offing. The report states later "meanwhile Ontario and western Quebec can expect another sunny day." This prognosis "lifts" the voice into a higher register: the lower E is exchanged for one an octave higher, which persists for a while, giving the voice a near jubilant character with the allusion that this melodic change might also be symbolic of a political change toward an improved relationship between the two jurisdictions. The song, and with it the entire piece, comes at this point to a peaceful and contemplative conclusion through a gradual thinning out of its texture, ending with a *morendo* on a single sustained B.

CENTO[4]

In an earlier commentary on this work, I wrote the following: "*Cento* ... evokes situations in which groups of people interact with each other; in other words, it is an expression of urban existence. It speaks of the inhabitants, the machines, the physical environment of a large city, and on the part of the people about a striving for identity in opposition to forces which would make them both anonymous and interchangeable."[5]

The sociopolitical context for the idea of composing a work like *Cento* (and thus also fulfilling a centennial commission of the University of British Columbia Chamber Singers and their conductor Cortland Hultberg) was that of Montreal in the mid-1960s, a city which, at that time, alongside its many attractive features, was also the terrain in which the Québécois versus English-Canadian tension and contest for power played itself out in the most intense way. At that time (one can conclude in hindsight), the province of Quebec experienced the early stages of what soon became known as the Quiet Revolution. Some persons resident in Montreal, neither French- nor English-Canadian in ethnic origin, watched anxiously, often helplessly, as the province's public arena became an ever louder and at times violent contesting ground. The outcome of this was difficult to see then. It is still difficult to see today, over thirty years later. (But one feels the need to add that the great changes, including the migration of many, often involving economic hardship, took place peacefully and within a legal framework, with only a minimal loss of life under violent circumstances.)

This was, then, the public context of situation in my apperception of Montreal in 1966. It was my aim that *Cento* should enact that mood, that chronotope. This, I felt, would exclude the *bel canto* singing style. Rather, I intended the piece to express itself through the means of a highly inflected declamation, in which consonants were to play an important role. In addition to the live vocal sounds, I planned to have tape-recorded voices, as well as additional electronic sounds. The ensemble was to suggest a technologically sophisticated urban milieu. My text for this consisted of an "assembly" (hence the title, *Cento*) of ninety-nine words taken from a long and powerful poem by Eldon Grier. Individual voices emerge rarely in this work, which emphasizes the group as the principal carrier of meaning. (An exception to this comes toward the end when we hear a single male voice saying repeatedly, "We have come to say nothing ... Let us hear our voices again.") The group utterances are diverse in character and their degree of intelligibility varies also. They symbolize social structures in contexts of situations. Unlike *Comments* there are no individual heroes here; alternatively, one could say that the only possible hero here is the urban mass of people, who jostle along a crowded sidewalk in a metropolis at rush hour, elbowing their collective selves toward the nearest subway (or, rather, I should say metro) entrance.

The preceding descriptions of *Comments* and *Cento* included references to societal groupings and ethnicity. In each the diversity of ethnicity was numerically "limited," which of course did not preclude vast cleavages (e.g., Balinese vs Western culture). In the next piece I shall comment on, the chronotopes to be visited will be different when considering the work as a whole.

FOCI[6]

This work, composed in 1969 for the Contemporary Music Performing Ensemble at the State University of New York (SUNY), Buffalo, is multilingual and "visits" a broader cultural terrain both as to space and time period. Elsewhere, I described certain facets of this work: the ideas that gave impetus to its composition, how its details emerged from the overall plan, and how they were eventually realized.[7] In that text, I commented about the contexts of *Foci* and the societies that provided the framework for them. Through this considerable cultural diversity and detail, I tried to assemble a heterogeneous picture of corresponding scope. Allusions to a series of concepts are enacted here, and they coexist with references to world religions. The modalities for representing these range from the quasi realistic to the poetic-dramatic and the surreal.

Was I concerned, at the time of composing, with the task of integrating all this diversity into a unified whole? No, I was not. I took it for granted that the compositional instinct would look after that. In other words, I did not want to rein in the push and pull of the ideas and materials; I let them influence me as if I were a sleepwalker. And the result? From the perspective of the present I see the work as an arrested moment in time in the multidirectional roamings of a mind that was attracted by all the work's contents, which it visits in an arbitrary order, a work whose "key" and "timetable" is not sufficiently known, not even by the one who is in the centre of it all.

Foci is not a succession of free associations; neither is this an instance of "automatic composition." Instead, one senses a purpose in the choices and order of presentation, but one is not certain what logic they follow, if any. Could the whole be but a picture of a world in transition, perhaps also in some turmoil, in which idea chases idea, concepts lose credibility without being supplanted by more credible ones? Is this a showing of a state of affairs that is characterized by a lack of cohesion, which nevertheless does not seem to stand in the way of persistence in time? Ideas simply coexist in time, or in close succession, and there appears to be no concern about how they hold together. There seems to be but a single common element to it all: they were thought of and put together in this order/disorder by a single mind that, while doing this, exercised its sovereign right to roam, to dream, to consider, to judge, to take or reject, and through this process define an extended moment in his life. That may be all. A long arrested moment, perhaps, and the desire to share it with whomever wants to eavesdrop ...

One of the "continuing threads" in the work is a set of four definitions taken from a dictionary of psychological and psychoanalytical terms.[8] These define coping behaviour, the soul, interaction, and lying. The first three are enacted by multilingual assemblies of voices, synthesized on tape, using a certain process of recruiting, rehearsing, recording, editing, and assembling in conjunction with a simultaneously sounding instrumental complement provided by a modest chamber orchestra. More than once the semantic content of a definition was placed in conflict with the modalities of the setting. For example, the dictionary discredits the notion of "the soul." In contrast, the setting (through the use of a saccharin-flavoured sequence) gives the lie to this, implying perhaps an inability, or unwillingness, to jettison a supposedly discredited concept. When the setting of the definition of "interaction" comes up, the setting features the voices of a French woman and an English man talking past each other, each oblivious of the other's presence, or pretending not to have noticed the "other." In the context of the situation in Montreal in the late 1960s this was an altogether possible event. The nature of the eerie accompaniment enhances this "reality in unreality" effect. In the movement entitled "Measures," one hears an assortment of words, all of which denote one aspect or another of quantification. The complementary instrumental and electronic sounds enact modalities of quantifying time or acoustical space. One might sense that the burden here lies in the allusion to the pervasiveness of quantification in our civilization.

The movements entitled "Icons" and "Individuals," respectively, touch on facets of religious experience in a number of faiths. The voices that enact these were selected with some care, in order to convey a sense of authenticity. The movement "Group" enacts a furious quasi cocktail party where a multiplicity of people talk simultaneously, and from this din the hearer tries, and succeeds, to snatch a word or two, wondering about their context, purpose, and relevance to the one who overheard them. Could this movement also stand as an enactment of trying to make sense of a context of situation under difficult conditions? In the course of the next movement, in which a court clerk administers an oath to a witness, the sole live vocalist, a mezzo-soprano, has meanwhile entered through the auditorium. During this the music gradually takes on a manic, obsessive character. The text of the final movement, an aria for the singer, consists of the four definitions in the order indicated above. At the conclusion of this the musicians leave the stage, one by one, uttering a single parting word in the direction of the singer, whose delivery by now has turned into incoherent mumbling, while the lights dim to near darkness. The last sounds heard offstage are those of an Indian elephant bell and two toy harmonicas.

LA TOURANGELLE[9]

Following the multihued world of *Foci* I found myself engaged in the composition of a kind of opera entitled *La Tourangelle* ("The Woman of Tours"). The impetus to write the piece which eventually became my first opera came through a commission, offered to me in person by John P.L. Roberts, then head of CBC Radio-Music, in 1970. He asked me to write a piece, about twenty to twenty-five minutes in duration, that would express "the search for order and meaning in life through the focus of religion – the search for God, in other words." My first re-action to this was to look for a Canadian historical figure whose life would have exemplified this theme. Through the advice of Laurier La Pierre I was led to Marie de l'Incarnation, Ursuline, a pioneer figure in the early history of La Nouvelle France.

The way I came to tell Marie's story came about, once again, organi-cally. While assembling the text and composing the music I constantly found myself questioning Marie, members of her family, her contem-porary associates, and historical personages. I looked for evidence of prevailing societal customs, laws, attitudes, church dogma, and more. I also looked for persons and books in whose example and teaching Marie had found inspiration. I also looked into Marie's legacy. I "heard" the voices of teachers teaching about Marie's doings. I looked for, and found, information about the cult of Marie among today's Ursulines. I visited the convent on rue Parloire in Quebec City, and also looked for Marie's "traces" in Tours. I sought out persons for whom Marie's life is still a central concern.

What was the result of all this? At one moment I felt that, in a way, I was beginning to know Marie's mind. This gave me the confidence necessary for "inventing" her voice and what may be expressed through that voice. Of course, it was but an illusion of authenticity. Nevertheless, to invent even a pseudo-Marie I needed the temerity that only that kind of questioning could begin to "authorize." After reaching that phase all I needed to do was to listen to my inner voices (in this I had the splendid example of Marie herself, whose closest models dwelt in her own "inner voices.") This advised me also about diverse contexts and situations. It allowed me to hear "voices," first of all those of Marie herself. At one moment the idea came to me that Marie should have "triple" voice, synthesized through the polyphony of three sopranos, enabling me to portray a complex mind at times in conversation within itself. The two live male voices were to take on a series of different roles. Many recorded voices (French as well as En-glish) were to populate the scenes, enact roles, and help create the contexts of situations. Responding to a clause in the commission, the work is bilingual (French/English) in character. I liked this proviso, because I thought Marie had a message for the entire country. That message ought to become comprehensible to all in the land.

A few more comments about one of the work's seven movements, "Isaac," might be useful here. The context of situation is the following: Marie, a single, widowed mother of a twelve-year-old son, decides to obey a "call" and join the Ursuline convent in Tours as a novice. She is about thirty-two years old at the time. Her decision evokes strenuous objections from her family and the town. People are aware that her step was taken (and authorized) despite the canon law that stipulates that no parent of a young child may enter religious orders. (But church authorities regarded Marie as an exception, on account of her extraordinary talents and religious fervour.) This section, "Isaac," enacts the complex situation in Tours to which Marie's decision gave rise. We hear the voices of gossiping townsfolk, and the voice of Marie behind the convent's door, under the double burden of fear and anguish. Stern voices cite the text of the canonical law. The collective voices of bands of children are also heard. They seem to be having a fun time, while making a nuisance of themselves, both in French and in English. Surprisingly a voice anachronistically cites the words "fight ... flight." The scene turns from tense to ugly. The voices become menacing and nearly incoherent. Marie, in a state of extreme agitation, emits piercing, wailing vocalises. The choral-orchestral texture is realized through a polyphony of polyphonies. All seems to be progressing toward a "dense" climax. After this has been achieved, the movement gradually calms down and reaches an expression of exhaustion ... At the very end one hears a deep sigh of relief – a physiological-semiotic signal indicating the end of a crisis and perhaps also the resolution of a conflict. Marie is now free to pursue her chosen vocation, without undue pangs of conscience, as she had taken steps, earlier, to secure admission of her son to a Benedictine institution.

CODA

The whole of *La Tourangelle* and the dramatic works that followed, each and every one, owes a debt to its predecessors (as well as to the relevant broader repertoire). *Winthrop, Thisness, Traces* (*Tikkun*), and now the work-in-progress, *Millennial Mall* (*Lady Diotima's Walk*),[10] all sought means by which to express individual character as well as depict groups through their choral expression. In so doing, they create context and situation that inform about the mind and the heart as engaged in the ongoing process of coping, making judgments, and decisions based on them, or to reflect a more modest yet no less difficult objective of persisting in the world with as much integrity as possible. I am at peace with an assessment that would allege that these pieces explore an imaginary boundary line between "reality" (what *is* reality?) and a more or less abstract representation.

There is no need to be concerned with a possible dearth of projects, given the infinite diversity of contexts one can "visit" transported on the magic carpet of Bakhtin's notion of the chronotope. Each of these, in turn, is populated with people representing an immense psychosocial diversity. And all of them move along in the streams of time. They meet, form associations, act in relation to people, to ideas, to agendas, displaying their share of freedom and power, joys as well as frustrations, and pain that can and does, at times, threaten – even destroy – cohesion.

Most of my vocal and choral works sample this vast reservoir of topics. Their individual ways of doing this developed in their own manner within the framework of my experience. Through this shared orientation, and through the particularities of my ways of working, these pieces appear to me to constitute a kind of "continuing thread." Whether they will appear likewise to others, I cannot claim to know.

NOTES

1 See B. Malinowski, "The Problem of Meaning in Primitive Languages," suppl. 1 in *The Meaning of Meaning*, ed. C.K. Ogden and I.A. Richards (London: Kegan Paul, 1921).

2 M.M. Bakhtin, *The Dialogic Imagination*, ed. Michael Holquist and trans. Caryl Emerson and Michael Holquist (Austin: University of Texas Press, 1981).

3 The score of *Comments* is available from the Canadian Music Centre.

4 *Cento* (Toronto: Berandol Music, 1968).

5 "Making of *Cento*," *The Canada Music Book* 1 (spring-summer 1970): 81–89; ellipsis added.

6 *Foci* (Toronto: Berandol Music, 1972).

7 "About *Foci*," *Artscanada* 28 (April-May 1971): 57–9.

8 Horace B. English and Ava Champney English, *A Comprehensive Dictionary of Psychological and Psychoanalytical Terms: A Guide to Usage* (New York: David McKay Co., 1958).

9 *La Tourangelle* (Toronto: Berandol Music, 1977).

10 [The score of *Millennial Mall (Lady Diotima's Walk)* was completed in February 1999. Eds.]

17 Millennial Mall (Lady Diotima's Walk): A Voice-Drama for the Imagination

1 Enter Lady Diotima

Finally here ... I'm late ... came from a distance ... My name ... Lady Diotima – Diotima for short ... At one time I was called "Diotima the sorceress," but I never cared for that tag. Others remembered me as the noted courtesan, a friend of the wise ... Oh love! They treated me with respect when it came to this theme ... They also listened raptly when I discoursed about ambivalence ... about feeling to be *in* a thing and *out* of it *at one and the same time.* Take, for example, this mall, which we are about to enter ... They call it the Millennial Mall now ... a bustling place this ... and while there, I know, I shall feel a part of it and also apart from it, *at one and the same time* ... You, too, have known this before, I'm certain ... Let us then move on ... We are now at the gate ... Do you hear the murmur of the crowd inside? They are at their usual games, which they play with a new twist, I hear ... We also played them before ... but perhaps not with the same flair. Are you ready to enter?

I now see people approaching ... They seem to have a message ... Let us hear what they have to say ...

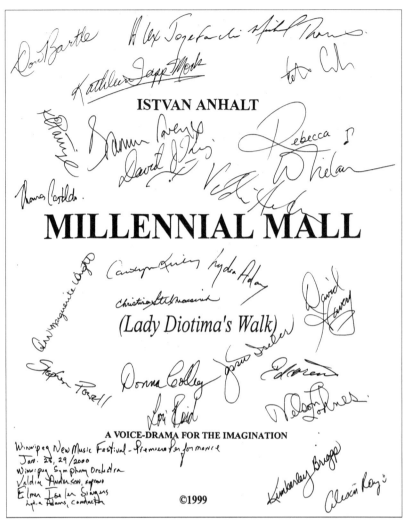

ISTVAN ANHALT

MILLENNIAL MALL

(Lady Diotima's Walk)

A VOICE-DRAMA FOR THE IMAGINATION

©1999

Title page of the score; signed by Valdine Anderson, Bramwell Tovey, Lydia Adams, Jessie Iseler, and the twenty members of the Elmer Iseler Singers; a surprise present to the composer.

2   The Mall Flag Song no. 1
We are the Mall People,
the Traders of the Mall.
Our "World" you ask ...
Yes, a "Global Carnival"!
Our flag? Blood-red, yellow, and purple.
Our "Emblem" for the "Task"?
Some say: the "Mask."
Wrong! The "Demand" is all!
The "Demand of Life" is all!

3   Reality Check (Mall Style)
Life is short! So
we live for the day!
Freedom in seeking pleasure
is our way ...
All the way.

Life is brief! Very brief! So
we live for the hour!
Hope for the sweet;
avoid the sour.
Deprecate our doubt,
and play up the need.

Life passes fast! So
to our sense
time is the presence;
it is the essence!
And when all boils down,
night turning to dawn,
what's left is dollars and cents.

We hold that
everything has its price;
try once, or even thrice,
at the end you will find
money is the ultimate prize.

So, like it or not,
everything it can buy:
separation ... a closer tie ...

loyalty ... betrayal ...
on the way to when we die ...

But for now we say:
Live for the day!
Live for the hour!
By the fountain of youth,
the source of all power,
you shall bend, bow,
and we all shall pray.

4 The Mall Workout and Spa
Youth-cult, youth-cult,
young body cult.
Youth-cult, youth-cult,
youth beauty cult.
Young beautiful body-cult.
The Mall Workout and Spa
Body-work, body-work.
Youth, health, and pleasure;
long life to treasure.
We work on body beautiful,
long life!
Body-work, body-work.
We exercise. We exercise.
Youth work, young body work, beauty work.
Position!
Fall into line!
Obey and follow the command, the beat!
Obey the whip-crack,
the rat-pack, the lead!
Bend now; sway now;
Swing to the beat
Sway now; bow now;
Stay with the beat.
Obey the whip-crack;
follow the rat-pack.
Pump, thump.
Rap – yell; rap – grunt.
Unlimited health benefit.
Beautiful life!
A long life!
A youthful, pleasure-filled life!

A beautiful, delightful life!
Sway and swing.
Stretch stream, body lean, in a dream.
Jump now! Jump now!
Hang on the beat!
Drum, yeah! Drum, yeah!
Once more; twice more.
Slow down, slow down now.
Tread water now.
Freely pant …
Gently walking, strolling … slowly …
A few more steps …

and now to the showers.
Soothing jet-stream.
More jet-stream.
Body lean.
Slapping, tapping.
Now the warm towels;
gentle soft hands …
kneading the skin …
caress … soft music,
and fragrant, balmy air …
balmy air … air …

5 *The Scent Shop (Many Scents)*
Here are scents, many scents …
lures …
in the best sense,
to enhance allures
with fragrance
that lingers … endures.

Scents … many scents …
to accent presence,
to imprint a memory-trace
that stands for a face.

With this device
a promise of paradise
wafts through the air …
on drifting atoms of rare
oils and balms.

The choice is vast! These
vials hold flower
extracts: rose, lavender,
hyacinth, and the tender
scents of orange-blossoms and lime,
fine barks, woods … and many more.

The South sends creams:
vanilla, almond paste;
Tibet, for the exotic taste
The Tonkin – musk perfume.
The sperm whale's gift:
ambergris … to induce dreams.

The cosmetic art
of Egypt's priests: a part
of this trade …
And so, the mysterious aid
Araby's beauticians of old
exchanged for fortunes in gold.

Ageless science, indeed …
Fantasy – dream turning to deed …
irresistible …
fuelling attraction,
binding, bonding us,
leading to action …
intoxication …
coupling, enjoyment …
wild … wild love,
mixing with torment
to release and gentle embrace
to caress in a wonder-filled daze.

6 *The Mall Flag Song no. 2*
We are the Mall People, Yes!
The magicians of the Mall.
Our "World," you ask …
a timeless, tireless Carnival!
Our flag?
Still blood-red, yellow, and purple.
Our task: to work

as well as need be ...
for your next return call.

And now:

7 *The Fashion Show*
Here they come! Here they come!
Birds of Paradise ... on the runway ...
gliding, swaying, sliding ...
spring gait ... dance steps ...
exquisite ... delicate ... fragile ...
weightless ... in soft silks,
ribbons and lace ...
pulsing, waving ...
sumptuous sculpted gowns ...
dresses ... belts ... and shawls ...
to enhance these shapes ...
skin tone and face ...
ivory, pale, dusky, or dark ...
centuries-old genetic designs ...
from all corners of the world ...
The choicest, bejewelled,
beautiful daughters of men ...
here on display ...
with hair in rainbow hues ...
tossed and teased into fantasy ...
to flutter ...
the brightest plumage of
faraway birds ...
with eyes high and far ...
gliding and sliding,
swaying, sashaying,
ambling, dissembling,
enticing ...
their premise: all promise ...
these Birds of Paradise ...
known since time immemorial ...
so the hearsay ...
they tempted and lured the sons of the gods,
who fell ... fell ...
from their mountain-peak fastness
at their feet ...

to worship those feet ... irresistible ...
Then children born from this union
became the demons of the world ...
to watch over our spells, games, and magic ...
All this is plain enough to see,
as the old-young beautiful daughters of men ...
still at the old routine ...
this timeless trance ...
glide ...
stride ... all pride ...
into eternal destiny ...

*

Hey!
Somebody got shot. Quick!
Call an ambulance ... !
The police ...!

8 Bamboozle Video
Now you see it ... now you don't ...
a car within a water-spray,
the ground rushes away
under the wings of a hurtling plane ... a skirt
flashing ... intimate
flesh ... a diver in flight ...
a soaring bird ... choice shots of scenery
hurry by ... a close embrace ...
a snarling dog ...
dissolve in a blur ... to ape
grooming ape ... an alligator yawn ...
a school of fish careening
by a reef ... now tundra ...
desert ... a glimpse of rain forest
from the air ... balloons ...
no reason at all
for the before or the aft ...
to startle and delight
is the name of the game ...
with all the world's fame at the fingertips
of the one in front of the tube,
or so ... it seems to say ...
All illusion ... con-game ... sleight of hand ...
Yes, we know ... the aim of it all ...

is to anchor the eye ... the mind ...
to delay ... delay the moment
when a jaded finger ends
it all ... with a flick ... Enough!
But ... but not as yet ... because ...

9 *Advertising Unlimited (Lesson in Magic)*
Now hear the trumpet-call.
Pay attention!
Attention please!
Attention to us, the poets of the Mall:
the magicians of soft words
who know how to awaken desire
and fuel the fire
in the mind.

We offer all kinds of release,
possession, symbolic hints,
to spring you to ease
in fantasy, dream-work, fetish ...
and promise the fulfillment
of your most secret wish.

Pay attention! Attention to us ...
See how it's done ...

Example:
Young males chasing athletic prowess
to attract females with reckless dare ...
We give them fantasy footwear
With the name of the victory-goddess,
and our promise: the rank of an ace
and success in this age-old race.

Example:
Young women who primp and prime,
as many flowers to attract the worker bees.
Sheer enchantment, magic and mimes,
enhanced by finery, pomp, tease ...
and our choicest rhymes.

Yes ... we know how to sway.

Pay attention to what we say.

We are Society's Engineers!

Watch us as we sway!
Our product: success, success, success!
All goals attained, no less!

What?
What did you say?
We didn't hear you well ...
Repeat! Repeat!
What?
You ask *us, here*
About "moral value"?

Ha!
The wrong stress!
The wrong address!
... and irrelevant!

We view
that such concerns belong
to pulpit and pew!

Yeah ...

10 The Mall Flag Song no. 3
We are the Mall People,
the Merchants of the Mall.
We work hard. Very hard.
This place never sleeps ...
Its commitment:
to anticipate
your myriad material needs;
to help you participate
in the good life;
to find happiness
of a certain kind.
It's Your Demand!
But be aware ...
Let the buyer beware ...
the voice is yours

which is responsible
for the final choice.

11 Millennial Tanking Now (The Global Carnival)
The Global Tank Machine! The Global Tank Machine!
Millennial Tanking Now!
The Ultimate Faceless Tank Trade!
Global, No-Face Tank Trade!
Our Ultimate Total Carnival!
Transactional Pulse Code Carnival!
Paradigm Shift! Paradigm Shift!
Paradise Gift!
Join Now This Total Tank Train!
This Ultimate Marvel of Techno-Brain!
So Place Your Trust in This Techno-Creed!
This Is Almost All That You'll Ever Need!
Irresistible! Irresistible!
Ambivalence Is Out, Is Finally Out!
No More Doubt! No More Doubt!
We Are the Top of the Line!
Watch Out for Our Every Sign!
The Ultimate Harpax Eidolon!
The Glitch-Free, Forever-New Obsolon!
Millennial Tanking Now!
Fully Operational! Our Global Carnival!
Then Turn On the Greed-Grid!
Switch On the Grid-Greed!
Techno-Creed! Techno-Creed!
Join the Worldwide Data Storm!
We Give the Form!
We Set the Norm! We *Are* the Norm!
Then Push 1, Push 2, 3, and 4!
And Get Our Online Perks Galore!
Now Is the Time! Now Is the Time!
Many New Options On the Line!
The Cost Is Slight!
The Price Is Right!
Service Assured Day and Night!
Don't Be Left Out!
Join the Crowd!
Share the Shout!
For Us All! For Us All!
This Is the Global …

The Total ...
The Millennial Carnival!
Our Carnival!

12 Diotima Leaves the Mall[1]

(Dialogue)
The head reels ... it needs a pause to look for
the aim of this busy scene ... with its appeals,
stresses and strain ...
One is left with questions ...
To the point? ... Or are they in vain?
Who are the masters of this game?
Who set the rules? In whose name?
Who ends rejoicing? Who's left with pain?

And now the time to go is near. One leaves
this place with relief, yet also with regret ...
Yes, this Mall is an enticing place ... a bustle,
for sure ... also delicate ... It needs care ...
watching ... (Did you notice the dense smoke yesterday? It hung like a threat in the air ...) And
now I hear a voice ... it calls me back home ...
I shall go in peace ... back to my garden ... to the
stillness of a long-dormant past in the shadows
of memory ... This scene for now ... (pulpit and pew, perhaps) ... yes
... as the shades descend ... slowly descend ... into the embrace of
sleep ...
Then ... as if in a dream ... I hear myself singing
the song of

Love's Gifts
The gift of silence
reserved for words of a friend ...

The gift of touch
for someone in need of re-assurance ...

The gift of a smile
to one who is short of hope ...

The gift of support
by an unseen hand ...

The gift of selfless love for a child
... and the love of a child
for someone who is ripe with years ...

Companions for life in love ...

The awe in sight of
nature's wonders ...

marvelling at the
mystery of existence ...

surrender to the
enigmas of the cosmos ...

and of thought thinking itself ...

ABOUT THE LIBRETTO OF *MILLENNIAL MALL (LADY DIOTIMA'S WALK)*

The title of the work, which came in response to certain things accumulating in my mind, was the first indication of the potentiality of a new piece: it sounded "good," it had the right kind of connotative dimensions, and it was ever so uncomplicated, that is to say, "direct" in allusion. This last characteristic suited the central idea of a work that would aim to get at the essence of contemporary North American society through certain kinds of probings, enactments, and the like, all expressed in ways that could be expected to be intelligible to and accepted by the listeners whom one would want to reach.

The inclusion of a Lady Diotima figure came for these reasons. While I knew that the piece would be in large measure a choral work (I was inspired by having heard some superb Scandinavian choirs in June 1997), I felt that I should balance this choral component with a solo lyric soprano voice. Ever since the completion of *Traces*, I was longing to compose for such a voice. In doing this I was influenced by two Diotima figures in literature. The first of these is the Viennese beauty Diotima Tuzzi, one of the central figures of Robert Musil's novel, *The Man Without Qualities*. The second was the Diotima in Plato's *Symposium*, the wise woman of Mantinea who had commented on love in such a way that Socrates himself accepted her as an authority on the subject. I only found out about the third Diotima (Hölderlin's) after the first draft of the libretto was finished, from the Germanist Anthony Riley, a friend and colleague at Queen's University. My Diotima was to be somewhat different from these predecessors. She was to take the role of a "pyschopomp," who will, figuratively, be holding the hand of those who venture into the "lower regions" of this Millennial Mall. At the outset I didn't know how I would depict her. She had to (and did) evolve in the course of writing and, subsequently, in the course of the composition of the score.

The choice and the nature of places to visit in this mall offered themselves readily. The dominant points of view in the selection were the degree of relevance and strength of focus. As a result of these considerations, places such as the Mall Workout and Spa, the Scent Shop, the Fashion-Show, Advertising Unlimited, and the like, demanded inclusion, so to say. The section entitled "The Global Tank Machine" was made to be a climactic part of the whole, as it represents (enacts) the spirit of one of the most dynamic aspects of the environment and the era of the theme. To make it capable of achieving this objective I found that the language that imposed itself came close in places to the affects that express brutality, coarseness, and a certain kind of banality of a manipulative sort.

The question of what axiological background to convey was uppermost in my thoughts throughout the writing. All along I found myself constantly having to question my preferences, discovering propensities that, in places, came close to being prejudices. I had to battle my own implicatures, the unwanted ones, that kept on oozing into the work whenever the "control" slackened. I wanted the piece to be strong, forthright, and not too difficult to understand (at those levels that I could identify). Yet its directness was to reveal numerous "floors" below its surface, allowing the discerning reader/listener exposure to it at a variety of levels, each intended to yield insight and, I hope, also a certain kind of pleasure. Indeed, pleasure is a central theme in this work, as it is within the North American society depicted in the work as a whole. (It was after the completion of the score that I learned to perceive this orientation as also close to that which is known as the Cyrenaic school of thought that flourished in the fourth century B.C.E.) One of the potentially puzzling elements in Diotima's opening aria is the unexpected reference to her ambivalence of "feeling to be *in* a thing and *out* of it *at one and the same time.*" What could she mean by this? The answer becomes evident in the course of the work, and perhaps a full understanding of it might only be attainable through the creative act of subsequent reflection. If so, this would aptly suggest the way this detail found its way into the text, almost like an imperative afterthought. It could be (should be?) taken as reference to my own feeling of being a part of this whole, yet in a sense also "apart" from it, so that I could be in a position to see it from various points of view, from a distance, so to say.

Like her inventor, the guide – enacted by Diotima – also becomes a participant, or to put it a different way, she shifts back and forth between "acting participant" on the one hand and "commentator" on the other, demanding constant alertness on the part of the audience (or the reader) to follow her as she moves from one posture to the other. This process is in ready evidence in "The Scent Shop" and "The Fashion Show" sections. And where is the evidence of Diotima's authority as an exceptional commentator on love? One hears the answer in the two sections just mentioned. Yet this cannot be taken as an adequate substantiation. These are the sections that emphasize pleasures, love for the senses, and perhaps also the demands of the "selfish gene," to invoke current parlance. But where are the other manifestations of love? It seems the work is close to its conclusion when Diotima, *this* Diotima, reveals the modalities and range of her understanding of the word "love."

The four Diotima arias (nos. 1, 5, 7, 12), the three flag songs, for a six-part chamber vocal ensemble, and the five sections for the large choral group (nos. 3, 4, 8, 9, 11) align themselves in a nearly symmetrical plan and follow each other in a closely integrated sequence. The subtitle "Voice-Drama for the Imagination" implies that I am aiming here at an ideal, imaginary enactment suggested by the words – and even more strongly by the music – that would take place in the mind of the reader/listener who is unfettered by visual cues, apart from the presence of the performers on the stage who distract only minimally from the acoustical channel. What follows is a commentary on the individual sections.

1 Enter Lady Diotima

The reader is not told where Diotima comes from in such great haste that she seems to be out of breath. With tongue in cheek she reveals some of the ways she has been referred to in times gone by. Where is this visitor coming from? History? World literature? Legend? Magic lore? Another place? She prefers to leave us in uncertainty about this. The implication is that she could have come from here, there, everywhere ... whatever the distance may be. Yet she is also obviously a contemporary, with an intimate understanding of what is being enacted in this mall. We readily accept her as an informed guide as we enter the "premises."

2 The Mall Flag Song no. 1

We now encounter a small group of the mall's professionals. These are the ones who work behind the scenes. They look after the displays, always keeping in mind the visitors, us. They are there to serve us and while doing this they are mindful of our responses, reactions. They convey a sense of realism and objectivity.

3 *Reality Check (Mall Style)*

This is the first statement by a large group of visitors expressing the mindset that is behind their presence in the mall. This statement might even be taken as their contribution to the very existence of *this* mall. What do they say, perhaps even emphasize? (a) We live for the moment; (b) let us have as much pleasure as possible; (c) everything can be purchased with money.

4 *The Mall Workout and Spa*

Suddenly the scene changes to that of the Mall Workout and Spa. The themes here are: the cult of the body; the ideal of the beauty of young bodies; people past their youth also aiming at the body-ideal of this youth cult; the body beautiful as an axiological objective; and there is a hint that behind all this striving there might be a potential loss of concern with other aspects of existence. To what extent might such a driven attitude be related to the destructiveness of a chimerical quest for perpetual youth and a yearning for an unrealistically extended lifespan?

5 *The Scent Shop (Many Scents)*

This Scent Shop conjures up the ambience of the "gardens of Adonis," the substances and sensations that have been a part of civilization since time immemorial across diverse cultures. It points to one of the most potent magical devices for the living as well as for the dead. Fragrance is closely related to sexuality and procreation. It is a part of early science and medicine and serves also as a central element of olfactory charms. As a key element in cosmetics perfume is a powerful economic agent as well. Diotima tells us about these connections and at the end of the section even demonstrates the effects of such enhancing aids in an implied personal encounter. All this doesn't prevent us from considering ancient censuring voices (for example, that of Tertullian in his *De Idololatria*) that warn about the supposed dangers that certain religious beliefs attributed to the use of such olfactory devices.

6 *The Mall Flag Song no. 2*

This section calls attention once again to the "professionals" of this mall.

7 *The Fashion Show*

Here we focus once again on Diotima. With the help of a women's chorus, she both describes and comments on what happens in this fashion show. The dual appeals of feminine and material beauty are displayed here in a play of bewitchment. The material means and the choreography are different, but the purpose behind this scene and that of the Scent Shop is identical. Perhaps to our surprise, midway we are reminded of a legend that is part of the Hebrew Bible: the story of the "beautiful daughters of men" and their attraction for the "sons of God." From this union children were born, supposedly a race of "supermen" (the Jerusalem Bible, Genesis 6, translates the Hebrew *nephilim* as "the heroes of days gone by, the famous men"; "supermen" appears in a note). Right after the reference to this tale follows the account of the Flood, and one is left free to decide whether or not there might be a causal link between the two events, but one thing seems certain – the practice of "powerful men" (the sons of God?) marrying the "beautiful daughters of men." The reference here to this ancient legend has antecedents; one of the most notable can be found in the *Book of Enoch* (dating from the second and first centuries B.C.E.), which embellishes the story with much detail. The concluding event is meant to function as a startling and shocking surprise, yet it is also a reminder of the gradually decreasing force of surprise in connection with such shootings, which are becoming more and more common in certain parts of North American society. (The presence of this episode *within* a fashion show calls to mind the murder of the Italian-American fashion designer, Giovanni Versace, which occurred two or three years ago.)

8 Bamboozle Video
There is a blatant discontinuity in the text of "Bamboozle Video." Each and every image called up stands by itself, unrelated to what precedes and what follows. The notions of cause and consequence are irrelevant here, with the possible exception of their rigorous exclusion. The content-repertoire is fact-oriented and refers solely to the visual domain at a superfast pace. (The viewer is expected to concentrate, in an effort to identify the images that hurtle by at the limit of perceptual speed, and often beyond, in the television sequences this section imitates.) Why the rush? Why the constant surprise? Why the unconnectedness? What is being referred to? Are some symbolic references hinted at here? Is this a carnival ride? Are the "champions" those who manage to hang on and not fall off this senseless merry-go-round?

9 Advertising Unlimited (Lesson in Magic)
Social engineering is the theme here, through a look at one of its central domains. This is the territory of Peitho, the goddess of persuasion, the core component of rhetoric. The masters of this art speak here with authority and candour. They offer insight into their workshop, and there is an obvious sense of pride in what they regard as their accomplishment. The recitation is forceful and near celebratory. Then the

discourse is unexpectedly brought to a halt by some questions from someone who remains unidentified, questions that bring up considerations that these masters of persuasion regard as being out-of-place and wholly irrelevant. The tone of the narrative turns sour here and even roughly dismissive, to the point of a thinly camouflaged insult. One must conclude that the unwelcome questions probe deeply.

10   The Mall Flag Song no. 3

This is the most explicitly candid of the three flag songs. It shows practitioners of fair, honest trade who feel a pride in serving the buyer while making a well-earned living for themselves. They warn, "buyer beware ... / the voice is yours / which is responsible / for the final choice." Suddenly we start to feel that these professionals of the mall just *might* refer here to something more important than the purchase of a dress or a car. Isn't there a more momentous warning hidden here? Are we not reminded here of choices that are more vital? Is this merchants' voice perhaps the voice of a spiritual counsellor? If this is indeed taken as such, then the following section constitutes a jarring contrast, to which the reader/listener is invited to respond.

11   Millennial Tanking Now! (The Global Carnival)

Here we are in the superfast, driven world of contemporary technology. This is the message of electronic wonders perhaps not yet invented, but sure to be on the market in a few months' time. The narrative is robust and contains not a shadow of doubt of being the only valid option for the foreseeable future. The obsolescence of certain vocations, certain human temperaments, and certain choices as to "being in the world" is implied here. The proselytizing language employed tolerates no doubt. Everything touched upon is presented as being inevitable, "according to plan." The controllers of this vast system remain unidentified, though. One doesn't learn where the orders are coming from, nor what is in store in the short and long terms. It is not possible to extrapolate from the "here" to what may be coming the day after tomorrow. The wisest option seems to be to grab and hold on to a handle as one tries to leap on board this hurtling bandwagon. But wait ... can one, should one, trust without the most careful reflection on what is being enacted here? Could one ask for respite? Or a brief pause, which could provide for sober reflection as to what to take and what to decline for the time being, or altogether? This insistent goading, for example; this fevered language, which seems to be contrary to what some souls need, at least in the long run, or as a steady diet. Yes, it can be great fun to spend time in the fairground at carnival time ... but at some point one gets sated and longs for a change, which might be sought as intimate face-to-face contact, or a leisurely stroll in a park far from the insistent appeals of near anonymous giant organizations that manage to "intrude" in surprising ways ... One longs to be allowed to entertain dissent *and* be secure at one and the same time ... And now, one sees Diotima turning ... is Diotima leaving the mall? Let's follow her ... Perhaps she has more to tell us outside the "gates" of this Millennial Mall ...

12 Diotima Leaves the Mall (Dialogue)
Diotima stops at the gate of the mall, asks a few difficult-to-answer questions, hesitates ... and then resolves to go. We follow her ... She appears to be oblivious of us ... Now she appears to be speaking to herself. Perhaps we can overhear this interior dialogue ... She seems to be still ambivalent in her feelings regarding this mall ... She voices concern about its prospects, but now we see her turning her back to the mall, as if putting it "behind her" ... We snatch a word or two of what she says: "my garden ... the past ... memory ... shadows ... descend ... into sleep." Then, surprisingly, she mentions singing in her sleep ... What would she want to sing about? Of Love's Gifts ... Of course! Love! This is the missing clue to Diotima's character, her personhood. She almost *owes* us the unveiling of her secret knowledge about love, which made her the unique historic/fictional figure in the imagination and memory of so many people over many centuries ... And as we listen to this song we become aware of why she was revered as a key figure whenever thoughtful people started to question and probe, in their own souls preferably, what love is all about.

Afterword

There are numerous voices implied in this text. Often they can be readily attributed to one person or another, or a group. But here and there one becomes aware of choices, alternative apperceptions and the like. Diotima herself is easily identifiable in most places. But whenever she changes roles from commentator-guide to one who participates in the enactment of a scene, the shift is not always self-evident. At places, the choral voices of the larger ensemble set the stage, the background, and elsewhere they are the ones who *show* what is being enacted and how. They are the people who make up the populace in this mall. Then there are the specialists: the Mall's professionals; and elsewhere a group appears that identifies itself as being "society's engineers." The technicians who bring us the "Bamboozle Video" form yet another subgroup. Most of this is easy enough to attribute. But now and then there suddenly appears a commentary that could rightly be taken as the voice of the author speaking. This play of voices constitutes a channel in itself. How much attention one wants to give to it will depend on the preferences of the individual reader/hearer as s/he conducts a personal dialogue with this Millennial Mall.

A Post-Premiere Note

To my ears, the music of *Millennial Mall (Lady Diotima's Walk)*, as performed by the group of outstanding interpreters in Winnipeg under the direction of Bramwell Tovey, featuring Valdine Anderson as Diotima, the Elmer Iseler Singers, and the Winnipeg Symphony Orchestra, on 28–29 January 2000, confirmed my expectations: it expressed a positive, hope-filled message through melody, rhythm, harmony, tone colour and form. It implied that much of the world of the mall is brimming with vigour, is enticing and deeply rooted, eventhough these characteristics had to be allowed to remain compatible with occasional allusions to ambivalence, questioning, or doubt. In light of this, the supposed "truth" of the work might be best thought of residing in the very interplay of all these elements and their potential reciprocal conciliation in the mind of an imaginary listener.

19 February 2000

NOTES

1 After having heard me read an earlier version of this work, Christopher and Adele Crowder, James and Carol Leith, and Anthony and Maria Riley expressed constructive criticism, which resulted in my changing the ending of section 12. I thank them for their help.

APPENDIX

List of Istvan Anhalt's Compositions and Writings[1]

COMPOSITIONS

The date in the left-hand column refers to the date of completion. Revised versions and publication dates, where applicable, follow in square brackets. [Lost and incomplete works are not included in this list.]

1942 *Ünnepek (Feasts)* (SATB chorus) (text: Bible, Gábor Devecseri, Homer)
1946 Capriccio (piano)
1946 *Concerto in stilo di Handel* (oboes, bassoons, horns, strings)
1947 String Quartet
1947 Piano Sonata [revised version 1951]
1947 *Six Songs from Na Conxy Pan* (Hat Dal Na Conxy Panból) (voice and piano) (text: Sándor Weöres) [Eng. version, 1984]
1949 Interludium (strings, timpani, piano)
1951 *L'Arc-en-ciel* (The Rainbow) (ballet in three lights for two pianos)
1951 *Funeral Music* (flute, clarinet, bassoon, horn, 2 violins, 2 violas, 2 cellos)
1951 "Journey of the Magi" (baritone and piano) (text: T.S. Eliot)
1951 "Psalm XIX – A Benediction" (baritone and piano) (text: A.M. Klein)
1951 "Son Scheorim" (SATB chorus, organ) (text: traditional)
1951 "Sonnet" (mezzo-soprano, piano) (text: Beatrice R. Hayes)
1951 *Three Songs of Love* (SSA chorus) (text: Walter de la Mare; folk poetry) [revised version, SSA chorus, flute, clarinet, 1997]
1952 *Three Songs of Death* (SATB chorus) (texts: William Davenant, Robert Herrick)

1953 Piano *Trio* (violin, cello, piano)

1954 *Comments* (contralto, violin, cello, piano) (text: *Montreal Star* press clippings)

1954 Fantasia (piano) [Toronto: Berandol Music, 1972]

1954 Violin Sonata (violin, piano)

1955 *Chansons d'aurore* (soprano, flute, piano) (text: André Verdet)

1958 Symphony (orchestra) [Toronto: BMI Canada, 1963]

1959 *Electronic Composition No. 1 ("Sine Nomine I")*

1959 *Electronic Composition No. 2 ("Sine Nomine II")*

1960 Electronic Composition No. 3 ("Birds and Bells")

1961 *Electronic Composition No. 4* ("On the Beach")

1967 *Symphony of Modules* (orchestra)

1967 *Cento* ("Cantata Urbana") (12-part mixed chorus and tape) (text: Eldon Grier) [Toronto, BMI Canada, 1968]

1969 *Foci* (mixed media: soprano, chamber orchestra, and tape) (libretto: collage by I. Anhalt) [Toronto: Berandol Music, 1972]

1974 "La Fuite" from *La Tourangelle* (piano)

1975 *La Tourangelle* (opera) (libretto: collage by I. Anhalt) [Toronto: Berandol Music, 1982]

1980 "The Bell-Man" [from *Three Songs of Death*] (chorus, organ, and bells) (text: Robert Herrick)

1983 *A Little Wedding Music* (soprano and piano or organ) (text: Gerard Manley Hopkins) [Toronto: Berandol Music, 1985]

1983 *Winthrop* (opera) (libretto: collage by I. Anhalt)

1985 *A Wedding Carol* (soprano and piano or organ) (text: I. Anhalt)

1985 *Thisness* (duo-drama for mezzo soprano and piano) (text: I. Anhalt)

1986–87 *Simulacrum* (orchestra)

1987 *SparkskrapS* (orchestra)

1989 *Sonance•Resonance (Welche Töne?)* (orchestra)

1992 *Doors … shadows (Glenn Gould in memory)* (string quartet movement)

1995 *Traces (Tikkun)* (opera) (libretto: I. Anhalt)

1996 *Galambabmalag: the Halloween Witch and 24 Other Easy Pieces for Recorder (Solos and Duets)* [Toronto: Berandol Music, 1996]

1999 *Millennial Mall (Lady Diotima's Walk)* (opera) (libretto: I. Anhalt)

PUBLISHED WRITINGS

1961 "Electronic Music: A New Experience in Sound." *JMC [Jeunesses musicales of Canada] Chronicle* 7, 4 (February): 3

1970 "The Making of *Cento.*" *Canada Music Book* 1 (spring-summer): 81–9

1971 "About *Foci.*" *Artscanada* 28 (April-May): 57–8

1971 "La musique électronique" and "L'Histoire de *Cento.*" In *Musiques du Kébèk*, ed. Raoul Duguay, 13–17; 21–8. Montreal: Éditions du jour

1972 "Composing with Speech." *Proceedings of the Seventh International Congress of Phonetic Sciences*, 447–51. Paris: Mouton

1973 "Luciano Berio's *Sequenza III*." *Canada Music Book* 7 (autumn-winter): 23–60

1977 "About One's Place and Voice." In *Identities: The Impact of Ethnicity on Canadian Society*, ed. W. Isajiw, 39–45. Toronto: Peter Martin Associates Ltd.

1979 "På spaning efter rösten I dag – reflexioner av en tonsättare," *Artes* 2 (Stockholm): 58–74

1981 "John Beckwith." In *Encyclopedia of Music in Canada*, ed. Helmut Kallmann, Gilles Potvin, Kenneth Winters, 90–1. Toronto: University of Toronto Press. Updated entry in 2nd ed. (1992), 98–100

1983 "*Winthrop*: The Work, the Theme, the Story." *Canadian University Music Review* 4: 184–95; reprinted in this volume, 375–84

1984 *Alternative Voices: Essays on Contemporary Vocal and Choral Composition.* Toronto: University of Toronto Press

1985 Liner notes for *Anthology of Canadian Music – István Anhalt*. Vol. 22. Radio Canada International, sound recording; excerpt reprinted in this volume, 371–4

1985 "What Tack to Take? An Autobiographical Sketch (Life in Progress ...)." *Queen's Quarterly* 92, 1 (spring): 96–107

1986 "Pst ... Pst ... Are You Listening? Hearing Voices from Yesterday." *Queen's Quarterly* 93, 1 (spring): 71–84. Also in *Companion to Contemporary Musical Thought*, ed. John Paynter et al. Vol. 2, 977–92. London: Routledge, 1992

1988 "Thisness: Marks and Remarks." In *Musical Canada: Words and Music Honouring Helmut Kallmann*, ed. John Beckwith and Frederick A. Hall, 211–31. Toronto: University of Toronto Press

1989 "Text, Context, Music." *Canadian University Music Review* 9, 2:1–21. Also in *Companion to Contemporary Musical Thought*, ed. John Paynter et al. Vol. 1, 272–89. London: Routledge, 1992

1989 "Music: Context, Text, Counter-text." *Contemporary Music Review* 5:101–35

1989 "Remembrance" in *George Whalley Remembrances*, ed. Michael D. Moore, 142–7. Kingston: Quarry Press

PUBLISHED REVIEWS

1957 *The Technique of My Musical Language*, by Olivier Messiaen. *The Canadian Music Journal* 2, 1:67–71

1957 *Introduction to the Theory of Music*, by H. Boatwright. *The Canadian Music Journal* 3, 4:83–5

1960–61 *Experimental Music: Composition with an Electronic Computer*, by L.A. Hiller and L.M. Isaacson, *The Canadian Music Journal* 5, 2:61

1962   "New Records." *The Canadian Music Journal* 5, 2:34–9
1996   *Taking a Stand: Essays in Honour of John Beckwith* (Toronto: University of Toronto Press), ed. Timothy J. McGee. *University of Toronto Quarterly* 67, 1:113–16

UNPUBLISHED WRITINGS²

1990   *Oppenheimer: An Opera-Fantasy in Three Acts* [libretto]
1991   The Bridge: A parable
1992   Indictment (An Old Story) [9 handwritten pages]
1992   A Weave of Life Lines. [528 handwritten pages with addenda; a detailed description of Anhalt's life experiences from childhood through to the 1990s; includes "The Bridge" and "Indictment (An Old Story)"]
1995   An Interim Account of My Search for Genealogical Information Pertaining to My Family's Background [95 handwritten pages]
1995   An Austro-Hungarian Journey, Sept. 24–Oct. 25, 1995 [139 handwritten pages in the format of a travel journal]
1995   A Brief Account of Four Escapes (or Were There Five?) [24 handwritten pages]
1995   *Traces (Tikkun)* [libretto]
1999   *Millennial Mall (Lady Diotima's Walk)* [libretto]
1999   About the Libretto of *Millennial Mall (Lady Diotima's Walk)* [printed in this volume, part 4]
1999   About the "Unidentifiable Righteous among the Nations" (A Personal Account)

NOTES

1 In addition to this list, the reader should consult "István Anhalt: An Inventory of Archival Fonds Held in the Music Division of the National Library of Canada" (Ottawa: National Library of Canada, 1994, typescript). See also Helmut Kallmann's essay in this volume on the Anhalt fonds at the National Library of Canada.
2 Part 4 of this volume contains previously unpublished writings on the operas, the libretto of *Millennial Mall (Lady Diotima's Walk)* followed by commentary, as well as essays on other topics pertaining to Anhalt's music.

Index

Brott, Alexander, 37, 42, 46
Brown, Earle, 116
Brown, Ted, 41
Buber, Martin, 337, 371,
    401
Budapest, xvii, 113; Dániel
    Berzsenyi Secondary
    School, 7–9, 28n29;
    Dohány Street syna-
    gogue, 3, 26n5, 78;
    Franz Liszt Academy of
    Music, xvii, 10–12, 26n9,
    28n33, 70, 77, 80,
    89n25, 135, 435; Hun-
    garian State Opera
    House, 18, 414; Jewish
    community, 3, 5, 26n6,
    76–7, 417; Margaret
    Island, 4, 7, 9, 27n15,
    27n25, 428; Pázmány
    University, 12; Salesian
    Order of St John Bosco,
    15, 67, 79, 373; Soviet
    capture of, 14–15;
    Spring Festival, 113,
    354n26
Bunyan, John, 319

Cage, John, 51, 75, 116,
    313, 326, 346
Calgary Symphony Orches-
    tra, 76
Campbell, J., 138–9
Canada Council, 52, 134,
    141
Canadian Association of
    University Schools of
    Music, 63n74, 73
Canadian Broadcasting
    Corporation, 45–6, 66–7,
    87n8, 132, 348, 369,
    371, 413, 441; Canadian
    Catalogue of Compos-
    ers, 348; CBC Symphony
    Orchestra, 45; Radio
    Canada International,
    45, 74, 137, 302n4,
    412–13
Canadian Jewish Congress,
    24, 44, 114–15
Canadian League of Com-
    posers, 52, 103

Canadian Music Centre,
    53, 96, 108n15, 305n26,
    322n2
Canadian Opera Com-
    pany, 79, 90n34, 412
Canadian University Music
    Society. See Canadian
    Association of University
    Schools of Music
Cardew, Cornelius, 141
Carter, Elliott, 238,
    304n16, 307n40
Cavanagh, Beverley, 72
CBC. See Canadian Broad-
    casting Corporation
Champagne, Claude, 45,
    347
Chapman, Norman B., 102
Charbonneau, Louis, 38
Chmura, Gabriel, 75,
    121–3, 347, 413–14, 420
Chopin, Fryderyk Fran-
    ciszek, 229
Clark, Alan, 110n49
Clarke, Douglas, 36–7, 40,
    42, 59n31
Clarke, F.R.C., 69–71
Clarkson, Ross, 24
Cologne, xviii, 46–7, 134–
    6, 141
Columbia-Princeton Elec-
    tronic Music Centre, 47,
    143–4, 145, 152, 161n53
Congress of Experimental
    Centers for Electronic
    Music, 52
Conrad, Doda, 21–2
Craig, Gordon, 72–3
Crawley, Clifford, 70
Crory, Neil, 105
Crumb, George, 75, 288,
    317, 346
Crystal, David, 68
Csipkay, Károly de, 15

D'Albert, François, 42, 103
Davenant, William, 41, 312
Davies, Meredith, 53
Davies, Peter Maxwell, 75,
    238, 288, 326, 339
Davis, Henriette, 24, 39,
    59n21, 112; Lady Davis

Fellowship, xvii, 24–5,
    38, 40, 112; Lady Davis
    Foundation, 24–5, 34, 44
Debussy, Claude, 283, 284
De Gaulle, Charles, 47
Delvincourt, Claude, 20
Depraz, Raymond, 22
Desjardins, Jeanne, 38
Devecseri, Gábor, 12
Devecseri-Huszar, Klára, 12
Dixon, Gail, 71
Dohnányi, Ernö, 10–11
Donald, Merlin, 82
Duchow, Marvin, 37, 42–3,
    45, 50, 60n38, 147
Duplessis, Maurice, 35,
    57n8
Duschenes, Mario, 42

Eastman School of Music,
    42–3
Easton, David, 82
Eichmann, Adolf, 14
Eimert, Herbert, 134–6
Einstein, Albert, 24
El-Dabh, Halim, 152
Eliade, Mircea, 79, 84
Eliot, T.S., 38, 312–14, 316
Ellis, Gordie, 136, 141
Elmer Iseler Singers, 67,
    82, 464
Encyclopedia of Music in
    Canada, 114
Epp, Robert, 75
Erkel, Ferenc, 10
Esprit Orchestra, 75,
    121–2, 305n26, 413–14,
    423

Falk, Géza, 10, 29n49
Fallis, Mary Lou, 72
Farley, René, 136, 141
Fauré, Gabriel, 207
Feldbrill, Victor, 115
Ferencsik, János, 12, 18
Ferneybough, Brian,
    307n40
Földesi, Tamás, 9, 351
Forrester, Maureen, 39,
    41–2, 347
Foss, Lukas, 53, 115, 346
Fourestier, Louis, xvii, 22, 25